MA

P9-CRJ-385

BAR REVIEW

Massachusetts

Table of Contents

THOMSON
™
BAR/BRI

celebrating over
35 **Y**EARS
*of preparing
law students
for the bar exam*

BAR REVIEW

Agency

celebrating over
35 YEARS
of preparing
law students
for the bar exam

AGENCY

TABLE OF CONTENTS

I. CREATION OF AGENCY

A. INTRODUCTION

Agency is generally defined as the relationship that arises when one person (the *principal*) manifests an intention that another person (the *agent*) shall act on his behalf. A principal may appoint an agent to do any act except an act which, by its nature, by public policy, or by contract, requires personal performance by the principal.

B. CREATION OF AGENCY RELATIONSHIP

Agency is a consensual relationship, but not all contract formalities are required to create an agency.

1. Capacity

To create an agency relationship, the respective parties must have capacity. However, the degree of capacity required for a principal differs from that required for an agent.

a. Principal Must Have Contractual Capacity

As a general rule, one who has contractual capacity himself may be a principal and enter into a contract through an agent. Thus, an incompetent cannot validly appoint an agent.

1) Minors

Because a minor generally cannot bind himself absolutely in contract, his appointment of an agent is *voidable* and can be disaffirmed before reaching majority. However, a minor probably can appoint an agent to contract for "necessaries."

2) Unincorporated Organizations

Unincorporated organizations such as churches and clubs cannot be principals. However, members of such organizations may be held *jointly liable* as principals if they have authorized or assented to the act giving rise to the litigation.

b. Agent Needs Only Minimal Capacity

Any person may be an agent, even if she has no contractual capacity herself. Thus, minors may be appointed as agents, as may incompetents. Nonetheless, a minimal mental capacity is usually required.

c. Disqualification of Agents

A person is disqualified from being an agent in the following situations:

1) Representing Both Parties

An agent cannot represent both parties to an agreement unless both parties are fully advised of the facts and agree to the dual representation.

2) Self-Dealing

The agent may not secretly act for her own account.

3) Not Licensed

If the law requires the agent to have a license, she cannot act without one, *e.g.*, brokers, insurance agents.

2. Formalities

a. Consent of Principal and Agent

Consent must be manifested by *both* the principal and the agent to create an agency relationship.

b. No Consideration Required

Consideration is not necessary for the creation of an agency relationship.

c. Writing Generally Not Required

Generally, absent an express statutory provision to the contrary, the existence of an agency does not have to be evidenced by a writing. This is true even when the Statute of Frauds requires a writing for the agreement that the agent is entering into on behalf of the principal. However, a number of states do have express provisions (*i.e.*, equal dignities rules) requiring agency agreements to be in writing when the agent is to enter into certain contracts within the Statute of Frauds—most notably, contracts involving the disposition of land.

3. Modes of Creating Agency Relationship

An agency relationship may be created by an act of the parties or by operation of law.

a. By Act of the Parties

An agency relationship may be created by an act of the parties in three different ways: (i) the agent and principal can *agree* that the agency shall exist (actual authority situation); (ii) the principal may *hold another out* as his agent to a third party (apparent authority situation); or (iii) the principal may *agree to be bound by the previously unauthorized acts* of another (ratification situation). These modes of creating the agency relationship will be examined in greater detail below.

b. By Operation of Law

1) Estoppel

An agency relationship may be created through estoppel; *i.e.,* a principal may be estopped from denying the existence of the agency. There is almost no difference between estoppel and apparent authority; they both depend on a third party's reliance on a communication from the principal. They differ only in application. Apparent authority makes the principal a party to the contract—with contractual rights and liabilities—whereas estoppel is merely a remedy to protect the innocent third party against loss.

2) Statute

An agency may be created by statute; such statutes are usually designed to accomplish a limited purpose.

Example: A, a resident of State Y, was involved in an automobile accident while driving in State X. The State X nonresident motorist statute provides that the driving of a vehicle on the highways of State X amounts to an appointment of the secretary of state as the agent of the nonresident driver for service of process in any action arising out of the operation of the vehicle. The secretary of state for State X will be deemed to be A's agent for this purpose.

C. RIGHTS AND DUTIES BETWEEN PRINCIPAL AND AGENT

1. Duties of Agent to Principal

The agent, of course, has whatever duties are expressly stated in her contract with her principal. In addition, in the absence of anything contrary in the agreement, the agent has three major duties implied by law: loyalty, obedience, and care.

a. Duty of Loyalty

The fiduciary duty of an agent to his principal is one of undivided loyalty. If an agent has interests adverse to the interests of his principal (*e.g.,* self-dealing or obtaining secret profits), he breaches this duty by failing to disclose them. A breach of the duty of loyalty also may occur where the agent acts on behalf of two different principals with adverse interests.

b. Duty of Obedience

1) In General—Liable for All Reasonable Directions

An agent must obey all reasonable directions of his principal. While the principal may well be liable for the agent's acts in violation of directions (apparent authority), the agent will be liable to the principal for any loss that the principal suffers.

2) What Constitutes Reasonable Directions

Reasonableness depends on the nature of the work, the contractual understanding, and custom. A janitor, for example, would be expected to follow minute instructions regarding his daily work effort, while an attorney would not normally be expected to follow her client's directions as to how to draft a complaint.

c. Duty of Reasonable Care

1) Compensated Agent

An agent owes a duty to her principal to carry out her agency with reasonable care, in light of local community standards and taking into account any special skills of the agent.

2) Gratuitous Agent

The modern trend is to hold a gratuitous or uncompensated agent to the degree of care customary in the community for one undertaking similar tasks without compensation. In most situations, this results in no difference between the standard for paid and unpaid agents.

3) Duty to Notify

The duty of care includes a duty to notify the principal of all matters that come to the agent's knowledge affecting the subject of the agency. The effect of this rule is that notice of all such matters coming to the attention of the agent is ***imputed*** to the principal. However, the majority of states will not impute such knowledge under certain circumstances, *e.g.,* where the agent acts in his own interest and adversely to the principal, or where the agent and the third party attempt to commit a fraud on the principal.

2. Remedies of Principal

The principal has a variety of remedies against the agent for breach of duty.

a. Action for Damages

An agent may be liable to her principal either for breach of contract or in tort.

1) Breach of Contract—Compensated Agents

A compensated agent may be held liable for damages suffered by the principal as a result of breach of contract. All of the remedies and methods of calculating damages that apply in normal breach of contract situations apply here. Note that an uncompensated agent cannot be held liable for breach of contract because there is no contract to perform.

2) Tort—All Agents

Any agent, whether compensated or gratuitous, may be held liable for damages resulting from her misuse of her principal's property, intentional or negligent misperformance, or failure to perform.

b. Action for Secret Profits

Where an agent breaches her fiduciary duty and secretly profits, the principal may recover the actual profits or property held by the agent.

Examples: 1) A is employed full-time by P to purchase timberland for P in a designated area. A purchases some land in the designated area for herself with her own money. A holds the land as constructive trustee for P and must convey to P at cost.

2) A is employed as a clerk in P's retail store. All goods are marked with a fixed price. A sells a $20 radio to a customer for $25. A must give P the additional $5 even though P has suffered no injury.

c. Accounting

The principal may bring an action in equity in complicated situations to have the court determine the exact amount of the principal's funds that the agent has that must be returned to the principal.

d. Withholding of Compensation

Where the agent has committed an intentional tort or intentionally breached her fiduciary duty, the principal may, in addition to any other remedies he has, refuse to pay the agent for any unapportioned compensation.

Examples: 1) A is employed on a commission basis by P to act as agent for the sale of P's land. A breaches her fiduciary duty to P by accepting additional compensation from the buyer. A is not entitled to receive her commission.

2) A is employed by P to act as agent for the sale of three parcels of P's land. A is to receive $1,000 for the sale of each parcel. After properly selling the first two parcels, A breaches her fiduciary duty when selling the third by accepting additional compensation from the buyer. A is entitled to $2,000. However, if A's agreement with P was that she was to receive $3,000 for the sale of all the land, she would be entitled to nothing because the compensation was not apportioned.

3. Duties of Subagent to Principal and Agent
Where a subagent has been appointed with proper authority, she too will owe the principal the same duties as would the agent.

   a. Liability of Agent for Subagent Breaches
   Note that the agent will also be held liable to the principal for breaches of the subagent. This is so even though the agent exercised diligence and good faith in appointing the subagent.

   b. Liability of Subagent to Agent

      1) General Rule—Subagent Liable to Agent
      The subagent owes the agent the same duties she owes the principal; thus, she will be liable to the agent for her breaches.

      2) Unauthorized Subagent
      Where the subagent has been appointed without authority, the subagent owes no duties to the principal. The agent alone will be responsible to the principal for performance of the agency duties and for any loss sustained because of the subagent's conduct, with the agent's only recourse being against the subagent.

4. Duties of Principal to Agent

   a. Duties Imposed by Operation of Law

      1) Compensation
      The principal owes the agent a duty to compensate her reasonably for her services unless, of course, the agent has agreed to act gratuitously. Note that a principal has no duty to compensate a subagent, even if the agent was authorized to hire subagents, unless the principal agrees otherwise.

      2) Reimbursement
      The principal owes the agent (and any authorized subagent) a duty to indemnify her for all expenses or losses reasonably incurred in discharging any authorized duties, including any legal liability incurred by the agent in acting for her principal unless the loss was due solely to the agent's fault.

   b. Duties Imposed by Contract
   Of course, the principal also has a duty to comply with the terms of any contract between him and the agent. Obviously, such a contract could vary the terms of the common law duties.

   c. Duty to Cooperate
   As a general rule, the principal should cooperate with his agent to help her carry out agency functions. Thus, he must provide the agent with the requisite opportunities and not unreasonably interfere with the agent's performance. Generally, the scope of the duty is measured by what is reasonably contemplated by the parties.
   Examples: 1) If P hires A for $500 a month to sell widgets, P has no obligation to provide A with widgets to sell. However, if A is to be paid by commission (or A's compensation is otherwise based on the results of her work), it is reasonable for A to assume that P will provide her with an opportunity to work, and so P must provide A with widgets to sell.

            2) If P hires A to sell his empty factory building on commission, P cannot then lease the building to a third party.

5. Remedies of Agent

   a. Breach of Contract
   A compensated agent has the usual remedies for breach of contract. The most important thing to remember is that the agent has a ***duty to mitigate*** damages.
   Example: A is employed by P under a 10-year written contract which provides for a salary of $40,000 per year. P fires A after two years. A cannot spend the next eight years in Acapulco on vacation and collect her money. She must actively seek other employment.

   b. Agent's Lien
   An agent has a possessory lien (*i.e.,* a claim against any property of the principal that

the agent holds) for any money due to the agent, including compensation for services, unless the contract provides otherwise.

Example: A purchases coins for P with his own funds. P does not reimburse A for the cost of the coins. If A still has possession of the coins, A has a lien on those coins and may retain them until P reimburses him.

6. Real Estate Brokers' Contracts

a. Nonexclusive Contract (Subject to Prior Sale)

A nonexclusive contract normally entitles a real estate broker to compensation when she has produced a buyer who is ready, willing, and able to buy, provided the property has not already been sold. In this case, the broker is entitled to her commission even though the sale is not consummated. However, occasionally a nonexclusive contract will specifically provide that the commission is due only when the sale is consummated. In such a case, the broker is not entitled to compensation until the *conveyance* (not the contract of sale) has been made.

b. Exclusive Contract

An exclusive contract entitles a real estate broker to her commission if she or anyone else (*e.g.,* the owner or another broker) produces a buyer who is ready, willing, and able to buy.

II. CONTRACT LIABILITY—AGENCY POWER

A. INTRODUCTION

Generally speaking, a person is not responsible for the acts of another who assumes to represent him. He will be held liable only if he has made the other his representative and given her the power to bind him. Such power can arise in three ways: (i) through *actual authority* granted by the principal to the agent; (ii) through *apparent authority* arising from the principal's holding out of another as his agent to third parties; and (iii) through *ratification authority*—power given by the principal after the act has been performed.

B. ACTUAL AND APPARENT AUTHORITY

When deciding whether a principal will be bound on a contract that an agent entered into on his behalf, it should first be determined whether the agent had actual authority. If she did, the principal will be bound regardless of whether the third party knew of the agent's authority, and the agent cannot be held liable to the principal for breach because she acted within the scope of her authority. If the agent lacked actual authority, it should then be determined whether she had apparent authority. Although apparent authority will bind the principal to the contract, the agent may be held liable by the principal for acting outside the scope of her authority.

1. Actual Authority

Actual authority is authority that the agent reasonably thinks she possesses based on the principal's dealings with her. In determining whether the actor had actual authority, you should ask yourself: (i) whether the requisite formalities, if any, have been complied with; (ii) what type of actual authority (express or implied) is present; and (iii) whether the authority has been terminated.

a. Types of Actual Authority

There are two basic types of actual authority: express and implied.

1) Express Authority

Express authority is that authority contained within the "four corners" of the agency agreement, *i.e.,* the communication, whether written or oral, from the principal to the agent.

a) Construction of Authority

In general, the grant of authority given to an agent will be interpreted in a fashion similar to interpretation of offers under contract law.

####### (1) Extravagant Language Usually Limited

Grants of authority often contain "extravagant" language that would appear to give extremely broad powers to the agent, *e.g.,* "to conduct any business on principal's behalf." Courts will generally limit application of such broad grants to what appears to be the business actually intended by the parties.

(2) Specific vs. General Language
Specific language in the grant of authority will prevail over general language.

(3) Reasonable Belief of Agent
The agent is free to act upon her grant of authority as she reasonably believes the principal intended. In construing the intent of the principal, the agent may look to the principal's words and acts when he conveyed authority.

b) Express Authority Granted Mistakenly
Express authority may exist even though the principal did not intend to convey such authority but did so by mistake. Mistakes may involve: (i) the person to whom the authority is given or (ii) the subject matter.

Examples: 1) Peter wishes Chauncey to enter into a transaction on his behalf but mistakenly tells Mary to do it. Mary has actual express authority to act on Peter's behalf.

2) Peter wishes Mary to buy Blackacre on his behalf. Mistakenly, he tells Mary to purchase Whiteacre. Mary has actual express authority to purchase Whiteacre.

c) Express Authority Granted Because of Misrepresentation
The fact that an agent induces the principal to grant authority by misrepresentation will *not* affect the extent of the authority actually granted.

2) Implied Authority
Implied actual authority is authority that the agent (not the third party) reasonably believes she has as a result of the actions of the principal. Implied authority may arise in the following ways:

a) Implied from Express Authority
Express authority granted to an agent to accomplish a particular result necessarily implies authority to use all means reasonably necessary for its accomplishment.

Example: P authorizes A to manage his apartment building. The express grant of authority states quite simply that A is "to manage"— nothing more. To manage the building, A must employ a janitor, purchase fuel for heating, arrange for the painting and repair of screens as needed, and occasionally redecorate an apartment. The authority of A to do these things, while not expressly granted, is implied because these acts are necessarily incidental to the proper management of the building.

b) Implied from Custom and Usage
Unless specifically directed otherwise, an agent has implied authority to act in accord with general custom or usage. However, the agent must have *knowledge* of the custom or usage.

c) Implied by Acquiescence
Authority by acquiescence is implied authority that results from the principal's acceptance of, or failure to object to, a series of unauthorized acts (*i.e.,* a series of ratifications) that *reasonably* leads the agent to believe that she has authority to do the same acts in the future.

Example: Mary, the office manager for Peter's company, has regularly bought its office supplies without previous authorization. Peter has never objected. Mary has implied authority by acquiescence to continue these purchases.

d) Implied Because of Emergency or Necessity
When the agent has no specific instructions on what to do in case of an

emergency, she has implied authority to take reasonable measures that are necessary until she can contact her principal.

Example: In case of a railroad accident, the highest ranking trainman can bind the railroad to pay for emergency medical expenses.

e) Specific Situations

(1) Authority to Delegate

In general, an agent's authority will not be construed to permit her to delegate any of her authority. The courts reason that an agency relationship is a consensual relationship, and the principal has not consented to someone else performing the agent's functions. However, the principal will be held to have impliedly consented to a delegation of authority by the agent in the following cases:

(a) Ministerial Acts

An agent may employ a subagent to execute ministerial acts, *i.e.,* purely mechanical acts.

Example: P employs A to manage his shoe store. A hires several college students to help her take an annual inventory. Authority to delegate these functions will be implied.

(b) Delegation Required by Circumstances

Often circumstances may indicate that the employment of a subagent would be necessary. If so, authority to delegate will be implied.

Example: P hires A, a contractor, to build a high-rise apartment building for him. A hires an electrician to install the wiring of the building. A has implied authority to delegate under these circumstances because P would be held to be aware of the fact that such delegation is necessary to build the apartment building.

(c) Custom

An agent may delegate to subagents when it is the custom of a particular business.

Example: P hires A to manage his new high-rise apartment building. Authority to hire janitors, doormen, etc., will be implied.

(d) Impossibility

A principal will be held to have impliedly consented to subdelegation where those acts being performed could not, by definition, be performed by the agent herself.

Example: P employs A to transact business that requires a license. P is fully aware that A does not have the requisite license nor can A procure one. A has implied authority to appoint a duly licensed subagent.

(2) Authority to Purchase

Authority to purchase on behalf of the principal will generate certain implied authority.

(a) Authority to Pay

An agent will be deemed to have authority to pay for the goods she is authorized to purchase. She may do this either out of the principal's funds or on credit if such funds are unavailable.

(b) Authority to Accept Delivery

An agent with authority to purchase goods will also be deemed to have authority to accept delivery of the goods.

(3) Authority to Sell

Similarly, an agent with authority to sell her principal's property will be deemed to have certain implied authority.

(a) Authority to Warrant
An agent having authority to sell personal property may give general warranties respecting quality and quantity; for real property, the agent may grant the customary covenants.

(b) Authority to Collect

1] Only If Agent Has Possession of Goods
An agent with authority to sell the principal's property has authority to collect payment if the property sold is in her possession.

2] Can Collect Only Cash
Payment for property sold must be in cash; the agent may not accept a check or extend credit (unless, of course, implied consent, *e.g.,* custom, past practices between the parties, etc., can be found).

(c) Authority to Deliver
An agent having authority to sell the principal's property generally is deemed to have authority to deliver possession of such property upon receipt of proper payment.

(4) Authority to Manage Investments
An agent having authority to manage investments will have her authority construed in accordance with a "prudent investor" standard. Also, when the agent is investing for the principal, the agent should take title to investments in the principal's name; if title is taken in the agent's name, her position as agent must be clearly designated.

b. Termination of Actual Authority
Once having determined that the requisite formalities exist and that there is express or implied actual authority, you should ask whether the authority has been terminated. Termination of actual authority may occur in the following ways:

1) By Lapse of Time

a) Specified Time
If the agency relationship is to last for a set period of time, the agent's authority will terminate upon expiration of this period.

b) Time Not Specified
If there is no set period of time specified in the agreement between a principal and an agent, then the courts will imply termination within a *reasonable* time period.

2) By Happening of an Event
The agency agreement may specify that it is to last until a specified event happens. When that event takes place, authority will be terminated.
Example: A is hired to work on public relations for the space exploration program until an astronaut has successfully been landed on Mars. With the first landing of an astronaut on Mars, the agency relationship terminates.

3) By Change of Circumstances
A change of circumstances that should cause an agent to realize the principal would not want the agent to exercise her authority terminates her authority. A change of circumstances sufficient to bring about termination would include the following:

a) Destruction of the subject matter of the authority;

b) A drastic change in business conditions;

c) A change in relevant laws; and

d) Insolvency of the agent or principal, if relevant.

4)   By Breach of Agent's Fiduciary Duty
A breach of fiduciary duty by the agent terminates her authority.

5)   By Unilateral Act of Principal or Agent
Either the principal or the agent can unilaterally terminate the agency relationship. Communication of a declaration that the agency is at an end is sufficient. Note well that the power to unilaterally terminate the relationship exists even though the party who exercises that power may be in breach of the agency contract when he does so. The breaching party could, of course, be liable for damages.

6)   By Operation of Law
An agency relationship may be terminated without regard to the will of either party by operation of law under certain circumstances, *e.g.,* death or loss of capacity of either party, such as a dissolution of a corporation or partnership or the insanity of a person.

a)   Exception—Durable Powers of Attorney
Most states have adopted some form of "durable power of attorney" statute. A power of attorney is a written instrument authorizing an agent ("attorney in fact") to perform specific acts, and is usually used by the agent to evidence his authority to third parties. A regular power of attorney—like any other agency—is terminated by operation of law upon the incapacity or death of the principal. However, typical durable power of attorney statutes provide that the power of the agent does ***not*** terminate on the ***incapacity*** of the principal if the power indicates that it will not be affected by the principal's incapacity. Although the power terminates at the principal's death, it continues if it is uncertain whether the principal is alive.

c.   Irrevocable Agencies
There are two types of agency relations that may not be unilaterally terminated by the principal and generally are not terminated by operation of law; *i.e.,* where: (i) the agent has an interest in the subject matter of the agency or (ii) a power is given for security.

1)   Definitions

a)   Agency Coupled with an Interest
An agent has an "interest" when she has been given immediately exercisable rights in the property.
Example: P owes A $20,000. P gives A a written power of attorney authorizing A to sell Blackacre, which P owns, and to remit to P any money received in excess of $20,000. A accepts this as a discharge of the debt. P cannot revoke A's power to sell Blackacre.

b)   Power Given as Security
A power given as security is normally exercisable by the agent only upon a subsequent default by the principal. These types of transactions normally involve a loan to the principal who posts collateral and gives the agent authority to sell in the event of default.

Note: Powers given as security involve a principal-agent relationship where the agent is really acting for her own benefit. Therefore, even though agency is involved, the agent has her own interest in the subject matter of the agency power.

2)   Restatement View
The Restatement (Second) of Agency ("Restatement") does not distinguish between these two types of interests—it treats them both as powers given as security. Under the Restatement view, the power is absolutely irrevocable other than in accord with the agreement. There are two other requirements that must be met.

a)   Purpose of Grant
The grant of authority must have been given in order to protect a debt, other duty, or title of the agent or third person.

b)   Consideration
The grant must be supported by consideration.

Example: Chauncey lends $2,000 to Bullwater in exchange for Bullwater's promissory note. Two weeks later, at Chauncey's request, Bullwater secures his obligation to repay Chauncey the $2,000 by giving Chauncey a security interest in his car. The security interest provides that Chauncey may sell the car upon Bullwater's default on the promissory note. Chauncey's authority to sell the car upon Bullwater's default is revocable because at the time Bullwater gave Chauncey the security interest there was no consideration.

2. Apparent Authority (Ostensible Authority)

Even if the agent lacks actual authority, the principal can still be held liable on contracts entered into on his behalf if the third party seeking to hold the principal liable can show that the agent had apparent authority to act.

a. Basic Theory

Where the principal "holds out" another as possessing certain authority, thereby inducing others reasonably to believe that authority exists, the agent has apparent authority to act, even though as between herself and the principal such authority has not been granted. Note that apparent authority differs from actual authority in that apparent authority arises out of reasonable beliefs of third parties, whereas actual authority arises out of reasonable beliefs of agents.

1) "Holding Out" by Principal

The mere assertion by an agent of her powers is not sufficient to bind the principal—the agent cannot "bootstrap" her own authority; the principal must have done or failed to do something that causes the third party's belief.

a) Affirmative Action

The "holding out" may be by word or conduct on the part of the principal.
Example: P tells T that A is P's agent and has the power to contract for P. A, in fact, has no actual authority to contract for P. If A contracts with T on P's behalf, P is bound.

b) Inaction

The "holding out" may also be by inaction on the part of the principal. Note, however, that there must be some *duty to act, i.e.,* to disclose.
Example: A, in P's presence, tells T that she is P's agent when in fact she is not. Under these circumstances, P has a duty to correct A's representation; if he does not, A will have apparent authority to act on P's behalf.

2) Reasonable Reliance by Third Party

In addition to the requirement that some "holding out" must be traceable to the principal, the third party must reasonably rely on the "holding out." Thus, unusual circumstances surrounding an agent's actions, or extraordinary transactions entered into by the agent, may create a duty on the third party to inquire into the agent's authority to act.

b. Types of Apparent Authority

1) When Agent Has No Actual Authority of Any Type

There are certain situations in which, at the time the agent acts, she has no actual authority to do anything at all for the principal, yet nonetheless, the principal may be bound by the agent's acts.

a) Impostors

When the principal *negligently* permits an impostor to be in a position where the impostor appears to have authority to act for the principal, the principal will be held liable for the impostor's act undertaken with such authority.
Example: P, a hotel corporation, employs one person as a night clerk. While the night clerk is away from the desk, a stranger goes behind the desk, poses as the clerk, accepts valuables for placement in the hotel safe from a guest who is registering, and absconds with them. P is liable to the guest for the stolen valuables.

b) Lingering Apparent Authority

(1) General Rule—Notice May Be Necessary

An agent's actual authority terminates when she knows or should have known of the termination. What about a third party who has had a pattern of dealing with the agent while she had actual authority? If the principal knows of the dealings between his past agent and the third party, he must give notice to the third party that the agent's actual authority has been terminated. If he fails to do so and if the third party did not know nor reasonably should have known of the termination of the agent's actual authority, the agent will continue to have apparent authority.

Example: A has been employed as P's agent for 10 years. During that period she has regularly purchased office supplies from T within the scope of her actual authority. P notifies A that her actual authority is terminated. T, however, has no notice of this termination. A purchases office supplies from T after termination. P will be held liable to T for the supplies because A had apparent authority to purchase the supplies.

Sufficient notification of termination may come either directly or indirectly and either from the principal or from some other source. The test is whether the third party knows or reasonably should have known of the termination of the agent's authority.

(2) Writing Manifesting Agent's Authority

If the principal has given the agent a writing manifesting her authority that is meant to be shown to third parties, the agent's apparent authority will not be terminated with respect to third parties who see and rely on such writing after termination of her authority.

(3) Death or Incompetency

Death or incompetency of the principal *terminates all authority* of the agent without notice to either the agent or third parties. This rule has been changed with respect to banks by Uniform Commercial Code ("U.C.C.") section 4-405, which provides that a bank can continue to honor transactions for a customer's account until it learns of his death or adjudication of incompetency and has a reasonable time to act. Even with knowledge, a bank can continue for 10 days after the date of death to pay or certify checks drawn on or prior to the date of death, unless ordered to stop payment by a person claiming an interest in the account.

2) When Agent Has Some Present Actual Authority

There are situations in which the agent exceeds her authority to act on behalf of the principal, yet the principal is still bound by the agent's acts.

a) Prior Acts

When the principal has previously allowed the agent to act beyond her authority and the principal knows that a third party is aware of this fact, the principal is bound by the agent's unauthorized act.

Example: A, a janitor in P's employ, has no authority to employ other people for P. On two prior occasions, A hired T, a painter, to do some painting in P's building. P paid T's invoices without protest. If A hires T to do another paint job, P is liable to T for his services.

b) Position

(1) In General

When the principal places the agent in a position that carries with it certain *customary responsibilities*, the principal is liable for the agent's acts that come within these customary responsibilities even though the agent had no actual authority to perform the acts.

Example: P, a country club, hires A to be the food service manager with the understanding that A will personally pay for all expenses of the dining room and will split the profits with P. A orders $10,000 worth of food from T, but A does not pay. P is liable for the food A purchased from T because food service managers customarily have authority to order food on behalf of their principals.

(2) General vs. Special Agent
In determining whether the agent's position customarily includes the act that she has performed, courts often rely on the distinction between a general and special agent. A general agent is one who is authorized to engage in (i) a series of transactions (ii) involving a continuity of service. A special agent is authorized to engage in one or more transactions not involving a continuity of service. A general agent's apparent authority is considerably broader than a special agent's.

c) Secret Limiting Instructions
When a principal secretly limits the actual authority of his agent to act, and the agent, when dealing with a third party, acts beyond the scope of the limitation, the principal will be bound by the agreement made between the third party and agent.

Example: P owns an antique store. A shipment of antique clocks arrives from London. P tells A, his sales associate, not to sell a special grandfather clock because the value has not been determined. P goes to lunch. A enters into a sales contract with T for the grandfather clock. P is bound on the sales contract even if the value of the clock is greater than the sales price.

3) Inherent Authority (Inherent Agency Power)
Inherent authority, or inherent agency power, as it is called in the Restatement, results in a principal being bound by his agent's acts in certain situations even though the agent has no actual authority.

a) Basic Rationale—Protection of Innocent Third Parties
The principal will sometimes be held liable on inherent authority grounds because, in balancing interests, courts normally tend to want to protect innocent third parties as opposed to the principal, who in fact gave *some actual authority* to the agent—in effect the principal turned the agent loose on the world and should have some responsibility for her misdeeds.

b) Examples

(1) Respondeat Superior
A principal is held liable for the torts that an employee commits within the scope of her employment even though there is no actual authority.

(2) Conduct Similar to that Authorized
Where a general agent exceeds her actual authority but the act performed is similar to the act authorized, the principal will be held liable.

c. Improper Disposition of Goods—Apparent Ownership
One recurring problem is the improper disposition of goods by a person to whom they have been entrusted.

1) General Rule—Mere Possession Insufficient
Generally, the fact that the agent has possession of the principal's goods does not entitle the agent to sell them or transfer good title.

Example: P loans his watch to A with the understanding that A will return it in one week. A sells the watch to T. P may recover the watch from T.

For the possessor of goods to have authority to transfer good title without authority, she must have either some indicia of ownership or be a dealer in the goods.

2) Indicia of Ownership
Where the principal transfers possession of property to the agent and gives the

agent some document of title or other indicia of ownership, the agent has the
power to transfer good title even though the transfer is unauthorized.

Example: P borrows money from A and gives A, for security, 100 shares of Texas Instruments stock along with a blank assignment of title signed by P. A improperly sells the stock to T. T takes good title.

3) Dealer in the Goods
Under the U.C.C. (section 2-403), where a dealer in goods of the type sold improperly sells the principal's goods to a third party in the ordinary course of business, the third party takes good title.

Example: P takes his watch to Acme Watch Store to have it repaired. Acme, which also sells watches, sells P's watch to T. T takes good title. P's remedy is to sue Acme.

C. RATIFICATION
There are situations where an individual ("agent") will purport to act on behalf of another person ("principal") without any type of authority. In such a situation, "principal" may still be bound by "agent's" act if "principal" subsequently ratifies "agent's" act.

1. Effect of Ratification

a. "Principal" Bound
When a "principal" ratifies an unauthorized transaction by an "agent," the "principal" becomes bound on the contract.

b. "Agent" Relieved of Liability for Breach of Warranty
Generally, an "agent" who acts without authority breaches the implied warranty of authority. (*See* D.2.a.2)b), *infra*.) An "agent" is relieved of this liability if the "principal" ratifies.

c. Contract Given Retroactive Effect
If ratified, a transaction will be treated as if it had originally been entered into with authority. However, there are several situations in which the ratification is considered effective on the date of ratification and does not relate back. In such cases, the "principal" is deemed to have ***adopted*** the contract rather than to have ratified.

1) Incapacity
If the "principal" has capacity at the time of the ratification, but did not have capacity at the time that the "agent" entered into the unauthorized transaction, then there will be no retroactive effect. The contract will be considered valid from the time of adoption.

2) Intervening Rights
Ratification will not have retroactive validity where it would operate to the prejudice of third persons who have, in the meantime, acquired rights that would be jeopardized if the transaction were valid retroactively.

Example: A, without authority, contracts to sell P's automobile to T for $2,500. P, without knowledge of A's purported transaction, contracts to sell the automobile to X for $2,000. Subsequently, finding out about A's transaction at the higher price, P decides to affirm it. X's intervening rights in the subject matter of the transaction will prevent this.

2. What Constitutes Ratification

a. Prerequisites

1) "Principal" Must Know Material Facts
There can be ratification only where the "principal" has or reasonably should have knowledge of the material facts at the time of the alleged affirmance.

2) "Principal" Must Accept the Entire Transaction
Ratification must be of the entire transaction. The "principal" may not merely ratify a portion of the transaction (unless, of course, the transaction(s) are severable).

3) "Principal" Must Have Capacity
The "principal" must be competent and of legal age to ratify.

4) No Consideration Needed
Ratification is a unilateral act of the "principal" and requires no consideration.

b. Methods of Ratifying

1) Express Affirmance
A transaction may be expressly affirmed by the "principal."

2) Implied Affirmance
Conduct on the part of the "principal" that would be consistent with approval of the heretofore unauthorized act may be taken as a ratification.

a) Acceptance of Benefits
If the "principal" accepts the benefits of the transaction when it is still possible to decline, he will be deemed to have ratified.
Example: P's part-time gardener contracted with T, without authority of P, to have P's trees pruned. P is not deemed to have accepted the benefits because there is no way P could reject or return them.

b) Silence
If the "principal" is silent where he would otherwise have a duty to disaffirm the transaction, it will act as a ratification.

c) Lawsuit
If the "principal" brings a lawsuit involving the transaction, it will be construed as a ratification.

3. What May Be Ratified

a. General Rule—Anything "Principal" Could Have Legally Done
As long as the "agent's" act could have legally been performed or authorized by the "principal" at the time the "agent" acted, the "principal" may ratify.
Example: On June 1, A, without any authorization, contracts on P's behalf to establish an off-track betting parlor. On December 1, the legislature legalizes off-track betting. P may *not* ratify after December 1 because A's original act was illegal.

b. Exceptions

1) Performance Illegal
Where performance of the contract would be illegal *at the time of ratification,* it may not be ratified.
Example: Assume same off-track betting example as above, except that off-track betting was legal on June 1 and outlawed on December 1; P may not ratify after December 1.

2) Withdrawal by Third Party
If, prior to ratification, the third party indicates that she will not be bound by the contract, the "principal" may not ratify.

3) Material Change of Circumstances
Where there has been a material change of circumstances so that it would not be equitable to hold the third party to the contract, there can be no ratification.
Example: A sells P's house to T. Before ratification, the house is destroyed by fire. P may not ratify.

4. Who May Ratify

a. Majority Rule—Only "Principal"
The majority rule is that the "principal" alone can ratify. An "agent" may *not* elect to treat the contract as her own.

b. **No Ratification by "Undisclosed Principal"**
Because the act must be entered into by the "agent" on behalf of her "principal," an "undisclosed principal" cannot ratify because the third party never relied upon his existence. (Compare with ratification in tort situations, however. There it is not necessary that the third party have knowledge of the "principal" as long as the "agent" *intended* to act on his behalf.)

D. LIABILITIES OF THE PARTIES
Having established that there is a valid contract entered into by an agent for her principal, the next step is to determine who the parties to the contract are and what their rights and liabilities are under the contract.

1. Third Party vs. Principal
The general rule is that if the agent had authority, the principal is liable to the third party.

2. Third Party vs. Agent
Whether an agent can be held liable on a contract the agent enters into on behalf of the principal depends on whether the principal was disclosed, partially disclosed, or undisclosed.

a. Disclosed Principal Situation
A disclosed principal is one whose *existence* and *identity* are known to the third party.

1) Disclosed Principal Liable
A disclosed principal is always liable on a contract entered into by an authorized agent.

2) Agent Generally Not Liable
A third party generally has no action against an agent in a disclosed principal situation because the contract is with the principal. There are, however, certain well-recognized exceptions to this rule:

a) Intent of Parties
Where the intent of the parties is that the agent shall be a party to the contract, she will be held liable. The intent of the parties may be determined by examining the contract itself, but if that is ambiguous, then parol evidence of the parties' intent may be introduced.
Example: A signs a contract: "P by A." The "by" indicates that A signed in a representative capacity and did not intend to be bound. If A signed "P, A," parol evidence would be admissible to prove the intent of the parties.

b) Agent's Implied Warranty of Authority
When an agent enters into a contract purportedly on behalf of a principal, the agent makes an implied warranty of authority—*i.e.,* a warranty that she has the authority that she purports to have. Thus, although the agent generally is not liable in contract when she contracts for a disclosed principal, she may nevertheless be held liable to the third party *for breach of her implied warranty* if she acted without authority. Damages for breach of the warranty generally are limited to the actual damage caused, which may be different from what could be recovered using a contract damages measure.

b. Partially Disclosed and Undisclosed Principal Situations
A *partially disclosed* principal is one whose existence, but *not* identity, is known to the third party. (*Note:* If the third party should have reasonably known that the person with whom he was dealing was acting for a principal, he would be deemed to have known of the principal's existence.) An *undisclosed* principal is one whose existence *and* identity are unknown to the third party.

1) Both Agent and Principal Liable
Both the agent and the principal are liable on a contract entered into by an authorized agent on behalf of a partially disclosed or undisclosed principal.

2) Election to Bind Principal or Agent
The majority of courts permit the third party to file suit against both the principal and agent but, upon objection of either defendant, the third party must elect *prior to judgment* which party he wishes to hold liable.

Note: If the third party obtains a judgment against the agent without knowledge of the principal's identity, he can later sue the principal when her identity is discovered if the judgment has not been satisfied.

3. **Right to Hold Third Party Liable on Contract**

   a. **Disclosed Principal Situation—Principal May Enforce Contract**
   In a disclosed principal situation, only the principal, not the agent, may enforce the contract and hold the third party liable.

   b. **Partially Disclosed and Undisclosed Principal Situations—Principal or Agent May Enforce Contract**
   In partially disclosed and undisclosed principal situations, either the principal or agent may enforce the contract and hold the third party liable. However, if the agent enforces the contract, the principal is entitled to all of the rights and benefits thereunder.

      1) **Situations Where Principal May Not Enforce Contract**
      Some situations exist, however, where the principal will not have a right to specifically enforce the contract against the third party.

         a) **Fraudulent Concealment of Principal's Identity**
         Where the agent has fraudulently concealed the identity of the principal, the contract will not be specifically enforceable by the principal and, indeed, the third party has a right to rescission. The majority of courts hold that there must have been an *affirmative misrepresentation* by the agent for this exception to operate.
         Example: Smidget Company wishes to enter into a licensing agreement with T respecting a process that T has developed, but knows that T would never deal with it. Thus, Smidget employs A to enter into the agreement. A enters into the agreement with T in her own name and represents that she is acting on her own behalf. Smidget Company may not get specific performance on the contract unless T waives his right of rescission.

         b) **Increase of Burden to Third Party**
         Where performance by the principal would impose an undue burden on the third party (by virtue of the fact that it is the principal and not the agent to whom performance must be made), the contract may not be specifically enforced and the third party will have a right to rescission.
         Example: A, on behalf of an undisclosed principal, P, enters into a "requirements" contract with T. In fact, the requirements of P are substantially greater than T believed the requirements of A to be. T may avoid this contract.

III. TORT LIABILITY—RESPONDEAT SUPERIOR

A. **IN GENERAL**
A principal may also be liable to third parties for torts committed by her agent under the doctrine of respondeat superior. In general, the rules governing imposition of tort liability are more limited in scope than those governing contractual liability.

1. **Elements Necessary to Establish Liability**
In analyzing a bar examination question concerning the liability of a principal under the doctrine of respondeat superior, two basic elements must be established.

   a. **Employer-Employee Relationship**
   First, there must have been an employer-employee (*i.e.,* master-servant) relationship between the party whose act caused the injury and the person sought to be held liable therefor.

   b. **Conduct Within Scope of Employment**
   Second, if the employer-employee relationship did exist, the employee's wrongful conduct must have been committed within the scope of the employment relationship.

2. **Nature of Employer's Liability**

a. **Liability Is Derivative**
The liability of the employer is derivative (respondeat superior). Thus, the nonliability or release from liability of the employee precludes recovery from the employer. By contrast, however, a personal defense of the employee that does not go to liability (*e.g.*, marital immunity) does not bar recovery from the employer.

b. **Liability Is Joint and Several**
The liability of the employer for the torts of her employee is joint and several inasmuch as the victim may recover in full from *either* the employer or the employee.

c. **Direct Liability**
In addition to derivative liability under the doctrine of respondeat superior, a principal may be liable for her *own negligence* in hiring or retaining an employee. An employer may also be negligent in supervising or entrusting the employee with specific responsibilities if the employee acts beyond the scope of his employment and the employer knows of dangerous tendencies of the employee.

B. THE EMPLOYER-EMPLOYEE RELATIONSHIP

A principal is liable only for those torts committed by a certain kind of agent—"employee" or "servant." He is not generally liable for torts committed by an agent functioning as an independent contractor. Therefore, the first determination to be made in each case is whether, in fact, an employer-employee relationship did exist.

1. **Independent Contractor or Employee?**

a. **Definitional Standards**

1) **Independent Contractor**
A clear example of an independent contractor is one who has a calling of her own, is hired to do a particular job, is paid a given amount for that job, and who follows her own discretion in carrying out the job. A principal has no right to control the manner and method in which an independent contractor performs the job.

2) **Employee**
A clear example of an employee is one who works full-time for his employer, is compensated on a time basis, and is subject to the supervision of the principal in the details of his work. An employer has the right to control the manner and method in which an employee performs the job.

b. **Determination of Right to Control**
There are many cases where it is not clear whether the relationship is one of employer-employee or principal-independent contractor. The single overriding factor in determining whether a person is an employee is whether the principal (employer) has the *right to control* the manner and method by which the person performs his tasks. [*See, e.g.*, Community for Creative Non-Violence v. Reid, 490 U.S. 730 (1989)] The following factors should be considered in determining right to control:

1) **Characterization by Parties**
The way the parties characterize their relationship (employer-employee vs. principal-independent contractor) is significant, but not dispositive.

2) **Distinct Business**
Is the person hired engaged in a distinct business or occupation of her own? A person who has her own business or occupation is more likely to be an independent contractor.

3) **Custom Regarding Supervision**
What are the customs of the locality regarding supervision of the type of work to be performed? If, in the locality, the type of work involved is usually performed under the supervision of the principal, the relationship is more likely to be employer-employee. However, if, in the locality, the type of work is usually performed without supervision, the relationship is more likely to be principal-independent contractor.

4) **Skill Required**
What degree of skill is required in the particular endeavor? Where great skill is required, the individual hired is more likely to be deemed an independent contractor.

      5)   Tools and Facilities
Does the worker or the principal supply the tools and facilities used to perform the job? If the principal supplies them, the relationship is more likely to be employer-employee; if the worker supplies her own tools and facilities, the relationship is more likely to be principal-independent contractor.

      6)   Period of Employment
What is the length of the employment period? If the period is definite and/or short, the relationship is more likely to be principal-independent contractor; if the period is indefinite and/or long, the relationship is more likely to be employer-employee.

      7)   Basis of Compensation
What is the basis of compensation? If the compensation is on the basis of time, the relationship is more likely to be employer-employee; if the one hired is paid on a job basis, the relationship is more likely to be principal-independent contractor.

      8)   Understanding of the Parties
Do the parties believe they have entered into an employer-employee relationship?

        a)   Contract Gives Right to Control
Where the contract gives the employer the right to control, it is conclusive.

        b)   Contract Gives No Right to Control or Is Silent
Where the contract is silent or specifically states that there is no right to control, evidence regarding exercise of actual control may be introduced.

      9)   Business Purpose
Was the person hired to perform an act in furtherance of the principal's business? If the principal does not hire the person for business purposes (*e.g.,* to mow the principal's lawn), then the hired person is more likely to be an independent contractor.

2.   Liability for Acts of Subservants
A principal may also be liable for the torts committed by a duly authorized subservant. In determining whether a subservant is authorized, you have to determine whether the person who hired him had authority to do so. A bar examination analysis should revolve around the existence or nonexistence of such authority.

    a.   Express Authority to Hire Subservant
A principal may expressly authorize an agent to hire a subservant on her behalf. Where such hiring takes place, the employer-employee relationship comes into being and the doctrine of respondeat superior will apply.
Example: Assume A authorizes B to hire employees on her behalf. Pursuant to this authorization, B hires C. The employer-employee relationship exists between A and C, and *not* between B and C. Under respondeat superior, A is liable for C's torts.

    b.   Implied Authority to Hire Subservant
Authority to hire a subservant can be implied from the circumstances, including past practices of the employee.

      1)   Emergency Situation
If an emergency situation arises and it is reasonably necessary to hire a subservant to protect the principal's interest, the authority to do so will be implied.

      2)   Reasonable to Achieve Result
Under the modern cases, where an employer directs her employee to achieve a result, there is implied authority to use reasonable means to accomplish the task, including the hiring of a subservant.
Example: P hires X to lay bricks, compensating X on the basis of the number of bricks laid. X hires a helper, Y. Nothing has been said about whether X can have a helper, but X is an employee (*i.e.,* he is subject to P's control). P is liable for Y's torts.

c. **No Authority to Hire Subservant**

As a general rule, an employer is not liable for the torts of a subservant engaged without authority.

Example: Sam is hired to drive a delivery truck. Sam is busy one day, so he asks his friend George to drive it for him without permission from his boss. George negligently causes an accident and injures Ted. The boss is not liable for Ted's injuries.

3. **Employer-Employee by Estoppel**

Even though no employer-employee relationship actually exists, a principal may still be held liable on an estoppel theory. Where the principal creates the appearance that an employer-employee relationship exists (though no such relationship actually exists), and a ***third person relies*** upon this appearance, the principal may be estopped from denying the existence of the relationship. If she is so estopped, she can be held liable under respondeat superior.

Example: Assume a shoe repair department in a department store is run by an independent contractor, but the department is run in such a manner that appearances indicate that its operator is an employee of the store. In a tort situation, the store will be estopped from denying the employer-employee relationship; *i.e.,* the store can be found liable for the torts of the department operator. This is a reliance situation. If the department store makes the true relationship known to the public (*e.g.,* by sign, etc.), no liability will be imposed.

4. **Liability for Acts of Borrowed Employees**

An employer may lend the services of her employee to another. If the employee commits a tort while performing in his loaned role, who is liable—*i.e.,* who is the employer? The key issue in determining liability for the employee's torts is whether the borrowing principal or the loaning principal has the primary right of control over the employee. In most situations, the employee remains under the right of control of the ***loaning principal***, and thus he is the only one liable for the employee's torts. However, if the ***borrowing principal directs*** the actions of the employee, she will be liable for those actions if they are performed tortiously.

Example: A owns a snowplow and employs B to operate it. A, either for compensation or without compensation, loans the plow and B to C. While plowing for C, B commits a tort. Is A or C liable under respondeat superior for B's tort? The initial and controlling question continues to be: Who has the right to control the manner in which the job is performed? If the borrowing principal (C) directs the employee's actions, then she is the employer and she is liable under respondeat superior for the employee's tort. If she does not direct the employee's actions, then the loaning principal (A) remains the employer with the right to control and is liable for the employee's tort.

5. **Liability for Acts of Independent Contractors**

It is important to note that there are situations where a principal may be ***directly*** liable in tort without regard to the existence of the employer-employee relationship. These are situations where, as a matter of public policy, liability for the negligence or wrongdoing of an independent contractor will be imposed upon the principal.

a. **Inherently Dangerous Activities**

Where the acts to be performed by the independent contractor are of an inherently dangerous nature, the principal will be held liable for resultant injury (*e.g.,* blasting, demolition, etc.).

b. **Selection of an Incompetent Independent Contractor**

1) **Knowing Selection**

If a principal who hires an incompetent independent contractor has knowledge of his incompetence, she will be liable for the ***contractor's negligence.***

2) **Negligent Selection**

If a principal negligently selects an incompetent independent contractor, she will be liable to the injured party for her ***own negligence*** in selection.

c. **Nondelegable Duties**

There are certain situations in which a principal has a nondelegable duty to act; *e.g.,* a land occupier has a duty to keep land safe for business invitees. When a principal delegates such a duty to an independent contractor and the independent contractor performs negligently, the principal will be liable for the independent contractor's negligence.

C. SCOPE OF EMPLOYMENT

The employer is *not* liable for the torts of her employee *unless* the tort occurred within the scope of the employee's employment. If the tortious conduct was in a "common sense" way associated with the employment, the courts will usually find that it was within the scope of employment. The distinction may be phrased: Was the employee about the employer's business? Three tests generally are used:

(i) Whether the conduct was of the same general nature as, or incident to, that which the employee was employed to perform;

(ii) Whether the conduct was substantially removed from the authorized time and space limits of the employment; and

(iii) Whether the conduct was actuated at least in part by a purpose to serve the employer.

1. Authorization Not Required—Same General Nature as Job

To be within the scope of employment, the employee's conduct does *not* have to be actually authorized. Furthermore, the fact that an act was forbidden by the employer or performed in a manner forbidden by the employer does not necessarily remove it from the scope of employment. There is no easy formula for determining whether conduct is of the same general nature (or incident thereto) as that which the employee was employed to perform. In each instance it is a question of fact. However, serious criminal acts are normally considered to be outside the scope of employment.

2. Frolic and Detour—Time and Space Limitation

Cases involving vehicle accidents are quite often analyzed on the basis of whether the employee was on a frolic or detour. Small or minor deviations from an employer's directions (detour) fall within the scope of employment, while major deviations (frolic) fall outside the scope.

a. Ownership of Vehicle Not Conclusive

1) Employer Ownership

The mere fact that the employee is driving the employer's vehicle at the time the employee commits a tort does not impose liability upon the employer for the employee's tort. For liability to be imposed on the employer, it must be shown that the tort occurred while the employee was within the scope of employment, rather than on his own affairs.

2) Employee Ownership

In some jurisdictions, the fact that the employee was driving his own vehicle at the time he committed a tort creates a *rebuttable presumption* that the employee was not acting within the scope of employment. Thus, if the presumption is not rebutted, the employer would not be liable for the employee's tort.

b. Substantial Departure

Where an employee engages in his own personal affairs while ostensibly at work for the employer, there must be a substantial departure from employment before a court will hold that the employee was on a *frolic*.

c. Proof of Return

Once it is shown that the employee left the scope of employment, there must be proof of return before the employer will be held liable for the employee's tort. For purposes of finding the employer liable, a court will generally require stronger proof that the employee has reentered the scope of employment than that he has remained within the employment once begun.

3. Motivation to Serve Employer

At the time of the act, the employee must be motivated, at least in part, by a desire to serve the purposes of the employer.

a. Passengers

Unless expressly authorized by the employer, the employee's invitation to a third party to ride in the employer's vehicle is generally held to be *outside* the scope of the employment relationship.

1) Unauthorized—Employer Not Liable
Where the employee, without authority, invites a third party to ride in the employer's vehicle and that party is injured by reason of the employee's negligence, the employer is not liable for the third party's injuries.

2) Trespasser—Employer Not Liable
The employer also is not liable for a passenger's injuries where the passenger is riding without an invitation from the employee.

b. Unauthorized Instrumentalities
The employer is generally not liable for torts caused by the employee in the use of an instrumentality *substantially different* from that authorized. The gauge of "substantially different" will be whether the instrument used created a greater risk of harm.
Example: P authorizes X to deliver messages by bike. If X uses a car instead and strikes a pedestrian, P will *not* be liable for the pedestrian's injuries.

c. Trips with Two Purposes
Often, the facts will reveal that the employee is serving two objectives on a trip: one his employer's, one his own. The question of whether he is within the scope of employment is one of fact. A number of courts will generally find that he is within the scope of employment where *any* substantial purpose of the employer is being served.

4. Intentional Torts

The employer is usually not liable for the intentional torts of her employee on the simple ground that an intentional tort is clearly outside the scope of employment. An employee is not, after all, hired to commit intentional torts. However, where the intentional tort occurs as a natural incident to the carrying out of the employer's business, or if any benefit may be found running to the employer, courts tend to hold the employer liable.

a. Physical Injuries

1) Force Is Authorized
Torts that occur in the course of a job such as that of a bouncer will cause an employer to be liable for those torts because the employer has authorized the use of force in the performance of the job at hand.

2) Promotion of the Employer's Business
If the employee intentionally chooses a wrongful means to promote the employer's business, the employer will be held liable for any torts that result.
Example: S, M's employee, is the manager of a store whose employees are on strike and picketing. S, without M's knowledge, hires some thugs to beat up picketers, one of whom is injured. M is liable for the picketer's injuries.

3) Friction Generated by Employment
An employer will be liable for torts that result from friction naturally engendered by the employer's business, such as the friction inherent in bill collection.

b. Fraud
A principal will be liable for the misrepresentations of her agent if the agent had authority (actual, apparent, or inherent) to make statements concerning the subject matter involved.

5. Ratification

An employer may ratify the unauthorized tortious acts of her employee. The same rules previously discussed under ratification of contracts apply. In tort ratification situations, pay particular attention to the requirement that the employer have *knowledge of all material facts*.

BAR REVIEW

Civil Procedure

celebrating
35 YEARS
*of preparing
law students
for the bar exam*

CIVIL PROCEDURE—MASSACHUSETTS

TABLE OF CONTENTS

I. INTRODUCTION

The adoption of the Massachusetts Rules of Civil Procedure ("Massachusetts Rules") substantially changed civil practice in Massachusetts. The Massachusetts Rules are patterned after the Federal Rules of Civil Procedure ("Federal Rules"), and the Massachusetts Supreme Judicial Court looks to federal court decisions construing the Federal Rules for guidance in interpreting the state rules. The Massachusetts Rules of Appellate Procedure are likewise patterned on the Federal Rules of Appellate Procedure. As a result, Massachusetts practice now resembles the federal civil procedure customarily taught in law school courses, making the subject easier to review. Indeed, you may find that the only new and unfamiliar material is set out in the following section, describing the organization and subject matter jurisdiction of the Massachusetts courts.

The Massachusetts Rules principally govern procedure before the superior court, single justice sessions of the supreme judicial court, and district court actions commenced after or pending on July 1, 1996. The Massachusetts Rules of Appellate Procedure govern the appellate process in both the supreme judicial court and the appeals court.

It should be noted that each court in Massachusetts also has its own set of rules that apply to that court. For example, the Superior Court is also governed by the Rules and Standing Orders of the Superior Court. This outline does not attempt to cover each and every rule that applies to each individual court.

You will likely have one bar exam question that deals solely with procedural issues. Additionally, be alert for procedural issues in any question that refers to a lawsuit.

Note: For your convenience, references will sometimes be included in these materials in brackets. It is not suggested that you memorize the references for the bar examination.

The bar commonly uses the pre-Court Reorganization Act names of the state trial courts, and the "old" names will sometimes be used in these materials. In most cases the formal (or "new") name is the "old" name with "department" appended to it, *e.g.,* the "Boston Municipal Court" is officially the "Boston Municipal Court Department" of the Trial Court of Massachusetts.

II. ORGANIZATION OF THE MASSACHUSETTS COURTS

A. OVERVIEW
Massachusetts has a familiar three-tier court system consisting of:

(i)   Supreme judicial court;

(ii) Appeals court; and

(iii) Trial court (consisting of departments).

Lawsuits go to trial in a department of the trial court, and the final judgment may be appealed to the appeals court with a further discretionary appeal to the supreme judicial court. Two of the most important variations on this theme—developed below—are (i) the trial de novo (in some circumstances) in the superior court department of the trial court of lawsuits initially heard by the district court department, and (ii) the exercise of original (*i.e.,* trial as opposed to appellate) jurisdiction by the single justice session of the supreme judicial court.

B. THE TRIAL COURTS OF THE COMMONWEALTH
The 1978 Court Reorganization Act created the trial court. Unfortunately, confusion is likely to arise from the fact that the legislation did not actually establish a new court. The Court Reorganization Act's principal goal was to improve the administration of the judicial system, and the trial court is the administrative "umbrella" created for the various state trial courts. These courts are now formally denominated "departments" of the trial court, but the change has little jurisdictional significance. (More significant changes were made in criminal practice.)

C. SELECTING A COURT—SUBJECT MATTER JURISDICTION

1. Introduction
Subject matter jurisdiction determines which court can hear the case. After the attorney has determined the substantive law theory (or theories) on which the plaintiff's lawsuit will be

based, the next task is to determine which court (or courts) is competent to hear the case. The inquiry, in conceptual terms, is which court(s) has "jurisdiction over the subject matter." The inquiry focuses on the legal claim asserted by the plaintiff—not on the parties to the lawsuit (*cf.* jurisdiction over the person, F., *infra*). State statutes (and occasionally the state constitution) creating the courts and vesting them with jurisdiction to decide certain types of cases answer this question. (The exceptions to this principle are cases over which the United States Congress has vested exclusive jurisdiction in the federal courts, *e.g.,* patent and copyright litigation.)

The next segment of the materials briefly summarizes the subject matter jurisdiction over civil cases of each of the departments in the trial court. The first two departments described (superior court and district court) have general civil jurisdiction. The remaining departments have more specialized functions.

2. Superior Court Department

    a. Generally
    The superior court is the principal trial court in the Massachusetts judicial system. There is one superior court in each county. It has subject matter jurisdiction over most (but not all) civil actions. [Mass. Gen. L. ch. 212] Generally, this means that the subject matter jurisdiction of the other departments in the trial court is *concurrent* with the superior court's jurisdiction. Two significant examples of this principle are that the superior court's subject matter jurisdiction is:

        1) Concurrent with the district court department in actions at law; and

        2) Concurrent with the probate and family court department in equity (but not in law actions).

    b. Distinctive Features
    Two distinguishing features of the superior court's jurisdiction are that parties can obtain both jury trials (in law actions) and equitable relief (*i.e.,* injunctions). The other tribunals are more limited in one or both of these respects.

    c. Jurisdiction
    Illustrations of the superior court's jurisdiction include:

        1) Actions at law (*e.g.,* personal injury and contract actions);

        2) Equity actions (*e.g.,* specific performance of contracts and injunctions);

        3) Declaratory judgment actions;

        4) Judicial review of adjudicatory proceedings before administrative agencies (this jurisdiction is exclusive of the other courts—exceptions are the supreme judicial court reviews of utility ratemaking proceedings and the district court reviews of unemployment compensation decisions);

        5) De novo trials in actions originally decided by the district court (*see* 3.d., *infra*);

        6) Review of zoning boards of appeal;

        7) Injunctive relief in labor controversies (exclusive original jurisdiction); and

        8) Injunctive relief against unfair trade practices pursuant to the Consumer Protection Act. [Mass. Gen. L. ch. 93A]

3. District Court Department and Municipal Courts
There may be more than one district court in each county. The district courts (including the Boston Municipal Court) have *concurrent* jurisdiction with the superior court over all civil actions in which money damages are sought. The district court can also award equitable relief in certain circumstances. [Mass. Gen. L. ch. 218, §19] The second principal distinction between the district and superior courts is that jury trials are not always available in the district court. There are, however, exceptions to this rule. For example, in recent years, many counties have experimented with a system permitting six-person jury trials in district court.

a.   **Concurrent Jurisdiction**
The district court has concurrent jurisdiction with the superior court over individual consumers' claims under the General Laws of the Commonwealth of Massachusetts ("Massachusetts General Laws") chapter 93A, section 9 for money damages arising out of the use of unfair and deceptive trade practices. However, only the superior court may adjudicate class actions or enjoin the use of deceptive practices under this statute.

b.   **De Novo Review of District Court Judgments**
The superior and district courts, as noted above, have concurrent jurisdiction over civil actions seeking money damages without regard to the amount in controversy. This means, for example, that a tort action may be filed in either court no matter how great or how slight the injury. Although this is an accurate statement of the concurrent subject matter jurisdiction over civil actions, there is a more complex relationship between the two courts which can result in a de novo trial before the superior court of cases initially decided by the district court. Under the applicable procedure, the superior court may transfer the action back to the district court if it appears that the plaintiff will not be able to recover more than $25,000 exclusive of interest and costs. In addition, as discussed below (*see* e., *infra*), a defendant may attempt to remove a case from district to superior court if the plaintiff's alleged damages exceed $25,000.

c.   **Removal and Remand**
The discussion of the trial de novo system is divided into two categories: (i) the removal of district court cases to the superior court, and (ii) the remand of cases from the superior court to the district court. The principal issues in each category are:

1)   Which court will initially hear and decide the case?

2)   How can the parties preserve the right to have the case heard and decided a second time before the superior court (the trial de novo)?

d.   **De Novo Trial**
In a trial de novo, the superior court actually hears all the evidence again (but the prevailing party can use the district court judgment to establish a prima facie case). The superior court, in other words, is not exercising appellate jurisdiction in the conventional sense of the word. Instead, the superior court is conducting a second trial.

e.   **Removal of District Court Cases to Superior Court**

1)   **Civil Actions**
A plaintiff who elects to bring a civil action in district court that could have been brought in superior court will be deemed to have waived a trial by jury and her right to appeal to the superior court, unless she files in the district court, within 30 days of commencement of the action or service of a responsive pleading, a claim to a jury trial in superior court. [Mass. Gen. L. ch. 231, §103]

A defendant may remove a civil action from district court to superior court if the action involves an amount in excess of $25,000 and the defendant follows the procedure outlined below. [Mass. Gen. L. ch. 231, §104]

2)   **Procedure**
Removal is accomplished by filing in the district court a written claim of trial before the superior court (with a fee and bond) within 25 days after service of the pleading which triggers the removal right (here the complaint or counterclaim). The same rules apply to claims filed by or against third parties.

Note that as discussed above, exercise of the removal right means that a lawsuit initially filed in the district court is transferred to the superior court at the pleading stage of the case (*i.e.,* the district court will never hear the case), and that the failure to exercise the removal right means the case will be decided by the district court without any further review (trial de novo) before the superior court. Contrast this situation with example 1), below, in which essentially the same process takes place *after* the district court trial.

Examples: 1) The plaintiff files a case in the district court in which the amount in controversy is $25,000 or *less*. If she does not file a claim to a jury trial, she waives a jury trial and trial de novo before the superior court. The defendant *cannot remove* the case to the superior court *prior* to trial in the district court. The defendant may remove the case to the superior court for a trial de novo after notice of the decision or finding. [Mass. Gen. L. ch. 231, §104]

2) The same basic rules apply if the defendant files a counterclaim against the plaintiff. The plaintiff may remove the case from the district court *prior* to trial if the amount claimed in a permissive or compulsory counterclaim *exceeds* $25,000. The plaintiff may remove the case *only after* the district court trial if the amount claimed in the permissive or compulsory counterclaim is for *less* than $25,000 (*see* example 1), above). The defendant may remove the case *prior* to the district court trial if the defendant's *compulsory* counterclaim is for an amount in excess of $25,000—even if the plaintiff's claim is for $25,000 or less (a variation of example 1), above). [Mass. Gen. L. ch. 231, §104]

f. **Remand of Cases from Superior Court to District Court**
The superior court may, either on its own motion or on the motion of the plaintiff or defendant, transfer a civil action for trial to the district court from which it was removed or in which it could have been brought originally, if the superior court determines that there is no reasonable likelihood that the plaintiff's recovery will exceed $25,000 if she prevails. [Mass. Gen. L. ch. 102C]

4. **Supreme Judicial Court—Single Justice**
One member of the supreme judicial court regularly sits in the single justice session and exercises trial-type jurisdiction. [Mass. Gen. L. ch. 214, §1] The single justice has jurisdiction—concurrent with the superior court—over all civil actions seeking equitable relief (except injunctions in labor disputes). The single justice can, and frequently does, transfer cases in its concurrent original jurisdiction to lower courts. [Mass. Gen. L. ch. 211, §4A] The single justice (as well as the full bench of the supreme judicial court) also has power to issue writs of superintendence to all inferior courts [Mass. Gen. L. ch. 211, §3]—a power exercised only in exceptional circumstances. The single justice session is *not* a department of the trial court—it is described here for organizational simplicity.

5. **Probate and Family Court Department**
The probate court exercises three principal kinds of subject matter jurisdiction:

(i) Probate of wills, administration of estates, trusts, and the appointment of guardians and conservators;

(ii) Divorce, separate support, adoption, change of names, and annulment; and

(iii) The execution and validity of health care proxies pursuant to Massachusetts General Laws chapter 201D.

The probate court has *exclusive original* jurisdiction over these matters. As noted above, the probate court also has concurrent original jurisdiction with the superior court and supreme judicial court over actions seeking equitable relief. [Mass. Gen. L. ch. 215, §6]

6. **Land Court Department**
The subject matter jurisdiction of the land court is limited to actions relating to title to land. [Mass. Gen. L. ch. 185]

a. **Exclusive Jurisdiction**
The land court has exclusive original jurisdiction over actions to:

1) Register title to land;

2) Foreclose tax titles;

3) Discharge mortgages; and

4) Determine municipal boundaries.

b. **Concurrent Jurisdiction**
The land court also has concurrent original jurisdiction with the superior court and supreme judicial court to grant equitable relief in actions concerning any right, title, or interest in land. (*Exception:* The probate courts have the power to distribute real property incident to a divorce action.)

Note: The land court lacks jurisdiction to order specific performance of contracts to convey land.

7. Housing Court Department

a. Five Housing Courts

The five housing court divisions serve the following areas: the city of Boston, Worcester County (including some towns in Norfolk and Middlesex Counties), Hampden County, southeastern division (including cities and towns of Bristol and Plymouth Counties), and northeastern division (including Essex County, and some cities and towns in northern Middlesex County). The housing courts have jurisdiction over all actions which involve the health, safety, and welfare of the occupants or owners of real property in Massachusetts. [Mass. Gen. L. ch. 185C, §3]

b. Miscellaneous

The housing court may grant money damages or equitable relief and conduct jury trials. Its subject matter jurisdiction is concurrent with the superior and district courts, *except* that a party may not transfer a case pending before the housing court to another trial court. However, a party can, prior to trial, transfer an action from another trial court to the housing court. There is no de novo trial before the superior court (or elsewhere) of cases decided by the housing court.

8. Juvenile Court Department

The juvenile court department was expanded in 1993 to include divisions in Suffolk County (Boston), Barnstable County, including the town of Plymouth, and Plymouth, Norfolk, Middlesex, Essex, Worcester, Franklin, Hampshire, Berkshire, Hampden, and Bristol Counties, with several sessions at different locations within each division. [Mass. Gen. L. ch. 218, §57] The juvenile courts (or sessions) exercise exclusive original jurisdiction over delinquency (violations of criminal statutes by offenders between seven and 17 years of age) and jurisdiction in equity concurrent with the supreme judicial court and the superior court department over children in need of services ("CHINS") cases. [Mass. Gen. L. ch. 119, §§39E, 55]

9. Small Claims

Small claims is a special session of the district court designed to hear civil actions (except libel and slander) where the amount in controversy does not exceed $2,000, exclusive of interest and costs. [Mass. Gen. L. ch. 218, §21] The court may award double or triple damages (where provided by statute) even if the total judgment then exceeds $2,000. (*Exception:* There is no amount in controversy limitation for motor vehicle property damage claims; and any judgment in such actions can have no collateral estoppel or res judicata effect in later personal injury claims arising from the same motor vehicle accident. [Mass. Gen. L. ch. 218, §23])

a. Distinctions

Small claims provides *informal procedures*. The rules of pleading are modified, there is no discovery, and summary judgment is not available. Choice of small claims by the plaintiff waives all rights to appeal, jury trial, and trial de novo. The district court has discretion to move a case from small claims to its regular civil docket, and unsuccessful *defendants* may obtain a de novo jury trial.

10. Declaratory Judgments

Where an actual controversy has arisen and is set forth in the pleadings, the supreme judicial court, the superior court, the land court, and the probate court may make binding declarations of right, duty, status, and other legal relations. [Mass. Gen. L. ch. 231A; Mass. R. Civ. P. 57] The procedure is also available to test the legality of certain administrative practices and procedures. It is essential for maintenance of a suit for declaratory relief that there be factual allegations showing an actual controversy; the court may refuse to render a declaratory judgment where it would not terminate the controversy giving rise to the proceedings. The procedure is applicable to secure declaratory determinations in questions concerning deeds, wills, or written contracts. Where the construction or validity of a statute or administrative regulation is in issue, the procedure for declaratory judgment is also permitted. The rule that declaratory judgment is intended to resolve an actual controversy is particularly pertinent where judgment is sought on the constitutionality of a statute. [Quincy City Hospital v. Rate Setting Commission, 406 Mass. 431 (1990)]

D. APPELLATE COURTS

The organization of the Massachusetts appellate courts is discussed in detail in section IX., *infra*.

E. SELECTING A COURT—VENUE

1. Introduction

Venue presents a related but narrower issue in selecting the proper court. Venue rules exist to allocate cases among the courts that have subject matter jurisdiction over a particular controversy. Venue rules are not jurisdictional (*i.e.,* objections to the venue of a lawsuit in a particular court are waived if they are not seasonably asserted by the defendant).

Example: The plaintiff intends to file a $15,000 breach of warranty suit in the superior court which (along with the district court) has subject matter jurisdiction. The superior court is a statewide court system sitting in each of the 14 counties in Massachusetts. The venue rules define the county or counties (*i.e.,* the division of the superior court) in which the lawsuit may be filed.

2. Venue Rules

The foundation of *all* venue rules is the geographic organization of the judicial system, which is based on:

a. *Counties* for the superior, probate, and land courts; and

b. *Judicial districts* for the district courts (judicial districts are subdivisions of counties).

3. General Venue Rules

a. Local Actions

Local actions must be brought in the county or the judicial district for the district court where the property is located. [Mass. Gen. L. ch. 223, §4] Local actions for title or possession of land, summary process [Mass. Gen. L. ch. 239], zoning appeals, and petitions in the probate court for the partition of land are examples of actions in this category.

b. Replevin Actions

Replevin actions constitute a very small category of actions in which the plaintiff seeks redelivery of personal property. Replevin actions must be brought in the county where the property is located. [Mass. Gen. L. ch. 223, §4] (The district court lacks subject matter jurisdiction over replevin actions. [Mass. Gen. L. ch. 214, §3])

c. Transitory Actions

1) Defined

Transitory actions are best defined as all actions which are *not local actions*. Most lawsuits, including tort and contract actions, belong in this category. By statute, actions for rent, use and occupation, or breach of covenant arising out of the use of real property are classified as transitory actions. [Mass. Gen. L. ch. 223, §3]

2) Venue Rule

Transitory actions may be filed in the county or the judicial district for the district court where *either party* (plaintiff or defendant) *resides* or has a *usual place of business*. [Mass. Gen. L. ch. 223, §1] "Usual place of business" does not include the place where an employee works.

A corporation may also sue or be sued in the county or judicial district where it usually holds its annual shareholders' meetings or where it held its last meeting. [Mass. Gen. L. ch. 223, §8] For actions in the district court only, a lawsuit may also be filed in a judicial district that *adjoins* the judicial district in which either party resides or has a usual place of business. [Mass. Gen. L. ch. 223, §2]

d. Special Venue Rules

1) Action by the Commonwealth

An action by the Commonwealth must be brought in *Suffolk* County, or in the county or judicial district where the *defendant* lives or has a usual place of business. [Mass. Gen. L. ch. 223, §5]

2) Trustee Process Actions

a) Generally

Trustee process actions must be brought in the county or judicial district where the *trustee* (not the plaintiff or defendant) resides or has a usual place of business. [Mass. Gen. L. ch. 246, §2] However, if the approval of trustee process is sought in connection with a transitory action in a district court, the action should be brought in the judicial district where one of the parties or any person alleged to be trustee lives or has a usual place of business, or in a district adjoining one where a party or alleged trustee lives or has a usual place of business. [Mass. Gen. L. ch. 223, §2]

b) Nonsupport Cases
Nonsupport actions must be brought in a probate and family court, in the court which issued the judgment of divorce or support, or where an action for divorce or support is pending. [Mass. Gen. L. ch. 208, §36A]

3) Actions by or Against Counties
Actions by or against counties must be brought in the county where the defendant lives or an adjoining county. Where the plaintiff is a county and the defendant lives in that county, venue lies only in an adjoining county. Where a county is the defendant, the plaintiff may bring the action in the county where the plaintiff lives, in the defendant county, or in an adjoining county. [Mass. Gen. L. ch. 223, §6]

4) Small Claims Actions
Small claims actions can be brought in the judicial district where either the plaintiff or defendant resides or has a usual place of business (district court has exclusive subject matter jurisdiction). [Mass. Gen. L. ch. 218, §21] *Note:* If the action is brought against a residential landlord, the action may also be brought in the judicial district where the property is located.

5) Supplementary Process Actions
Supplementary process actions may be brought only in the judicial district in which the *defendant* lives, has a usual place of business or employment, *or was arrested* (district court has exclusive original jurisdiction). [Mass. Gen. L. ch. 224, §6]

6) If Neither Party Lives in the Commonwealth
If neither party resides in the Commonwealth, venue lies in any county (but beware of jurisdictional problems). [Mass. Gen. L. ch. 223, §§1, 2]

e. Change of Venue
If venue is erroneous, the court may transfer the case to an appropriate court or dismiss the action without prejudice to a future filing. Venue may also be changed to assure an impartial trial (*e.g.,* for prejudicial pretrial publicity).

f. Consolidation of Actions
If actions arising out of the same transaction or occurrence are pending before several Massachusetts courts, they may, in the court's discretion, be consolidated for trial in one court.

g. Forum Selection Clauses
A forum selection clause is a contract provision requiring that any suit to enforce the contract be brought in a specific venue. Massachusetts recently decided that forum selection clauses would be given full effect absent fraud, duress, abuse of economic power, or other unconscionable behavior. [Jacobson v. Mailboxes Etc. U.S.A., Inc., 419 Mass. 572 (1995)] Note, however, that such clauses do not govern precontractual behavior.

F.   SELECTING A COURT—JURISDICTION OVER THE PERSON
To recapitulate, at this point the plaintiff's attorney has: (i) determined a legal claim for the forthcoming lawsuit; (ii) identified the proper parties to the plaintiff's claim; (iii) identified the state court(s) with subject matter jurisdiction to adjudicate the plaintiff's claim; and (iv) refined the identification of the court(s) to those which also have proper venue over the parties.

The final step before commencing the lawsuit is to determine whether the Massachusetts judiciary can exercise jurisdiction over the defendants. (In practice, the attorney will consider jurisdiction over the person and service of process on the defendant simultaneously. Discussion of service of process is postponed because service is not made until the complaint is filed.)

1.   Subject Matter Jurisdiction Distinguished
At the outset, it is important to distinguish the concepts of jurisdiction over the subject

matter and jurisdiction over the person. Subject matter jurisdiction looks to the nature of the *legal claims* asserted in the lawsuit. The purpose is to determine: first, whether the state (or sovereign) permits its courts to adjudicate the claim; and second, which court (or courts) within the state judicial system may decide the claim. Jurisdiction over the subject matter, in other words, is a matter of state law (except where federal courts have exclusive jurisdiction); its principal function is to allocate lawsuits among the component courts within the state judicial system.

Jurisdiction over the person, by contrast, assumes that a Massachusetts court has jurisdiction over the subject matter; the question is whether the subject matter jurisdiction can be exercised in this *particular case* with respect to a particular defendant. Analysis of jurisdiction over the person focuses on the *parties* to the lawsuit—not on the nature of the legal claim presented. The function of jurisdiction over the person is to allocate litigation among the 50 states' judicial systems. It ensures that traditional notions of fair play are not offended by requiring or forcing a particular defendant to defend the lawsuit in the courts of the forum state selected by the plaintiff.

2. Foundation of Jurisdiction Over the Person

a. Background

Traditionally, personal jurisdiction over an individual or over property was premised on physical presence in the state. [*See* Burnham v. Superior Court, 495 U.S. 604 (1990)—upholding personal jurisdiction over a transient defendant served within a state for a cause of action unrelated to his brief presence in the state] The state's courts had sovereignty over persons within its boundaries, but no power to affect the rights of individuals outside the state. [Pennoyer v. Neff, 95 U.S. 714 (1877)] Thus, service of process on a defendant in the state was the only, and remains today the most common, basis for obtaining personal jurisdiction. However, the *Pennoyer* approach proved unsatisfactory because of the inability to reach individuals located out of state who had significant effects on and relationships with the state and its citizens. The interesting questions about personal jurisdiction today relate to the ability of the state courts to reach defendants who are beyond its boundaries.

b. Personal Jurisdiction Issues

Analysis of personal jurisdiction focuses on two principal questions:

(i) Does Massachusetts law authorize its courts to exercise jurisdiction over the person in this particular case?

(ii) Does the state law authorization transgress the federal constitutional limits imposed on the exercise of jurisdiction over the person by the Due Process Clause of the Fourteenth Amendment?

Each of these two questions, in turn, breaks down into two subsidiary questions, which can be stated in terms of the requirements imposed by the Due Process Clause:

(i) Are the *minimum contacts* between the defendant and the forum state such that the "maintenance of the suit does not offend 'traditional notions of fair play and substantial justice' "? [International Shoe Co. v. Washington, 326 U.S. 310 (1945)]

(ii) Has the defendant received reasonable *notice* that the suit has been brought? [Mullane v. Central Hanover Bank & Trust Co., 339 U.S. 306 (1950)]

As we shall see, Massachusetts law always requires notice to the defendant that a lawsuit has been filed against him. Usually, this is done by *service of process* (*see* H., *infra*); on occasion a form of "substituted" service of process is permitted (*e.g.,* registered mail or publication). Constitutional questions are unlikely to arise in this area as long as the plaintiff strictly adheres to the state law requirements (unless the defendant is out of state and does not receive actual notice of the action).

The "minimum contacts" between the defendant, the subject of the litigation, and the forum state required to exercise jurisdiction over the person present more substantial questions, however. The remainder of this section will focus on this topic.

3. **Residence, Domicile, and Consent**

    a. **Residence and Domicile**
    A Massachusetts court can exercise jurisdiction over the person if the defendant resides, has a usual place of business, or has a place of domicile within the state. Domicile or residence satisfies the Due Process Clause's minimum contacts requirement. (Of course, the defendant must also receive notice of the action.)

    b. **Consent**
    A party may also consent to the exercise of jurisdiction over the person. However, recall that, by contrast, the parties *cannot* consent to the exercise of jurisdiction over the *subject matter*.

        1) **Plaintiff Consents by Filing**
        The plaintiff consents merely by the act of filing suit in a Massachusetts court, and this consent extends to counterclaims filed by the defendant. [Mass. Gen. L. ch. 227, §2]

        2) **Defendant Consents by Appearing**
        The defendant consents if she appears in the action (*e.g.,* by filing a responsive pleading, including an answer) and does not object to the court's exercise of jurisdiction over her person.

        3) **Incorporation Is Consent**
        Massachusetts law also provides that the act of incorporation in Massachusetts establishes jurisdiction over the person. [Mass. Gen. L. ch. 223A, §2]

        4) **Consent by Contract**
        Parties to a commercial contract may consent in advance to the jurisdiction of a Massachusetts court as to claims arising out of breach of that contract. Such may be accomplished by appointing an in-state resident as an agent for purposes of service of process. [National Equipment Rental v. Szukhent, 375 U.S. 311 (1964)]

    c. **Lack of Consent**
    There is no consent to jurisdiction over the person if:

        1) The plaintiff procured the defendant's presence in the state by *fraud* or *duress*; or

        2) The defendant is present in the state merely to participate in *unrelated litigation*.

    d. **Summary for Bar Exam**
    In sum, you should be alert to a jurisdiction over the person issue in any bar examination question involving a defendant who is not an inhabitant of Massachusetts or who does not have a usual place of business here.

4. **Long Arm Statute**

    a. **Generally**
    Massachusetts has enacted a "long arm" statute [Mass. Gen. L. ch. 223A], which permits its courts to exercise jurisdiction over the person of certain individuals and businesses even though they lack a Massachusetts domicile, residence, or principal place of business. The supreme judicial court has held that the long arm statute confers jurisdiction over the person to the limits allowed by the federal Due Process Clause. [Splaine v. Modern Electroplating, Inc., 391 Mass. 1106 (1984)]

    b. **Application**
    The long arm statute provides that a Massachusetts court (which has subject matter jurisdiction) may exercise jurisdiction over a person who commits an actionable act while performing one or more of the following activities:

        1) Transacting any business in Massachusetts (defendant need not be physically present in the state);

        2) Contracting to supply services or things in Massachusetts;

        3) Causing tortious injury in Massachusetts by an act or omission in Massachusetts;

4) Causing tortious injury in Massachusetts by an act or omission elsewhere, provided that the defendant regularly does or solicits business, engages in any other persistent course of conduct, or derives substantial revenue from goods used or consumed or services rendered in Massachusetts;

5) Holding an interest in, using, or possessing real property in Massachusetts;

6) Contracting to insure any person, property, or risk located within the Commonwealth at the time of contracting [*see* McGee v. International Life Insurance Co., 355 U.S. 220 (1957)]; or

7) Living as one of the parties in a marriage where the marital domicile has been in the Commonwealth for at least one year within the two years prior to the commencement of the action; the action being valid as to all obligations or modifications of alimony, custody, child support, or property settlement orders relating to said marriage or former marriage, if the plaintiff continues to live within the Commonwealth regardless of the defendant's departure from Massachusetts.

c. **Scope of Long Arm Statute**

A good example of the expansive reading given to the long arm statute is *Good Hope Industries v. Ryder Scott Co.,* 378 Mass. 1 (1979). A corporation incorporated in Massachusetts, and with its principal place of business there, solicited a Texas corporation to appraise the value of its natural gas holdings in Texas. The supreme judicial court upheld the exercise of jurisdiction over the defendant Texas corporation for a claim arising out of the appraisals. The court pointed to the fact that the contract called for the defendant to deliver the appraisals in Massachusetts plus the existence of invoices, telephone calls, etc., in this state.

The *Good Hope Industries* decision defines the outermost reach of the long arm statute. One facet of the decision is particularly significant: The court's statement that the constitutional and statutory inquiry is whether there was "some minimum contact with the Commonwealth which resulted from an affirmative, intentional act of the defendant, such that it is fair and reasonable to require the defendant to come into the state to defend the action." The supreme judicial court as well as many federal courts in Massachusetts have reaffirmed this notion in several decisions. Essentially, the courts have sought to protect Massachusetts plaintiffs in their dealings with out-of-state defendants. As long as a defendant has engaged in activities having commercial ramifications in Massachusetts, it is likely to be subjected to the in personam jurisdiction of the Massachusetts courts.

5. **Federal Constitution**

Assertion of personal jurisdiction pursuant to the Massachusetts long arm statute is subject to limitations set by the Due Process Clause of the Fourteenth Amendment. The 1945 Supreme Court decision in *International Shoe* expanded the permissible reach of state courts beyond state boundaries to allow jurisdiction over out-of-state defendants when there are "minimum contacts" between the defendant and the forum state such that maintenance of the suit does not offend "traditional notions of fair play and substantial justice." Application of this standard leads to a highly fact-based analysis of the relationship between the parties, the underlying transaction, and the forum state, and often does not produce clear-cut, predictable results. The factors which have been given most weight by the Supreme Court in its recent decisions are:

(i) The level of activity or effects caused by the defendant in the forum state;

(ii) The nexus or relationship between the cause of action and those activities or effects;

(iii) Whether the defendant has purposefully availed himself of the privilege of conducting activity within the state, thus involving the benefits and protections of its laws;

(iv) Whether the defendant's conduct and connection with the forum state are such that he should reasonably anticipate being haled into court there;

(v) The inconvenience to the defendant of litigating in the forum state;

(vi) The interest of the forum state in providing a remedy for the plaintiff; and

(vii) The availability of other more convenient forums.

Since the Supreme Court's decision in *World-Wide Volkswagen Corp. v. Woodson,* 444 U.S. 286 (1980), it appears that greater emphasis is placed on the contacts between the defendant and the forum state (factors (i)-(iv), above) than on considerations of fairness and inconvenience. However, in analyzing a personal jurisdiction question on the bar exam, you should note that if the state long arm statute is satisfied, the contacts requirement of the constitutional test will presumably also be met. The long arm statute requires that the claim against the defendant arise out of one of the enumerated activities, any one of which would be "minimum contacts" under the constitutional standard. Thus, it will usually be the case that you only need to consider, in addition, the "fair play and substantial justice" factors in order to conclude whether due process has been satisfied.

6. Traditional Classifications Abolished

Traditionally, analysis of jurisdiction over the person was commonly divided into three subheadings according to the type of jurisdiction which was being exercised:

(i) In personam;

(ii) In rem; and

(iii) Quasi in rem.

a. In Personam

Briefly stated, in personam jurisdiction involves the typical lawsuit where the plaintiff seeks to recover money damages (*i.e.,* a "personal" judgment) against the defendant. The *International Shoe* case (5., *supra*) required "minimum contacts" between the defendant and the forum state to exercise in personam jurisdiction—residence, domicile, or consent meets this test. The Full Faith and Credit Clause requires other states' courts to honor a judgment rendered in personam.

b. In Rem and Quasi In Rem

In rem and quasi in rem jurisdiction could be exercised even where the court did ***not*** have in personam jurisdiction over the defendant. For example, a court could exercise in rem jurisdiction to adjudicate a case involving title to land (the res) if the land were located in the state. Quasi in rem jurisdiction was a hybrid. For example, it permitted the court to render a money judgment in the plaintiff's favor by attaching the defendant's land (or other property) in Massachusetts, but the judgment could be satisfied only out of the attached property (*i.e.,* it was not a personal judgment against the defendant). A judgment rendered quasi in rem was not entitled to full faith and credit against the defendant in other states.

c. Decision in *Shaffer v. Heitner*

These separate categories are no longer significant in analysis of personal jurisdiction problems. In *Shaffer v. Heitner,* 433 U.S. 186 (1977), the Supreme Court abolished the distinction, applying the "minimum contacts" test of the *International Shoe* decision to all three of the traditional jurisdictional classifications. The result is that actions classified as in rem and quasi in rem must meet a higher standard to pass constitutional muster than under the overruled doctrine of *Pennoyer v. Neff, supra.*

7. Forum Non Conveniens

A court may dismiss a lawsuit under the doctrine of forum non conveniens, even where the constitutional and statutory tests for jurisdiction over the person are satisfied, if the court determines that ***the ends of justice would be better served by trial of the action in another state***. In so determining, the court will consider such factors as (i) the location of the parties, (ii) the expense of litigation (*e.g.,* of securing attendance of witnesses), (iii) the availability of witnesses, (iv) the ease of access to proof, (v) the enforceability of the judgment, and (vi) described by many courts as possibly the "most important" factor, the ability to bring the suit in another state (*i.e.,* one in which the suit is not barred by a statute of limitations). [New Amsterdam Casualty Co. v. Estes, 353 Mass. 90 (1967); Green v. Manhattanville, 40 Mass. App. Ct. 76 (1996)]

G. COMMENCING THE ACTION

1. Generally

A civil action is commenced when the plaintiff *files the written complaint* (*see* III.B.2., *infra*) and the entry fee with the clerk of court. [Mass. R. Civ. P. 3]

2. Certified Mail

Alternatively, the action is commenced when the ***plaintiff mails*** the complaint and entry fee to the clerk by certified or registered mail. [Mass. R. Civ. P. 3]

3. Regular Mail

The plaintiff may also use ordinary mail, but then the action is not commenced until the clerk actually ***receives*** the complaint and entry fee.

4. Tolling

Commencement tolls the statute of limitations. Thus, the method of mailing assumes significance only when the statute of limitations is about to expire.

H. SERVICE OF PROCESS

1. Mechanics

a. The Summons

Service of process provides notice to the defendant of the pendency of the lawsuit. The summons directs the defendant to appear and defend within the time set by the rules, and notifies the defendant that failure to appear and defend may result in a default judgment for the relief requested in the complaint. The summons should identify the court and the parties, bear the signature or facsimile of the clerk of the court, and state the name and address of the plaintiff's attorney, if any, otherwise it should state the plaintiff's address. The summons needs to be obtained from the court in which the complaint is filed.

b. Service

The plaintiff must deliver a summons and a copy of the complaint to a process server (sheriff or person specially appointed by the court) who then serves the summons and complaint on each defendant. A "return of service" (*i.e.,* the officer's written statement of when, where, and how the complaint and summons were served) is then filed with the clerk of the court. [Mass. R. Civ. P. 4]

2. Timing

The service of the summons and complaint must be made on the defendant, and the filing of the return of service with the court, within 90 days after filing the complaint. If this is not done, the court can dismiss the complaint upon its own initiative, with notice, unless the party required to serve process can show good cause why it was not served. [Mass. R. Civ. P. 4(j)]

3. Service Within Massachusetts

Service of the summons and complaint is made within Massachusetts in the following manner [Mass. R. Civ. P. 4(d)]:

a. On an Individual

An individual may be served by:

(i) Delivery to the defendant personally.

(ii) Leaving the papers at the defendant's last and usual place of abode. If the case is in district court, a copy must also be mailed to the defendant. [Mass. Gen. L. ch. 223, §31] *Note:* Unlike under the Federal Rules, service at a defendant's last and usual place of abode does not require that service be left with a person of suitable age and discretion.

(iii) Delivery to the defendant's agent.

If after a diligent search service cannot be made as above, the plaintiff may apply to the court to issue an order of notice by alternative means.

b. On a Corporation

A corporation can be served by delivery to:

(i) A corporate officer;

(ii) A managing or general agent; or

(iii) The person in charge at the corporation's principal place of business.

If none of the foregoing can be found, the court can order service on the corporation itself by delivery of an order of notice to the secretary of state who forwards it by registered mail, return receipt requested, to the corporation. [Mass. Gen. L. ch. 223, §§37, 38]

c.   On a Partnership
Generally, a partnership may be served by serving each of the partners as individuals.

d.   On the Commonwealth or a State Agency
The Commonwealth or a state agency may be served by delivery (or by certified or registered mail) to the attorney general (in Boston) and to the agency's office, or to the agency's chairman, one of its members, or its secretary or clerk.

e.   On Cities, Towns, and Counties
Cities, towns, and counties may be served by delivery (or by certified or registered mail) to the treasurer or clerk or their office.

4.   Service Outside Massachusetts
Service is made outside Massachusetts (assuming jurisdiction over the person) pursuant to the long arm statute (*see* F.4., *supra*) by the following methods, "when reasonably calculated to give actual notice" [Mass. Gen. L. ch. 223A, §6; *and see* Mass. R. Civ. P. 4(e)(1) - (5)]:

a.   Delivery in the same manner as process is served in Massachusetts;

b.   Service in the manner prescribed by the law of the place where the defendant is located;

c.   Mail, return receipt requested, to the defendant;

d.   On a nonresident motorist, by delivery to the registrar of motor vehicles, and by registered or certified mail, return receipt requested, to the defendant [Mass. Gen. L. ch. 90, §3c]; or

e.   A method ordered by the court (or as directed by a foreign authority in response to a letter rogatory).

5.   Service of Process and Commencement of Action
Service of process (as opposed to commencement of the action) starts the clock running on the 20-day time period within which the defendant has to file a responsive pleading with the court. Note that service also satisfies the Due Process Clause's "notice" requirement for jurisdiction over the person. (*See* F.2., *supra*.)

Each pleading or motion after the complaint must also be filed with the clerk of the court with copies served on every other party in the case. Here, however, service may be made simply by mailing a copy of the pleading or motion to the opponent's attorney who has filed a written appearance in the lawsuit. [Mass. R. Civ. P. 5, 11(b)] If no attorney has filed an appearance on behalf of a party, service should be made directly on the party.

I.   JURY CLAIM
To preserve the right to trial by jury (in courts where jury trial is available), the plaintiff (or defendant) must file a "demand therefor in writing at any time after the commencement of the action and not later than 10 days after service of the last pleading directed to such issue." [Mass. R. Civ. P. 38] This is generally done by requesting a jury trial in the complaint or answer. If a case is removed to the superior court from the district court either before or after trial (C.3.e., *supra*), it is likewise necessary to file a jury demand.

III.   PLEADING STAGE OF THE LAWSUIT

A.   INTRODUCTION

1.   General Rules of Pleading
The principal function of the pleadings is to inform the court and the opposing party of the

pleader's claims (or defenses) in the lawsuit. The Massachusetts Rules adopt the "notice pleading" system embodied in the Federal Rules. Pleadings, accordingly, should be "simple, concise, and direct." Technical forms of pleading are not required; rather, pleadings are construed to do "substantial justice." [Mass. R. Civ. P. 8(e), (f)]

a. Categories
Pleadings fall into three general categories [Mass. R. Civ. P. 7(a)]:

1) Plaintiff—complaint;

2) Defendant—answer; and

3) Plaintiff—reply (used only if the defendant's answer includes a counterclaim).

b. Cross-Claims
The above sequence is replicated whenever a defendant adds a new claim to the lawsuit. For example, a cross-claim and third-party complaint are each answered by the defending party.

c. Motions
The above three pleadings are supplemented by motions, which are written requests to a court for an order related to the lawsuit (*e.g.,* motion to dismiss for failure to state a claim) and discovery requests. A motion, however, is not technically a pleading. [Mass. R. Civ. P. 7(a)]

d. Requirements
A pleading that sets forth a claim for relief (a complaint, counterclaim, cross-claim, or third-party complaint) must contain:

(i) A short and plain statement of the claim showing that the pleader is entitled to relief; and

(ii) A demand for judgment for the relief to which she deems herself entitled.

[Mass. R. Civ. P. 8(a)]

Note: The requirement that a pleading contain a statement of the amount of damages sought in civil suits has been ***statutorily*** eliminated, except where damages are liquidated or ascertainable by calculation. [Mass. Gen. L. ch. 231, §13B] (Previously the legislature had prohibited specific monetary claims in medical malpractice cases. [Mass. Gen. L. ch. 231, §60C]) However, a ***district court rule*** requires a statement of the amount of damages on a form prescribed by the district court, and complaints cannot be filed without the form. The rule is designed to inform the court and the parties of the amount in controversy for purposes of removal and remand of cases between the district court and superior court.

Unlike under the Federal Rules, the complaint need not state the basis for the court's jurisdiction.

e. Formal Requirements
There are certain formal requirements for all pleadings and motions. They must contain:

(i) The name of the court and the docket number;

(ii) The names of the parties (and their residences or places of business in the initial pleading);

(iii) The caption (*e.g.,* complaint, answer);

(iv) Numbered paragraphs;

(v) Separate counts for different claims or defenses whenever it facilitates "clear presentation"; and

(vi) The signature of the attorney filing the pleading, with the attorney's address and telephone number, and Board of Bar Overseers registration number. The party's signature is not required, unless he is not represented by an attorney.

If a pleading does not contain all of the above, a court, in its discretion, can return the pleading to the attorney who filed it.

1) Purpose
The attorney's signature certifies that "he has read the pleading; that to the best of his knowledge, information, and belief there is good ground to support it; and that it is not interposed for delay." An attorney may be sanctioned for a willful violation of this rule. [Mass. R. Civ. P. 11(a)]

f. Service of Papers and Pleadings Other than Process
(Service of process is governed by Massachusetts Rule 4 and is discussed at II.H., *supra.*)

1) Papers Required to Be Served
Each of the parties must be served with:

(i) Every order required by its terms to be served;

(ii) Every pleading subsequent to the original complaint;

(iii) Every paper relating to discovery required to be served on a party;

(iv) Every written motion except those which may be heard ex parte; and

(v) Every written notice, notice of change of attorney, appearance, demand, brief or memorandum of law, offer of judgment, designation of record on appeal, and similar papers.

[Mass. R. Civ. P. 5(a)]

2) Procedure
Service must be made on the party's attorney unless the court orders otherwise. Service may be made by (i) delivery, (ii) mailing the papers to the attorney's last known address, or (iii) leaving the papers with the clerk of the court if no address is known.

Note: Delivery means handing the paper to the recipient or leaving it at her office with a person in charge, or, if no one is in charge, leaving it in a conspicuous place therein. If the office is closed or if there is no office, pleadings may be delivered to the attorney's home and left with some person of suitable age and discretion residing therein. Service by mail is complete upon mailing. [Mass. R. Civ. P. 5(b)]

3) Filing in Court
The attorney must file with the court a copy of any papers drafted after the complaint that are required to be served. By this filing the attorney represents that all parties have been or will be properly served. [Mass. R. Civ. P. 5(d)(1)] However, the following are **not** to be filed with the court absent a specific court order: notices of taking depositions, transcripts of depositions, and requests and responses thereto for production of documents under Massachusetts Rule 34 (production of documents). [Mass. R. Civ. P. 5(d)(2)] It should be noted that each court has different requirements as to when certain papers must be filed with the court. For example, in the superior court, pursuant to Superior Court Rule 9A, motions (with the exception of emergency motions) must be served on counsel, and counsel must have an opportunity to respond to the motion before the motion may be filed with the court.

g. Time Computation

1) Computation
In computing time periods specified by rule, court order, or statute:

a) The day the period begins to run is not included;

b) The last day is included unless it is a Saturday, Sunday, or holiday; and

c) If the period is less than seven days, Saturdays, Sundays, and holidays are excluded.

2) Enlargement

Before expiration of the time in question, the court may allow an extension for cause shown if requested. After expiration of the time, the court may still grant an extension if the failure to act was the result of excusable neglect.

2. Pleading Special Matters

The basic rules for all pleadings are set forth above, but there are seven rules for pleading "special matters" that require separate attention. [Mass. R. Civ. P. 9(a)] The unifying theme of *most* of these rules is to assume the regularity of certain matters and not to require supporting proof at trial unless the opposing party gives specific notice that the matter is contested.

a. Capacity

Capacity or authority to sue or be sued need not be alleged. The opposing party must raise the issue by specific negative averment, including supporting particulars within his knowledge.

b. Fraud, Mistake, Duress, Undue Influence, or Condition of Mind

Circumstances that establish fraud, mistake, duress, or undue influence must be stated with particularity. Malice, intent, or knowledge may be alleged generally. The test as to fraud is whether the complaint adequately notifies defendant of the particular statements constituting the alleged fraud so that she can prepare her defense, and whether the complaint shows sufficient aspects of reliance and damage.

c. Conditions Precedent

The performance of conditions precedent may be alleged generally. Denial of performance or occurrence must be made specifically and with particularity.

d. Official Document or Act

When dealing with an official document or act, it is sufficient to aver that the document was issued or the act was done in compliance with law.

e. Judgment

The judgment or decision of a court or quasi-judicial body (within or outside Massachusetts) can be pleaded without allegations sufficient to demonstrate the jurisdiction of the tribunal that issued the judgment or decision.

f. Time and Place

Averments of time and place in a pleading are material for the purpose of testing the pleading's sufficiency (*e.g.,* to determine whether the statute of limitations has run).

g. Special Damages

Special damages (damages which do not normally flow from the opponent's acts) must be specifically stated.

B. THE PLAINTIFF'S PERSPECTIVE

1. Overview

One way to organize and remember the rules governing the commencement of litigation by the plaintiff is to consider the tasks confronting the plaintiff's attorney:

a. Select a legal theory (complaint).

b. Decide who has been injured and by whom (parties).

c. Select the proper court (subject matter jurisdiction; jurisdiction over the person).

d. Decide whether to seek a trial before a jury (jury demand) or a judge ("jury waived" or "bench trial").

e. Notify the court of the claim (commencement).

f. Notify the defendant of the claim (service of process).

2. Complaint

The complaint sets forth the plaintiff's legal theory of the lawsuit. The basic rules for the preparation of complaints were set forth in the preceding section. *Joinder* rules permit the plaintiff to include in the complaint all legal or equitable claims against each defendant, whether the claims are independent or alternative. [Mass. R. Civ. P. 18]

3. Parties

a. Permissive Joinder

Broad scope is given to the joinder in one lawsuit of multiple plaintiffs or defendants; each of the parties does not even have to be interested in obtaining (or defending against) all the relief sought in the complaint. The test for permissive joinder is whether any right to relief (i) is sought jointly, severally, or alternatively; (ii) arises out of the same (or same series of) transactions or occurrences; and (iii) presents common questions of fact or law. [Mass. R. Civ. P. 20]

In contrast to compulsory joinder (below), the plaintiff's attorney need not join as plaintiffs or defendants all parties who qualify for permissive joinder. Where multiple parties have been joined, the court may order separate trials to prevent delay, prejudice, or undue expense. It may also order that parties be dropped or added.

b. Compulsory Joinder (Indispensable Parties)

In certain situations, a plaintiff must join all interested parties or face dismissal of the lawsuit. [Mass. R. Civ. P. 19] Compulsory joinder problems usually arise when the plaintiff cannot serve process on the absentee party. The court must then decide whether the absent party is "indispensable," *i.e.*, that the suit should not proceed in his absence.

Analysis of a compulsory joinder issue follows a three-step process:

(i) Should the party be joined?

(ii) Can the party be joined?

(iii) If not, should the action proceed in his absence?

1) A party should be joined when:

    a) Complete relief cannot be accorded among the other parties to the lawsuit in the party's absence; or

    b) The absentee party has such an interest in the subject matter of the lawsuit that a decision in his absence will:

        (1) As a practical matter, impair or impede his ability to protect the interest; or

        (2) Leave any of the other parties subject to a substantial risk of incurring multiple or inconsistent obligations.

2) Assuming that a party should be joined under the analysis above, the next question is whether he can be joined, *i.e.*, whether the court can obtain jurisdiction over him. If it can, then he is joined as a party by court order.

3) If the absent party cannot be joined, the court must determine whether "in equity and good conscience" the action should proceed among the parties before it, or should be dismissed, the absent person thus being regarded as indispensable. The decision requires consideration of:

    a) The extent of prejudice to the absentee or available parties of a judgment;

    b) The extent to which the prejudice can be reduced or avoided by means of protective provisions in the judgment, the shaping of relief, or other measures;

    c) The adequacy of a judgment rendered without the absentee party; and

    d) Whether the plaintiff will have an adequate remedy (*e.g.*, in another forum) if the case is dismissed for nonjoinder.

c. Class Actions

1) **In General**
   A class action is a procedural device that permits one party (or more) to sue or be sued as a *representative* of a larger group of potential plaintiffs or defendants who are not personally named as parties to the lawsuit. Thus, the class action is an *exception* to the general principle that an in personam judgment rendered in a lawsuit does not bind (*i.e.,* has no res judicata effect on) persons who are not parties.

2) **Prerequisites to a Class Action**
   The court must find that six requirements are satisfied for a case to proceed as a class action [Mass. R. Civ. P. 23(a), (b)]:

   a) The class is so *numerous* that joinder of all members is impracticable;

   b) There are questions of law or fact *common* to the class;

   c) The claims or defenses of the representative parties are *typical* of the claims or defenses of the class;

   d) The representative parties will fairly and *adequately protect* the interests of the class;

   e) The *questions of law or fact common* to the members of the class *predominate* over any questions affecting only individual members; and

   f) The class action is *superior* to other available methods for the fair and efficient adjudication of the controversy.
      Example: The supreme judicial court upheld the refusal to certify a class action where all but the sixth requirement (superior method of adjudication) were satisfied. The trial court determined that a "test case" between the named plaintiff and defendant was superior to a class action lawsuit, because a class action lawsuit is often more time-consuming and expensive. The basic distinction is that the decision of the underlying legal issue in a test case will have only stare decisis effect in subsequent litigation, while the decision in a class action bars further litigation altogether due to the res judicata effect of the judgment. [Carpenter v. Suffolk Franklin Savings Bank, 370 Mass. 314 (1976)]

3) **Restrictions on Dismissals**
   An important consequence of the court's certification of a lawsuit as a class action is that the parties cannot thereafter dismiss or settle the action without the court's approval, and the attorney's professional responsibilities as counsel for both the named party and absentee members of the class are greatly increased. (Indeed, some federal courts have concluded there may even be an obligation to appeal the denial of class certification.) Another consequence is that a defendant cannot moot a class action merely by ceasing the complained of conduct with respect to the named plaintiff. [Santana v. Registrars of Voters of Worcester, 384 Mass. 487 (1981), *aff'd,* 398 Mass. 862 (1986)]

4) **Differences Between Massachusetts and Federal Rules**

   a) **Notice**
      The Federal Rules require individual notice to the class of the pendency of a Federal Rule 23(b)(3) type class action (common questions of fact or law), but not in Federal Rule 23(b)(1) or 23(b)(2) type class actions. The state rule does not distinguish types of class actions; type of notice is discretionary. Similarly, the Federal Rules require notice to the class of any proposed dismissal or settlement, while notice is discretionary under the state rule.

   b) **"Opt Out" Provisions**
      Absentee members may "opt out" or appear through their own counsel after receiving notice in a Federal Rule 23(b)(3) type class action; there is no "opt out" provision in the state rule.

c) Hearing

A federal court must conduct a class certification hearing as soon as practicable after the commencement of an action under Federal Rule 23(c) and enter an "order" whether it can be maintained as a class action. The state rule omits this requirement as such, but it is clearly necessary that the court determine at some point whether the six requirements (*see* 2), *supra*) are satisfied.

d) Failure to Give Notice

The failure to give notice to absentee members of the class under Massachusetts Rule 23 may make the judgment vulnerable to attack under the Fourteenth Amendment Due Process Clause. [*See* Eisen v. Carlisle & Jacquelin, 417 U.S. 156 (1974)]

d. Unincorporated Associations

Massachusetts Rule 23.2 permits unincorporated associations to sue or be sued by naming certain members of the association as representative parties, paralleling the class action rule in many respects. A labor union is a typical example of an unincorporated association given "entity" treatment under Rule 23.2. An action under this rule may be maintained only if it appears that the representative parties will fairly and adequately protect the interests of the association and its members.

e. Death of a Party

1) Contract Action

A contract action *survives* the death of either the plaintiff or defendant.

2) Tort Action

Massachusetts has, by statute, modified the common law rule that tort actions *do not* survive the death of either the plaintiff or defendant. [Mass. Gen. L. ch. 228, §1] Tort actions that survive include:

(i) Actions for assault, battery, false imprisonment, or other damage to the person;

(ii) Actions for consequential damages arising out of personal injury to the decedent (*e.g.,* medical expenses); and

(iii) Actions for damages to real or personal property or conversion of goods.

a) "Or Other Damage to the Person"

In *Harrison v. Loyal Protective Life Insurance Co.,* 379 Mass. 212 (1979), the supreme judicial court gave an expansive reading to the statutory words "or other damage to the person," holding that a suit for intentional infliction of emotional distress survives the plaintiff's death. The opinion appears to reject earlier decisions that only tort actions involving "damage of a physical character" survive the death of a party (*e.g.,* libel, slander, malicious prosecution, and alienation of affections actions were held not to survive). However, the court has determined that a cause of action for an alleged violation of the wiretap statute did not seek to recover for damage to the person; no actual damage was sustained, and therefore the action did not survive the plaintiff's death. [Pine v. Rust, 404 Mass. 411 (1989)]

b) Procedure

If an action survives the death of a party, the proper procedure is to file a motion for substitution of parties (*e.g.,* the executor or administrator of the deceased party's estate). If the action is one which does not survive, a suggestion of death is filed and the court dismisses the action (except that the action may proceed between any remaining parties). [Mass. R. Civ. P. 25(a)]

3) Death of Defendant

Massachusetts continues to follow the "nullity doctrine," whereby suits against deceased defendants are of no effect. The doctrine has a narrow scope, however. Where the plaintiff sues a living defendant who later dies while the action is pending, *the plaintiff may simply substitute the executor or administrator of the estate as the defendant*. If the defendant is already dead at the time the suit is commenced, the executor or administrator must be named in the complaint. Note, however, that if the plaintiff mistakenly commences an action against a deceased person rather than the executor or administrator, the suit is of no effect, and an amendment to name the proper party does not relate back to the original filing. Thus, the plaintiff must start over, and if the statute of limitations has expired in the interim, the suit is time-barred. An exception to the nullity doctrine exists where the administrator or executor had already been appointed when the suit began, and where she had actual knowledge of the pending suit. [Nutter v. Woodard, 34 Mass. App. Ct. 596 (1993)]

4) Death of Public Officials

If a public official sued in his official capacity subsequently dies or leaves office, the successor official is substituted as a party. [Mass. R. Civ. P. 25(d)]

C. THE DEFENDANT'S PERSPECTIVE

1. Overview

The defendant's perspective of the pleading stage of a lawsuit begins when the defendant is served with the summons and complaint (*see* II.H., *supra*). The defendant has 20 days to file a responsive pleading with the court. Failure to comply with this rule results in the entry of a default judgment against the defendant for failure to plead.

a. Defendant's Tactical Decisions

The tasks confronting the defendant's attorney at this point are, in most respects, the mirror image of the tasks before the plaintiff's attorney (*see* B., *supra*). The defendant's attorney must:

1) Determine whether to raise issues such as lack of subject matter jurisdiction or jurisdiction over the person, among others, in a motion to dismiss (threshold defenses);

2) Ascertain the legal and factual basis for the defense (answer); and

3) Determine whether the defendant has any claims for relief against the plaintiff (counterclaims), against co-defendants (cross-claims), or against others not joined as parties by the plaintiff (third-party complaints).

b. Response

Each defendant must also notify the court and all parties of his position by filing the responsive pleading with the clerk and serving a copy on each party in the case as discussed in A.1.f., *supra*.

c. Jury Demand

The defendant must also file a jury demand (typically with the answer) if trial by jury is desired.

2. Threshold Defenses—Motion to Dismiss

a. Introduction

1) Generally

The motion to dismiss and the answer are two mechanisms available to the defendant at the inception of a lawsuit. Their functions are virtually identical to practices under the Federal Rules. Regardless of which one is filed, the first response to the plaintiff's complaint is due within 20 days after service of the complaint on the defendant.

2) Motion to Dismiss vs. Answer

The motion to dismiss is narrower in scope than the answer, and the defendant has the option of raising in the answer all matters that can be raised in a motion to dismiss. The principal advantage of the motion to dismiss is that it permits the defendant to make a preliminary test of the sufficiency of the plaintiff's action without requiring the defendant to respond to the factual allegations in the complaint or to plead defenses addressed to the merits of the plaintiff's claims. [Mass. R. Civ. P. 12(b)]

3) Post-Motion Answer
If the defendant elects to file a motion to dismiss, an answer may still be filed within 10 days after the court decides the issues presented in the motion. [Mass. R. Civ. P. 12(a)]

b. Motion to Dismiss
The motion to dismiss tests the legal sufficiency of the plaintiff's action on its face. This means that the defendant (i) admits—for purposes of the motion only—all the factual allegations in the plaintiff's complaint, and (ii) cannot introduce evidence to support the defendant's contentions.

Motions to dismiss are best understood if they are grouped into two categories according to the type of issue the defendant seeks to raise.

1) Grounds for Motion—Jurisdiction/Procedure
Massachusetts Rule 12(b) lists eight jurisdictional or procedural issues which the defendant may raise by motion:

a) Lack of jurisdiction over the subject matter;

b) Lack of jurisdiction over the person;

c) Improper venue;

d) Insufficiency of process;

e) Insufficiency of service of process;

f) Failure to join a party under Massachusetts Rule 19;

g) Misnomer of a party; and

h) Pendency of a prior action in a court of the Commonwealth.

2) Waiver
The defendant waives the above defenses if they are omitted from the motion to dismiss (or answer). The *exception* to this principle is that the defendant does not waive:

a) Lack of jurisdiction over the *subject matter*, or

b) Failure to join an *indispensable* party.

3) Motion to Dismiss—"Failure to State a Claim upon Which Relief Can Be Granted"
A motion to dismiss based on Rule 12(b)(6) asserts that even if the plaintiff were to succeed at trial in proving all the factual allegations in the complaint, the plaintiff still would not be entitled to relief because the law does not recognize the plaintiff's claim (or cause of action). (The demurrer served this function in common law pleading.)

In ruling on motions to dismiss under Rule 12(b)(6), Massachusetts courts have adopted the same liberal notice pleading standard as the federal courts—that a complaint should not be dismissed "unless it appears beyond doubt that the plaintiff can prove no set of facts in support of his claim which would entitle him to relief." [Spence v. Boston Edison, 390 Mass. 604 (1983)—*quoting* Conley v. Gibson, 355 U.S. 41 (1957)]

4) Motion to Dismiss—Anti-SLAPP Suit Statute
There is a special motion to dismiss available to a party who presented a written or oral statement to a legislative, executive, or judicial body and who is sued based on that statement. This motion is available to counter strategic lawsuits against public participation ("SLAPP" suits). The court must grant this special motion to dismiss unless the nonmoving party can show that:

(i) The moving party's exercise of its right to petition was devoid of any reasonable factual support or any arguable basis in law, and

(ii) The moving party's acts caused actual injury to the nonmoving party.

[Mass. Gen. L. ch. 231, §59H]

5) Other Matters

Although Massachusetts Rule 12(b) does not say so, the motion to dismiss may also be used to raise defenses such as failure to exhaust administrative remedies, lack of ripeness, etc. (subject, of course, to the general limitation that the defect must appear on the face of the pleadings).

Sometimes the attorney encounters a complaint (or counterclaim) which is so poorly drafted that compliance with the foregoing rules is difficult. The attorney may resort to two rarely used motions to remedy the situation before filing the answer:

(i) Motion for more definite statement where the complaint is so vague or ambiguous that the defendant cannot frame a responsive pleading [Mass. R. Civ. P. 12(e)]; or

(ii) Motion to strike where the complaint contains redundant, immaterial, impertinent, or scandalous material [Mass. R. Civ. P. 12(f)].

Successful use of either of these motions by the defendant merely requires the plaintiff to amend the complaint before a responsive pleading is filed.

c. Conversion into Summary Judgment Motion

Extrinsic evidence cannot be considered as part of a motion to dismiss. If the court receives evidence—*e.g.,* by affidavit—the motion to dismiss is treated as a motion for summary judgment. Note, however, that it is an abuse of discretion for a judge to convert a motion to dismiss into a motion for summary judgment without first giving the plaintiff a reasonable opportunity to obtain and submit additional evidentiary material to counter the defendant's affidavits.

3. Answer

a. Generally

The answer is the primary defensive pleading. If no motion to dismiss is filed, the answer must be filed within 20 days of service of the complaint upon the defendant. It may be used to assert:

(i) The threshold defenses (including failure to state a claim) described in the preceding sections;

(ii) Denials of the events alleged by the plaintiff;

(iii) Affirmative defenses;

(iv) Counterclaims;

(v) Cross-claims; and

(v) Third-party claims.

The purpose of the answer is to frame issues for trial.

b. Admits, Denies, or States Insufficient Knowledge or Information

The formal requirements for the answer (as well as the motion to dismiss) were set forth in A.1.d., *supra.* The answer must, in addition, respond to each of the allegations in the complaint by:

(i) *Admitting* the allegation;

(ii) *Denying* the allegation; or

(iii) Stating the defendant has ***insufficient knowledge or information*** to form a belief as to the truth of the allegation (which has the effect of a denial).

[Mass. R. Civ. P. 8]

Special pleading requirements are established by court rule or statute in some circumstances. One example is that the genuineness of a signature to a written instrument is admitted unless the party *specifically* denies its genuineness. Another is that an allegation that a street is a public way (*e.g.,* in motor vehicle cases) is admitted unless specifically denied. [Mass. R. Civ. P. 8(b)] Rules for pleading special matters (set forth in Massachusetts Rule 9) were summarized in A.2., *supra*.

c. **Affirmative Defenses**

1) **In General**
    In addition to paragraph-by-paragraph responses to the complaint (*see* B.2., *supra*), the answer must specifically plead any "affirmative defenses" the defendant may have to the plaintiff's claim for relief. [Mass. R. Civ. P. 8(c)] Affirmative defenses are the modern version of the "confession and avoidance" in common law pleading. They are, in other words, legal defenses to the claim asserted by the plaintiff—whether or not the defendant denies the plaintiff's factual allegations or the plaintiff succeeds in proving the facts at trial.

    Massachusetts Rule 8(c) sets forth an illustrative list of 20 affirmative defenses, including:

    (i)   Accord and satisfaction;

    (ii) Assumption of risk;

    (iii) Statute of Frauds;

    (iv) Res judicata and collateral estoppel;

    (v)   Statutes of limitations;

    (vi) Payment; and

    (vii) Release (including an unexecuted offer by the party's attorney to compromise litigation which did not amount to an accord and satisfaction [Peters v. Wallach, 366 Mass. 622 (1975)]).

    The affirmative defenses most commonly tested are res judicata and collateral estoppel (*see* VIII., *infra*), and statutes of limitations.

2) **Statutes of Limitations**

    a) **Introduction**
        A statute of limitations is an arbitrary limitation imposed by the legislature on the time for pursuing a legal claim. The period begins to run when the claim for relief accrues. The lawsuit must be ***commenced*** (II.G., *supra*) within the period specified by the applicable statute of limitation or it is time-barred, unless the statute is tolled or extended. Massachusetts General Laws chapter 260 provides a number of limitations periods.

    b) **Affirmative Defense**
        The statute of limitations is an affirmative defense. If the defendant fails to plead the defense that the plaintiff's action is barred by the statute of limitations, the defense is ***waived*** and the action proceeds as if it were commenced in a timely manner.

    c) **When Claim Accrues**
        In general, a claim for relief (or cause of action) accrues when the plaintiff's right to sue is complete. Massachusetts courts, however, have adopted a discovery rule that states that a cause of action accrues when the plaintiff learns or reasonably should have learned that he has been harmed.

(1) Contract Actions

Contract actions accrue at the time of breach, regardless of whether the plaintiff then had knowledge of the breach.

(2) Actions on Promissory Notes

Actions on promissory notes accrue the day after the note matures. For a demand note, the date the note was executed is the operative date.

(3) Medical Malpractice Claims

Medical malpractice claims accrue on the date the physician committed the act complained of, unless there is no way the patient was aware of the physician's negligent act, in which case the claims accrue on the date the injured patient learns, or in the exercise of reasonable diligence should have learned, of the facts giving rise to the cause of action.

(4) Legal Malpractice Claims

Legal malpractice claims accrue on the date of the attorney's act or omission, unless there is no way the client was aware of the attorney's act or omission, in which case the claims accrue on the date the injured client learns, or in the exercise of reasonable diligence should have learned, of the facts giving rise to the cause of action. [Cantu v. Saint Paul Cos., 401 Mass. 53 (1987)]

(5) Personal Injury Claims

Claims for personal injury based on negligence, including manufacture of goods, accrue only when the plaintiff knows or reasonably should know of the harm. [Massachusetts Electric Co. v. Fletcher, Filton & Whipple, P.C., 394 Mass. 265 (1985)] In situations in which the injury is not discernible, or is discernible but the cause is not ascertainable, a cause of action does not accrue until knowledge of it may reasonably be imputed to the plaintiff. [Lijoi v. Massachusetts Bay Transportation Authority, 28 Mass. App. Ct. 926 (1990)]

d) Counterclaims

Counterclaims are also governed by statutes of limitations. However, a counterclaim is not time-barred if the limitations period for a permissive or compulsory counterclaim had not expired when the plaintiff's action was commenced. In addition, even where the statute of limitations has expired on a counterclaim, the defendant may still interpose a compulsory counterclaim to defeat or diminish the plaintiff's claim (*i.e.,* the counterclaim can be used as a setoff against the complaint but it cannot be the basis for an affirmative recovery of damages by the defendant). [Mass. Gen. L. ch. 260, §36]

e) Tolls and Extensions of Statute of Limitations

(1) Definition

A toll postpones the running of a statute of limitations. An extension enlarges the time in which the action may be filed.

(2) Illustrative Tolls and Extensions

(a) Nonresidence

The limitations period does not start to run if the defendant resides outside Massachusetts when the claim accrues; the statute is tolled if the defendant leaves the state after the claim accrues but before the limitations period expires. [Mass. Gen. L. ch. 260, §9]

Exception: There is no toll if the defendant can be reached under the long arm statute (II.F.4., *supra*). [Walsh v. Ogorzalek, 372 Mass. 271 (1977)]

(b) Incapacity

If the plaintiff is a minor (under 18), insane, incapacitated by reason of mental illness, or imprisoned at the time the claim *accrues*, the limitations period does not begin to run until the disability is removed. [Mass. Gen. L. ch. 260, §7]

1] Not Applicable to Medical Malpractice Claims
A plaintiff's disability does not toll the statute for medical malpractice claims. The statute allows for some flexibility by allowing an action to be brought until a minor reaches age nine where the claim accrued when the minor was under age six. However, all malpractice claims must be brought within seven years of the negligent act or omission, regardless of the plaintiff's age at the time of the negligent act or omission. [Mass. Gen. L. ch. 231, §60D; Plummer v. Gillieson, 44 Mass. App. Ct. 578 (1998)] This exception does not apply, however, to actions based on leaving a foreign object in the body.

(c) Death
If a party dies before the limitations period expires or within 30 days thereafter, the executor or administrator of the decedent's estate has two years (after giving bond) to commence the action or three years from the date that the executor or administrator knew or should have known the factual basis for the cause of action (if the claim is one which survives death). [Mass. Gen. L. ch. 260, §10]

(d) Fraudulent Concealment
If the defendant fraudulently conceals the claim from the plaintiff, the statute does not start to run until the plaintiff learns of the claim. [Mass. Gen. L. ch. 260, §12]

(e) Reinstatement of Debt
A written promise to pay or partial payment of a debt starts the statute of limitations running again from that point. [Mass. Gen. L. ch. 260, §§23, 14]

(3) Renewal Statute
If an action, commenced within the statute of limitations, is dismissed for insufficient service of process, death of a party, or for any matter of form, or if the judgment is vacated or reversed, the plaintiff may commence a new action for the same cause within one year even though the statute of limitations has expired. [Mass. Gen. L. ch. 260, §32] This statute applies to claims dismissed in federal court together with dismissal of the federal question. [Liberace v. Conway, 31 Mass. App. Ct. 40 (1991)]

(4) Continuing Representation Doctrine
A cause of action for legal malpractice does not begin to run until the attorney's representation of the plaintiff ends. This doctrine, recently adopted in Massachusetts, assumes that a client is not expected to evaluate the services of her lawyer and that she may rely on her lawyer's good faith. [Murphy v. Smith, 411 Mass. 133 (1991)]

(5) Discovery Rule
Under the "discovery rule," the statute of limitations begins to run only from the time that the plaintiff knew or reasonably should have known of any alleged injuries. This rule has been applied in malpractice actions against physicians, psychotherapists, and attorneys (negligent title search), and in actions for fraudulent misrepresentation in the sale of real estate. The running of the statute of limitations is not suspended where the plaintiff knows of the harm but does not know who caused the harm until much later. [Bowen v. Eli Lilly Co., 408 Mass. 204 (1990)]

f) Selected Statutes of Limitations

(1) Fifty Years
Foreclosure of mortgage. [Mass. Gen. L. ch. 260, §33]

(2) Twenty Years

(i) Actions on contract under seal;

(ii)   Actions on notes issued by banks;

(iii) Actions brought by original payee on an attested-to promissory note;

(iv)   Actions on court judgments (*Note:* There is a rebuttable presumption of payment of a judgment upon the passage of 20 years after the judgment was rendered. [Mass. Gen. L. ch. 260, §20]); and

(v)   Actions for the recovery of real property [Mass. Gen. L. ch. 260, §§21-23].

[Mass. Gen. L. ch. 260, §1]

(3) Six Years

(i)   Actions on contracts (other than those to recover for personal injury); and

(ii)   Actions on judgments not rendered by courts of record or judgments of courts outside the United States.

[Mass. Gen. L. ch. 260, §2]

(4) Four Years
Consumer protection actions [Mass. Gen. L. ch. 260, §5A; *see also* Mass. Gen. L. ch. 93A].

(5) Three Years

(a)   Tort actions (*e.g.,* malpractice, assault, battery, false imprisonment, libel, slander) [Mass. Gen. L. ch. 260, §§2A, 4];

(b)   Replevin actions [Mass. Gen. L. ch. 260, §2A];

(c)   Actions in tort or contract to recover for personal injury [Mass. Gen. L. ch. 260, §2A];

(d)   Claims against the Commonwealth [Mass. Gen. L. ch. 258, §4];

(e)   Actions for breach of warranty [Mass. Gen. L. ch. 229, §2];

(f)   Actions against hit-and-run motorists (but within six months of identification of the defendant if two years have elapsed since the accident) [Mass. Gen. L. ch. 260, §4B];

(g)   Wrongful death actions [Mass. Gen. L. ch. 260, §4];

(h)   Actions for damages arising out of neglect in design, construction, or improvement to real property (must be brought within three years after cause of action accrued but not later than six years after date of design or performance) [Mass. Gen. L. ch. 260, §2B];

(i)   Actions arising on account of any law intended for the protection of civil rights, including actions alleging employment, housing, and other discrimination on the basis of race, color, creed, national origin, sex, sexual orientation, age, ancestry, or handicap [Mass. Gen. L. ch. 260, §5B];

(j)   Actions for assault and battery alleging sexual abuse of a minor. (Note that the statute of limitations is tolled until the victim reaches the age of 18 and until the victim discovers or reasonably should discover that an emotional or psychological injury was caused by the abusive actions.) [Mass. Gen. L. ch. 260, §4C]; and

(k)   Actions for value of property taken by eminent domain. [Mass. Gen. L. ch. 79, §16]

(6) Two Years
Actions against trustees on their contracts [Mass. Gen. L. ch. 260, §11]

(7) One Year

(a) Actions against banks for payment on unauthorized signatures [Mass. Gen. L. ch. 106, §4-406];

(b) Actions against executors on their contracts [Mass. Gen. L. ch. 260, §11]; and

(c) Actions by a creditor of a decedent (must be commenced against the estate within one year after the date of the deceased's death) [Mass. Gen. L. ch. 197, §9].

g) Amendments and Relation Back
An amendment to a pleading raising a new claim or defense arising out of the conduct, transaction, or occurrence set forth in the original pleading "relates back" to the original pleading. [Mass. R. Civ. P. 15(c)] This means that such an amendment is not barred by the statute of limitations as long as the original pleading was filed in a timely manner. (*See* E.6., *infra*.)

d. Counterclaims
The answer may also assert, as counterclaims, any claims the defendant has against the plaintiff. (The caption should then be "defendant's answer, affirmative defenses, and counterclaim.") A counterclaim may seek money damages in an amount greater than the plaintiff's claim, and it may also seek relief different in kind from that demanded by the plaintiff (*e.g.,* the defendant's counterclaim may be for injunctive relief where the plaintiff seeks only money damages). [Mass. R. Civ. P. 13]

Note: The counterclaim rules apply to any party against whom a claim for relief is stated (*e.g.,* the third-party defendant's answer could contain a counterclaim). The rules are stated in terms of the complaint and answer for simplicity.

1) Compulsory Counterclaims
The answer must assert any compulsory counterclaim or the claim is waived (*i.e.,* the defendant cannot file an independent lawsuit against the plaintiff).

a) Definition
Compulsory counterclaims are claims the defendant has:

(1) At the time the answer is filed; *and*

(2) That arise out of the same transaction or occurrence which is the subject of the complaint.

b) Exceptions
The exceptions to the compulsory counterclaim rule are that the defendant may elect to omit the counterclaim from the answer if:

(1) The claim was already the subject of another lawsuit;

(2) By statute, the subject matter of the counterclaim must be brought in a different court than the original;

(3) The court is exercising in rem (or quasi in rem) jurisdiction rather than in personam jurisdiction, *e.g.,* the plaintiff is proceeding by attachment or trustee process; or

(4) The counterclaim is based upon property damage arising out of a collision, or personal injury, including actions for consequential damages, or death.

2) Permissive Counterclaims
Here the defendant is given a choice between asserting the claim as an independent lawsuit or including it in the answer as a counterclaim. Simply stated, permissive

counterclaims are claims the defendant has against the plaintiff which do ***not*** arise out of the same transaction or occurrence as the complaint.

D. THIRD-PARTY ACTIONS

The preceding discussion was set in terms of the typical two-party lawsuit (including suits which join multiple plaintiffs versus multiple defendants). This section will briefly describe pleadings which do not fit in this mold. The basic pleading rules remain the same.

1. Cross-Claims

A cross-claim is a claim by one party against a co-party. It must ***arise out of the same transaction or occurrence as the original claim (or counterclaim),*** or it must ***relate to property that is the subject of the original action.*** Cross-claims are permissive. [Mass. R. Civ. P. 13(g)]

Example: P sues two defendants, D1 and D2. D1 must file a responsive pleading to P's complaint. D1 may also file a cross-claim against D2. D2 then must file a responsive pleading to both P's complaint and D1's cross-claim. (The compulsory counterclaim rule, *supra,* applies to D2's answer to D1's cross-claim.)

2. Third-Party Practice (Impleader)

A defendant may assert a claim against a third person who was not joined as a party to the original two-party action. This is done by serving a summons, third-party complaint, and all the original pleadings on the third-party defendant (*i.e.,* by commencing an action). The third-party defendant must then file a responsive pleading in the same manner as a party originally named as a defendant and may also file claims against the original plaintiff. The third-party defendant may in turn proceed against any person who is or may be liable to her for all or part of the claim made against her. [Mass. R. Civ. P. 14]

Third-party complaints are used where the third-party defendant stands in some relationship to the original defendant that requires the third-party defendant to answer to the defendant for any or all of the liability which the original plaintiff seeks to impose on the defendant. Examples include:

    a.   Contractual indemnity (including insurance policies); and

    b.   Contribution among joint tortfeasors [Mass. Gen. L. ch. 231B, §1].

3. Intervention

Intervention [Mass. R. Civ. P. 24] is the process by which one who is not named as a party to a lawsuit may seek to become a party. It is, in some sense, the counterpart to the rules on compulsory and permissive joinder of parties (*see* B.3.a., b., *supra*).

There are three types of intervention:

a. Intervention as of Right

A court must allow a timely application for intervention where:

    (i)   A state statute unconditionally confers the right, or

    (ii)   The disposition of the lawsuit, as a practical matter, may impair or impede the intervenor's ability to protect his interest in the property or transaction that is the subject of the lawsuit.

If a motion to intervene as of right is made after entry of final judgment, the court may allow the motion after consideration of the following factors: (i) whether applicant could have intervened earlier, (ii) whether delay would prejudice the central parties, and (iii) the force of the need to intervene. [Peabody Federation of Teachers v. Peabody School Committee, 28 Mass. App. Ct. 410 (1990)]

b. Permissive Intervention

The court has discretion to permit intervention where:

    (i)   A state statute confers a ***conditional*** right to intervene;

    (ii)   The intervenor and the parties raise a common question of law or fact; or

(iii) A government official or agency seeks to participate in a lawsuit in which the parties' claim or defense is based on a statute or regulation administered by the intervenor.

In exercising its discretion, the court must consider whether there will be undue delay and whether an original party will be prejudiced.

c. **Intervention by Attorney General**
Whenever the constitutionality of a state statute or municipal ordinance is drawn into question, the party asserting the unconstitutionality must give notice to the attorney general who may intervene (*e.g.,* this rule applies in cases in which a state agency or official is not a party).

4. Interpleader
Interpleader protects a party (the stakeholder) from having to pay double or multiple damages. A typical example involves a claim by several beneficiaries of an insurance policy. Interpleader permits the insurance company to bring an action to determine (i) whether the policy proceeds are owed to any of the claimants and (ii) to which claimants proceeds are owed. Note, however, that if the controversy concerns whether an insured's policy requires the insurance company to pay for losses or to provide the insured with a defense, the appropriate action is for a declaratory judgment. (*See* II.C.10., *supra.*) [Mass. R. Civ. P. 22]

5. Derivative Actions
A derivative action permits shareholders (*i.e.,* third parties) in a corporation—or members of an association—to commence an action to enforce a right belonging to the corporation, which the corporation has failed to enforce in a lawsuit brought in its own name. A derivative action has many of the characteristics of a class action (*see* B.3.c., *supra*). The complaint in a derivative action must allege the efforts made by the plaintiff to obtain the action she desires from the directors or comparable authority, and the reasons for her failure to obtain the action or for not making the effort. [Mass. R. Civ. P. 23.1]

E. AMENDMENTS TO PLEADINGS

1. In General
The court may at any time allow amendments (i) adding or deleting a party; (ii) changing the form of the action; or (iii) changing anything else to allow the plaintiff to sustain the action or the defendant to make a legal defense.

2. Amendments as of Course

a. **Responsive Pleading Permitted**
Where a responsive pleading is permitted, a party may amend her pleading once as a matter of course at any time before the responsive pleading is served as long as an order of dismissal has not been entered. [Mass. Gen. L. ch. 231, §51; *and see* Mass. R. Civ. P. 15(a)]

Note: A motion under Rule 12 is not considered a responsive pleading. Accordingly, a party may amend her complaint after the court rules favorably on a motion for failure to state a claim upon which relief can be granted.

b. **Responsive Pleading Not Permitted**
If the pleading does not permit a responsive pleading and the pleading has not been placed on the trial calendar, a party may amend the pleading within *20 days* after it has been served.

3. Amendments Not as of Course

a. **By Motion**
Where an amendment does not meet the requirements for an amendment as of course, a party may amend her pleading by leave of court, and "leave shall be freely given when justice so requires." [Mass. R. Civ. P. 15(a); *and see* Foman v. Davis, 371 U.S. 178 (1962)] The court considers such factors as undue delay, undue prejudice, and bad faith.

b. **By Written Consent**
Amendments not as of course may also be made if the adverse party consents in writing to the amendment.

4. Response to Amended Pleading
A party must respond to the amended pleading within the time allowed for response to the original pleading or *10 days*, whichever is longer.

5. Amendments to Conform to the Evidence
Rule 15(b) provides that if issues are tried by express or implied consent of the parties, they are treated as if they had been raised in the pleadings. If an opponent objects to evidence because it is outside the pleadings, the court may allow the pleadings to be amended, and it shall do so freely when the presentation of the merits of the action will be served and the opposing party will not be prejudiced.

6. Relation Back
An amendment barred by a statute of limitations may relate back to the date of the original pleading if (i) the claim or defense asserted in the amended pleading arose out of the same conduct, transaction, or occurrence set forth or attempted to be set forth in the original pleading, *and* (ii) the original pleading was filed within the limitations period.

a. Exceptions

1) Action Barred by Statute of Repose
An action barred by a statute of repose may not be revived by an amendment to the pleadings, even if the amendment would have met the requirements of the relation back rule, *supra*. A statute of repose completely eliminates a claim within its scope after a certain period of time, whereas a statute of limitations bars a claim after a certain period of time unless the claim relates back to a timely pleading. [Casco v. Warley Electric Co., 37 Mass. App. Ct. 701 (1994)]

2) Nullity Doctrine
Under the nullity doctrine, a complaint brought against a deceased person is one brought against nobody, and because such an action is void, any subsequent amendment of the complaint does not relate back to the date of the initial filing. (*See* B.3.e.3), *supra*.)

a) When the Nullity Doctrine Does Not Apply
The nullity doctrine does *not* apply where a legal representative was in existence when the complaint was filed; the representative had notice of the complaint; and no showing was made of any prejudice resulting from not applying the doctrine. [Nutter v. Woodard, B.3.e.3), *supra*]

F. SUPPLEMENTATION OF PLEADINGS
The court may allow a party upon motion to supplement pleadings with transactions or occurrences that happened after the filing of the pleadings. Such action shall be taken by filing a motion to amend and/or supplement the pleadings.

IV. INTERLOCUTORY ORDERS

A. INTRODUCTION
Upon filing a complaint, a plaintiff may seek preliminary relief, or interlocutory orders, which are designed to preserve the status quo or maintain assets of the defendant until a final judgment is rendered. The most common forms of preliminary relief are temporary restraining orders ("TROs"), preliminary injunctions, attachment, and trustee process.

B. INJUNCTIONS
A court may grant TROs and preliminary injunctions to prevent irreparable injury at any point between the commencement of the action and the entry of final judgment. Rule 65(c) requires that an applicant for a TRO or preliminary injunction post security in an amount determined by the court, unless the court decides otherwise for good cause shown. [Mass. R. Civ. P. 65] (The injunctive power is covered in the Equity outline.)

1. Temporary Restraining Order
A TRO may be granted without notice (written or oral) to the adverse party or attorney if specific facts in the verified complaint (or supporting affidavit) demonstrate that immediate and irreparable injury will occur before the opponent can be heard.

  a. The TRO may not last for a period exceeding 10 days (unless the opponent consents).

    b.   A hearing on a preliminary injunction must occur within the 10-day period.

    c.   The opponent, on two days' notice, may secure a hearing to dissolve or modify a TRO granted without notice.

2.   Preliminary Injunction
A preliminary injunction serves the same purposes as a TRO, but a preliminary injunction may be granted only after notice to the opponent and an opportunity to be heard. It also:

    (i)   Remains in effect until entry of final judgment (unless the court orders otherwise); and

    (ii) May be consolidated by the court for hearing with the trial on the merits.

[Mass. R. Civ. P. 65(b)]

3.   Standard for Granting Preliminary Injunction
A plaintiff seeking relief must establish that:

    a.   There is a substantial likelihood that he will succeed on the merits;

    b.   There is a substantial threat that the plaintiff will suffer irreparable injury if relief is not granted; and

    c.   A balancing of the equities favors issuance of the injunction (weighing the threatened injury to the plaintiff, harm inflicted on the defendant if an injunction is issued, and the public interest).

4.   General Requirements and Characteristics
A TRO or preliminary injunction may be requested in either:

    (i)   The demand for judgment (prayers) portion of a verified complaint; or

    (ii) A separate motion.

    a.   Verified Complaint
    A verified complaint (*i.e.,* signed by the plaintiff, rather than the attorney) setting forth specific facts showing the basis for relief or a complaint or motion supported by an affidavit of a person having knowledge of the facts is typically required. The plaintiff (except the government) may be required to post a bond or other security to cover damage sustained by wrongfully enjoining the defendant.

    b.   Counterclaim
    A TRO or preliminary injunction is likewise available to the defendant in connection with a counterclaim.

    c.   Appealability
    The grant or denial of a preliminary injunction is an exception to the general rule that interlocutory orders are not appealable. [Mass. Gen. L. ch. 231, §118]

    d.   Form and Scope
    An injunction or restraining order must be specific in its terms and describe in reasonable detail the conduct to be restrained. It is binding only on the parties to the action; their officers, agents, servants, employees, and attorneys; and those persons in active concert with them who receive actual notice of the order.

C. ATTACHMENT

1.   Introduction
At the commencement of the action (or thereafter) the plaintiff (or a counterclaimant) may attempt to attach another party's real or personal property. [Mass. R. Civ. P. 4.1] The purpose of an attachment is to ensure that the property will be available at the end of the lawsuit to satisfy the judgment, if the moving party prevails.

2.   Procedure
The plaintiff must file the complaint, a motion for approval of attachment, and supporting

affidavits with the court and serve them on the defendant with a notice setting the date and time for a court hearing on the motion for approval of attachment.

a. Court Approval
The court may approve an attachment only on a finding that:

1) There is a "reasonable likelihood" the plaintiff will recover a judgment in an amount greater than the attachment; and

2) The defendant has inadequate liability insurance to satisfy the judgment.

b. Writ of Attachment
The court then issues a writ of attachment, which a sheriff or constable must serve on the party whose property is being attached.

3. Ex Parte Attachment
An attachment may be approved ex parte (*i.e.,* without notice to the defendant) if the court makes the foregoing findings and also finds:

a. "Clear Danger"
There is a "clear danger" the defendant will conceal or remove the property from the state or damage or destroy the property if notified in advance;

b. In Rem Jurisdiction
The court can exercise only in rem (or quasi in rem) jurisdiction over the action—as opposed to in personam jurisdiction (*but see* II.F., *supra*). The defendant may move to dissolve an ex parte attachment on two days' notice.

4. Effecting the Attachment

a. Real Estate

1) **Unregistered Land**
The sheriff attaches all unregistered land in the defendant's name by recording the writ of attachment in the registry of deeds for the county in which the land lies. The defendant must also receive notice of the writ of attachment within 60 days or the attachment is dissolved.

2) **Registered Land**
For registered land, the attachment must be recorded directly on the registration certificate.

3) **Attachment Period**
Real estate attachments are good for six years. At that point, they dissolve unless rerecorded.

b. Personal Property
Personal property is generally attached either by the sheriff taking physical possession of it, by placing a keeper on it, or by filing the writ of attachment with the town clerk in the city or town where the property is located.

5. Time Limits
An attachment is automatically dissolved:

(i) If the final judgment is for the defendant—at the expiration of the plaintiff's appeal period (30 days) or upon affirmance of the judgment by an appellate court; or

(ii) If the final judgment is for the plaintiff—30 days after the plaintiff can secure an execution on the judgment (*i.e.,* after the defendant's appeal period expires or the judgment is affirmed) unless the attachment is levied upon in this period (but the sheriff's sale of the property does not have to be completed in this period).

Caveat: The reader should be aware that this is a simplified summary of a detailed and complex area of law. [*See* Mass. R. Civ. P. 4.1(a) - (i)]

6. Property Not Attachable

a.   **Exempt Property**
Property that is exempt from seizure on execution to satisfy a judgment cannot be attached. (*See* VII.J., *infra.*) [Mass. Gen. L. ch. 223, §42; ch. 235, §34]

b.   **Shares of Stock**
Shares of stock cannot be attached in an action where money damages are sought.

c.   **Mortgaged Personal Property**
Personal property subject to a mortgage cannot be attached unless the attaching creditor pays off the mortgage within 10 days.

d.   **Goods Covered by Negotiable Instrument**
Goods delivered to a carrier or other bailee are not attachable if a negotiable instrument of title is issued.

D.   TRUSTEE PROCESS

1.   Introduction
Trustee process is the method by which the plaintiff, at the commencement of the action (or thereafter), can attach the defendant's property in the hands of a third person (the trustee). It is principally used to attach debts owed to the defendant by the trustee (*e.g.,* bank accounts). Trustee process cannot be used in the following types of actions:

(i)   Libel or slander;

(ii)   Malicious prosecution;

(iii)   Assault and battery; or

(iv)   Specific recovery of goods and chattels.

[Mass. Gen. L. ch. 246; Mass. R. Civ. P. 4.2]

2.   Procedure
The court must give prior approval to the use of trustee process pursuant to the attachment procedure (*supra*). The court then issues a "trustee summons," which the plaintiff serves on the trustee to effect the attachment. The trustee thereafter files an answer in court describing the property being held for the benefit of the parties.

The plaintiff must also post a bond if the damages claimed are over $1,000, **unless** the action is on a:

(i)   Judgment;

(ii)   Contract for personal service;

(iii)   Contract for goods sold and delivered;

(iv)   Money due under a contract in writing;

(v)   Tort for operation of an unregistered motor vehicle; or

(vi)   Order for alimony, maintenance, or child support.

This is a *jurisdictional* requirement; if it is not complied with, the action will be dismissed.

3.   Exemptions

a.   **Wages**
Wages are usually exempt from trustee process unless the plaintiff first obtains a judgment against the defendant. The plaintiff must then follow the procedure (described above) **and** give the employer 10 days' advance notice of the application for court approval. [Mass. Gen. L. ch. 246, §32(8)] However, these restrictions do not apply to proceedings to enforce alimony or child support obligations. [Mass. Gen. L. ch. 208, §36A]

The first $125 of each week's wages are exempt from trustee process, except in proceedings to enforce support orders. [Mass. Gen. L. ch. 246, §28] Federal law imposes a further restriction that no more than 25% of weekly wages may be reached by trustee process. [15 U.S.C. §1673]

Additionally, money held by a defendant in a payroll account is exempt from trustee process. [Mass. Gen. L. ch. 246, §20] The statute provides both civil and criminal sanctions for deposits made to a payroll account by a defendant with the intent to evade trustee process.

b. Annuities; Pensions
Annuities, pensions, and retirement allowances of members of state or municipal retirement systems are exempt from trustee process, except in actions to enforce alimony or support orders. [Mass. Gen. L. ch. 32, §19]

c. Monies on Deposit
In a natural person's bank account, $500 is exempt from trustee process. If the account is a joint account, each depositor is considered to hold one-half of the amount. [Mass. Gen. L. ch. 246, §28A]

d. Aid to Families with Dependent Children
Aid given to a family with dependent children is exempt from trustee process. [Mass. Gen. L. ch. 118, §10]

E. REACH AND APPLY

1. Introduction
A much less common prejudgment device is "reach and apply," an equitable action combining features of both attachment and trustee process to secure intangible property or an equitable interest in property (*i.e.,* property not subject to either attachment or trustee process). Where the intangible property sought to be secured is in the possession of the defendant, reach and apply operates like an attachment; where it is in the hands of a third party, reach and apply functions like trustee process. The existence of a debt to the creditor must be established before the clerk will seek to reach and apply the asset in question. [Mass. Gen. L. ch. 214]

2. Property Subject to Reach and Apply
Property subject to reach and apply includes:

a. Negotiable instruments;

b. Investment securities;

c. Accounts payable;

d. Intangibles such as goodwill, literary rights, copyrights, trademarks, and patents;

e. Equitable interests in property (*e.g.,* options to purchase real estate; property fraudulently conveyed by the defendant; interests in a trust); and

f. Any property, right, title, or interest of the debtor.

3. Procedure
The general rule, derived from case law (no Massachusetts procedural rule governs specifically), is that the plaintiff may obtain security in the property by means of a preliminary injunction enjoining the sale or transfer of the property. Where the property is evidenced by a writing (*e.g.,* negotiable instrument), the plaintiff may need to acquire possession of the writing as well in order to prevent conveyance to a bona fide purchaser. Note that the complaint in an action to reach and apply must clearly indicate on its face that the property, right, title, or interest of the defendant is in existence and cannot be attached by ordinary means.

F. LIS PENDENS
Where the subject matter of an action involves the title to or use of real property, a party may move that the court make a finding to that effect. The party may then record a lis pendens at the registry of deeds, which will notify persons checking the record that an action involving the

property is pending. Until this is done, the action has no effect except against the parties involved in the action. [Mass. Gen. L. ch. 184, §15]

V. DISCOVERY

A. INTRODUCTION

Discovery may take place at any point after the commencement of the action until the beginning of the trial. The basic purposes of discovery are to narrow issues for trial (supplementing the "notice pleading" in the complaint and answer) and to prevent surprise at trial. Parties may gather further information in support of their own case, preserve testimony where a witness may not be available to testify at trial, and secure evidence to impeach the opponent's witnesses at trial.

Discovery may also be instrumental in avoiding trial altogether. Materials obtained through discovery may be used to support a motion for summary judgment (*see* VI.A., *infra*). Also, the exchange of information during discovery provides the parties with a common basis for evaluating the claims and defenses and promotes reasonable settlements.

B. SCOPE OF DISCOVERY

Parties may obtain discovery of *any matter not privileged* that is *relevant* to the subject matter of the lawsuit, including information which will be inadmissible at trial if it is reasonably calculated to lead to the discovery of admissible evidence. [Mass. R. Civ. P. 26]

1. Discoverable Matters

a. Individuals
The identity and location of persons (including experts) with knowledge of discoverable matter may be discovered.

b. Expert Testimony
A party may also discover, through the use of interrogatories, the identity of each person the other party expects to call to testify as an expert witness at trial, the subject matter on which the expert is expected to testify, the substance of facts and opinions to which the expert is expected to testify, and a summary of the grounds for each opinion. Further discovery by deposition is limited by requiring leave of court (or agreement of the parties) and allocation of the expert's time. [Mass. R. Civ. P. 26(b)4(A)] Where an expert has been retained by a party but is *not* expected to testify at trial, no discovery is permitted unless "exceptional circumstances" are demonstrated, such as the inability of the party seeking discovery to obtain facts or opinions on the same subject by other means. [Mass. R. Civ. P. 26(b)4(B)]

c. Books and Records
The existence, location, and custody of books or records may be discovered.

d. Insurance Agreements
Subject to certain restrictions, the existence and contents of an insurance agreement may be discovered, but such information does not by reason of disclosure become admissible at trial.

2. Work Product Rule
Documents (and tangible things) prepared by a party or its representative (including the attorney) in anticipation of litigation generally may *not* be discovered.

a. "Substantial Need" Exception
A court may order discovery if the opposing party has "substantial need" of the material and cannot obtain the "substantial equivalent" without "undue hardship."

b. Exception Not Applicable to Attorney's Work Product
The attorney's work product (mental impressions, opinions, or conclusions) cannot be discovered under the exception.

3. No Need to Supplement
There is no general duty to supplement answers to discovery if the original response was complete when made, *except* that a party must supplement:

a. Requests for the identity of witnesses, or experts, or the subject and substance of expert testimony;

b. Responses that were incorrect when made;

c. Responses that are no longer true when the circumstances are such that a failure to supplement is "in substance a knowing concealment"; and

d. Where supplementation is required by court order or by agreement of the parties.

C. DISCOVERY DEVICES

Any party to a lawsuit may elect to use any, all, or none of the discovery devices provided by the Massachusetts Rules of Civil Procedure. Discovery may be conducted simultaneously by all the parties, and the various discovery devices may be used in any sequence.

Two categories of discovery devices are available: those only against other parties to the lawsuit and those against nonparties (witnesses and documents) as well as parties.

1. Discovery Against Parties and Witnesses

a. Oral Depositions
Oral depositions are governed by Massachusetts Rule 30.

1) Definition
An oral deposition usually takes place in the attorney's office before a stenographer (who must have qualified as an officer competent to give oaths). The attorney asks questions of the deponent—the opposing party or a witness—who is under oath, and a stenographic transcript is made of both the questions and the deponent's responses. The deponent may also be compelled to produce documents at the deposition, although documents are usually exchanged between parties before depositions. Attorneys for both parties attend the deposition, and a nonparty deponent may also be represented by counsel. Cross-examination of the deponent is permitted.

2) Notice

a) In General
Seven days' advance written notice to the attorney for the opposing party—stating the time, place, and name (where available) of the deponent—is required. If the deposition notice requires that documents be brought to the deposition, the deponent must have at least 30 days' notice. The notice of deposition compels the attendance of a party.

A subpoena (or subpoena *duces tecum*) may be used to compel the attendance of a witness who is not a party. The subpoena must be served directly on the nonparty witness. If the opposing party is a corporation, association, or government agency, the notice of deposition may state with "reasonable particularity" the subjects for examination and require the party to designate the appropriate deponent(s).

b) Leave of Court Generally Not Required
Leave of court is *not* required to take a deposition, *except:*

(1) Where there is no reasonable likelihood the recovery will exceed $5,000;

(2) Where the case is in superior court after a trial in the district court;

(3) Where there has been a previous hearing before a master;

(4) In divorce, separate support, and child custody cases;

(5) Where the plaintiff seeks to take a deposition prior to the expiration of 30 days after service of the summons and complaint upon any defendant (unless the defendant has already initiated discovery); or

(6) Where the deponent is confined in prison.

3) Formalities
The stenographer prepares a verbatim transcript of the deposition which is then submitted to the deponent to be read, corrected if necessary, and signed. The stenographer then certifies it and returns it to the party taking the deposition.

4) Objections
Evidentiary objections to questions must be made in the deposition, and they are noted in the transcript. However, the deponent must still answer the deposition question (*i.e.,* the objection reserves the matter for decision by the trial judge if the deposition is used at trial). Parties frequently modify this rule by stipulation to reserve the making of all objections until the trial, except for objections to the form of questions (*i.e.,* objections which can be "obviated" by restating the question in a proper form).

A deponent sometimes refuses to answer a question (*e.g.,* to protect privileged information). In this situation, if the opposing attorney believes the objection is improper, the deposition may be suspended, and the parties can go before a judge (in either the court where the lawsuit is pending or the locality where the deposition is taking place) for a ruling on the objection.

Objection to matters such as the qualifications of the stenographer, the manner of taking the deposition, the conduct of a party, etc., must also be made at the deposition and placed in the transcript.

5) Use at Trial

    (i) The deposition of a *party* may be used for *any purpose* if it satisfies the rules of evidence.

    (ii) A deposition of a *witness* may *not* be used *unless* it satisfies the rules of evidence *and*:

        i. The deposition is used to *impeach* the witness's trial testimony (*e.g.,* by prior inconsistent statement); or

        ii. The witness is *not available* to testify at trial (*e.g.,* death, sickness, infirmity, could not be served with subpoena, more than 100 miles from the place of trial).

[Mass. R. Civ. P. 32]

b. Depositions upon Written Questions
Deposition upon written questions [Mass. R. Civ. P. 31] is an uncommon form of discovery. It is principally used where distance makes an oral deposition inconvenient, or where the deponent is not a party so interrogatories (2.a., *infra*) are not an available choice. Written questions are delivered to an officer who then asks the questions and transcribes the deponent's responses under oath.

c. Audiovisual Depositions

1) Authorization

    a) Treating Physicians and Expert Witnesses
    A party intending to call a treating physician or an expert as that party's own witness may depose that person audiovisually, and the audiovisual deposition may be used at trial in lieu of oral testimony unless the court orders otherwise.

    b) All Other Witnesses
    A party may audiovisually depose witnesses other than treating physicians and experts if the court allows (or if the parties stipulate). The other party must be given notice and an opportunity to be heard in opposition.

2) Timing
Notice of the taking of an audiovisual deposition cannot be served before six months after commencement of the action except by leave of court.

3) Procedure for Physician and Expert Audiovisual Depositions

a) Initial Notice
An initial notice must be given concerning an audiovisual deposition involving a party's own treating physician or experts stating that it is to be used in lieu of oral testimony. Other parties have 14 days after receiving this notice to file a motion opposing the deposition by audiovisual means.

b) Written Report
In addition to the six-month limitation discussed in c.2), above, notice to take audiovisual depositions of treating physicians and expert witnesses cannot be given until 30 days after a written report has been furnished to all parties. The written report must contain a curriculum vitae of the witness and shall detail the subject matter, substance, and support for all matters about which the witness will testify.

4) Evidentiary Objections

a) Experts
Objections to statements of treating physicians and experts must be made, to the extent practicable, during the deposition. The objections must be filed in court within 21 days before trial and responded to within 14 days of receipt. If these deadlines are not met, the objections are deemed waived.

b) All Other Witnesses
For nonexpert audiovisual depositions, objections must be made, if practicable, before the trial begins.

5) Use at Trial
Generally, audiovisual depositions may be used to the extent stenographic depositions are used. Additionally, unless the court orders otherwise, a party may use an expert audiovisual deposition at trial in lieu of oral testimony whether or not the witness is available to testify.

d. Depositions by Telephone
A deposition may be taken by telephone with leave of court on motion with notice and an opportunity to be heard or by stipulation of all parties. [Mass. R. Civ. P. 30]

2. Discovery Against Parties Only

a. Interrogatories

1) Definition
Interrogatories are written questions propounded by one party to the opposing party and are governed by Massachusetts Rule 33.

2) Time
The opponent must serve written answers—signed by the party under the penalties of perjury—on the party who served the interrogatories within 45 days. If a party fails to respond to interrogatories within this time, the clerk of the court, on request and after prior notice to the parties, will dismiss the action for failure to answer interrogatories only after the party who has served the interrogatories complies with a number of procedural requirements.

3) Number
No more than 30 interrogatories may be served without leave of court, but a party can divide the 30 interrogatories into more than one set (*e.g.,* a party can serve three sets of interrogatories, each consisting of 10 questions). The court on motion for good cause shown may allow additional interrogatories.

4) Objections
An objection may be made to an interrogatory by stating the objection (signed by the attorney) in the answers to the interrogatories. However, an interrogatory is "not necessarily objectionable" because the answer involves an opinion or the application of law to fact, but the court may order that it need not be answered until after a pretrial conference or until after designated discovery is complete.

If an objection is made, the party does not answer the interrogatory (*cf.* depositions, *supra*). Instead, the party serving the interrogatories may file a motion for an order compelling answers to interrogatories and get a court ruling on the objection.

5) Use at Trial

Interrogatories may be used at trial to the extent permitted by the rules of evidence.

b. Production of Documents and Things

1) Definition

A party may require the opposing party to produce documents for inspection and copying. [Mass. R. Civ. P. 34] This discovery device extends to:

a) Other forms of data, charts, photographs, computer records, etc.; and

b) Entry on land to inspect, measure, photograph, or test the property or any object or operation.

2) Procedure

The party seeking production serves a written request itemizing the documents (or things) to be produced and specifying a reasonable time, place, and manner for production. The opponent has 30 days to file a written response, either acceding to the request or stating objections to production. Each item or category requested must be described with reasonable particularity.

c. Request for Admissions

Requests for admissions are governed by Massachusetts Rule 36.

1) Definition

A party may request the opposing party to admit or deny—solely for the purpose of the lawsuit—the truthfulness of:

a) Statements;

b) Opinions of facts;

c) The application of law to fact; and

d) The genuineness of documents.

2) Procedure

Written requests for admissions (usually declaratory sentences setting forth factual propositions) are served on the opposing party. The matters are taken as admitted **unless**, within 30 days, the opponent serves a written response:

(i) Denying the truthfulness of the requested admission;

(ii) Objecting to the requested admission; or

(iii) Setting forth in detail why the matter cannot truthfully be admitted or denied.

The response must be signed by the party under penalties of perjury. Objections may be signed by the attorney.

3) Use at Trial

Facts admitted under this procedure are taken as "conclusively established" at trial. Any admission made pursuant to Rule 36 is for the purpose of the pending action only.

If a party proves at trial a matter denied in a response to a request for admissions, the court will order the opposing party to pay the expenses incurred in making the proof. [Mass. R. Civ. P. 37(c)]

    d. Physical or Mental Examination of a Party
    Mental and physical examinations of a party are governed by Massachusetts Rule 35.

        1) Definition
        With leave of court, a party may obtain a physical or mental examination (including the determination of blood group) of another party when her physical or medical condition is in controversy. For example, a defendant may seek the examination of the plaintiff in a personal injury suit by an expert of the defendant's choosing. Of course, the plaintiff can also agree to the examination, thus eliminating the need for court involvement.

        2) Procedure
        Because of the intrusiveness of this method of discovery, a party seeking a physical or mental examination must present a motion to the court and establish good cause for the examination. If an examination is ordered, the examined party may obtain a copy of the written report of the examining physician. The court may order delivery of the report "on such terms as are just" and may exclude a physician's testimony if the physician fails to deliver the report.

D. CONDUCT OF DISCOVERY AND SANCTIONS

Discovery is conducted by the parties without court supervision. A party may, however, invoke the court's aid to compel responses to discovery or to protect against unwarranted discovery.

    1. Sanctions
    A party may apply for an order compelling a response to a discovery request or a complete and unevasive response. [Mass. R. Civ. P. 37] The court may invoke a wide range of sanctions for failure to comply with discovery rules including:

        a. Payment of costs;

        b. Contempt;

        c. Dismissal of the action;

        d. Taking certain facts as admitted; and

        e. Refusing the introduction of certain evidence at trial.

    2. Limiting Answer (Protective Order)
    A party seeking to avoid disclosure of information requested in discovery may seek a protective order from the court to:

        (i) Confine discovery to its permissible scope (B., *supra*);

        (ii) Protect privileged information; or

        (iii) Generally prevent annoyance, embarrassment, oppression, or undue burden or expense.

    The range of choices available to the court is again quite broad, including:

        (i) Forbidding discovery;

        (ii) Specifying the terms and conditions under which the discovery will be conducted;

        (iii) Limiting discovery to specified topics; and

        (iv) Prescribing the discovery devices that can be used.

    [Mass. R. Civ. P. 26(c)]

    3. Stipulations
    The parties may, by written stipulation, vary the discovery provisions in the Massachusetts Rules (unless the court orders otherwise). [Mass. R. Civ. P. 29]

VI. METHODS FOR TERMINATING LITIGATION WITHOUT TRIAL

A. SUMMARY JUDGMENT

Summary judgment is governed by Massachusetts Rule 56. The topics covered below apply to both superior courts and district courts. Differences in summary judgment procedures between the two courts are not covered in this outline.

1. Introduction

    a. When Available

    A judge may decide a lawsuit on a motion for summary judgment if the case presents *no genuine issue as to any material fact* for trial. A *defendant* may move for summary judgment at any time after commencement of the action. The motion may be made before filing a timely answer or after the due date of an answer. A *plaintiff* may move for summary judgment at any time after 20 days from commencement of the action or after service on the plaintiff of a motion for summary judgment by the defendant. The moving party must establish two matters to prevail:

    1) That the case presents no genuine issue of material fact; and

    2) That the moving party is entitled to judgment as a matter of law.

    b. Final Judgment

    If the judge allows the motion for summary judgment on all of the issues presented by the moving party, a final judgment may be entered (*i.e.,* the judgment has full res judicata effect and may be appealed). On the other hand, if the judge denies the motion for summary judgment (*i.e.,* decides there is a genuine issue of material fact), the case stands for trial. Summary judgment may be entered either for or against the moving party.

2. Procedure

A motion for summary judgment is typically filed after discovery is complete. The moving party may rely on two categories of documents to establish that there is no genuine issue of material fact:

    (i) The *pleadings* and any *discovery* (depositions, answers to interrogatories, and admissions) already on file with the court; and

    (ii) *Affidavits* (*see* 3., *infra*) filed with the motion for summary judgment.

Although Massachusetts Rule 56 does not say so, three additional documents may be used to support a motion for summary judgment:

    (i) A master's report [DeVaux v. American Home Assurance Co., 387 Mass. 814 (1983)];

    (ii) The district court judgment (in a trial de novo before the superior court) [O'Brion, Russell & Co. v. Lemay, 370 Mass. 243 (1976)]; and

    (iii) A foreign judgment where the plaintiff seeks a Massachusetts judgment under the Full Faith and Credit Clause [*see* Shapiro Equipment Corp. v. Morris & Son Construction Co., 369 Mass. 968 (1976)].

Where the opposing party has the burden of proof at trial, the proponent of a motion for summary judgment need only show that the party opposing it has no reasonable expectation of proving an essential element of that party's case. Affirmative evidence to negate the opposing party's claim need not be submitted. [Kourovacilis v. General Motors Corp., 410 Mass. 706 (1991)]

3. Affidavits

Affidavits are often filed in support of and in opposition to a motion for summary judgment. The *form* of the affidavits is critical.

Massachusetts Rule 56(e) requires that the affidavit:

    (i) Be made on personal knowledge;

(ii) Show affirmatively that the affiant is competent to testify under the rules of evidence;

(iii) Set forth such facts as would be admissible in evidence at the trial; and

(iv) Have attached sworn or certified copies of all documents referred to in the affidavit.

In particular, affidavits made on "information and belief" are insufficient. [Shapiro Equipment Corp. v. Morris & Son Construction Co., *supra*]

4. **Opposing Summary Judgment**
The opponent must file affidavits establishing a genuine issue of material fact for trial in order to avoid decision of the case on a motion for summary judgment. The opposing affidavit must set forth *specific* facts and satisfy all the form requirements (3., *supra*).

The opponent cannot rely on denials in the pleadings (usually the answer). The opposing affidavit cannot merely assert that there is a triable issue of fact, nor can it merely set forth "ultimate" facts or conclusions. [Community National Bank v. Dawes, 369 Mass. 550 (1976)] Note that when the intent of one of the parties is at issue in the lawsuit, a motion for summary judgment is unlikely to succeed for either party. [Gurry v. Cumberland Farms, Inc., 406 Mass. 615 (1990)]

5. **Unavailability of Affidavits**
The court may deny summary judgment or grant a continuance if the opponent sets forth in an affidavit sufficient reasons why the opponent cannot file opposing affidavits. In this situation, the summary judgment hearing is frequently postponed to permit further discovery. [Mass. R. Civ. P. 56(f)]

6. **Partial Summary Judgment**
A motion for summary judgment may be used to dispose of only part of the lawsuit. For example, the court may enter summary judgment on liability alone, leaving damages for trial. Where multiple claims or parties have been joined in one lawsuit, the court may grant summary judgment as to some claims or parties but not others.

7. **Bad Faith or Delay**
If affidavits are filed in bad faith or for purposes of delay, the court may:

a. Order payment of costs, including attorneys' fees; and

b. Adjudge the attorney or party in contempt.

B. OTHER DEVICES

1. **Motion to Dismiss for Failure to State a Claim on Which Relief Can Be Granted**
The Massachusetts Rule 12(b)(6) motion to dismiss—discussed in connection with the defendant's pleadings (III.C.2.b.3), *supra*—is the other principal device for terminating litigation prior to trial. The motion to dismiss:

(i) Hypothetically admits the allegations in the complaint; and

(ii) Tests the legal sufficiency of the complaint.

The motion to dismiss, in other words, does not look to either the defenses to the complaint or to the facts underlying the claim or defense. The motion for summary judgment is broader in scope. It comes at a point when the issue is joined by the complaint and answer, and it permits use of undisputed facts in deciding the legal claims. (Remember that a motion to dismiss is treated as a motion for summary judgment if the court does receive evidence.)

2. **Motion for Judgment on the Pleadings**
A motion for judgment on the pleadings [Mass. R. Civ. P. 12(c)] is principally addressed to the rare occasion when the answer admits all the facts in the complaint (or the plaintiff's reply admits allegations in a counterclaim), leaving only an issue of law for decision. It may be filed as early as 20 days after the complaint (or counterclaim) has been served on the defendant. A plaintiff who files this motion usually argues that the answer has failed to controvert any material issue in the complaint and that the defendant has failed to raise any legally sufficient affirmative defenses.

C. DISMISSALS

1. Rule 41
Massachusetts Rule 41 governs voluntary dismissals and certain involuntary dismissals.

a. Voluntary Dismissals
An action will be dismissed if counsel for all parties sign and file a written stipulation of dismissal with the court. The plaintiff alone also may also dismiss an action by filing a notice of dismissal at any time before the defendant files an answer or motion for summary judgment. [Mass. R. Civ. P. 41(a)(1)]

b. Involuntary Dismissals
The court may grant the defendant's motion for dismissal due to the plaintiff's failure to prosecute the action. There must be at least convincing evidence of unreasonable conduct or delay, and the court should consider other penalties. [Monahan v. Washburn, 400 Mass. 126 (1987)]

2. Fraud on the Court
In addition to its power to dismiss certain actions under Massachusetts Rule 41, the court also has the inherent power to dismiss a complaint where it appears by *clear and convincing evidence* that the plaintiff has attempted to commit fraud upon the court. Destruction of evidence and proffering a forged document or perjured deposition testimony are examples of fraud that may, in the exercise of the court's discretion, justify dismissal. [Rockdale Management Co. v. Shawmut Bank, 418 Mass. 596 (1994)]

3. Refusal to Comply with Judicial Orders
A court may also dismiss a complaint where a plaintiff persistently refuses to comply with a judicial order. [Friedman v. Globe Newspaper Co., 38 Mass. App. Ct. 923 (1995)—case dismissed where pro se plaintiff refused to follow court's order requiring him to delete the inclusion of a demand for $7 million in damages from his complaint]

VII. TRIAL

A. PRETRIAL CONFERENCE
Massachusetts Rule 16 provides that a court, in its discretion, may direct the attorneys for the parties to appear at a pretrial conference for the following purposes:

1. Simplification of issues;

2. Necessity or desirability of amendments to pleadings;

3. Obtaining admissions of fact and documents to avoid needless proof;

4. Limitation of the number of expert witnesses;

5. Advisability of a preliminary reference of issues to a master;

6. Possibility of settlement;

7. Agreement on damages;

8. Similar matters that may aid disposition of the action; and

9. Establishment of a firm trial date for the case.

B. MASTERS
A master is a person appointed by the court to hear evidence and report facts. A case or specified issues in the case may be referred to a master prior to trial before a judge or jury, either by consent of the parties or by order of the court. [Mass. R. Civ. P. 53]

Note: In district court, a master may not be appointed without assent of all parties.

1. Purpose
The function of the master is to conduct evidentiary proceedings and, in the usual case, to

make findings of fact and conclusions of law which the master files with the court in a "report" (after submitting a draft to the parties for their suggestions). A transcript of the evidence produced before the master is reported in a jury-waived case.

2. Use at Trial

In a jury trial, the master's findings may be read to the jury and constitute prima facie evidence. In a jury-waived action, the court accepts the master's findings of fact unless they are clearly erroneous. In order to contest the master's findings, a party must file written objections to the master's report within 10 days after it is filed in court.

C. JURY TRIAL

1. Availability—Law Actions

The Massachusetts Constitution preserves the right to trial by jury in law actions (*i.e.,* where the relief claimed is money damages). Under Massachusetts Rule 38, a party must file a written demand for a jury trial within 10 days after service of the last pleading which presents the issue on which a jury trial is sought. The jury demand may specify the issues on which a jury trial is requested or the demand may be for all the issues in the case triable to a jury.

The right to trial by jury is *waived* if a timely demand is not filed. In this event, the case is tried by the court (*i.e.,* the judge sitting without the jury). Remember that a jury demand must be filed in the superior court in a case removed from the district court for trial de novo; otherwise the case will be tried by the court. A party cannot withdraw a jury demand without the consent of the other parties. [Mass. R. Civ. P. 38(d); Vaught Construction Co. v. Bertonazzi Buick Co., 371 Mass. 553 (1976)]

2. Availability—Equity Actions

Jury trials are *not* available in equity actions (*i.e.,* where the relief claimed is an injunction or specific performance). The dichotomy between law and equity actions requires one to ask whether the claim for relief was one traditionally tried to a jury at common law at the time the Massachusetts Constitution was adopted (1780) or whether the state legislature has provided a jury trial by statute.

Note that these same issues arise under the Federal Rules. [*See, e.g.,* Beacon Theatres, Inc. v. Westover, 359 U.S. 500 (1959)]

3. Jury Size and Verdict

Twelve jurors sit on civil actions in the superior court, but the parties may stipulate to fewer jurors. [Mass. R. Civ. P. 48] If 12 jurors are impaneled and jurors subsequently die, become ill, or are otherwise unable to complete the trial, the trial may proceed before 10 jurors. [Mass. Gen. L. ch. 234, §34B]

Only five-sixths of the jurors need agree to return a verdict in a civil action. [Mass. Gen. L. ch. 234, §34A]

4. Jury Instructions

Jury instructions are governed by Massachusetts Rule 51.

a. Requests for Instructions

After the close of all the evidence and before the closing arguments begin, any party may file written requests for instructions to the jury. The judge will then inform the attorneys of the instructions that will be given to the jury after the closing arguments.

b. Objections to Instructions

To preserve an issue for appeal, an objection must be made to the judge's proposed instructions out of the presence of the jury. The objection must be raised before the jury retires to consider its verdict, and must state distinctly the grounds for the objection.

1) Compare Federal Practice in First Circuit

Massachusetts demands only that counsel make any objections to jury instructions clearly known to the judge at some point before the jury begins deliberations. If the judge indicates to counsel that she understands the basis for the objections, counsel need not renew them immediately before the jury retires to deliberate. In contrast, federal practice in the First Circuit strictly requires that counsel restate all objections to the judge immediately before the jury retires; failure to do so waives all previously stated objections. [Flood v. Southland Corp., 416 Mass. 62 (1993)]

D. BURDENS OF PROOF

1. Preponderance of Evidence
In a civil action, the trier of fact (judge or jury) must be persuaded by a preponderance of the evidence of the truth of each fact necessary for recovery. Usually both the burden of producing the evidence and the burden of persuasion are on the plaintiff.

2. Burden on Defendant
Sometimes the burden is shifted to the defendant—*affirmative defenses* are a prime illustration. The burden of proof and the burden of pleading a matter do not necessarily go hand in hand, however. Examples are the Statute of Frauds and the statute of limitations; they must be pleaded by the defendant, but the burden of proof remains with the plaintiff.

3. Clear and Convincing Evidence
In some civil cases, clear and convincing evidence is required—a burden of persuasion higher than the usual preponderance of the evidence test, but less than the criminal test of beyond a reasonable doubt. Examples include proof of mental illness for involuntary commitments, of the irregularity of official proceedings, and of a gift causa mortis.

E. DIRECTED VERDICT
A directed verdict withdraws the case (or a particular issue) from the jury for decision by the judge. Directed verdicts are governed by Massachusetts Rule 50(a). While a verdict may be directed for either party, a motion for directed verdict is usually filed by the defendant, either at the close of the plaintiff's case in chief or at the close of all the evidence.

1. Directed Verdict Test
In ruling on a motion for directed verdict, a judge:

(i) Views the evidence in the light most favorable to the plaintiff (*i.e.,* the party opposing the motion);

(ii) Does not weigh the credibility of the witnesses; and

(iii) Determines whether reasonable jurors could reach different conclusions from the evidence in the case.

The issue, in sum, is whether the case should be submitted to the jury for decision or whether there is no basis on which a reasonable juror could conclude that the plaintiff has established a claim for relief against the defendant. In the latter situation, the judge should direct a verdict against the plaintiff. [*See* Foley v. Kibrick, 12 Mass. App. 382 (1981)]

2. Effect of Making Motion
The defendant does not waive the right to present evidence by moving for a directed verdict at the close of the plaintiff's evidence. The denial of the motion at this point likewise does not preclude the defendant from renewing the motion for directed verdict at the close of all the evidence.

3. Motion After Opening Statement
A verdict may also be directed at the conclusion of the opening statement if the attorney's opening statement does not adduce evidence which (if believed) would establish a claim or defense.

4. Motion in Case Tried Before a Judge
The directed verdict is not available in a case tried to a judge; the defendant may make a motion for a directed finding. Where there is no jury, the judge:

a. Does not have to view the evidence in the light most favorable to the plaintiff; and

b. May weigh the credibility of witnesses.

F. JUDGMENT NOTWITHSTANDING THE VERDICT
The judgment notwithstanding the verdict ("JNOV") [Mass. R. Civ. P. 50(b)] serves essentially the same function, but at a different point, as the directed verdict.

1. **When It Is Made**
   A motion for JNOV may be granted in the following situation:

   a. The defendant (or plaintiff) originally moved for a directed verdict at the close of all the evidence (not just at the close of the plaintiff's case);

   b. The judge submitted the case to the jury;

   c. The jury returned a verdict in favor of the plaintiff (or defendant); and

   d. Within 10 days after the entry of judgment on the jury's verdict, the defendant (or plaintiff) filed a motion for JNOV.

2. **Test**
   The judge must decide whether a reasonable juror, considering the evidence, the law (jury instructions), and the burden of proof, could have reached the verdict in question. If the answer is yes, the motion for JNOV must be denied. If the answer is no, then the judge will set aside the jury's verdict and enter judgment in favor of the party who filed the motion for JNOV. [Rubel v. Hayden, Harding & Buchanan, Inc., 15 Mass. App. 252 (1983)]

G. POST-VERDICT MOTIONS

1. **Motion for New Trial**

   a. **Time**
      A motion for new trial must be *served* (not merely filed in court) within 10 days after the entry of judgment. [Mass. R. Civ. P. 59(b)]

   b. **Grounds**
      The trial judge may grant a new trial for any of the following reasons:

      1) Jury verdict is against the weight of the evidence. The court should set aside the verdict and grant a new trial if the jury failed to exercise honest and reasonable judgment pursuant to controlling principles of law. [Robertson v. Gaston Snow & Ely Bartlett, 404 Mass. 515 (1989), *cert. denied*, 493 U.S. 894 (1990)]

      2) Damages awarded are either (i) excessive, and the prevailing party has been given an opportunity to accept a reduction (remittitur), or (ii) inadequate, and the defendant has been given an opportunity to accept an addition to the award (additur).

      3) Newly discovered evidence (which was not available at trial, despite due diligence by the party, and which may affect the result).

      4) Jury misconduct.

      5) Errors of law in the trial.

   c. **Effect of Motion**
      A decision granting a new trial is an interlocutory order that cannot be appealed until after the new trial.

      A motion for new trial may be joined with a motion for JNOV. If the court allows a motion for JNOV, the opposing party may serve a motion for new trial within 10 days. [Mass. R. Civ. P. 50]

2. **Motion to Alter or Amend the Judgment**
   A party may move to alter or amend a judgment by serving a motion on all parties not later than 10 days after entry of judgment. Such motions include motions for rehearing, reconsideration, and vacation for want of jurisdiction. The appeal clock is tolled until after disposition of a motion to alter or amend judgment. [Mass. R. Civ. P. 59(e)]

H. JUDGMENT

1. **Introduction**
   A judgment (or final judgment) is a separate written document entered on the court docket that signifies the final adjudication by the trial court of all the issues presented by all parties

to the lawsuit. The judgment is prepared and entered by the clerk where the judge or jury has denied all relief or awarded relief for a specified sum of money. In other cases, the clerk enters the judgment after the court has approved the form of judgment (*e.g.,* an injunction). The judgment entered may differ in kind or amount from the demand for judgment in the pleadings (except where entered by default).

2.   Entry of Judgment

a.   Against Some Parties or on Some Claims

Although a court sometimes resolves certain issues or renders decisions affecting certain parties prior to the conclusion of trial (*e.g.,* on a motion for partial summary judgment), these decisions are usually interlocutory, and no judgment is entered until the conclusion of the litigation. The exception to this general principle occurs in cases involving multiple claims or multiple parties where judgment may be entered as to some parties or claims if the court makes:

(i)   An express determination that there is no just reason for delay; *and*

(ii)   An express direction for entry of judgment.

[Mass. R. Civ. P. 54(b)]

b.   By Default

The clerk may enter a default judgment against a party:

(i)   For failure to file a responsive pleading (*e.g.,* answer) or otherwise defend the action as required by the Massachusetts Rules (*e.g.,* to file timely answers to interrogatories); or

(ii)   Upon application to the clerk by the opposing party.

[Mass. R. Civ. P. 55]

1)   Effect of Default Judgment

Entry of a default precludes the party from defending the case further on the merits. (Defaults are most commonly entered against defendants. Defaults against plaintiffs are frequently called "nonsuits" but the term is not used by the Massachusetts Rules.)

2)   Requirements for Default Judgment

a)   General Rule

Judgment may be entered on the default by the clerk if the:

(i)   Claim is for a "sum certain" or an amount ascertainable by calculation (*e.g.,* recovery on a promissory note);

(ii)   The plaintiff files an affidavit that the defendant is not an infant or incompetent person; and

(iii)   Pursuant to the Soldiers' and Sailors' Civil Relief Act, the plaintiff files an affidavit that the defendant is not in the military service. [50 U.S.C. §§520 *et seq.*]

Otherwise, the party must apply to the court for entry of judgment by default. A defaulted party who filed an appearance in the lawsuit must be served with the application for judgment at least seven days before the court hears the matter.

The court, after seven days' notice to defendant, will hold an assessment of damages hearing. At the hearing, plaintiff will introduce evidence to prove the amount of damages. Defendant may also offer evidence on the damages issue. The court will not receive evidence on the underlying issue of liability (*e.g.,* negligence).

b)   Special Rule

A special rule applies where the defendant failed to appear and the judgment is secured by a motor vehicle insurance policy. Here the insured is still entitled to four days' notice before damages can be assessed. [Mass. Gen. L. ch. 231, §58A]

c) Limitations
A judgment by default *cannot:*

(1) Be different in kind than that asked for in the demand for judgment in the pleadings; or

(2) Exceed the amount set forth in the demand for judgment.

[Mass. R. Civ. P. 54]

c. Confession of Judgment
A provision in a contract, promissory note, or other written instrument whereby a party agrees in advance to confess judgment if a lawsuit is brought to enforce the instrument is *void*. [Mass. Gen. L. ch. 231, §13A] After a lawsuit is filed, however, both parties (or their attorneys) may agree to entry of judgment by signing and filing a written stipulation with the court.

3. Interest and Costs

a. Included Interest
The judgment may include 12% annual interest from the date the action was commenced (or in contract actions, from the date of breach or demand). [Mass. Gen. L. ch. 231, §§6B, 6C] Costs (*e.g.,* filing fees) may also be recovered by the prevailing party. The clerk will include interest in the judgment. Every judgment for the payment of money shall bear interest up to the date of payment of the judgment. [Mass. R. Civ. P. 54(f)]

b. Applying for Costs
The prevailing party must apply to the clerk for costs, which will be allowed as a matter of course. Only the court, however, may allow the award of costs for depositions, and it must find that the deposition was "reasonably necessary" (whether or not the deposition was used at trial). [Mass. R. Civ. P. 54(e)]

c. Not Available Against Commonwealth
Costs and interest are generally not available against the Commonwealth. [Mass. R. Civ. P. 54(d); Broadhurst v. Director of Division of Employment Security, 373 Mass. 720 (1977)] One example of a statutory exception is that the Commonwealth waives its sovereign immunity against the payment of costs by the act of commencing a lawsuit. [Mass. Gen. L. ch. 261, §14]

I. RELIEF FROM JUDGMENT
It is important to distinguish entry of a default from entry of judgment (including judgment by default) because it is more difficult to secure relief in the latter situation. *Note:* Motions for relief from judgment do not toll the appeal time.

1. Relief from Default
A default may be set aside by the court for "good cause shown." [Mass. R. Civ. P. 55(c)]

2. Relief from Judgment
The court in its discretion may set aside a judgment on motion by a party [Mass. R. Civ. P. 60(b)]:

(i) Within *one year* for:

i. Mistake, inadvertence, surprise, or excusable neglect;

ii. Newly discovered evidence (which due diligence could not have uncovered in time for a motion for a new trial) (G.1.b.3), *supra*); or

iii. Fraud, misrepresentation, or other misconduct of an adverse party; or

(ii) Within a *reasonable time* because:

      i.   The judgment is void;

      ii.   The judgment has been satisfied, released, or discharged; or

      iii. Of any other reason justifying relief from the judgment.

The court's decision will not be set aside except where there is an abuse of discretion.

J. EXECUTION

An execution is the process which issues from the court, at the request of the prevailing party, to enforce the court's judgment. The clerk will not issue an execution until the time for appeal (30 days) has expired, and court permission is required to issue execution more than one year after judgment is entered. [Mass. Gen. L. ch. 235, §§17, 19; Mass. R. Civ. P. 69]

The execution is used by a sheriff, acting at the request of a party, to seize and sell property to satisfy the judgment. Certain property is *exempt* from execution: *e.g.,* $3,000 of household furniture; $500 of tools and fixtures to carry out the debtor's trade; a homestead declared in the debtor's residence and $75 per month for utility service (or $200 per month for rent); $125 in cash, savings, or wages; and an auto necessary for personal transportation or to secure or maintain employment, not exceeding $700 in value. [Mass. Gen. L. ch. 235, §34] Retirement benefits may be exempt from execution, unless the underlying debt is to: (i) support a spouse or children, (ii) satisfy a monetary penalty, or (iii) make restitution to a victim of a crime. [Mass. Gen. L. ch. 235, §34A]

VIII. RES JUDICATA AND COLLATERAL ESTOPPEL

A. INTRODUCTION

The res judicata and collateral estoppel doctrines both present questions of the binding effect in a subsequent lawsuit of a judgment entered in a prior action. The principal distinction is that res judicata concerns the *legal claim* adjudicated in the prior action, while collateral estoppel concerns the preclusive effect of *issues* determined in the prior action.

B. RES JUDICATA/CLAIM PRECLUSION

Res judicata, also known as "claim preclusion," bars relitigation in a later action of every claim that was raised in the first action or that *could have been* raised as long as the parties in the later action are identical (or in privity with) the parties to the prior action. [Harker v. City of Holyoke, 390 Mass. 555 (1983)] There are four prerequisites to the application of res judicata/claim preclusion:

1. Same Claim

Massachusetts courts, like the federal courts, have adopted a broad concept of the "same claim" in applying res judicata. The traditional common law approach was that suits raising different legal theories to justify relief were not the same "cause of action," and judgment on the first did not bar the subsequent action. Thus, a judgment on a contract claim did not preclude a second action by the same plaintiff for the same work on a quantum meruit theory. The current approach adopts a transactional view of the "same claim" for purposes of preclusion—does the second suit arise out of the same transaction or occurrence as the first, involve the same or similar evidence of liability and damages, and would it promote judicial economy to try the two together?

2. Same Parties

Res judicata/claim preclusion will only apply in a suit between the same parties or someone in *privity* with the same parties. The concept of "privity" is that two parties stand in such a relationship that they have identical interests and that it is fair to hold both to the outcome of the prior suit. Privity is commonly found between employer and employee, successors in interest in property, and an agent and principal. Privity may also be found when no such legal relationship exists but a party in fact had its interests represented in the prior suit, *e.g.,* through its control or financing of the prior litigation even though not named as a party.

3. Raised or Could Have Been Raised

To promote judicial economy, res judicata precludes not only claims that were litigated in the prior suit, but also claims that could have been joined, but were not. Given the liberal rules permitting joinder of claims by a plaintiff, res judicata acts as strong pressure on a party to litigate in a single suit all claims arising out of the same transaction or occurrence.

A party seeking to litigate the related claim in a subsequent suit will have to establish that it could not have been joined, *e.g.,* because of a jurisdictional limitation of the first forum.

> *Example:* Plaintiff brought suit in federal court under federal question jurisdiction and appended state law claims. After the state claims were dismissed for lack of subject matter jurisdiction and summary judgment was entered against plaintiff on his federal question claim, he tried to bring the state claims back into federal court based on diversity. The court held that since plaintiff could have initially brought his state claims in federal court under diversity jurisdiction, those state claims were barred by the doctrine of res judicata. [Kale v. Combined Insurance Co. of America, 736 F. Supp. 1183 (D. Mass. 1990), *aff'd,* 924 F.2d 1161 (1st Cir. 1991)]

4. Judgment on the Merits

In order to have res judicata effect, the prior judgment must have been rendered on the merits of the claim for relief. Included in this category are judgment after trial, dismissal for failure to state a claim, and summary judgment.

In addition, certain procedural dismissals or judgments which are not truly on the merits are given res judicata effect in order to give "teeth" to the sanction, *e.g.*, judgment by default, dismissals for failure to comply with discovery rules, and dismissals with prejudice.

The following prior decisions do ***not*** have res judicata effect:

a. Dismissals for insufficient service of process;

b. Dismissals for improper venue;

c. Dismissals without prejudice; and

d. Cases where the defendant demonstrates that the court lacked jurisdiction over the person (unless the defendant appeared in the prior action and either unsuccessfully litigated the jurisdictional issue or consented to the exercise of jurisdiction).

C. COLLATERAL ESTOPPEL/ISSUE PRECLUSION

1. Defined

Under the collateral estoppel doctrine, also known as "issue preclusion," an issue that was actually litigated and was necessary to the decision of the prior action is conclusive in a subsequent action between the same parties. Collateral estoppel applies even when the legal theory in the later action is different from that of the prior action (and res judicata does not apply) if both actions present a common issue of fact or law.

2. Component Parts

a. **Same Issue**

Collateral estoppel/issue preclusion applies to issues which are the same as ones adjudicated in a prior action, even though the causes of action (claims) are different. Collateral estoppel does not preclude suit altogether, but compels the second court to adopt the same finding on identical issues.

b. **Actually Litigated and Determined**

Unlike res judicata/claim preclusion, when a claim may be barred which could have been raised, but was not, collateral estoppel/issue preclusion only applies when the same issue was actually litigated and decided in the prior action. Thus, a default judgment which does not adjudicate any contested issues has no collateral estoppel effect. Similarly, if there are alternative grounds which might justify granting of a general verdict, and it is not clear which was the basis for the verdict, then collateral estoppel may not be applied to either ground.

c. **Necessary to Decision in Prior Action**

To assure that the issue was given the full attention of the parties and the court in the prior suit, it is required that the finding was necessary to the outcome of that action. Thus, if a court makes findings on matters tangential or collateral to the judgment, no preclusion applies to those findings.

d. **Same Parties**

The traditional rule, the "mutuality" requirement, limited the use of collateral estoppel to parties (or those in privity with parties) to the first suit. However, Massachusetts has followed the lead of the federal courts in permitting nonmutual use of collateral estoppel, both "offensively" and "defensively." The key requirement in both situations is that the party against whom collateral estoppel is asserted must have had a full and fair opportunity to litigate the issue in the prior proceeding.

Example: In *Aetna Casualty and Surety Co. v. Niziolek*, 395 Mass. 737 (1985), an insurance company brought a civil action against defendant to recover money paid on a fire insurance policy. Defendant had previously been convicted of arson in a criminal action which established that he had intentionally set fire to the building. In the subsequent civil suit, the insurance company was able to invoke the doctrine of collateral estoppel to preclude him from relitigating issues decided in the criminal trial. Although the insurance company had not been a party to the criminal proceeding, it was fair to hold defendant to those findings because he had ample opportunity and incentive to litigate them in the prior action. Another decision held that a convicted defendant will be collaterally estopped from relitigating issues already disposed of in her criminal case in a subsequent federal forfeiture action. [Commonwealth v. Koulouris, 406 Mass. 281 (1989)]

Note: Collateral estoppel/issue preclusion may **never** be applied against one who was not a party to the prior suit. As a matter of due process, a nonparty cannot be bound by prior findings without her "day in court."

IX. APPELLATE PROCESS

A. INTRODUCTION
The Massachusetts Bar Exam tests appellate procedure tangentially, as in questions that ask how an appellate court would rule.

Appeals to the supreme judicial court and appeals court are governed by the Massachusetts Rules of Appellate Procedure, which are patterned on the Federal Rules of Appellate Procedure. There are two methods—appeal and report—by which a case may reach the appellate courts.

B. APPELLATE COURTS

1. Appeals Court
The appeals court was created as an intermediate appellate court. It reviews final judgments entered by the superior, probate, and land courts. It also has special statutory authority to review preliminary injunction decisions by the superior and housing courts. [Mass. Gen. L. ch. 231, §118] The appeals court consists of a chief justice and 21 associate justices who sit in panels of three to hear cases. [Mass. Gen. L. ch. 211A]

2. Supreme Judicial Court
The supreme judicial court is the state's highest appellate court. It has concurrent appellate jurisdiction with the appeals court. It also hears appeals from judgments rendered by the single justice session of the supreme judicial court and, by special statutory provisions, from some agencies (*e.g.,* appellate tax board, department of public utilities rate decisions). The supreme judicial court also issues advisory opinions to the legislature, governor, and council. [Mass. Gen. L. ch. 211]

There are seven justices on the supreme judicial court (one chief justice and six associate justices). Five justices customarily hear oral argument in appeals; four constitute a quorum.

3. Special Problem—Appeals Court/Supreme Judicial Court Relationship
As noted above, most appeals go to the appeals court in the first instance. A party has no right to a further appeal to the supreme judicial court. Instead, most cases get to the supreme judicial court by one of two methods: direct appeal or further appellate review.

a. Direct Appeal
Direct appeal means that the appeal moves from the trial court to the supreme judicial court without first being decided by the appeals court. This happens when either: (i) two supreme judicial court justices order direct review (on their own initiative or at the request of a party) and the case presents constitutional questions or questions of first

impression or public importance which should be decided by the supreme judicial court, or (ii) a majority of the appeals court certifies that direct review by the supreme judicial court is in the public interest. [Mass. Gen. L. ch. 211A, §10]

b. Further Appellate Review
Further appellate review involves supreme judicial court review of appeals court decisions. It occurs where either (i) three supreme judicial court justices authorize further review for substantial reasons affecting the public interest or the interests of justice, or (ii) a majority of appeals court justices or a majority of the justices deciding the case certifies that further review is required by the public interest or the interests of justice. [Mass. Gen. L. ch. 211A, §11]

C. INITIAL APPEAL

1. Standard of Review on Appeal
The appeals court and supreme judicial court review rulings of law made by the trial judge. Findings of fact will not be set aside unless they are "clearly erroneous," *i.e.,* when, although there may be some evidence to support the finding, the reviewing court, on the entire evidence, is left with the firm and definite conviction that a mistake has been committed. [Mass. R. Civ. P. 52(a)]

2. Preserving Right to Appeal
If a party has an opportunity to object to a ruling at trial, the party must do so to preserve the issue for appeal. [Mass. R. Civ. P. 46] Likewise, a party must object to jury instructions before the jury begins its deliberations. [Mass. R. Civ. P. 51(b)] These requirements apply only to the party who is claiming error on appeal. Note that a decision may be upheld on appeal even on grounds not raised or argued before the lower court.

3. Notice of Appeal

a. Deadlines

1) Filed with the Trial Court Clerk
A party appeals from a final civil judgment entered by a trial court (except the district court) by filing a notice of appeal with the clerk of the trial court within 30 days after the entry of judgment (60 days if the Commonwealth or a state agency is a party). Filing may be accomplished by mail, but it is not timely unless received by the clerk within the 30- or 60-day period. [Mass. R. App. P. 4] On a showing of excusable neglect, the time to appeal may be extended an additional 30 days. The request for extension must be made by motion if the original 30 or 60 days have expired.

2) Appeal Erroneously Filed in Appellate Court
If the appeal is erroneously filed in the appellate court, the clerk must note when the appeal is filed and transfer the notice of appeal to the lower court. The appeal is deemed to be filed on the date the appellate court clerk noted on the notice.

b. Form of Notice
The notice of appeal must specify the parties taking the appeal and designate the judgment, order, or part thereof appealed from.

c. Service of Notice
The clerk serves the notice of appeal on other parties to the lawsuit, who then can file cross-appeals within either 14 days from the date on which the first notice of appeal was filed, or the original 30 or 60 days, whichever is later. Failure of the clerk to serve notice of the appeal does not affect the validity of the appeal.

d. Effect of Motion on Appeal Period
Timely filing of a motion for JNOV, for a new trial, or to amend the judgment tolls the running of the 30-day appeal period. Any notice of appeal filed before the court rules on these motions has no effect and must be refiled. The full 30- or 60-day period starts to run again after the court acts on the motion. Note that a motion for relief from judgment under Massachusetts Rule 60(b) does *not* toll the running of the appeal period. [Mass. R. App. P. 4]

e. **Stay of Judgment**
A notice of appeal *does not stay* the trial court's judgment. A stay may be sought in the trial court and subsequently in the appellate court. [Mass. R. App. P. 6] In civil cases, relief from judgment may be conditioned on the filing of a bond or other appropriate security.

f. **Extensions of Time**
Generally, the appellate court may extend any time period on a showing of good cause. The time within which a party may file a notice of appeal, however, may not be extended in any case beyond one year from the date of judgment.

4. **Direct Appellate Review by the Supreme Judicial Court**
Where the supreme judicial court and the appeals court have concurrent appellate jurisdiction, an appeal must first be entered in the appeals court. Within 20 days of docketing in the appeals court, any party may apply to the supreme judicial court for direct appellate review if the appeal presents: (i) questions of first impression or novel questions of law; (ii) questions concerning the Massachusetts or United States Constitution; or (iii) questions of sufficient public interest. Within 10 days of filing an application, any other party may but need not file and serve an opposition thereto. The parties must file one copy of the application or opposition with the appeals court and 14 copies with the supreme judicial court.

Note: The filing for direct appellate review by the supreme judicial court does not extend the time for filing of briefs or for doing any other action for which the rules call.

And note: If the supreme judicial court grants direct appellate review, either party may still request that the appeal be transferred to the appeals court.

5. **Record**

a. **Trial Recorded by a Stenographer**

1) **The Record**
The record on appeal consists of:

(i) A certified copy of the docket entries in the trial court;

(ii) The original papers and exhibits filed in the trial court; and

(iii) Designated portions of the trial transcript, if the case proceeded to trial before the appeal.

The clerk assembles these documents, except that the appellant must, within 10 days after filing the notice of appeal, order the transcript (or portion thereof) from the stenographer. If the entire transcript is not ordered, the appellant at the same time must serve a statement of issue on appeal and a designation of portions of the transcript on the opposing party. The opponent then has an opportunity to designate other portions of the transcript for inclusion in the record. [Mass. R. App. P. 8(b)]

2) **Assembling the Record**
Within 40 days after filing the notice of appeal, the appellant must file with the clerk of the lower court either (i) any transcript that the appellant deems necessary to the appeal, or (ii) a signed statement certifying that the transcript has been ordered. If the appellant fails to do so, the appellee may move with notice that the appeal be dismissed. The appellant has until the hearing to comply.

b. **Trial Electronically Recorded**

1) **Transcript of the Trial Already Produced**
If the court has already produced a copy of the transcript, the procedure that applies to stenographically recorded trials is followed, except that the appellant's time for ordering the transcript is extended to 10 days from the time she was informed of the name of the preparer of the transcript.

2) **Transcript Not Yet Produced**
If the transcript has not yet been produced, the appellant must order from the

clerk, simultaneously with filing the appeal, a cassette copy of the electronic recording. Within 15 days of receiving the cassette, the appellant must file in court and serve on the appellee a notice that details the portion of the cassette that is to be transcribed. The appellee then has 15 days to designate any additional portions that she wishes to have transcribed. The court selects who will transcribe the cassette if the parties cannot mutually select someone.

c. Proceedings Not Recorded
If the trial court proceedings were not recorded, the appellant must, within 30 days of filing a notice of appeal, file with the court and serve on the appellee a statement of the proceedings as he remembers them. The appellee then has 10 days to file any objections or amendments. The lower court settles any discrepancies and then files an approved statement. [Mass. R. App. P. 8(c)]

6. Agreed Statement
In lieu of the record on appeal, the parties may file an agreed statement of the facts and issues. This statement must be approved by the lower court.

7. Docketing the Appeal
The trial court clerk next notifies the parties that the record has been assembled. The appellant then has 10 days to pay the docket fee to the appellate court clerk, and the case is entered on the docket. [Mass. R. App. P. 10(a)(1)] If the appellant does not comply, the appellee may move to dismiss (with notice), but the appellant has until the hearing to comply.

8. Briefs

a. Timing

1) Appeals to the Appeals Court
The appellant's brief must be filed within 40 days after the appeal is docketed. The appellee then has 30 more days to file her brief. Any reply brief must be filed within 14 days of the receipt of the appellee's brief and at least three days before the first day of the sitting at which the case is in order for argument.

2) Direct Review Appeals to the Supreme Judicial Court

a) All Briefs Filed
If all briefs have been filed at the time of transfer, any reply brief may be served within 10 days after the date on which the appeal is docketed in the supreme judicial court or within the original time allowed had the case not been transferred, whichever period is longer.

b) Only Appellant's Brief Filed
If only the appellant's brief has been filed at the time of transfer, the appellant may file an amended brief within 20 days. The appellee then has 50 days from docketing or 30 days after service of any amended brief to file her brief, whichever period is longer.

c) No Briefs Filed
If at the time of transfer no briefs have been filed, the appellant has 20 days after the docketing to file a brief or 40 days after the original docketing in the appeals court, whichever period is longer.

b. Number

1) Appeals Court
Seven copies of each brief must be filed with the appeals court, unless the court orders a lesser number, and two copies must be served on counsel for each party separately represented. [Mass. R. App. P. 19(b)(1)]

2) Transfer to Supreme Judicial Court
If an appeal is transferred to the supreme judicial court after briefs were filed in the appeals court, an *additional 11 copies* must be filed with the supreme judicial court, unless the court orders a lesser or greater number. [Mass. R. App. P. 19(b)(3)]

3) **Direct Appeal to Supreme Judicial Court**
On appeal to the supreme judicial court, the *original and 17 copies* of each brief must be filed with the supreme judicial court, unless the court orders a lesser or greater number, and two copies must be served on counsel for each party separately represented. [Mass. R. App. P. 19(b)(2)]

c. **Length**
Unless the court grants permission, principal briefs may not exceed 50 pages, excluding the table of contents, table of citations, and any addendum. Reply briefs are limited to 20 pages, with the same exclusions. The brief must follow a prescribed format, and nonconforming briefs may be stricken from the record. [*See* Mass. R. App. P. 16]

d. **Form**
All briefs must include a table of contents; a table of cases, statutes, and other authorities; a statement of issues; a statement of the case; an argument section; and a short conclusion. [Mass. R. App. P. 16(a)(1) - (5)]

e. **Filing by Mail**
Briefs are considered docketed when mailed if accompanied by an affidavit signed by counsel of record certifying that the day of mailing was within the time fixed for filing.

f. **Failure to File Brief**
If the appellant fails to file a brief, the appellee may move for dismissal. If the appellee fails to file a brief, the appellee may not be heard on oral argument except by leave of the court.

9. **Appendix**
The appellant must prepare and file with its brief an appendix that reproduces the portions of the record on which both parties rely in the briefs and oral arguments on appeal. [Mass. R. App. P. 18]

10. **Service**
Parties must serve on the other parties copies of all papers that they file except those the rules require the clerk to file. Service may be personal or by first class mail. If a party is represented by counsel, service must be on counsel by leaving the papers with a clerk or other responsible person at counsel's office. Service by mail is complete on mailing. Papers presented for filing must contain an acknowledgment of service unless the clerk allows the acknowledgment or proof to be filed promptly thereafter.

11. **Prehearing Conference**
The appellate court may direct the parties to appear for a prehearing conference to consider simplification of the issues and any other matters that might aid in the disposition of the proceedings.

12. **Argument**
The appellant argues first and is allowed 15 minutes; then the appellee argues for 15 minutes. Note that an attorney who has been a witness for his client may not argue a case except by leave of court.

13. **Decision**
The appellate court sends an opinion and rescript to the parties notifying them of its decision. Judgment is then entered in the trial court pursuant to the rescript.

14. **Costs**
If an appeal is determined to be frivolous, the court may award whatever damages are just, double costs, and any interest allowed by law to the appellee. The loser on appeal is taxed costs unless the parties agree otherwise or the court orders otherwise.

D. **REPORT**
A trial court (except the district court) may report a case to the appeals court prior to a decision by the trial court. (The single justice of the supreme judicial court may report the case either to the supreme judicial court or to the appeals court.) The trial court may also report an interlocutory order to an appellate court if in its opinion the matter ought to be reviewed before further proceedings in the trial court. [Mass. R. Civ. P. 64]

For a case to be reported, either the trial court must find the facts or the parties must stipulate the facts. The judge's report serves as the notice of appeal. The report then follows the appellate process set forth above.

E. APPEALS TO SUPREME JUDICIAL COURT

1. Timing
Parties may appeal from an appeals court judgment within 20 days after the date of rescript. Other parties may oppose the application by filing and serving an opposition within 10 days after the filing of the appeal. The supreme judicial court will accept appeals "founded upon substantial reasons affecting the public interest or the interests of justice."

2. Briefs
Within 10 days of the supreme judicial court granting further appellate review, any party may apply for permission to file a separate or supplemental brief. If such permission is denied or not sought, the case is argued on the briefs and appendix filed in the appeals court.

F. APPEALS FROM DISTRICT COURT JUDGMENTS

Decisions of the district court are not reviewed by the appeals process outlined above. In some situations, such judgments may be reviewed in a trial de novo by a superior court, depending upon the amount in controversy and whether the right to jury trial has been preserved. (*See* II.C.3., *supra,* on the relationship between district and superior courts.)

Rulings on issues of law by the district court may be reviewed by the appellate division of the district court, based on a report by the trial judge. Decisions of the appellate division may be appealed to the supreme judicial court.

G. INTERLOCUTORY ORDERS

The traditional but eroding rule is that the appellate courts review only final judgments. Interlocutory orders, such as preliminary relief, discovery orders, and other nondispositive rulings are usually not subject to immediate appeal. Note that while orders granting motions to dismiss and motions for summary judgment are final, orders denying such motions are interlocutory. Since the effect of denial is simply to proceed with a trial on the merits, such orders are considered nondispositive.

1. To Preserve for Appeal
To preserve interlocutory orders for appeal, a party must object to the order (if there is an opportunity to object) and designate the order in the notice of appeal. It is not necessary to notice an appeal at the time the interlocutory order is entered. [Mass. R. App. P. 3(a)] However, a party should comply with lower court rules as to exceptions to rulings or orders of the court. [Mass. R. Civ. P. 46]

2. Exceptions

a. In General
There are three principal exceptions to the rule against piecemeal review by immediate appeal of interlocutory orders:

1) Chapter 231, section 118 of the Massachusetts General Laws provides for review by a single justice of the appeals court of orders granting or denying preliminary injunctions. (An appeal pursuant to this provision must be taken within 30 days of the date of entry of the interlocutory order and in accordance with the Massachusetts Rules of Appellate Procedure.)

2) The trial court judge may report an interlocutory order to an appellate court (D., *supra*).

3) The doctrine of present execution.

b. Present Execution
The doctrine of present execution determines when an order is "final." An order may be the subject of immediate appellate review under this doctrine if the order is to be executed presently so that any appeal would be futile unless the execution of judgment is stayed by appeal. [*See* Borman v. Borman, 378 Mass. 775 (1979)]

In *Borman,* the court granted immediate appellate review of an order disqualifying the defendant's law partners from representing him in the litigation, a divorce action. The disqualification order was effective immediately; it would affect the defendant's right to counsel throughout the proceedings, and the effect of the disqualification could not be undone on appeal. On the other hand, the court refused to grant immediate appellate review of an order that the plaintiff's alimony claim *would* be stricken if she refused to answer deposition questions which she claimed violated her constitutional privilege against self-incrimination. The court noted that the order had no impact on the case unless the defendant resumed the deposition of the plaintiff, and it treated the trial court's ruling as a prediction which the court might still modify. The court recognized that the plaintiff's confidentiality claim would be lost forever if she answered the deposition questions, but it stated that she, unlike the defendant, could preserve the issue for appeal by refusing to answer. The court suggested that an order striking a claim as a discovery sanction could be the subject of an immediate appeal under the doctrine of present execution.

H.   MISCELLANEOUS

1.   Voluntary Dismissal

a.   Before Docketing
If an appeal has not been docketed, the parties may dismiss an appeal by signing a stipulation for dismissal and filing it in the lower court. The appeal may also be dismissed by the appellant alone upon motion and notice.

b.   After Docketing
To dismiss a case that has been docketed in the appellate court, the parties must file with the clerk of the appellate court an agreement that the case be dismissed, specifying the terms as to payment of costs. The parties must also pay all fees due. The appeal may also be dismissed on motion of the appellant upon either terms that the parties agree on or terms fixed by the court.

2.   Substitution of Parties

a.   Public Parties
If a public officer dies or is separated from office, her successor is automatically substituted as a party.

b.   Non-Public Parties

1)   Necessity Arising Before Notice of Appeal Is Filed
If a party dies before taking an appeal, her personal representative may file the appeal. If a party against whom an appeal may be taken dies before an appeal is taken, the appellant proceeds as if the death had not occurred; the appellee may move for substitution after the appeal is filed.

2)   Necessity Arising After Notice of Appeal Is Filed
If substitution is necessary because of death or any other reason after the notice of appeal is filed, the party may be substituted by motion of any party.

3.   Petition for Rehearing
A petition for rehearing must be filed with the clerk of the appellate court within 14 days of the date of the rescript opinion unless the court shortens or enlarges the time. The appellate court may decide to allow oral argument or an answer to the petition. The petition, which cannot be longer than 10 pages without permission of the court, must state with particularity the points of law or fact that the appellate court overlooked or misapprehended and must be supported by an argument the petitioner desires to present. The petition and seven copies must be filed and a copy must be delivered or mailed to all other counsel.

X.   MISCELLANEOUS MATTERS

A.   MEDICAL MALPRACTICE TRIBUNALS
Medical malpractice tribunals are governed by Massachusetts General Laws chapter 231, section 60B.

1. **Purpose**
   Every damages action for malpractice by a "health care provider" must undergo initial screening by a tribunal consisting of an attorney, superior court judge, and a physician to determine whether the case presents a "legitimate question of liability appropriate for judicial inquiry" or merely an "unfortunate medical result." The tribunal is supposed to be convened within 15 days after the defendant's answer is filed (although this frequently does not occur), and the plaintiff is required to produce substantial evidence that such a "legitimate question" exists. The tribunal applies a directed verdict standard (VII.E., *supra*) to decide this issue.

2. **Trial**
   If the tribunal decides that a legitimate question of malpractice exists, the lawsuit proceeds in the ordinary manner. If the tribunal rules against the plaintiff, however, the case may go to trial only if the plaintiff posts a $6,000 bond within 30 days. The bond is to cover the defendant's costs (specifically including attorneys' fees and expert witness's fees) in the event the plaintiff does not recover a judgment, and the judge has discretion to increase the amount of the bond. The bond may be reduced but not eliminated—if the judge finds the plaintiff is indigent.

   The tribunal's finding is admissible as evidence at trial. The testimony before the tribunal of any impartial physician appointed by the tribunal to examine the plaintiff is also admissible at trial. As a result of 1986 legislative reforms, copies of findings of the medical malpractice tribunal and copies of judgments and other trial court dispositions must be sent to the Board of Registration in Medicine and are available for public inspection.

3. **Appeals**
   The plaintiff has two avenues of appeal from an adverse decision by a medical malpractice tribunal:

   a. **Immediate Appeal**
      The plaintiff may immediately appeal the decision—if the plaintiff loses an appeal, the plaintiff is precluded from subsequently going to trial on the underlying malpractice claim; or

   b. **Trial**
      The plaintiff may post the bond (2., *supra*) and go to trial on the underlying malpractice claim and preserve the alleged error for appeal from the court's final judgment. [McMahon v. Glixman, 379 Mass. 60 (1979)]

B. REVIEW OF ADMINISTRATIVE AGENCIES

1. **Rulemaking Proceedings**
   Regulations promulgated by administrative agencies pursuant to the State Administrative Procedure Act [Mass. Gen. L. ch. 30A] may be reviewed by the superior court or a single justice of the supreme judicial court (and possibly the probate or land courts) by filing a declaratory judgment action (unless a special statute provides an exclusive mode of review). [Mass. Gen. L. ch. 30A, §7]

2. **Adjudicatory Hearings**
   A final decision rendered by an administrative agency in an adjudicatory hearing may be reviewed by filing a complaint in the superior court within 30 days, pursuant to the procedure set forth in Massachusetts General Laws chapter 30A, section 14.

3. **Primary Jurisdiction and Exhaustion of Administrative Remedies**
   Two related doctrines—primary jurisdiction (or prior resort) and exhaustion of administrative remedies—operate to postpone judicial review of administrative agencies. The exhaustion doctrine requires the plaintiff to complete the process before the agency before seeking judicial review, while the primary jurisdiction doctrine requires the plaintiff to first invoke any remedial processes available before the agency prior to seeking judicial relief. The basic purpose underlying both doctrines is to preserve the proper relationship between the judiciary and the agencies to which the legislature has delegated regulatory powers.

   The doctrines do not bar initial judicial decision of (i) cases presenting issues of law not committed to agency discretion, (ii) some cases presenting questions of the agency's jurisdiction, or (iii) some cases of first impression which present issues of law and will affect large numbers of cases before the agency. [*See, e.g.*, McKenney v. Commission on Judicial Conduct, 380 Mass. 263 (1979)]

C. **SUING PUBLIC OFFICIALS—MASSACHUSETTS TORT CLAIMS ACT**
In response to the abrogation of common law sovereign immunity by the supreme judicial court, the legislature enacted a tort claims act [Mass. Gen. L. ch. 258] modeled after the Federal Tort Claims Act. It permits recovery for up to $100,000 per claim, for "injury or loss of property or personal injury or death caused by the neglect or wrongful omission of any public employee (state or local) while acting within the scope of his office or employment . . . ." [Mass. Gen. L. ch. 258, §2]

The waiver of immunity under Massachusetts General Laws chapter 258 has important procedural aspects, including:

(i) Suit may be filed only against the public employer (not employee) in the superior court.

(ii) Prior to filing suit, the plaintiff must first present a claim in writing to the public employer, who has six months to act on the claim.

(iii) The written presentment of the claim to the public employer must be made within two years and the lawsuit filed within three years after the cause of action arose.

   Note: Presentment is not required for claims raised by means of a third-party action. [McGrath v. Stanley, 397 Mass. 775 (1986)]

(iv) The public employer may settle or compromise the claim (subject to certain limitations).

(v) Lawsuits are defended by the attorney general, district attorney, or town counsel (as appropriate), and service of process is usually made on the public attorney, although Massachusetts General Laws chapter 258, section 4 provides for service upon the mayor, city or town manager, or chairperson or executive secretary of the board of selectmen.

Note that the presentment letter is not jurisdictional in nature. Thus, the public employer must affirmatively raise the claimant's failure to write a timely presentment letter or the defense is waived. In addition, the letter must describe the wrongful acts or omissions that form the basis of the plaintiff's claim, and it must set forth all applicable theories of recovery.
Example: Where a student injured on a playground wrote a presentment letter alleging negligent supervision of the playground but not negligent treatment by the school physician, the negligent treatment claim was barred.

D. **FRIVOLOUS LITIGATION**
A trial court (except the district court), upon motion of a party after decision of the case, may order the losing party (represented by counsel) to pay for the costs of defending against claims which the court determined were:

(i) Wholly unsubstantial;

(ii) Frivolous; and

(iii) Not advanced in good faith.

The costs include reasonable attorneys' fees and 12% interest. [Mass. Gen. L. ch. 231, §6F]

The appeals court and the supreme judicial court may award double or treble costs for frivolous appeals. [Mass. Gen. L. ch. 211, §10; ch. 211A, §15]

E. **IN FORMA PAUPERIS**
If a court determines a litigant is indigent, it must waive payment of all the normal fees associated with litigation (*e.g.*, filing fee) and order the state to pay certain related costs (*e.g.*, service of process). The state may also be ordered to pay for such costs as subpoena and witness fees, expert testimony, etc. The indigent person must repay the fees or costs out of the judgment if recovery exceeds three times the fees and costs. [Mass. Gen. L. ch. 261, §§27A-27G]

F. **UNIFORM FRAUDULENT CONVEYANCE ACT**
Massachusetts has adopted the Uniform Fraudulent Conveyance Act [Mass. Gen. L. ch. 109A], which provides a mechanism by which a creditor may reach real or personal property transferred by a debtor in fraud of creditors. (*See also* Massachusetts Real Property Supplement.)

1. **Presumptions**
The Act provides that every conveyance made and every obligation incurred by a person

who is or will be thereby rendered insolvent is fraudulent as to creditors without regard to actual intent if the conveyance is made or the obligation incurred without fair consideration.

2. Remedies

A creditor whose claim has *matured* may seek to have the conveyance set aside or the obligation annulled to the extent necessary to satisfy his claim, or he may seek to attach or levy execution on the property conveyed.

A creditor whose claim has *not matured* may seek a restraining order to prevent the defendant from disposing of her property, or he may request the appointment of a receiver to take charge of the property.

BAR REVIEW

Commercial Paper

COMMERCIAL PAPER

TABLE OF CONTENTS

INTRODUCTION

The law of Commercial Paper is set out in Article 3 of the Uniform Commercial Code. Because the Code is highly specific, the answers to bar questions in this area tend to turn on the application of these specific rules with practically no room for argument as to what is the correct answer. That is why the materials on Commercial Paper are somewhat longer than those in some other areas. The questions do not turn on the application of central, broad rules to the facts but rather on the *application of narrow rules,* any one of which is likely to be the subject of a question. The questions seem to range fairly evenly across all areas of Commercial Paper except that Presentment and Notice of Dishonor (*see* VII., *infra*) are often assumed out of the question, and Documents of Title and Investment Securities (*see* XI., *infra*) are rarely touched.

Having offered that discouraging fact, let us quickly point out two important offsetting factors. First, because the questions tend to turn on the straightforward application of narrow rules, Commercial Paper is an area where you can easily pick up full credit (and almost none if you have no idea what the rules are). If you correctly *state the rule and apply it to the facts*, there is little that can be faulted in your answer. As a result, the gains from mastering the Commercial Paper area may be somewhat greater than from mastering other areas that, even when mastered, retain a "looser" quality (*i.e.*, you can't be as completely right or as completely wrong).

Second, *and most important*, the central concepts of Commercial Paper are simple indeed. The narrow rules of the area are for the most part logical corollaries of the central concepts. Thus, in studying this area, you should constantly attempt not only to learn the rules, but to relate those rules to the central concepts. If you understand these central principles, you should be able to work out acceptable answers to all the questions whether or not you remember the specific applicable rule.

I. IN GENERAL

A. INTRODUCTION

It is often inconvenient or unsafe to use cash as payment in certain transactions (*e.g.,* involving large sums of money), but ordinary promises to pay are unsuitable as a substitute because of difficulties in transferring ordinary contract rights (*e.g.,* the assignee would take subject to defenses good against the transferor). The law of negotiable instruments arose, in part, to provide a convenient and safe substitute for cash in such situations.

To facilitate a freely transferable but safe substitute for cash, a central theme of Article 3 of the Uniform Commercial Code (which governs negotiable instruments) is that if an instrument is in a special form (*i.e.,* it is *negotiable*) and it is transferred in a special way (*i.e.,* it is *negotiated*) to a person who takes the instrument for value, in good faith, and without notice of any defenses to or claims on the instrument (*i.e.,* a holder in due course or "*HDC*"), the person will be able to enforce the instrument subject to very few defenses.

B. APPLICABILITY OF ARTICLE THREE

All of the states (including Louisiana and the District of Columbia) have adopted Article 3 of the Uniform Commercial Code.

C. TERMINOLOGY

There are basically two kinds of instruments to which Article 3 applies: a "note" and a "draft." There are also subclasses of notes and drafts (*e.g.,* checks) for which the Code contains special rules.

1. Notes

a. General Definition
A note is *two-party* commercial paper. It is simply a written and signed promise (undertaking) by one party (the *"maker"*) to pay money to another party (the *"payee"* or bearer). [*See* U.C.C. §§3-103(a)(9), 3-104(e)]
Example:

> ### PROMISSORY NOTE
>
> I, Max Maker, promise to pay to the order of Peter Payee one hundred dollars ($100).
>
> *Max Maker*

b. Certificates of Deposit
A certificate of deposit ("CD") is like a note in that two parties are involved. But the Code specifically defines a CD as an instrument made by a bank containing: (i) *an acknowledgment* that a sum of money has been received by the bank; and (ii) *a promise* by the bank to repay the sum of money. [U.C.C. §3-104(j)]

c. Maker Makes a Note
Note that the name given to the physical act of creating an instrument differs, depending on whether the instrument is a note or a draft. A maker makes a note; a drawer (*see* below) draws a draft.

2. Drafts
A draft is *three-party* commercial paper. It is a written and signed instruction by one person (the *"drawer"*) to another person (the *"drawee"*) demanding that the drawee pay money to still a third person (the *"payee"* or bearer). [U.C.C. §3-104(e)] In practice, the term "bill of exchange" is synonymous with the term "draft."

a. Checks
A "check" is a specific type of draft, namely one drawn on a bank and payable on demand. An instrument will be deemed a check if it meets these requirements, *even if the instrument is described on its face by another term* (*e.g.,* a "money order"). [U.C.C. §3-104(f)]

2. COMMERCIAL PAPER

Example:

```
Drew Drawer                                          101
123 Elm                                        7/24/2004
Elmwood, Ohio


Pay to the order _____ Peter Payee _____   | $100 |
One hundred and 00/100 ------------------------- _ dollars


First Bank of Erehwon

                                          Drew Drawer
memo  _____
```

b. Instrument Qualifying as Draft or Note
If an instrument falls within the definition of both "note" and "draft," a person entitled to enforce the instrument may enforce it as either. [U.C.C. §3-104(e)]

3. Other Instruments
There are other kinds of negotiable instruments dealt with in separate articles of the U.C.C. *Investment securities* (stocks and bonds) are made negotiable by Article 8, and *documents of title* (warehouse receipts and bills of lading) are made negotiable by Article 7. Each is governed by a special set of rules. If you see one of these instruments on your exam, remember that they are negotiable even though they do not meet the formal requisites of Article 3 for negotiability. Answer any other questions that you may have about them by analogy to Article 3.

4. Money
The U.C.C. does *not* apply to money.

5. Issue
"Issue" means the first delivery of an instrument by the maker or drawer for the purpose of giving rights on the instrument to any person. The maker or drawer is the "issuer." [U.C.C. §3-105]

II. FORMAL REQUISITES OF NEGOTIABILITY

A. NEGOTIABILITY DEFINED
Whether an instrument is negotiable depends on its *form*; it must meet the very technical formal requisites of negotiability listed in the U.C.C. Therefore, the following definition of negotiability should be memorized for the bar exam. The meaning of its terms will be detailed below.

A negotiable instrument means a written and signed:

(i) *Unconditional*

(ii) *Promise or order*

(iii) *To pay a fixed amount of money*, with or without interest or other charges described in the promise or order, that:

    i. *Is payable to order or to bearer* at the time it is issued or first comes into possession of a holder;

    ii. *Is payable on demand or at a definite time*; and

    iii. *Does not state any unauthorized undertaking or instruction* by the person promising or ordering payment.

[U.C.C. §§3-103, 3-104]
Example: The promissory note at I.C.1.a., *supra,* is negotiable. It is written and signed by Max Maker, and it: (i) states no conditions, (ii) contains a promise ("I, Max Maker, promise"), (iii) to pay a fixed amount of money ("to pay $100"), and is (a) payable to order ("to the order of Peter Payee"), (b) on demand (since no time for payment is stated; *see* F.1., *infra*), and does not state any unauthorized undertaking or instruction.

B. UNCONDITIONAL

A goal behind negotiable instruments law is to provide a convenient substitute for cash that can pass freely in commerce. To facilitate this goal, Article 3 restricts the conditions that may be placed on payment and limits placing terms relevant to payment in other documents so that a purchaser will be able to tell what he is getting merely by examining the instrument.

1. When Promise or Order Conditional

An instrument will be conditional and therefore will not be negotiable if it:

(i) **Expressly** states a condition to payment (*e.g.*, "I promise to pay *if* the Chicago Bears win the Super Bowl"); or

(ii) States that the promise or order (or rights and obligations subject thereto) is **subject to or governed by** another writing (*e.g.*, "This note is subject to the sales agreement between the parties dated August 1").

Note, however, that merely referring to or stating that the promise or order arises out of a separate writing (*e.g.*, "this instrument is given as a down payment on a contract to rent a building") does not condition the promise or order. [U.C.C. §3-106(a)]

2. When Promise or Order Not Conditional

Article 3 specifically provides that a promise or order will not be deemed conditional merely because it:

a. **Refers to another writing for a statement of rights regarding collateral, prepayment or acceleration**;

b. **Limits payment to a particular source or fund** (*e.g.*, "I promise to pay out of the funds from my next wheat crop"); or

c. **Requires as a condition to payment a countersignature** by a person whose specimen signature appears on the promise or order (such conditions are commonly placed on traveler's checks).

3. Effect of Reference to Separate Writing

As noted above, a negotiable instrument cannot be subject to another writing, but it may refer to another writing. What is the effect of the other writing referred to? If the negotiable instrument merely refers to a separate writing, the contents of the separate writing are irrelevant to negotiability and the rights of HDCs are not limited by the terms of the separate writing (unless the HDC happens to know the terms of the separate writing). However, as between the two parties, the terms of the negotiable instrument may be modified and controlled by the separate writing. [*See* U.C.C. §3-117] Watch out for parol evidence rule issues, however.

C. PROMISE OR ORDER TO PAY

A note must contain a promise to pay. A draft must contain an order to pay. A promise is a **written** undertaking to pay money **signed** by the person undertaking to pay (*e.g.*, "I promise to pay . . ."). An order is a **written** instruction to pay money **signed** by the person giving the order (*e.g.*, "Pay to the order of John Smith").

1. Writing Required

The U.C.C. is very liberal as to what constitutes a writing. It may be printing, typing, or "any other intentional reduction to tangible form." [U.C.C. §1-201(46)]

2. Signature Required

The U.C.C. is very liberal as to what constitutes a signature. A signature may be handwritten, typed, printed, or made in any other manner (*e.g.*, a mark by a machine or a thumbprint). It may be made in any name (trade or assumed) adopted for the purpose of being a signature. The signature need not be at the end of the instrument; it may be in the body. [U.C.C. §3-401, comments 1, 2]

Example: Alice Wonderland is the proprietor of Carroll Book Store and signs all of the store's checks "Carroll Book Store." Wonderland is bound on the checks as if she had signed her own name.

For a discussion of problems raised by agent's signatures, *see* VII.D., *infra*.

D. FIXED AMOUNT OF MONEY

1. What Is Money?
Money includes any medium of exchange authorized or adopted by a government. [U.C.C. §1-201(24)] "Currency" and "current funds" are synonymous with money. Thus, an instrument may still be negotiable if it is payable in "currency."

a. Foreign Currency Proper
An instrument may be negotiable even if it calls for payment in foreign money. Unless the instrument otherwise provides, it is payable in the specified foreign money *or its equivalent* in United States dollars at the current bank exchange rate at the time and place the instrument is paid. [U.C.C. §3-107]

b. Other Consideration Improper
An instrument will not be negotiable if it calls for payment with something other than money (*e.g.*, an ounce of gold) or allows such payment in the alternative (*e.g.*, "$400 or an ounce of gold").

2. What Is Fixed?

a. Principal Must Be Fixed
To be negotiable, the principal due under the instrument must be fixed.

b. Interest Need Not Be Fixed
No interest will be due unless the instrument provides for the payment of interest. [U.C.C. §3-112]

1) Specified Interest Rate
It is not necessary that the amount of interest be fixed. A variable interest rate or indexed rate may be used. The interest rate need not be determinable from the face of the instrument; the rate may require reference to information not contained in the instrument (*e.g.*, "3% over prime, adjusted each six months based on the then prevailing bank rates in New York City" is negotiable).

2) Unspecified Interest Rate
If the instrument says that it is payable *with interest* but does not state how much interest, the judgment rate (the rate on a court judgment) will be implied.

E. PAYABLE TO ORDER OR TO BEARER
To be negotiable, an instrument must be payable to order or to bearer. Order paper is payable only to the person named or his order. Bearer paper is payable to anyone legitimately possessing the instrument.

1. To Order
A promise or order is payable to order if it is payable to the order of an identified person (*e.g.*, "pay to the order of John Smith") or to an identified person or order (*e.g.*, "pay John Smith or his order"). [U.C.C. §3-109(b)]

2. To Bearer
A promise or order is payable to bearer if it:

(i) States that it is payable to bearer, to order of bearer, to order or bearer, to order and bearer, or otherwise indicates that the person in possession of the promise or order is entitled to payment (*e.g.*, "I promise to pay Bearer");

(ii) Does not state a payee (*e.g.*, "pay to the order of _____"; note that while this is payable to bearer, it is also an incomplete instrument, which is discussed at VII.F., *infra*); or

(iii) States that it is payable to cash or otherwise indicates that it is not payable to an identified person (*e.g.*, "I promise to pay to the order of Merry Christmas").

[U.C.C. §3-109(a)]

3. **Identification of Payee**
    The person to whom an instrument is payable is governed by the intent of the person signing as or on behalf of the issuer (maker or drawer). If more than one person issues the instrument, any person intended by any signer may properly be paid. [U.C.C. §3-110(a)]
    Example: If the president of Big Corp. draws a corporation check to be payable to "John Smith," the president's intention controls which of the many John Smiths in the world is to be paid. If the check is signed by the president and the secretary and each intended a different John Smith, payment to either John Smith is proper.

    a. **Signature by Machine**
        If the signature of the issuer is made by machine (*e.g.,* a check drawn by a computer), the instrument is payable to the person intended by the person who supplied the name of the payee. [U.C.C. §3-110(b)]

    b. **Means of Identification**
        A payee may be identified by any means, including name, office, account number, etc. An instrument payable to an account number is payable only to the person named on the account. An instrument payable to a trust or estate is payable to the representative. An instrument payable to an agent or other representative is payable to the represented person or the representative. [U.C.C. §3-110(c)]

    c. **Multiple Payees**
        An instrument may name more than one payee. For rules regarding to whom such instruments are payable, *see* III.B.2.c., *infra*.

4. **Checks Missing "Magic Words" Still Negotiable**
    There is a special rule for checks—a check (*see* I.C.2.a., *supra*) that is not payable to order or to bearer is still negotiable. [U.C.C. §3-104(c)]

F. **ON DEMAND OR AT A DEFINITE TIME**
    To be negotiable, an instrument must be payable on demand or at a definite time.

    1. **Demand**
        An instrument is payable on demand if it states that it: (i) is payable "on demand" or "at sight" or otherwise indicates that it is payable at the will of the holder; or (ii) does not state a time for payment. [U.C.C. §3-108(a)]

    2. **Definite Time**
        An instrument is payable at a definite time if it is payable: (i) on a fixed date (*e.g.,* "April 1, 2008"); (ii) on elapse of a specified period of time after sight or acceptance (*e.g.,* "60 days after presentment for payment"); or (iii) at some time *readily ascertainable* at the time the instrument is issued. Note that the time stated may be subject to rights of prepayment, acceleration, extension at the option of the holder, or extension to a further definite time either automatically or at the option of the maker or acceptor. [U.C.C. §3-108(b)]

        a. **Events Certain to Happen But Uncertain as to Time**
            If the instrument is payable on or after a stated time or event certain to happen but *uncertain as to time*, it is *not negotiable* because the time for payment is not readily ascertainable and, therefore, there is no definite time for payment.
            Example: An instrument "payable on my uncle Sam's death" or "payable 30 days after my uncle Sam's death" is not negotiable.

        b. **Acceleration Clauses**
            Any clause that accelerates the time of payment upon the occurrence of an event or at the option of the maker or holder is *permissible*; *i.e.,* an acceleration clause does not destroy negotiability.
            Example: An instrument "payable 100 years from date, but if my uncle Sam should die, payable on his death" is *negotiable*.

        c. **Extension Clauses**
            Extension clauses (*i.e.,* clauses that extend rather than shorten the time when payment is due) present a more complicated situation. There are three types: extensions at the option of the maker, extensions that are automatic upon the happening of an event, and extensions at the option of the holder.

1) At Option of Maker or On Happening of Event
The first two types of extension clauses may be included without affecting nego-tiability *if* the extension is *to a further definite time* stated in the instrument. For example, an instrument containing the clause, "This instrument can be extended at the option of the maker," is *not negotiable* because it does not specify when it is due. In contrast, an instrument providing that it "may be extended by the maker for one month after the original due date," is negotiable because the instrument will be payable no later than one month after the due date.

2) At Option of Holder
The third type of extension (at the option of the holder) is always permitted because the holder always has the option of giving extra time for payment. Note, however, that the holder may not exercise this option if the maker or drawer objects and at the same time tenders payment.

G. NO UNAUTHORIZED UNDERTAKING OR INSTRUCTIONS

To be negotiable, an instrument generally cannot contain any unauthorized undertakings or prom-ises. However, the Code explicitly permits three undertakings or instructions that may be included:

(i) An undertaking or power to give, maintain, or protect collateral;

(ii) An authorization or power to the holder to confess judgment or realize on or dispose of collateral; and

(iii) A waiver of the benefit of any law intended for the advantage or protection of the obligor (*e.g.*, waiver of presentment, notice of dishonor, homestead exemption, trial by jury, etc.).

Any other promise or undertaking will destroy negotiability. [U.C.C. §3-104(a)(3)]

H. MISCELLANEOUS PROVISIONS

1. Rules of Construction
If an instrument contains contradictory terms, typewritten terms control printed terms and handwritten terms control both. Words control figures unless the words are ambiguous or uncertain (*e.g.*, illegible), in which case the figures control. Thus, "pay five hundred dollars ($5,000)" is construed as an order to pay $500.

2. Opting Out
A promise or order that otherwise meets the requirements of a negotiable instrument will not be negotiable if when issued it contains a conspicuous statement that it is not a nego-tiable instrument or that Article 3 is not applicable. Note, however, that this rule does not apply to checks. [U.C.C. §3-104(d)] Such instruments are often used in advertisements offering a discount.

Example:

Jack Smith Oldsmobile	444
1 Main Street	
Erehwon, PA	

Pay to the order of _____*Peter Payee*_____ ⎹$1,000⎸
One thousand and 00/100 ---------------------------------- dollars

NONNEGOTIABLE

memo on purchase of an Olds _____*Jack Smith*_____

The above instrument is not a check since it is not drawn on a bank (in fact, it is not even a draft since there are only two parties), and it is not negotiable because the maker has clearly said so.

3. Two or More Signers in Single Capacity
Unless the instrument otherwise specifies, two or more persons who have the same liability on an instrument as makers, acceptors, drawers, or indorsers who indorse as joint payees or anomalous indorsers are jointly and severally liable in the capacity in which they sign. [U.C.C. §3-116(a)] For example, if two people sign as makers of a note, either one can be held liable for the full value of the note.

4. **Incomplete Instruments**
   Under Article 3, an incomplete instrument may be enforced according to its incomplete terms or as augmented by an authorized completion. This is true even if the instrument would not qualify as an instrument but for the completion. [U.C.C. §3-115] If an instrument is completed *without* authority, it is treated as a fraudulently altered instrument. (*See* VII.F.2., *infra*.)

III. NEGOTIATION—BECOMING A HOLDER

A. **INTRODUCTION**
   As stated in I.A., *supra*, the key to the protection of Article 3 is HDC status. To become an HDC, one must first become a holder of a negotiable instrument; to become a holder of a negotiable instrument requires proper negotiation. Negotiation is nothing more than the process specified by Article 3 for transferring a negotiable instrument.

B. **THE NEGOTIATION PROCESS**
   The Code's definition of negotiation is somewhat confusing. It provides that:

   (i) Negotiation is a *transfer of possession*, whether voluntary or involuntary, by a person other than the issuer to a person who thereby becomes its holder [U.C.C. §3-201(a)] (recall that transfer of possession by the issuer is deemed an "issue"); and

   (ii) A holder is a person in possession of the instrument if the instrument is payable to bearer; if the instrument is payable to an identified person, that person is the holder as soon as she gets possession [U.C.C. §1-201(20)].

   For exam purposes, it is best to think of a holder as a person *in possession* of an instrument *with a right to enforce it*. Holder status (and the right to enforce an instrument) and what is needed for negotiation depend on whether the instrument is bearer paper or order paper.

   1. **Bearer Instruments**
      A negotiable instrument that is issued as bearer paper or subsequently converted into bearer paper (*e.g.,* by blank indorsement; *see* B.3.a.2), *infra*) is negotiated simply *by transferring possession* of the instrument. Once the transferee has possession, she technically qualifies as a "holder." [U.C.C. §3-201(b)]
      Example: Drawer writes a check payable to "Cash," which makes the check a bearer instrument. If Drawer transfers the check to Grocer, Grocer becomes a holder.

   2. **Order Instruments**

      a. **Negotiation to Specific Payee**
         An instrument that is payable to an identified person is negotiated by *transferring possession* of the instrument along with the indorsement of the identified person. [U.C.C. §§3-201(b), 3-205(a)]
         Example: Dan Drawer writes a check payable to the order of Paula Payee. Upon receiving the check, Paula qualifies as a "holder." If Paula subsequently wishes to negotiate the check, she must indorse it and deliver possession to her transferee, who will then also qualify as a "holder."

      b. **Payee's Indorsement Must Be Valid**
         Generally, the right to enforce an order instrument will not pass unless the payee's indorsement is *authorized* and *valid*. In most cases, forging the payee's name breaks the chain of title and no subsequent possessors of the instrument can qualify as "holders." (In certain situations, however, an unauthorized signature can be made "effective" under the principles of ratification or estoppel. *See* VII.D.1.b., *infra*.)
         Example: Dan Drawer writes a check payable to the order of Paula Payee. Before indorsement by Paula, the check is stolen from her by Harry Thief, who signs "Paula Payee" on the back and deposits the check in his account at Forgers National Bank for collection from Big Bucks Bank (the "drawee bank"). Title to this check stops with Paula Payee, and the check is still her property. No one taking the check after the forgery has the right to enforce the instrument and therefore *no one* (neither Harry, Forgers National, nor subsequent innocent transferees) can qualify as a "holder." *Note:* Technically, Harry's forgery of Paula's name is treated as if he had signed his *own* name. (*See* VII.E., *infra*.)

1) Genuine Signature Obtained by Fraud or from Infant Is Effective

A signature is effective for the purpose of negotiation even if it is made by an infant or anyone else without legal capacity, obtained by mistake, fraud, or other illegality, part of an illegal transaction, or made in breach of duty. [U.C.C. §3-202(a)]

2) All Necessary Signatures Must Be Included

The right to enforce an instrument will pass only if all necessary signatures of all payees and special indorsees are on the instrument.

c. Multiple Payees

An instrument may be made payable to more than one payee. If the names on the payee line are connected by an "and," the instrument is payable to the payees *jointly*, and any subsequent negotiation is effective only if *all* indorse the instrument. However, if the names are connected by "or" or "and/or," the instrument is payable to the payees *severally*, and the valid indorsement of any *one* of them is sufficient to pass the right to enforce to a subsequent transferee. [U.C.C. §3-110(d)]

Examples: 1) A check payable to the order of "George and Martha Washington" requires that *both* payees indorse the check in order to negotiate it further. If only one signs, the subsequent transferee would not qualify as a "holder" because an indorsement necessary to his right to enforce is missing.

2) On the other hand, a check payable to "George or Martha Washington," or a check to "George and/or Martha Washington" can be negotiated by the indorsement of *either* payee—and that single signature is sufficient to establish the right to enforce in the transferee.

d. Location of Indorsement

An indorsement (any signature other than as maker, drawer, or acceptor) must be written on the instrument. Typically, the indorsement is placed on the reverse side of the instrument, but it may also properly be placed on the front or on a paper affixed to the instrument (an "allonge"). [U.C.C. §3-204(a)]

e. Effect of Transferring Order Instrument Without Indorsement

The delivery of an order instrument without indorsement (or with one of several indorsements missing) may be effective to transfer possession, but it does not constitute a negotiation until the indorsement is made. [U.C.C. §3-203(c)]

1) Rights of Transferee Without Indorsement

Unless and until he obtains the indorsement, the transferee of the instrument does *not* have the status of a "holder," and certainly cannot qualify as an HDC. Therefore, he cannot negotiate the instrument (because "negotiation" requires a transfer of the right to enforce, which the transferee will be unable to provide until the missing indorsement is procured). However, the transferee is not entirely without rights:

a) Suit to Compel Indorsement

If the transferee paid value for the instrument, he has "a specifically enforceable right to the unqualified indorsement of the transferor." [U.C.C. §3-203(c)] What this means, however, is that the transferee would have to sue in equity for a decree ordering the transferor to indorse.

b) Suit to Enforce Instrument

Similarly, if the instrument is due, the transferee can bring suit to enforce it even though it lacks an indorsement. However, he would have to prove his ownership rights in the instrument (*i.e.*, that he was entitled to the missing indorsement).

2) Different Rules for Banks

Traditional concepts governing negotiable instruments give way to the rules governing bank collections under Article 4 of the U.C.C. A depositary bank (a bank in which an item is first deposited) that takes an instrument *for collection* becomes a holder of the instrument if the customer was a holder at time of delivery, even if the customer has not indorsed the instrument. [U.C.C. §4-205(1)]

(i) This rule applies only as to instruments taken for collection. Thus, for example, if the bank held an instrument as collateral for a loan to a customer, it would have no power to supply the customer's indorsement.

    (ii)   This rule does not insulate the bank for mishandling the funds represented by the instrument.

       Example: Check drawn payable jointly to A and B; Bank cashes check on A's signature only and forwards check for collection (supplying B's indorsement). Bank is liable to B for conversion of her interest in the check. It makes no difference that Bank was acting in good faith.

3) When Indorsement Later Obtained

a) Transferee Becomes a Holder
Upon obtaining the transferor's indorsement, the right to enforce is thereupon vested in the transferee, who now becomes a holder—having both the right to enforce and possession. And, the transferee may qualify as an HDC if other requirements for due course holding are met.

b) Notice of Adverse Claim or Defense
For the purpose of determining whether the transferee lacked "notice" of any adverse claim or defense to the instrument (an essential element for due course holding), her knowledge is measured as of the time she *obtains the missing indorsement*. [*See* U.C.C. §3-203, comment 3] This means that if the transferee finds out about some defense or claim in the interval between the time she paid for and obtained possession of the instrument and the time the missing indorsement was obtained, she cannot qualify as an HDC.

f. Indorsement of Partial Interests Not a "Negotiation"
If an indorsement attempts to convey less than the complete amount of the instrument, it is *not a negotiation* and the transferee does not qualify as a "holder." [U.C.C. §3-203(d)] The rationale is that a cause of action on a negotiable instrument cannot be split up.

    Example: Dan draws a check payable to the order of Paula Payee, who indorses it: "Pay George Washington two-thirds and Martha Washington one-third, /s/ Paula Payee." Neither George nor Martha qualifies as a holder.

           If Paul writes "pay George and Martha Washington, /s/ Paula Payee," a negotiation has occurred; *i.e.,* this indorsement transfers the entire interest to George and Martha as joint owners of the whole amount, and they both become "holders."

1) Partial Payment of Instrument
If an instrument has been partially paid (*e.g.,* an installment note), an indorsement of all that remains will be an effective negotiation.

3. Types of Indorsements
There are several types of indorsements, each having certain qualities and each affecting further negotiation. Every indorsement must be either special or blank, qualified or unqualified, *and* restrictive or unrestrictive.

a. Special or Blank

1) Special Indorsement
A "special" indorsement is one that names a particular person as "indorsee" (*e.g.,* "pay John Smith"). The indorsee must sign in order for the instrument to be further negotiated. [U.C.C. §3-205(a)]

a) Words of Negotiability Not Required
Words of negotiability (*e.g.,* "pay to the order of . . .") are not required in an indorsement, and lack thereof does not affect the negotiability of the instrument. Thus, a special indorsement reading "pay to John Smith" is as freely negotiable as one indorsed "pay to the order of John Smith."

b) Extra Words in Indorsement Do Not Impair Validity
Occasionally, out of an abundance of caution or otherwise, an indorser will include extra words in the indorsement (*e.g.,* "I hereby assign . . ."; or "I hereby guarantee payment . . ."). Such words generally do not impair the validity of the indorsement.

2) Blank Indorsement

A "blank" indorsement is a signature that is not accompanied by the naming of a specific indorsee. Blank indorsements create bearer paper, which may then be negotiated by *delivery* alone. [U.C.C. §3-205(b)]

Examples: 1) Dan Drawer writes a check to the order of Paula Payee, who signs the check on the back "/s/ Paula Payee" (a "blank indorsement"). The check blows out the window and is recovered by Frank Forger. Frank is a holder.

2) If in the previous example Paula had written, "Pay to Mark Money, /s/ Paula Payee," there would have been a special indorsement, and the check would have remained order paper. Thus, if it had blown out the window and was recovered by Frank, he would not qualify as a holder.

3) Indorsements of Names Not Necessary to Chain of Title

Forgery of names *not* necessary to the chain of title will not keep later takers from becoming holders.

Example: Same facts as in Example 1), above. If Forger takes the check to Gullible Grocery and indorses it as "Mark Money" (the town's wealthiest citizen) in payment for groceries, Gullible then becomes a "holder" because the instrument was bearer paper at the time of Frank's forgery and could have been negotiated by delivery alone. However, a forgery of Money's name in Example 2), above, would *break* the chain of title, because good title requires the valid signatures of the payee *and* all special indorsees. Thus, Gullible or other subsequent transferees could not qualify as "holders."

4) Forgery of Drawer's Name

Forgery of the drawer's name does *not* break the chain of title, and, thus, subsequent transferees may qualify as holders. This is because the forgery operates as the genuine signature of the *forger*.

5) Multiple Indorsements—Last Indorsement Controls

If the instrument has been indorsed several times, some in blank and some specially, the *last indorsement controls* what is necessary for further negotiation.

b. Qualified Indorsements

An indorsement that adds the words "*without recourse*" is a "qualified" indorsement. The effect is to limit the legal liability otherwise imposed on indorsers under the U.C.C. (*See* VII.B.2.a., *infra*.)

c. Restrictive Indorsements

Any other language added to an indorsement creates a "restrictive" indorsement. Examples would include *conditions* ("pay Flora Flowers only if she has paid her daughter all the money still owing under her father's will"), *trust indorsements* ("pay John Doe in trust for Jane Doe"), and indorsements restricting further negotiation to the check collection system ("for deposit only," "pay any bank," etc.). [U.C.C. §3-206]

1) Limiting Transfer or Negotiation

An indorsement limiting payment to a particular person or otherwise prohibiting further transfer or negotiation is *not* effective to prevent further transfer or negotiation of the instrument. [U.C.C. §3-206(a)] Thus, for example, even if a check is indorsed "Pay Pete Payee only," Pete can indorse and further negotiate the check.

2) Conditional Indorsement

An indorsement stating a condition to payment (*e.g.*, "pay John Jones if he fixes my car") is *ineffective* to condition payment. [U.C.C. §3-206(b)]

3) "For Deposit" or "For Collection"

If an indorsement includes words that indicate the purpose of having the instrument collected by a bank for the indorser (*e.g.*, "for deposit" or "for collection"), a person or depositary bank (bank in which an instrument is first deposited) must pay the instrument consistently with the indorsement or will be deemed to have converted the instrument. Intermediary banks and the payor bank (unless it is also the depositary bank) may disregard the restrictive indorsement. [U.C.C. §3-206(c)]

> *Example:* Pete Payee received his paycheck at work. He indorsed it "Pete Payee, For Deposit," since he was planning to go to his bank immediately after work to deposit the check. While Pete was going to his car, Hot Check Harry picked Pete's pocket and liberated Pete's paycheck. Harry took the check to a nearby off-track betting parlor where he lost it on a long shot. The off-track betting parlor deposited the check in its bank, Gambler's National. Gambler's National credited the parlor's account and forwarded the check to Employer's National, the bank on which the check was drawn. Employer's National paid the check. The parlor and Gambler's National can be held liable for converting the check because it was not deposited in Pete's account. Employer's National—the payor bank—is not liable, however.

d. Anomalous Indorsements

An anomalous indorsement is an indorsement made by a person who is not a holder of the instrument. This usually is done for purpose of accommodation. (*See* VII.B.7., *infra*.) Such an indorsement does not affect the manner in which the instrument may be negotiated, but it does make the signer liable on the instrument. [U.C.C. §3-205(d)]

IV. HOLDERS IN DUE COURSE

A. INTRODUCTION

Whether the transferee of a negotiable instrument qualifies as an HDC affects his liability on the instrument and the claims or defenses that may be asserted against him. It is therefore important to understand how one becomes an HDC and the basic attributes of that status. The U.C.C. provides that a holder in due course is a *holder* who takes the instrument:

(i)   For *value*;

(ii) In *good faith*; and

(iii) *Without notice* that:

> i.   The instrument *is overdue or has been dishonored*, or that there is an uncured default with respect to payment of another instrument issued as part of the same series;
>
> ii.   The instrument *contains an unauthorized signature* or has been altered;
>
> iii. *There is a claim* to the instrument; or
>
> iv.   *Any party has a defense or claim in recoupment* (a claim that reduces the amount payable) on the instrument.

Note also that the instrument must not bear apparent evidence of forgery or alteration, or be so irregular as to call into question its authenticity. [U.C.C. §3-302]

B. TWO-STEP PROCESS

As can be seen from the U.C.C. definition, determining whether a person is an HDC is a two-step process. First, you must determine whether the person is a "holder," and second, you must determine whether the person holds in "due course."

C. HOLDER

The first requirement of due course holding is that the person in possession of the instrument *be* a "holder." [U.C.C. §3-302] In other words, the transferee must have possession, and the instrument must be payable either to bearer or to the person in possession. [U.C.C. §1-201(20)] The instrument must be free of forgeries of those names necessary to the chain of title (the payee and any special indorsees). (*See* III.B.2.b., *supra*.)

D. DUE COURSE

"Due course" requires the holder to take for value, in good faith, and without notice of the circumstances described in A.(iii), above.

1. **Value**
   There are several things to note about "value" as it is used in the definition of HDC. [U.C.C. §3-303]

   a. **Types of Value**
      Any one of five things constitutes value:

      (i) Performance of the agreed *consideration*;

      (ii) Acquisition by the holder of a lien or a *security interest* in the instrument;

      (iii) Taking the instrument as *payment of* or security for an *antecedent debt*;

      (iv) Trading *a negotiable instrument* for another instrument; or

      (v) Giving the instrument in exchange for the incurring of an *irrevocable obligation* to a third person by the person taking the instrument.

      1) **Executory Promise Is Not "Value"**
         Section 3-303 makes it clear that an executory promise—a promise to give value in the future—is not itself "value." Hence, if that is all the holder gave for the instrument, he is *not* an HDC.
         Example: Ben promises to make improvements to Jerry's house in exchange for Jerry's transferring to Ben a $3,000 bearer note due in two months. Even though Ben's promise to make the improvements would be consideration under contract law, it is not value for Article 3 purposes. Not until the agreed consideration has been *performed* has value been given.

      2) **Antecedent Debt Is "Value"**
         Taking an instrument in payment of or as collateral for a preexisting indebtedness amounts to the giving of value, even though it would not qualify as consideration under contract law.
         Example: Jerry is indebted to Ben for $2,500. In payment of that debt, Jerry negotiates to Ben a $3,000 bearer note payable to Jerry. Ben has given value for the note.

   b. **Value Need Not Be Equivalent to Face Amount**
      It is important to note that the value given in exchange for commercial paper need not be equivalent to the face amount of the instrument. An instrument purchased for less than its face value is said to be purchased "at a discount," but as long as the full price agreed upon is given, full value has been paid.
      Example: Ben agrees to buy from Jerry for $2,500 a $3,000 bearer note due in two months. As soon as Ben gives Jerry $2,500, he has given full value.

      1) **Compare—Partial Failure of Consideration**
         If one pays less than the agreed-upon value, one becomes a *partial HDC* in proportion to the percentage of the value paid.
         Example: Ben agrees to buy from Jerry for $2,500 a $3,000 bearer note due in two months. Ben gives Jerry $1,250 and promises to pay the remaining $1,250 in a week. Before Ben pays the remaining $1,250, he is an HDC only to the extent of half the value of the note ($1,500) since he has given only half the agreed-upon value.

   c. **Time of Payment Important**
      The time that value is given is important because whether one takes an instrument in good faith and without notice is measured at the time the instrument is negotiated or at the time value is given, whichever is later. Thus, if a holder gets notice of a claim or defense after paying only partial value, the holder can be only a partial HDC even if the holder pays the rest of the agreed-upon value.
      Example: Same facts as in the example in 1), above, but before Ben gives Jerry the remaining $1,250, Ben discovers that the maker of the note has a defense to payment. Ben cannot be an HDC for more than $1,500, even if he pays Jerry the remaining $1,250.

d.   Bank Deposits

Merely crediting the depositor's account—a bookkeeping transaction—is not "value," since the bank certainly would have the right to set aside the credit if the instrument were returned unpaid. However, the bank *becomes* a holder for "value" to the extent that it *permits withdrawals* of the amount credited to the depositor's account—using the "first-money-in, first-money-out" ("FIFO") rule to determine if the particular item credited has been reached. Under the FIFO rule, money is considered to be withdrawn from an account in the order in which it is deposited. For example, Bank gives Depositor a provisional credit in the $100 amount of a check deposited to Depositor's account. Depositor then adds $50 to the account. Depositor then withdraws $100 from the account. Has the bank full value or only half? Answer: Full. The first money in is the first money out. [*See* U.C.C. §§4-210, 4-211]

2.   Good Faith

Good faith means honesty in fact and the observance of *reasonable commercial standards* of fair dealing. [U.C.C. §3-103(a)(4)]

a.   Honesty in Fact

The honesty in fact component of good faith is *subjective* (*i.e.*, what the actor actually believed). Thus, it has been referred to as the "pure heart, empty head" test. It is not a reasonable person standard.

b.   Reasonable Commercial Standards of Fair Dealing

The fair dealing component of good faith is *objective* (*i.e.*, the actor must proceed fairly in light of the facts and commercial standards). Note that the standard is different from ordinary care.

3.   Notice to Purchaser

The holder must purchase the instrument without notice of a number of things, as detailed below.

a.   What Constitutes Notice?

1)   Actual Knowledge and Reason to Know

Notice includes both actual knowledge (a subjective standard) and reason to know from the facts surrounding the transaction (an objective standard). [U.C.C. §1-201(26)] Thus, a purchaser cannot shut his eyes to the obvious or purposefully avoid finding out the truth.

Example: A cashier's check bears the indorsement "Deposit to A-B Partnership Account," signed by both partners. Bank officer observes Partner A strike the quoted words and then deposit the check in his personal account. Bank's failure to make inquiry from Partner B under such circumstances may be held commercial bad faith—motivated by a belief that inquiry would have disclosed that Partner A was acting without authority.

2)   Facts Constituting Notice

a)   Instrument Overdue

The purchaser has notice that an instrument is overdue *if she has reason to know any of the following* [U.C.C. §3-302(a)(2)]:

(1)   Any Part of Principal Overdue

Any part of the *principal* amount is overdue or there is an uncured default in payment of another instrument of the same series. This means that the purchaser of a time instrument must purchase before midnight of the due date. Likewise, if the principal is payable in installments, notice that the maker has defaulted on *any installment* of principal makes it impossible for a subsequent purchaser to be an HDC.

(2)   Acceleration Made

Acceleration of the instrument has been made.

Example: Ira Investor buys a promissory note having a maturity date of February 1, 2010, but payable earlier if the Enron Corporation files for bankruptcy. Enron filed for bankruptcy in 2001. If Ira purchased the note in 2003, he cannot qualify as an HDC because he has reason to know that the note is overdue.

(3) Demand Made
Demand has been made or more than a reasonable time has elapsed after issue. If the instrument is a check, it becomes overdue 90 days after its date; the check is stale and no taker may become a holder in due course. [*See* U.C.C. §3-304(a)(2)]

b) Notice of Unauthorized Signatures or Alteration
To be an HDC, a holder cannot have notice of any unauthorized signatures or that the instrument has been altered.

c) Claims to Instrument
To be an HDC, a holder cannot have notice of any claim to the instrument. A claim is a defense to the obligation of payment. Thus, the holder cannot have notice that another has a property or possessory right in the instrument or its proceeds (*e.g.*, the instrument was wrongfully taken from the other's possession) or that negotiation is rescindable (*e.g.*, negotiation from an infant may be rescinded if other law so provides [U.C.C. §3-202(b)]). [*See* U.C.C. §3-306]

(1) Knowledge of Breach of Fiduciary Duty
If the purchaser has knowledge that a fiduciary has negotiated the instrument in payment of or as security for the fiduciary's own debt or in any transaction for the fiduciary's own benefit or has otherwise breached his duty, the purchaser has notice of a claim.

d) Defenses or Claims in Recoupment
To be an HDC, the holder must not have notice of any defense available to the obligor (*e.g.*, infancy, duress, failure of consideration, etc.) or claim in recoupment (*i.e.*, a claim that reduces the amount payable) by the obligor. [*See* U.C.C. §3-305]

3) When and How Notice Must Be Received
To be effective, notice must be received at such time and in such manner as to give a *reasonable opportunity to act* on it. [U.C.C. §3-302(f)] This is relevant for large organizations (*i.e.,* notice received by a bank officer one minute before the bank's teller cashes the check is not effective to prevent the bank from becoming an HDC). In the institutional setting, a reasonable time is allowed for the person receiving notice to transmit it to the proper persons.

b. Facts Not Constituting Notice
Knowledge of the following facts does not of itself give the purchaser notice of a defense or claim.

1) Date or Lack Thereof
That the instrument is antedated, undated, or postdated does not constitute notice.

2) Executory Promise
That the instrument was issued or negotiated in return for an executory promise or accompanied by a separate agreement does not constitute notice unless the purchaser has notice that a defense or claim has arisen from the terms thereof.

3) Accommodation Party
The mere fact that a party has signed for accommodation does not of itself constitute notice.

4) Incomplete Instrument
A purchaser does not have notice merely because an incomplete instrument has been completed, unless the purchaser has notice of any improper completion.

5) Fiduciary Negotiated
That any person negotiating the instrument is or was a fiduciary does not constitute notice of a defense unless the purchaser also knows that the negotiation constituted a breach of trust.

6) **Default on Interest or Other Instrument**

That there has been default in payment of interest on the instrument or in payment of any other instrument is not notice of a defense unless the default was on an instrument of the same series.

7) **Public Filing or Recording**

The filing or recording of a document does not of itself constitute notice to a person who would otherwise be an HDC.

Example: The fact that a security agreement on the paper has been made and a financing statement filed under Article 9 of the Code, thus perfecting a security interest in the paper, does not prevent a subsequent holder for value without actual notice of the security interest from becoming an HDC.

8) **Purchase at a Discount**

When the payee sells the instrument to a later holder, the later holder sometimes buys the instrument for less than the face amount, the difference being referred to as the "discount." The existence of a discount does not mean that the holder has not given full value for the instrument, nor does a large discount in and of itself constitute lack of good faith or a reason to be suspicious. However, a very large discount together with other suspicious circumstances may lead courts to find lack of good faith and/or notice and thus deny HDC status to the holder.

9) **Notice of Discharge of a Party**

Notice of discharge of a party, other than a discharge in an insolvency proceeding, does not of itself constitute notice of a defense or claim. [U.C.C. §3-302(b)] For example, if a note is signed by two co-makers and a holder crosses out the name of one co-maker, the crossing-out does not constitute notice to subsequent holders that the remaining co-maker has a defense on the note.

4. **Transactions Precluding HDC Status**

A holder does not become an HDC of an instrument taken by:

(i) *Legal process* or purchase at a *creditor's sale* or similar proceeding;

(ii) Acquiring it as a successor in interest to *an estate or other organization*; or

(iii) Purchasing it as part of a *bulk transaction* not in the regular course of business of the transferor.

[U.C.C. §3-302(c)]

5. **Time at Which HDC Status Determined**

Whether a holder qualifies as an HDC is an issue determined at the *moment* the instrument is *negotiated* to the holder *and* she gives *value* therefor, whichever occurs later. Thus, if the transferee of a negotiable instrument acquires notice of a claim or defense to the instrument *prior* to negotiation or the giving of value, the transferee will not qualify as an HDC.

Example: Payee tricks Drawer into giving him a check, which Payee indorses over to his bank. The bank is now a "holder" but not an HDC until it gives value. If Drawer notifies the bank of the fraud prior to the bank's parting with value (*e.g.,* cashing the check), Drawer may reclaim the check from the bank or stop payment. However, if the bank has given value before Drawer gives notice of the fraud, it is an HDC—meaning that Drawer cannot reclaim the check and must pay it if the bank sues him.

6. **Holder of Security Interest**

If the person entitled to enforce an instrument has only a security interest in the instrument, and the person obliged to pay the instrument has a defense or claim that may be asserted against the person who granted the security interest, the person entitled to enforce the instrument may assert HDC rights only to the extent of the unpaid secured obligation. [U.C.C. §3-302(e)]

Example: Paul Payee borrows $500 from Heather Holder, promising to repay Heather in six months. As security for the debt, Heather takes possession of a $1,000 note on which Paul is the payee. The note is due in 12 months, and Marty Maker is its maker. Paul fails to pay Heather the $500. When the note from Marty is due, Heather presents it to Marty for payment. It turns out that Paul breached the contract for which Marty gave Paul the $1,000 note, so Marty has a defense against Paul. Because Heather took the note as security, she is treated as an HDC—and takes free of Marty's defense—only to the extent of the unpaid security obligation ($500).

7.   Payees as HDCs
A payee of an instrument might qualify as a holder in due course [*see* U.C.C. §3-302, comment 4], but generally because the payee is involved in the transaction giving rise to the instrument and has dealt with the person he wishes to sue (*e.g.,* the maker or drawer of the instrument), the payee will be subject to that person's defenses.

8.   Successors to Holders in Due Course

a.   Shelter Rule

1)   Transferee Acquires Transferor's Rights
It is a basic rule of commercial law that a transferee acquires whatever rights her transferor had. [U.C.C. §3-203] The transferee is said to take "shelter" in the status of her transferor; and the principle is known as the "shelter" rule. Subject to the fraud/illegality exception noted below, this rule allows any transferee to "step into the shoes" of the HDC who formerly held the instrument and to obtain the rights of an HDC, even though she otherwise clearly fails to meet the requirements of due course holding.

Example: A promissory note is held by H, who qualifies as an HDC. H makes a gift of the note to his daughter, D. Because D did not give value for the note, she obviously would not otherwise qualify as an HDC; but because her father had that status, D succeeds to the rights of an HDC too. The result would be the same even if D *knew* of some defense to the instrument.

2)   Protects Free Negotiability of Commercial Paper
The underlying reason for the shelter rule is to protect the free negotiability of commercial paper. Once the instrument comes into the hands of an HDC, defenses that could not be asserted against the HDC cannot be allowed against any transferee. Otherwise, the obligor could, by putting all potential transferees on notice of claimed defenses, vastly restrict the HDC's market for the instrument and thereby interfere with the free passage of commercial paper.

b.   Exceptions to the Shelter Rule
The shelter rule never grants HDC rights to ***persons who were parties to fraud or illegality affecting the instrument***. A party so implicated cannot sell the instrument to an HDC and reobtain it in order to free herself from a defense of fraud or illegality.

Note: Under section 3-203(b), apparently a person who is not an HDC merely because she has notice of a claim, defense, etc., who then transfers the instrument to another who qualifies as an HDC, and then reacquires the instrument can take shelter in the interim HDC's status.

c.   HDC Rights and Remote Transferees
Once a person has qualified as an HDC, all subsequent transferees will acquire the same HDC rights no matter how far down the chain of transferees they may be, *unless* they are transferees after the holder failed to obtain HDC rights because she was a party to fraud or illegality affecting the instrument.

Example: M signs a promissory note payable to A, who negotiates it to B, an HDC. B makes a gift of the note to C, who makes a gift of it to D, who in turn donates the note to E. Neither C, D, nor E qualifies as an HDC in her own right, since none paid value. Nevertheless, C obtained B's HDC rights under the shelter rule; and when C gave the note to D, D likewise received all of C's rights (which include B's HDC rights). E then took shelter in D's status, which included acquisition of B's HDC rights.

V. CLAIMS AND DEFENSES ON NEGOTIABLE INSTRUMENTS

A. IN GENERAL

As stated above, the heart of Article 3 is the HDC rule—an HDC takes an instrument free from personal defenses and claims and is subject only to real defenses. The rule comes into play when a holder of an instrument attempts to collect on it from an obligated party (such as a maker, drawer, or indorser; *see* VII., *infra*). In most cases in the real world, the obligated party will pay the holder, but that will not happen on your exam. Instead, the obligated party will refuse to pay, claiming that he has a defense to payment. Whether the obligated party will be forced to pay depends on whether the holder is an HDC and on the nature of the defenses the obligated party asserts. If the holder is not an HDC, the obligated party can successfully assert *any* defense that an obligor under an ordinary contract could successfully assert against a transferee (*e.g.*, failure of consideration). If the holder is an HDC, the obligated party's defenses against payment are limited—he can successfully assert only the defenses commonly called *real defenses*. [U.C.C. §3-305(b)]

1. "Claim" Defined

A claim is an affirmative right to a negotiable instrument because of *superior ownership*. For example, if a check is stolen from the payee and the payee's name is forged thereon, the payee is still the true owner of the check and may bring a replevin action to claim it from the person who now possesses it. In this case, the possessor cannot be an HDC because he cannot qualify as a "holder."

B. REAL DEFENSES

The following defenses (commonly called "real" defenses) may be asserted against *both* HDC and non-HDC transferees of the instrument in question. Other defenses (commonly called "personal" defenses) cannot be asserted against an HDC.

1. Forgery

a. Forgery of Names Necessary to Title—Precludes HDC Status

If the name of the *payee* or any *special indorsee* is unauthorized (*i.e.*, forged or signed by a nonagent), no subsequent taker can be an HDC because no one can obtain the right to enforce necessary to qualify as a "holder." However, if the person whose name was forged *ratifies* the unauthorized signature or is *estopped* from denying it, subsequent takers can qualify as HDCs (provided they meet the other requirements for due course holding).

b. Forgery of Names Not Necessary to Title—May Be HDC Subject to Real Defense of Unauthorized Signature

The names necessary to the chain of title on an instrument are those of the payee and any special indorsee. The forgery of any other name (*e.g.*, maker, drawer, acceptor, or indorsers on a bearer instrument) does not affect the right to enforce; and subsequent takers may qualify as HDCs if they meet the usual tests. Even so, a party whose name was either forged or placed on the instrument by a nonagent has a real defense of *unauthorized signature* unless he has ratified the signature or is estopped from denying it.

Example: Fingers Fagin steals a blank check from Ronald Rich and forges Rich's name as drawer. The check ends up in the possession of Collecting Bank, an HDC. If Rich is sued for payment by Bank, he may defend on the basis that he is not a "party to the instrument." Collecting Bank will have to sue Fagin, who is liable under section 3-403(a) just as if he had signed his own name instead of "Ronald Rich."

2. Fraud in the Factum (Real Fraud)

Under the U.C.C., there are two kinds of fraud: real and personal. "Real" fraud (fraud in the factum) is assertable against an HDC and is defined in section 3-305(a)(1)(iii) as "fraud that induced the obligor to sign the instrument with neither knowledge nor reasonable opportunity to learn of its character or its essential terms." Any other type of fraud—which would encompass *most* types—is a personal defense not assertable against an HDC.

Example of Fraud in the Factum: Hans Immigrant, who cannot read English, signs a promissory note after his attorney tells Hans that it is a credit application. Even in the hands of an HDC unaware of this lie, the note is not enforceable against Hans if he asserts fraud in the factum.

Example of *Personal Fraud:*	Honest John tells Cathy Consumer that the car he is selling has been driven only by a little old lady to Sunday church services. After paying for the car by check, Cathy discovers that the auto was formerly a police car and stops payment on the check. If the check is now held by an HDC, Cathy's defense cannot be asserted: She knew she was signing a negotiable instrument, so the fraud defense is personal only.

a.   Requirement of Excusable Ignorance
Even where the defendant was unaware that he was signing a negotiable instrument, fraud in the factum cannot be asserted if he failed to take *reasonable steps* to ascertain the nature of the transaction.

3.   Alteration of Instrument
An alteration is a change in the terms of the instrument. For example, a thief may alter the amount of a check from $10.00 to $1,000 by eliminating the decimal point. In certain circumstances discussed below (*see* VII.F.2.a., *infra*), an HDC may be able to collect only the original amount, so that the material alteration is a partial "real" defense. In other situations, the HDC may be able to collect on the instrument as altered.

4.   Incapacity to Contract
Under the state law, certain persons may lack the capacity to contract. For example, persons *declared incompetent* by judicial proceedings and *corporations* that have failed to take the necessary legal steps to transact business within the state may lack such capacity. [U.C.C. §3-305(a)(1)(ii)]

Note that before such incapacity will constitute a real defense, however, state law must render the contract *void* from its inception, rather than merely voidable. If the obligations of the incompetent are merely voidable at the option of the incompetent, incompetency is a personal defense and cannot be raised against an HDC. [U.C.C. §3-305, comment 1]

5.   Infancy
Infancy is a real defense (and therefore assertable against an HDC) if it would be a defense *under state law* in a simple contract action. If state law does *not* make the contracts of an infant void or voidable, infancy would be only a personal defense (not assertable against an HDC). [U.C.C. §3-305(a)(1)(i)]

6.   Illegality
If some illegality in the underlying transaction renders the obligation *void* (as opposed to merely voidable), this is a real defense assertable against an HDC even if the HDC had nothing to do with the illegality. (If the obligation is merely voidable under state law, the illegality becomes a *personal* defense.) [U.C.C. §3-305(a)(1)(ii)]

Example:	Minnesota Chubby loses a game of pool to Paul Hustler and pays off his gambling wager with a check. State law makes gambling debts void from their inception. Minnesota Chubby stops payment on the check after it has been negotiated to Hustler's bank. Even if the bank qualifies as an HDC, Chubby can assert the illegality to avoid payment.
Compare:	A state consumer protection law provides that notice of the fabric content of all garments must be firmly affixed to the garments. B buys four shirts from Shirt Mart, a retail store, and pays by check. The shirts do not have the required fabric content labels. The illegality here merely renders the contract voidable (B can keep the shirts if he wants to), and so the illegality is only a personal defense.

7.   Duress
Duress occurs in a contract situation where one party *acts involuntarily.* It is sometimes a real and sometimes a personal defense. Article 3 provides that duress is a matter of degree. It is a real defense if state law would render the contract *void*, but not if the contract is merely voidable. Thus, an instrument signed at the point of a gun is void, even in the hands of an HDC. However, one signed under threat to prosecute the son of the maker for theft may be merely voidable, so that the defense is cut off against an HDC. [U.C.C. §3-305(a)(1)(ii)]

8.   Discharge in Insolvency Proceedings
Insolvency proceedings include an assignment for the benefit of creditors (a state liquidation

proceeding) and any other proceeding intending to liquidate or rehabilitate the estate of the person involved. [U.C.C. §3-305(a)(1)(iv)]

Example: Douglas Debtor borrows $10,000 from Nightflyer Finance Company, signing a promissory note for that amount. The following day, Douglas files a petition in bankruptcy, listing the promissory note as an unpaid debt; shortly thereafter, the court discharges the debts in bankruptcy. One year later, National Bank presents the note to Douglas for payment. Even if the bank is an HDC, Douglas has a real defense based on his discharge in bankruptcy.

9. **Statute of Limitations**
If the statute of limitations has run on the instrument, even an HDC cannot enforce the instrument—the statute of limitations is a valid defense. Article 3 provides two general statutes of limitations: three years and six years. [U.C.C. §3-118]

a. **Three Years**
Actions on *unaccepted drafts* (*see* VII.B.6., *infra*) must be brought within three years after the date of dishonor or within 10 years after the date of the draft, whichever is earlier. Actions against the acceptor of certified checks (*see* VII.B.6., *infra*) or the issuer of teller's, cashier's, or traveler's checks must be brought within three years after demand for payment is made to the acceptor or the issuer, as the case may be. Actions for conversion of an instrument and the like, for breach of warranty, or to enforce other obligations or rights arising under Article 3 must be brought within three years after accrual.

b. **Six Years**
Actions on *notes* payable at a definite time or on demand must generally be commenced within six years after the due date or demand, respectively. Actions on certificates of deposit must be brought within six years after demand is made, but the limitations period does not commence before any stated due date.

10. **Accommodation (Suretyship) Defenses**
An accommodation party is one who signs an instrument for the purpose of incurring liability on the instrument without being a direct beneficiary of the instrument. [U.C.C. §3-419] In essence, the accommodation party is a surety. If an HDC knows of the accommodation when he takes the instrument, he takes subject to the accommodation party's suretyship defenses (*i.e.*, discharge to the extent of loss caused by: (i) an extension of the due date; (ii) a material modification of the obligation; or (iii) impairment of collateral). [U.C.C. §3-605] (*See* VII.B.7., *infra*, for a discussion of accommodation parties; *see* IX.E., *infra*, for further discussion of suretyship defenses.)

11. **Discharges Known to HDC**
An HDC takes a negotiable instrument subject to any discharge of which he has notice when he acquires HDC status. The word "discharge" here means the discharging events included in Article 3 and any other act that would discharge an obligation to pay money under a simple contract. [U.C.C. §3-601] Discharging events are discussed in detail at IX., *infra*.

a. **Discharge Usually a Personal Defense**
Unless the discharge of a prior party is apparent from the face of the instrument (as in the case of a line drawn through an indorsement) or the HDC knows of the discharge, discharge is a personal defense and therefore not assertable against an HDC. For example, payment by a party discharges that party, but unless the payment was apparent on the instrument, a later HDC could compel payment again.

Example: After 20 years, Peter Pumpkin finally pays off the mortgage on his house. He asks the mortgagee, National Bank, for his promissory note and is very upset to learn that National Bank sold it long ago but failed to tell Peter. If the note is later presented to Peter by an HDC for payment, Peter must pay again—since his discharge by payment is only a personal defense. However, Peter should be able to pass his additional liability on to National Bank in a quasi-contract action for money had and received.

C. **PERSONAL DEFENSES**
Personal defenses cannot be asserted against one having the rights of an HDC, and may be viewed as all defenses other than the real defenses discussed above. These include every defense

available in simple contract actions. Any transferee of a negotiable instrument without HDC rights takes the instrument subject to all such personal defenses. [U.C.C. §3-305(a)(2)]

Example: Personal defenses available on a negotiable instrument include lack of consideration, failure of consideration, theft ("nondelivery"), breach of warranty or contract, failure of a condition precedent, and other defenses available in a simple contract action (such as mistake, unconscionability, duress, impossibility of performance, or waiver).

1. Consideration and Negotiable Instruments

A negotiable instrument must be supported by sufficient consideration. However, the existence of consideration is not technically a prerequisite to negotiability. Rather, its absence (lack or failure of consideration) is a valid defense to an instrument in the hands of anyone *other than an HDC*. [U.C.C. §3-303(b)] Where there is only a *partial* failure of consideration, the failure is a pro tanto defense, whether or not the failure is in an ascertained or liquidated amount.

2. Claims or Defenses of Another

a. Must Rely on One's Own Defenses

In defending a lawsuit, one must rely on his own defenses and cannot use the claims or defenses of third parties as a defense (subject to the exception noted below). [U.C.C. §3-305(c)]

Example: Martha signs a promissory note as maker. Years later, the current holder, Panther Finance, presents the matured note to Martha and demands payment. Martha receives a phone call from Harry Holdit, a prior indorser of the instrument, who asks Martha not to pay on the note because Panther Finance defrauded him when he negotiated the note to them. Unless Harry is willing to defend Panther's lawsuit against Martha himself, she may not raise the rights of Harry if she is sued.

b. The "Payment" Rule

The liability of any party obligated to pay on an instrument is discharged by payment to a person entitled to enforce the instrument unless:

(i) Payment is made with knowledge that it is prohibited by an injunction (*e.g.*, a party has obtained a court order to prevent payment);

(ii) In cases not involving a cashier's, teller's, or certified check, the party making payment has accepted (from a person with a claim to the instrument) indemnity against loss for refusal to pay the person entitled to enforce the instrument; or

(iii) The person making payment knows the instrument is stolen and that the person being paid is in wrongful possession.

[U.C.C. §3-602(b)]

c. Exception to Relying on One's Own Defenses—Theft

The above payment rule provides the only exception to relying on one's own defenses—theft. A defense that the non-HDC acquired the instrument by theft and the person holding the instrument is in wrongful possession must be raised if known by the person making payment. Payment without raising this issue will not result in discharge of liability.

Example: In the example in a., above, if Harry Holdit tells Martha that Panther Finance *stole* the bearer note from him, she should raise this issue before paying Panther (unless Panther is an HDC). One possibility would be to pay the money into court in an *interpleader* action.

VI. TRIAL PROCEDURE

A. IN GENERAL

Article 3 specifies the procedure to be followed for the trial of a case involving negotiable paper.

B. WHO MAY ENFORCE?

The following persons are entitled to enforce an instrument:

(i)   A holder of the instrument;

(ii) A nonholder in possession of the instrument who has the rights of a holder (*e.g.*, a person who obtained the instrument through subrogation); and

(iii) A person not in possession of the instrument but who is entitled to enforce it (*e.g.*, lost, stolen, or destroyed instrument situation).

[U.C.C. §3-301]

C. BURDEN OF PROOF

To make out a prima facie case for payment, the person presenting the instrument for payment need only prove that:

(i)   Signatures on the instrument are genuine; and

(ii) She is a person entitled to enforce the instrument as discussed above.

If these elements are proved, the person presenting the instrument is entitled to payment unless the defendant proves a defense or claim in recoupment (*i.e.*, a claim reducing the amount owed; *see* IV.D.3.a.2)d), *supra*). [U.C.C. §3-308(b)] Note that the issue of whether the person presenting the instrument for payment has the status of an HDC is irrelevant unless the defendant raises defenses.

1. Proof of Signatures—Presumption of Validity

Unless the defendant specifically denies the validity of any signature in his pleadings, its validity is deemed admitted. If the defendant specifically denies the validity of a signature, the person claiming the signature valid has the ultimate burden of proof; however, a presumption of validity still applies, and so no evidence of validity is necessary until the defendant presents evidence of invalidity, unless the action is to enforce the liability of the purported signer, who is now dead or incompetent. [U.C.C. §3-308(a)]

a. Undisclosed Principal Case

If the plaintiff is seeking to enforce the instrument against an undisclosed principal (*e.g.*, the instrument was signed by an agent in his own name on behalf of and with authority from a principal whose name does not appear on the instrument), the plaintiff has the burden of establishing that the principal is liable on the instrument as a represented person. (*See* VII.D., *infra*.)

2. Proof of Defenses

If the person presenting the instrument has made out a prima facie case, she is entitled to payment unless the defendant raises a defense or claim in recoupment. If a defense or claim in recoupment is made, the plaintiff can cut off the defense by proving that she is entitled to HDC status. [U.C.C. §3-308(b)]

3. Where Instrument Is Lost, Destroyed, or Stolen

If the person entitled to enforce the instrument cannot produce it because it is lost, stolen, or destroyed, she is nevertheless entitled to maintain an action on the instrument as though she could produce it, providing she can prove her ownership, the terms of the instrument, and the facts that prevent her production of it. The court in such a case is entitled to require protection indemnifying the defendant against loss by reason of additional claims on the instrument. Adequate protection may be provided by any reasonable means; it need not be by security bond. [U.C.C. §3-309]

a. Procedure for Missing Certified, Cashier's, or Teller's Check

A drawer or payee of a certified check (*see* VII.B.6.d., *infra*) or the remitter (a person who purchases an instrument from its issuer payable to a third party) or payee of a cashier's or teller's check may claim a right to payment if the check is lost, destroyed, or stolen. The claimant must inform the bank that the check is missing, giving the bank a reasonable time to prevent payment to another, and must provide reasonable identification if the bank requests. The claim is enforceable at the later of the time it is asserted or 90 days after the date of the check (90 days after acceptance for certified checks). In the interim, the check may be paid if a person entitled to enforce the check presents it, and such payment discharges liability to the claimant. If the claim becomes enforceable (*i.e.*, the check has not been presented for payment in the interim), the bank is obliged to pay the claimant and need not pay a person later presenting the check for payment. However, if the later presenter has the rights of an HDC, the claimant must refund the money to the bank or pay the HDC. [U.C.C. §3-312]

D. ACTION FOR CONVERSION

A person entitled to possession of an instrument may bring an action for conversion of the instrument. Conversion generally is governed by the law applicable to the conversion of personal property. Note, however, that neither the issuer nor a payee or indorsee who never received delivery of the instrument may maintain an action for conversion. [U.C.C. §3-420]

Example: Cola Corp. sends Mark Drinker a rebate check of $5. The check names Mark as payee but is delivered to Thad Thief's house, who lives next door to Mark. Thad takes the check, forges Mark's name, and deposits the check in his own account. The check is then forwarded through the check collection system to the drawee bank. Neither Cola Corp. nor Mark can maintain an action for conversion against the drawee bank since Cola Corp. was the issuer and Mark never received delivery of the instrument. However, if the check were delivered to Mark's house and then was stolen, Mark could maintain an action for conversion against the bank. *Rationale*: If the payee never receives an instrument, he never becomes a holder and never has a right to enforce the instrument. Once the payee receives an instrument, he becomes a holder and the obligation for which the instrument was taken is suspended (*see* IX.A.2.b.2), *infra*).

E. VOUCHING IN

As an aside, it should be noted that it is possible to "vouch in" parties to an instrument who may be liable to the party sued. The procedure works as follows:

1. If a defendant to a suit on an instrument has a right of recourse against someone else if he is required to pay, then he may give that third person written notice of the litigation.

2. The notice will say that the person notified may come in and defend, and that if he does not do so, he will nevertheless be bound by any determination of fact common to a suit against him by the party giving the notice.

3. If the person does not come in after receipt of such a notice, then he will be so bound if in a subsequent lawsuit he is sued by the party who gave the notice. Again, he will be bound by the facts found in the first suit that are common to both suits.

4. Any person "vouched in" under this procedure may in turn "vouch in" any person who may be liable to him, and so on.

VII. LIABILITY OF PARTIES

A. INTRODUCTION

The rights of persons entitled to enforce negotiable instruments were discussed above. This section discusses who may be held liable on a negotiable instrument. There are a number of parties who may be held liable on an instrument simply because their names appear on the instrument, including makers, drawers, indorsers, and drawees. As a preliminary rule, remember that no one may be held liable on a negotiable instrument unless her signature or the signature of an authorized representative appears thereon. [U.C.C. §3-401] (For a discussion of the effect of agents' signatures, *see* D., *infra*.)

B. PARTIES WHO MAY BE LIABLE ON AN INSTRUMENT

1. Maker of Note, Issuer of Cashier's Check

The maker of a note or issuer of a cashier's check, merely by signing her name, becomes obligated to pay the instrument according to its terms at the time it was issued, or if the instrument was not issued, at the time it first came into possession of a holder. [U.C.C. §3-412] Her promise is unconditional—she must pay the instrument on the due date, although she is permitted to assert the defenses as described in V., *supra*.

Note: If a note is payable at a bank ("I promise to pay to the order of Pete Payee at Payee National Bank"), the person entitled to enforce the note must take the instrument to the bank and present it for payment. [U.C.C. §3-501(a)]

2. Indorser—Secondary Liability

An indorser is a person who signs his name other than as maker, drawer, or acceptor, usually on the back of an instrument, for the purpose either of negotiating the instrument, restricting payment of the instrument, or incurring indorser's liability on the instrument. [U.C.C. §3-204] An indorser is considered to be secondarily liable on an instrument, meaning that a person entitled to enforce an instrument looks to the maker or drawee first for payment, and will look to the indorser for payment only if the maker or drawee does not pay. An indorser can be held liable in two separate ways—for the basic obligation of indorsers (*i.e.,* indorser's contract) or in warranty.

a. Basic Obligation—Indorser's Contract

The basic obligation of an indorser arises merely from signing one's name. The obligation is to pay according to the terms of the instrument at the time of the indorsement (or if the indorser indorsed an incomplete instrument, according to its terms as completed). [U.C.C. §3-415(a)] The obligation can be negated if the indorsement is *qualified* (*i.e.,* signed "without recourse"). Generally, there are three prerequisites to the indorser's obligation (*i.e.,* an indorser cannot be held liable unless three things happen first): presentment, dishonor, and notice of dishonor.

1) Presentment

Presentment simply is a demand for payment made by a person entitled to enforce an instrument. The demand usually is made to the drawee of a draft or the maker of a note. [U.C.C. §3-501(a)]

a) Time Requirement for Checks—Thirty Days

An indorser's liability on a check will be discharged unless it is presented for payment or given to a depositary bank for collection within *30 days* after the indorsement was made. [U.C.C. §3-415(e)]

b) How Presentment Made

Presentment can be made by any commercially reasonable means, including oral, written, or electronic communication, and can be made at any contemplated place of payment (but if the instrument is payable at a bank in the United States, presentment must be made at that bank). [U.C.C. §3-501(b)(1)]

c) When Presentment Excused

Presentment for payment or acceptance is excused if:

(i) The person entitled to present the instrument cannot with reasonable diligence present;

(ii) The maker or acceptor has repudiated the obligation to pay or is dead or insolvent;

(iii) By the terms of the instrument presentment is unnecessary;

(iv) The obligor has waived presentment; or

(v) The drawer instructed the drawee not to pay or the drawee was not obligated to pay.

[U.C.C. §3-504(a)]

2) Dishonor

Dishonor occurs when the maker of a note or the drawee of a draft does not pay or accept (*see* 6., *infra*) the instrument within the allowed time after presentment. Note the following timing rules:

a) Demand Instruments Other than Checks

Generally, demand instruments (*i.e.,* instruments not stating a date for payment) other than checks will be considered dishonored if they are not paid on the date they are presented for payment. [U.C.C. §3-502(a)(1), (b)(2)]

b) Time Instruments

Time notes *payable at or through a bank* and most time drafts payable on a specific date are considered dishonored if they are not paid on the date they become payable according to their terms or the date they are presented, whichever is later. A time note *not* payable at or through a bank is dishonored if it is not paid on the date it is payable. [U.C.C. §3-502(a)(2), (b)(3)] A time draft presented for acceptance rather than payment is dishonored if it is not accepted on the date it is presented. [U.C.C. §3-502(b)(3), (4)]

c) Checks
If a check is presented to a bank other than for immediate payment over the counter (*e.g.*, a customer deposits a check to be credited to his account), it is dishonored if the bank returns the check or sends written notice of dishonor or nonpayment before final payment has been made or before its midnight deadline (*see* below). [U.C.C. §§3-502(b)(1), 4-301]

(1) Final Payment
If the bank in which a check is deposited (the depositary bank) is not the bank on which the check is drawn, the depositary bank will usually provisionally credit its customer's account (*i.e.*, make a bookkeeping entry that the account is to be credited) and wait to see whether the check will be paid by the bank obligated to pay. The check usually is sent to a clearinghouse to facilitate payment. The provisional credit becomes final payment when the check is settled through clearinghouse rules. (Payment is also final if payment is made in cash over the counter.) [U.C.C. §4-215]

(2) Midnight Deadline
If final payment is not made, the depositary bank has until its midnight deadline to dishonor. The midnight deadline is midnight of the next banking day following the day on which an instrument is received. [U.C.C. §4-104(a)(10)]

3) Notice of Dishonor
Notice of dishonor simply is notification that the instrument was dishonored. It may be given by any commercially reasonable means of communication. The obligation *of an indorser* is discharged if he is not given a notice of dishonor. [U.C.C. §3-503]

a) Generally Not Required for Maker or Drawer Liability
Note that notice of dishonor does not have to be given to a maker of a note (because he knows that he did not pay it) or the drawer of a draft unless the draft was accepted by an acceptor.

b) Timing—Thirty Days
Generally, notice of dishonor must be given within *30 days* after dishonor. For instruments taken for collection by collecting banks, notice of dishonor must be given before the midnight deadline. [U.C.C. §3-503(c)]

c) When Delay in Giving Notice Is Excused
A delay in giving a notice of dishonor is excused if the delay is caused by circumstances beyond the control of the person giving notice *and* the party exercised reasonable diligence after the cause of the delay ceased to exist. [U.C.C. §3-504(c)]

d) When Notice Entirely Excused
Notice of dishonor is excused entirely if the terms of the instrument make notice unnecessary or the obligor has waived notice. [U.C.C. §3-504(b)]

4) Multiple Indorsers
Where more than one indorsement appears on an instrument, any indorser is severally liable for the *full amount* to any holder or *later* indorser of the instrument.
Example: Maker's note is indorsed by four indorsers before coming into the possession of Harold Holder. When Maker dishonors the note at maturity, Holder demands payment from Indorser Number 4, who pays. Number 4 may now recover the full amount from any of the indorsers before her. She need not proceed in any particular order, but may select any prior indorser.

If Number 4 collects from Number 2, Number 2 gets the note and may seek repayment from Number 1. However, Number 2 may **not** sue Number 3 because (as to Number 2) she is a later indorser. Liability moves **up** the chain of indorsements; and indorsers are presumed to have indorsed in the order in which their names appear on the instrument (unless the contrary is shown).

5) Summary Example of Indorser Liability

Dan gives Pete a $1,000 check as payment for a car. Pete owes Ivana $950 for a ring Pete purchased from Ivana, and so he indorses his name on the back of the check and gives the check to Ivana. Three things must happen before Pete will be liable to Ivana on the check: (i) Ivana must present the check for payment or deposit the check for collection within 30 days after Pete indorsed; (ii) the drawee bank must refuse to pay (dishonor); and (iii) Ivana must give Pete notice of dishonor within 30 days after the dishonor.

b. Warranty Liability of Indorser

When an indorser transfers an instrument, the indorser becomes a transferor and can be liable for the transfer warranties discussed below.

3. Transferor

a. The Five Transfer Warranties

Whenever a person (i) *transfers an instrument* (*i.e.*, any movement of possession of the instrument other than issuance or presentment) (ii) *for consideration*, the transferor makes the following five transfer warranties [U.C.C. §3-416]:

1) Entitled to Enforce

The transferor warrants that he is a person entitled to enforce the instrument. Effectively, this is a warranty that all indorsements necessary to the chain of title (that of the payee and any special indorsees) are genuine. It is likewise a warranty that the transferor is a proper person (in her own right or as an agent) to make presentment and obtain payment (or acceptance), and that the transfer is "otherwise rightful."

Example: Drawer writes a check to the order of Payee and gives it to Payee. Before Payee can sign it, the check is stolen from her and her name is forged on the back by Forger. Forger then transfers the check to Gullible Grocery, who deposits it at Grocer's State Bank ("GSB"). GSB in turn sends the check to the drawee ("payor") bank, Antitrust National Bank. At the moment they transferred the check, both Forger and Gullible Grocery breached the transfer warranty that they are persons entitled to enforce. GSB did not breach a transfer warranty when it sent the check to the drawee, because the act is a *presentment* (as opposed to transfer).

2) Signatures Are Authentic and Authorized

The transferor warrants that all signatures are authentic and authorized.

3) No Alteration

The transferor warrants that the instrument has not been altered.

4) No Defenses

The transferor also warrants that no defense or claim of any party is good against her.

Example: Payee defrauds Maker into giving Payee a promissory note, which Payee promptly negotiates to Loan Company. Because Maker could successfully defend a suit on the note by Payee, transfer of the note to Loan Company breached the warranty that there was no defense good against Payee.

5) No Knowledge of Insolvency Proceedings

Finally, the transferor warrants that she has no knowledge of any insolvency proceeding that has been instituted against the maker, acceptor, or drawer of an unaccepted instrument.

b. Made to Immediate Transferee (and Subsequent Transferees If Indorsed)
If the transfer is not by indorsement (*i.e.*, transfer by delivery alone, as in the case of a bearer instrument), the warranties run *only to the immediate transferee*. But if the transferor indorses, the warranties run to *all subsequent transferees*.

c. Presentment and Notice of Dishonor Not Needed
Presentment, notice of dishonor, etc., are *irrelevant* to warranty liability.

d. Liability Can Be Negated
Other than on checks, warranty liability can be negated by the transferor if she places the proper words on the instrument (*e.g.*, "without warranty"). [U.C.C. §3-416, comment 5] The words "without recourse" probably are *not* sufficient.

4. Drawer
Generally, if a draft is dishonored (*i.e.*, the drawee refuses to pay), the drawer of the draft is obliged to pay the draft according to its terms when the drawer signed the instrument (or if the instrument was incomplete, according to its terms as completed, as controlled by the rules regarding incomplete instruments; *see* F., *infra*). Thus, like an indorser, a drawer has secondary liability. [U.C.C. §3-414]

a. Drafts Accepted by a Bank—Drawer Discharged
If the draft has been accepted by a bank (signed by the bank so that the bank has primary liability on the draft; *see* 6., *infra*), the *drawer is discharged* from his obligation on the draft *regardless of when* the draft was accepted *or by whom* acceptance was obtained.

5. Drawee

a. In General
Because no one is liable on an instrument unless her signature appears thereon, the drawee of a draft cannot have any liability on an instrument unless and until the drawee signs the instrument. In other words, the drawee has no direct liability to the holder of a draft—the holder cannot force the drawee to pay unless the drawee signs. When the drawee does sign, it becomes an acceptor (discussed in 6., *infra*). [U.C.C. §3-408]

b. Rights and Duties of Parties
When a bank is the drawee (as in the case of a check), the bank may well be liable to its customer for failure to accept the draft. This is because of the contractual relationship between a bank and its customer. This contract imposes various duties on the bank and the customer, and governs the relationship between the parties.

1) Duties of Drawee Bank to Customer

a) Must Honor Customer's Check
The bank is obligated to honor its customer's check if there are sufficient funds on deposit to cover the draft. If the bank wrongfully dishonors the draft, the customer can recover damages for whatever harm is proximately caused by the wrongful dishonor. If a check is more than six months old, the bank may refuse to pay unless again ordered by the drawer. [U.C.C. §§4-402, 4-404]

(1) Insufficient Funds
If the customer has insufficient funds at the bank to cover a check, the bank may nevertheless choose to honor the check. In such a case, the customer is liable to the bank for the overdraft. [U.C.C. §4-401(a)]

b) When Bank Cannot Charge the Account
The bank must honor a check as drawn. Therefore, it cannot charge the account:

(i) If there is no order by the depositor (*forged* signature of drawer);

(ii) For more money than the original order (*alteration* of amount by third party);

(iii) If the bank pays the wrong person (*forgery* of payee or indorsee's signature); or

(iv) If the item is postdated, the customer *gives the bank notice of the postdating*, and the bank pays the item *before* the stated date.

If the bank pays a check in violation of these principles, the customer is entitled to a re-credit on her account.

2) Duties of Customer to Bank

The customer must be careful, however, or she might lose this right. Upon receipt of her bank statement, the customer has a duty to the bank to exercise *reasonable care and promptness* to discover any unauthorized payments resulting from an alteration or forgery of the drawer's signature and to notify the bank promptly after any such discovery. [U.C.C. §4-406]

a) When Customer's Account Can Be Charged

The bank can successfully charge the customer's account if it can show:

(i) That the customer failed to comply with this duty; *and*

(ii) That the bank suffered loss by reason of the failure.

[U.C.C. §4-406(d)]

b) Defense of Customer

The customer may answer such proof by showing that the *bank was negligent* in paying the item. If the bank was negligent, the loss will be allocated between the customer and the bank in proportion to the fault of each. [U.C.C. §4-406(e); *see* E.4., *infra*]

c. Death of a Customer

Death of the customer does not revoke the bank's authority to pay a check until the bank (i) knows of the death and (ii) has a reasonable time to act on such knowledge. Even with such knowledge, the bank may keep paying checks for 10 days after the date of death, unless a person claiming an interest in the account orders that payment be stopped. [U.C.C. §4-405]

d. Subrogation

A bank that pays a check is subrogated to the rights of the person it pays against the customer. Thus, if a bank pays an HDC, it can assume the position of an HDC in attempting to charge its customer's account. [U.C.C. §4-407] This is important because if the customer would have had to pay the HDC, the bank can charge the customer's account because the customer will have suffered no loss from the bank's payment. (*See* e.2), below.)

e. Stop Payment Orders

1) Requirements of Reasonable Notice

Under the U.C.C., a written stop payment order is binding on the bank for *six months, but an oral stop payment order lapses after 14 days* if it is not confirmed in writing within that period. [U.C.C. §4-403(b)] Of course, if the bank pays over a valid stop payment order, then it has not honored the orders of its customer and cannot charge her account. The bank must be given reasonable time to act, and is under no obligation to honor a stop payment order on a cashier's check.

2) Customer Has Burden of Proving Loss

If the bank pays an item in spite of a stop payment order, the *customer* has the burden of proving that a loss occurred and the amount of the loss. [U.C.C. §4-403(c)] If there is an HDC in the chain of transferees of the item, the customer cannot recover—because even if payment *had* been stopped, the customer would have had to pay the HDC.

f. Bank's Right to Recover Payment from Party Paid

1) Generally Payment Is Final

If the bank erroneously pays out on a forged instrument to an HDC, it generally may not recover payment back from the party paid unless there has been a breach of either a transfer warranty or a presentment warranty (*e.g.*, forged indorsement). (*See* VIII.C., *infra,* for a detailed discussion of finality of payment.) Recognize, however, that the holder could *not* have initially forced the bank to pay.

2) Recovery Before "Final Payment"
The bank can recover for any item paid up until it has made "final payment." Thus, if instead of paying cash (final payment) the bank makes a provisional settlement by crediting the holder's account, it can revoke this payment any time prior to its midnight deadline (midnight of the next banking day). [*See* U.C.C. §4-215]

6. Acceptor
Acceptance is a process whereby the acceptor (usually a drawee bank) signs a draft and thereby becomes primarily bound to pay the instrument. [U.C.C. §3-409] In essence, the acceptor enters into a contract that it will pay the draft when due according to its terms when accepted.

a. Purpose and Procedure
Accepted drafts often are required where a payee does not want to rely on the credit of a drawer unknown to it (*e.g.*, the payee will not accept a personal check, requiring instead a certified check, which is a form of an accepted draft). The draft is usually presented to the acceptor, which signs the draft and returns it to the party presenting the draft for acceptance. At this point, the bank will usually charge its customer's account for the amount of the draft, because after acceptance, the customer is no longer liable on the draft. This process is called "*presentment for acceptance*." Acceptance may be sought at any time and by any party entitled to enforce the instrument.

b. Variance
It is permissible for the *acceptor* to change the terms of the draft. This is called a variance. The draft will apparently remain negotiable even if by such a device the acceptor makes the promise to pay expressly conditional or changes the sum to an uncertain amount. However, if the acceptor wants to do this: the *holder may refuse to take the varied acceptance*, and may then treat the instrument as *dishonored* and pursue other parties on it [U.C.C. §3-410(a)]; or (ii) the holder may accept the variance, in which case by so doing he will *discharge* all prior nonconsenting parties to the instrument; *i.e.,* he will release the drawer and all prior indorsers from liability [U.C.C. §3-410(c)].

d. Certification of Check
Certification of a check is the equivalent of an acceptance; it is the acceptance of a check by the bank on which it was drawn. [U.C.C. §3-409(d)] Certification has the effect of discharging the drawer and all prior indorsers. [U.C.C. §3-310] The bank need not certify a check if it does not want to, absent some special agreement with its customer. When it does certify, it is putting its own credit on the line, which is why certified checks are so good and why the bank will charge the customer's account upon certification rather than waiting until after the item has been paid. A bank's failure to certify may constitute a dishonor. [U.C.C. §3-502(b)(3)]

Example: Bob wants to buy a piano from neighbor Tom, but Tom will not sell unless Bob's personal check is certified. Bob draws a check payable to Tom and presents it to his own bank for certification (acceptance). After the bank certifies the check, the bank returns it to Bob, who gives it to Tom in return for the piano.

1) Alteration After Certification
If the certification of a check does not state an amount, and the amount of the check is subsequently raised before the check is negotiated to a holder in due course, the obligation of the acceptor is the amount at the time it was taken by the holder in due course. [U.C.C. §3-413(b)] Thus, a bank can avoid liability for the altered amount only by stating on the check the amount the bank agrees to pay.

e. Refusal to Pay Certified, Teller's, or Cashier's Checks
If the acceptor of a certified check or the issuer of a teller's check or a cashier's check wrongfully refuses to pay, the person asserting the right to enforce the check generally is entitled to expenses and interest resulting from the failure to pay. If the bank receives notice of particular circumstances, it will also be liable for consequential damages arising from those circumstances. [U.C.C. §3-411(b)]

7. **Accommodation Parties**

An accommodation party is one who signs an instrument for the purpose of lending her name and credit to another party to the instrument. She is in essence a surety. If the accommodation party pays the instrument, she will have an action on the instrument against the party accommodated, irrespective of their formal positions on the instrument. An accommodation maker can thus recover from an accommodated indorser on the instrument. [*See* U.C.C. §3-419]

Example: "Hot Check" Harry wants to buy an auto, but Honest John Used Cars will not accept his check. Harry then persuades his friend Gloria to write the check for him, payable to Honest John. Harry signs as an indorser, and obtains the car. When Honest John collects the amount of the check from Gloria (the accommodation party), she may seek reimbursement from Harry (the accommodated party) even though check drawers usually may not sue indorsers (*i.e.,* because indorsers sign subsequent to drawers). Similarly, if Honest John collected the money from Harry, Harry would have no right to sue Gloria on her drawer's contract (although indorsers usually have this right). Both of these results occur because Gloria was in fact a surety for Harry, even though Harry signed as the indorser of her check.

a. **Liability**

An accommodation party is never liable to the party accommodated. An accommodation party is, however, liable on the instrument *in the capacity in which she signs* (maker, indorser, drawer, etc.), even where the taker is aware of the accommodation. An HDC's awareness of accommodation status merely allows the accommodation party to raise her special suretyship defenses; it does not release the accommodation party from her liability as a maker, indorser, etc. (The suretyship defenses are discussed at IX.E., *infra*.)

Note: Because the accommodation party will usually not be a transferor, she will normally not have any warranty liability.

b. **Proof of Accommodation Status**

1) **Presumption from Anomalous Indorsement**
A person signing an instrument is presumed to be an accommodation party and there is notice of the accommodation status if the signature is anomalous (*i.e.,* made by a person who is not a holder; *see* III.B.3.d., *supra*) or otherwise indicates that the signer is acting as a surety or guarantor with respect to the instrument. [U.C.C. §3-419(c)]

2) **Oral Proof Generally Allowed**
As a general rule, the fact of accommodation can be shown by parol evidence in order to give the accommodation party the benefit of any discharge relating to her character as a surety. The one *exception* to this rule is in the case of an *HDC,* who took *without notice* of the accommodation.

c. **Collection Guarantee**
"Collection guaranteed" or the equivalent means that the signer enters into a contract that she will be liable on the instrument *only if* the person entitled to enforce the instrument has reduced his claim to judgment against the maker or acceptor and execution has been returned unsatisfied, or only if the maker or acceptor has become insolvent or it otherwise appears that it is useless to proceed against the maker or acceptor.

Example: A surety's promise to "guarantee against loss by reason of the nonpayment of this note" has been held to be a guarantee of collection only, so that the surety could not be sued unless full efforts at collection had first been taken against the maker.

C. **EFFECT OF PERSONS SIGNING JOINTLY**

If parties to an instrument sign jointly (*e.g.,* a note signed by Max Maker and Mary Maker or an indorsement of a check payable to Irwin Indorser and Ingrid Indorser), they have *joint and several* liability on the instrument, so either one or both can be sued for the entire amount due. If one party pays more than his share, he generally has a right of contribution against the other jointly liable party. A release of one jointly liable party by a third party does not affect the right of contribution. [U.C.C. §3-116]

D. EFFECT OF REPRESENTATIVE OR AGENT SIGNING

Article 3 provides that no one can be liable on an instrument unless her signature or the signature of an authorized agent appears on the instrument. [U.C.C. §3-401(a)] Article 3 has adopted much of the law of agency concerning signatures by representatives or agents.

1. Liability of Represented Person ("Principal")

a. General Rule—Principal Liable If Agent Authorized

If a representative ("agent") signs an instrument with her own name or the name of the represented person ("principal"), the principal is bound to the same extent as if the signature were on a simple contract. [U.C.C. §3-402(a)] On a simple contract, a principal is bound if the agent had authority.

Example: Paul appoints Alice to be his purchasing agent and gives her authority to issue negotiable instruments for the purchases made. Paul can be held liable for the instruments Alice signs on his behalf whether or not Paul's name appears on the instrument.

b. When Principal Liable Despite Lack of Agent's Authority

There are two situations where the principal might be liable even though the agent signed the instrument without authority.

1) Ratification

The principal can ratify the signature. Ratification occurs when a principal knowingly adopts a signature as his own or when, with full knowledge of the circumstances, he appropriates the benefit of the unauthorized signing or fails to deny the validity of the signature, knowing his silence may mislead others. Note that ratification does not relieve the forger of criminal liability or insulate him from civil liability to the person whose name was forged.

2) Estoppel

The principal can be precluded from denying authority if by his negligence he contributed to the making of the unauthorized signature (the same rule would apply to forgeries); the preclusion operates in favor of one who is otherwise an HDC or one who in good faith pays the instrument in accordance with the reasonable commercial standards of his business.

2. Liability of Representative ("Agent")

Whether an authorized agent who signs an instrument for a principal will be liable on the instrument depends on whether the fact of agency and the principal's identity were disclosed. [U.C.C. §3-402]

a. Agent Signs Principal's Name Only

If the agent simply signs her principal's name without putting her own name on the instrument, as indicated above, the principal will be liable if the agent was authorized, but the agent will not be liable because neither her name nor that of her authorized agent appears on the instrument. (For a discussion of the effect of unauthorized signatures, *see* E., *infra*.)

b. Agent Signs Own Name But Discloses Principal

If the agent signs her own name to the instrument and the principal has given her authority, the agent is not bound if the signature unambiguously shows that it was made on behalf of the principal who is identified in the instrument.

Example: If Joan Smith, the treasurer of Blue Corporation, signs a corporate instrument "Blue Corporation, by Joan Smith, Treasurer," she will not be liable on the instrument if she had authority to sign the instrument.

c. Agent Signs Own Name But Does Not Disclose Principal's Name and/or Agency Relationship

If the signature does not show that it was made in a representative capacity or the principal is not identified in the instrument, the agent will be liable to any HDC who takes the instrument without notice that the agent was not intended to be liable, but will not be liable to non-HDCs if she can prove that the original parties did not intend her to be liable.

Example: Peter has appointed Ann as his purchasing agent and has given her authority to issue instruments for him. Ann buys radios from Supplier for Peter and gives Supplier a negotiable promissory note for payment signed simply "Ann," or "Ann, Agent," or "Peter, Ann." Supplier knows that the note is actually for Peter and that Ann is not meant to be personally liable on the note. Supplier transfers the note to Manufacturer as payment for radios Supplier purchased from Manufacturer. Manufacturer does not know that Ann was not intended to be personally bound. Neither Supplier nor Manufacturer are HDCs because they know the radios sold to Peter are defective. If Manufacturer attempts to force Ann to pay on the note, she may raise the defense that she was not intended to be bound since Manufacturer is not an HDC. Suppose instead that Manufacturer transfers the note to Harry, a raw materials supplier who does not know of the defects in the radios and so qualifies as an HDC. Harry will be able to enforce the note against Ann if he does not have notice that Ann was not to be bound on the note.

d. Check Cases

An agent with authority who signs her name to her principal's check cannot be held liable on the check if it is drawn on the principal's account and indicates the identity of the principal. It does not matter whether the agent indicates her representative capacity.

Example: In the example in c., above, if Ann had issued a check drawn on Peter's account and naming Peter as the drawer (most checks are personalized and indicate the name of the drawer), she could not be held liable on the check regardless of how she signed.

E. EFFECT OF UNAUTHORIZED SIGNATURES

The general rule is that an unauthorized signature is wholly ineffective as the signature of the person whose name is signed but is effective as the signature of the signer. [U.C.C. §3-403(a)] Unauthorized signatures include both forgeries and signatures by persons exceeding their authority. However, the Code specifies *five circumstances* in which a forgery or unauthorized signature will be validated because the person whose name is used has done something to preclude her from raising the forgery issue.

1. Fictitious Payee

The carelessness of the drawer or maker in *issuing* an instrument may make it very likely that the payee's name will be forged. In such cases, the Code treats the resulting forgery as *effective to pass the right to enforce the instrument* to later transferees.

a. Issuance to Impostor

An impostor is one who pretends to be someone else. The U.C.C. requires that drawers and makers be careful with whom they deal; and if they are duped into issuing an instrument to an impostor, the resulting forgery of a name substantially similar to the payee's name is effective to pass the right to enforce. [U.C.C. §3-404(a)]

Example: Lisa Liar tells Mr. Jones that she is Meredith Money, the town's wealthiest resident, and that she is collecting money for a new public library. Mr. Jones thereupon writes out a $50 check payable to "Meredith Money." Liar's subsequent forgery of that name to the instrument is effective to pass the right to enforce to her transferees. If Mr. Jones finds out the truth, he has no complaint to his bank that the check was not "properly payable" due to the forgery of the payee's name.

1) Applies to Misrepresentation of Agency

The impostor rule also applies where the person to whom the instrument is issued merely misrepresents that she is an *agent* of the payee named on the instrument.

2) Identity of Actual Forger Irrelevant

Once the drawer or maker has issued an instrument to an impostor, the resulting "indorsement" of the payee is validated regardless of who actually forges it (*i.e.,* it need not be forged by the original impostor).

b. Issuance to Payee Not Intended to Have Interest in Instrument

If the drawer, maker, or other person whose intent determines to whom an instrument is payable does not intend the person identified to have any interest in the instrument, or the person identified in the instrument as the payee is fictitious:

(i) Any person in possession of the instrument is a holder; and

(ii) Any indorsement in a name substantially similar to the name of the payee stated in the instrument is effective as an indorsement of the named payee as to anyone who takes the instrument in good faith and for value.

[U.C.C. §3-404(b)]

Examples: 1) Every week, Lawyer Brown signs the checks for bills typed for her by her secretary, Mr. White. One week, White draws up five checks payable to actual creditors of Brown but to whom Brown currently owes no money. Brown signs the checks, whereupon White forges the creditors' indorsements and cashes them. The forgeries are effective.

2) Darren Stephens, the treasurer of Tate Advertising, draws 50 checks on the corporation payable to phony employees, forges the names of the payees thereto, and cashes the checks at the drawee bank. Tate Advertising has no recourse against its bank for the proceeds.

c. Requirement of Ordinary Care

A person paying or taking an instrument involving a fictitious payee must use ordinary care in paying or taking the instrument. If ordinary care is not exercised, the person bearing the risk of loss on the instrument may recover from the party that failed to exercise ordinary care to the extent that the failure contributed to the loss.

Example: In example 2), above, if the court determined that the drawee bank failed to exercise ordinary care when it allowed Darren to cash 50 checks in names other than his own, Tate Advertising can recover from the bank to the extent of the loss caused by the bank's failure to exercise ordinary care.

2. Fraudulent Indorsements by Employees

If an employer *entrusts* an employee (including independent contractors) with responsibility with respect to an instrument and the employee makes a fraudulent indorsement on the instrument, the indorsement is effective (although a person who takes the instrument and fails to exercise ordinary care may be held liable to the extent of loss caused by the failure). [U.C.C. §3-405]

Examples: 1) Bob works in the billing department of a law firm. His duties include receiving checks and posting them to the firm's accounts. If Bob steals a check made out to the firm, forges the firm's name, and transfers the check to an HDC, the firm will bear the risk of loss. However, if instead of Bob stealing a check, a night watchman steals a check while making his rounds, the firm would not bear the risk of loss under section 3-405 since presumably the watchman was not entrusted with the instrument (although the firm might have liability under section 3-406, below, for negligently contributing to a forged signature).

2) Assume Ted is the treasurer of Big Corp. He draws a check on the company's accounts to pay a supplier. Subsequently, he decides to steal the check. He takes the check, forges the supplier's signature, and transfers the check to an HDC. Under section 3-405, the employer and not the HDC will bear the risk of loss resulting from the forgery. Note that liability does not arise under section 3-404 (the fictitious payee rule), above, since Ted intended a current supplier to be paid when he drew the check.

3. Failure to Exercise Ordinary Care—Negligence Rule

A person whose failure to exercise ordinary care substantially contributes to an alteration or forged signature on an instrument is precluded from asserting the alteration or forgery against a person who in good faith paid the instrument or took it for value or for collection. [U.C.C. §3-406(a)]

a. What Constitutes "Negligence"?

Actions that would usually constitute negligence under the Code include: (i) leaving blanks or spaces on the instrument; (ii) mailing an instrument to a person having the same name as the payee; (iii) failing to follow internal procedures designed to avoid forgeries (*e.g.*, keeping a rubber signature stamp in the same unlocked drawer as blank checks).

b. Later Parties Not Completely Protected

A prior person's failure to exercise due care does not relieve later persons from exercising due care regarding the instrument. Thus, if the person asserting preclusion has failed to exercise ordinary care in taking the instrument himself, the loss is allocated between both parties according to the share of the loss that resulted from each party's failure. [U.C.C. §3-406(b)]

Example: Jane Joker signs her name on all her blank checks and throws them out of her car window. One of the checks is picked up by Easy Money, a convicted thief, who fills it out for $8,000 and presents it for payment to the drawee bank. The teller who pays the check knows both Joker and Money, and observed Money fill out the check. The loss will be allocated according to the fault of each party.

4. Bank Statement Rule

Once a month (typically), a bank will return canceled checks to its customers, along with a statement of account. Failure to examine this statement is a form of negligence that can preclude the defenses of forgery and alteration.

a. Customer's Duty to Examine Statement

After receiving a statement, the customer must promptly use reasonable care in examining it for two things: (i) an unauthorized signing of the customer's *own* name as a drawer; and (ii) any alteration (*e.g.*, a change in amount) on the item. [U.C.C. §4-406(c)]

b. Effect of Failure to Examine

If the customer fails to promptly report a forgery or alteration, she is precluded (estopped) from complaining to the bank that the item in question was not "properly payable." Moreover, where the statement has been available to the customer for a reasonable period (not more than 30 calendar days) and she does not complain about an unauthorized signature or alteration, the customer is *estopped* from demanding recredit on any other items forged or altered by the same wrongdoer and subsequently paid by the bank (until the customer gives notice). [U.C.C. §4-406(d)]

c. Result Where Bank Is Also Negligent

If the bank itself fails to exercise ordinary care in paying a check—as where a forgery is sloppy or an alteration is obvious—the loss is allocated between the bank and the customer according to the extent that each contributed to the loss. However, if the customer proves that the bank did not pay in good faith, the bank will bear the entire loss. [U.C.C. §4-406(e)]

d. One-Year Limit for Alteration or Forged Drawer's Signature

No matter which party was negligent, a customer is precluded from asserting an alteration or a forgery of his signature if he does not notify the bank of the alteration or the forgery within *one year* after the bank has made the instrument available to him. [U.C.C. §4-406(f)]

e. Three-Year Limit for Forged Indorsement

A customer is precluded from asserting a forged indorsement more than *three years* after the cause of action accrues. [U.C.C. §4-111]

5. Estoppel by Certification

A bank that certifies a check has the opportunity of checking identification and the bona fides of the transaction with the person seeking certification. If the bank certifies the check, it is therefore estopped as against subsequent parties from claiming that the named payee was not the original payee.

Example: Drawer makes out a check for $1,000 payable to John Doe. Thief steals the check, uses chemicals to change the designated payee to himself ("Harry Thief"), and has the check certified by the payor bank. If the check is later presented for payment by a subsequent holder in due course, the bank is estopped from raising the defense that the indorsement of the original payee is missing.

F. EFFECT OF ALTERATION AND INCOMPLETE INSTRUMENTS

An alteration is an unauthorized change in an instrument that purports to modify the obligation of any party in any respect. [U.C.C. §3-407(a)] The effect of an alteration depends on whether the alterer's intent was fraudulent or nonfraudulent.

1. **Nonfraudulent Alteration**

Nonfraudulent alterations do not discharge any party, and the instrument may be enforced according to its original terms.

Example: Antonin has made a promissory note payable to the order of Sandra in installments with a stated interest rate of 8%. Sandra mistakenly but in good faith believes the interest rate stated should be 10% according to the underlying agreement. Sandra speaks to an attorney who has represented Antonin and who advises Sandra to change the rate on the note to 10%, but the attorney does not in fact have authority from Antonin to make that change. Nevertheless Sandra in good faith makes a handwritten change on the note raising the rate to 10%. Because this is not an alteration made fraudulently, Antonin is not discharged and the note can be enforced according to its original 8% interest term.

2. **Fraudulent Alteration**

A fraudulent alteration has the effect of discharging every party obligated on the instrument unless the party assents to or is precluded from asserting the alteration. [U.C.C. §3-407(b)]

    a. **Limitation—HDCs**

However, a payor bank or drawee paying a fraudulently altered instrument or a person who takes it for value, in good faith, and without notice of the alteration *may enforce the instrument*:

      (i) According to its *original terms*; or

      (ii) In the case of an incomplete instrument altered by an *unauthorized completion*, according to its *terms as completed*.

[U.C.C. §3-407(c)]

Examples: 1) Dave draws a check to pay his monthly rent on his apartment and drops the check in the mail. Dave's landlord Larry is a little short on funds and decides to raise Dave's rent without telling Dave. Larry accomplishes this feat by changing the amount on Dave's check from $500 to $5,000. Larry cashes the check at a local currency exchange. Dave is discharged to the extent of the alteration, but if the currency exchange is an HDC, it will be able to enforce the check to the extent of its original terms ($500).

2) Alex agrees to buy 100 widgets from Becky at a price to be determined at the time of delivery based on the then current market price of widgets. As payment, Alex sends Becky a negotiable promissory note with a blank amount line. If Becky fills in an amount three times higher than the then current market price for widgets and the note is transferred to an HDC, the HDC will be able to enforce the instrument to the full extent of the altered terms, since this is an unauthorized completion case.

VIII. PAYMENT

A. **INTRODUCTION**

The issues for treatment here fall into three general categories of questions:

1. When can the maker or acceptor of a note or draft safely pay it without worrying about having to pay it again?

2. What can the maker or acceptor do if she pays the instrument by mistake—if she pays it and she later wants to get her money back?

3. What can an acceptor do if she finds out after acceptance that she should not have accepted the draft—under what circumstances can she get out of her acceptance obligations?

B. **WHEN CAN MAKER SAFELY PAY AND AVOID FURTHER LIABILITY?**

1. **Determine If Party Seeking Payment Is a Holder**

The maker must first determine that the party seeking payment is a holder. If he is a holder, the maker may safely pay him, even if she knows that a third party has a claim to the instrument. It is up to the third party to protect his own interests; the primary obligor has no obligation to do that for him. If she pays a holder, the primary obligor is safe; if she pays someone not a holder, she will have to pay the true holder when he comes along.

2. **Actions of Third Party to Protect Claim**
   What can the third party do to protect his claim to the instrument in such a context? One of two things:

   a. *Offer to indemnify* the maker or acceptor in an amount deemed sufficient by the maker or acceptor while the other two parties fight it out; or

   b. *Seek an injunction* in an action in which the maker or acceptor, the holder, and the third party are parties.

3. **Do Not Pay Holder Where There Has Been a Theft**
   The maker or acceptor may *not* safely pay the holder of an instrument where she knows that the holder acquired the instrument by theft or that he holds through one who acquired it by theft. If the holder is an HDC (there was a theft further up the chain of title), then the maker may pay him (the HDC would cut off the defense of theft in a lawsuit anyway; in fact, it should be noted in general the extent to which the rules set forth here parallel the rules as to the defenses that can be raised against a holder).

C. FINALITY OF PAYMENT—RECOVERY FOR INSTRUMENTS MISTAKENLY PAID OR ACCEPTED

1. **General Rule—Payment Is Final**
   The general rule is that payment of a negotiable instrument to an HDC or one who in good faith changed her position in reliance on the payment is final—*i.e.*, the payor cannot recover payment back from the party paid. There are two exceptions to the general rule: The payor can recover from the party paid if (i) that party neither took for value nor in good faith, nor detrimentally relied on the payment or (ii) the party paid breached a transfer warranty (*see* VII.B.2.b., *supra*) or a presentment warranty (*see* below). [U.C.C. §3-418]

2. **Presentment Warranties**
   Section 3-418 specifically provides that it does not affect a payor's rights pursuant to the presentment warranties. There are two sets of presentment warranties: those made to a drawee on an unaccepted draft and those made to a payor of any other instrument. [U.C.C. §3-417]

   a. **Presentment Warranties on Unaccepted Draft**
      A drawee can recover for breach of the presentment warranties, even from an HDC or one who detrimentally relied on payment. On unaccepted drafts, the person obtaining payment and previous transferors of the draft make the following warranties.

      1) **Entitled to Enforce**
         The first warranty is that the warrantor is a person entitled to enforce the draft or is authorized to act on behalf of one who is entitled to enforce. In essence, this is a warranty of good title—that there are no unauthorized or missing indorsements.

         a) **Forged Drawer Signature—Title Good**
            A forgery of the drawer's name does *not* destroy good title. The forgery operates as the signature of the forger, so that the presenter has good title to the *forger's instrument*. The fact that the forger is not the drawer whom the drawee *meant* to deal with is the drawee's own responsibility.

            Example: Forger steals Drawer's checkbook and writes a check payable to himself, signing Drawer's name. Forger then indorses the check as payee and deposits it with Forger's State Bank ("FSB"), which in turn receives payment from the drawee, Antitrust National Bank ("ANB"). When FSB presented the check for payment, it warranted that it was a person entitled to enforce the check, and this warranty has not been breached. FSB is the holder of a check drawn by Forger, payable to the order of *Forger* and properly indorsed by him as payee. ANB arguably should have been more careful in checking the drawer's name, but that is a *drawee's problem.* If ANB does not have the time for careful examination of the drawee's name, it can obtain forgery loss insurance.

b) Forged Indorser Signature—Title Not Good
The forged signature of a necessary indorser (payee or special indorsee) *destroys* good title.

Example: Suppose that Drawer writes a check payable to the order of May Doe. The check is stolen and May Doe's name is forged on the back by Forger, who cashes it at Forger's State Bank ("FSB"). FSB then presents the check to the drawee, Antitrust National Bank ("ANB"). Here, ANB may recover money paid on the check because both Forger and FSB have breached the warranty that they are persons entitled to enforce the instrument. Doe was a holder, and for Forger to become a holder requires Doe's indorsement. Since the forgery is not effective as Doe's indorsement, neither Forger nor FSB can be a holder. ANB may recover from FSB or Forger on the presentment warranty of good title; and FSB may use any of a number of *transfer warranties* to recover from Forger.

2) Instrument Not Altered
The second warranty is that the instrument is not altered.

3) No Knowledge that Drawer's Signature Is Unauthorized
The third warranty is that the warrantor has no knowledge that the drawer's signature is unauthorized.

b. Presentment Warranties on Other Instruments
If any instrument other than an unaccepted draft is presented to any party obligated to pay (*e.g.*, a note is presented to its maker; a dishonored draft is presented to its drawer) and the instrument is paid, the party receiving payment and prior transferors warrant that they were parties entitled to enforce the instrument or were representatives of one so entitled. The other transfer warranties (no alteration or unauthorized signature) are inapplicable since the obligated party—*i.e.*, the drawer, maker, or acceptor—should know whether its signature has been forged or whether the instrument has been altered.

c. Who Makes the Warranties?
The presentment warranties are made by: (i) any person who obtains payment or acceptance and (ii) any prior transferor. Note that these warranties on presentment are similar but *not* identical to the transfer warranties made by an indorser. (*See* VII.B.2.b., *supra.*)

d. To Whom Are They Made?
The presentment warranties are made to any person who in good faith pays or accepts.

Example: Drawer writes a check to the order of Payee, who loses the check. Payee's name is forged thereto by Forger, who transfers the check to Gullible Grocery ("GG"). GG cashes the check at Grocer's State Bank ("GSB"), which sends it to the Federal Reserve Bank ("FRB"). FRB in turn presents the check to the payor bank, Antitrust National Bank ("ANB"), and receives payment. At the moment FRB made presentment, *all* prior transferors made the presentment warranties. Thus when ANB learns that Payee's name was forged, it must repay the money to Drawer and may then sue FRB, GSB, GG, or Forger for breach of the presentment warranty of entitlement to enforce. If it sues and recovers from GSB, GSB may in turn recover from GG for breach of the *transfer* warranty of entitlement to enforce (etc.). The loss proceeds up the chain until it rests with Forger (or, if he is unavailable or insolvent, with the first person to trust him).

IX. DISCHARGE

A. IN GENERAL

1. Statutory Provisions on Methods of Discharge
The extent of the discharge of any party from liability on an instrument is governed by the sections on:

a.   Payment [U.C.C. §3-602];

b.   Tender of payment [U.C.C. §3-603];

c.   Cancellation or renunciation [U.C.C. §3-604];

d.   Impairment of right of recourse or of collateral [U.C.C. §3-605];

e.   Reacquisition of instrument by a prior party [U.C.C. §3-207];

f.   Fraudulent alteration [U.C.C. §3-407];

g.   Certification of a check [U.C.C. §3-409];

h.   Acceptance varying a draft [U.C.C. §3-410]; or

i.   Unexcused delay in presentment or notice of dishonor [U.C.C. §3-503].

2.   **Other Important Factors**

a.   **Instrument Itself Never Discharged**
Note that instead of speaking of the instrument being discharged, the Code speaks of the discharge of the parties from their obligation. This is because discharge of a party is a personal defense that is cut off when a subsequent HDC takes the instrument without notice of the defense. No discharge of any party is effective against a subsequent HDC *unless he has notice* thereof when he takes the instrument. [U.C.C. §3-601(b)]
Example: Suppose Peter Payee indorsed his paycheck and then lost it. He tells his employer that he lost his paycheck, but that he had not indorsed it before losing it, so the employer pays Payee in order to discharge its obligation to him. Subsequently, Rick Ruthless finds the indorsed check and cashes it at a nearby currency exchange, making the currency exchange an HDC. The currency exchange presents the check for payment. The check has not been discharged; Payee's employer will be obligated to pay out on the check.

b.   **Effect of Instrument on Obligation for Which It Was Taken**

1)   **Certified, Cashier's, or Teller's Check Generally Discharges Obligation**
Unless otherwise agreed, if a certified, cashier's, or teller's check is given in satisfaction of an obligation, the *obligation is discharged* to the same extent that it would be discharged if cash were given. However, this discharge does not affect any indorser liability that the obligor might have on the instrument. [U.C.C. §3-310(a)]

2)   **Other Instruments Generally Suspend Obligation**
If any negotiable instrument other than the ones listed in 1), above, is given to satisfy an obligation, unless otherwise agreed the *obligation is suspended* to the same extent as if cash were given. [U.C.C. §3-310(b)]

a)   **Duration of Suspension**
Suspension of the obligation continues until the instrument is paid (which results in discharge) or is dishonored. An obligation for which a check was given may also be discharged by subsequent certification.

b)   **Rights On Dishonor**

(1)   **Instrument in Hands of Obligee**
If the instrument is dishonored and the obligee of the obligation for which the instrument was taken is the person entitled to enforce the instrument, he may enforce either the instrument or the obligation.
Example: Steve sells a car to Bob, and Bob pays with a personal check naming Steve as payee. Bob's obligation to pay for the car is suspended. Steve takes the check to the drawee bank, and the bank refuses to pay because Bob does not have sufficient funds on deposit. Upon the bank's dishonoring the check, Bob's obligation to pay

for the car revives, and Steve can hold Bob liable on either the obligation or the check.

(2) Instrument in Hands of Third Party

If the instrument is dishonored but the person entitled to enforce the instrument is not the obligee of the obligation for which the instrument was given, the obligee may not enforce the obligation.

Example: In the example above, suppose Steve negotiated Bob's check to Dealer as a down payment on Steve's new car, and the drawee bank refused to pay Dealer. Dealer cannot hold Bob liable on the original sale contract; his remedies are limited to those available on the instrument.

3) Lost, Stolen, or Destroyed Instruments

If the obligee is a person entitled to enforce the instrument but is no longer in possession of the instrument because it was lost, stolen, or destroyed, the obligation remains suspended to the extent of the instrument, and the obligee's rights are limited to enforcement of the instrument (*see* VI.C.3., *supra*).

Example: Suppose in the example in (1), above, that Steve lost the check after Bob issued it to Steve. Steve may not enforce the original contract; his remedy is limited to enforcement of the instrument.

4) Tenders "in Full Satisfaction"—Accord and Satisfaction

If a claim is unliquidated or subject to dispute, the claim can be discharged in full if the person against whom the claim is asserted tenders an instrument that conspicuously states that it is tendered in full satisfaction of the claim (*e.g.*, the memo line says "Payment in Full"). However, if the claimant is an organization, it can, by notice sent before the instrument is tendered, require that such instruments be tendered to a designated person, office, or place to be effective. If the claimant sends no such notice or is not an organization, the discharge will not be effective if the claimant returns the payment within 90 days. [U.C.C. §3-311]

B. DISCHARGE BY PAYMENT

1. Generally Party Discharged Even If She Has Knowledge of Claim

Under the Code, the liability of any party is discharged to the extent of her payment or satisfaction to a person entitled to enforce the instrument even if payment is made with knowledge of a claim of another person to the instrument, *unless* prior to payment the person making the claim either (i) *supplies indemnity* deemed adequate by the party seeking the discharge, *i.e.,* the one tendering payment, or (ii) *enjoins* payment or satisfaction by order of a court of competent jurisdiction in an action in which the adverse claimant and the holder are parties. Neither is there a discharge if the person making payment knows that the instrument is stolen and pays a person who she knows is in wrongful possession of the instrument. [U.C.C. §3-602]

a. Payment Prior to Maturity

On the holder's request, the Code permits payment prior to maturity and dispenses with the requirements that the payment be made in good faith and without notice that the title of the holder is defective.

Example: If Hoenes, the holder of a negotiable promissory note, presents it to Morgan, the maker, before maturity and requests payment, Morgan is at liberty to pay Hoenes even if she knows that Hoenes improperly acquired the instrument from the payee, as long as the payee has not enjoined payment or posted indemnity that Morgan feels is sufficient to cover any possible loss that she may incur from refusal to pay.

C. DISCHARGE BY TENDER OF PAYMENT

If payment of an obligation on an instrument is tendered to a person entitled to enforce the instrument, the effect of the tender is governed by principles of law applicable to tender of payment under a simple contract. [U.C.C. §3-603(a)]

1. Discharges Duty to Pay Interest After Due Date

A tender of the amount due on an instrument discharges any duty to pay interest after the due date. [U.C.C. §3-603(c)]

2. **Who Is Discharged?**
Any person who has a right of recourse against the party making tender is discharged to the extent of the amount tendered, whether the person is a prior party or a subsequent one who has been accommodated. [U.C.C. §3-603(b)]

Example: Mary is the maker of a promissory note; Phil is the payee; Alex, Becky, and Chloe have all in turn indorsed the note. It is now due and in the hands of Hanna. Phil tenders payment but Hanna refuses to accept it. Because Alex, Becky, and Chloe are indorsers and have recourse against Phil, they are discharged. This operates as a complete discharge—not just a discharge as to liability for interest, costs, and attorneys' fees.

D. DISCHARGE BY CANCELLATION OR RENUNCIATION

The person entitled to enforce an instrument may, *even without consideration*, discharge a party: (i) by an *intentional* voluntary act, such as surrender of the instrument to the party, destroying the instrument, or striking out a party's signature; or (ii) by agreeing in a signed writing not to sue or by otherwise renouncing rights against the party. [U.C.C. §3-604(a)] Recall, however, that in connection with HDCs, no discharge of any party is effective against a subsequent HDC unless the HDC has notice thereof when she takes the instrument. [U.C.C. §3-601]

Example: Mary was maker; Phil was payee and indorser of a negotiable promissory note held by Hanna, an HDC. Prior to maturity and before the negotiation to Hanna, Phil agreed in a separate writing to release Mary in consideration of her promise to render certain services that were performed by her. Hanna, who purchased the note without knowledge of the separate agreement, now sues Mary, who refused to pay the note at maturity. Mary's defense is discharge as a result of renunciation. The defense is not good against Hanna. Even though the renunciation is in writing as prescribed by the Code, it is not effective against a subsequent HDC who takes without knowledge of its existence.

E. DISCHARGE BY IMPAIRMENT OF RECOURSE OR COLLATERAL—SURETYSHIP DEFENSES

1. **Discharge of an Obligated Party**
A discharge of an obligated party *does not discharge* the obligation of an indorser or accommodation party who has a right of recourse against the obligated party. [U.C.C. §3-605(b)]

2. **Extension of Due Date or Other Material Modification**
An *extension of the time* an instrument is due or other material modification of an obligation on an instrument *discharges* an indorser or accommodation party having a right of recourse against the party whose obligation was modified to the extent of the loss caused by the modification. In the case of an extension, the party whose right of recourse was affected has the burden of proving the loss. In the case of *other modifications*, the loss is *presumed* and is deemed to be the value of the recourse unless the person enforcing the instrument proves that the loss was less. [U.C.C. §3-605(c), (d)]

3. **Impairment of Collateral**
Impairment of collateral securing a party's obligation on an instrument discharges an indorser or accommodation party having a right of recourse against the obligor to the extent of the impairment. The burden of proving the extent of the impairment is on the party claiming discharge. [U.C.C. §3-605(e)]

   a. **What Constitutes Impairment?**
   The value of an interest in collateral is impaired if (i) there is a failure to perfect a security interest or otherwise file; (ii) the collateral is released without obtaining substitute collateral; (iii) there is a failure to do any act required by agreement or law to preserve the value of collateral; or (iv) there is a failure to dispose of the collateral as the law requires. [U.C.C. §3-605(g)]

4. **Limitations on Discharge**

   a. **Accommodation Parties**
   An accommodation party is not discharged as provided above unless the person entitled to enforce the instrument knows of the accommodation. [U.C.C. §3-605(h)]

   b. **Consent**
   A party will not be discharged if he consented to the event or the conduct that is the

basis of the ground for discharge or he has waived his defenses based on suretyship or impairment of collateral.

5. Illustration

Sonny wants to buy a hot dog cart for $5,000. He does not have the money for the cart and so he goes to Friendly Bank and asks for a loan. Since Sonny has little money, Friendly tells Sonny that it will give him a loan only if he executes a negotiable installment promissory note, gives Friendly a security interest in the cart, and gets his father ("Father") to sign the note as an accommodation party. Sonny complies. Since Sonny's loan is for such a small amount, Friendly never files its Article 9 financing statement and the security interest never becomes perfected. Sonny's business is unsuccessful and he falls behind in payments to Friendly and to Supplier, Sonny's hot dog supplier. Friendly allows Sonny to take two extra months in making one of his payments in hope that Sonny's business will pick up. In the meantime, Supplier obtains a judgment lien against Sonny, attaches Sonny's cart, and sells it at a judicial sale for $2,000. Sonny then offers Friendly $500 in return for a release of his liability. Friendly takes the $500 and gives Sonny a written release. Friendly now seeks payment from Father. How do these facts affect Father's liability?

a. Father was not discharged merely because of the release given to Sonny, since the release is not effective to discharge Sonny's obligation to Father.

b. If Father wants a discharge due to the extension of time for payment, he will have to prove that the extension caused him damage. If he proves resulting damage, he will be discharged to the extent of the damage.

c. Father will be discharged to the extent of the value of the hot dog cart due to the bank's failure to file and perfect its security agreement (which failure allowed Supplier to get an interest superior to Friendly's interest in the cart).

F. DISCHARGE BY REACQUISITION

A reacquisition occurs if an instrument is transferred to a former holder. Upon reacquisition, the reacquirer may cancel indorsements that were made between the time she formerly held the instrument and the present. This cancellation has the effect of discharging the indorsers whose signatures were canceled, and the discharge is effective against *any subsequent holder*, including an HDC. [U.C.C. §3-207] Of course, reacquisition has the automatic effect of canceling intervening indorsers' liability to the reacquirer since the intervening indorsers would have an action back against the reacquirer based on her prior indorsement.

Example: Alex, the payee of a promissory note, negotiates the note to Becky by special indorsement as payment for some widgets. Alex immediately discovers that the widgets are defective and returns the widgets to Becky. Becky has already indorsed the note, but offers to return it to Alex if he promises to strike Becky's indorsement. Alex agrees and does in fact strike Becky's indorsement. He then negotiates the note to Chloe, another widget supplier. Becky has no liability on the note because her indorsement was canceled. If Alex had not canceled Becky's indorsement, she would owe indorser liability to Chloe, but not to Alex.

G. DISCHARGE BY ANY ACT THAT WILL DISCHARGE A SIMPLE CONTRACT

A party is discharged from his liability to another party on an instrument by any act of or agreement with that party that would discharge an obligation to pay money under a simple contract. [U.C.C. §3-601(a)]

H. DISCHARGE BY DELAY IN PRESENTMENT OF A CHECK

1. Indorsers

If a check is not presented for payment or given to a depositary bank within *30 days* after the date of the indorsement, the indorser is discharged. [U.C.C. §3-415(e)]

2. Drawers

If a check is not presented for payment or given to a depositary bank for collection within *30 days* after its date and because of the delay the drawer is deprived of funds with which to pay the obligation (*e.g.*, the bank has gone bankrupt in the interim), the drawer is discharged to the extent of the loss caused by the delay if he assigns his drawer's rights against the drawee to the party entitled to enforce the check. [U.C.C. §3-414(f)]

I. DISCHARGE BY FAILURE TO GIVE NOTICE OF DISHONOR

If a notice of dishonor is required (*see* VII.B.2.a.3), *supra*) and notice is not given, the indorser is discharged from his indorsement obligation. [U.C.C. §3-415(c)] Recall that, ordinarily, a drawer or maker is not entitled to notice.

J. DISCHARGE BY ACCEPTANCE OF A DRAFT BY A BANK

1. **Indorsers**
   If a draft is accepted by a bank after an indorsement is made, the indorser is discharged. [U.C.C. §3-415(d)]

2. **Drawers**
   If a draft is accepted by a bank, the drawer is discharged regardless of when or by whom acceptance is obtained. [U.C.C. §3-414(c)]

K. DISCHARGE BY ALTERATION

A fraudulent alteration discharges every party obligated on the instrument unless the party assents to or is precluded from asserting the alteration. However, HDCs may enforce the instrument according to its original terms or, if the instrument was altered only by an unauthorized completion, according to its terms as completed. [U.C.C. §3-407; *and see* VII.F., *supra*]

X. STATUS OF BANK IN COLLECTION PROCESS

(For definitions applicable to the bank collection process, *see* U.C.C. section 4-105.)

A. THE PROBLEM

Article 4 of the U.C.C. covers bank deposits and collections. Much of that article is beyond the scope of the subject of negotiable instruments. Some of it has already been referred to at various points where it has become relevant. There is one particular feature of bank collections that should be noted. It relates to the debate that occurred under the Negotiable Instruments Law as to the status of a bank in the collecting process. The situation is this: D presents to Bank A a check drawn on Bank B by C. What is the status of Bank A with relation to the check while it is in the collection process? Bank A would like to be an agent of D, so that if the check is lost while being forwarded to Bank B, D will bear the loss and not itself. On the other hand, suppose Bank A gave D cash for the check, and now D has absconded. Now Bank A would like to be a purchaser and if it satisfies all of the other requirements, an HDC. As such, of course, it could cut off most defenses that C might assert in an attempt to recover on his drawer's contract. How does the Code handle this situation?

B. BANK IS AGENT FOR COLLECTION

Unless it is made clear to the contrary, the bank is an agent for collection. As such, it owes its customers the duty of "ordinary care" and is liable only for its negligence. [U.C.C. §4-202] The risk of loss is thus on the depositor. [U.C.C. §4-201] Such depositor is considered to be a customer as is anyone in the collection process dealing with a bank, including another bank.

C. BANK MAY BECOME AN HDC

However, if the bank *advances money* for the item, it acquires a *security interest* in the instrument and to the extent of that security interest can become an HDC. [U.C.C. §4-211] In other words, the security interest satisfies the "value" requirement and if the bank can satisfy the other HDC requirements, it can become an HDC to the extent that it has advanced cash on the item. The bank is thus both an agent when it wants to be and a purchaser when it needs to be.

D. BANK'S RIGHT OF CHARGE BACK

When a customer deposits a check in her bank account, her bank is not required to allow her to draw funds against the check until the check has had sufficient time to be presented to the drawer's bank for payment or dishonor. The deposit results in a *"provisional settlement"*—the depositor's account is credited, but the credit may be reversed until *"final settlement"* occurs. [U.C.C. §4-214] Final settlement occurs when the drawer's bank makes "final payment" (*i.e.,* when the drawee actually pays the check or fails to dishonor it by its midnight deadline—midnight of the banking day following the banking day of receipt). [U.C.C. §4-215]

Note: Federal law provides specific time limits regarding the availability of funds, which are beyond the scope of both this outline and the bar examination.

1. **Prior Use of Credit Irrelevant**
   The fact that the depositary bank allowed the depositor to draw against a deposited check

which is later dishonored by the drawee does not affect the depositary bank's right to reverse the provisional settlement; the customer must repay the money in the event of an overdraft. [U.C.C. §4-214]

XI. DOCUMENTS OF TITLE AND INVESTMENT SECURITIES

A. WAREHOUSE RECEIPTS AND BILLS OF LADING

Warehouse receipts and bills of lading are governed by Article 7 of the Code on "Documents of Title." A warehouse receipt is a document of title issued by a warehouse entitling a named person, or his order, or the bearer to delivery of stored goods. Similarly, a bill of lading is a document of title issued by a carrier for shipped goods. Documents of title may be either *negotiable or nonnegotiable*. The basic rules for determining what documents are negotiable and who is an HDC are the same as in commercial paper generally; *i.e.*, the document must be payable to bearer or to order on demand or at a time certain. The one important difference is, of course, that a negotiable document of title is not payable in "money" but in the delivery of identified goods. Article 7 labels the "holder in due course" of a document of title as a "holder to whom a negotiable document of title has been *duly negotiated*." [U.C.C. §7-502]

1. Form and Terms of Warehouse Receipt

a. No Particular Form
A warehouse receipt need not be in any particular form. [U.C.C. §7-202(1)]

b. Certain Terms Required
Unless a warehouse receipt embodies within its written or printed terms each of the following, the warehouseman is liable for damages caused by the omission to a person injured thereby [U.C.C. §7-202]:

1) **Location**
   The location of the warehouse where the goods are stored;

2) **Date**
   The date of issue of the receipt;

3) **Number**
   The consecutive number of the receipt;

4) **Person to Whom Delivery Due**
   A statement whether the goods received will be delivered to the bearer, to a specified person, or to a specified person or his order;

5) **Charges**
   The rate of storage and handling charges, except that where goods are stored under a field warehousing arrangement a statement of that fact is sufficient on a nonnegotiable receipt;

6) **Description**
   A description of the goods or the packages containing them;

7) **Signature**
   The signature of the warehouseman, which may be made by his authorized agent;

8) **Warehouseman's Ownership, If Any**
   If the receipt is issued for goods of which the warehouseman is the owner, either jointly, solely, or in common with others, the fact of such ownership; and

9) **Lien or Security Interest**
   A statement of the amount of advances made and of liabilities incurred for which the warehouseman claims a lien or security interest. If the precise amount of such advances made or of such liabilities incurred is, at the time of the issue of the receipt, unknown to the warehouseman or to his agent who issues it, a statement of the fact that advances have been made or liabilities incurred and the purpose thereof is sufficient.

c. **Other Terms Permitted**
A warehouseman may insert in his receipt other terms that do not impair his obligation of delivery or his duty of care. Any provision contrary to these duties is ineffective. [U.C.C. §7-202]

2. **Form and Terms of Bill of Lading**
A bill of lading is similar to a warehouse receipt, except that it must also specify *point of shipment and destination.* The carrier and the shipper have the following obligations with respect to the description of the goods at the time of shipment [U.C.C. §7-301]:

a. **Misdating, Nonreceipt, or Misdescription**
A consignee of a nonnegotiable bill who has given value in good faith or a holder to whom a negotiable bill has been duly negotiated relying in either case upon the description therein of the goods, or upon the date therein shown, may recover from the issuer damages caused by the misdating of the bill or the nonreceipt or misdescription of the goods. An exception exists to the extent that the document indicates that the issuer does not know whether any part or all of the goods in fact were received or conform to the description, as where the description is in terms of marks or labels of kind, quantity, or condition or the receipt or description is qualified by "contents or condition of contents of package unknown," "said to contain," "shipper's weight, load, and count," or the like, if such indication is true.

b. **Duty to Ascertain Kind and Quantity**
When goods are loaded by an issuer who is a common carrier, the issuer must count the packages of goods if package freight and ascertain the kind and quantity if bulk freight. In such cases "shipper's weight, load, and count" or other words indicating that the description was made by the shipper are ineffective except as to freight concealed by packages.

c. **Shipper's Guarantee**
The shipper is deemed to have guaranteed to the issuer the accuracy at the time of shipment of the description, marks, labels, number, kind, quantity, condition, and weight as furnished by him; and the shipper shall indemnify the issuer against damage caused by inaccuracies in such particulars.

3. **Liability Limited**
A bailee who in good faith, including observance of reasonable commercial standards, has received goods and delivered or otherwise disposed of them according to the terms of the document of title, or pursuant to Article 7, is not liable therefor. This rule applies even if the person from whom he received the goods had no authority to procure the document or to dispose of the goods, and even if the person to whom he delivered the goods had no authority to receive them.

B. **FINANCIAL ASSETS**
Article 8 of the U.C.C. regulates some aspects of the purchase and sale of financial assets. "Financial assets" is a broad term that includes securities (*e.g.*, stocks and bonds) and other interests in persons or enterprises commonly dealt in as investment mediums (*e.g.,* brokerage accounts, mutual fund interests, etc.). [U.C.C. §8-102] Article 8 originally had rules concerning only certificated securities (*i.e.*, stocks or bonds represented by pieces of paper), but in the late 1970s the Article was amended to govern aspects of uncertificated securities as well (*i.e.*, securities not represented by a certificate but the ownership of which is recorded in the issuer's books).

1. **Direct vs. Indirect Holding Systems**
Certificated and uncertificated securities are part of the system of direct holdings (where the owner holds ownership directly), but today, most investment devices are not held this way; rather, most financial assets are held indirectly. For example: Purchaser instructs Broker, a member of a national brokerage house, to purchase 100 shares of MegaCorp stock and to hold the stock in "street name" (the name of the brokerage house) to facilitate a quicker sale when the time comes. On that same day, the brokerage house has another customer who wants to sell 100 shares of MegaCorp stock held in street name. The brokerage house merely adjusts its records to reflect who is entitled to the shares. If the brokerage house had to purchase shares for Purchaser from an outside source, a similar process often is used. Many brokers and banks belong to a trust company (the Depository Trust Company or "DTC") that holds shares in its own name and merely adjusts its account records to record what bank or broker is entitled to the shares DTC holds as trustee. Thus, corporations are not constantly issuing new share certificates each time a share is traded; rather, entries are

made in intermediaries' books to reflect who is entitled to the securities the intermediary holds or has a right to hold.

2. Direct Holding System Rules Analogous to Article 3 Rules

The Article 8 system of rules to protect purchasers of security investments is similar to the system Article 3 develops to protect holders in due course of negotiable instruments.

a. Protected Purchaser

The purchaser who is protected under Article 8's rules is not called an HDC, but rather a "protected purchaser." Article 8 defines a protected purchaser as a purchaser of a certificated or uncertificated security who: (i) gives value, (ii) does not have notice of any adverse claim to the security, and (iii) obtains control of the security. A protected purchaser acquires whatever rights the transferor had and takes the security free of any adverse claim. [U.C.C. §8-303]

b. Control

Control is analogous to the Article 3 concept of negotiation.

1) Certificated Securities

As under Article 3, a purchaser has control of a certificated *bearer* security as soon as the security is delivered to the purchaser. [U.C.C. §8-106(a)] A person has control of a certificated security in *registered form* (*i.e.*, a security certificate that specifies the person entitled to the security, similar to an instrument "payable to order" under Article 3) if the instrument is delivered to the purchaser and is either indorsed to the purchaser in blank or registered by the issuer in the name of the purchaser. [U.C.C. §8-106(b)]

2) Uncertificated Securities

A purchaser has control of an uncertificated security if it is delivered to the purchaser or the securities intermediary (*i.e.,* a person who maintains securities accounts for others in the regular course of business) has agreed that it will comply with instructions originated by the purchaser without further consent from the registered owner. [U.C.C. §8-106(c)]

3. Indirect Holding System Rules

Many of the rules in Article 8 regard the rights and duties of the securities intermediary and are very loosely analogous to the rules governing the relationship between a drawer and a drawee bank. The intermediary has a duty to obey the orders of the person entitled to the security (the beneficial owner, known as the "entitlement holder") [U.C.C. §8-507], the duty to maintain securities sufficient to cover entitlement holders' ownership interests [U.C.C. §8-504], and other duties, but these rules are outside the scope of the bar exam. If anything is tested in this area, it will most likely be the rules—similar to the HDC rules of Article 3— protecting the purchaser of a security entitlement.

a. Security Entitlement

A security entitlement is the ownership interest of an "entitlement holder" in a financial asset. An entitlement holder is the person identified in the records of a securities intermediary as the person having rights in securities of the intermediary. [U.C.C. §§8-102(a)(7), 8-503]

b. Rights of Purchaser of Securities Entitlement from Entitlement Holder

A person who purchases a security entitlement from an entitlement holder takes free of any adverse claim to the financial asset or security entitlement if the purchaser gives value, does not have notice of the adverse claim, and obtains control. [U.C.C. §8-510]

c. Control

Generally, a purchaser has control of a security entitlement if the purchaser becomes the entitlement holder or the securities intermediary has agreed that it will obey the purchaser's orders without further consent from the entitlement holder. [U.C.C. §8-106(d)]

4. Statute of Frauds Inapplicable

A contract or modification of a contract for the purchase or sale of a financial asset is not within the Statute of Frauds; no writing is necessary, even if the contract or modification by its terms cannot be performed within one year. [U.C.C. §8-113]

U.C.C. ARTICLE 4A—FUNDS TRANSFERS

I. INTRODUCTION

A. IN GENERAL

To speed up banking processes such as check collection, many banks use electronic funds transfers (*e.g.*, wire transfers). It is useful to think of an electronic funds transfer as commercial paper encoded into electronic signals: credit and debit instructions wired between banks. U.C.C. Article 4A governs electronic funds transfers **between banks** (the federal Electronic Funds Transfers Act governs consumer electronic funds transfers, such as ATM machine transactions). An exam question concerning Article 4A is unlikely, but you should be familiar with the following basic material just in case it does appear.

B. TERMINOLOGY

In a typical funds transfer, someone (the "sender") asks a bank (the "originator") to send an instruction (a "payment order") to another bank (the "receiving bank"), instructing the receiving bank to pay money to someone else (the "beneficiary"). Payment orders can pass through a number of banks before the money reaches the beneficiary. The last bank is the "beneficiary's bank" and any bank between the originator and the beneficiary's bank (usually a federal reserve bank) is called an "intermediary" bank. Note that the originator is also a sender.

II. ACCEPTANCE AND REJECTION

A. ACCEPTANCE

The U.C.C. never requires a bank to accept a payment order; banks are free to choose whether or not to pay out on another bank's order. However, a bank may contractually agree with other banks to honor orders. In any case, once a bank "accepts" a payment order, it must pay the funds to the recipient of the order. What constitutes acceptance depends on whether a bank is the beneficiary's bank.

1. Acceptance by Bank Other than Beneficiary's Bank

A receiving bank other than the beneficiary's bank accepts a payment order when it *executes the order*, *i.e.*, when it passes on the payment order it received to the next receiving bank.

2. Acceptance by Beneficiary's Bank

A beneficiary's bank accepts by doing any of the following:

(i) Paying the beneficiary in cash;

(ii) Notifying the beneficiary that the money is available;

(iii) Receiving full payment of the funds from the sender of the payment order; or

(iv) Failing to object before or within an hour after the opening of its funds-transfer business day (*i.e.*, the part of the day that the bank is open to receive and process funds transfers).

Note: If the payment order states a payment date (it is not required to), acceptance cannot occur before the payment date, and the beneficiary's bank may reject within one hour after the opening of the *sender's* business day following the payment date.

B. REJECTION

A receiving bank can reject a payment order by giving the sender notice (oral, electronic, or written), within one hour after the opening of the receiving bank's funds-transfer business day, that the receiving bank will not accept. No particular words are necessary.

C. EFFECT OF ACCEPTANCE

Once the beneficiary's bank accepts a payment order, it must pay the funds to the beneficiary even if it does not receive them from the sender. The beneficiary's bank must make the funds available to the beneficiary on the next banking day and must dispatch notice of the funds' availability to the beneficiary before midnight of its next funds-transfer business day (*see* A.2.(iv), above) following the payment date. Notice may be mailed. If the beneficiary's bank refuses to pay, it is liable for all damages caused by its refusal unless the bank can show that it had reasonable doubt concerning the right of the beneficiary to the payment (*e.g.*, that the beneficiary is not really the intended beneficiary).

D. SENDER'S DUTY TO PAY

Once the receiving bank accepts a payment order, the sender has a duty to pay the amount involved. A sender can cancel or amend a payment order only if it has not yet been accepted. If a sender or receiving bank becomes insolvent after acceptance, the payment order is still effective, and whoever chose the sender or receiving bank will bear the loss.

III. LIABILITY FOR PAYMENT

A. MISDESCRIPTION OF BENEFICIARY

A funds transfer can describe the beneficiary both by name and by an account number. If a funds transfer refers to a nonexistent or unidentifiable person or account, no one acquires the rights of a beneficiary and a technical acceptance cannot occur. Note that banks are permitted to ignore the beneficiary's name and rely solely on the account number. If the beneficiary's account number is wrong, the beneficiary's bank is not liable if it put the money into the identified account, and generally the person who made the mistake will bear the loss. (Of course, if the beneficiary's bank becomes aware of the mistake before payment, it must investigate to find the right beneficiary or the bank will bear the loss.)

B. ERRONEOUS PAYMENT ORDERS

If an error is made during the transmission of a payment order (*e.g.*, the order is sent twice), the entity that made the mistake will bear the loss.

C. LIABILITY FOR CRIMINAL WIRE FRAUD

If a bank fails to follow procedures to thwart wire transfer fraud, the bank will be liable for resulting losses (*e.g.*, the bank and the customer agree that payment orders from the customer will be considered valid only if they include a certain "password," and the bank sends a payment order despite lack of the password). If the bank and its customer have developed security procedures and despite adherence to those procedures fraud occurs, the customer is liable if the criminal gained access through the customer's system, and the bank is liable if the criminal gained access through the bank.

IV. PAYMENT TO WRONG BENEFICIARY

A. WHEN IMPROPER PAYMENT ARISES

A payment may be made to an improper party as a result of either the improper execution of the payment order or a mistake in the terms of the payment order. Liability for the error must be borne by the party responsible for the error.

B. SENDER'S RECOVERY

A sender may recover all damages, expenses, and those consequential damages of which the mistaken party had notice, as well as the full amount of the transfer where the sender was not at fault for the improper payment.

C. WRONG ACCOUNT NUMBER

A receiving bank may ignore the name of the beneficiary and deal only in account numbers; a bank has no duty to "match" a beneficiary's name with a given account number. Thus, where a payment order incorrectly supplies the wrong account number, the liability rests with the party responsible for the error.

Exception: Where the sender incorrectly writes the wrong account number, the sender bank will bear the loss unless it gave prior notice to the sender that the payment would be made on the basis of the account number alone.

V. CRIMINAL ACTS

A. SECURITY PROCEDURE NOT FOLLOWED

Most banks have developed security procedures to thwart criminal interference with funds transfers. If a loss results from a party's failure to follow a security procedure, that party must bear the loss.

B.   CRIMINAL ACTIVITY IN SPITE OF SECURITY PROCEDURE

Where the bank and the customer have agreed to a security procedure and a fraudulent fund transfer occurs in spite of compliance with that procedure, the *customer bears the loss* if the criminal gained access though a *breach of the customer's system. Otherwise, the bank responsible* must bear the loss.

BAR REVIEW

Consumer Protection

celebrating over

35 YEARS

of preparing law students for the bar exam

CONSUMER PROTECTION—MASSACHUSETTS

TABLE OF CONTENTS

I. OVERVIEW

A. INTRODUCTION

The Massachusetts Consumer Protection Act [Mass. Gen. L. ch. 93A] gives public and private remedies to those injured as the result of "unfair methods of competition and unfair or deceptive acts or practices in the conduct of any trade or commerce." [Mass. Gen. L. ch. 93A, §2(a)] The remedies provided by the act are in addition to the relief available through traditional tort and contract actions.

B. SCOPE

1. "Trade or Commerce" Defined

Trade or commerce includes the advertising, the offering for sale, rent or lease, or the actual sale, rent, lease, or distribution of:

(i) Any services and any property, tangible or intangible, real, personal or mixed;

(ii) Any security and any contract of sale of a commodity for future delivery; and

(iii) Any other article, commodity, or thing of value, wherever situated.

This shall include any trade or commerce directly or indirectly affecting the people of Massachusetts. [Mass. Gen. L. ch. 93A, §1(b)]

2. Examples

The following cases have been held to fall within the statute:

a. Landlord-tenant disputes;

b. Claims against attorneys by clients;

c. Breach of implied warranties;

d. Landlord harassment of tenants;

e. Employers vicariously liable for unfair or deceptive acts of employees acting within the scope of employment;

f. Automobile sellers sued by buyers;

g. Real estate brokers sued by purchasers; and

h. Contractors sued by homeowners.

3. Actions Not Within Statute

Business transactions that are completely private and not undertaken in the normal course of trade or business are not covered by Chapter 93A. These include the following:

(i) Suit by a buyer against a noncommercial seller of a house;

(ii) Claims by employees against their employers regarding the employer/employee relationship;

(iii) Disputes relating to the private action of trustees;

(iv) Disputes between parties in the same venture or between members of the same legal entity, such as actions between partners; shareholder derivative suits; or actions between equal shareholders in a closely held corporation; and

(v) Securities transactions between two businesses. (Note that with Chapter 93A consumer actions, damages incurred in a securities transaction are recoverable but only to the amount of actual damage.)

Chapter 93A also does not apply to suits involving state-based claims that would be preempted by federal law. [Pariseau v. Albany International Corp., 822 F. Supp. 843 (D. Mass. 1993)]

C. PROHIBITED CONDUCT

1. Defined Through Other Sources

Two types of conduct are held unlawful by Chapter 93A: (i) unfair or deceptive acts or practices and (ii) unfair competition. However, neither term is defined in the statute. Instead, Chapter 93A directs that the interpretation of its terms be guided by decisions of the Federal Trade Commission ("FTC") and the federal courts interpreting the Federal Trade Commission Act [15 U.S.C. §45L(a)(1)], regulations of the FTC, and regulations of the Massachusetts Attorney General [Mass. Gen. L. ch. 93A §2(a), (b)]. This allows the statute the flexibility to address a wide range of business practices.

2. Unfair or Deceptive Acts or Practices

The Massachusetts courts have defined deceptive practices as conduct that "could reasonably be found to have caused a person to act differently from the way he otherwise would have acted." [Lowell Gas Co. v. Attorney General, 377 Mass. 27, 51 (1979)] Deciding whether a particular action is unfair is also determined by analyzing the effect of the conduct on the public. [Schubach v. Household Finance Corp., 375 Mass. 133 (1978)] The courts rely heavily on the regulations of the FTC and the Massachusetts Attorney General in making these determinations.

a. Federal Trade Commission Regulations

In its regulations, the Federal Trade Commission sets forth three factors to consider in determining whether a particular practice or conduct is deceptive or unfair:

(i) Whether the conduct, while not necessarily having been previously considered unlawful, offends public policy as established by statutes, the common law, or otherwise (*i.e.*, whether it comes within at least the penumbra of some common law, statutory, or other established concept of unfairness);

(ii) Whether the conduct is immoral, unethical, oppressive, or unscrupulous; or

(iii) Whether it causes substantial injury to consumers (or competitors or other businesspersons).

[29 Fed. Reg. 8325, 8355; *see* PMP Associates Inc., v. Globe Newspaper Co., 366 Mass. 593 (1975)]

b. Attorney General's Regulations

The Attorney General is authorized to issue regulations defining specific conduct constituting unfair methods of competition or unfair or deceptive acts or practices. Because these regulations have the "force of law," violation of such regulations constitutes a violation of Chapter 93A. [Dorgan v. Loukas, 19 Mass. App. Ct. 959 (1985)]

1) General Regulations

A regulation of the Attorney General prohibits claims or representations concerning any product or service that directly, or by omission, serve to deceive a buyer in any material respect. [940 C.M.R. §3.05(1)] Another regulation deems a practice or act to be unfair or deceptive if:

(i) It is oppressive or unconscionable in any respect;

(ii) Any person or other legal entity subject to this act fails to disclose to a buyer or prospective buyer any fact the disclosure of which may have influenced the buyer or prospective buyers not to enter into the transaction;

(iii) It fails to comply with existing statutes, rules, regulations, or laws meant for the protection of the public's health, safety, or welfare, or violates any statute, rule, regulation, or law which is intended to protect the public's health, safety, or welfare promulgated by the Commonwealth or any of its political subdivisions; or

(iv) It violates the Federal Trade Commission Act, the Federal Consumer Credit Protection Act, or other federal consumer protection statutes within the purview of Chapter 93A.

[940 C.M.R. §3.16]

2) **Specific Regulations**
Specific regulations govern transactions concerning:

a)   Business and career schools;

b)   Debt collection;

c)   Deceptive price claims or representations;

d)   Door-to-door sales;

e)   Employment agencies and business schemes;

f)   Failure to deliver goods or services;

g)   False advertising and bait-and-switch schemes;

h)   Home improvement transactions;

i)   Landlord-tenant relations;

j)   Layaway plans;

k)   Mail orders;

l)   Mail subscriptions;

m)   Misrepresentation that a product or any part thereof is new, and failure to disclose that a product is used or contains used or reconditioned parts;

n)   Motor vehicle advertising, services, sales, and repairs;

o)   Nursing homes;

p)   Price gouging on petroleum products in a market emergency by any petroleum-related business;

q)   Repairs and services, and service contracts;

r)   Refunds, returns, and cancellations;

s)   Retail advertising; and

t)   Substitution of products.

c.   **Public Protection Statutes**
As discussed above (2.b.1)(iii), *supra*), a violation of a statute enacted to protect the public's health, safety, or welfare constitutes an unfair or deceptive act or practice under Chapter 93A. Statutes included within this category are the following:

1)   New and leased car "lemon law" [Mass. Gen. L. ch. 90, §7N½];

2)   Right to cancel agreements consummated at a place other than seller's place of business within three days [Mass. Gen. L. ch. 93, §48P];

3)   Debt collection in an unfair, deceptive, or unreasonable manner [Mass. Gen. L. ch. 93, §49];

4)   Consumer credit reporting [Mass. Gen. L. ch. 93, §§50-68];

5)   Certification of title to mortgaged premises by lender's attorney [Mass. Gen. L. ch. 93, §70];

6)   Regulation of sale of hearing aids [Mass. Gen. L. ch. 93, §§71-75];

7)   Health club services contracts [Mass. Gen. L. ch. 93, §§78-88];

8) Plaintiff personal injury listings [Mass. Gen. L. ch. 93, §§95-100];

9) Consumer credit cost disclosure [Mass. Gen. L. ch. 140D];

10) Bad faith insurance practices [Mass. Gen. L. ch. 176D];

11) Retail installment sales of motor vehicles [Mass. Gen. L. ch. 255B]; and

12) Retail installment sales and services [Mass. Gen. L. ch. 255D].

3. Unfair Competition

In an unfair competition action by one businessperson against another under section 11 of the Act, "unfair competition" is defined according to the Massachusetts Antitrust Act, which in turn is interpreted according to federal antitrust law. [Action Ambulance v. Atlanticare Health Services, 815 F. Supp. 33 (D. Mass 1993)] An unfair competition action may also be brought by a consumer under section 9 of the Act. In that case, the term is defined by its ordinary meaning with reference to the regulations and statutes discussed above.

D. EXEMPTIONS

Transactions or acts permitted under other laws or regulations of federal or Massachusetts agencies are exempt from Chapter 93A. The burden of proving an exemption is upon the person claiming the exemption. [Mass. Gen. L. ch. 93A, §3; Bierig v. Everett Square Plaza Associates, 34 Mass. App. Ct. 354 (1993)]

E. WAIVER

Generally, consumer rights acquired by law in Massachusetts cannot be waived by agreement or otherwise, unless specifically permitted by the law creating the rights. [Mass. Gen. L. ch. 93, §101]

II. CONSUMER RIGHTS

A. IN GENERAL

The Consumer Protection Act provides remedies for persons who are harmed as a result of unfair competition or unfair or deceptive acts or practices. "Persons" are defined to include natural persons, corporations, trusts, partnerships, incorporated or unincorporated associations, and any other legal entity. The Act contains both public relief provisions available to the Attorney General (sections four through eight) and private relief provisions available to businesspersons and consumers (sections nine through eleven).

B. PUBLIC REMEDIES

1. In General

Actions by the Attorney General to enforce Chapter 93A are done on behalf of all persons of the Commonwealth; thus, it is like a private class action. [Commonwealth v. DeCotis, 366 Mass. 234 (1974)] The Attorney General may make investigations, resolve problems informally, obtain an assurance of discontinuance from the wrongdoer, or file a legal action to enjoin the conduct and obtain restitution.

2. Investigations

The Attorney General may conduct investigations whenever she believes a person has engaged in conduct violating Chapter 93A. Investigations may include the taking of testimony and the examination of documentary evidence. Failure to comply subjects a person to civil penalties of up to $5,000. [Mass. Gen. L. ch. 93A, §§6, 7]

3. Informal Resolution

If a complaint does not involve either a substantial financial loss or numerous consumers, the Consumer Protection Division of the Attorney General has established procedures for attempting an informal resolution of the problem.

4. Assurance of Discontinuance

In lieu of instituting an action, the Attorney General may accept an assurance that the violator will discontinue any unlawful method, act, or practice. Such an assurance may include a stipulation for voluntary payment. Any assurance must be in writing and must be filed in Superior Court.

5. **Injunctions**

The Attorney General may file actions to restrain unfair methods of competition or unfair or deceptive practices if to do so would be in the public interest. [Mass. Gen. L. ch. 93A, §§4-5] The restraint may be by temporary restraining order, preliminary injunction, or permanent injunction.

6. **Restitution**

If a person has been injured as a result of an act or practice that violated Chapter 93A, the Attorney General may file an action to force the violator to provide restitution. In addition to ordering restitution, a court may order the violator to pay a civil penalty of up to $5,000 for each violation if the court finds that the unlawful actor knew or should have known that his actions were a violation of Chapter 93A. The court may also compel the violator to pay the reasonable costs of investigation and litigation, including attorneys' fees.

7. **Notice Required**

Except where a temporary restraining order is sought, the Attorney General must give a person five days' notice prior to the commencement of an action. The notice must be by mail, postage prepaid, and sent to the person's usual place of business (or the person's last known address if the person does not have a usual place of business). The person must be given the opportunity to confer with the Attorney General.

8. **Habitual Violations**

If a corporation habitually violates injunctions issued pursuant to the Act, the court may, upon petition of the Attorney General, order the dissolution of the corporation or the suspension or forfeiture of its franchise. In the case of individuals or foreign corporations, the court may suspend their right to do business in Massachusetts. [Mass. Gen. L. ch. 93A, §8]

C. PRIVATE REMEDIES

1. **In General**

The Consumer Protection Act permits private civil actions by persons injured by unfair competition or by unfair or deceptive acts or practices. Actions by businesspersons (persons engaged in any trade or commerce) are governed by section 11 of the Act. Actions by consumers (all persons who are not businesspersons) are governed by section 9. Note that a section 9 plaintiff need not be a *purchaser* of goods or services; he need only be a person who is not a businessperson. [Murphy v. Charlestown Savings Bank, 380 Mass. 738 (1980)]

2. **Actions by Consumers**

a. **Thirty-Day Demand Letter**

As a jurisdictional requirement, a demand letter must be mailed or delivered to all defendants in a section 9 claim at least 30 days prior to the filing of a civil action. The failure to send or deliver the required letter will result in dismissal of the Chapter 93A claim. [Spring v. Geriatric Authority, 394 Mass. 274 (1985)] The statute provides two exceptions to the demand letter requirement: (i) where a section 9 claim is asserted by way of a counterclaim or cross-claim, or (ii) where the respondent does not maintain a place of business or keep assets in the Commonwealth. [Mass. Gen. L. ch. 93A, §9(3)]

1) **Purpose**

The purpose of a demand letter is to encourage negotiation and settlement. It also functions to control the amount of damages a plaintiff might ultimately recover because, if a reasonable settlement offer was rejected by the plaintiff, recovery is limited to the amount of that offer.

2) **Contents**

To avoid dismissal of the claim, the demand letter should be specific and include:

(i) The identity of the claimant;

(ii) An express reference to Chapter 93A;

(iii) An express reference to the Consumer Protection Act;

(iv) An assertion that the claimant's rights as a consumer were violated;

(v) An assertion that the defendant acted in an unfair or deceptive manner;

(vi) A reasonable description of the unfair or deceptive act or practice that the claimant alleges;

(vii) A reasonable description of the injuries suffered as a result of the act or practice alleged;

(viii) The relief requested;

(ix) Notice that the claimants expect an offer of settlement within 30 days; and

(x) An assertion that the claimant will pursue multiple damages and attorneys' fees should relief be denied.

[Spring v. Geriatric Authority, *supra*; Cassano v. Gogos, 20 Mass. App. Ct. 348 (1985)]

3) Defendant's Response to the Demand Letter

As a practical matter, a defendant should always respond to a Chapter 93A demand letter, because a court finding that the defendant's settlement offer was reasonable in light of the injury will limit the plaintiff's recovery to that offer. Otherwise, the plaintiff may be able to recover multiple damages, attorneys' fees, and costs. [Mass. Gen. L. ch. 93A, §9(3)] The defendant has the burden of proving that the settlement offer was reasonable. [Bachman v. Parkin, 19 Mass. App. Ct. 908 (1984)]

b. Relief Available

A court may award damages and equitable relief, including injunctions. Damages are actual damages or $25, whichever is greater.

1) Statutory Damages

A plaintiff in a section 9 action does not need to prove financial loss; it is sufficient for her to prove that another's unlawful actions caused her to suffer "injury," which has been defined as "the invasion of any legally protected interest of another." [Leardi v. Brown, 394 Mass. 151 (1985)] Thus, even in the absence of harm for which actual damages may be awarded, statutory damages in the amount of $25 may be recovered. [Mass. Gen. L. ch. 93A, §9(1), (3)]

2) Multiple Damages

If the defendant made an offer of settlement that the court finds was reasonable in relation to the injury actually suffered by the plaintiff, the plaintiff's recovery is limited to the relief tendered. Otherwise, the plaintiff may recover up to three times but not less than two times actual damages if the court makes one of the following findings:

(i) That the use or employment of the act or practice was a willful or knowing violation of Chapter 93A; or

(ii) That the refusal to grant relief upon demand was made in bad faith with knowledge or reason to know that the act or practice complained of violated Chapter 93A.

The amount of actual damages to be multiplied by the court is the total amount of the judgment of all claims arising out of the underlying transaction or occurrence, and is calculated without regard to the existence or nonexistence of insurance coverage. [Mass. Gen. L. ch. 93A, §9(3)]

3) Attorneys' Fees and Costs

A successful plaintiff is entitled to reasonable attorneys' fees and costs unless the court finds that the defendant tendered a timely and reasonable offer of settlement. [Mass. Gen. L. ch. 93A, §9(4)] Attorneys' fees for appellate work are also recoverable under Chapter 93A and will be awarded only to the party who prevails. [Yorke Management v. Castro, 406 Mass. 17 (1989)] A party requesting an award of attorneys' fees for appellate work should petition the appellate court in her brief. The appellate court rules on the request. [Jacobs v. Yamaha Motor Corp., U.S.A., 420 Mass. 323 (1995)]

c. **Failure to Exhaust Remedies Not Bar**
    The failure to exhaust administrative or other judicial remedies is not a bar to filing a lawsuit under section 9. [Mass. Gen. L. ch. 93A, §9(6), (8)]

d. **Damages Where a Demand Letter Is Not Required**
    As noted above, a demand letter need not be sent where a section 9 claim is asserted by way of a counterclaim or cross-claim, or where the respondent does not maintain a place of business or keep assets in the Commonwealth. In the absence of a demand letter, the defendant may prevent the imposition of multiple damages by making a written offer of relief and paying the rejected tender into the court.

3. **Actions by Businesspersons**
    Section 11 of the Consumer Protection Act provides for private civil actions by businesspersons injured by unfair or deceptive acts or practices or unfair competition. Unlike under section 9, a section 11 plaintiff need not send a demand letter. Should the plaintiff do so, the defendant is not prejudiced by failing to send any response.

    a. **Exhaustion of Remedies Required**
        Under section 11, plaintiffs must exhaust administrative remedies before bringing a claim.

    b. **Actual Loss Required**
        Section 11 plaintiffs must show actual loss of money or property as a result of the unfair or deceptive act or practice. [Bump v. Robbins, 24 Mass. App. Ct. 296 (1987)] However, if the plaintiff is seeking an *injunction*, he only needs to show that the defendant's act or practice may cause a loss of money or property.

    c. **"Rascality" Required**
        When a case involves sophisticated business entities engaged in arms-length transactions, the section 11 plaintiff has a more difficult burden to establish a violation of the Act than a less sophisticated consumer plaintiff does under section 9. [Knapp Shoes, Inc., v. Sylvania Shoe Manufacturing Corp., 72 F.3d 190 (1st Cir. 1995)] Not only must a plaintiff show that the defendant's conduct constituted an unfair or deceptive practice (*see* I.C.2., *supra*), but also that it reached "a level of rascality that would raise an eyebrow of someone inured to the rough and tumble world of commerce." [Levings v. Forbes & Wallace, Inc., 8 Mass. App. Ct. 498 (1979)]

    d. **Transaction Must Occur Primarily in Massachusetts**
        For purposes of bringing an action under section 11, the transactions constituting the unfair or deceptive act or practice or unfair method of competition must occur primarily and substantially within the Commonwealth. [Mass. Gen. L. ch. 93A, §11; Nickerson v. Matco Tools Corp., 813 F.2d 529 (1st Cir. 1987)] However, this is not a jurisdictional requirement but a defense; thus, the burden of proof is on the defendant to show that the transactions did not occur primarily in Massachusetts. The factors considered are:

        (i)   Where the defendant committed the deceptive practices or acts;

        (ii) Where the plaintiff received and acted upon the deceptive statements or acts; and

        (iii) Where plaintiff's losses occurred due to the deceptive acts of the defendant.

        [Central Massachusetts Television, Inc. v. Amplicon, Inc., 930 F. Supp. 16 (D. Mass. 1996)]

    e. **Recovery Available**
        Generally, recovery is limited to actual damages and any necessary equitable relief.

        1) **Multiple Damages for Willful or Knowing Violations**
            If the court finds that the defendant's actions were a willful or knowing violation of Chapter 93A, the court can award up to three times but not less than two times actual damages. As in section 9 claims, the amount of actual damages to be multiplied by the court is the total amount of the judgment of all claims arising out of the underlying transaction or occurrence, and is calculated without regard to the existence or nonexistence of insurance coverage.

2) Tender of Reasonable Offer Precludes Multiple Damages

The defendant may tender with her answer a written offer of settlement for single damages. If the tender was rejected by the plaintiff and the court finds that the offer was reasonable in relation to the injury actually suffered, the court may not award more than single damages.

4. Forum Selection

a. Superior Court

Chapter 93A actions are generally brought in superior court, which has the power to provide monetary damages as well as equitable relief.

b. District Court

The district court has concurrent jurisdiction with the superior court over claims brought under Chapter 93A for money damages. In a case filed in district court, however, the claim must be limited to money damages (*i.e.*, no equitable relief can be sought) and cannot be made on a class action basis; district courts do not have general jurisdiction in equity.

c. Small Claims

Actions may also be brought in the small claims court if actual damages do not exceed $2,000. Note that the small claims court can award appropriate double or triple damages even if the total judgment then exceeds $2,000. [Mass. Gen. L. ch. 218, §21]

d. Housing Court

The Housing Court Department has subject matter jurisdiction to try Chapter 93A actions related to housing (*e.g.*, landlord-tenant disputes) and to laws concerned directly or indirectly with the "use of any real property and activities conducted thereon as such use affects the health, welfare, and safety of any resident, occupant, user, or member of the general public and which is subject to regulation by local cities and towns under the state building code, state specialized codes, state sanitary code, and other applicable statutes and ordinances." [Mass. Gen. L. ch. 185C, §3; Patry v. Liberty Mobilhome Sales, Inc., 15 Mass. App. Ct. 701 (1983)]

e. Federal Court

Chapter 93A claims may also be brought under the doctrine of pendant jurisdiction in the federal district court. [Kaminski v. Shawmut Credit Union, 416 F. Supp. 1119 (D. Mass. 1976)]

5. Class Actions Permitted

Both consumers and businesspersons having a cause of action under Chapter 93A may bring class action suits if the statutory requirements are met. To make her action a class action, the plaintiff must:

(i) Show that the use or employment of the unfair or deceptive act or practice has caused similar injury to numerous other persons similarly situated;

(ii) Obtain a finding from the court in a preliminary hearing that the plaintiff adequately and fairly represents such other persons; and

(iii) Comply with the order of the court regarding the manner of giving notice of the action to the unnamed plaintiffs in the most effective, practicable manner.

[Mass. Gen. L. ch. 93A, §§9(2), 11(3); Fletcher v. Cape Cod Gas Co., 394 Mass. 595 (1985)]

6. No Right to a Jury Trial

There is no right to a jury trial in a Chapter 93A case. [Spring v. Geriatric Authority, 394 Mass. 274 (1985)] Nevertheless, if a jury trial is desired, a demand should be made because the court does have the discretion to submit a Chapter 93A case to the jury. [Travis v. McDonald, 397 Mass. 230 (1986)] Because most Chapter 93A cases are accompanied by causes of action for which a jury right does exist, a court may be more disposed to permit the jury to decide the Chapter 93A claim as well.

7. Four-Year Statute of Limitations

The statute of limitations for laws that are "intended for the protection of consumers" is four years. [Mass. Gen. L. ch. 260, §5A] This statute applies to claims under Chapter 93A.

[Kusek v. Family Circle, Inc., 894 F. Supp. 522 (D. Mass. 1995)] However, where the claim is based on misrepresentation or breach of warranty, the accrual of a Chapter 93A claim is determined by the same principles governing the underlying cause of action. [Hanson Housing Authority v. Dryvit System, Inc., 29 Mass. App. Ct. 440 (1990)] Also, the right of action in tort by a tenant against a landlord is subject to the three-year statute of limitations applicable to tort actions rather than the four-year statute applicable here. [Mahoney v. Baldwin, 27 Mass. App. Ct. 778 (1989)]

BAR REVIEW

Corporations

celebrating over
35 YEARS
*of preparing
law students
for the bar exam*

CORPORATIONS—MASSACHUSETTS

TABLE OF CONTENTS

PART ONE—CHARACTERISTICS AND FORMATION OF CORPORATIONS

I. TYPES OF CORPORATIONS AND OTHER
BUSINESS ORGANIZATIONS

A. INTRODUCTION

The threshold issue in any Massachusetts bar examination question concerning business organizations is: What type of corporation has been described?

B. GENERAL BUSINESS CORPORATION

Effective July 1, 2004, Massachusetts business corporations are created and operated under chapter 156D of the Massachusetts General Laws—the Massachusetts Business Corporation Act ("MBCA"). The basic attributes of a Massachusetts business corporation (hereinafter, simply "corporation") include:

1. **Creation by State**

    A corporation may only be organized in compliance with a state statute.

2. **Distinct Legal Personality**

    A corporation is a legal entity separate from its shareholder-owners and may sue or be sued and hold property in its own name.

3. **Limited Liability**

    Shareholders usually are not personally liable for corporate debts.

4. **Perpetual Life**

    A corporation may enjoy perpetual existence unless it is incorporated for a specified period or its articles of organization are revoked.

5. **Centralized Management**

    The management and control of a corporation are centralized in a board of directors. Shareholders elect the board and approve fundamental transactions, such as mergers or amendments to the articles of organization.

6. **Transferability of Ownership**

    A corporation is owned by its shareholders, whose shares usually may be freely transferred.

C. CLOSE CORPORATIONS

Close corporations (*i.e.,* corporations with relatively few shareholders; *see* below) are also formed under the MBCA and are subject to exactly the same statutory and common law requirements as other business corporations, with the crucial exception that case law demands a higher duty of loyalty from the controlling shareholders in a close corporation than is demanded from controlling shareholders in other corporations.

1. **Definition**

    The landmark case of *Donahue v. Rodd,* 367 Mass. 578 (1975), "deemed" a close corporation to be typified by (i) a small number of shareholders; (ii) no ready market for the corporate stock; and (iii) substantial majority shareholder participation in the management, direction, and operations of the corporation. Accordingly, a close corporation typically would have between two and 30 shareholders, stock not publicly traded on a securities market, such as the New York Stock Exchange or the over-the-counter market, and a single individual or family who controls the election of the board of directors.

2. **High Duty of Loyalty**

    Shareholders in a close corporation owe one another the same duty of loyalty that partners owe to one another. This standard of "utmost good faith and loyalty" is more stringent than the duty of loyalty generally applied to business corporations. *Examples:*

    a. **Purchase of Shares from Shareholders**

        Because of the high duty of loyalty, when a close corporation offers to purchase shares from a controlling shareholder, it must make an equal pro rata offer to purchase minority shareholders' shares.

    b. **Misappropriation of Goodwill Prohibited**

        The high duty of loyalty prohibits a shareholder from using his superior voting power over another shareholder to cause the corporation to be dissolved and starting a new business dealing with the dissolved corporation's customers, occupying the dissolved corporation's premises, using the dissolved corporation's staff and telephone number, etc. This constitutes misappropriation of the corporation's goodwill. [Donahue v. Draper, 397 Mass. 1104 (1986)]

c. Termination of Employment of Minority Shareholder
Because of the high duty of loyalty, controlling shareholders may be held liable for damages caused to a minority shareholder-employee if the shareholder-employee is fired without a legitimate business reason. [Merola v. Exergen Corp., 423 Mass. 461 (1996)]

3. Less Harmful Alternatives
The minority shareholders in close corporations are entitled to argue (unlike shareholders in ordinary corporations) that the majority had an alternative course of action that could have been taken that would have been less harmful to the minority's interests. This reduces the discretion available to the controlling groups in such matters as declaring or withholding dividends, or dismissing employees. The court will weigh the legitimate *business purpose* of the particular corporate action against the practicality of less harmful *alternatives.* [Zimmerman v. Bogoff, 402 Mass. 650 (1988)]

4. Direct Suits
Because of the small number of shareholders in a close corporation, the heightened fiduciary duties of corporate officers and directors run directly to the shareholders as well as to the corporation itself. Thus, shareholders in close corporations may sue directly rather than derivatively for breach of those duties. However, direct suits are limited to actions where traditional corporate law does not provide a complete remedy or where recovery on the corporation's behalf does not provide a just measure of relief to the complaining shareholder. (*See* V.F., *infra.*)

D. PROFESSIONAL CORPORATIONS
Professional corporations are organized under chapter 156A of the Massachusetts General Laws and are subject to all of the statutory and common law requirements as other business corporations except where that chapter so provides.

1. Definition
A professional corporation is a corporation organized to provide "the personal services performed by registered physicians and surgeons, chiropractors, podiatrists, engineers, electrologists, physical therapists, psychologists, certified public accountants, public accountants, dentists, veterinarians, optometrists, acupuncturists, and attorneys-at-law . . . ."

2. Statutory Distinctions

a. Each incorporator, officer, director, and shareholder of a professional corporation must be *licensed* to practice the relevant profession.

b. A professional corporation may engage in two or more *types* of professional service only to the extent permitted by other regulating laws.

c. Professional incorporation *does not shield* a professional from personal liability relating to professional services rendered.

E. FOREIGN CORPORATION
A foreign corporation is a corporation formed under the law of another jurisdiction.

1. Filing Requirements
Foreign corporations are required to file a certificate with the secretary of state within 10 days after commencing business in Massachusetts. The certificate must include information such as: (i) the name of the corporation, (ii) its state and date of incorporation, (iii) the street address of the corporation's principal office, (iv) a statement of the activities the corporation will carry on in Massachusetts, and (v) the name and address of the corporation's registered agent for service of process in Massachusetts. Foreign corporations are also required to file a report of condition each year. [MBCA §15.03]

2. Requirements of Registered Agent
The registered agent may be a Massachusetts resident, a domestic corporation, or a foreign corporation properly registered in Massachusetts and having an office in Massachusetts. [MBCA §15.07]

3. **What Constitutes Doing Business?**
A corporation will be considered to be doing business in Massachusetts if it owns or leases real estate in Massachusetts; engages in construction, alteration, or repair of any structure, railway, or road in Massachusetts; or engages in any other activity in Massachusetts requiring the performance of labor. Note that the following activities alone *do not constitute doing business*: (i) maintaining a bank account within the state; (ii) maintaining or appointing trustees, depositories, or agencies for the purpose of holding, transferring, exchanging, or registering the corporation's securities in Massachusetts; (iii) holding directors' or shareholders' meetings in the state; or (iv) participating or appearing in any judicial, administrative, or other dispute settlement proceeding. [MBCA §15.01]

F. OTHER FORMS OF BUSINESS ORGANIZATIONS
Technically, the Massachusetts bar examination tests knowledge of "business organizations," not "corporations." Although it is highly improbable that a question would concern an unincorporated business organization other than a partnership, you should be familiar with three such business organizations.

1. **Business Trust ("Massachusetts" Trust)**
A "business trust" has the participants transfer property of the business to trustees, who manage and control it for the benefit of the beneficiaries. The interests of the beneficiaries are represented by transferable shares. The trust is established by a written declaration of trust by which the beneficiaries (unless they act as trustees) avoid personal liability for the organization's debts. Unlike directors of a corporation, the trustees are *personally liable* for trust debts unless creditors consent to look only to the trust corpus. Suits are prosecuted by the trustees instead of the entity itself, and the business is not interrupted by death or withdrawal of a beneficiary. The trustees are not subject to election or recall unless otherwise agreed.

2. **Joint Stock Company**
A joint stock company is an association of persons, formed for the purpose of making profits, that possesses a common capital contributed by the members, which is divided into transferable shares. It is commonly created by written articles of agreement. By agreement in the articles, members may limit their liability to third persons who know of the restriction and consent to it. Since the association is *not a complete legal entity* like a corporation, with such attributes as the right to sue or be sued and to hold or deal in property in the business's name, suits are prosecuted for the association by its managers and property is held and disposed of in their names.

The business of the company is not disrupted by the death or withdrawal of the managers or owners, so its continuity is similar to that of a corporation or business trust. Management, not subject (unless otherwise agreed) to annual election or recall, can be self-perpetuating.

3. **Examination Strategy with Business Trusts or Joint Stock Companies**
Pay particular heed to the different liability rules for a business trust or joint stock association. Generally, the officers of both organizations are subject to the same duties of care and loyalty as a corporation.

4. **Limited Liability Companies**
Massachusetts has adopted legislation permitting the formation of limited liability companies ("LLCs") [Mass. Gen. L. ch. 156C, hereafter the "Massachusetts Limited Liability Company Act" or "MLLCA"], and the Supreme Judicial Court has authorized attorneys to form LLCs to practice law [Supreme Judicial Court Rule 3:06].

   a. **In General**
   An LLC is an entity designed to be taxed like a partnership while offering its owners (called "members") the limited liability that shareholders of a corporation enjoy (*i.e.*, members of the LLC are *not personally liable* for any obligations of the LLC). Under current tax law, an LLC will be taxed like a partnership (*i.e.*, profits and losses flow through the entity and are attributed to the owners personally) unless the LLC elects to be taxed as a corporation.

      1) **Compare—S Corporations and Limited Partnerships**
      If a person is seeking a business format that offers limited personal liability and an opportunity to control the business, an LLC may be better than a Subchapter S corporation (a corporation that elects to be taxed as a partnership under the Tax

Code) in that an LLC is not subject to the limitations of Subchapter S (*e.g.*, S corporations are limited to 75 or fewer shareholders). Similarly, an LLC may be better than a limited partnership because the limited partnership act requires that there be at least one general partner who is personally liable for the partnership's obligations; the LLC statute does not require that a member of the LLC be personally liable.

2) Statute vs. Operating Agreement
Although LLCs are governed by statute, the statute provides that members of an LLC may enter into *oral or written* operating agreements. [*See* MLLCA §2(9)] Most of the statute's provisions regarding members' rights may be varied by such operating agreements. In other words, with respect to members' rights, the statute provides a default set of rules which the members are free to vary.

3) Distinct Legal Entity
Like a corporation, an LLC has a legal existence distinct from its members. It may sue and be sued in its own name, hold property in its own name, its debts are its own and not the debts of its members, etc. [*See* MLLCA §§6, 22, 55]

b. Formation
An LLC is formed by filing a certificate of organization with the secretary of state. Although the certificate may be executed by one person, an LLC must have *at least two members*. [MLLCA §§2(5), 12]

1) Contents of Certificate
The certificate of an LLC must include the following:

a) The *name of the LLC*, which must include an indication that it is an LLC;

b) The street address of the LLC's *registered office and name of its registered agent*;

c) The *name and address of at least one person who is authorized to execute documents* to be filed with the state; and

d) A statement of the *general nature of the LLC's business*.

2) Required Records
LLCs must keep the following records:

(i) A current list of the *name and address of each member and manager*;

(ii) A copy of the *certificate of organization and any written operating agreement*;

(iii) Copies of *tax returns and financial statements* for the three most recent years; and

(iv) Unless contained in a written operating agreement: (a) a description of *each member's contribution* and its agreed value, (b) the *times at which additional* contributions are to be made, (c) the *rights of the members and managers to receive distributions*, and (d) any *events that will trigger dissolution*.

These records may be inspected and copied by the members. [MLLCA §9]

c. Management
An LLC will be managed by all of the members unless the articles provide that management is to be vested in managers. [MLLCA §24]

1) Management by Members
Unless an operating agreement provides otherwise, if the members are managing the LLC, management decisions must be approved by members owning a majority of the unreturned contributions to the LLC (*i.e.*, the members' voting power is proportional to the members' contributions). [MLLCA §21(d)]

2) Management by Managers

The members may elect to have the LLC run by managers. [MLLCA §23] If the LLC is to have managers, the name and address of each manager must be included in the certificate. [MLLCA §§12(a)(5), 13(c)] A manager need not be a member of the LLC. [MLLCA §25] Unless an operating agreement provides otherwise, decisions are to be made by a majority of the managers. [MLLCA §26(d)]

d. Members' Liabilities

As indicated above, members generally are *not* personally liable for the LLC's obligations, but rather are only liable to make the contributions that they agree to make to the LLC. [MLLCA §28]

e. Contributions

To obtain their interests in the LLC, members may contribute cash, property, services, or a promissory note or other obligation to contribute cash, property, or services. [MLLCA §27]

f. Sharing of Profits and Losses

Profits and losses of an LLC are allocated *on the basis of contributions* unless an operating agreement provides otherwise. [MLLCA §29]

g. Transfers of Interest

An assignment of a member's interest in an LLC transfers only the member's right to receive profits and losses. Management rights are not transferred. [MLLCA §39] One can become a member (*i.e.*, management rights can be transferred) only with the consent of *all* members unless an operating agreement provides otherwise. [MLLCA §41]

h. Dissolution

An LLC will be dissolved and its affairs must be wound up on the first to occur of the following:

(i) Reaching the *date of dissolution specified in an operating agreement*;

(ii) *Occurrence of an event* that an operating agreement specifies will cause dissolution;

(iii) *All members consent in writing* to dissolution; or

(iv) *Death, retirement, or any other event terminating the membership of a member* unless remaining members agree to a different arrangement within 90 days after the event or another course of action is directed by an operating agreement.

Upon dissolution, the LLC's assets are distributed first to creditors and then to the members. Unless an operating agreement provides otherwise, the members' contributions are returned first, and any remaining money is distributed in the same proportion as other profits are allocated (on the basis of contributions, absent an operating agreement otherwise). [MLLCA §46]

G. APPLICABLE LAW

The Massachusetts bar examination requires knowledge only of Massachusetts statutory and case law concerning business organizations. Do *not* apply federal securities law, including such well-known provisions as rule 10b-5 or the federal proxy rules.

II. FORMATION AND STATUS OF THE CORPORATION

A. FORMATION TERMINOLOGY

A corporation formed in accordance with all applicable laws is a de jure corporation and its owners generally will not be personally liable for the corporation's obligations. However, if all applicable laws have not been followed, a business may still be treated as a corporation under the de facto corporation doctrine if there was a good faith attempt to incorporate. Even if no attempt to incorporate was made, under some circumstances, a business may be treated as a corporation for the purposes of a particular transaction under an estoppel theory.

B. FORMATION OF A DE JURE CORPORATION

To form a de jure corporation under the MBCA, incorporators (*i.e.*, the persons who undertake to form a corporation) must sign and file a document called the "articles of organization" with the secretary of state.

1. Incorporator Defined
An incorporator is simply a person who signs the articles of organization. Under the MBCA, only one incorporator is necessary, but there may be more than one. [MBCA §2.01] Incorporators may be either natural persons or artificial entities, such as a corporation. Before the initial issuance of shares, incorporators have the same powers as shareholders.

2. Contents of Articles
The articles are required to set out certain basic information about the corporation and may contain any other provision that the incorporators deem appropriate.

a. Mandatory Provisions
The articles must set out:

(i) The *name of the corporation,* which must include the word "corporation," "incorporated," "company," "limited," or the like (or an abbreviation of such words) and generally may not be similar to the name of another business entity qualified to do business in the state, unless the other business consents;

(ii) The *number of shares* the corporation is authorized to issue; and

(iii) The *name and address of each incorporator.*

[MBCA §2.02(a)]

1) Required Supplemental Information
In addition to the above information, the articles must be accompanied by a *supplemental form* including:

(i) The name and address of the corporation's *initial registered agent and office*; and

(ii) The names and addresses of the corporation's *initial directors, president, treasurer, and secretary.*

The supplemental form is not considered to be part of the articles, so it can be easily amended should information change. [MBCA §2.02(d)]

b. Optional Provisions
The articles may set forth any other provision not inconsistent with law regarding managing the business and regulating the affairs of the corporation. [*See* MBCA §2.02(b)] However, it should be noted that the MBCA includes a number of features that a corporation need not adopt, but if they are adopted they must be provided for in the articles. For example, a corporation may choose to limit directors' liability for damages in certain circumstances, but if a corporation wants to so limit liability, it may do so only by including the limitation in the articles. A number of these conditionally mandatory provisions will be discussed later in this outline.

1) Business Purposes
Traditionally, the articles had to include a statement of the business purposes of the corporation, and the corporation was limited to activities pursuing the stated purposes. However, this rule has been abandoned. The MBCA *presumes* that a corporation is formed for *any lawful business* unless the articles provide a more restricted business purpose. [MBCA §3.01]

a) Ultra Vires Acts
Generally, a corporation is allowed to undertake any action necessary or convenient to carry out its business or affairs. [MBCA §3.02] If a corporation includes a narrow purpose statement in its articles of organization, it may *not* undertake activities unrelated to achieving the stated business purpose (*e.g.,* if the articles state that the corporation's purpose is to operate restaurants, the corporation may not undertake to run a mink farm). If a corporation undertakes activities beyond the scope of its stated purpose, it is said to be acting "ultra vires."

(1) Effect

At common law, if a corporation acted ultra vires, the action was void; no one could enforce the action. Modern laws and the MBCA have changed this dramatically. Generally, an ultra vires act is enforceable, and the ultra vires nature of an act may be raised in only three circumstances:

(i) A *shareholder* may sue the corporation to enjoin a proposed ultra vires act;

(ii) The *corporation* directly, derivatively, through a receiver, etc., may sue an incumbent or former officer, director, employee, agent, etc., for damages arising from the commission of an ultra vires act authorized by such person; and

(iii) The *state* may bring an action against the corporation to have it dissolved for committing an ultra vires act.

[MBCA §3.04(b)] Note that if an officer, director, employee, or agent is found liable for committing an ultra vires act, such person may be held *personally* liable for damages.

(2) Charitable Donations

At one time, charitable donations were thought to be outside the scope of any business purpose, but most states and the MBCA now allow corporations to make charitable donations. [MBCA §3.02(13)]

(3) Loans

Formerly, some courts held that corporations did not have the power to make loans to employees, officers, or directors. Today, most states and the MBCA allow such loans. [MBCA §3.02(11)] However, a corporation may not lend money to a director (or guarantee a director's obligation) unless: (i) the loan is approved by the holders of a majority of the outstanding voting shares, excluding the shares of the benefited director; or (ii) the board determines that the loan benefits the corporation and specifically approves it. [MBCA §8.32(a)]

3. Corporate Existence Begins on Filing by the State

The articles must be submitted to the secretary of state. If the secretary of state's office finds that the articles comply with the requirements of law, it will file the articles. [MBCA §§2.03, 1.23] This filing of the articles by the state is conclusive proof of the beginning of the corporate existence unless a delayed effective date is specified.

4. Additional Procedures to Make De Jure Corporation Operative

After the articles are filed, the incorporators or initial directors will hold an organizational meeting to adopt bylaws, elect officers, and transact other business.

a. Bylaws

Bylaws may contain any provision for managing the corporation that is not inconsistent with law or the articles of organization. [MBCA §2.06] Initial bylaws are adopted by the incorporators or directors, but can be modified or repealed by the shareholders. Directors can modify the bylaws only if the articles or a bylaw so provides. [MBCA §10.20]

C. RECOGNITION OF CORPORATENESS WHEN CORPORATION IS DEFECTIVE

One of the main reasons to incorporate is to avoid personal liability for obligations of a business enterprise. This veil of protection generally is available when a de jure corporation is formed (*i.e.*, when all the steps required by statute for incorporation have been followed). The veil of protection may also be available in some circumstances even when all of the steps necessary under the incorporation statute have not been followed—under the de facto corporation or corporation by estoppel doctrines.

1. De Facto Corporation

A de facto corporation has all the rights and powers of a de jure corporation at common law, but it remains subject to direct attack in a *quo warranto* proceeding by the state.

a. Common Law Requirements
Traditionally, the requirements for establishing a de facto corporation are:

1) Statute for Valid Incorporation Available
There must be a corporate law under which the organization could have been legally incorporated, such as the MBCA.

2) Colorable Compliance and Good Faith
There must be colorable compliance with the incorporation laws. "Colorable" compliance means a *good faith attempt to comply* with the state law.

3) Exercise of Corporate Privileges
Finally, the corporation must act like a corporation, *i.e.,* conduct the business in its corporate name and exercise corporate privileges.

b. Limitation on De Facto Doctrine
The MBCA provides that persons who purport to act as or on behalf of a corporation *knowing* that there was no incorporation are liable for all liabilities created in so acting. [MBCA §2.04] It follows under the common law maxim *expressio unius est exclusio alterius* (expression of one thing is the exclusion of another) that persons who do not know that there was no incorporation will not be liable (*i.e.,* the de facto corporation doctrine probably is available for such persons).

Examples: 1) Andrea and Bart agree to form AbbeyCorp. They properly draw up the necessary papers and Bart tells Andrea that he will file them the next day. Bart forgets to file the papers and forgets to tell Andrea of his failure. The following week, Andrea enters into a contract with a supplier on behalf of AbbeyCorp. Andrea probably can avoid personal liability on the contract under the de facto corporation doctrine.

    2) Same facts as above, but the day after Andrea and Bart draw up the articles, Bart mails them to the secretary of state, and a few days after Andrea entered into the contract with the supplier, Andrea and Bart receive a letter from the secretary of state indicating that the articles were not filed because they were missing the incorporators' signatures. Andrea probably can avoid personal liability on the contract under the de facto corporation doctrine.

2. Corporation by Estoppel
A business might also be treated as a corporation despite the lack of de jure status under the corporation by estoppel doctrine. Under the doctrine, persons who treat an entity as a corporation will be estopped from later claiming that the entity was not a corporation. The doctrine can be applied either to an outsider seeking to avoid liability on a contract with the purported corporation, or to a purported corporation seeking to avoid liability on a contract with an outsider.

Examples: 1) Suppose X, an outsider, deals with the entity as though it were a valid corporation. Upon discovering a defect in formation, X seeks to hold the shareholders personally liable. A shareholder without prior knowledge of the defect may successfully assert that X is estopped to deny the corporation's existence, since X always treated the corporation as though it were properly formed.

    2) Z, an improperly formed corporation, contracts to buy supplies from W. If Z tries to avoid the contract on the basis of its formation defects so that the "shareholders" can purchase goods elsewhere, Z would be treated as a corporation by estoppel.

3. Application of De Facto and Estoppel Doctrines
When an organization is considered to be a de facto corporation, it is treated as if it were de jure, except in a direct attack by the state. That is, its shareholders enjoy limited liability and it has perpetual life, ability to buy and sell property, etc. Estoppel, on the other hand, is applied on a case-by-case basis between two parties to equitably resolve a dispute.

a. Contracts
In contract cases, both doctrines are easily applied. When the parties have previously dealt on a corporate basis, or have assumed there to be a valid corporation, corporate status is generally upheld.

b. Torts

The de facto doctrine has been applied in tort cases [*see* Kardo Co. v. Adams, 231 F. 950 (6th Cir. 1916)], but normally there is little room for an estoppel argument when a tort claim is involved, because recognition of corporateness has no relevance to the commission of the tort (*i.e.,* the plaintiff did not allow herself to be injured in reliance on the fact that the defendant was acting as a corporation). Thus, parties with tort claims are generally free to sue the shareholders of an improperly formed corporation.

c. Liability of Associates

Generally, when the court finds no corporate status, the associates will be held liable as partners. The MBCA imposes joint and several liability on such persons. [MBCA §2.04] There is little Massachusetts law on this topic, but courts are prone to hold "*active*" associates (those participating in the particular transaction involved) personally liable, and absolve inactive associates from personal liability.

D. DISREGARD OF CORPORATE ENTITY (PIERCING THE CORPORATE VEIL)

In some circumstances, even though a corporation has been validly formed, the courts will hold the shareholders, officers, or directors *personally liable* for corporate obligations because the corporation is abusing the legislative privilege of conducting business in the corporate form. This is frequently called "piercing the corporate veil." This doctrine counterbalances the de facto corporation and corporation by estoppel doctrines, for here a *valid corporate existence is ignored* in equity to serve the ends of justice.

1. Elements Justifying Piercing the Corporate Veil

As a general rule, a de jure corporation will be treated as a legal entity until sufficient reason to the contrary appears. Each case is different, but there are three recurring situations in which the veil is often pierced: (i) when corporate formalities are ignored; (ii) when the corporation is inadequately capitalized at the outset; and (iii) to prevent fraud.

a. Alter Ego (Ignoring Corporate Formalities)

If a corporation is the "alter ego," "agent," or "instrumentality" of a sole proprietor or of another corporation, its separate identity may be disregarded.

1) Individual Shareholders

If the shareholders treat the assets of the corporation as their own, use corporate funds to pay their private debts, fail to keep separate corporate books, and fail to observe corporate formalities (such as holding meetings, issuing stock, and conducting business by resolution), courts often find that the corporate entity is a mere "alter ego" of the shareholders. However, sloppy administration alone may not be sufficient to warrant piercing the corporate veil. The operation of the corporation must result in some *basic injustice* so that equity would require that the individual shareholders respond to the damage they have caused.

Note: As will be discussed later, the MBCA allows the shareholders to vest power to run the corporation in themselves, rather than in a board of directors. Their doing so is *not* a ground for disregarding the corporate veil, even if it results in a failure to keep corporate records. [MBCA §7.32; *and see* V.C.3., *infra*]

2) Parent-Subsidiary Corporations

A subsidiary or affiliated corporation will not be deemed to be a separate corporate entity if the formalities of separate corporate procedures for each corporation are not observed. For example, both corporations must be held out to the public as separate entities; separate meetings of directors and officers should be held; identical or substantially overlapping directors and officers should be avoided; and corporate policies should be significantly different.

3) Affiliated Corporations

If one person owns most or all of the stock in several corporations, a question may arise as to whether one of the corporations, although not formally related to the other, should be held responsible for the other's liabilities. Dominating stock ownership alone is not enough in such a case, unless the majority shareholder dominates finances, policies, and practices of both corporations so that both are a business conduit for the principal shareholder.

b. Inadequate Capitalization

It is generally accepted that shareholders will be personally liable for their corporation's obligations if *at incorporation* they fail to provide adequate capitalization. The shareholders must "put at the risk of the business *unencumbered capital reasonably adequate for its prospective liabilities.*" Undercapitalization cannot be proved merely by showing that the corporation is now insolvent. However, if insolvency occurs soon after incorporation, it may be a primary indicator of undercapitalization.

1) One-Person or Close Corporation
No absolute test for adequate capitalization has been formed. In any case, the corporation should have enough capital "to pay debts when they become due." The scope of the contemplated operations of the corporation, and the potential liability foreseeable from the operations, are factors to consider.

2) Parent-Subsidiary Corporations
A parent corporation's inadequate capitalization of a subsidiary corporation may constitute constructive fraud on all persons who deal with that subsidiary. One additional test should be applied in the parent-subsidiary situation: whether the subsidiary may reasonably expect to achieve independent financial stability from its operation.

c. Avoidance of Existing Obligations, Fraud, or Evasion of Statutory Provisions
The corporate entity will be disregarded any time it is necessary to prevent fraud or to prevent an individual shareholder from using the corporate entity to avoid his *existing* personal obligations.

1) Avoiding Liability
The mere fact that an individual chooses to adopt the corporate form of business to avoid personal liability is not, of itself, a reason to pierce the corporate veil. A shareholder must engage in other acts that seem inequitable, such as forming a corporation to run a public swimming pool without sufficient funds to buy accident insurance, or inducing a creditor to deliver goods and services under a long-term payment contract by showing the creditor a financial statement that deliberately misstates the firm's assets or income.

2) Fraud
The corporate veil will be pierced whenever the avoidance of personal liability through the formation of a corporation operates as a fraud on creditors or other outsiders.
Example: If A is bound by a covenant not to compete with B, he cannot avoid the covenant by forming a corporation and having it compete with B.

2. Who Is Liable?
When the corporate entity is ignored and the shield of limited liability is pierced, the persons composing the corporate entity may be held personally liable.

a. Active-Inactive Tests
Normally, only the persons who were active in the management or operation of the business will be held personally liable. In other words, passive investors who acted in good faith will not be held liable for corporate obligations.

b. Theories of Liability

1) Joint and Several
When shareholders are held liable, they will be held liable for the entire amount of the claim (even if it exceeds the amount that would have been considered "adequate capitalization"). Liability for obligations of the corporation is extended to the shareholders as joint and several liability.

2) Property Cases
If a corporation has conveyed its assets to a shareholder in fraud of creditors, upon piercing the corporate veil the assets may be reached on principles of fraudulent conveyance.

3. Types of Liability

    a. Tort
    A tort victim is often a successful plaintiff under the theory of piercing the corporate veil, since he usually has not been involved with the corporation in a transactional sense, and should not be forced to sue an insolvent corporate shell for his damages.

    b. Contract
    Courts are reluctant to pierce the corporate veil in contract cases, since the contracting party has an opportunity to investigate the financial condition of the corporation and, in the absence of misrepresentation or fraud, has a less equitable claim for relief. When the creditor deals at arm's length with the corporation, the court will most likely effect the reasonable expectation of the parties and force the creditor to look only to the corporation for satisfaction of the contract.

    c. Bankruptcy and Subordination of Claims
    When the corporation is insolvent and some of the shareholders have claims as "creditors," the shareholders' claims may be subordinated to those of the other creditors *if equity so requires* (*e.g.,* because of fraud). This is an application of "piercing the corporate veil" by refusing to recognize the shareholders as creditors of a separate legal entity—the corporation.

    In the subordination situation, called the "Deep Rock" doctrine from the case that first applied it, a court has discretion to subordinate the shareholder's claim to any class of creditors, including subordinating the claim even as to unsecured creditors.

4. Who May "Pierce"?

    a. Creditors
    The creditors of a corporation are the most likely persons to pierce the corporate veil, and the cases involving disregard of corporateness primarily involve creditors.

    b. Shareholders
    Generally, those who choose to conduct business in the corporate form may not disregard the corporate entity at their will to serve their own purposes. Courts virtually never pierce the corporate veil at the request of the shareholder.

III. CAPITAL STRUCTURE

A. TYPES OF CORPORATE SECURITIES
Corporate capital comes from the issuance of many types of "securities." The word "security" is used generically to describe many obligations, including equity obligations (*e.g.,* shares of stock) and debt obligations (*e.g.,* bonds).

1. Debt Securities
A debt security represents a creditor-debtor relationship with the corporation, whereby the corporation has borrowed funds from an "outside creditor" and promises to repay the creditor. A debt security holder has *no ownership interest* in the corporation.

2. Equity Securities
An equity security is an instrument representing an investment in the corporation whereby its holder becomes a part *owner of the business*. Equity securities are shares of the corporation, and the investor is called a shareholder.

B. DEBT SECURITIES
A debt obligation usually has a stated maturity date and a provision for interest. Debt obligations may be secured (a "mortgage bond") or unsecured (a "debenture"), and may be payable either to the holder of the bond (a "coupon" or "bearer" bond) or to the owner registered in the corporation's records (a "registered bond"). A debt obligation may also have special features; *e.g.,* it may provide that it is convertible into equity securities at the option of the holder, or it might provide that the corporation may redeem the obligation at a specified price before maturity of the obligation.

C. EQUITY SECURITIES (SHARES)

1. **Terminology**
   The shares that are described in a corporation's articles are called the "*authorized shares*." The corporation may not sell more shares than are authorized. Shares that have been sold to investors are "*issued and outstanding*." Shares that are reacquired by the corporation are no longer issued and outstanding, and so revert to being "authorized shares" (in some states, reacquired shares are called "treasury shares"). [*See* MBCA §6.03] Shares may be "certificated" (*i.e.,* represented by share certificates) or "uncertificated" (*i.e.,* not represented by certificates, but described in a written statement of information). [MBCA §§6.25, 6.26]

2. **Classification of Shares**
   As stated above, equity securities represent an ownership interest in the corporation. A corporation may choose to issue only one type of shares, giving each shareholder an equal ownership right (in which case the shares are generally called "*common shares*"), or it may divide shares into *classes*, or *series within a class*, having varying rights, as long as one or more classes together have unlimited voting rights and one or more classes together have a right to receive the corporation's net assets on dissolution. [MBCA §6.01]

   a. **Classes and Series Must Be Described in Articles**
      If shares are to be divided into classes, the articles must (i) prescribe the number of shares of each class, (ii) prescribe a distinguishing designation for each class (*e.g.,* "Class A preferred," "Class B preferred," etc.), and (iii) either describe the rights, preferences, and limitations of each class or provide that the rights, preferences, and limitations of any class or series within a class shall be determined by the board of directors prior to issuance. [MBCA §§6.01, 6.02]

      1) **Authorized Rights, Preferences, and Limitations**
         The MBCA provides a *nonexhaustive* list of rights, preferences, and limitations that can be used to vary classes and series:

         (i) Shares may have special, conditional, or limited *voting rights*, or no right to vote;

         (ii) Shares may provide that they may be *redeemed or converted* for cash, indebtedness, securities, or other property (the redemption or conversion can take place at the option of the corporation or the shareholder, or on the occurrence of a specified event);

         (iii) Shares may entitle the holders to *distributions, including dividends*; or

         (iv) Shares may have *preference over any other class of shares with respect to distributions*, including on dissolution of the corporation.

         [MBCA §6.01(c)]

      2) **Blank Stock**
         The shareholders or, if the articles so provide, the directors may reclassify any *unissued* shares into shares of a different class or series or into shares of a new class or series—with rights different from those of the outstanding shares. [MBCA §6.02(b)] Thus, the shareholders (and directors) have power to vary the capital structure of the corporation as needed. Shares subject to such power are sometimes referred to as "blank stock."

3. **Fractional Shares**
   A corporation may: (i) issue certificates representing fractions of a share or pay in money the fair value of fractions of a share as determined by the board; (ii) arrange for the disposition of fractional shares by those entitled to the fractional shares; or (iii) issue scrip that entitles the holder to a full share on surrendering enough scrip to equal a full share. [MBCA §6.04(a)]

   a. **Rights of Holders of Fractional Shares and Scrip**
      A certificate representing fractions of a share entitles the holder to exercise the rights of a shareholder. In contrast, the holder of scrip may not exercise any rights of a shareholder unless otherwise provided in the scrip. [MBCA §6.04(c)]

4. **Subscription Agreements**
   A subscription is an offer to purchase shares from a corporation. Subscriptions can be made to existing corporations or to corporations to be formed. Subscriptions between an existing

corporation and a subscriber generally are governed by the law of contracts. Preincorporation subscriptions are governed by the following rules:

a. **Acceptance and Revocation**
Under the MBCA, a *preincorporation* subscription is irrevocable by the subscriber for *six months* from the date of the subscription unless otherwise provided in the terms of the subscription, or unless all subscribers consent to revocation. [MBCA §6.20(a)]

b. **Payment**
Unless otherwise provided in the subscription agreement, preincorporation subscriptions for shares are payable on demand by the board of directors.

1) **Discrimination Not Allowed**
The board of directors may not discriminate among subscribers in calling for payment of subscriptions. As far as is practicable, any demand for payment must be uniform as to all shares of the same class or as to all shares of the same series. [MBCA §6.20(b)]

2) **Penalties for Failure to Pay**
If a subscriber fails to pay under a preincorporation subscription agreement, the corporation may collect the amount owed as it would any other debt. Alternatively, the subscription agreement may set forth other penalties for failure to pay. However, the corporation may not effect a rescission or forfeiture unless the subscriber fails to cure the default within 20 days after the corporation sends *written notice* of default to the subscriber. Note that rescission is the corporation's (not the subscriber's) option. A subscriber may not escape her liability by voluntarily rescinding. Also, the board of directors may release, settle, or compromise any subscription or dispute arising from a subscription, unless otherwise provided in the subscription agreement. [MBCA §6.20(d)]

5. **Consideration for Shares**
The MBCA prescribes rules regarding the types and amount of consideration that may be received in exchange for stock issued by the corporation.

a. **Forms of Consideration**
Traditionally, states limited the type of consideration that could be received by a corporation issuing stock (stock could be issued only in exchange for cash, property, or services already rendered). The MBCA has virtually abandoned such limitations and allows stock to be issued in exchange for *any tangible or intangible property or benefit to the corporation.* [MBCA §6.21(b)]

b. **Amount of Consideration**

1) **Traditional Par Value Approach**
Traditionally, the articles of organization would indicate whether the corporation's shares were to be issued with a stated par value or with no par value. Stock with a par value could not be issued by the corporation for less than the par value (although this rule did not apply to stock repurchased by the corporation and held as treasury shares). Furthermore, in many states the money received from the issuance of par value stock had to go into a special account—called stated capital. The stated capital account could not be reduced below the aggregate par value of all the stock that had been issued. The idea was to guaranty creditors that the corporation would be capitalized at a certain level.

2) **MBCA Approach**
The MBCA generally does not follow the traditional par value approach and instead allows corporate directors to issue stock for whatever consideration they deem adequate. The MBCA also provides that the board of directors' *determination* as to the adequacy of the consideration received is *conclusive* as to whether the stock exchanged for the consideration is validly issued, fully paid, and non-assessable. [MBCA §6.21(c)]
Example: Roger and Tony form Genie Carpets, Inc. ("Genie") to manufacture faux Persian rugs. Genie's articles authorize the issuance of 1,000 shares of stock. The corporation issued its first 500 shares at

a price of $1,000 each. Bellows approached Roger and Tony and offered to sell to the corporation his carpet manufacturing facility in exchange for 500 shares of Genie stock. Although a six-month-old appraisal found the property to be worth $400,000, other factors made Roger and Tony believe the property to be worth more, so they agreed to the transaction. One of Genie's shareholders thinks the facility was not sufficient consideration and brings suit to have the issuance to Bellows declared invalid. The suit will fail. The board's good faith determination of value is conclusive as to whether the stock exchanged for the consideration is validly issued, fully paid, and nonassessable.

a) Optional Limitation

The articles of organization may limit the amount or type of consideration for which shares may be issued. [MBCA §6.21(c)] Presumably, directors would breach their duty owed to the corporation if they authorized the sale of shares for a lesser amount and be liable for the difference. Note that the articles may also provide for a par value for shares. [MBCA §2.02(b)(1)(iv)] Historically, par value shares could not be sold for less than par. If they were, they were considered "watered" and the directors could be held liable. However, the MBCA and its comments make clear that merely referring to par value in the articles will not itself be deemed to be a specification of a minimum amount required for the issuance of shares. Such a provision is a limitation only if other provisions (*e.g.*, a contract or other provisions in the articles) give it effect. [MBCA §6.21(d)] This appears to mean that if the articles merely state that "the shares shall have a par value of $10," they may be sold for any amount; but if the articles state that "the shares shall have a par value of $10 and may not be sold for less than par," the $10 amount will then be considered an effective limitation.

c. Unpaid Stock

A shareholder is liable to pay the corporation the full consideration for which her shares were authorized to be issued. [MBCA §6.22] If the shareholder fails to pay the full consideration, the shares are referred to as "unpaid stock." If the corporation is insolvent, a trustee in bankruptcy can enforce the corporation's claim for unpaid stock.

PART TWO—INTRACORPORATE PARTIES

IV. PROMOTERS

A. PROMOTERS PROCURE CAPITAL AND OTHER COMMITMENTS

The first step in forming a corporation is the procurement of commitments for capital and other instrumentalities that will be used by the corporation after formation. This is done by promoters. Generally, promoters enter into contracts with third parties who are interested in becoming shareholders of the corporation once it is formed (*i.e.*, "stock subscriptions"). Promoters might also enter into contracts with others for goods or services to be provided to the corporation once it is formed. Usually, the promoters will go on to serve as incorporators, but this is not necessary.

B. PROMOTERS' RELATIONSHIP WITH EACH OTHER

Absent an agreement indicating a contrary relationship, promoters are considered to be joint venturers, and they occupy a *fiduciary relationship to each other*. As fiduciaries, promoters are prohibited from secretly pursuing personal gain at the expense of their fellow promoters or the corporation to be formed.

Example: Arnie and Barb have agreed to form a corporation to engage in a real estate business. Arnie tells Barb that he can acquire a piece of land suitable for subdividing for $100,000. Arnie acquires the land for $70,000 and pockets the difference. Arnie is liable to Barb for breach of a fiduciary duty, since the promotion began when Arnie and Barb agreed to form the corporation.

C. PROMOTERS' RELATIONSHIP WITH CORPORATION

Upon incorporation, the promoters owe fiduciary duties to the corporation and to those persons investing in it. The promoters' duty in this respect is one of fair disclosure and good faith. Promoters are not permitted to retain a secret profit resulting from transactions with, or on behalf of, the corporation. Promoters' liabilities will arise under one of three theories: (i) breach of fiduciary duty; (ii) fraud or misrepresentation; or (iii) obtaining unpaid stock.

1. Breach of Fiduciary Duty Arising from Sale to Corporation
A promoter who profits on the sale of property to the corporation may be liable to the corporation for the profit, or may be forced to rescind the sale, unless the promoter has disclosed all of the material facts of the transaction.

a. Independent Board of Directors
If the transaction is disclosed to an independent board of directors (not under the control of the promoter) and approved, there is no breach of a fiduciary duty.

b. Disclosure to Subscribers or Shareholders
If the board of directors is not completely independent, the promoter's transaction must be approved by the shareholders or subscribers to the stock of the corporation. The promoter is insulated from a breach of fiduciary duty if the subscribers knew of the transaction at the time they subscribed or, after full disclosure, unanimously ratified the transaction. Disclosure must be to all shareholders, not merely to the controlling shareholders. In addition, disclosure must include those *persons contemplated as part of the initial financing scheme*. [Old Dominion Copper Mining & Smelting Co. v. Bigelow, 203 Mass. 159 (1909)]

Example: Alex, Becky, and Chloe decide to form a corporation with 200,000 shares of authorized common stock. They plan to sell 50,000 shares to the public. Prior to formation they obtain subscriptions to 20,000 shares. Alex, Becky, and Chloe contribute property in exchange for 150,000 shares and they "profit" on the transaction. They obtain approval of the transaction from the subscribers for the 20,000 shares. The remaining 30,000 shares are sold within three weeks after formation of the corporation, but the promoters do not disclose their profit to the new shareholders. Under the *Bigelow* rule, the promoters are liable to the corporation because the transaction was not approved by all shareholders who were contemplated as part of the original promotion plan.

c. Promoters' Purchase of All the Stock
If the promoters purchase all the stock of the corporation themselves, with no intention to resell the stock to outsiders, but subsequently do sell their individual shares to outsiders, they *cannot be liable* for breach of a fiduciary duty with respect to their promoter transactions, since at the time they purchased the stock there was no one from whom the profit was kept secret.

2. Fraud
Promoters may always be held liable if plaintiffs can show that they were defrauded by the promoters' fraudulent misrepresentations or fraudulent failure to disclose all material facts. The basis of this liability can be either common law fraud or the state and federal securities acts.

D. PROMOTERS' RELATIONSHIP WITH THIRD PARTIES—PREINCORPORATION AGREEMENTS

1. Promoter's Liability
The MBCA provides that if a person acts on behalf of a corporation, knowing that there has been no incorporation, the person is jointly and severally liable for any obligations incurred. [MBCA §2.04] Thus, as a general rule, if a promoter enters into an agreement with a third party to benefit a planned, but as of yet unformed, corporation, the promoter is personally liable on the agreement.

Example: Fred and Barney agree to pool their money to form a corporation ("Dyno, Inc.") to run a rock quarry. Fred approaches Mr. Slate, explains his plans, and enters into a contract to purchase a small quarry from Slate for $100,000—$50,000 to be paid at closing and an additional $50,000 to be paid six months later. The contract provides that the closing will not be held for 45 days so that Fred and Barney will have time to incorporate Dyno, Inc. before the closing. Fred signs the contract, "Fred, on behalf of Dyno Inc." Subsequently, Fred and Barney have a falling out, and Dyno, Inc. is never formed. Fred probably will be found to be personally liable on the contract with Mr.

Slate since he entered the contract knowing that Dyno, Inc. had not yet been formed.

a. Liability Continues After Formation Absent Novation

A promoter's liability on preincorporation agreements continues after the corporation is formed, even if the corporation adopts the contract and benefits from it. The promoter's liability can be *extinguished only if there is a novation*—an agreement among the parties releasing the promoter and substituting the corporation. To clearly establish a novation, the third party should expressly release the promoter after the corporation has adopted the contract, although some cases have implied a novation from the conduct of the third party and the corporation.

Example: Same facts as in the example in 1., above, but Fred and Barney do not have a falling out, Dyno, Inc. is formed, and a few days later the parties close on the quarry. At the closing, title to the quarry is transferred to Dyno, Inc. Despite Dyno, Inc.'s adoption of the purchase contract, Fred remains personally liable for the remainder of the purchase price unless the parties agreed to a novation at the closing.

b. Exception—Agreement Expressly Relieves Promoter of Liability

If the agreement between the parties expressly indicates that the promoter is not to be bound, there is no contract. Such an arrangement may be construed as a revocable offer to the proposed corporation. The promoter has no rights or liabilities under such an arrangement.

c. Promoter Indemnification

When a promoter is liable on a preincorporation contract and the corporation thereafter adopts the contract but no novation is agreed upon, the promoter may have the right of indemnification from the corporation if he is subsequently held liable on the contract.

2. Corporation's Liability

a. General Rule—No Liability Prior to Incorporation

Since the corporate entity does not exist prior to incorporation, it is not bound on contracts entered into by the promoter in the corporate name. A promoter cannot act as an agent of the corporation prior to incorporation, since an agent cannot bind a nonexistent principal.

b. Adoption

Unlike the majority rule, in Massachusetts a corporation cannot be bound to a promoter contract by resolution of the corporation's board of directors. However, the corporation can be bound under a continuing offer theory if the promoter contract is deemed to be a continuing offer to the corporation that the corporation accepted by accepting the benefits. The corporation could also be bound on an implied contract theory merely by accepting the benefits of the promoter contract, at least to the extent of the fair market value of the benefits received. In any case, the promoter remains liable on his contract absent a novation.

E. UNIFORM SECURITIES ACT

Massachusetts has enacted a Uniform Securities Act ("U.S.A.") similar in its approach to the 1933 Federal Securities Act. [Mass. Gen. L. ch. 110A]

1. Registered Securities

All corporations making sales of securities to more than 25 persons whose shares are not listed on a national securities exchange (such as the American, Boston, Midwest, New York, or Pacific Stock Exchange) must file with the state secretary a detailed registration statement describing the firm, the security, and the issuing process. The state secretary may issue a stop order barring sale of the security in the Commonwealth if there is fraud in the preparation of the registration statement or if the statement was not filed or fully completed.

2. Antifraud Provision

The U.S.A. also contains a section similar to rule 10b-5 of the 1934 Securities Exchange Act. Section 101 of the U.S.A. makes it unlawful for any person in connection with the offer, sale, or purchase of any security, directly or indirectly: (i) to employ any device, scheme, or artifice to defraud; (ii) to make any untrue statement of a material fact, or omit to state a fact necessary in order to make the statements made, in the light of the circumstances under which they are made, not misleading; or (iii) to engage in any act, practice, or course of business that operates or would operate as a fraud or deceit on any person.

3.   Elements of Action Under Section 101

a.   All Securities Offered, Purchased, or Sold
Section 101 applies to *all* securities, both those registered under Massachusetts law and those not. It is broader than rule 10b-5 because it applies to "offers" to sell securities as well as to purchases or sales. Hence any person who bought, sold, or was even offered a security in a Massachusetts corporation may be a plaintiff against a promoter, the corporation, or any outsider who sells, buys, or offers to sell stock.

b.   Fraud
The plaintiff must prove a fraud. Typically the fraud will be a material misrepresentation or material omission concerning the corporation's worth.

c.   Knowledge
The plaintiff must also prove that the defendant knowingly engaged in the fraudulent conduct—a negligent misstatement or omission is not sufficient.

4.   Partial Preemption by Federal Law
In 1996 federal law was changed to preempt most state regulation of securities *except* with regard to: (i) penny stocks (generally, stock selling for less than $5 per share and not listed on a national securities exchange); (ii) intrastate offerings exempt under the 1933 Act; (iii) actions against brokers for fraud; and (iv) notice filing requirements for stocks sold within the state.

F.   ENFORCEMENT THROUGH CHAPTER 93A
The Massachusetts Consumer Protection Act [Mass. Gen. L. ch. 93A] prohibits the use of unfair or deceptive practices in the conduct of any trade or business. This includes the sale of stock.

1.   Misleading Disclosure
Chapter 93A is generally applied where the corporation fails to disclose information that a purchaser would consider material, particularly information regarding the corporation's net worth. Note that a stock offering where disclosure goes beyond legal requirements must still be accurate in all material respects. That is, the corporation cannot release misleading information and then defend on the grounds that the information provided was not required by law.

2.   Not Applicable to Governance Issues
Chapter 93A is not available for corporate governance issues. Once stock has been purchased, the existence of fiduciary duties between the shareholder and the corporation's officers and directors precludes a chapter 93A suit. The rationale is that such disputes are principally private in nature and chapter 93A only governs transactions between legally separate persons dealing at arm's length. [Puritan Medical Center v. Cashman, 413 Mass. 167 (1992)]

3.   Damage Limitations
Generally, chapter 93A provides for double or treble damages and attorneys' fees where the deceptive conduct is particularly egregious or willful. By statute, however, recovery for the sale of any security is limited to the plaintiff's *actual damages*. [Mass. Gen. L. ch. 93A, §9(3)]

4.   Formalities Required for Suit
Certain formalities are required before a plaintiff may bring a chapter 93A suit, including the writing of a demand letter to the corporation. If the corporation replies to the demand letter within 30 days with a reasonable settlement offer, the plaintiff cannot recover more than the offer.

G.   THIRD-PARTY LIABILITY
Stock offerings are often accompanied by statements from law firms attesting to the legality of a particular offering or certifying the truth of the information disclosed by the offeror. Although actions for malpractice generally require that the plaintiff be a client of the firm sued, Massachusetts has implied a cause of action sounding in negligence against such firms on behalf of the stock purchaser if (i) the information supplied is untruthful or misleading, (ii) the shareholder relies on the information in the purchase, and (iii) the firm could foresee that the shareholder

would rely on the information. [Norman v. Brown, Todd & Heyburn, 693 F. Supp. 1259 (D. Mass. 1988)] Although there are as yet no cases directly imputing such a duty to an accounting firm, case law in other states suggests that the cause of action might extend to them as well.

V. SHAREHOLDERS

A. SHAREHOLDER CONTROL OVER MANAGEMENT

1. Direct Control

At common law, shareholders have no right to directly control the day-to-day management of their corporation. Instead, the right to manage is vested in the board of directors, who usually delegate their day-to-day management duties to officers. This is still the general rule under the MBCA. However, the MBCA also allows a departure from the general rule: Shareholders may enter into agreements concerning management of the corporation, including an agreement to vest the powers that the board would ordinarily have in one or more shareholders. The requirements for such agreements are discussed at C.3., *infra*.

2. Indirect Control

Even absent a shareholder agreement vesting direct control of the corporation in shareholders, shareholders have indirect control over their corporation through their power to elect directors, amend the bylaws, and approve fundamental changes to the corporation.

a. Shareholders Elect and May Remove Directors

Shareholders have the right to elect directors. [MBCA §8.03(d)] The shareholders may also remove a director, *with or without cause*, at any time. [MBCA §8.08]

b. Shareholders May Modify Bylaws

As discussed above (II.B.4.a., *supra*), shareholders have the power to adopt, amend, or repeal bylaws.

c. Shareholders Must Approve Fundamental Corporate Changes

Changes to the fundamental structure of a corporation cannot be made without the approval of the shareholders. Shareholder approval is required in cases of merger, sale of corporate assets outside the ordinary course of business, dissolution, and for other extraordinary corporate matters. Similarly, amendments to the articles of organization may require shareholder approval. (*See* IX., *infra*.)

B. SHAREHOLDERS' MEETINGS AND VOTING POWER

1. Convening Meetings

a. Annual Meetings

Corporations must hold annual meetings, the primary purpose of which is the election of directors. [MBCA §7.01] If a meeting is not held within the earlier of six months after the end of the corporation's fiscal year or 15 months after the last annual meeting, the superior court in the county where the corporation's registered office is located may order an annual meeting to be held on the application of any shareholder entitled to participate in an annual meeting. [MBCA §7.03(a)]

b. Special Meeting

The board of directors, or those persons authorized to do so by the articles or bylaws, may call special meetings during the year to conduct business that requires shareholder approval. A special meeting may also be called by the holders of at least 10% of all the votes entitled to be cast at the meeting. [MBCA §7.02(a)]

2. Place of the Meeting

Shareholders' meetings may be held *anywhere* within or outside the state, at the place stated in, or fixed in accordance with, the bylaws. If no place is so stated or fixed, annual meetings are held at the corporation's principal office. [MBCA §§7.01(b), 7.02(c)]

3. Notice

Generally, written notice of the shareholders' meetings—special or annual—must be sent to the shareholders entitled to vote at the meeting. [MBCA §7.05] Delivery may be by mail, messenger, or electronic transmission. [MBCA §1.41]

a.   **Time Within Which Notice Must Be Sent**
Under the MBCA, the notice must be delivered not less than seven days or more than 60 days before the meeting. [MBCA §7.05(a)]

b.   **Contents of Notice**
The notice must state the place, day, and hour of the meeting. For special meetings, the purpose(s) for which the meeting is called must also be stated in the notice. [MBCA §7.05(a)]

c.   **Notice May Be Waived**
Action taken at a meeting can be set aside if notice was improper. However, a shareholder will be held to have waived any defects in notice if the shareholder (i) waives notice in a *signed writing* either before or after the meeting or (ii) *attends the meeting* and does not object to notice at the beginning of the meeting (or, if the defect is that the notice did not identify a special purpose, when the purpose is first brought up). [MBCA §7.06]

4.   **Eligibility to Vote**

a.   **Record Date**
A corporation's bylaws may fix, or provide the manner of fixing, a *record date* to determine which shareholders are entitled to notice of a meeting, to vote, or to take any other action. If the bylaws do not so provide, the board may specify a date as the record date. The record date may not be more than *70 days* before the meeting or action requiring a determination of shareholders. [MBCA §7.07(a)]

   1)   **If Record Date Not Set**
   If there is no fixed record date, the record date will be the day before the first notice of the meeting is sent to the shareholders, or, if no notice is sent, on the day before the meeting. [MBCA §7.05(a)]

b.   **Shareholders' List for Meeting**
After a record date for a meeting has been fixed, the corporation must prepare an alphabetical list of all shareholders entitled to notice of a shareholders' meeting. The list must show each shareholder's address and the number of shares held by each shareholder. [MBCA §7.20(a)]

   1)   **List Available for Inspection**
   Beginning two business days after notice of the meeting for which the list was prepared is given, and continuing through the meeting, the shareholders' list must be made available for inspection by any shareholder or her agent at the corporation's principal office or at another place identified in the notice. The shareholder may, by written demand, inspect and copy the list during regular business hours. [MBCA §7.20(b)]

      a)   **Refusal to Allow Inspection**
      If the corporation refuses to allow inspection of the list, the superior court in the county where the corporation's principal office (or if none, its registered office) is located may, on application by the shareholder, order the inspection or copying at the corporation's expense. The court may postpone the meeting for which the list was prepared until completion of the inspection or copying, but a refusal or failure to prepare or make available the shareholders' list otherwise does *not* affect the validity of actions taken at the meeting. [MBCA §7.20(e), (f)]

c.   **Voting Entitlement of Shares**
Unless otherwise provided in the articles, each outstanding share, regardless of class, is entitled to one vote on a matter to be voted on at a shareholders' meeting. Shares held by one corporation in a second corporation generally may be voted like any other outstanding shares, unless the second corporation owns a majority of shares entitled to vote for directors of the first corporation (*e.g.*, a subsidiary holding shares of its parent usually cannot vote those shares). [MBCA §7.21(a), (b)] Note that shares held by the corporation in a fiduciary capacity (*e.g.*, under an employee stock ownership plan) can be voted by the corporation. [MBCA §7.21(c)]

d. Corporation's Acceptance of Votes

If the name signed on a vote, consent, waiver, or proxy appointment corresponds to that of a shareholder, the corporation is entitled to accept the vote, consent, etc., if the corporation is acting in good faith. The corporation may also accept signatures from representatives (*e.g.,* an executor, an officer of an entity that holds the shares, a guardian of the owner of the shares, etc.). However, if the corporate officer authorized to tabulate votes has a good faith, reasonable doubt about the validity of a signature or about the signatory's authority to sign for the shareholder, the corporation may reject the vote, consent, waiver, or proxy appointment. [MBCA §7.24]

5. Proxies

A shareholder may vote his shares either in person or by proxy executed in writing by the shareholder or his attorney-in-fact. [MBCA §7.22]

a. Duration of Proxy

A proxy is valid for only 11 months unless it provides otherwise.

b. Revocability of Proxy

An appointment of a proxy generally is revocable by a shareholder and may be revoked in a number of ways (*e.g.,* in writing, by the shareholder's showing up to vote himself, or by later appointment of another proxy). A proxy will be irrevocable only if the appointment form *conspicuously states that it is irrevocable* and the appointment is *coupled with an interest*. Appointments coupled with an interest include the appointment of any of the following:

(i) A *secured party*;

(ii) A *person who purchased* or agreed to purchase the shares;

(iii) A *creditor* of the corporation who extended credit to the corporation under terms requiring the appointment;

(iv) An *employee* of the corporation whose employment contract requires the appointment; or

(v) A *party to a voting agreement*.

[MBCA §7.22(d)]

1) Death or Incapacity of Shareholder

Death or incapacity of a shareholder appointing a proxy does *not* affect the right of the corporation to accept the authority of the proxy unless the corporate officer authorized to tabulate votes receives *written notice* of the death or incapacity prior to the time the proxy exercises her authority under the appointment. [MBCA §7.22(e)]

6. Mechanics of Voting

a. Quorum

A quorum must attend a meeting before a vote may validly be taken. A *majority of the votes entitled to be cast* on the matter by a particular voting group (*see* below) will constitute a quorum unless the articles provide *greater* quorum requirements. Once a share is represented at a meeting, it is deemed present for quorum purposes for the remainder of the meeting; thus, a shareholder cannot prevent a vote by leaving before the vote is taken. [MBCA §§7.25, 7.27]

1) Voting by Group

The articles may, and the MBCA does, require approval by certain groups of shares separately under some circumstances. For example, an amendment to the articles must be approved by a share group when the share group will be significantly affected if the amendment is approved. (*See* IX.B.2.a., *infra.*)

b. Voting—In General

Generally, each outstanding share is entitled to one vote unless the articles provide otherwise. [MBCA §7.21] (The articles may provide that a certain class or classes shall have more than one vote—weighted voting—or no vote. [MBCA §§6.01, 6.02]) If a quorum exists, an action will be deemed approved by the shareholders (or appropriate shareholder group) if the ***votes cast in favor of the action exceed the votes cast against the action***, unless the articles provide for a greater voting requirement. [MBCA §§7.25, 7.27]

c. **Director Elections**

Unless the articles provide otherwise, directors are elected by a ***plurality*** of the votes cast at a meeting at which there is a quorum. In other words, as long as a quorum is present, the candidates receiving the most votes—even if not a majority—win.

1) **Cumulative Voting Optional**

Instead of the normal one share, one vote paradigm, the articles may provide for ***cumulative voting*** in the election of directors. [MBCA §7.28] Cumulative voting is a device that gives minority shareholders a better chance to elect a director to the board than the shareholders would have using the ordinary voting procedure described above. In cumulative voting, each share may cast as many votes as there are board vacancies to be filled. Thus, if three directors are to be elected, each voting share is entitled to cast three votes. The votes may be cast for a single candidate, or they may be divided among the candidates in any manner that the shareholder desires.

Example: Tammy owns 300 voting shares of Circle X stock. Nine directors are to be elected at the next annual meeting. Tammy is entitled to cast 2,700 votes (300 shares x 9 vacancies). She may cast all 2,700 votes for one candidate or divide her 2,700 votes in any manner she desires.

2) **Classification of the Board**

The articles may grant certain classes of shares the right to elect a certain director or number of directors. Only shareholders of that class may vote to fill the specified position(s). [MBCA §8.04]

d. **Class Voting on Article Amendments**

Whenever an amendment to the articles of organization affects only one class of shares (Class A common, preferred, etc.), that class generally has the right to vote on the amendment ***even if the class would not otherwise be permitted to vote*** at a shareholders' meeting. Typical situations where class voting may occur include:

(i) A ***change in the designation, preferences, rights*** (including preemptive and dividend rights), ***or aggregate number of shares of a class;***

(ii) An ***exchange, reclassification, or cancellation of some of the shares*** of the class or a change of the shares of the class into a different class; and

(iii) The ***creation of a new class having superior rights*** to the shares of this particular class.

[MBCA §10.04] Generally, it may be said that class voting should be used if a proposed amendment has any effect—adverse or advantageous—on holders of the class.

7. **Shareholders May Act Without Meeting**

Shareholders may take action without a meeting by the unanimous written consent of all shareholders entitled to vote on the action. Alternatively, the articles may allow shareholders to take action through consents submitted by shareholders having at least the number of votes that would be required to approve the action if it were voted on at a meeting at which all shareholders entitled to vote on the matter were present and voting. All consents must be filed with the corporation within 60 days of the first consent. [MBCA §7.04]

C. **SHAREHOLDER AGREEMENTS**

Shareholders may enter into several types of agreements in an effort to protect their voting power, proportionate stock ownership, or other special interests in the corporation. Although most shareholder agreements are encountered in the close corporation (where stock is held by a few individuals and is not actively traded), most of these agreements can be used in any corporation.

1. **Voting Trusts**

To ensure that a group of shares will be voted a particular way in the future, one or more shareholders may create a voting trust by (i) entering into a signed agreement setting forth the trust's terms and (ii) transferring legal ownership of their shares to the trustee. The trust may contain any lawful provision not inconsistent with the trust purposes, and the trustee must vote the shares in accordance with the trust. A copy of the trust agreement and the names and addresses of the beneficial owners of the trust must be given to the corporation. The trust is valid for the period stated in the trust and may be extended. [MBCA §7.30]

2. Voting Agreements

Rather than creating a trust, shareholders may enter into a written and signed agreement that provides for the manner in which they will vote their shares. Unless the voting agreement provides otherwise, it will be *specifically enforceable*. Unlike a voting trust, such an agreement need not be filed with the corporation. [MBCA §7.31]

3. Shareholder Agreements

The shareholders may enter into an agreement among themselves regarding almost *any aspect of the exercise of corporate powers or management*. For example, an agreement may:

(i) *Eliminate* the board of directors or *restrict* the discretion or powers of the board;

(ii) *Govern the authorization or making of distributions*;

(iii) *Establish who shall be directors or officers*, as well as their terms and conditions of office, or the manner of selection or removal; or

(iv) *Transfer* to one or more shareholders or other persons the *authority to exercise the corporate powers* or to manage the business and affairs of the corporation.

[MBCA §7.32(a)]

a. Statutory Requirements

To be valid, the agreement must either (i) be set forth in the *articles or bylaws*, and be approved by all persons who are shareholders at the time of the agreement or (ii) be set forth in a *written agreement signed by all persons who are shareholders* at the time of the agreement, and be filed with the corporation. Unless otherwise provided, the agreement is valid for 10 years. The agreement is subject to amendment or termination only by *all* persons who are shareholders at the time of the amendment, unless the agreement provides otherwise. The existence of the agreement must also be noted conspicuously on the corporation's share certificates. [MBCA §7.32(b)]

b. Enforceability

Any party to the agreement may enforce it against any other party. One who purchases shares without knowledge of the agreement is entitled to rescind the purchase. [MBCA §7.32(c)]

c. Termination of Agreement's Effectiveness

The agreement ceases to be effective when shares of the corporation are listed on a national securities exchange or are regularly traded in a market maintained by a member of a national or affiliated securities association. [MBCA §7.32(d)]

d. Agreement Does Not Impose Personal Liability on Shareholders

Even if the agreement treats the corporation as a partnership or results in failure to observe corporate formalities, the agreement does not constitute a ground for imposing personal liability on any shareholder for the acts or debts of the corporation. [MBCA §7.32(f)]

4. Restrictions on Transfer of Shares

Another way shareholders may control the destiny of their corporation is by imposing restrictions on transfers of outstanding shares. The articles, the bylaws, an agreement among shareholders, or an agreement between shareholders and the corporation may impose restrictions on the transfer of the corporation's shares for *any reasonable purpose* (*e.g.*, to preserve the corporation's eligibility for S corporation status or for a securities law exemption). [MBCA §6.27]

a. Permissible Restrictions
The MBCA permits restrictions that:

(i) Obligate the shareholder to *first offer* the corporation or other persons an opportunity to acquire the restricted shares;

(ii) Obligate *the corporation or other persons to acquire* the restricted shares;

(iii) Require the corporation, the holders of any class of its shares, or another person to *approve the transfer* of the restricted shares, if the requirement is not manifestly unreasonable; or

(iv) *Prohibit transfer* of the restricted shares to designated persons or classes, if the prohibition is not manifestly unreasonable.

[MBCA §6.27(d)]

b. Enforceability
A permitted stock transfer restriction is enforceable against the holder of the stock or a transferee of the holder only if (i) the restriction's existence is *noted conspicuously on the certificate* (or is contained in the information statement, if the shares are uncertificated) or (ii) the holder or transferee *had knowledge* of the restriction. [MBCA §6.27(b)]

5. Agreements Affecting Action by Directors
The board has the authority to exercise corporate powers and to manage the business and affairs of the corporation. However, limitations may be imposed on this authority by the articles or by a shareholders' agreement, as discussed above. [MBCA §8.01(b)]

D. SHAREHOLDERS' INSPECTION RIGHTS
At common law, shareholders had a qualified right to inspect corporate books and records: They could inspect upon request if they had a *proper purpose* for the inspection. Proper purposes include purposes such as waging a proxy battle, investigating possible director or management misconduct, seeking support for a shareholder initiative, etc. Improper purposes are purposes aimed primarily at personally benefiting the inspecting shareholder, such as to obtain the names and addresses of the shareholders in order to create a commercial mailing list to sell to third parties.

1. MBCA Approach—In General
The MBCA generally continues the common law approach. Under the MBCA, a shareholder may inspect the corporation's books, papers, accounting records, shareholder records, etc. To exercise this right, the shareholder must give *five days' written notice* of his request, stating a *proper purpose* for the inspection. The shareholder need not personally conduct the inspection; he may send an attorney, accountant, or other agent. [MBCA §16.02]

a. Unqualified Right
The MBCA also includes an exception to the general rule. It provides that any shareholder may inspect the following records *regardless of purpose*: (i) the corporation's articles and bylaws, (ii) board resolutions regarding classification of shares, (iii) minutes of shareholders' meetings from the past three years, (iv) communications sent by the corporation to shareholders over the past three years, (v) a list of the names and business addresses of the corporation's current directors and officers, and (vi) a copy of the corporation's most recent annual report. [MBCA §§16.02(a); 16.01(e)]

b. Right May Not Be Limited
The right of inspection may not be abolished or limited by the articles or bylaws. [MBCA §16.02(d)]

c. Inspection by Court Order
If a corporation does not allow a required inspection, a court may order that the inspection and copying take place. Where a court so orders, it must also order the corporation to pay the shareholder's costs incurred in obtaining the order, unless the corporation proves that its refusal to allow inspection was in good faith. [MBCA §16.04]

E. PREEMPTIVE RIGHTS
When the corporation proposes to issue additional shares of stock, the current shareholders often

want to purchase some of the new shares in order to maintain their proportional voting strength. The common law granted shareholders such a right, known as the "preemptive right." Under the MBCA, a shareholder *does not have any preemptive rights* except to the extent provided by the articles or a contract to which the corporation is a party. [MBCA §6.30]

F. SHAREHOLDER SUITS

Shareholders enjoy a dual personality. They are entitled to enforce their own claims against the corporation, officers, directors, or majority shareholders by *direct* action. Shareholders are also the guardians of the corporation's causes of action, provided no one else in the corporation will assert them. In this sense, shareholders may sue *derivatively* to enforce the corporate cause of action, as long as they meet the requirements specified by law and they have made necessary demands on the corporation or the directors to enforce the cause of action. In either capacity, direct or derivative action, the shareholder may sue for herself and for others similarly situated.

1. Direct Actions

a. Nature of Action
A breach of a fiduciary duty *owed to the shareholder* by an officer or director of a corporation is a proper subject for a shareholder's direct action against that officer or that director. However, be careful to distinguish breaches of duty owed to a shareholder from duties owed to the corporation. If the duty is owed to the corporation rather than to an individual shareholder, the cause of action is derivative rather than direct. The basic tests are: (i) who suffers the most immediate and direct damage? and (ii) to whom did the defendant's duty run?

b. Recovery
In a shareholder direct action, any recovery is for the benefit of the individual shareholder, or, if the action was a class action, for the benefit of the class.

2. Derivative Actions

a. Nature of Action
The derivative action is often described as a "representative" action, since the shareholders are enforcing the rights of another—*i.e.,* the corporation. Recovery in a derivative action generally goes to the corporation rather than to the shareholder bringing the action.

b. Standing—Ownership at Time of Wrong
To commence or maintain a derivative proceeding, a shareholder must have been a shareholder of the corporation *at the time of the act or omission* complained of, or must have become a shareholder through *transfer by operation of law* from one who was a shareholder at that time. Also, the shareholder must fairly and adequately represent the interests of the corporation. [MBCA §7.41]

c. Demand Requirements
The shareholder must make a *written demand* on the corporation to take suitable action. A derivative proceeding may not be commenced until 90 days after the date of demand, unless: (i) the shareholder has earlier been notified that the corporation has rejected the demand; or (ii) irreparable injury to the corporation would result by waiting for the 90 days to pass. [MBCA §7.42]

1) If Demand Futile
In a number of states, demand is excused if it would be futile (*e.g.*, where a shareholder is seeking damages from the entire board for breach of duty, they are unlikely to approve the action). However, the MBCA does not provide for such an excuse.

d. Corporation Named as Defendant
In a derivative action, the corporation is named as a party defendant. Although the cause of action asserted belongs to the corporation (so the corporation is the real plaintiff in interest), the failure of the corporation to assert its own claim justifies aligning it as a defendant.

e. Dismissal If Not in Corporation's Best Interests
If a majority of the directors (but at least two) or shareholders who have no personal

interest in the controversy found *in good faith after reasonable inquiry* that the suit is not in the corporation's best interests, but the shareholder brings the suit anyway, the suit may be dismissed on the corporation's motion. [MBCA §7.44] Good business reasons for the directors' refusal might be the fact that there is no likelihood of prevailing, or that the damage to the corporation from litigating would outweigh any possible recovery.

1) Burden of Proof

To avoid dismissal, in most cases the *shareholder* bringing the suit has the burden of proving to the court that the decision was *not* made in good faith after reasonable inquiry. However, if a majority of the directors had a personal interest in the controversy, the *corporation* will have the burden of showing that the decision was made in good faith after reasonable inquiry. [MBCA §7.44(e)]

f. Discontinuance or Settlement Requires Court Approval

A derivative proceeding may be discontinued or settled only with court approval. [MBCA §7.45]

g. Court May Order Payment of Expenses

Upon termination of a derivative action, the court may order the corporation to pay the plaintiff's reasonable expenses (including attorneys' fees) incurred in the proceeding if it finds that the action has resulted in a substantial benefit to the corporation. If the court finds that the action was commenced or maintained without reasonable cause or for an improper purpose, it may order the plaintiff to pay reasonable expenses of the defendant. [MBCA §7.46]

G. DISTRIBUTIONS

1. Types of Distributions

Distributions of the corporation's assets to shareholders may take a number of forms: Dividends can be paid to shareholders in the form of cash or indebtedness while the corporation is operating. Shares can be redeemed from shareholders where there is a redemption right (*i.e.,* a built-in right of the corporation to repurchase the shares in a forced sale at a particular price) or repurchased (a voluntary sale by a current shareholder and purchase by the corporation). Finally, liquidating distributions can be paid to the shareholders when the corporation is dissolved. [MBCA §1.40(a)]

2. Rights to Distributions

At least one class of stock must have a right to receive the corporation's net assets on dissolution. [MBCA §6.01(b)] Beyond this rule, the articles may provide for distributions in any manner.

a. Declaration Generally Solely Within Board's Discretion

Even if the articles authorize distributions, the decision whether or not to declare distributions generally is *solely within the directors' discretion* (recall, however, that a shareholder agreement can change this rule; *see* C.3., *supra*), subject to any limitations in the articles and statutory solvency requirements (*see* below). The shareholders have no general right to compel a distribution; it would take a very strong case in equity to induce a court to interfere with the directors' discretion.

1) Limitations

a) Solvency Requirements

No distribution of any kind (*i.e.,* dividend, share repurchase, etc.) is permitted if, after giving it effect, either:

(i) The corporation would *not be able to pay its debts as they become due* in the usual course of business (*i.e.,* the corporation is insolvent in the bankruptcy sense); or

(ii) The corporation's *total assets would be less than the sum of its total liabilities plus* (unless the articles permit otherwise) the amount that would be needed, if the corporation were to be dissolved at the time of the distribution, *to satisfy the preferential rights* on dissolution of shareholders whose preferential rights are superior to those receiving the distribution (*i.e.,* the corporation is insolvent in the balance sheet sense).

[MBCA §6.40(c)]

b) **Restrictions in the Articles**
The articles may restrict the board's right to declare dividends. For example, to assure repayment, a creditor might be able to have the corporation include in its articles a provision prohibiting payment of any distributions unless the corporation earns a certain amount of profits.

c) **Share Dividends**
Distributions of a corporation's own shares (*i.e.,* "share dividends" or "stock dividends") to its shareholders are excluded from the definition of "distribution" under the MBCA. [MBCA §1.40] Therefore, the above solvency rules are inapplicable to share dividends. However, shares of one class or series may not be issued as a share dividend with respect to shares of another class or series unless one of the following occurs: (i) the articles so authorize; (ii) a majority of the votes entitled to be cast by the class or series to be issued approves the issuance; or (iii) there are no outstanding shares of the class or series to be issued. [MBCA §6.23]

d) **Equitable Limitations on Share Repurchases**
Before adoption of the MBCA, courts placed equitable limitations on share repurchases in certain situations. These limitations will probably still apply, even under the MBCA.

(1) **Close Corporations**
Shares may not be repurchased from some shareholders in a close corporation unless an identical offer is made to all shareholders.
Example: The ACB Corp. has three shareholders, each of whom owns 50 shares. Ms. A and Ms. C dominate the board. They could not cause the board to offer to buy half of their shares at $100 per share unless an equal offer was made for Ms. B's shares.

Note: In the absence of a shareholder agreement, corporate provision, or oppressive conduct, a close corporation is not required to purchase the shares of minority shareholders upon their death. [Goode v. Ryan, 397 Mass. 84 (1986)]

(a) **"Freeze-Outs"**
Since shareholders in close corporations may have no ready market for their stock, Massachusetts law has been particularly sensitive to attempts by directors—who generally are also the majority shareholders—to compel a minority shareholder to sell his shares back to the corporation at less than fair market value. Thus, a minority shareholder in a close corporation who merely *receives an inadequate offer* to repurchase his shares may have a cause of action against the directors *if* the minority shareholder can show that the offer is part of an attempt to freeze him out of the financial benefits he would ordinarily receive from the corporation. The most common indicia of a freeze-out are: (i) a refusal to declare dividends; (ii) draining corporate earnings through excessive salaries to majority shareholder-officers and their relatives; (iii) depriving minority shareholders of corporate offices or employment, particularly where there is no valid business purpose for doing so; and (iv) causing the corporation to sell its assets at an inadequate price to the majority shareholders. Shareholders who are frozen out may compel the corporation to repurchase their shares at a fair market price.

(2) **Maintaining Control**
Case law in other jurisdictions has limited directors' powers to cause the corporation to repurchase its own shares when the repurchase is intended to maintain incumbent directors in office. A share repurchase

to maintain control will not be permitted unless the directors (i) found there was a justifiable business purpose served by preventing a particular outsider from gaining control and (ii) adequately investigated the threat. Typically, share repurchases to maintain control are permitted if the challenging shareholder has a past record of looting or liquidating firms, or would significantly change the corporation's business policies.

(3) Duty of Disclosure

Directors and majority shareholders have an independent duty to exercise complete candor with minority shareholders when they negotiate stock repurchases. Thus, all material circumstances surrounding a proposed transaction must be fully disclosed. If this duty is breached and the minority shareholder sells at an inadequate price, the minority shareholder can recover damages based on the difference between the offered price and the fair value of the stock. Note that such damages are available *only to the shareholder who accepts* the inadequate offer.

2) Abuse of Discretion

If directors do not act in good faith in omitting a dividend, shareholders may sustain a suit to compel a dividend. A court may find an abuse of discretion when there is a conflict of interest between the shareholders who control the board of directors and the shareholders seeking a dividend, and there is no business justification for the omission of the dividend.

Example: XYZ Corp. has rising earnings and the majority shareholder would like to buy all the minority's shares. The minority refuses to sell and dividends are promptly stopped. Under such circumstances, unless the board could present a persuasive reason why the corporation needed to retain earnings (*e.g.,* monies needed to retire debt security then due; or monies needed for essential expansion), shareholders probably could sustain an abuse of discretion suit for the failure to pay dividends.

a) Abuse of Discretion in Close Corporation

Massachusetts courts will subject the failure to pay a dividend in a close corporation to closer scrutiny. Even if the plaintiffs cannot identify a conflict of interest, the courts will balance the business purpose offered to justify the omitted dividend against the practicality of a less harmful alternative (as explained in I.C.3., *supra*).

3) Historical Note—Par Value and Capital Accounts

Under traditional corporate laws, distributions were also prohibited unless there was sufficient money in a particular account or accounts. Generally, dividends could be paid only from accounts containing "surplus," such as an account containing retained earnings; dividends could not be paid out of the "stated capital account," which had to contain at least the aggregate par value of all outstanding par value shares. Such limitations do not apply in Massachusetts.

b. Contractual Rights in Regard to Distributions

1) Limitations and Preferences

As discussed previously, a corporation need not give each shareholder an equal right to receive distributions. Shares may be divided into classes with varying rights (*e.g.,* some classes may be redeemable, others not; some may have no right to receive distributions, others could have preferences; etc.). The following are common preference terms with which you should be familiar:

a) (Noncumulative) Preferred Shares

Shares that have a preference usually are entitled to a fixed amount of money (*e.g.,* $5 each year if the preference is a dividend preference, $5 on dissolution if the preference is a liquidation preference) before distributions can be made with respect to nonpreferred shares. Note that the right is not absolute; the directors must still declare a dividend before the preferred shareholder has any right to receive it. Unless the dividend is cumulative (*see infra*), the right to a dividend preference for a particular year is extinguished if a dividend is not declared for that year.

b) Cumulative Preferred Shares

Cumulative preferred shares are like noncumulative preferred shares, but if a dividend is not declared in a particular year, the right to receive the preference accumulates and must be paid before nonpreferred shares may be paid any dividend.

Example: NavaCorp has 1,000 shares of $5 cumulative preferred stock outstanding. The directors did not declare a dividend in 1999 or 2000. If the directors want to declare a dividend in 2001, they will have to pay the cumulative preferred shareholders $15,000 (1,000 shares x $5 x 3 years) before any payment can be made to shares without a preference.

c) Cumulative If Earned Shares

If shares are "cumulative if earned," dividends for any one year cumulate only if the corporation's total earnings for that year exceed the total amount of the preferred dividends that would have to be paid out for that year.

d) Participating Shares

Generally, preferred shares are entitled only to their stated preference. However, preferred shares may be designated as "participating," in which case they have a right to receive whatever the nonpreferred shares receive in addition to the preference.

2) Rights After Declaration—Same as a General Creditor

As established above, shareholders have no general right to receive distributions. However, once a distribution is lawfully declared, the shareholders generally are treated as creditors of the corporation, and their claim to the distribution is equal in priority to claims of other unsecured creditors. [MBCA §6.40(f)] Note, however, that a distribution can be enjoined or revoked if it was declared in violation of the solvency limitations, the articles, or a superior preference right.

c. Who May Receive—Shareholder of Record on Record Date

Once declared, dividends are payable to the persons named as shareholders in the corporate records on a particular date—known as the record date. If shares have been sold prior to the record date but have not been transferred on the corporation's books, the corporation pays the record owner (*i.e.,* the seller), and the beneficial owner (*i.e.,* the purchaser) must look to the seller for payment.

3. Liability for Unlawful Distributions

a. Directors

A director who votes for or assents to a distribution that violates the above rules is personally liable to the corporation for the amount of the distribution that *exceeds what could have been properly distributed*.

1) Good Faith Defense

A director is not liable for distributions approved in good faith (i) based on financial statements prepared according to reasonable accounting practices, or on a fair valuation or other method that is reasonable under the circumstances [MBCA §6.40(d)] or (ii) by relying on information from officers, employees, legal counsel, accountants, etc., or a committee of the board of which the director is not a member [MBCA §8.30(b)].

2) Contribution

A director who is held liable for an unlawful distribution is entitled to contribution from (i) *every other director* who could be held liable for the distribution; and (ii) *each shareholder*, for the amount she accepted *knowing that the distribution was improper*. [MBCA §6.41(c)]

b. Shareholder Liability

In addition to the shareholder's liability for contribution to a director noted above, the MBCA provides that a shareholder who receives a distribution *knowing that it was made improperly* is directly liable to the corporation for the amount he received in excess of what could have properly been distributed to him. Moreover, if the distribution was a *liquidating distribution* made within three years after the effective date of the corporation's dissolution, the shareholder is liable to the corporation on account of any claim against the corporation that the corporation cannot pay, even if the shareholder did not know that the distribution was improper. In any case, the shareholder's liability is limited to his pro rata share of the claim and cannot exceed the amount that the shareholder received at liquidation. [MBCA §§6.41(c), (d), (e); 14.06; 14.07]

H. SHAREHOLDERS' LIABILITIES

1. General Rule—No Fiduciary Duty
Generally, shareholders may act in their own personal interests and owe no fiduciary duty to the corporation or their fellow shareholders except as outlined above concerning shareholder liability for:

1) Unpaid stock;

2) A pierced corporate veil; and

3) Absence of de facto corporation when the shareholder knew that there was no incorporation.

2. Liability Pursuant to Shareholder Agreement
As discussed above, shareholders may enter into agreements that vest some or all of the right to manage the corporation in one or more shareholders. When such agreements exist, the shareholder(s) in whom the management power is vested have the liabilities that a director ordinarily would have with respect to that power. [MBCA §7.32(e)]

3. Close Corporations
Shareholders in a close corporation (*i.e.,* a corporation owned by a few persons) owe each other the same duty of loyalty and utmost good faith that is owed by partners to each other. [Donahue v. Rodd Electrotype Co., 328 N.E.2d 505 (Mass. 1975)] Whether acting as shareholders or directors, the controlling shareholders may not pursue *any* corporate policy that will harm a minority shareholder when a less harmful alternative is available. This principle even applies to minority shareholders if they are in a position to control corporate actions. [Smith v. Atlantic Properties, Inc., 13 Mass. App. Ct. 9 (1981)]

a. Limitations on Sale of Control
A controlling shareholder or controlling shareholder group is under certain fiduciary limitations when selling control of a corporation to a new control group.

1) Sale of Offices Alone Forbidden
A controlling shareholder group may not sell seats on the board of directors. Control of the board may be purchased only by a group that purchases a stock interest sufficient to elect a majority of the board.

2) Looters
Controlling shareholders who sell the controlling interest to individuals who subsequently loot the company to the detriment of the minority shareholders will be liable for damages, unless reasonable measures were taken to investigate the character and reputation of the buyers.

VI. DIRECTORS

A. GENERAL POWERS
Unless the articles or a shareholder agreement provides otherwise, the board of directors of the corporation has general responsibility for the management of the business and the affairs of the corporation. [MBCA §8.01]

B. QUALIFICATIONS
The articles of organization or bylaws may prescribe qualifications for directors. A director need not be a resident of the state or a shareholder of the corporation unless so required by the articles or bylaws. [MBCA §8.02]

C. NUMBER, ELECTION, AND TERMS OF OFFICE

1. **Number of Directors**
   The board of directors may consist of one or more individuals, as the articles or bylaws provide. However, a Massachusetts corporation must have at least three directors if there are three or more shareholders and two directors if there are two shareholders. In lieu of a set number of directors, the articles or bylaws may provide a variable range for the size of the board by fixing a minimum and maximum number of directors. If a variable range is established, the number may be fixed or changed from time to time, within the specified minimum and maximum, by the shareholders or the board. [MBCA §8.03]

2. **Election of Directors**
   The directors are elected at the first annual meeting of the shareholders, and at each annual meeting thereafter unless the directors' terms are staggered. [MBCA §8.03(d)]

3. **Terms of Directors**
   Directors' terms expire at the annual shareholders' meeting following their election, except for directors with staggered terms. [MBCA §8.05(a), (b)] Even if a director's term expires, she remains in office until her successor is elected and qualifies. [MBCA §8.05(e)]

   a. **Staggering Director Terms**
      In nonpublic corporations (*i.e.*, corporations whose shares are not registered under federal securities laws), the articles may divide the directors into two or three groups (as close to equal in size as is possible) to serve staggered two- or three-year terms. Thus, only one-half or one-third of the board is elected each year. Such staggering of terms ensures some continuity in the board, but it also lessens the effect of cumulative voting because fewer directors are elected at each annual meeting. Publicly held corporations are *required* to stagger directors into three groups. [MBCA §8.06]

4. **Resignation of Director**
   A director may resign at any time by delivering written notice to the board, its chairperson, or the corporation. The resignation takes effect when notice is delivered, unless the notice specifies a later effective date or event. [MBCA §8.07]

5. **Vacancies May Be Filled by Directors or Shareholders**
   Absent a contrary provision in the articles, a vacancy on the board may be filled by either the shareholders or the board. If the directors remaining in office constitute fewer than a quorum, they may fill the vacancy by the affirmative vote of a majority of all the directors remaining in office. [MBCA §8.10(a)]

   a. **Where Director Elected by Voting Group**
      If the vacant office was held by a director elected by a voting group of shareholders, only holders of shares of that voting group, or the remaining directors elected by that group, may vote to fill the vacancy if it is filled by shareholders. [MBCA §8.10(b)]

D. **REMOVAL OF DIRECTORS**
   Directors may be removed *with or without cause* by the shareholders, unless the articles provide that removal may be only for cause. [MBCA §8.08]

1. **Cumulative Voting Limitation**
   If less than the entire board is to be removed, a director elected by cumulative voting may not be removed if the votes cast against her removal would have been sufficient to elect her if cumulatively voted at an election of the board.

2. **Where Director Elected by Voting Group**
   If a director is elected by a voting group of shareholders, only shareholders of that group may vote to remove the director.

3. **Removal by Directors**
   A director may also be removed by a majority vote of the other directors—but *only for cause*; and if the director was elected by a voting group, only the directors elected by that voting group may participate in the vote to remove the director.

E. **DIRECTORS' MEETING**
   The board may hold regular or special meetings either within or outside the state. Unless otherwise provided in the articles or bylaws, the board may permit any or all directors to participate in a regular or special meeting by, or conduct the meeting through, the use of any means of communication by which *all directors participating may simultaneously hear each other* (*e.g.*, a conference call). [MBCA §8.20]

1. **Notice of Meetings**
   Regular board meetings may be held *without notice*. Special meetings require at least *two days' notice* of the date, time, and place of the meeting, but a purpose need not be included in the notice. [MBCA §8.22]

   a. **Notice May Be Waived**
      A director may waive notice by a signed writing, filed with the minutes or corporate records. Attendance at or participation in a meeting waives notice unless the director, at the beginning of the meeting or promptly on her arrival, objects to holding the meeting or transacting business at the meeting, and does not thereafter vote for or assent to action taken at the meeting. [MBCA §8.23]

2. **Quorum**
   A majority of the board of directors constitutes a quorum for the meeting unless a higher or lower number is required by the articles of incorporation or the bylaws, but a quorum may be *no fewer than one-third* of any fixed number of directors provided for in the articles. [MBCA §8.24]

   a. **Breaking Quorum**
      A quorum must be present *at the time the vote is taken* for the vote to constitute valid action. Thus, even if a quorum is present at the beginning of a meeting, a group of minority directors may break quorum by leaving a meeting before a vote is taken. This is not true of shareholders at shareholders' meetings. Once a shareholder is present for a shareholders' meeting, he is deemed present even if he leaves.

3. **Approval of Action**
   If a quorum is present, resolutions will be deemed approved if approved by a *majority of directors present* unless the articles or bylaws require the vote of a greater number. [MBCA §8.24(c)]

   a. **Right to Dissent**
      A director who is present at a board meeting when corporate action is taken is deemed to have assented to the action taken unless:

      (i) *The director objects at the beginning of the meeting*, or promptly on her arrival, to holding it or transacting business at the meeting;

      (ii) *The director's dissent or abstention* from the action taken is *entered in the minutes* of the meeting; *or*

      (iii) *The director delivers written notice* of her dissent or abstention to the presiding officer of the meeting before its adjournment or immediately thereafter.

      [MBCA §8.24(d)]

   b. **Action May Be Taken Without Meeting by Unanimous Written Consent**
      Action required or permitted to be taken at a directors' meeting may be taken without a meeting if the action is taken by *all directors*. Each director must sign a *written consent*, or send such consent electronically, that describes the action taken. [MBCA §8.21]

F. **MAY DELEGATE AUTHORITY TO COMMITTEES OR OFFICERS**
   The board of directors is not expected to participate in the daily business affairs of the corporation. Rather, they usually delegate management functions for daily business affairs to executive committees or to officers.

1. **Executive Committees**
   The board may create one or more committees, each made up of *one or more members* of the board. [MBCA §8.25]

   a. **Selection**
      Creation of a committee and appointment of its members must be approved by the greater of (i) a majority of all directors in office when the action is taken or (ii) the number of directors required to take action under the articles or bylaws. [MBCA §8.25(b)]

    b. **Powers**
    Subject to the following limitations, each committee may exercise the authority granted to it by the board. However, a committee may *not* do any of the following:

    (i)   Authorize *distributions*;

    (ii) Approve or *submit to shareholders* any action that requires shareholder approval;

    (iii) *Change the size of the board*, remove directors, or fill vacancies on the board;

    (iv) *Amend articles* of organization;

    (v) *Adopt, amend, or repeal bylaws*; or

    (vi) *Authorize reacquisition of shares*, except according to a formula or method prescribed by the board.

    [MBCA §8.25(d), (e)]

2. **Officers**
The officers have whatever duties the board prescribes. The board remains responsible for supervision of the officers despite the delegation of duty.

G. **DIRECTORS' RIGHT TO INSPECT**
Directors have a right to inspect corporate books. [MBCA §16.05]

H. **DIRECTORS' DUTIES AND LIABILITIES**
The directors' management duties are typical fiduciary duties, including the duty of due care, the duty of loyalty, and the duty to protect the interests of the other intracorporate parties.

1. **Personal Liability of Directors May Be Limited**
The articles of organization can limit or eliminate directors' personal liability for money damages to the corporation or shareholders for action taken, or failure to take action, as a director. However, no provision can limit or eliminate liability for (i) any breach of the director's duty of loyalty to the corporation or its shareholders; (ii) any acts or omissions not in good faith or that involve intentional misconduct or knowing violation of the law; (iii) improper distributions; or (iv) any transaction from which the director derived an improper personal benefit. [MBCA §2.02(b)(4)]

2. **Duty of Care**
Directors are vested with the duty to manage the corporation to the best of their ability; they are not insurers of corporate success, but rather are merely required to discharge their duties:

    (i)   In *good faith*;

    (ii) *With the care that an ordinarily prudent person in a like position* would exercise under similar circumstances; and

    (iii) In a manner the directors *reasonably believe to be in the best interests of the corporation* (the director may consider interests of employees, suppliers, customers, and society when making this determination).

[MBCA §8.30(a)] Directors who meet this standard of conduct will not be liable for corporate decisions that, in hindsight, turn out to be poor or erroneous. At common law, this was known as the *"business judgment rule."*

    a. **Director May Rely on Reports or Other Information**
    In discharging her duties, a director is entitled to rely on information, opinions, reports, or statements (including financial statements), if prepared or presented by any of the following:

    (i)   *Corporate officers or employees* whom the director reasonably believes to be reliable and competent;

(ii) *Legal counsel, accountants, or other persons* as to matters the director reasonably believes are within such person's professional competence; or

(iii) A *committee* of the board of which the director is not a member, if the director reasonably believes the committee merits confidence.

[MBCA §8.30(b)]

b. Doctrine of Waste
As part of their duty of care, directors have a duty not to waste corporate assets by overpaying for property or employment services (*e.g.,* by paying someone an amount substantially above market value for services or property).

c. Typical Violations of Duty of Care

1) Irrational Decisions
Directors violate their duty of care by grossly negligent decisions, such as failing to buy fire insurance or hiring an embezzler to be a bank teller. Such decisions are "irrational" in the sense that there is no plausible business justification for them.

2) Failure to Know Facts
Directors may violate their duty of care when they fail to take reasonable steps to learn facts they should have known; *e.g.,* a director who neither attends board meetings nor studies corporate records may be held liable if the corporate chief executive officers have been withdrawing corporate funds for personal use.

3) Failure to Heed Warnings
Directors are not omniscient and are not expected to know every decision made by every executive in the corporation, but they may be held liable if they are put on notice that something is wrong in the corporation and they take no steps to investigate or correct the wrong.
Example: After he has been hired, it is discovered that a new bank teller has been convicted of embezzlement. If the directors do nothing and the bank teller later embezzles some of the bank's money, the directors may be held liable.

4) Failure to Supervise
Directors may not only be liable for negligent decisions they personally make, but also may be liable for negligent decisions made by officers that they reasonably should have supervised. The *pivotal fact* in a failure to supervise case often is the *size of the corporation*. In a small corporation, directors are expected to know more about the day-to-day decisions of managing executives than they would in a giant corporation. Thus, if a corporation had only one executive and he was engaged in criminal price-fixing, the board might be liable for a violation of the duty of care for failure to learn about and stop this practice. In a large corporation with 1,600 executives, if one low-level executive was fixing prices, the board probably would not be liable unless it actually knew that the subordinate executive was fixing prices.

3. Duty of Loyalty (Common Law)
A director owes a duty of loyalty to her corporation and will not be permitted to profit at the expense of the corporation. The problems in this area involve the director's dealings with the corporation and her potential conflict of interest; her dealings with third parties and her usurpation of a corporate opportunity; and her dealings with shareholders, which may raise insider trading issues.

a. Conflicting Interest Transactions
At common law in a number of states, if a corporation entered into a transaction in which a director had a personal interest (*e.g.,* where the director sells property to the corporation or hires his son as an officer), the transaction was considered automatically voidable at the option of the corporation. That common law rule has been changed by statute or case law in virtually every state. Under the MBCA, a transaction is not voidable by the corporation *solely* because a director had a material personal interest in the transaction if any of the following is true:

(i)   The transaction was approved by a *majority* (but at least two) *of all of the directors* (not just those present at the meeting) *without a conflicting interest* after all material facts have been disclosed to the board;

(ii) The transaction was approved by *a majority of all of the votes entitled to be cast* (not just those represented at the meeting) *by shareholders without a conflicting interest* in the transaction after all material facts have been disclosed to the shareholders (notice of the meeting must describe the conflicting interest transaction); or

(iii) The transaction, judged according to circumstances at the time of commitment, was *fair to the corporation*.

[MBCA §8.31] If a transaction is approved by a vote of the directors or shareholders after full disclosure, it is not automatically valid—the vote only means that the transaction is not automatically voidable. A person can still have the transaction set aside upon proving some ground for setting it aside (*e.g.,* waste). If disclosure was inadequate or proper approval was otherwise lacking, the transaction is subject to automatic voidability unless the interested director proves that the transaction was fair.

1) **Interested Director's Presence at Meeting Irrelevant**
    The presence of the interested director(s) at the meeting at which the directors or shareholders voted to approve the conflicting interest transaction does not affect the action. [MBCA §8.31(c)]

2) **Special Quorum Requirements**
    Because the director with a conflicting interest has no right to vote whether to approve the transaction, quorum requirements are changed for purposes of the vote on the transaction. *For purposes of a directors' meeting*, a majority of the directors without a conflicting interest, but not less than two, constitutes a quorum for purposes of the vote on the transaction. [MBCA §8.31(c)] *For purposes of a shareholders' meeting*, a quorum consists of a majority of the votes entitled to be cast, not including shares owned or controlled directly or beneficially by the director with the conflicting interest. [MBCA §8.31(d)]

3) **Factors to Be Considered in Determining Fairness**
    In determining whether a transaction is fair, courts traditionally look to factors such as adequacy of the consideration, corporate need to enter into the transaction, financial position of the corporation, and available alternatives.

4) **Remedies**
    Possible remedies for an improper conflicting interest transaction include enjoining the transaction, setting aside the transaction, damages, and similar remedies.

b. **Directors May Set Own Compensation**
    Despite the apparent conflict of interest, unless the articles or bylaws provide otherwise, the board may set director compensation. [MBCA §8.11] Of course, setting an unreasonable compensation will breach the directors' fiduciary duties.

c. **Corporate Opportunity Doctrine**
    A director's fiduciary duty of loyalty prohibits his personal diversion of a business opportunity in which the corporation may reasonably be interested without first giving the corporation an opportunity to act.

1) **Majority "Unfairness" Rule**
    Most states will hold that a director has diverted a corporate opportunity only when (i) the opportunity was in the same line of business as the corporation, (ii) the corporation had the financial resources to undertake it, and (iii) the opportunity was presented to an officer or director in his capacity as a corporate officer or director.

2) **Massachusetts "Unfairness" Rule**
    By contrast, Massachusetts employs the *less precise* standard of "unfairness." In Massachusetts, a director will be held to have misappropriated a corporate opportunity when a court of equity finds that the corporation justly called for protection. In the leading case, a director formed a new firm to sell a new type of oil rather than allowing the oil distribution corporation he served to sell the oil, arguing that

the corporation he directed lacked the financial resources to distribute the new oil. The court held for the plaintiff on the theory that under the circumstances of the case, the defendant-director's duty was to present the opportunity to his corporation. Only if the corporation formally declined the opportunity would the director have been free to pursue it himself. [Energy Resources Corp. v. Porter, 14 Mass. App. Ct. 296 (1982); BBF, Inc. v. Germanium Power Devices Corp., 385 Mass. 1103 (1982)]

3) Extent of Liability
A director who fails to give the corporation a chance to act and diverts the opportunity for his personal gain is liable to the corporation for any profits made, and the corporation may attach a constructive trust upon the opportunity.

4) Timing
When the director's opportunities existed prior to the director's involvement with the corporation, the director probably is free to exercise the opportunity despite the fact that it is a suitable opportunity for the corporation. [*See* Puritan Medical Center v. Cashman, 413 Mass. 167 (1992)]

d. Competing Business

1) While Directing a Corporation
A director may not engage in a business in direct competition with the corporation he directs. However, absent a contractual prohibition, a director may engage in an *unrelated* business.

2) After Resigning
A director may create or join a business in direct competition with the corporation he directed after completely dissociating himself from the corporation, if acting in good faith.

3) Covenants Not to Compete
Even after resigning, a director may not create or join a competitive firm if he has signed a covenant not to compete and the covenant is reasonable in its definition of the business, term, and geographic area.

4) Trade Secrets and Know-How
A director may never wrongfully appropriate a corporation's patents, copyrights, trade secrets, or legally protected confidences. However, after resigning, in the absence of a reasonable covenant not to compete, the director may employ skill or "know-how" learned at a former corporation for the advantage of a new firm.

VII. OFFICERS

A. IN GENERAL
In Massachusetts, a corporation *must* have a president, treasurer, and secretary. It may also have any other officers described in its bylaws or appointed by the board pursuant to the bylaws. An officer may appoint other officers or assistant officers if so authorized by the bylaws or the board. One person may simultaneously hold more than one office. [MBCA §8.40]

B. DUTIES
Officers' duties are determined by the bylaws or, to the extent consistent with the bylaws, by the board or an officer so authorized by the board. [MBCA §8.41]

C. POWERS
The officers are agents of the corporation and receive their power to manage from the directors. The ordinary rules of agency determine the authority and powers of the officers and agents. Authority may be actual or apparent. If authority exists, actions taken by an officer or agent (such as entering into contracts) bind the corporation.

1. Actual Authority
An officer's actual authority includes not only the authority expressly granted to the officer by the directors, the bylaws, the articles, and statutes, but also any authority that may be implied by the express grant.

a. **President**

In Massachusetts, the implied authority of a president is *extremely limited*. Usually, the president may not sign a contract with a third party in the absence of authorization from the board.

b. **Secretary**

The secretary usually has implied authority only to keep the corporate records.

c. **Treasurer**

The treasurer usually has implied authority to receive and keep corporate funds and to execute checks and promissory notes if the corporation is engaged in trading or manufacturing.

d. **Exception—Land Conveyance**

A recordable instrument purporting to affect an interest in real estate signed by the president or vice president *and* the treasurer is binding in favor of the purchaser and other persons relying on it in good faith, notwithstanding the fact that execution was not authorized by the board. [Dolan v. Airpark, Inc., 24 Mass. App. Ct. 714 (1987)]

2. **Apparent Authority**

When the corporation "holds out" an officer as possessing certain authority, thereby inducing others reasonably to believe that the authority exists, the officer has apparent authority to act and to bind the corporation even though actual authority to do so has not been granted. Apparent authority may be found when the officer once possessed actual authority to perform an act and the authority has been terminated without a third party's knowledge.

Example: Apparent authority would exist when a corporation gave an officer a written resolution to buy heating oil and verbally told her to buy up to $100,000 if the officer showed the resolution to an oil firm and bought $150,000 of oil. Apparent authority would also exist if the officer showed the oil firm the resolution and bought oil after the resolution had been rescinded.

3. **Ratification**

Unauthorized acts of officers may be ratified by express resolution of the board or shareholders or through the acquiescence or acceptance of the benefits, but only with *full knowledge of the facts*.

D. **STANDARD OF CONDUCT**

Officers' standard of conduct is similar to the standard for directors: If an officer has any discretionary authority with respect to any duties, the officer must carry out her duties *in good faith*, *with the care an ordinarily prudent person in a like position* would exercise under similar circumstances, and in a manner she *reasonably believes to be in the best interests of the corporation*. [MBCA §8.42(a)]

E. **RESIGNATION AND REMOVAL**

Despite any contractual term to the contrary, an officer has the power to resign at any time by delivering notice to the corporation, and the corporation has the power to remove an officer at any time, *with or without cause*. If the resignation or removal constitutes a breach of contract, the nonbreaching party's rights to damages are not affected by the resignation or removal, but note that mere appointment to office itself does not create any contractual right to remain in office. [MBCA §§8.43, 8.44]

VIII. INDEMNIFICATION OF DIRECTORS, OFFICERS, AND EMPLOYEES

A. **IN GENERAL**

If a person is made a party to a legal proceeding because of his status as a director, officer, employee, or agent of the corporation, depending on the circumstances, the corporation may be required to indemnify the person, may have discretion to indemnify the person, or may be prohibited from indemnifying the person.

B. **MANDATORY INDEMNIFICATION**

A corporation *must* indemnify a director or officer who *prevailed* (on the merits or otherwise) in defending the proceeding against him for reasonable expenses, including attorneys' fees incurred in connection with the proceeding. [MBCA §§8.52, 8.56(c)]

C. DISCRETIONARY INDEMNIFICATION
A corporation *may* indemnify a director for reasonable expenses incurred in *unsuccessfully defending* a suit brought against the director on account of the director's position if:

(i) The director acted in *good faith*; and

(ii) Believed that her conduct was:

     i. In the *best interests of the corporation* or at least *not opposed to the best interests of the corporation*; and

     ii. In the case of a criminal proceeding, *not unlawful*.

[MBCA §8.51(a)]

1. Exceptions
A corporation does not have discretion to indemnify a director who is unsuccessful in defending a suit: (i) for *breach of the director's duty of loyalty*; (ii) for *improper distributions;* or (iii) for any transaction from which the director derived an *improper personal benefit*. [*See* MBCA §§8.51(a)(2); 2.02(b)(4)]

2. Who Makes Determination?
Generally, the determination whether to indemnify is to be made by a disinterested majority of the board (if there are two or more disinterested directors) or a board committee, or by special legal counsel selected by disinterested board members. The shareholders may also make the determination (the shares of the director seeking indemnification are not counted). [MBCA §8.55(b)]

3. Officers
Officers generally may be indemnified to the same extent as a director. [MBCA §8.56]

D. COURT-ORDERED INDEMNIFICATION
A court may order indemnification whenever it is appropriate (*e.g.*, grounds for mandatory indemnification exist or, in view of all relevant circumstances, it is *fair and reasonable* to do so). [MBCA §8.54]

E. ADVANCES
A corporation may advance expenses to a director defending an action as long as the director furnishes the corporation with a statement that she believes she met the appropriate standard of conduct and that she will repay the advance if she is later found to have not met the appropriate standard. [MBCA §8.53]

F. LIABILITY INSURANCE
A corporation may purchase liability insurance to indemnify directors for actions against them even if the directors would not have been entitled to indemnification under the above standards. [MBCA §8.57]

G. AGENTS AND EMPLOYEES
The MBCA does not limit a corporation's power to indemnify, advance expenses to, or maintain insurance on an agent or employee. [MBCA §8.58(e)]

PART THREE—CHANGES IN STRUCTURE

IX. FUNDAMENTAL CHANGES IN CORPORATE STRUCTURE

A. INTRODUCTION
The MBCA permits corporations to undertake fundamental changes to their structure, but because it would be unfair to force a person to remain an owner of a fundamentally changed corporation, the Act provides special procedures that allow shareholders to vote whether to adopt a fundamental change, and in some cases provides dissenting shareholders a right to have the corporation purchase their shares after a fundamental change has been approved.

1. **Types of Fundamental Corporate Changes**
   The MBCA provides special procedures for the following corporate changes: most amendments of the articles, mergers, share exchanges, dispositions of substantially all property outside the usual and regular course of business, and dissolution.

2. **General Procedure for Fundamental Change**
   The basic procedure for adopting a fundamental corporate change is the same for all fundamental changes:

   a. *A majority of the board of directors adopts a resolution* recommending the fundamental change;

   b. *Notice* of the proposed change is sent to *all shareholders* (whether or not entitled to vote). The notice must (i) describe the change and inform the shareholders that a vote will be taken on the matter at a shareholders' meeting, and (ii) be given not less than seven or more than 60 days before the meeting;

   c. The change is *approved by two-thirds of all votes entitled to be cast and by two-thirds of any voting group entitled to vote as a group*; and

   d. The change is formalized in *articles* (*e.g.*, articles of amendment, articles of merger, etc.), which are *filed* with the state.

B. **AMENDMENTS OF THE ARTICLES OF ORGANIZATION**
   A corporation may amend its articles at any time to add or change a provision that is required or permitted, or to delete a provision that is not required. [MBCA §10.01]

   1. **Amendments Before Shares Are Issued**
      The board of directors (or the incorporators if the corporation does not yet have directors) may make any amendment to the articles before any shares are issued. [MBCA §10.05]

   2. **Amendments After Shares Are Issued**
      Once shares have been issued, amendment of the articles generally requires implementation of the general fundamental change procedure as discussed *supra* (*i.e.*, resolution of the board, notice to the shareholders, approval by the shareholders, and filing articles of amendment with the state). [MBCA §10.03] However, certain amendments can be made with the approval of only a majority of the shares (*e.g.*, a change in the corporation's name; a change in the authorized number of shares).

      a. **Class Vote**
         Classes of stock otherwise not entitled to vote must approve the articles' amendment by the requisite majority whenever their rights, privileges, or powers will be impaired or diminished; *e.g.*, eliminating dividend or liquidation rights of otherwise nonvoting preferred stock can only be done by a two-thirds vote of the nonvoting preferred stock as well as a two-thirds vote of the voting class (or classes) of stock. [MBCA §10.04]

C. **MERGER AND SHARE EXCHANGE**
   The MBCA provides that the basic procedure for fundamental corporate changes must be followed to approve a merger or share exchange. A merger involves the blending of one or more corporations into another corporation, and the latter corporation survives while the merging corporations cease to exist following the merger. A share exchange involves one corporation purchasing all of the outstanding shares of one or more classes or series of another corporation.

   1. **Not All Shareholders Need Approve**
      Mergers and share exchanges vary a little from the basic fundamental change procedure in that not all shareholders have a right to approve these procedures under all circumstances.

      a. **No Significant Change to Surviving Corporation**
         Approval by shareholders of the *surviving* corporation on a plan of merger, or purchasing corporation on a plan of share exchange, is *not* required if *all* the following conditions exist:

         (i) The articles of organization of the surviving corporation will *not differ* from the articles before the merger or share exchange;

    (ii) Each shareholder of the survivor whose shares were outstanding immediately prior to the effective date of the merger or share exchange will hold the *same number of shares*, with identical preferences, limitations, and rights; and

    (iii) The *voting power* of any class of shares issued as a result of the merger or share exchange will comprise more than *20%* of the voting power of the same class of shares of the surviving corporation that were outstanding immediately prior to the merger.

[MBCA §11.04(7)]

b.   Short Form Merger of Subsidiary
A parent corporation owning at least 90% of the outstanding shares of each class of a subsidiary corporation may merge the subsidiary into itself *without the approval of the shareholders or directors of the subsidiary*. [MBCA §11.05] This is known as a "short form merger." The parent must give the subsidiary's shareholders notice that the merger has become effective within 10 days after its effective date.

2.   Effect

a.   Merger
Where there is a merger, every other corporation that is a party to the merger merges into the surviving corporation, and the separate existence of every corporation except the survivor ends. All property owned by the separate entities, and all obligations of the separate entities, become the property and obligations of the surviving corporation. A proceeding pending against a party to the merger may continue as if the merger did not occur, or the surviving corporation may be substituted.

b.   Share Exchange
When a share exchange takes effect, the shares of each acquired corporation are exchanged as provided in the plan, and the former holders of the shares are entitled only to the exchange rights provided in the plan. The corporations remain separate.

3.   Freeze-Out Mergers
It is permissible for the surviving corporation in a merger to issue cash in exchange for the stock of a nonsurviving corporation. This provides an avenue for controlling shareholders to freeze out minority shareholders: The controlling shareholders arrange a merger into a corporation that they own. They receive stock in exchange for their shares, and give the minority shareholders money in exchange for their shares. The Supreme Judicial Court has held that a court can assess the fairness of such freeze-out mergers and has held such a merger unfair where the controlling shareholder/director precipitated the merger solely for his own personal benefit (to gain sole control of the corporation). [Coggins v. New England Patriots Football Club, Inc., 397 Mass. 525 (1986); *appeal after remand*, 406 Mass. 666 (1990)]

D.   DISPOSITION OF PROPERTY OUTSIDE THE USUAL AND REGULAR COURSE OF BUSINESS
A sale, lease, exchange, or other disposition of *all or substantially all* (*i.e.*, nearly all) of a corporation's property outside of the usual and regular course of business is a fundamental corporate change *for the corporation disposing of the property*. Thus, the corporation disposing of the property must follow the fundamental change procedure. [*See* MBCA §12.02] Note that the corporation *purchasing* the property is not undergoing a fundamental corporate change, and so approval from that corporation's shareholders is not required.

1.   Compare—Dispositions Within Usual and Regular Course of Business
A disposition of a corporation's property within the usual and regular course of business is not a fundamental change and need not be approved by the shareholders. [MBCA §12.01(a)(1)]

2.   Compare—Mortgages, Pledges, Etc.
The fundamental change procedure need not be followed to approve the grant of a mortgage, pledge, or similar security interest, even if the security interest is in all or substantially all of a corporation's assets, and even if the grant is not within the usual and regular course of the corporation's business. [MBCA §12.01(a)(2)]

3.   Effect on Purchaser
Generally, the purchaser of another corporation's property does not become liable for the

seller's obligations; the seller remains solely liable. However, if the disposition of property is really a disguised merger, a court might treat it as a merger under the de facto merger doctrine and hold the purchaser liable for the seller's obligations just as if a merger had occurred.

a. Factors Contributing to De Facto Merger
To determine if a de facto merger has occurred, the courts look to whether:

(i) There is a *continuation of the enterprise*;

(ii) There is a *continuation of shareholders*;

(iii) The seller corporation *quickly ceases to exist* as a legal entity; and

(iv) The purchasing corporation *assumes the obligations* of the seller that are necessary for the uninterrupted continuation of normal business.

[Cargill, Inc. v. Beaver Coal & Oil Co., 424 Mass. 356 (1997)]

E. DISSENTING SHAREHOLDERS' APPRAISAL REMEDY
Shareholders who are dissatisfied with the terms of a fundamental corporate change usually are permitted to compel the corporation to buy their shares at a fair value by following a special statutory procedure. In most cases, absent fraud, misrepresentation, or improper procedure, a shareholder entitled to appraisal rights may not challenge a completed corporate action for which appraisal rights are available (*i.e.*, the appraisal right generally is a shareholder's exclusive remedy for completed corporate action). [MBCA §13.02(d)]

Example: XYZ Corp., a major conglomerate, owns 95% of the stock of ABC, Inc. XYZ effects a short form merger with ABC and offers ABC's shareholders $100 per share. P, an ABC shareholder, believes the stock is worth $200 per share. May P seek to enjoin ABC from being merged into XYZ? *No.* P's dispute solely concerns the value of XYZ's offer. The only available remedy would be an appraisal.

Compare: 1) D, owner of 95% of the shares of BCD, Inc., causes BCD to sell all of its assets to PQR Corp., in return for cash equal to $100 per share. Also, D personally is hired by PQR to be a part-time consultant for five years at $100,000 per year. P, owner of the remaining 5% of BCD's shares, believes the assets have value equal to $200 per share. Must P demand an appraisal or could P seek an injunction to block the sale of the assets? P may allege that D fraudulently agreed to a low price for the assets in return for a personal "payoff" and may seek an injunction to prevent the sale of assets.

2) Controlling shareholders attempt to freeze out minority interests in the corporation by forcing a merger. Minority shareholders may seek an injunction to block the proposed merger.

1. Who May Dissent?

a. Merger
Generally, any shareholder *entitled to vote* on a plan of merger and *shareholders of the subsidiary* in a short form merger have the right to dissent. [MBCA §13.02(a)(1)]

b. Share Exchange
Generally, shareholders of the corporation whose shares are being *acquired* in a share exchange have the right to dissent. [MBCA §13.02(a)(2)]

c. Disposition of Property
A shareholder who is *entitled to vote* on a disposition of all or substantially all of the corporation's property outside the usual and regular course of business is entitled to dissent. This does not include a sale pursuant to court order, or a cash sale pursuant to a plan by which the net sale proceeds will be distributed to the shareholders within one year of the date of sale. [MBCA §13.02(a)(3)]

d. Amendment of Articles
A shareholder has a right to dissent from an amendment of the articles that *materially and adversely affects the shareholder's rights* (*e.g.*, changes preferential redemption

or preemptive rights, limits voting rights, or reduces the shareholder's shares to fractional shares to be purchased by the corporation). [MBCA §13.02(a)(4)]

2. Procedure

a. Corporation Must Give Shareholders Notice

If a proposed corporate action will create dissenters' rights, the notice of the shareholders' meeting at which a vote on the action will be taken must state that the shareholders will be entitled to exercise their dissenting rights. [MBCA §13.20(a)] If the action may be taken without a vote of the shareholders (*e.g.*, in a short form merger), they must be given notice within 10 days after the action was taken and of their right to dissent. [MBCA §13.20(b)]

b. Shareholder Must Give Notice of Intent to Demand Payment

If the shareholder will be entitled to vote and wishes to exercise her dissenting rights, she must, *before a vote is taken*, deliver *written notice of her intent to demand payment* for her shares if the proposed action is taken. Also, she cannot vote in favor of the proposed action. Failure to satisfy these requirements means that the shareholder is not entitled to payment for her shares. [MBCA §13.21]

c. Corporation Must Give Dissenters Notice

If the proposed action is approved at the shareholders' meeting, the corporation *must notify, within 10 days* after the vote, all shareholders who filed an intent to demand payment. The notice must tell the shareholders when and where they must submit their shares and state the other terms of the repurchase. The corporation cannot set the time for receiving the payment demands less than 40 or more than 60 days after the date the corporation's notice is delivered. [MBCA §13.22]

d. Shareholders Must Demand Payment

A shareholder who is sent a dissenter's notice must then *demand payment* in accordance with the notice given by the corporation. [MBCA §13.23]

e. Corporation Must Pay

When the proposed action is taken, the corporation must pay the dissenters the *amount the corporation estimates as the fair value* of the shares, plus accrued interest. Along with the payment, the corporation must send the corporation's balance sheet and income statement, and a statement that the shareholder has a right to demand further payment if she is dissatisfied with the corporation's payment. [MBCA §13.24]

f. Notice of Dissatisfaction

If the shareholder is dissatisfied with the corporation's determination of value, the shareholder has 30 days in which to send the corporation her *own estimate of value* and demand payment of the difference between her estimate and the amount sent by the corporation. [MBCA §13.26]

g. Court Action

If the corporation does not want to pay what the shareholder demanded, *the corporation* must file an action in court within 60 days after receiving the shareholder's demand, requesting the court to determine the fair value of the shares. If the corporation fails to file suit within 60 days, it will be required to pay the shareholder the amount the shareholder demanded. [MBCA §13.30]

X. DISSOLUTION AND LIQUIDATION

A. INTRODUCTION

Dissolution is the termination of the corporate existence. To dissolve the corporation, some act must be taken, which may be voluntary by the corporation or its aggregate members, or may be involuntary through judicial proceedings.

B. VOLUNTARY DISSOLUTION

Dissolution by corporate action without judicial proceedings is termed voluntary dissolution and may be accomplished in the following ways:

1. **Dissolution by Incorporators or Initial Directors**
   A majority of the incorporators or initial directors may dissolve the corporation if *shares have not yet been issued or business has not yet been commenced* by delivering articles of dissolution to the secretary of state. All corporate debts must be paid before dissolution, and if shares have been issued, any assets remaining after winding up must be distributed to the shareholders. [MBCA §14.01]

2. **Dissolution by Corporate Act**
   The corporation may dissolve voluntarily by an act of the corporation, involving both board of directors and shareholder approval. The standard procedure for *fundamental corporate change* is followed. [MBCA §14.02]

3. **Effect of Dissolution**
   A corporation that has been dissolved continues its corporate existence, but is not allowed to carry on any business except that which is appropriate to *wind up and liquidate its affairs*. Permissible activities include collection of assets, disposal of property that will not be distributed in kind to shareholders, discharging liabilities, and distributing remaining property among shareholders according to their interests. Dissolution does not transfer title to the corporation's property, change quorum or voting requirements, suspend proceedings pending against or by the corporation, or prevent commencement of a proceeding by or against the corporation. [MBCA §14.05]

   a. **Director and Shareholder Liability**
      In Massachusetts, corporations are prohibited from distributing their assets to shareholders in liquidation unless adequate provision has been made to satisfy the corporation's reasonably foreseeable obligations to both known and unknown creditors (*e.g.*, setting aside adequate reserves or purchasing insurance for possible claims [*see* MBCA §14.08]). A director who authorizes a liquidating distribution in violation of this rule can be held personally liable for the amount improperly distributed. Moreover, a shareholder who receives a liquidating distribution made within three years of dissolution may be required to return it to a creditor whose claim cannot be satisfied by the corporation, to the extent of the shareholder's pro rata share of the claim. [MBCA §§6.40(h), 6.41(d), (f)]

4. **Revocation of Voluntary Dissolution**
   A corporation may revoke a voluntary dissolution within 120 days of its effective date by using the same procedure that was used to approve the dissolution. The revocation relates back to and takes effect as of the effective date of the dissolution, so that the corporation may resume carrying on its business as if there had never been a dissolution. [MBCA §14.04]

C. ADMINISTRATIVE DISSOLUTION

1. **Grounds for Administrative Dissolution**
   The secretary of state may bring an action to administratively dissolve a corporation: (i) for failure to file required reports or to file or pay taxes for two consecutive years; or (ii) if satisfied that the corporation has become inactive or that dissolution would otherwise be in the public interest. [MBCA §14.20]

2. **Procedure and Effect**
   If grounds for dissolution exist as set forth above, the secretary of state must serve the corporation with written notice. If the corporation does not correct the grounds for dissolution or show that the grounds do not exist within *90* days after service of notice, the state effectuates the dissolution by signing a certificate of dissolution. [MBCA §14.21]

3. **Reinstatement May Be Retroactive**
   A corporation that is administratively dissolved may apply for reinstatement *at any time*. The application must state that the grounds for dissolution did not exist or that they have been eliminated. *Reinstatement relates back* to the date of dissolution but is subject to such terms and conditions as the secretary of state directs. [MBCA §14.22]

D. JUDICIAL DISSOLUTION

1. **Action by Attorney General**
   The attorney general may seek judicial dissolution of a corporation on the ground that the

corporation *fraudulently obtained its articles* of organization or that the corporation is *exceeding or abusing its authority*. [MBCA §14.30(1)]

2. **Action by Shareholders**
   Shareholders holding at least 40% of all voting power may seek judicial dissolution on any of the following grounds:

   (i)   The *directors are deadlocked* in the management of corporate affairs, the shareholders are unable to break the deadlock, and *irreparable injury* to the corporation is threatened, or corporate affairs cannot be conducted to the advantage of the shareholders because of the deadlock; or

   (ii) The *shareholders are deadlocked* in voting power and have *failed to elect one or more directors* for a period that includes at least two consecutive annual meeting dates, and irreparable injury to the corporation is threatened or being suffered.

   [MBCA §14.30(2)]

3. **Action by Creditors**
   Creditors may seek judicial dissolution if: (i) the creditor's claim has been reduced to judgment, execution of the judgment has been returned unsatisfied, and *the corporation is insolvent*; or (ii) the corporation has admitted in writing that the creditor's claim is due and owing and *the corporation is insolvent*. [MBCA §14.30(3)]

4. **Action by Corporation—Court Supervision of Voluntary Dissolution**
   A court may dissolve a corporation in an action by the corporation to have its voluntary dissolution continued under court supervision. [MBCA §14.30(4)]

BAR REVIEW

Domestic Relations

celebrating over
35 YEARS
*of preparing
law students
for the bar exam*

DOMESTIC RELATIONS—MASSACHUSETTS

TABLE OF CONTENTS

I. BEFORE MARRIAGE—CLAIMS AND ACTIONS

A. "HEART BALM" ACTIONS ABOLISHED

1. Breach of Promise to Marry; Deceit
Massachusetts has abolished actions for breach of contract to marry and actions in tort for deceit when connected with a breach of promise to marry. Moreover, the Commonwealth will not enforce such causes of action accruing in other jurisdictions. [Mass. Gen. L. ch. 207, §47A]

2. Third-Party Actions Abolished
Third-party actions, such as alienation of affection or criminal conversation, have also been abolished.

3. Recovery of Gifts
An action is available to recover a gift (typically, an engagement ring) made in "consideration" of marriage if the marriage did not occur by reason of the mutual consent of the parties or by the action of the donee. However, a suit to recover a gift cannot be maintained if the donor is the one responsible for the marriage not taking place or if the gift was made under circumstances indicating an unconditional gift (*e.g.*, Christmas or birthday present).

B. ANTENUPTIAL CONTRACTS
Premarital contracts between prospective spouses, other than contracts to marry, are termed "antenuptial" contracts and typically pertain to *property.* Written antenuptial agreements that vary the rights at law in the estates of prospective spouses are valid and enforceable in Massachusetts. [Mass. Gen. L. ch. 209, §§25, 26]

1. Requisites of Validity

    a. Absence of Duress and Fraud
    To be enforceable, an antenuptial contract must have been freely made. Both parties to the agreement have the duty to fully disclose their total assets to each other, so that there will be no fraud, deceit, or overreaching. The agreement must be "fair and reasonable" at the time of its execution. [Upham v. Upham, 36 Mass. App. Ct. 295 (1994)]

    b. Preservation of Certain Marital Obligations
    The contract may neither "alter or dissolve" the marriage, nor relieve the parties of their respective support obligations to minor children.

    c. Statute of Frauds
    The contract will be unenforceable unless it is in writing and subscribed by the party to be charged.

    d. Consideration
    The *impending marriage* is sufficient consideration for an antenuptial agreement.

    e. Fair and Reasonable at the Time of Divorce
    An antenuptial agreement will be enforced only if the agreement is also fair and reasonable at the time of entry of the judgment nisi. It may be modified in certain situations, such as where one spouse is or will become a public charge or where a provision affecting the right to custody is not in the best interests of the child. [Osborne v. Osborne, 384 Mass. 591 (1981); Upham v. Upham, *supra*]

2. Effect
If the marriage does not take place, the parties to an antenuptial agreement are discharged. Once the marriage takes place, the antenuptial agreement survives. Note that an otherwise valid antenuptial agreement survives a subsequent annulment.

II. GETTING MARRIED

A. WHO MAY MARRY

1. Sufficient Mental Capacity
To marry, a person must be capable of giving the consent needed to enter into such a contract. If a person understands: (i) the nature of his acts; (ii) the significance of marriage; and

(iii) the duties and responsibilities imposed by marriage, then such a person is deemed to be of sufficient mental capacity to marry. [Mass. Gen. L. ch. 207, §5]

a. Consent Required
The consent of the parties capable in law of making a contract is essential to a valid marriage. Lack of such consent, if objected to in direct (not collateral) proceedings during the lifetime of both parties, vitiates the marriage.

b. Conservator to Manage Property Not Conclusive as to Capacity to Marry
A party may have a conservator because of inability to manage his property yet have sufficient capacity to marry.

2. Sufficient Age
The clerk or registrar will not receive a notice of intention of marriage of a person under age 18 except when the appropriate court, after a hearing, issues an order allowing the marriage of such person. Parents or the guardian must consent to such order, unless the parent has deserted her family or is otherwise unfit. Absent the requisite court order, a magistrate or minister will not solemnize a marriage if he has reasonable cause to believe that a party to the intended marriage is under age 18. [Mass. Gen. L. ch. 207, §§24, 25]

3. Lack of Incestuous Relationship (Consanguinity or Affinity)
Marriages between persons "too closely" related by blood (consanguinity) or marriage (affinity) are prohibited. [Mass. Gen. L. ch. 207, §§1-3] (*See* IV.A.2.b., *infra*.)

4. No Prior Marriage in Effect (Bigamy)
A person who is already married may not enter into another valid marriage unless: (i) the first marriage has been terminated by a valid divorce or by death of the former spouse; or (ii) the former spouse has been missing, without indication of being alive, for seven years.

5. Same-Sex Couples
Same-sex couples can marry in Massachusetts. In Massachusetts, a civil marriage is construed as the voluntary union of two persons as spouses, to the exclusion of all others.

B. PROCEDURAL REQUIREMENTS

1. License
Massachusetts requires persons intending to marry to obtain a license. [Mass. Gen. L. ch. 207, §§28-37] To obtain a license, persons must file a notice of intention to marry with the town clerk or registrar, who will request documentary proof of several requirements, including age, parental consent (or court order, if necessary), and blood test results for syphilis and rubella. Note that if blood test results indicate the presence of the AIDS antibody or antigen, the results are governed by statutory confidentiality requirements. [Mass. Gen. L. ch. 111, §70F] If the clerk or registrar finds the requirements have been met, she delivers the license to the parties, on or after the third day from the filing of notice of intention of marriage, but not later than 60 days after such filing.

a. Scope of Clerk's Authority
The clerk's duty is partly mandatory and partly discretionary. Before issuing the license, the clerk may ask questions about the parties' capacity and may require substantiation of answers.

b. License Is Mandatory
The license requirement is mandatory, although, in exigent circumstances, a certificate may be granted by the probate or district court stating that it is expedient that the intended marriage be solemnized without delay. Also, a license must issue at once upon the request of a minister or attending physician on the ground that either party's death is imminent.

2. Ceremony
A marriage must be solemnized by a ceremony performed by a judicial officer or a member of the clergy (*see* d., below).

a. Time
The ceremony must occur not more than 60 days after filing notice of intention to marry.

b. Notice
No fewer than three days before the ceremony, the parties must file a notice of marriage with the clerk or registrar.

      c.   **Form**
          If the marriage is performed by clergy or a magistrate, no particular form of ceremony is ordinarily required. No form of words is necessary, as long as the words employed are sufficient to complete the contract of marriage.

      d.   **Officiant**
          A civil ceremony is as binding as a religious ceremony. Solemnization may be by a minister of the gospel, justice of the peace, meeting of Quakers, a leader of a duly authorized ethical society, or the Imam of the Orthodox Islamic religion. Catholic, Jewish, and Protestant ceremonies are recognized.

      e.   **Irregularities**
          Lack of authority in the officiant or irregularity in the license will not render the marriage invalid if it is consummated with the belief of *either party* that the marriage is legal. [Mass. Gen. L. ch. 207, §42]

C.   COMMON LAW MARRIAGE
Common law marriages cannot be contracted in Massachusetts. The only common law marriages recognized in Massachusetts are those validly contracted elsewhere by the parties, who then reside in Massachusetts. The elements of a common law marriage in those jurisdictions that permit them are as follows:

1.   The parties *agree* to become husband and wife immediately;

2.   The parties to a common law marriage *contemplate a permanent marital relationship* to the exclusion of all others;

3.   The purported marriage must be *open and notorious*; and

4.   The parties *cohabit* as husband and wife.

D.   PROXY AND CONTRACTUAL MARRIAGES—NOT VALID IN MASSACHUSETTS
One cannot marry by proxy or purely by contract (*i.e.*, no license and ceremony) in Massachusetts.

E.   RECOGNITION OF FOREIGN MARRIAGES
Massachusetts will not recognize a marriage when the state of the parties' residence (and where they intend to continue to reside, *i.e.*, their domicile) would consider the marriage void if contracted in the state of domicile. Thus, Massachusetts residents marrying in another state to avoid the laws of Massachusetts are not considered married when they return to Massachusetts. [Mass. Gen. L. ch. 207, §10]

III.   BEING MARRIED

A.   MARRIAGE IN GENERAL
Marriage is the creation of the status of husband and wife. Once this legal status has been formed, the law imposes various obligations and liabilities upon the parties.

B.   CAPACITY OF SPOUSES

   1.   **Removal of Traditional Disabilities on Wife**
      Each spouse is treated as an individual under the law, with individual capacity to own and sell property, to contract, to sue and defend, and to commit torts, without dependence on or imputation to the other spouse.

   2.   **Interspousal Immunity**
      Spouses may sue each other in connection with contracts. [Mass. Gen. L. ch. 209, §2] Moreover, Massachusetts case law has effectively abolished tort immunity between spouses.

   3.   **Business Certificate for Married Woman—Requirement Abolished**
      A married woman formerly had to file a business certificate to show that she was engaging in business on her own account; failure to comply with this requirement gave her spouse's creditors the right to seize assets of the business and made her spouse liable for her debts. This requirement has been abolished. [Mass. Gen. L. ch. 209, §9]

C. SUITS AGAINST THIRD PARTIES

1. Alienation of Affection—Abolished in Massachusetts
Alienation of affection is the action of a third party that results in the loss of love and affection of one spouse for the other. This cause of action was abolished by the legislature in 1985.

2. Criminal Conversation—Abolished in Massachusetts
Criminal conversation is the action of a third party causing the loss to one spouse of the *exclusive* right of sexual intercourse with the other spouse. Lack of knowledge by the third party that the spouse was married is no defense. The only requirement is the intercourse with the spouse; loss of consortium is presumed. This cause of action was abolished by the legislature in 1985.

D. SUPPORT OBLIGATIONS
Each spouse owes the other a duty of support.

1. Breach of Support Obligation
A spouse who is not being supported may seek support in district court. [Mass. Gen. L. ch. 273, §2] The support order may include provision for necessary shelter, food, clothing, care, medical attention, expense of confinement, expenses for educating a minor, funeral expenses, and other "proper and reasonable expenses." The order may be enforced by contempt proceedings, which require notice and a hearing. Note that *fault* or misconduct on the part of the spouse may influence the courts in deciding whether to enforce the right to support.

2. Joint Liability for Necessaries
Spouses are jointly and severally liable for debts incurred for necessaries by the other spouse or by their children. [Mass. Gen. L. ch. 209, §1]

3. Desertion
Criminal liability may be imposed on any spouse or parent who, without just cause, deserts his spouse or minor child without making reasonable provision for that spouse's or child's support. [Mass. Gen. L. ch. 273, §1]

4. Neglect
Also subject to liability is any spouse or parent who unreasonably neglects or refuses to provide for the support and maintenance of his spouse or minor child, and any spouse or parent who abandons or leaves his spouse or minor child in danger of becoming a burden upon the public.

E. WIFE'S DOMICILE

1. Voting and Office-Holding
For purposes of voting and holding office, Massachusetts law establishes the domicile of a married woman in Massachusetts by reference to the same rules and types of fact as would establish the domicile of any other class of person.

2. As Plaintiff in Matrimonial Action
If a wife commences a matrimonial action while living in Massachusetts, the fact that her husband lives elsewhere will not prevent her from being deemed a Massachusetts domiciliary.

F. WIFE'S NAME

1. Adoption of Husband's Name Optional
If a married woman takes her husband's name in Massachusetts, she does so as a matter of custom; she is not required to do so as a matter of law.

2. Procedures for Change of Name
If the wife takes her husband's name and subsequently seeks to change it, two procedures are available.

a. Custom and Usage
A name change may be effected by usage and habit, provided that there is no fraud, misrepresentation, or interference with the rights of others.

b.   Judicial
The name may be changed by court order in a divorce proceeding or other action in accordance with statutory law. [Mass. Gen. L. ch. 210, §§12-14]

G.   MASSACHUSETTS EQUAL RIGHTS AMENDMENT
Not all statutes that make different provisions for husband and wife have been challenged under the Equal Rights Amendment. Bear in mind the possible impact of the amendment in answering bar exam questions.

IV.   TERMINATION OF MARRIAGE

A.   ANNULMENT
An annulment is a declaration that a marriage is invalid; *i.e.,* that due to an impediment at the time of the marriage, no marriage ever occurred. Thus, a decree of annulment generally treats the parties as if they had never been married. Two types of marriage are subject to annulment: void marriages and voidable marriages.

1.   Void/Voidable Distinction

a.   Void Marriage
A void marriage is one that never existed for any purpose; it is a complete nullity. Generally, parties may walk away from void marriages without court order; the reason for bringing an annulment action in this situation is usually to have the court determine property distribution and child custody. Any interested party may seek annulment of a void marriage, and the marriage is subject to collateral attack (*i.e.,* in actions other than for annulment, such as probate actions) even after the death of one of the parties.

b.   Voidable Marriage
If a marriage is voidable, *one of the spouses* may bring an action to have the marriage declared invalid because of an impediment existing at the time of the marriage. This type of marriage cannot be attacked collaterally or by third parties. A voidable marriage is deemed valid unless one spouse seeks to have it annulled. If the spouse with the cause of action *ratifies* the marriage by continuing the relationship, or if one spouse dies, the marriage can no longer be invalidated.

2.   Grounds for Void Marriage

a.   Bigamy or Polygamy
If either party to the marriage has another living spouse (*i.e.,* a prior marriage not terminated by death or divorce, and spouse not missing for seven years), the marriage is void. [Mass. Gen. L. ch. 207, §8] A bigamous marriage *may become valid if and only if all three* of the following elements are present:

(i)   *Good faith on spouse's part as to lack of impediment* (*i.e.,* at the time of the second marriage, one of the parties believed that the "former" spouse was dead, the prior marriage was terminated by a valid divorce, or the prior parties were never validly married);

(ii)   *Cohabitation* (*i.e.,* after the second marriage, the parties lived together as husband and wife, and continued to do so after the impediment was removed); *and*

(iii)   *Good faith on spouse's part as to marriage* (*i.e.,* one of the parties believed the second marriage was valid at the time the impediment was removed).

[Mass. Gen. L. ch. 207, §§4, 6] Note that a divorce nisi judgment is not a dissolution of the marriage. As a result, if another marriage is contracted during the time between the judgment nisi and the judgment absolute, the new marriage is void. [Ross v. Ross, 385 Mass. 30 (1982)]

b.   Incest (Consanguinity or Affinity)
Marriages where the parties are too closely related are void. [Mass. Gen. L. ch. 207, §8]

1) **Relationships Rendering Marriage Void**
The parties' relationship must not be so close as to render the marriage incestuous by blood or affinity. In Massachusetts, marriages between a male and any female who bears one of the following relationships to him are deemed incestuous and therefore void:

(i) Consanguinity (blood)—Grandmother, mother, aunt, sister, niece, daughter, granddaughter; or

(ii) Affinity—Step-grandmother, stepmother, grandmother-in-law, mother-in-law, stepdaughter, step-granddaughter, granddaughter-in-law.

Likewise, a female is barred from marrying the male who bears the equivalent relationship to her by blood or affinity except that a woman may marry her father-in-law, but not her son-in-law.

2) **Incestuous Affinity Survives Dissolution of Marriage Creating It**
Once the affinity has been created it continues in effect even though the marriage by which the affinity was created is subsequently dissolved by death or divorce, unless the divorce is granted because the marriage was originally unlawful or void.

3) **Massachusetts Incest Law Applies to Valid Out-of-State Marriages**
Massachusetts does not recognize out-of-state marriages between siblings or between direct lineal descendants, even if valid where contracted.

c. **Nonage**
The marriage of a party under age 18 at the time of the marriage who married in violation of the statute (*i.e.,* without getting required parental and/or judicial consent) is void. Of course, the underage spouse, upon reaching the specified age, may ratify the marriage by continuing in the relationship.

3. Grounds for Voidable Marriage

a. **Lack of Mental Capacity**
A marriage may be annulled because a party was incapable of consenting to a marriage for lack of understanding due to mental infirmity or because of alcohol or drugs.

b. **Duress**
If either party entered the marriage as a result of duress, the marriage is voidable and subject to an annulment action by the aggrieved party. Duress is present when the party is acting out of fear of harmful consequences (often fear of physical violence against the party or those close to the party).

c. **Fraud**
In Massachusetts, the false allegation of facts that induce a person to enter into the marital relationship, or the concealment of facts which, if known, would prevent a person from entering into the marriage constitutes fraud, provided that it is the type of fraud that goes to the *essence* of the marriage contract. To establish fraud, the moving party must prove the tort elements of deceit (*i.e.,* that there has been a knowing misrepresentation of a material fact with the intention that the party rely on the fact and that the party has so relied to his detriment, with the marriage itself usually constituting the detriment). [Mass. Gen. L. ch. 207, §14]
Examples: 1) If one of the parties marries solely for marital status without intent to live together as husband and wife, the marriage may be voidable on grounds of fraudulent inducement.

2) Concealment of an advanced state of syphilis with no consummation of the marriage constitutes fraud sufficient to render a marriage voidable.

The Massachusetts courts allow a man to obtain an annulment on the ground that he was fraudulently induced to marry a woman who asserted that: (i) he was the father of her unborn child; or (ii) she was not pregnant, when in fact she was pregnant by another man. [Symonds v. Symonds, 385 Mass. 540 (1982)]

4. **Defenses**

   a. **Void Marriages—No Impediment**

   Void marriages are of no legal effect. The only way to defend an action to annul a void marriage is to deny the existence of the defect that allegedly caused the marriage to be void.

   b. **Voidable Marriage—Equitable Defenses**

   In addition to denying the existence of the defect that allegedly caused the marriage to be voidable and the defense of ratification (*see* 1.b., *supra*), courts recognize the other equitable defenses, such as laches, estoppel, and unclean hands, as defenses to suits to annul voidable marriages. Note, however, that laches and estoppel will often be subsumed in the defense of ratification, and unclean hands (recrimination) is no longer applied by a majority of courts.

5. **Effect of Annulment**

   A decree of annulment renders the marriage void *ab initio*. The court, however, will not undo or reopen transactions done during the period of the supposed marriage. [Glazer v. Silverman, 354 Mass. 177 (1968)—court would not reimpose the obligation to pay alimony to a former spouse even though that spouse's remarriage was later annulled; Gleason v. Galvin, 374 Mass. 574 (1978)—property conveyed by husband during marriage to husband and wife as tenants by the entirety was not returned to husband but was treated as tenancy in common]

6. **Status of Child in Void Marriage**

   A court that renders a judgment of annulment has the power to issue orders pertaining to the custody and support of the parties' children. [Mass. Gen. L. ch. 207, §18]

   a. **Incest—Nonmarital Child**

   If a marriage is void for incest, any child of the relationship is considered to be a nonmarital child. [Mass. Gen. L. ch. 207, §15]

   b. **Nonage or Mental Incapacity—Marital Child of Capable Party**

   If a marriage is void for nonage or mental incapacity, any child of the relationship is considered the marital child of the party who was capable of contracting the marriage. [Mass. Gen. L. ch. 207, §16]

   c. **Bigamy—May Be Marital Child of Capable Party**

   If a marriage is void through bigamy, any resulting child is the marital child of the party capable of contracting the marriage, if that party believed that he was free to marry the spouse who was actually still married to another person. The child must have been born or begotten before the second marriage was declared void. [Mass. Gen. L. ch. 207, §17]

7. **Effect of Annulment on Property Owned as Tenants by the Entirety**

   When parties to a voidable marriage own a house as tenants by the entirety, a subsequent annulment will result in the parties' holding the property as tenants in common.

B. DIVORCE

A decree of divorce terminates a valid marriage relationship. Thus, a court must first determine that there has been a valid marriage.

1. **Jurisdiction**

   The *probate court* has exclusive original jurisdiction over divorce actions. [Mass. Gen. L. ch. 215, §3]

   a. **Residency Requirements**

   A divorce may not be adjudicated in Massachusetts if the parties have never lived together as husband and wife in Massachusetts or if the cause for divorce arose outside Massachusetts, *unless,* prior thereto, both parties resided in Massachusetts as husband and wife, and one party lived in Massachusetts at the time the cause arose. However, if: (i) a party resides in Massachusetts for one year prior to filing, and the cause for divorce occurred outside Massachusetts; or (ii) a party resided in Massachusetts at the time of filing, and the cause for the divorce occurred in the Commonwealth, there may be an adjudication as long as the party seeking the divorce did not move into Massachusetts for the purpose of securing a divorce. [Mass. Gen. L. ch. 208, §§4, 5]

b. Service

1) Local
Personal service is required. If personal service is not possible (*e.g.*, the whereabouts of the spouse are unknown) and the court so orders, service may be by publication. Any disinterested person may serve process.

2) Long Arm
Personal service may be obtained under the long arm statute if the parties were legally married *and* maintained a marital domicile in Massachusetts for at least one of the two years prior to commencement of the divorce action, even if the defendant has thereafter left the jurisdiction. Also, a defendant's suit to modify a support order can be characterized as a "business transaction" under the broader subsection of the long arm statute (Mass. Gen. L. ch. 223A). [Ross v. Ross, 371 Mass. 439 (1976)] The long arm statute now includes the exercise of jurisdiction over a defendant outside Massachusetts if (i) the action sought pertains to child support or maintenance, (ii) the plaintiff and child continue to reside in the Commonwealth, and (iii) the defendant is subject to the exercise of personal jurisdiction of a Massachusetts court, which resulted in the original order.

3) Publication
If the court grants the plaintiff's motion (*see supra*), service may be made by publishing a copy of the notice for three successive weeks in a newspaper designated by the court and mailing copies of such by registered or certified mail, if practicable, to the defendant's last known address.

4) Award Enforcement
Support awards may be enforced under the long arm statute and under the Uniform Interstate Family Support Act. [Mass. Gen. L. ch. 209D]

c. Venue
The proper venue is that county in which either party resides. However, if a party still resides in a county where the couple last resided as husband and wife, the action must be brought in that county. [Mass. Gen. L. ch. 208, §6]

2. Fault Grounds
There are several fault grounds upon which a divorce action can be based. [Mass. Gen. L. ch. 208, §1] Corroboration is *not* required to establish any of the grounds for divorce.

a. Adultery
Voluntary sexual intercourse with someone other than one's spouse is a ground for divorce. Adultery usually cannot be proven directly; circumstantial evidence is usually the only form of proof available. (Adultery is a crime in Massachusetts; therefore, the defendant might invoke the Fifth Amendment privilege against self-incrimination.) A showing of adulterous disposition and opportunity to commit adultery can suffice to prove this ground. The co-defendant is entitled to notice and an opportunity to defend. When a married woman is pregnant, third parties may testify to nonaccess of the spouse to prove adultery.

b. Cruel and Abusive Treatment
Cruel and abusive treatment consists of deliberate physical abuse or nonphysical conduct (words and/or actions) that the defendant knew would result in the impairment of the health of the spouse or does, in fact, impair the physical and/or mental health of the spouse. Usually, a resulting physical harm must accompany the nonphysical abuse in order to prove the existence of this ground. However, the Supreme Judicial Court has upheld the granting of a divorce in one case where there had not been any resulting physical harm, on the basis that the defendant knew or should have known that the harm was reasonably likely to follow from the defendant's conduct.

c. Desertion
The ground of desertion is available if there is a voluntary departure (i) without justification, (ii) without consent of the other spouse, and (iii) with the intent of not returning, so as to create a cessation of cohabitation for at least one year prior to the filing of the complaint for divorce. A temporary return is not a defense unless the temporary return is coupled with a good faith attempt at resuming cohabitation. Desertion may be

"actual" or "constructive," *i.e.,* as when one spouse bars the other from entering the marital home.

d.   Impotency
The inability of either spouse to perform sexual intercourse constitutes a ground for divorce. (Impotency should not be confused with sterility, which is the inability to bear or beget children and is **not** a ground for divorce.) Condonation is not a defense.

e.   Gross and Confirmed Intoxication by Use of Liquor or Drugs
For use of liquor or drugs to be a ground for divorce, the use must be voluntary, gross, and confirmed. It must continue until the complaint is filed. Use of drugs pursuant to a medical prescription is not sufficient to support this ground.

f.   Nonsupport
To show nonsupport, the refusal to support must occur at a time when the nonsupporting spouse is of sufficient ability to support, and it must be gross or wanton and cruel. This ground may be available to either the wife or husband, depending on the circumstances.

g.   Sentence of Confinement to Penal Institution for Five Years or More
A sentence of confinement to a penal institution for life or for five years or more is a valid ground for divorce. For purposes of divorce, the maximum term of a sentence is considered rather than the minimum term. The court has held an indeterminate sentence of four to six years sufficient. [Mass. Gen. L. ch. 208, §2]

3.   Affirmative Defenses to Fault Grounds

a.   Condonation
Condonation is forgiveness either expressed or implied, for a known breach of a marital duty coupled with the resumption of marital relations on the implied condition that the offense committed will not be repeated or that no other marital offense will be committed. If the same offense is repeated, or a different offense is committed, the condonation defense will dissolve. This defense is not available when impotency is the ground for divorce.

b.   Collusion
Collusion is agreement between or conduct by the spouses to commit or appear to commit a ground for divorce in order to obtain a divorce.

c.   Connivance
Connivance is conduct that facilitates commission of a matrimonial offense (usually adultery); *i.e.,* it is the willing consent of one spouse to the other's misconduct.

d.   Insanity
Acts committed by a spouse who is insane will not give rise to grounds for divorce. Usually, expert testimony is required. The standards applied are the same as the *M'Naghten* Rule. (*See* Criminal Law outline.)

e.   Recrimination—Not a Defense in Massachusetts
The recrimination doctrine precludes both the husband and wife from obtaining a divorce if the conduct of each has been sufficient to furnish grounds for divorce. This defense has been abolished in many states, including Massachusetts, with the enactment of "no-fault" statutes.

4.   Irretrievable Breakdown of Marriage—"No-Fault Divorce"

a.   Uncontested—Four-Month Wait for Final Divorce After Hearing
Upon the filing of the complaint, a sworn affidavit of an irretrievable breakdown, and a notarized separation agreement, the court holds a hearing to establish the breakdown and to approve the agreement. It uses the same criteria as in a contested divorce, except that it does not consider fault. Thirty days after initial approval of the agreement, a judgment nisi is entered, which becomes final 90 days thereafter. [Mass. Gen. L. ch. 208, §1A]

b.   Contested—Minimum Nine-Month Wait for Final Divorce After Filing
If the action is contested and there is no separation agreement, the parties file the

complaint and a hearing is held. No earlier than six months after the filing, the court may hold the hearing and issue the judgment nisi, which will become final 90 days thereafter. However, depending on the date of the hearing, the time from the date of filing to final judgment of divorce in a contested no-fault action may be substantially longer than nine months. Fault is considered only as one of the elements used in fixing alimony. [Mass. Gen. L. ch. 208, §1B]

c. Note—Total Waiting Periods
The nisi period in Massachusetts is 90 days (*see supra*). Therefore, a "no-fault divorce" with an agreement will become final no sooner than four months after the hearing. A "no-fault divorce" without an agreement will become final no sooner than nine months after filing.

5. Effective Date of Divorce (Nisi Period)
Three months after the judgment nisi is entered following the trial of a contested divorce matter, the divorce judgment becomes final, unless it is revoked or stayed for cause. The party in whose favor the judgment nisi is entered may have the judgment vacated before it becomes final. However, it does not appear that there is an absolute right to such relief.

a. Resumption of Marital Relations
A resumption of marital relations during the nisi period may be used by the defendant to attack the judgment.

b. Death
The death of a spouse before the judgment becomes final terminates the judgment, and it never becomes final.

c. Appeal
The filing of an appeal stays the running of the nisi period in a divorce case. [Mass. Gen. L. ch. 215, §24] However, the party appealing should be specific as to the purpose of the appeal, *i.e.,* that it is the divorce judgment itself that is being challenged. [Yanolis v. Yanolis, 402 Mass. 470 (1988)] Failure to designate that it is the divorce judgment being appealed will likely result in dismissal and entry of a retroactive divorce judgment absolute 90 days from the date of the judgment nisi. [Karp v. Amendola, 28 Mass. App. Ct. 929 (1990)]

6. Rights During Pendency of Divorce
As in a complaint for separate support (*see* F., *infra*), the court may enter **temporary orders** for custody, support, and use of the marital home and property. The court can order a spouse out of the marital home for up to 90 days. The 90 days may be extended upon a showing of good cause. [Mass. Gen. L. ch. 208, §34B] If a defendant becomes incapacitated by reason of mental illness during the pendency of a divorce action, the court will appoint a suitable guardian to appear and answer. [Mass. Gen. L. ch. 208, §15]

C. ALIMONY
Alimony is an award of support to **either spouse** sufficient to satisfy the needs of the parties. [*See* Mass. Gen. L. ch. 208, §34] Misconduct does not bar alimony. Rehabilitative alimony may be awarded to a spouse for a limited period of time to prepare the spouse for employment. [Gordon v. Gordon, 26 Mass. App. Ct. 973 (1988)]

1. Factors the Court Must Consider
The court considers the following factors in determining the amount of alimony, if any:

(i)   Length of marriage;

(ii)   Conduct of the parties during marriage;

(iii) Age of the parties;

(iv) Health of the parties;

(v)   Station in life of the parties;

(vi) Occupation of the parties;

(vii) Amount and sources of income available to each party;

(viii) Vocational skills of each party;

(ix) Employability of each party;

(x) Estate of each party;

(xi) Liabilities and needs of each party; and

(xii) Opportunities for future acquisition of capital assets and income.

Note: Alimony may not be awarded to compensate a spouse for time or money invested in the other spouse's business. [Heins v. Ledis, 422 Mass. 477 (1996); *but see* D.8., *infra*]

2. Form of Award
Alimony may be paid in the form of periodic payments or in the form of an assignment of part or all of the assets of one spouse to the other. In choosing the type and value of assets to be assigned to one spouse in lieu of alimony, the court is required to consider the needs of the dependent children of the marriage. Also, if the payor spouse has health insurance coverage available through an employer or otherwise at a reasonable cost, the court must order that spouse to provide health insurance for the payee spouse. Provision of health insurance will *not* result in a reduction of alimony. [Mass. Gen. L. ch. 208, §34]

a. Classifying Income Source
The court has discretion to determine whether an income source is a capital asset to be divided or a source for ongoing alimony. The alimony classification is an advantage to the recipient spouse because alimony is subject to modification to meet changing circumstances. [Andrews v. Andrews, 406 Mass. 1101 (1990)]

3. Modifiable While Both Parties Are Alive
The award and arrears are always modifiable by the court while both parties are alive. To modify, however, there must be a *material change in the circumstances* of the parties. Unless the decree provides otherwise, the death of either party terminates the right to alimony.

a. Remarriage
A recipient spouse's remarriage does not *automatically* terminate alimony unless such a termination was set forth in a court order or an agreement between the parties. However, remarriage makes a prima facie case for a material change in circumstances, unless the recipient spouse can demonstrate extraordinary factors warranting its continuation. [Keller v. O'Brien, 420 Mass. 820 (1995)] *But note:* The remarriage of either parent generally will *not* constitute a material change in circumstances sufficient to modify a child support order.

4. Unavailable for Annulment
Alimony is unavailable when there has been a judicial determination of annulment, although the trial court may make orders relative to the care, custody, and maintenance of the parties' minor children.

D. DIVISION OF PROPERTY
In addition to or in lieu of alimony, the court may order a division of *all* property held by each spouse. [Mass. Gen. L. ch. 208, §34] In dividing the property, the court *must* consider the *same statutory factors* considered with respect to alimony (*see* C.1., *supra*), as well as *the present and future needs of the dependent children of the marriage*. In addition, the court *may* consider: (i) the contribution of each party in the *acquisition*, *preservation*, *or appreciation* in value of the respective estates; and (ii) each party's *contribution as a homemaker* in the family unit. The court is not required to follow any specific formula, and the weight accorded each factor is within the court's discretion. [Bacon v. Bacon, 403 Mass. 1102 (1988)]

Note: The court may assign marital property only to the husband or the wife; the court may not assign marital property to the spouses' children. [Johnson v. Johnson, 425 Mass. 693 (1997)] However, the court may order marital property be put in trust for future child support. [Passemato v. Passemato, 427 Mass. 52 (1998)]

1. No Binding Arbitration
The judge may not delegate the division of property to binding arbitration. The judge may obtain a *recommendation* from an arbitrator, but the judge is responsible for promulgating

the final decision. [Gustin v. Gustin, 420 Mass. 854 (1995)] Moreover, even if the parties agree to submit to binding arbitration, any results are subject to judicial review. [Reynolds v. Whitman, 40 Mass. App. Ct. 315 (1996)]

2. Choses in Action
Choses in action may be distributed as marital property. If the present valuation is uncertain or impractical, the court may order that any future recovery or payment be divided according to a formula fixed in the property assignment. [Hanify v. Hanify, 403 Mass. 184 (1988)]

3. Contingent Fees
The interest of an attorney-spouse in a contingent fee agreement pertaining to a pending lawsuit is a property interest subject to equitable distribution. [Lyons v. Lyons, 403 Mass. 1003 (1988)]

4. Personal Injury Settlement
Proceeds from a personal injury suit compensating for loss of earning capacity and medical expenses are part of the divisible estate in a dissolution proceeding. [Dalessio v. Dalessio, 409 Mass. 821 (1991)]

5. Beneficial Interest in Real Estate
The beneficial interest in certain real estate trusts is subject to equitable division. For example, if such a trust allows a spouse to reside on the property, the spouse has a present, enforceable right to use the trust for his benefit, and that may be subject to division. [Lauricella v. Lauricella, 409 Mass. 211 (1991)]

6. Pension Benefits
Generally, pension benefits and other retirement benefits are included in the marital estate. Note, however, that Social Security old age benefits cannot be included in the marital estate pursuant to federal law. [Mahoney v. Mahoney, 425 Mass. 441 (1997)]

7. Inheritance Proceeds
A mere *expectancy* of an inheritance is not an interest subject to division upon divorce. The judge may, however, consider this expectancy as a factor ("opportunity of each [spouse] for future acquisition of capital assets and income") in determining how to divide other property that is subject to division. Because the Massachusetts statute provides for the division of *all* property held by each spouse, inheritance actually received is subject to division.

8. Investment in Spouse's Business
When a spouse has invested time or money in a business owned by the other spouse, the court may value the business as an asset and distribute it, or other assets based on the value of the business, to compensate for the spouse's contribution to the business. [Heins v. Ledis, *supra*—court ordered property division to compensate wife for her contribution to husband's veterinary business]

E. DIVORCE SETTLEMENT AGREEMENTS

1. Acceptance by the Court
Frequently, the parties enter into agreements that provide for custody, support, and division of assets. Such agreements are always subject to court approval. The court has the inherent power to modify any agreement if it is not fair, reasonable, and free from fraud. [Lavin v. Lavin, 24 Mass. App. Ct. 929 (1987)] For example, an agreement in which the wife transferred all marital assets to her husband prior to divorce was deemed unconscionable by the court in light of her role as primary caregiver to the couple's five children during a marriage of 19 years. [Brash v. Brash, 407 Mass. 101 (1990)] Note that when a no-fault divorce action is filed, a settlement agreement making proper provisions for custody, support, and disposition of property is required as part of the filing (*see* B.4.a., *supra*), and the court will make a determination as to whether the agreement is fair and reasonable. In fact, in these no-fault cases, the agreement is vulnerable to attack in the absence of an independent court finding that it is fair and reasonable. [Slaughter v. McVey, 20 Mass. App. Ct. 768 (1985)]

2. Modification
The ability of a court to modify an agreement depends on whether the agreement survives the decree or is merged with the decree.

a. Merger
If the parties agree, the settlement agreement is merged into the divorce decree. This means that the agreement is no longer an enforceable contract (*i.e.*, the original contract

is dissolved), but becomes part of a court order and is subject to enforcement and modification as such.

b. Survival of Agreement
The parties may agree that their separation agreement will be incorporated into the decree but survive the divorce judgment as an independent legal contract. In this case, if one party later seeks modification of a support order contrary to the terms of the contract, which has survived the judgment of divorce, the other party might raise the agreement/contract as a bar to the modification.

c. Merger vs. Survival
The Massachusetts courts apply different standards for the modification of a "merged" as opposed to a "surviving" divorce settlement agreement. A merged agreement may be modified on a showing of a material change in circumstances. An agreement that survives is modified only upon a showing of something more than a material change in circumstances (*e.g.,* a showing that the party seeking the modification was in danger of becoming a public charge or that the respondent failed to comply with the agreement). [Stansel v. Stansel, 385 Mass. 510 (1982)]

d. Modification of Specific Provisions of Agreement

1) Alimony
The court may modify an alimony provision in an incorporated agreement on a showing by the petitioning party of: (i) a *material change in circumstances*, if the agreement was *merged* in the judgment of divorce; or (ii) *something more than a material change of circumstances*, if the agreement was not merged, but *survived* as an independent binding contract (*see* c., above).

2) Child Support, Custody, and Visitation
The court will always retain jurisdiction over matters of child support, custody, and visitation, regardless of whether other provisions of a divorce settlement agreement are merged or survive. [Mass. Gen. L. ch. 208, §28] This is to protect children and prevent parents from bargaining away the rights of their children in a divorce agreement. A court may, therefore, modify the child support provisions of any divorce settlement agreement on a showing: (i) of a *material change of circumstances*; *and* (ii) that such a modification is necessary to promote the *best interests of the child* or children.

3) Property Division
Unlike alimony, property division is final and is *not modifiable*, regardless of whether the divorce agreement is merged or survives. [Drapek v. Drapek, 399 Mass. 240 (1987)]

e. Duty of Good Faith and Fair Dealing
The duty of good faith and fair dealing applies to settlement agreements, as well as all other contracts. Under the duty of good faith, neither party may deprive the other of the benefits of the contract. Thus, a spouse who is required to pay a certain percentage of income as alimony may not intentionally accept employment that pays far less than his earning capacity, since that would have the effect of depriving the recipient spouse of the bargained-for payments. [Larson v. Larson, 37 Mass. App. Ct. 106 (1994)]

F. SEPARATE SUPPORT
Separate support is a procedure whereby a party to a marriage obtains court protection without dissolving the marriage. Although it often is claimed in connection with a separation, separate support does not require physical separation of the spouses. [Mass. Gen. L. ch. 209, §32]

1. Grounds

a. Desertion
Desertion, a deprivation of physical presence, is a ground for separate support. (*See* B.2.c., *supra.*)

b. Living Apart for Justifiable Cause
Living apart for justifiable cause is a ground for separate support. Justifiable cause includes all grounds for divorce, as well as marital wrongs not sufficient of themselves to constitute grounds for divorce.

c. **Failure to Support**
Separate support may be granted on the ground that the defendant spouse neglects or refuses to provide for her spouse.

2. **Jurisdiction**
First, the court must adjudicate whether there is a valid marriage. Then the jurisdiction basis is satisfied by: (i) domicile of either party; (ii) physical presence of both parties; or (iii) conduct in the marital relationship qualifying for the long arm statute (*e.g.*, prior domiciliaries). *Note:* There is no requirement of living together as husband and wife in Massachusetts.

3. **Defenses**

a. **Condonation**
Forgiveness by the injured party operates as a defense to the injured party's action. However, since forgiveness may be conditioned on future proper behavior by the offending spouse, a breach of the condition may revive the original injury as a ground.

b. **Removal of Cause**
If the offending party removes the wrong, the injured spouse has no right to a judgment. Even after a judgment is entered, the offending spouse who has removed the wrong is entitled to have the court revoke the judgment.

4. **Effect of Separation Agreement or Divorce**
A separation agreement that is found to be fair, reasonable, and free from coercion *bars* a separate support judgment if both parties are in compliance. A subsequent divorce *terminates* the judgment of separate support.

5. **Nature and Effect of Judgment**

a. **Custody and Maintenance of Minor Child**
As in divorce actions, the *best interests of the child* is the standard in determining custody and support of a minor child. (*See* V.A.1., *infra.*) The spouse not receiving custody is usually awarded visitation rights.

b. **Support**
Factors to be considered by the court in awarding separate support are the needs, financial resources, and the standard of living of both spouses and minor children. For the most part, these are the same factors considered for alimony awards; however, the court cannot (as it can in divorce judgments) order a lump sum payment in final satisfaction of the obligation of support.

c. **Assets of Parties May Be Awarded**
The court may secure each party's performance under the judgment and enforce it by its contempt powers. The court has the power to use assets held in the name of one party for the benefit of the other (*e.g.*, it can order the husband to vacate the marital home for 90 days even though title is in him alone). [Mass. Gen. L. ch. 208, §34B]

d. **Offending Spouse Precluded from Inheritance Rights**
The offending spouse will not be entitled to his intestate share, the election to waive a will, and dower or curtesy.

e. **Judgment Is Modifiable**
The judgment of separate support is not designed to be a permanent adjudication of the parties' rights and responsibilities. It may be modified by the court.

V. CUSTODY AND SUPPORT OF CHILDREN

A. CUSTODY OF MINOR CHILDREN
[Mass. Gen. L. ch. 208, §§28, 31]

1. **Standard for Determining Custody**
The standard used in awarding custody of minor children in divorce matters is the *best interests of the child*. Absent lack of fitness on the part of either parent, the parents have equal rights to custody.

2. **Types of Custody Awards**

    a. **Legal Custody**
        Generally, in a divorce situation, both parents will share legal custody, which is defined under the statute as "continued mutual responsibility and involvement by both parents in major decisions regarding the child's welfare, including matters of education, medical care and emotional, moral, and religious development." [Mass. Gen. L. ch. 208, §31]

    b. **Physical Custody**
        Often, one parent will have physical custody of the children, meaning that the children will reside with and be under the supervision of that parent, subject to reasonable visitation by the other parent, unless such visitation is not in the best interests of the children.

    c. **Shared Custody**
        In some cases, the parents will seek or the court will award joint or shared legal and physical custody. Under a shared physical custody arrangement, the children have periods of residing with and being under the supervision of each parent. When the custody matter is heard on the merits, there is no presumption either for or against shared legal or physical custody. [Mass. Gen. L. ch. 208, §31]

3. **Effect of Custody on Disposition of Marital Home**
    The issue of custody of the minor children will often be considered together with the issue of which parent in a divorce proceeding will be awarded the use and occupancy of the marital home. Often the court will award the use and occupancy to the parent with the physical custody of the minor children, because in many cases, the best interests of the children will dictate this result. [*See* Hartog v. Hartog, 27 Mass. App. Ct. 124 (1989)]

4. **Evidence of Physical Abuse**
    If there is credible evidence of physical abuse to a family member by a person seeking custody, the trial judge must make findings that demonstrate that the effect of the abuse on the child has been evaluated and, if physical or legal custody is given to the abuser, how such an award is in the best interests of the child. [R.H. v. B.F., 39 Mass. App. Ct. 29 (1995)]

5. **Jurisdictional Basis**
    Massachusetts has adopted the Uniform Child Custody Jurisdiction and Enforcement Act ("UCCJEA").

    a. **Initial Custody Determination**
        Under the UCCJEA, the Massachusetts court has jurisdiction over a child for purposes of awarding custody or visitation if one of the following is true:

        (i) Massachusetts is the child's *home state* (the state in which the child lived with a parent, or a person acting as a parent, for at least six consecutive months immediately before the commencement of the proceeding), or was the child's home state within the past six months and the child is absent from Massachusetts, but a parent or person acting as a parent continues to live in Massachusetts. This is the most important jurisdictional test.

        (ii) *No other state has home state jurisdiction* or a court of the home state has declined to exercise jurisdiction on the "inconvenient forum" ground, *and* (i) the child and at least one parent (or person acting as a parent) have a *significant connection* with Massachusetts, and (ii) *substantial evidence* is available in Massachusetts concerning the child's care.

        (iii) *All other states having jurisdiction* under the "home state" or "significant connection" test have *declined jurisdiction* on the ground that a Massachusetts court is a more appropriate forum.

        (iv) *No other state has jurisdiction* under either the "home state" or "significant connection" test.

    [UCCJEA §201]

b. Exclusive Continuing Jurisdiction

The court that made the initial child custody or visitation determination has exclusive continuing jurisdiction over the matter until the court determines that: (i) neither the child nor the child's parents continue to reside in the state; *or* (ii) the child no longer has a significant connection with the state (*e.g.,* a close relationship with a parent who lives in the state), and substantial evidence relating to the child's care, protection, training, and personal relationships is no longer available in the state. [UCCJEA §202]

6. Removal of a Minor Child from Massachusetts

A child of divorced parents, who is a native of, or who has resided five years in, Massachusetts and over whose custody the Massachusetts court has jurisdiction, cannot be removed from the state without her consent. If the child is too young to consent, the agreement of both parents is required. If the child is too young and the parents cannot agree, application must be made to the court for an order allowing removal of the child from Massachusetts.

7. Visitation Rights of Grandparents

Under Massachusetts law, grandparents may be granted reasonable visitation rights if such rights would be in the best interests of the child. Such rights are not available if the child is adopted out of the family. Note, however, that neither *maternal nor paternal* grandparents have standing to obtain visitation when a child has been born out of wedlock and the child's paternity has not been adjudicated or acknowledged. [Enos v. Correia, 38 Mass. App. Ct. 318 (1995)]

Note: Portions of Massachusetts's current standards for grandparent visitation *may be unconstitutional* under the United States Constitution. The Supreme Court has held that, as long as a parent is fit, that parent's determination as to the appropriateness of grandparent visitation must be given "special weight." A judge may *not* override a fit parent's decision regarding third-party visitation merely because he feels a "better" decision could be made or visitation would be in the best interests of the child. [Troxel v. Granville, 530 U.S. 57 (2000)] It is not yet clear what effect this decision will have on how grandparents' visitation rights are determined in Massachusetts.

8. Parental Kidnapping Prevention Acts

The federal Parental Kidnapping Prevention Act ("PKPA") mandates the application of principles of full faith and credit to custody judgments by requiring each state to give effect to valid custody judgments entered by other states. [28 U.S.C. §1738A] The Massachusetts Parental Kidnapping Prevention Act makes it a crime for a noncustodial parent to entice or take a child under the age of 18 without lawful authority to do so. [Mass. Gen. L. ch. 265, §26A] However, the statute is not applicable to a parent who takes his child from the other parent prior to a court proceeding to determine custody. [Commonwealth v. Beal, 405 Mass. 550 (1989)]

9. State May Intervene in Extreme Cases

A state may intervene when the parents of a child decline to assent to potentially lifesaving treatment on the basis that the welfare of a child supersedes the parents' natural rights when the welfare involves a life or death situation. [Mass. Gen. L. ch. 119]

B. CHILD SUPPORT

In a divorce action or in an action for child support where paternity has been established, the court will, after examination of the financial conditions of both parents, make an order of child support to be paid by the noncustodial parent to the custodial parent.

1. Child Support Guidelines

Orders of support are made by the court in accordance with the provisions of the Child Support Guidelines promulgated by the chief administrative justice. The guidelines determine support payments by using a formula that weighs the parents' relative incomes as well as existing support orders, child care expenses, and health insurance costs. The guidelines do *not* apply if:

a. The noncustodial parent earns in excess of $75,000 per year;

b. The combined annual income of the parents exceeds $100,000;

c. The parties have entered into a child support agreement that the court finds is fair and reasonable and makes adequate provision for the support of the children;

d. The parents have either shared physical custody of the children or split physical custody (*i.e.,* each parent has custody of one or more children); *or*

e. The application of the guidelines would be unjust or inappropriate, and it would be in the best interests of the child not to apply the guidelines.

2. Duration of Support Obligation
The obligation of support runs from parent to child until the child turns 18 or becomes emancipated, but may be extended until the child reaches age 21 if the child resides at home and is principally dependent on his parents for maintenance. Additionally, the court may extend the parental support obligation until the child reaches the age of 23 under certain circumstances (*see* VII.D.2., *infra*).

a. Adult Child with Special Needs
Parents may be liable for the support of an adult child who is so physically or mentally impaired as to be incapable of supporting himself. [Viccaro v. Milunsky, 406 Mass. 777 (1990)]

3. Modification
Modification of a child support order is possible if there has been a *material change of circumstances and modification is in the best interests of the child*. Modification is also available upon a showing of a discrepancy of 20% or more between the established order and a proposed order calculated under the guidelines.

Note that the court will not enforce an agreement that prohibits modification of child support.

4. Attribution of Income
If a court determines that either or both parties are earning substantially less than they could through reasonable efforts, the court may consider potential earning capacity rather than actual earnings.

5. Health Insurance
If the payor parent has health insurance that may be extended at a reasonable cost to include the children covered by the support order, a court must order the payor parent to obtain the coverage unless the custodial parent prefers otherwise. When such an order is made, one-half of any additional cost to the payor is subtracted from the support order.

6. Death of the Payor Parent
A probate court judge has the jurisdiction to modify child support provisions after the death of the payor parent. [Clark v. Barba, 37 Mass. App. Ct. 322 (1994)—on former spouse's motion, court ordered that the assets of a deceased payor parent be available for child support]

7. Support Obligations of Stepparents
Generally, stepparents are not required to pay child support; however, some courts have required support payments when the stepparent provided support for a number of years. [A.R. v. C.R., 411 Mass. 570 (1992)]

8. No Recovery of Support Erroneously Paid
A man who either admits paternity or is adjudicated a father and who is later determined not to be the father is not entitled to the return of any support payments he has already made. [Richardson v. Department of Revenue, 423 Mass. 378 (1996)]

VI. CONFLICT OF LAWS

A. DIVORCES

1. Sister State Divorces
[Mass. Gen. L. ch. 208, §39]

a. Full Faith and Credit
Full faith and credit will be accorded to sister state divorces if they are final and unmodifiable, and the rendering court had an adequate jurisdictional base. The plaintiff's residence alone may be the basis for the state's granting a divorce, regardless of whether there is personal jurisdiction over the defendant in that state. The defendant is

entitled to due process rights of notice and opportunity to be heard, but as the divorce itself is viewed as an in rem action, certain kinds of constructive service, such as publication, may be allowed. In addition, a court in an *ex parte* divorce can even adjudicate the parties' rights as to marital property located within the forum state. However, to have jurisdiction over requests for certain other relief incident to divorce (*e.g.,* alimony and maintenance), there must be personal jurisdiction over the defendant.

b. Res Judicata

Res judicata compels recognition of a sister state divorce if the defendant appeared and participated in the divorce proceedings in the first forum, even if the defendant was not domiciled in the first forum. Any challenge to the allegations, including those of the rendering court's jurisdiction, could have been litigated by the defendant, and failure to do so collaterally estops later challenges.

c. Equitable Estoppel

Massachusetts cases have held that equitable estoppel may be invoked in the second forum against the party who is attacking the sister state divorce in a number of situations, such as when:

1) The party procured, ex parte, the divorce that she is attacking;

2) Though failing to appear in the divorce proceeding, the party then took advantage of the divorce decree by becoming remarried;

3) The party attacking the divorce married one of the parties to the divorce proceeding, with knowledge of the circumstances that created doubt about the validity of the divorce; or

4) The party deferred an attack on her former spouse's divorce, without acquiescing in or consenting to the divorce, until years later, when the former spouse became remarried.

2. Foreign Bilateral Divorces

The erstwhile "Mexican" divorce (now Haitian or Dominican), in which one party makes a personal appearance and the other appears by attorney, is deemed bilateral. However, since public policy is offended by the foreign nation's liberal requirements for establishing "domicile," many states refuse to recognize such divorces. Massachusetts, however, has recognized a Mexican divorce on estoppel grounds. The spouse in question had remarried in good faith, not knowing that the divorce attorney had provided a fraudulent and invalid Mexican divorce decree. Both the wronged spouse and her second husband married in good faith, and the dissolution of the first marriage was not challenged until the second husband died and his brother claimed the marriage was invalid to obtain the deceased's retirement benefits. [Suneson v. Suneson, 400 Mass. 1104 (1988)]

B. DIVISIBLE INCIDENTS OF DIVORCE

1. Alimony and Child Support

a. Enforcement

A valid foreign decree will be enforced in Massachusetts in accordance with the Uniform Interstate Family Support Act. [Mass. Gen. L. ch. 209D] In addition, the federal Full Faith and Credit for Child Support Orders Act requires that full faith and credit be given to another state's child support order where the parties had reasonable notice and an opportunity to be heard. Also, the federal Child Support Recovery Act makes it a federal criminal offense to willfully fail to pay past due child support to a child who resides in another state if the amount has been unpaid for more than one year, or if the amount due is greater than $5,000.

b. Modification

A foreign award may be modified when there are changed circumstances if the rendering court's decree on alimony or child support is not considered final (unmodifiable) in the rendering jurisdiction (and hence may be treated as modifiable by Massachusetts under the Full Faith and Credit Clause). An ex parte divorce decree may be enforced without enforcement of its order of alimony or child support (or lack of such), on the ground that there was no jurisdiction in the rendering court over the defendant to cut off such property rights. Furthermore, if a Massachusetts court has personal jurisdiction over both parties to a foreign decree or order of support and the foreign court also had personal jurisdiction over both parties, the Massachusetts court may modify the foreign decree—but only to the extent it is modifiable under the laws of the foreign jurisdiction. However, if both parties are Massachusetts *domiciliaries*, the court may modify the order as if it were rendered by a Massachusetts court. Note that a Massachusetts court may not modify a foreign decree concerning the *division of marital property* if the foreign jurisdiction had personal jurisdiction over both parties.

2. Custody

The UCCJEA (*see* V.A.5., *supra*) requires a court of one state to recognize and enforce the custody order of a court of another state if the other state had jurisdiction to enter or modify the order under the UCCJEA. However, a court that would otherwise not have jurisdiction may have temporary emergency jurisdiction if a child has been abandoned or if it is necessary in an emergency to protect the child.

VII. PARENTS AND CHILDREN

A. CUSTODY

Parents of minor children have custody unless the probate court finds them unfit to have such custody. A central element in determining custody is the best interests and welfare of the child. Upon divorce or separation, no parent has a better right than the other to the child's custody. [Mass. Gen. L. ch. 208, §§28, 31; *see* V.A.1., *supra*]

B. PATERNITY ISSUES

1. Presumption of Marital Child If Born in Wedlock

A child born to a married woman is presumed to be the marital child of the married woman and her spouse.

a. Overcoming Presumption—Adjudication of Paternity

A putative father who alleges that he is the father of a child born or conceived when the mother was married to another man may bring a common law action for adjudication of paternity in accordance with the probate court's equity jurisdiction. [Mass. Gen. L. ch. 209C, §5(a)] When such a complaint is filed, the probate court must conduct a preliminary hearing to determine if there is clear and convincing evidence of a substantial parent-child relationship such that the petitioner should be allowed to proceed with the paternity action. [C.C. v. A.B., 406 Mass. 679 (1990)] The court looks at the relationship as a whole and considers: existing bonds, economic support, custody of the child, extent of personal association, the consistency of the putative father's expressed interest, the names listed on the birth certificate, and any other factors that bear on the nature of the alleged parent-child relationship. [M.J.C. v. D.J., 410 Mass. 389 (1991)]

1) Child May Not Challenge Own Paternity

Neither a child represented by a guardian ad litem nor an adoption agency may bring an action to challenge the paternity of the husband of the child's mother. [Matter of Walter, 408 Mass. 584 (1990)]

b. Remarriage After Child's Conception

If there is a remarriage after the child's conception, but before his birth, then the first husband is presumed to have been the father. [*In re* J.S.V., 402 Mass. 571 (1988)]

2. Filiation

A child born out of wedlock whose parents marry after his birth is a marital child if his father recognizes him. [Mass. Gen. L. ch. 190, §7C] A person may be adjudicated to be the child's father; paternity must be established by clear and convincing evidence. [Mass. Gen. L. ch. 209C, §7] The court may order blood or genetic marker tests of the mother, child, and putative father, and the results, including statistical data as to probability of paternity, are admissible and are weighed together with other evidence of paternity. [Mass. Gen. L. ch. 209C, §17]

3. Rights of Non-Biological "Fathers"

A putative father who admits he is not the biological father of a child cannot establish his paternity or obtain visitation privileges, even though he stood in parental relation to the child and demonstrated a devotion to the child. [C.M. v P.R., 420 Mass. 220 (1995)]

C. ADOPTION

1. Adopting and Adopted Persons
Any person of majority age may adopt a person of a *younger* age, except a spouse, sibling, aunt, or uncle of whole or half blood. If married and a minor, one may adopt the child of a spouse, but the spouse must also sign the petition. [Mass. Gen. L. ch. 210, §1]

2. Consent
Written consent to the adoption is required of:

(i) The child, if over 12 years old;

(ii) The spouse, if any, of the person to be adopted;

(iii) The child's lawful parents (may be previous adoptive parents or surviving natural parent);

(iv) The mother only of a child born out of wedlock who has not been previously adopted. (*Note:* Although this provision is the current law, it appears open to challenge by the biological father in appropriate circumstances.)

Consent is void if given within three days of the adopted child's birth. Consent must be attested and subscribed before a notary public and in the presence of two competent witnesses.

a. Department of Social Services Consent
Consent is required of the Department of Social Services unless the adoptive parent is a blood relative, stepparent, or nominee of a deceased parent. The court may reverse the decision of the department. [Mass. Gen. L. ch. 210, §2A]

b. Circumstances Under Which Parental Consent Unnecessary
The consent of the child's biological parents is not necessary if the child is of majority age or the biological parents are unfit. [*See* Adoption of Sarah, 31 Mass. App. Ct. 906 (1991)] The court may also dispense with parental consent if the court finds that the child is in need of care and protection, and the best interests of the child are thereby served. In determining whether the child's best interests are served by dispensing with parental consent, the court must look to several factors, including:

(i) Any abandonment of the child;

(ii) Any abuse or neglect of the child;

(iii) The nature of parental conduct and support while the child has been temporarily placed in the care of another; and

(iv) The effect of any parental incarceration or substance abuse.

[Mass. Gen. L. ch. 210, §3]

3. Investigation
After a filing for adoption of a child under 14 years of age, the Department of Social Services must investigate the home of the adoptive parent.

4. Religion
Religion will be taken into account in adoption proceedings only if requested by the natural parent or parents. Otherwise, the court will consider only the need of the child for loving and responsible parental care and all factors relevant to the physical, mental, and moral health of the child. [Mass. Gen. L. ch. 210, §5B]

5. Effects of Adoption
The adopted child stands in the same relation for all purposes to the adoptive family as would their natural marital child. The family relationship with the adoptive child's natural family is terminated, except for prohibitions against incest with natural or former adoptive parents.

D. CONSEQUENCES OF MINORITY

1. Parent's Guardianship

a. Scope
Parents exercise joint guardianship with equal powers, rights, and duties. As such, they:

1) Are entitled to custody and control of the child's person;

2) May appoint successors for themselves; and

3) Control the child's property, but are not trustees absent court appointment.

b. Termination
Termination of parental rights may be effected by: (i) *emancipation*; (ii) *surrender* to an authorized adoption agency, by means of a signed and acknowledged written instrument; or (iii) *judicial termination* in the course of: a matrimonial action resulting in custody orders; a hearing to determine issues of neglect, abuse, juvenile delinquency, etc.; custody proceedings; adoption proceedings; or appointment of a guardian.

2. Parent's Support Obligation
As previously stated, the obligation of support runs from parent to child until the child turns 18 or becomes emancipated; however, this obligation may be extended until the child reaches the age of 21 if the child resides at home and is principally dependent on his parents for maintenance. The obligation may even be extended until the child reaches the age of 23 if: (i) the child is domiciled in a parent's house; and (ii) the child is principally dependent on his parents due to his enrollment in an educational program. This obligation does not, however, include educational costs beyond an undergraduate degree. [Mass. Gen. L. ch. 208, §28] A parent may also be liable for the support of an adult child who is so physically or mentally impaired as to be incapable of supporting himself. [Viccaro v. Milunsky, V.B.2.a, *supra*]

a. Child Who Is a Ward of the State
Parents or stepparents, to the extent that they are able, must support a child younger than 18 years old who is a ward of the state. Generally, however, a stepparent will not be liable for the support of such a child if the stepparent divorces the child's parent. (*See* V.B.7., *supra*.)

b. Child Support Obligations After Dissolution
Child support obligations continue after dissolution of the marriage and are imposed on both parents. [Mass. Gen. L. ch. 208, §28] Child support orders attempt to provide the child with the standard of living he would have enjoyed if the family had remained intact.

c. Enforcement
The child may bring a support proceeding in probate or district court. However, support rights are conditioned on obedience to reasonable demands by parents.

3. Torts
See Torts outline.

4. Crimes and Other Undesirable Behavior

a. Juvenile Delinquents
Children aged seven or older, but younger than age 16, who commit an act that would be a crime if committed by an adult are juvenile delinquents. [Mass. Gen. L. ch. 119, §52]

b. Children in Need of Supervision
Children younger than 16 years old who are truant, incorrigible, ungovernable, or habitually disobedient and beyond the lawful control of their parents are considered children in need of supervision. [Mass. Gen. L. ch. 119, §39E]

c. Presumptions of Criminal Incapacity
There is a conclusive presumption of incapacity for a person under seven years of age, a rebuttable presumption for a person between ages seven and 14, and no presumption

for a person over age 14. Proceedings involving children under age 17 are held in juvenile court. [Mass. Gen. L. ch. 218]

5. **Contracts that Are Valid Despite Infancy**
See Contracts outline.

6. **School**

a. **Eligibility for Free Public Schooling**
Persons more than five years old and less than majority, without a high school diploma, are entitled to attend the public schools maintained in the district where they reside, without tuition charge. [Mass. Gen. L. ch. 71]

b. **Mandatory Schooling**
Persons more than six and less than 16 years old must attend school.

VIII. ABUSE PREVENTION

A. **ABUSE PREVENTION STATUTE**
Under the abuse prevention statute [Mass. Gen. L. ch. 209A], any person who suffers abuse from a family member, household member, or other party with whom the abused has a significant relationship (*e.g.,* boyfriend or girlfriend) may seek the protection of the court. "Abuse" is defined as: (i) attempting to cause or causing physical harm; (ii) placing another in fear of imminent serious physical harm; or (iii) causing another to involuntarily engage in sexual relations by force, threat, or duress. (Note that courts have interpreted the second element broadly, requiring only that the plaintiff demonstrate a *reasonable apprehension of harm* under the circumstances. [Commonwealth v. Gordon, 407 Mass. 340 (1990)])

1. **Procedure**
The superior, probate and family, district, and municipal courts all have jurisdiction to hear an abuse prevention complaint. The action is commenced by filing a complaint with the court. If the plaintiff demonstrates a reasonable likelihood of an immediate danger of abuse, the court may immediately enter a temporary order without notice to the defendant (*see* 3., *infra*). No filing fee is charged for a 209A complaint.

2. **Remedies**
The court may order the alleged abuser to:

(i) *Refrain from abusing* the plaintiff;

(ii) *Refrain from contacting* the plaintiff;

(iii) *Vacate* and remain away from the household of the parties;

(iv) *Surrender custody* of children to the plaintiff;

(v) *Pay temporary support* to the plaintiff and/or children;

(vi) *Refrain from abusing the plaintiff's child* or a child in the plaintiff's care; or

(vii) *Pay monetary compensation* to the plaintiff.

Additionally, the court may order the suspension and surrender of the alleged abuser's license to carry firearms and may order that the plaintiff's address be impounded.

3. **Temporary Order Without Notice; Right of Defendant to Hearing**
The court may enter an order under the statute without notice to the alleged abuser if necessary to protect the plaintiff from abuse. However, the court must schedule another hearing *not later than 10 court business days* after such an order is entered and notify the defendant so the defendant has the opportunity to be heard. [Mass. Gen. L. ch. 209A, §4] If the plaintiff demonstrates a substantial likelihood of an immediate danger of personal abuse, the court must, as part of the temporary order, order the immediate suspension and surrender of any license to carry firearms held by the alleged abuser.

4.   Duration of Protection Order

Any order of relief shall be for a fixed period *not exceeding one year*. Every order is required to state the date of expiration, and if the plaintiff appears at the court on the date set for expiration, the court will determine whether to extend the order for an additional time reasonably necessary to protect the plaintiff or to enter a permanent order. [Mass. Gen. L. ch. 209A, §3(i)]

5.   Violations

Violation of a court order under the statute constitutes a criminal offense punishable by a fine of not more than $5,000 or by imprisonment in a house of correction for not more than two and one-half years, or by both a fine and imprisonment. The court may also order the offender to undergo treatment in a batterer's treatment program. [Mass. Gen. L. ch. 209A, §7]

6.   Modification of Relief Order

Any order entered by a court pursuant to chapter 209A may be modified at any subsequent time, after a hearing on a motion brought by either party.

B.   STALKING STATUTE

Massachusetts has enacted a statute making it a crime to: (i) willfully, maliciously, and repeatedly follow or harass another person, and (ii) threaten that person with the intent to place that person in imminent fear of death or serious bodily injury. [Mass. Gen. L. ch. 265, §43]

1.   Application to Domestic Relations Law

Under the stalking statute, restraining orders, which are common in family law proceedings, can give rise to criminal sanctions. Any party who is convicted of stalking in violation of an order to vacate or a restraining or no-contact order will be punished by imprisonment for a minimum of one year or a maximum of five years, with no possibility of a reduced sentence until one year is served. [Mass. Gen. L. ch. 265, §43(b)]

BAR REVIEW

Federal Jurisdiction and Procedure

celebrating over
35 YEARS
of preparing law students for the bar exam

FEDERAL JURISDICTION AND PROCEDURE

TABLE OF CONTENTS

INTRODUCTION

This outline is designed to acquaint you with commonly tested areas within the fields of federal jurisdiction and procedure. These are: personal jurisdiction, subject matter jurisdiction, venue, discovery, pleading and motion practice, and joinder of multiple parties.

1. Personal Jurisdiction

Personal jurisdiction refers to the ability of a court to exercise power over a particular defendant or item of property. It may be categorized as in personam, in rem, or quasi in rem. The primary limitations on a court's power to exercise personal jurisdiction are found in the United States Constitution and state statutes.

2. Subject Matter Jurisdiction

The subject matter jurisdiction of the federal courts is limited to that authorized by the Constitution as implemented by federal statute and decisional law. In general, it may be categorized as follows:

a. Diversity of Citizenship Jurisdiction

Diversity of citizenship jurisdiction under 28 U.S.C. section 1332 is grounded historically in the desire to protect out-of-state parties from local prejudice. Its main requirement is that there be complete diversity between opposing parties. Each plaintiff must be of diverse citizenship from each defendant. Also, the amount in controversy must exceed $75,000.

b. Federal Question Jurisdiction

Federal question jurisdiction under section 1331 presents fewer specific difficulties. The principal problem in this area is to determine when an action "arises under" federal law. A secondary problem is to know what types of actions are within the exclusive jurisdiction of the federal courts under other specific statutes.

c. Removal Jurisdiction

Removal jurisdiction allows defendants to remove an action brought in a state court to a federal court if the federal court would have had original jurisdiction over the action.

d. Supplemental Jurisdiction

The doctrine of supplemental jurisdiction is codified under section 1367 and includes under a single name the concepts of "ancillary" and "pendent" jurisdiction. In any form, supplemental jurisdiction allows a federal court to entertain certain claims over which it would have no independent basis of subject matter jurisdiction, *i.e.,* claims that do not satisfy diversity or federal question jurisdiction requirements. It is important to note that supplemental jurisdiction operates only after a claim has invoked federal subject matter jurisdiction, after the case is properly in federal court. Supplemental jurisdiction operates to bring additional claims into that case that arise from the same transaction or occurrence as the original claim, but cannot be used to get the case into federal court in the first instance.

3. Venue

Venue is the designation of the proper district in which to bring an action. Venue will depend on the nature of the jurisdiction (*i.e.,* whether federal question or diversity of citizenship), and on the nature of the parties (*i.e.,* whether corporate or natural persons).

4. Discovery

Discovery issues principally revolve around the scope of the examination allowed in discovery, the uses of depositions at trial, and the available methods of enforcing discovery rights.

5. Multiple Parties

Multiple party questions concern whether various types of joinder are permitted under federal law and, if so, whether there is a jurisdictional basis for a particular attempted joinder. The majority of the issues that arise in this area are grounded in the interpretation or application of statutes and the Federal Rules of Civil Procedure ("Federal Rules"), and also require knowledge of subject matter jurisdictional bases, especially supplemental jurisdiction.

I. PERSONAL JURISDICTION

A. OVERVIEW

There are two branches of jurisdiction: subject matter jurisdiction and personal jurisdiction. *Subject matter jurisdiction* involves the court's power over a particular *type of case*. *Personal jurisdiction* involves the ability of a court having subject matter jurisdiction to exercise power over a *particular defendant or item of property*. This section discusses personal jurisdiction.

1. Limitations on Personal Jurisdiction

Limitations on a court's personal jurisdiction arise from two sources: state statutes and the United States Constitution. An exercise of personal jurisdiction must not exceed the limitations of either source.

a. Statutory Limitations

States have the power to decide over whom their courts may exercise jurisdiction. Therefore, the first place to look to determine whether the court has properly exercised personal jurisdiction is state law. If no state statute grants the court the power over the parties before the court, then the court lacks personal jurisdiction. On the other hand, an exercise of jurisdiction will not be proper merely because it comports with a state statute; it must also be within the limitations set by the Constitution (below).

b. Constitutional Limitations

The Due Process Clause of the Constitution places two restrictions on the exercise of personal jurisdiction. First, the defendant must have such contacts with the forum state that the exercise of jurisdiction would be fair and reasonable. Second, the defendant must be given appropriate notice of the action and an opportunity to be heard. Note that these requirements are the outer limits to which a state may reach in exercising jurisdiction over a person. A state statute cannot exceed these constitutional boundaries, but is not required to exercise the full limit of constitutional power. Thus, in evaluating jurisdiction over a person, both constitutional and statutory limitations must be considered.

c. Personal Jurisdiction in Federal Courts

The main jurisdictional problem in state courts arises when the defendant over whom power is sought lives in another state. Since the federal borders encompass all states, one might expect that federal courts would encounter problems of personal jurisdiction only when the defendants were foreign nationals. However, Rule 4 of the Federal Rules provides that (absent some special federal provision) each federal court must analyze personal jurisdiction *as if it were a court of the state in which it is located*. Thus, in nearly every case, the assessment of whether the court has personal jurisdiction over the defendant will be exactly the same in federal court as it is in state court.

2. Three Types of Personal Jurisdiction

a. In Personam Jurisdiction

In personam jurisdiction exists when the forum has power over the person of a particular defendant. (Jurisdiction over a plaintiff is generally not an issue because the plaintiff accedes to the court's jurisdiction by bringing suit in that court.) In these cases, the court may render a money judgment against the defendant or may order the defendant to perform acts or refrain from acting. Such a judgment creates a personal obligation on the defendant and is entitled to full faith and credit in all other states; *i.e.,* if a defendant is ordered to pay a sum of money to a plaintiff, the plaintiff may enforce the judgment against the defendant's property in any other state where that property is located.

b. In Rem Jurisdiction

In rem jurisdiction exists when the court has power to adjudicate the rights of all persons in the world with respect to a *particular item* of property. This jurisdiction is limited to situations where the property is located within the physical borders of the state and where it is necessary for the state to be able to bind all persons regarding the property's ownership and use. This occurs with respect to actions for condemnation (eminent domain cases), forfeiture of property to the state (*e.g.,* when the property is used for the unlawful transportation of narcotics), and settlement of decedents' estates.

c. Quasi In Rem Jurisdiction

One type of quasi in rem jurisdiction exists when the court has power to determine whether particular individuals own specific property within the court's control. Unlike in rem jurisdiction, however, it does not permit the court to determine the rights of all persons in the world with respect to the property. A second type of quasi in rem jurisdiction permits the court to adjudicate disputes other than ownership based on the presence of the defendant's property in the forum (*see* E.2.a.2), *infra,* regarding applicable constitutional limitations).

1) Defendant Is Not Bound Personally

The basis of a court's power to exercise quasi in rem jurisdiction is the property within the state. (*See* E., *infra.*) The judgment does not bind the defendant *personally* and cannot be enforced against any other property belonging to the defendant.

B. STATUTORY LIMITATIONS ON IN PERSONAM JURISDICTION

Each state is free to prescribe its own statutory bases for personal jurisdiction. Of course, the exercise of jurisdiction in a given case must also satisfy the constitutional requirements. (*See* C., *infra.*) Most states have statutes granting their courts in personam jurisdiction in the following four situations:

(i) Where the defendant is present in the forum state and is personally served with process;

(ii) Where the defendant is domiciled in the forum state;

(iii) Where the defendant consents to jurisdiction; and

(iv) Where the defendant has committed acts bringing him within the forum state's long arm statutes.

Each of these bases of in personam jurisdiction will be discussed in detail below.

1. Physical Presence at Time of Personal Service

Most states grant their courts in personam jurisdiction over any defendant who can be served with process within the borders of the state, no matter how long he was present (*i.e.,* even if merely passing through). The Supreme Court has upheld this type of jurisdiction, allowing a transient defendant to be served with process for a cause of action unrelated to his brief presence in the state. [Burnham v. Superior Court, 495 U.S. 604 (1990)]

2. State Law Exceptions to Traditional Rule

Even though jurisdiction through presence at the time of service has been upheld under the Constitution, state statutes and court decisions have limited the power of their courts in certain situations.

a. Service by Fraud or Force Invalid

For example, if a plaintiff brings a defendant into a state by fraud or force to serve process, most courts will find the service invalid. [*See, e.g.,* Copas v. Anglo-American Provision Co., 73 Mich. 541 (1889)]

b. Immunity of Parties and Witnesses

Most states likewise grant immunity from personal jurisdiction to nonresidents who are present in the state solely to take part in a judicial proceeding, or who are passing through the state on their way to a judicial proceeding elsewhere.

3. Domicile

Most states grant their courts in personam jurisdiction over persons who are domiciliaries of the state, even when the defendant is not physically within the state when served with process.

a. Defined

Domicile refers to the place where a person maintains her permanent home. Where a person has legal capacity, her domicile is the place she has chosen through presence (even for a moment) coupled with the intention to make that place her home. If a person lacks capacity, domicile is determined by law (*e.g.,* infant is domiciliary of custodial parent's home state).

b. Citizenship

A United States citizen, even though domiciled abroad, is subject to personal jurisdiction in the United States. The scope of this basis for jurisdiction is unclear, because states have never attempted to enact laws or rules enabling their courts to obtain jurisdiction solely on the basis of citizenship. However, the power of federal courts to subpoena a United States citizen domiciled abroad to return to the United States to give testimony has been upheld by the Supreme Court.

4. Consent
Virtually every state provides for in personam jurisdiction through the defendant's consent. Such consent may be express or implied or through the making of a general appearance.

a. Express Consent
A party's express consent to the jurisdiction of local courts, whether given before or after suit is commenced, serves as a sufficient basis for in personam jurisdiction.

1) By Contract
A person can, by contract, give advance consent to jurisdiction in the event a suit is brought against him.

2) By Appointment of Agent to Accept Service of Process
A person can, by contract, appoint an agent in a particular state to receive service in that state in an action against him. The terms of the contract determine the extent of the agent's power and, thus, the scope of the jurisdiction conferred.

a) Appointment Required by State
When the state heavily regulates a type of business (*e.g.,* sale of securities) to protect its citizens, it can require a nonresident engaged in that business to appoint an agent for service of process in the state. *Note:* The state cannot require every nonresident businessperson to appoint such an agent, because the state lacks power to exclude individuals from the state. However, a state can require nonresident corporations to make such an appointment before doing business in the state.

b. Implied Consent
When the state has substantial reason to regulate the in-state activity of a nonresident of the state, it may provide that by engaging in such activity, the nonresident thereby appoints a designated state official as his agent for service of process. Thus, for example, the Supreme Court has upheld statutes that use such implied consent to subject a nonresident motorist to jurisdiction in any state in which he has an accident. [Hess v. Pawloski, 274 U.S. 352 (1927)]

c. Voluntary Appearance
A defendant may consent to jurisdiction by a voluntary appearance, *i.e.,* by contesting the case without challenging personal jurisdiction. Generally, any sort of appearance provides a sufficient basis for jurisdiction, but most states allow *"special appearances"* through which a defendant can object to the court's exercise of jurisdiction. The defendant usually must make this special appearance—by stating grounds for his objection to jurisdiction—in his initial pleading to the court; otherwise, the defendant will be deemed to have consented to jurisdiction.

5. Long Arm Statutes
Most states also grant their courts in personam jurisdiction over nonresidents who perform or cause to be performed certain acts within the state. In personam jurisdiction is granted regardless of whether the defendant is served within or outside the forum, but is limited to causes of action arising from the acts performed within the state.

a. Unlimited Long Arm Statutes
A few states, such as California, have long arm statutes that give their courts power over any person or property over which the state can constitutionally exercise jurisdiction. (*See* C., *infra.*) These are known as unlimited long arm statutes.

b. Limited (or Specific) Long Arm Statutes
Most states, however, have long arm statutes that specify in detail the situations in which their courts can exercise jurisdiction.

1) Limitations in Tort Cases
Some statutes permit jurisdiction when a "tort" occurs within the state, while others require a "tortious act." The latter language has caused problems where an

out-of-state manufacturer puts his products into the stream of commerce knowing that some items will end up in the forum state. When the gravamen of the complaint is negligent manufacture, some courts have read "tortious act" narrowly and confined jurisdiction to the place of manufacture; others have read it to mean "the place the tort occurred," interpreting that to be the place of injury.

2) Limitations in Contract Cases

Many statutes permit jurisdiction if the cause of action arises out of the "transaction of business" in the state. Some states require the defendant or his agent to have been physically present in the state at the time the transaction took place, but others have taken a broader view—*e.g.,* New York has upheld jurisdiction over a California resident who made telephone bids from California on paintings being sold in New York.

3) Limitations in Property Actions

Many state statutes permit jurisdiction over a nonresident defendant when the cause of action arises from ownership of property within the state—as in the case of a tort action based on negligent maintenance of realty or a contract action regarding the sale of the property. Some statutes include chattels, while others are confined to realty.

4) Limitations in Marital Dissolution Cases

All states provide that when a married couple last lived together in the state and one spouse then abandons the other, the remaining spouse may obtain personal jurisdiction over the absent spouse for divorce or legal separation proceedings. States vary on whether the plaintiff spouse must be living in the state at the time of abandonment (or other cause for dissolution) or whether jurisdiction may be acquired whenever the plaintiff has acquired domicile in the state.

C. CONSTITUTIONAL LIMITATIONS ON IN PERSONAM JURISDICTION

Once it is determined that a state has a statute that allows the court to exercise in personam jurisdiction over the parties before it, the constitutionality of the exercise must next be determined. As noted above, there are two components of the constitutional aspect: contacts with the forum and notice.

1. Sufficient Contacts with the Forum: Contact and Fairness

a. Traditional Rule: Physical Power

Traditionally, jurisdiction over a person (or res) was a consequence of the state's physical power to carry out its judgment; *i.e.,* it was based on the power to arrest the person to force compliance with a judgment. Accordingly, the Supreme Court upheld exercises of jurisdiction whenever the defendant was served with process within the forum state. [*See* Pennoyer v. Neff, 95 U.S. 714 (1878)] The Court later expanded states' physical power to extend not only to those defendants who were served within the state, but also to those defendants who consented to the state's power or who were domiciled in the state, regardless of where they were served.

b. Modern Due Process Standard: Contact and Fairness

The concept of power by which a state could enforce its judgments was greatly expanded by the Supreme Court in *International Shoe Co. v. Washington,* 326 U.S. 310 (1945). No longer was power controlled solely by whether one of the traditional bases of presence, residence, or consent was present. Instead, the focus became whether sufficient minimum contacts exist between the defendant and the forum so that maintenance of the suit against the defendant does not offend "traditional notions of fair play and substantial justice." The Supreme Court has listed a series of factors by which to assess the constitutionality of personal jurisdiction. In general, the factors fall under two headings: contact and fairness.

1) Contact

International Shoe requires that the defendant have "such minimum contacts" with the forum that the exercise of jurisdiction would be fair and reasonable. In considering whether there are such contacts, a court will look to two factors: purposeful availment and foreseeability.

a) Purposeful Availment

Defendant's contact with the forum must result from her purposeful availment with that forum. The contacts cannot be accidental. Defendant must reach out to the forum in some way, such as to make money there or to use the roads there. The court must find that through these contacts the defendant *purposefully availed* herself "of the privilege of conducting activities within the forum state, thus invoking the benefits and protections of its laws." [Hanson v. Denckla, 357 U.S. 235 (1958)]

Examples: 1) Defendants, Michigan residents, entered into a franchise contract with a Florida corporation. The agreement required, among other things, that fees be sent to the franchisor's home office in Florida, and provided that Florida law would govern any dispute. The Court held that the defendants could be sued in Florida; their contact with Florida resulted from their purposeful availment of that state. [Burger King v. Rudzewicz, 471 U.S. 462 (1985)]

2) Defendant manufactures widgets in Alabama and markets them to customers in Mississippi. Plaintiff, a resident of Mississippi, purchases a widget from Defendant. Defendant accepts the order and ships the widget to Plaintiff in Mississippi. If the widget explodes and injures Plaintiff, she can probably sue Defendant in Mississippi. Defendant purposefully availed itself of the market in Mississippi. [*See* International Shoe Co. v. Washington, *supra*]

Compare: 1) Father, in New York, agreed to give up custody of Daughter to Mother in California. Mother sued Father in California for additional support. Father's only contact with California was letting Daughter go there. The Court held that California could not obtain in personam jurisdiction over Father because, in acting in the interest of family harmony, Father could not be said to have purposefully availed himself of the benefits and protections of California laws. [Kulko v. Superior Court, 438 U.S. 908 (1978)]

2) Defendant, a New York car dealer, was sued in Oklahoma based on an injury that Plaintiff received from an accident in Oklahoma. The only basis for jurisdiction over Defendant was the sale of the allegedly defective car in New York by Defendant, who knew no more than that any vehicle sold might be driven elsewhere. The Court found that there was no purposeful availment of the privileges or protections of Oklahoma. [World-Wide Volkswagen Corp. v. Woodson, 444 U.S. 286 (1980)]

(1)   "Stream of Commerce" Cases
There is great difficulty, however, in assessing purposeful availment in a "stream of commerce" case—*e.g.,* Defendant manufactures valves in State A and sells them to a heater manufacturer in State B. The heater manufacturer incorporates Defendant's valves into its heaters and sells them to customers in States C, D, and E. If a valve explodes and injures Plaintiff in State E, can it be said that Defendant (who acted in State A and sold only to State B) purposefully availed itself of State E? The Supreme Court faced this type of fact pattern in *Asahi Metal Industry Co. v. Superior Court,* 480 U.S. 102 (1987), and failed to resolve it definitively. Four justices opined that placing the item in the stream of commerce, with the knowledge that it would end up in a particular forum, constituted purposeful availment. Four other justices opined that there would also have to be a showing that the defendant took some additional step to avail itself of the forum. Not surprisingly, lower courts have reached varying conclusions on such fact patterns.

b)   Foreseeability
In addition to purposeful availment, the contact requirement of *International Shoe* requires that it be foreseeable that the defendant's activities make her amenable to suit in the forum. The defendant must know or reasonably

anticipate that her activities in the forum render it foreseeable that she may be "haled into court" there.

Example: A national magazine is probably subject to in personam jurisdiction for libel cases in every state in which the magazine is marketed. Its publishers may reasonably anticipate causing injury in every state in which the magazine is sold, and thus should reasonably anticipate being haled into court in each state. [Keeton v. Hustler Magazine, 465 U.S. 770 (1984); Calder v. Jones, 465 U.S. 783 (1984)]

2) Fairness

In addition to the defendant's having relevant contacts with the forum, *International Shoe* requires that the exercise of jurisdiction not offend "traditional notions of fair play and substantial justice." The Court has listed several factors relevant to assessing whether jurisdiction would be fair. It is possible that an especially strong showing of fairness might make up for a lesser amount of contact (although minimum contacts are always required).

a) Relatedness of Claim to Contact

One important factor is whether the claim asserted against the defendant arises in some way from the defendant's contacts with the forum. If it does, the court is more likely to find that jurisdiction is fair and reasonable. This assessment requires the court to determine the nature and quality of the defendant's contacts with the state. Some authorities consider this factor to be part of the "contact" assessment; others consider it, as we do here, to be part of the "fairness and reasonableness" assessment. The important point is that you address the issue in your answer, whether under the contact prong or the fairness prong of the analysis.

(1) Claim Arising from Activity in the State

If the defendant's in-state activity is less than systematic or continuous (*e.g.,* isolated acts), in personam jurisdiction over the defendant will be proper only for causes of action arising from *that in-state activity*; *i.e.,* the court will have "specific jurisdiction."

(2) Systematic and Continuous Activity in the State

If the defendant engages in systematic and continuous activity in the forum state, the court could find this activity a sufficient basis for exercising in personam jurisdiction for *any* cause of action against the defendant, whether the cause of action arose from the in-state activity or from activity outside the state; *i.e.,* the court will have "general jurisdiction." However, casual, occasional, or indirect activities in the state are not sufficient bases for this general in personam jurisdiction.

Examples: 1) Statutes that grant in personam jurisdiction on the defendant's mere domicile, residence, or doing of business in the state would generally be valid since these constitute systematic and continuous activity in the forum.

2) Due process requirements for personal jurisdiction were not satisfied in Texas in a wrongful death case against a Colombian corporation whose contacts with the forum state consisted of only one trip to Texas by the corporation's chief executive officer to negotiate a contract, acceptance of checks drawn on a Texas bank, and purchases of helicopters and equipment from a Texas manufacturer and related helicopter training trips. The claims were not related to the defendant's activities in Texas, and defendant's contacts with Texas were not so continuous and systematic as to justify general jurisdiction. [Helicopteros Nacionales de Colombia v. Hall, 461 U.S. 955 (1984)]

b) Convenience

A defendant will often complain that the forum is inconvenient. The Supreme Court has emphasized, however, that the Constitution does not require that the forum be the best of several alternatives. The forum is constitutionally acceptable unless it is "so gravely difficult and inconvenient that a party is unfairly put at a severe disadvantage in comparison to his opponent." [Burger King v. Rudzewicz, *supra*] This is a very difficult standard to meet, and the defendant usually will not be able to meet it simply by showing that the plaintiff has superior economic resources.

c) Forum State's Interest
The forum may have a legitimate interest in providing redress for its residents.

Examples: 1) Decedent, a California resident, purchased a life insurance policy by mail from a Texas company. Decedent regularly mailed his premiums from California to the Texas company, which had no other contacts with California. In a suit brought by the beneficiary of the life insurance policy, the Supreme Court held that California had personal jurisdiction over the Texas company. Among other things, the Court noted that California had a strong interest in protecting its citizens from alleged misfeasance by insurance companies. [McGee v. International Insurance Co., 355 U.S. 220 (1957)]

2) Asahi, a Japanese manufacturer of tire valves, shipped valves to a Taiwanese manufacturer of motorcycle tire tubes. The valves were incorporated into tires and sold in California, where a resident was injured by a defective tire. The Taiwanese manufacturer was sued in a California court, where it sought to implead Asahi. The main case was settled, leaving only the indemnity claim by the tire manufacturer against Asahi pending. *Held:* Even though Asahi placed the defective goods in the stream of commerce knowing that some would be used in California, exercise of jurisdiction by the California court would be unreasonable considering the severe burdens of Asahi in defending in a foreign legal system, the slight interest of the Taiwanese manufacturer and California in the exercise of jurisdiction, and the international interest in not subjecting an alien corporation to United States jurisdiction. [Asahi Metal Industry Co. v. Superior Court, *supra*]

d) Other Factors
The Supreme Court has listed other factors relevant to the assessment of whether the exercise of jurisdiction would be fair and reasonable, but has not discussed these factors in detail: (i) the plaintiff's interest in obtaining convenient and effective relief, (ii) the interstate judicial system's interest in obtaining the most efficient resolution of controversies, and (iii) the shared interest of the states in furthering fundamental substantive social policies.

2. Notice
In addition to the requirement that the defendant have such minimum contacts with the forum to render the exercise of jurisdiction there fair and reasonable, due process also requires that a ***reasonable method be used to notify the defendant of a pending lawsuit*** so that she may have an opportunity to appear and be heard. Due process requires that notice be "reasonably calculated, under all the circumstances, to apprise interested parties of the pendency of the action and afford them an opportunity to present their objections." [Dusenbery v. United States, 534 U.S. 161 (2002)—*quoting* Mullane v. Central Hanover Bank & Trust Co., 339 U.S. 306 (1950)]

a. Traditional Methods of Personal Service Satisfy Due Process Notice Requirements
Any of the traditional methods of personal service satisfy due process notice requirements. These include personal delivery to the defendant; leaving papers with a responsible person at the defendant's residence or place of business; delivery to an agent appointed to accept service; or delivery by registered mail, return receipt requested. (*See* VII.B., *infra,* for discussion of methods of service of process.)

b. Requirement that Agent Notify Defendant
If an agent is appointed by contract, in a case where the plaintiff chose the agent for his

own benefit, or the agent is appointed by operation of law (as under a nonresident motor vehicle statute), the failure of the agent to notify the defendant will prohibit jurisdiction—since the defendant will in fact be deprived of an opportunity to be heard. (This is not true when the defendant voluntarily selects his own agent, since any failure of the agent can and will be attributed to the principal.)

c. **Requirements for Cases Involving Multiple Parties or Unknown Parties**
In *Mullane v. Central Hanover Bank & Trust Co.,* 339 U.S. 306 (1950), an action was brought against a vast number of trust beneficiaries, scattered throughout the world. The Supreme Court held that the Constitution did not require personal service on each beneficiary since the cost would have been prohibitive. However, every beneficiary had to be notified by the ***best practical means*** available. Thus, those whose addresses were known or could reasonably be ascertained had to be notified by ordinary mail, while those whose names or addresses were unknown could be notified by publication. Such methods of notice are valid only if all defendants have substantially identical interests.

D. IN REM JURISDICTION
As stated above, in rem actions adjudicate rights of all persons with respect to property located in the state. An in rem judgment does not bind the parties personally, but is binding as to the disposition of the property in the state.

1. Statutory Limitations
Most states have statutes providing for in rem jurisdiction in actions for condemnation, title registration, confiscation of property (such as vehicles used to transport narcotics), forfeiture of a vessel, distribution of the assets of an estate, and a grant of divorce when only the complaining spouse is present and subject to personal jurisdiction. In the last case, the "property" is the marital status of the complainant.

2. Constitutional Limitations

a. **Nexus**
In in rem actions the basis of jurisdiction is the presence of the property in the state. The state has a great interest in adjudicating the rights of all the world regarding this property. Therefore, the presence of the property in the state is constitutionally sufficient for the exercise of jurisdiction over the property.

1) **No Jurisdiction If Property Not Located in State**
A court has no in rem power over property outside the state; *e.g.,* in settling a decedent's estate, the court has no in rem power over property in other jurisdictions.

2) **No Jurisdiction If Property Brought in by Fraud or Force**
The exercise of in rem power is prohibited when the property is brought into the state by fraud or force.

b. **Notice**
The early view held that attachment of property, when supplemented by publication of notice in a local newspaper or by posting of notice on the property, would give all interested persons sufficient notice of the action. However, such procedures are no longer adequate, and the requirements of *Mullane v. Central Hanover Bank & Trust Co., supra,* apply to in rem actions. Thus, persons whose interests are affected and whose addresses are known must at least be notified by ordinary mail. [Walker v. City of Hutchinson, 352 U.S. 112 (1956)]

E. QUASI IN REM JURISDICTION
Quasi in rem jurisdiction permits a court without in personam jurisdiction to determine certain disputes between a plaintiff and defendant regarding property when the property is located in the forum state.

1. Statutory Limitations
Most states provide for two types of quasi in rem jurisdiction. The first type (type I) involves disputes between parties over their rights in property within the state. The second type (type II) involves disputes ***unrelated*** to the in-state property and has been severely limited by the Supreme Court. In quasi in rem cases, the plaintiff is unable to obtain personal jurisdiction over the defendant, but the defendant has property in the state that the

plaintiff attaches. The court then adjudicates the dispute between the parties on the basis of its power over the property. Since the court's sole basis of jurisdiction is the property, any judgment against the defendant can be satisfied only out of that property.

2. Constitutional Limitations

a. Nexus
Before 1977, a state clearly had power over all persons and property found within its borders. A defendant with no other connections with the state could be sued in the state for *any* dispute simply because he owned property there. However, in 1977, the Supreme Court held that the minimum contacts standard is applicable to *every* exercise of jurisdiction. And the Court found that the mere presence of property within a state is not itself sufficient to permit a court to exercise quasi in rem jurisdiction over property in a quasi in rem action. [Shaffer v. Heitner, 433 U.S. 186 (1977)—quasi in rem jurisdiction is proper only when minimum contacts exist making exercise of jurisdiction fair and just]

1) Quasi In Rem Type I
Thus, when the dispute involves the rights of the parties in the property itself (quasi in rem type I), jurisdiction based upon presence of the property in the state is proper. The close connection between the litigation and the property provides the necessary minimum contacts.

2) Quasi In Rem Type II
When the dispute is unrelated to the ownership of property (quasi in rem type II), jurisdiction cannot be based solely on the presence of property in the forum state; there must be minimum contacts between the defendant and the forum. Because contacts sufficient to exercise in personam jurisdiction under a long arm statute make it unnecessary to resort to quasi in rem jurisdiction, and given that in personam jurisdiction is preferable because it does not limit the source of the remedy to defendant's in-state property, use of quasi in rem jurisdiction type II will be rare.

Example: A, a Maine resident, flies to Ohio and enters into a contract with B, an Ohio resident. All performance is to occur in Ohio. A flies home. B breaches. A does not want to fly to Ohio to sue B, but he discovers that B has a boat docked in Maine. Traditionally, A could have sued on his contract claim in Maine by attaching the boat (his remedy being limited by the value of the boat). Today, he would have to show minimum contacts between B and Maine.

3) Procedural Requirements
To obtain quasi in rem jurisdiction, a plaintiff must "bring the asset before the court" by attachment (or garnishment). This will inhibit the sale or mortgage of the defendant's interest, since a new owner must take subject to the decision of the court. Serious questions have been raised as to whether such a pretrial interference with a defendant's property rights is constitutional unless the defendant is afforded a hearing on the necessity of such procedures. Most commentators think the process is valid, but the Supreme Court has thus far avoided the issue.

b. Notice
As in in rem cases, quasi in rem cases require the best practical notice. Therefore, posting of notice or notice by publication will be insufficient where the addresses of persons affected by the action are known or reasonably ascertainable.

II. DIVERSITY OF CITIZENSHIP JURISDICTION

Section 1332: Diversity of Citizenship; Amount in Controversy

(a) The district courts shall have original jurisdiction of all civil actions where the matter in controversy exceeds the sum or value of $75,000, exclusive of interest and costs, and is between—

(1) citizens of different States;

(2) citizens of a State and citizens or subjects of a foreign state;

(3) citizens of different States and in which citizens or subjects of a foreign state are additional parties; and

(4) a foreign state . . . as plaintiff and citizens of a State or of different States.

For the purposes of this section, section 1335, and section 1441, an alien admitted to the United States for permanent residence shall be deemed to be a citizen of the State in which such alien is domiciled.

(b) . . .

(c) For the purposes of this section and section 1441 of this title—

(1) a corporation shall be deemed to be a citizen of any State by which it has been incorporated and of the State where it has its principal place of business. . . .

(2) the legal representative of the estate of a decedent shall be deemed to be a citizen only of the same State as the decedent, and the legal representative of an infant or incompetent shall be deemed to be a citizen only of the same State as the infant or incompetent.

(d) The word "States," as used in this section, includes the Territories, the District of Columbia, and the Commonwealth of Puerto Rico.

The federal courts have been given subject matter jurisdiction over controversies between citizens of different states, even though the controversies do not involve questions of federal substantive law, in order to protect an out-of-state party from possible local bias in state courts.

A. DIVERSITY AMONG THE PARTIES

1. Complete Diversity When Action Is Commenced

a. Multiple Parties—Complete Diversity
Every plaintiff must be of diverse citizenship from every defendant. If one defendant and one plaintiff are co-citizens of the same state, there is no diversity jurisdiction. This is the rule of "complete diversity."

Example: A, B, and C bring an action against X, Y, and Z. A and B are citizens of New York; X and Y are citizens of Florida; and C and Z are citizens of Texas. Since no diversity exists between C and Z, the requirement of *complete* diversity is not satisfied, and, as structured, the case cannot be brought in federal court under diversity jurisdiction.

1) But Note
The rule of complete diversity does not require that every party be of diverse citizenship from every other party. It requires only that no plaintiff be a co-citizen with any defendant. Thus, two plaintiffs who are both citizens of Missouri may invoke diversity of citizenship jurisdiction against three defendants, all three of whom are citizens of Kansas.

2) Interpleader Exception

a) Federal Interpleader Statute—Minimal Diversity
The federal interpleader statute [28 U.S.C. §1335] requires only that among the parties there be "two or more adverse claimants, of diverse citizenship." Thus, "minimal diversity" is sufficient to confer jurisdiction under the statute. If there is diversity between *any two* of the claimants, all other claimants may be citizens of the same state. (Also, section 1335 only requires that the money or property at issue be valued at $500 or more.)

b) **Interpleader Under Federal Rules—Complete Diversity**
Interpleader pursuant to Rule 22 of the Federal Rules, on the other hand, requires the usual diversity between all the plaintiffs (stakeholders) and all the defendants (claimants).

b. **"Alienage" Jurisdiction**
Most bar exam questions in this general area involve basic diversity of citizenship jurisdiction, in which the dispute involves "citizens of different states," as discussed immediately above. However, section 1332(a)(2) grants subject matter jurisdiction over "alienage" cases, in which the dispute is between a citizen of a state, on the one hand, and an "alien"—meaning a citizen or subject of a foreign country. Alienage is occasionally tested on bar exams.

Examples: 1) A, a citizen of Venezuela, sues B, a citizen of New York. This dispute would invoke alienage jurisdiction (assuming the amount in controversy requirement was also met), because it is between a citizen of a state and a citizen of a foreign country.

2) A, a citizen of Venezuela, sues B, a citizen of France. This dispute would *not* invoke alienage jurisdiction, because it is *not* between a citizen of a state and a citizen of a foreign country. There is no citizen of a state involved here.

c. **Diversity When Action Is Commenced**
Diversity of citizenship (or alienage) must exist as of the time the suit is instituted. [Grupo Dataflux v. Atlas Global Group, 124 S. Ct. 1920 (2004)] It need not exist at the time the cause of action arose, and it is not defeated if, after commencement of the action, a party later becomes a citizen of the same state as one of his opponents.

2. **Questions of Citizenship**

a. **State Citizenship of an Individual—Domicile**
The determination of the state of citizenship of a natural person depends on the permanent home to which he intends to return. The concept is the same, except in name, as domicile. A new state citizenship may be established by (i) *physical presence* in a new place and (ii) the *intention to remain there*, *i.e.,* no present intent to go elsewhere. The citizenship of a child is that of her parents. In most cases, the citizenship of a party will be determined by the court, but it may be left to the jury.

b. **Citizenship of a Corporation—Multiple Citizenship**
For diversity purposes, a corporation's citizenship is defined by federal statute. Under this statute, a corporation is deemed a citizen of "any" state of its incorporation, which has been interpreted to mean *"every" state of its incorporation*, and also of *the one state in which it has its principal place of business*. Thus, although very few corporations incorporate in more than one state, many corporations have two citizenships (the state of incorporation *and* the state of the principal place of business). If an opposing party is a citizen of any of the corporate party's states of citizenship, there is no diversity.

1) **Multiple Incorporation**
There is no diversity between a citizen of State B and a corporation incorporated in States A and B. Note, however, that it is extremely rare to have a corporation incorporated in more than one state.

2) **"Principal Place of Business"**
A corporation's "principal place of business" is a fact question. Problems arise when a corporation has its executive offices in one state and its physical operations in another; which is considered the "principal place of business"? The courts have generally held that if a corporation has its executive offices in one state and its *physical operation wholly or predominantly* in another state, the principal place of business is the state where physical operations are conducted. When, however, the corporation performs its operational activities in many states, the courts have applied a "home office" or "nerve center" test and held that the principal place of business is the state where the executive offices are located. The Fifth Circuit applies the "total activities" test.

3) **Special Rule for Direct Actions**
The rules of corporate citizenship are subject to a special rule in direct action

cases. When a plaintiff sues an insurer on a policy or contract of liability insurance, and does not also join the insured, the insurer (whether incorporated or not) is treated as a citizen of all of the following: (i) the state in which the insurer is incorporated (if it is), (ii) the state in which the insurer has its principal place of business, and (iii) the state of which the *insured* is a citizen.

4) **Corporations Chartered in Foreign Countries**
A corporation is deemed a citizen of the foreign country of incorporation and is therefore an *alien for diversity purposes*. All of the circuits that have reached the issue have also held that when a foreign corporation has its principal place of business in this country, it is also a citizen of the state in which that principal place of business is located. [*See, e.g.,* Jerguson v. Blue Dot Investment, Inc., 659 F.2d 31 (5th Cir. 1981)]

c. **Unincorporated Associations**

1) **Citizenship**
In claims based on federal law for or against an unincorporated association, the association has entity capacity, but the question of its citizenship is normally irrelevant because the court will have federal question jurisdiction. When diversity jurisdiction is involved, an unincorporated association:

(i) May sue or be sued in its own name if local state law so permits; or

(ii) Is an aggregate of individuals if local state law follows the common law rule.

In either case, the unincorporated association's citizenship is that of *each and every one* of its members.

2) **Class Action**
If the association is large, a class action is possible. If a class action is brought, the relevant citizenship is that of the *named members* who sue or are sued on behalf of the members of the association. (*See* f., *infra.*)

3) **Partnerships**
The citizenship of a general partnership is that of each and every general partner. The citizenship of a limited partnership is that of each and every partner, both limited and general. [Carden v. Arkoma Associates, 494 U.S. 185 (1990)]

d. **Business Trusts**
The *trustees* of a business trust are the real parties in interest and their citizenship, not that of the individual shareholders, determines whether there is diversity. [Navarro Savings v. Lee, 446 U.S. 458 (1980)]

e. **Suits Brought by Legal Representatives**
A legal representative of an infant, an incompetent, or an estate of a decedent is deemed to be a citizen of the same state as the infant, incompetent, or decedent.

f. **Class Actions**
If suit is brought by several named persons on behalf of a class under Rule 23, diversity is determined on the basis of the citizenship of the *named members* of the class who are suing. Thus, there is considerable room for maneuvering to create diversity if the class has members who are citizens of several different states.

g. **Nonresident United States Citizens**
A United States citizen *domiciled abroad* is not a citizen of any state and also is not an alien. (Alien status depends on nationality, not domicile.)

h. **Aliens Admitted for Permanent Residence**
An alien admitted to the United States for permanent residence is deemed to be a citizen of the state in which the alien is domiciled. [28 U.S.C. §1332(a)] Nevertheless, it is generally accepted that at least one party to the suit must be a natural-born or naturalized United States citizen in order for jurisdiction under section 1332 to be proper. [*See* Saadeh v. Farouki, 107 F.3d 52 (D.C. Cir. 1997)]

3.   Collusion and Devices to Create or Defeat Diversity

The federal court does not have jurisdiction if a party "by assignment or otherwise, has been improperly or collusively made or joined to invoke jurisdiction." [28 U.S.C. §1359]

a.   Assignment of Claims

The assignment of a claim to another party for collection only is clearly within this section. [Kramer v. Caribbean Mills, Inc., 394 U.S. 823 (1969)] Thus, the assignment would be ignored in determining whether diversity exists. *But note:* There is no collusion if an absolute assignment of a claim is made and the assignor retains no interest in the assigned claim.

b.   Class Actions

No rule prevents achieving diversity by the adroit selection of named plaintiffs to bring a proper class action on behalf of others. The naming of only members of the class who are not co-citizens of the defendants will create diversity even though other unnamed members of the class are co-citizens who would defeat diversity if named.

c.   Voluntary Change of State Citizenship

A plaintiff can create diversity by changing his domicile after the cause of action accrued but before suit is commenced, but the change must be genuine. In other words, a true change of domicile can create diversity. The party's *motive* for changing domicile is *irrelevant.*

d.   Defeating Diversity to Prevent Removal

No rule prevents manipulation in choice of a representative or assignment of a claim to defeat diversity (and thus prevent removal from state to federal court). On the other hand, fraudulent joinder of an in-state defendant to defeat diversity is no bar to removal.

4.   Realignment According to Interest

a.   May Create or Destroy Diversity

In determining whether diversity exists, the court will look beyond the nominal designation of the parties in the pleadings and realign them according to their true interests in the dispute. Thus, realignment may create diversity or destroy it.

b.   Shareholder Derivative Actions

Taking the view that the shareholder's alignment of the corporation as a party plaintiff or defendant is not controlling insofar as diversity jurisdiction is affected by the citizenship of the corporation, the federal courts have established the rule (at least when alignment of the corporation in a shareholder's derivative suit is not specifically provided for by state law) that the corporation is to be aligned as a party *defendant.* Federal diversity jurisdiction is determined in accordance with that alignment, when, with respect to the claim sought to be enforced by the shareholder's derivative suit, the corporation is "antagonistic" to the shareholder. [*See* Smith v. Sperling, 354 U.S. 91 (1957)]

5.   Ancillary ("Supplemental") Jurisdiction

Occasionally, a claim may be joined that could not, by itself, invoke federal question jurisdiction or diversity jurisdiction (because, for example, it is a state claim between parties who are citizens of the same state or because it does not involve the requisite amount in controversy). (*See* B., *infra.*) The court may nonetheless entertain such claims under the doctrine of ancillary jurisdiction, now codified under the rubric "supplemental" jurisdiction, if they arise from the same transaction or occurrence as the underlying suit and, generally, are asserted by a party other than the plaintiff. Specific applications will be discussed below.

6.   Subsequent Addition of Parties

The Federal Rules permit numerous methods by which additional parties not originally named may become involved in an action. A claim by or against an additional party, like any claim in federal court, must satisfy some basis of federal subject matter jurisdiction, such as diversity of citizenship or federal question. If the claim does not satisfy either of those, the party asserting the claim might invoke supplemental jurisdiction.

a.   Joinder of Additional Parties

In cases of joinder of additional parties (either necessary under Rule 19(a) and (b) or permissive under Rule 20(a)), complete diversity must be maintained.

b. Intervention of Right

Intervention of right is given under Rule 24(a) where the intervenor claims an interest relating to the property or transaction that is the subject of the action and the disposition of the action may adversely affect that interest. Traditionally, intervention of right has not required any showing of independent jurisdiction; the intervenor's claim was considered to be within the court's ancillary jurisdiction if the requirements for intervention of right were met. Under the supplemental jurisdiction statute, however, there is no ancillary jurisdiction for claims by or against intervenors. Thus, such a claim could proceed only if there were an independent basis of jurisdiction, *e.g.,* diversity or federal question.

c. Permissive Intervention

Under Rule 24(b), permissive intervention may be permitted in the court's discretion where the intervenor's action and the main action have a claim or defense involving a *common question of law or fact*. The claim by a permissive intervenor must invoke either diversity of citizenship or federal question jurisdiction. It is unlikely to satisfy the "transaction or occurrence" requirement of supplemental jurisdiction.

d. Substitution of Parties

Substitution under Rule 25 involves changes in parties to a lawsuit necessitated by death, incompetency, etc., of an original party after an action has been commenced. The citizenship of the substituted party is disregarded; that of the original party controls. Substitution should be distinguished from an *amendment* that allows "replacement" of an original party by the party in whom or against whom the action properly lies. A "replacement" party must be diverse to the party or parties on the opposing side.

Example: A v. B. A dies and the administrator of his estate is substituted as plaintiff. Jurisdiction is not destroyed even though B and the administrator are co-citizens. However, if A sues B and subsequently discovers that C—not B—is the proper defendant, an amendment to the complaint by which B is replaced by C must show that diversity exists between A and C.

e. Third-Party Practice—Impleader

A third-party claim under Rule 14 is the joinder by the defendant in the original action (who is usually called the third-party plaintiff) of another person not originally a party to the action (who is called the third-party defendant). The impleader claim asserts that the third-party defendant is or may be liable to the defendant for all or part of the plaintiff's claim against the defendant. In other words, an impleader claim is for indemnity or contribution.

Example: P sues D for $500,000 for personal injuries allegedly inflicted by joint tortfeasors D and X. Applicable law provides that joint tortfeasors have a right of contribution against each other. D may implead X into the pending case. D is seeking to deflect her liability on P's claim, in part, to X. (If X owed D indemnity for some reason, then D could implead X to deflect her entire liability on the underlying claim to X.)

Under Rule 14, after the third-party defendant is impleaded, he may assert a claim against the plaintiff in the pending case if the claim arises from the same transaction or occurrence as the underlying suit. In addition, under Rule 14, after the third-party defendant is impleaded, the plaintiff may assert a claim against him if it arises from the same transaction or occurrence as the underlying suit.

1) Subject Matter Jurisdiction Required

Of course, every claim asserted in federal court must have a basis of subject matter jurisdiction.

Examples: 1) P, a citizen of Illinois, sues D, a citizen of Wisconsin, asserting a state law claim of more than $75,000. Thus, the case invokes diversity of citizenship jurisdiction and is properly brought in federal court. Now D impleads X, who is also a citizen of Illinois, on an indemnity claim of more than $75,000. That claim invokes diversity of citizenship jurisdiction, because it is asserted by a citizen of Wisconsin (D) against a citizen of Illinois (X) and exceeds $75,000. The fact that P is also a citizen of Illinois is irrelevant; the claim is not by or against her, so her citizenship does not affect the impleader claim. If P wanted to assert a claim against X in this situation, however, there would not be diversity because P and X are co-citizens of Illinois. In addition, the claim would not invoke supplemental jurisdiction, because in diversity of citizenship cases, the supplemental jurisdiction statute does not allow supplemental jurisdiction over claims asserted by plaintiffs (*see* III.D., *infra*). Thus, unless the claim by P against X invoked federal question jurisdiction, it could not be asserted in the pending case; it would have to be asserted in state court.

2) P, a citizen of Alabama, sues D, a citizen of Maine, asserting a state law claim of more than $75,000. Thus, the case invokes diversity of citizenship jurisdiction and is properly brought in federal court. Now D impleads X, who is also a citizen of Maine, on a state law contribution claim. The impleader claim does not invoke diversity of citizenship jurisdiction, because it is asserted by a citizen of Maine (D) against another citizen of Maine (X). It does not invoke federal question jurisdiction because it is based on state law. The claim invokes the ancillary form of supplemental jurisdiction, however, because it arises from the same transaction or occurrence as the underlying case and is asserted by the defendant, not the plaintiff.

f.   Cross-Claims
Rule 13(g) allows a party to assert a claim in a pending case against a co-party, but only if the claim arises from the *same transaction or occurrence* as the underlying dispute. So, in a lawsuit of A v. B and C, a claim by B against C (or C against B) that arises from the same transaction or occurrence as the underlying case would be a cross-claim.

1)   Subject Matter Jurisdiction Required
Cross-claims, like all claims in federal court, must invoke subject matter jurisdiction. Therefore, after determining that a cross-claim would be filed, assess whether that claim could invoke diversity of citizenship or federal question jurisdiction. If so, the claim may be asserted in federal court. *However*, if a cross-claim does not invoke diversity of citizenship or federal question jurisdiction, the cross-claim could nonetheless be asserted in federal court through the ancillary form of supplemental jurisdiction. By statute, there is supplemental jurisdiction in diversity of citizenship cases over claims that arise from the same transaction or occurrence as the underlying action (cross-claims do by definition) and are asserted by defendants (not plaintiffs).

B.   JURISDICTIONAL AMOUNT: IN EXCESS OF $75,000
Actions brought in a federal court under the diversity statute must meet the jurisdictional amount requirement. The matter in controversy must be *in excess of $75,000,* exclusive of interest and costs. [28 U.S.C. §1332] The amount is determined from what is claimed in the complaint, disregarding potential defenses or counterclaims. Usually, all that is necessary is a *good faith allegation* that the amount of the damages or injuries in controversy *exceeds*, exclusive of interest and costs, the sum of $75,000. Good faith means that there must be a legally tenable possibility that recovery will exceed the jurisdictional amount. The complaint can be dismissed only if it appears there is no legal possibility of a recovery exceeding the jurisdictional amount. Jurisdiction is not retroactively defeated by the fact that the amount actually recovered is less than the jurisdictional amount.

1.   What Is "In Controversy"?

a.   Collateral Consequences of the Judgment
Does the collateral effect of the judgment sought by the plaintiff bring into controversy the value of other claims that may be governed by the judgment? The Supreme Court has held that the collateral effects of a judgment may *not* be considered.

Examples: 1) If an insured asserts a claim for installments due under a disability policy, only the installments due may be considered, even though the judgment may control the insured's rights to payment of future installments. However, if the insurance company sues to cancel the contract for fraud, the value of the entire contract is brought into controversy.

2) If a bondholder sues to collect amounts due on coupons that have matured, only the amount of the coupons is in controversy, even though

the judgment will determine the validity of the entire bond issue. However, if the issuer of the bonds seeks a declaratory judgment that the bonds are properly issued, the value of the entire bond issue would be in controversy.

b. **Interest and Costs**
The statute excludes interest and costs in determining the jurisdictional amount. However, attorneys' fees that are recoverable by contract or by statute are considered part of the matter in controversy rather than as costs. Similarly, interest that constitutes a part of the claim itself, as distinguished from interest payable by virtue of a delay in payment, is part of the jurisdictional amount.

Example: Plaintiff sues on a three-year note with face value of $70,000 and interest at 5% (an additional $10,500). Since the interest on the note is part of the claim, the jurisdictional amount is satisfied. [*See, e.g.,* Brainin v. Melikian, 396 F.2d 153 (3d Cir. 1968)] But if the interest accrued between maturity and filing, the additional interest after maturity is not part of the claim.

c. **Equitable Relief**
There may be difficulty calculating an amount in controversy for a claim for equitable relief, given that the claimant does not seek money damages. For example, suppose P sues D for an injunction ordering D to remove part of D's house that blocks P's view. What is the value of the injunction and, therefore, the claim? Some courts look at the issue from the *plaintiff's viewpoint*, and ask what the value of the harm caused by the blocked view is. Other courts look at the issue from the *defendant's viewpoint*, and ask what it would cost the defendant to comply with the injunction if it were ordered. Some courts conclude that the amount in controversy requirement is satisfied if the amount under *either* test—plaintiff's viewpoint or defendant's viewpoint—exceeds $75,000.

d. **Punitive Damages**
If a punitive damage claim is permitted under state substantive law, it may be used in making the dollar amount requirement because there is "no legal certainty" that the amount will not be recovered.

2. **Aggregation of Separate Claims**

a. **One Plaintiff Against One Defendant**
For purposes of meeting the jurisdictional amount, the plaintiff may aggregate all her claims against a single defendant. This aggregation is permitted regardless of whether the claims are legally or factually related to each other.

b. **One Plaintiff Against Several Defendants**
A plaintiff who has an action against several defendants cannot aggregate claims based on separate liabilities. Thus, if P had a claim of $50,000 against D-1 and a separate claim of $30,000 against D-2, she may not aggregate those claims. Note, however, that there is no aggregation problem if plaintiff asserts a joint claim against multiple defendants. With a joint claim, courts look to the total value of the claim.

Example: P sues alleged joint tortfeasors X, Y, and Z for damages of $76,000. This claim satisfies the amount in controversy requirement. Because this is a claim based on *joint liability,* any of the three defendants might be held liable for the total amount of the claim. This is not a case of trying to aggregate three separate claims. Because of joint liability, courts see this as one claim. Because it exceeds $75,000, it meets the amount requirement.

c. **Several Plaintiffs Against One Defendant**
Several plaintiffs can aggregate their claims only where they are seeking "to enforce a single title or right in which they have a common or undivided interest . . . ."

Example: If joint owners of real estate file suit to quiet title, the right asserted is held jointly and the amount in controversy is the total value of the land. However, if several victims of the same accident sue for personal injuries, their claims are separate and distinct from one another and aggregation is not allowed.

This rule has special importance in class actions, in which the rule is that the claims of the class members cannot be aggregated if their rights are "separate" rather than "joint" or "common." [Snyder v. Harris, 394 U.S. 332 (1969)]

3. **Counterclaims**
A defendant's counterclaim cannot be combined with the plaintiff's claim to reach the jurisdictional amount; *e.g.,* if the plaintiff claims $20,000, there is no jurisdictional amount even though the defendant counterclaims for $100,000. Does a counterclaim itself have to meet the requirements of the jurisdictional amount?

a. **Compulsory Counterclaim Need Not Meet Jurisdictional Amount**
A compulsory counterclaim (arising out of the *same* transaction or occurrence) does not need to meet the jurisdictional amount requirement. The court has *ancillary* (supplemental) jurisdiction over such a counterclaim just as it does over a third-party claim under Rule 14 impleader.

b. **Permissive Counterclaim Must Meet Jurisdictional Amount**
A defendant's permissive counterclaim (arising out of an *unrelated* transaction) must have an independent jurisdictional basis, and thus *must meet the jurisdictional amount* requirement.

c. **No Removal to Federal Court Based on Counterclaim**
A plaintiff who claims $75,000 or less in a state court action who is met with a counterclaim for more than $75,000 may not remove the suit to federal court, regardless of whether the counterclaim is compulsory or permissive, because removal is permitted only to defendants. The weight of authority also holds that in a situation where the plaintiff has not met the jurisdictional amount, the *defendant* who must assert a compulsory counterclaim in the state suit *may not remove* the action, even though the counterclaim is over $75,000 and there is complete diversity. Thus, a plaintiff with a small claim can require a defendant with a large claim to litigate it in state court simply by being the first to file. *But note:* Even though this is the *traditional rule*, there is a *trend allowing removal*.

C. *ERIE* **DOCTRINE AND THE LAW APPLIED UNDER DIVERSITY JURISDICTION**
A federal court, in the exercise of its diversity jurisdiction, is required to apply the *substantive law of the state* in which it is sitting, including that state's conflict of law rules. [Erie Railroad v. Tompkins, 304 U.S. 64 (1938); Klaxon Co. v. Stentor Electric Manufacturing Co., 313 U.S. 487 (1941)] However, the federal courts apply *federal procedural law* in diversity cases.

1. **Is There a Federal Directive On Point?**
To determine whether federal law should be applied, the first question to ask is whether there is a federal law (*e.g.,* statute, Federal Rule of Civil Procedure) on point. If there is, the federal law will apply, provided that it is valid.
Example: Federal Rule 4 permits substituted service of process. Suppose that state law (of the state in which the federal court sits) does not permit substituted service. The court will apply the Federal Rule, because it is on point and is valid. A Federal Rule of Civil Procedure is valid if it is "arguably procedural." [Hanna v. Plumer, 380 U.S. 460 (1965)]

a. **Caution**
Sometimes it is difficult to determine whether a federal directive is on point. For example, Federal Rule 3 provides that a case is commenced when the complaint is filed. Many people thought that the rule thus was a directive that the statute of limitations would be tolled from the date of filing the complaint. The Supreme Court held, however, that Rule 3 did not address tolling at all, and thus did not constitute a federal directive on the tolling question. [Walker v. Armco Steel, 446 U.S. 740 (1980)]

2. **If There Is No Federal Directive on Point, Is the Issue Substance or Procedure?**
If there is no federal directive on point, can a federal judge refuse to follow state law on a particular issue? The answer depends on whether the law on that issue is substantive or procedural. If it is a matter of substance, the federal judge must follow state law in a diversity case. If it is a matter of procedure, the federal judge may ignore state law.

a. **Some Situations Are Clearly Established**
In some instances, the characterization as substance or procedure is well established. For example, the Supreme Court has established that *statutes of limitations and rules for tolling statutes of limitations* are substantive for *Erie* purposes; therefore, a federal judge in a diversity case must follow state law on those issues. [Guaranty Trust Co. v. York, 326 U.S. 99 (1945)] *Choice of law rules* are also substantive for *Erie* purposes, and a federal judge in a diversity case must follow state law on that issue as well.

[Klaxon v. Stentor Electric Manufacturing Co., 313 U.S. 487 (1941)] Finally, of course, *elements of a claim or defense* are substantive.

b. **Law Is Unclear in Other Situations**
Outside these areas, when there is no federal directive on point, it is often difficult to determine whether an issue is substantive or procedural for *Erie* purposes. The Supreme Court has given different "tests" at different times on this point, and has failed to integrate the tests comprehensively. One such test is *outcome determination*, which holds that an issue is substantive if it substantially affects the outcome of the case. [Guaranty Trust Co. v. York, *supra*] Another test is *balance of interests*, in which the court weighs whether the state or federal judicial system has the greater interest in having its rule applied. [Byrd v. Blue Ridge Electric Cooperative, Inc., 356 U.S. 525 (1958)] Yet another test is *forum shopping deterrence*, which directs that the federal judge should follow state law on the issue if failing to do so would cause litigants to flock to federal court. [Hanna v. Plumer, *supra*]

3. **Statutes Involving Both Substance and Procedure**
Sometimes, a state statute or rule may be both substantive *and* procedural. In one case, the state tort reform law relaxed the standard for granting a new trial, making it easier to grant a new trial than under the basic federal standard. Also, the state *appellate* court was charged with the responsibility to consider whether a new trial should be ordered. In a diversity case under this state law, the standard for granting a new trial was held to be substantive, so the federal court had to apply the state standard for granting a new trial. However, the requirement that the appellate court consider whether a new trial should be ordered was held to be procedural, so a federal *trial* court would determine whether a new trial should be ordered, using the aforementioned state standard, rather than an appellate court. [Gasperini v. Center for Humanities, Inc., 518 U.S. 415 (1996)—in diversity case, federal trial court applied New York "excessive damages" standard for new trial rather than federal "shock the conscience" standard]

4. **Interpreting State Law**
The federal court is bound to apply the substantive state law that would be applied by the highest court of the state. If the state courts have not decided the issue that is before the federal court, or if the decisions on point are old and no longer current with the decisions of other jurisdictions, the federal court may consider the law of other jurisdictions in reaching its decision. However, the focus of the federal court is to *determine what decision the highest court of the state would reach* if confronted with the issue.

a. **De Novo Review of District Court's Decision**
On appeal, the federal appellate court reviews the federal trial judge's decision as to state law *de novo*. [*See* Salve Regina College v. Russell, 499 U.S. 225 (1991)]

b. **Subsequent State Court Decisions**
If the highest state court renders a decision on an issue after the federal court has made its determination, the decision of the district court may be changed to conform to the new decision of the highest state court until the disposition of the final federal appeal. [*See* Thomas v. American Home Products, Inc., 519 U.S. 913 (1996)]

D. **EXCEPTIONS TO DIVERSITY OF CITIZENSHIP JURISDICTION**
For historical reasons, even though diversity may be present, federal courts will not exercise jurisdiction over domestic relations or probate proceedings.

1. **Domestic Relations**
The federal court will not take jurisdiction over actions "involving the issuance of a divorce, alimony or child custody decree." [Akenbrandt v. Richards, 504 U.S. 689 (1992)] Note that this exception is quite narrow. Federal courts may maintain actions upon state court decrees, such as those for alimony. They also may hear cases involving intra-family torts. They refuse only cases involving issuance of decrees of divorce, alimony, or child custody.

2. **Probate Proceedings**
Federal courts will not take jurisdiction over proceedings maintainable in probate courts, but will take jurisdiction over actions by and against fiduciaries maintainable in state courts of general jurisdiction.

E. **MULTIPARTY, MULTIFORUM TRIAL JURISDICTION ACT OF 2002**
The Multiparty, Multiforum Jurisdiction Act applies to accidents meeting the statutory definition that occurred after January 30, 2003. The principal points are these:

1.   **Requirements**

   a.   **The Action**
      The Act grants jurisdiction to federal district courts of civil actions that (i) arise "from a *single accident,* (ii) *where at least 75 natural persons have died* in the accident (iii) *at a discrete location.*" [28 U.S.C. §1369(a)]

   b.   **Minimal Diversity**
      Such jurisdiction attaches based on *minimal diversity of citizenship*; thus, all that is required is that at least one plaintiff be of diverse citizenship from at least one defendant.

   c.   **One Additional Condition**
      In addition, however, *one of three other conditions* must be satisfied: either (i) a defendant "resides" in a different state from the place where "a substantial part" of the accident took place (even if the defendant also resides where the accident took place); (ii) any two defendants "reside" in different states; or (iii) substantial parts of the accident took place in different states.

2.   **Intervention**
   Anyone "with a claim arising from the accident" is *permitted to intervene* as a plaintiff, even if she could not have maintained an action in the district where the case is pending. [28 U.S.C. §1369(d)]

3.   **Service of Process**
   Finally, the Act provides for *nationwide service of process*. [28 U.S.C. §1697]

III.   FEDERAL QUESTION JURISDICTION

Section 1331: Federal Question

The district courts shall have original jurisdiction of all civil actions *arising under the Constitution, laws or treaties of the United States.* . . .

It is difficult to formulate a summary of the case holdings as to when an action "arises under" federal law. The best one can do, perhaps, is the following: A case arises under federal law if the plaintiff is alleging a right or interest that is substantially founded on federal law, which consists of federal common law, federal constitutional law, federal statutory law, treaty law, and federal administrative regulations.

A.   FEDERAL QUESTION MUST APPEAR IN THE COMPLAINT
The federal question must appear as part of the *plaintiff's cause of action* as set out in a well-pleaded complaint. It is therefore sometimes necessary to determine whether certain allegations are proper in pleading the cause of action, and whether the federal element is essential to the plaintiff's case.

1.   **Defendant's Answer or Defense Is Irrelevant**
   The content of the defendant's answer is not relevant; the existence of a defense based on federal law will not give federal question jurisdiction. Likewise, the court may not look to a counterclaim asserted by the defendant to determine whether the plaintiff's complaint states a federal question claim. [Holmes Group, Inc. v. Vornado Air Circulation System, Inc., 535 U.S. 826 (2002)]

2.   **Anticipation of a Defense**
   Similarly, a complaint does not raise a federal question if it does so only in anticipation of some defense.
   Example: A sues B for specific performance of a contract and alleges that B's refusal to perform is based on B's erroneous belief that federal law prohibits his perfor-mance. No federal question jurisdiction exists because the federal question presented by the plaintiff's complaint is merely in anticipation of B's de-fense. [Louisville & Nashville Railroad v. Mottley, 211 U.S. 149 (1908)]

B.   IMPLIED FEDERAL RIGHT OF ACTION
It is not essential that the federal statute expressly provide for a civil cause of action for an

alleged violation. Thus, federal question jurisdiction was held to exist in an action involving an alleged violation of the Fourth and Fifth Amendments [Bell v. Hood, 327 U.S. 678 (1946)] and an alleged violation of the Securities Exchange Acts of 1934 [J. I. Case v. Borak, 377 U.S. 426 (1964)], although neither the Constitution nor the act involved created a "remedy" for the wrongs complained of. However, not all federal provisions creating duties are held to create an implied private right of action. [Cort v. Ash, 422 U.S. 66 (1975)]

C. FEDERAL CORPORATIONS
Federal question jurisdiction does not arise merely from the fact that a corporate party was incorporated by an act of Congress *unless* the United States *owns more than one-half* of the corporation's capital stock, in which case it is treated as a federal agency that can sue or be sued on that basis in federal court. [28 U.S.C. §1349]

D. PENDENT (SUPPLEMENTAL) JURISDICTION OVER STATE CLAIMS
As previously discussed (*supra* II.A.5.), claims asserted by parties other than the plaintiff can invoke supplemental jurisdiction in any case that arises from the same transaction or occurrence as the original claim, whether it got into federal court by diversity of citizenship or federal question jurisdiction. Claims asserted by the plaintiff, however, can invoke supplemental jurisdiction only in federal question cases.

1. Pendent Claims
In some cases, the plaintiff will have both federal and state claims against the defendant. Although there may be no diversity, the federal court has *discretion* to exercise pendent jurisdiction over the claim based on state law if the two claims "derive from a common nucleus of operative fact" and are such that a plaintiff "would ordinarily be expected to try them all in one judicial proceeding." [United Mine Workers of America v. Gibbs, 383 U.S. 715 (1966)] Essentially, this means that the two claims must arise from the same transaction or occurrence. The supplemental jurisdiction statute [28 U.S.C. §1367(a)] adopts this standard for the grant of supplemental jurisdiction. That statute permits assertion of supplemental jurisdiction over claims by plaintiffs only in federal question (not diversity of citizenship) cases.

Example: P, a citizen of Arkansas, asserts two claims against D, who is also a citizen of Arkansas, in federal court. Importantly, both claims arise from the same transaction or occurrence. Claim #1 is for violation of a federal statute, and thus invokes federal question jurisdiction. Claim #2 is based on state law, and thus does not invoke federal question jurisdiction (because it is based on state, not federal, law). Also, Claim #2 does not invoke diversity of citizenship (because P and D are citizens of the same state). Nonetheless, Claim #2 invokes supplemental jurisdiction because it arises from the same transaction or occurrence as the claim that invoked federal question jurisdiction.

a. Effect of Dismissal of Federal Claim on Pendent Claim
The court may exercise pendent jurisdiction over the state claim even though the federal claim is dismissed on the merits. However, the state claim should probably also be dismissed (without prejudice) if the federal claim is dismissed before trial. Indeed, the supplemental jurisdiction statute provides that the court may refuse supplemental jurisdiction if the federal claim is dismissed, if the state claims are complex or novel, or if the state claims predominate substantially over federal claims. Note also that a federal court may not award relief against a state official based solely on a state law claim. [Pennhurst State School & Hospital v. Halderman, 465 U.S. 89 (1984)]

2. Pendent Parties
Pendent parties jurisdiction is relevant only in cases in which the plaintiff sues more than one defendant, there is a federal question claim against one defendant, and the claim against the second defendant does not invoke federal question or diversity of citizenship jurisdiction. Under the supplemental jurisdiction statute, the claim against the second defendant invokes supplemental jurisdiction if it arises from the same transaction or occurrence as the federal question claim against the first defendant.

Example: P asserts a federal question claim against D-1 and joins a transactionally related state law (not federal question) claim against D-2. P and D-2 are citizens of the same state. The claim against D-1 invokes federal question jurisdiction. The claim against D-2 does not invoke federal question jurisdiction (because it is based upon state law) and does not invoke diversity of citizenship jurisdiction (because P and D-2 are citizens of the same state). The claim against D-2 invokes supplemental jurisdiction, however, because it arises from the same transaction or occurrence as the claim that invoked federal question jurisdiction and is asserted by the plaintiff in a federal question case. (Remember, *plaintiff's* claims can invoke supplemental jurisdiction only in *federal question cases*.)

E. SPECIFIC STATUTORY GRANTS

1. Amount in Controversy
There is no amount in controversy requirement in federal question cases, with the narrow exception for cases brought against defendants *other than* the United States, its agencies, or employees under section 23(a) of the Consumer Product Safety Act. That section authorizes action by any person who sustains injury by reason of a knowing violation of a consumer product safety rule, or any other rule issued by the Commission. In such actions, at least $10,000 must be in controversy. [15 U.S.C. §2072]

2. Exclusive Jurisdiction
Congress has expressly provided that the jurisdiction of the federal courts shall be exclusive of state courts in:

a. Bankruptcy Proceedings [28 U.S.C. §1334]

b. Patent and Copyright Cases [28 U.S.C. §1338]

c. Many Cases Where United States Is Involved
Cases involving fines, penalties, or forfeitures under the laws of the United States; crimes against the United States; tort suits against the United States; or customs review. (Because of the doctrine of sovereign immunity, there is no jurisdiction in the courts to hear lawsuits against the United States unless the United States has consented to be sued.)

d. Cases with Consuls and Vice-Consuls as Defendants [28 U.S.C. §1351]

e. Antitrust Cases
Although section 1337 does not expressly make federal jurisdiction exclusive in actions arising under laws regulating interstate commerce, the federal antitrust statutes are interpreted to place the remedy exclusively in the federal courts. [Freeman v. Bee Machine Co., 319 U.S. 448 (1943)]

f. Admiralty Cases—Caveat
Section 1333 grants exclusive jurisdiction in cases of admiralty and maritime jurisdiction, but since the same section has a clause "saving to suitors in all cases all other remedies," the result is that federal jurisdiction is exclusive only in limitation of liability proceedings and in maritime actions in rem.

g. Foreign State—Caveat
Section 1441(d) permits a foreign state (or agency thereof), if sued in state court, to remove the action to federal court.

h. Postal Matters [28 U.S.C. §1339]

i. Internal Revenue [28 U.S.C. §1340]

j. Securities Exchange Act [15 U.S.C. §78a]

IV. VENUE

Section 1391: Venue Generally

(a) A civil action wherein jurisdiction is founded *only on diversity* of citizenship may, except as otherwise provided by law, be brought only in (i) a judicial district where any defendant resides, if all defendants reside in the same State, (ii) a judicial district in which a substantial part of the events or omissions giving rise to the claim occurred, or a substantial part of property that is the subject of the action is situated, or (iii) a judicial district in which any defendant is subject to personal jurisdiction at the time the action is commenced, if there is no district in which the action may otherwise be brought.

(b) A civil action wherein jurisdiction is *not* founded *solely on diversity* of citizenship may, except as otherwise provided by law, be brought only in (i) a judicial district where any defendant resides, if all defendants reside in the same State, (ii) a judicial district in which a substantial part of the events or omissions giving rise to the claim occurred, or a substantial part of property that is the subject of the action is situated, or (iii) a judicial district in which any defendant may be found, if there is no district in which the action may otherwise be brought.

(c) For purposes of venue under this chapter, a *defendant* that is a *corporation* shall be deemed to reside in *any judicial district in which it is subject to personal jurisdiction* at the time the action is commenced. In a State which has more than one judicial district and in which a defendant that is a corporation is subject to personal jurisdiction at the time an action is commenced, such corporation shall be deemed to reside in any district in that State within which its contacts would be sufficient to subject it to personal jurisdiction if that district were a separate State, and, if there is no such district, the corporation shall be deemed to reside in the district within which it has the most significant contacts.

(d) An alien may be sued in any district.

Section 1392: Defendants or Property in Different Districts in Same State

(a) Any civil action, not of a local nature, against defendants residing in different districts in the same State may be brought in *any of such districts*.

Section 1404: Change of Venue

(a) For the convenience of parties and witnesses, in the interest of justice, a district court may transfer any civil action to any other district or division *where it might have been brought*.

Section 1406: Cure or Waiver of Defects

(a) The district court of a district in which is filed a case laying venue in the wrong division or district shall *dismiss*, or if it be in the interest of justice, *transfer* such case to any district or division in which it could have been brought.

(b) Nothing in this chapter shall impair the jurisdiction of a district court of any matter involving a party who does not interpose timely and sufficient objection to the venue.

Federal venue rules determine the judicial district in which an action within the jurisdiction of federal courts may be brought.

A. SUBJECT MATTER JURISDICTION DISTINGUISHED

Subject matter jurisdiction and venue are very often confused. Subject matter jurisdiction is the *power* of the court to adjudicate the matter before it. Venue relates to the *proper district* in which to bring the action. Subject matter jurisdiction is a question of power or authority; venue is a question of convenience. Subject matter jurisdiction cannot be conferred by agreement; venue can be. A court can have subject matter jurisdiction without having proper venue.

Example: Smith, a citizen of Georgia, brings a personal injury suit arising in Florida against Jones, a citizen of New York. Suit is brought in the federal district court in California. The amount in controversy exceeds $75,000. Under section 1332, the district court has diversity jurisdiction, but venue is improper because section 1391, the general venue statute quoted above, requires that actions founded solely on diversity be brought in a district satisfying one of the requisites of section 1391(a).

B. GENERAL RULES

1. General Rules for Most Civil Actions

Venue in civil actions in the federal courts is proper in:

(i) A judicial district where *any defendant resides*, if all defendants reside in the same state;

(ii) A judicial district in which *a substantial part of the events or omissions giving rise to the claim occurred*, or *a substantial part of property that is the subject of the action is situated*; or

(iii) If there is no district anywhere in the United States which satisfies (i) or (ii),

    i. For actions based *solely on diversity*, a judicial district in which *any defendant is subject to personal jurisdiction at the time the action is commenced*; or

ii.   For actions *not based solely on diversity*, a judicial district in which *any defendant may be found*.

[28 U.S.C. §1391]

2. **Actions Involving Both Diversity and a Federal Question**
   If an action satisfies the jurisdictional requirements for both federal question and diversity jurisdiction, the venue provisions for *federal question* cases govern, because such a suit is not "based solely on diversity."

3. **Special Venue Provisions**
   There are many venue provisions applicable only to specified types of actions. Two worth noting are:

   a.   An alien may be sued in any district [28 U.S.C. §1391(d)]; and

   b.   Where the defendant is the United States or an agency thereof, or an officer, employee, etc., of the United States acting in his official capacity, a civil action may be brought where: (i) a defendant resides; (ii) a substantial part of the events or omissions giving rise to the action occurred, or a substantial part of property that is the subject of the action is situated; or (iii) the plaintiff resides if no real property is involved in the action [28 U.S.C. §1391(e)].

C. RESIDENCE

1. **Individuals**
   Residence for federal venue purposes is usually determined by a *person's domicile*. Therefore, a person who maintains two homes usually will be deemed to reside only in the district of his domicile. It is possible, however, for a domiciliary of one state to reside for venue purposes in a different state.

2. **Corporations**
   For purposes of venue, a corporation is deemed to reside in *any judicial district in which it is subject to personal jurisdiction* at the time the action is commenced. If a state has more than one judicial district, the corporation is deemed to reside in any district in the state within which the corporation's contacts would be sufficient to subject the corporation to personal jurisdiction if the district were a state; if there is no such district, the corporation is deemed to reside in the district within which it has the most significant contacts. [28 U.S.C. §1391(c)]

3. **Unincorporated Associations**
   For venue purposes, an unincorporated association "resides" where it does business. [Denver & Rio Grande Western Railroad v. Brotherhood of Railroad Trainmen, 387 U.S. 556 (1967)—union could be sued in Colorado where doing business]

D. VENUE IN "LOCAL ACTIONS"
A "local action" (*e.g.,* an in rem action relating to real property) must be brought in the district where the property that is the subject matter of the action is located. Section 1392(b) provides that where the property is located in more than one district in the same state, venue is proper in any such district.

E. IMPROPER VENUE MAY BE WAIVED
Unlike jurisdiction over the subject matter, venue may be waived by the parties. Venue is considered to be waived unless timely objection (in a pre-pleading motion or, where no such motion is made, in the answer) is made to the improper venue.

F. TRANSFER

1. **Where Original Venue Is Proper**
   Section 1404(a) allows transfer to another district where the action *"might have been brought"* even though venue has been properly laid in the court before which the motion to transfer is made. The policy behind section 1404 is that while venue may be correct, the parties or the witnesses might be greatly inconvenienced by the trial in the original forum. By balancing the relative convenience offered by the alternative forums, the original court has discretion to transfer the action to a court in which the action "might have been brought" in conformity with the rules governing: (i) subject matter jurisdiction, (ii) in personam jurisdiction over the defendant, and (iii) where venue is proper.

   The presence of a *forum selection clause* in a contract, by which the parties have specified a particular forum as the appropriate place for litigation, *is a factor* to be considered along with convenience and the interest of justice in deciding whether to transfer the case. [Stewart Organization, Inc. v. Ricoh Corp., 487 U.S. 22 (1988)]

2. Where Original Venue Is Improper
Section 1406(a) is designed for situations where the venue is improper and the alternative to transfer is dismissal of the action. The standard for transfer is *"the interest of justice."* Transfer is more appropriate than dismissal except in extraordinary circumstances. The transferee forum must have subject matter jurisdiction and in personam jurisdiction over the defendant, and venue must be proper. Some courts have held that section 1406(a) applies when the original court is a proper venue but lacks personal jurisdiction over the defendant. This view seems contrary to the language and purpose of the statute.

3. Where Original Court Lacks Personal Jurisdiction
The Supreme Court has held that the original court's lack of personal jurisdiction over the defendant does not affect its power to transfer a case under section 1404(a). [Goldlawr, Inc. v. Heiman, 369 U.S. 463 (1962)] There is also authority to support the conclusion that the same is true in transfers under section 1406(a). [*See, e.g.,* United States v. Berkowitz, 328 F.2d 358 (3d Cir. 1964)]

G. LAW APPLICABLE UPON TRANSFER

1. Original Venue Proper
A transfer solely on convenience grounds (under section 1404(a)) carries to the transferee court the originally applicable (under *Erie*) rules (including choice of law); *i.e.,* the law of the state in which the transferor court sat. This is true even where the plaintiff initiates a transfer for convenience after initially choosing the inconvenient forum. [Ferens v. Deere Co., 494 U.S. 516 (1990)]
Example: P sued D in a federal district court in Pennsylvania. Upon the transfer to Massachusetts, the district court judge there must apply the law that would have been applied in Pennsylvania. [Van Dusen v. Barrack, 376 U.S. 612 (1964)]

2. Original Venue Improper
A transfer on the ground that the original choice of venue was improper (under section 1406(a)) generally results in a change of the law applicable under *Erie; i.e.,* the law of the state in which the transferee court sits.
Example: P sued D in the federal district court in Maryland. Upon transfer to New York under section 1406(a), the law applied in the transferee court (New York) would be its own law.

V. REMOVAL JURISDICTION

Section 1441: Actions Removable Generally

(a) Except as otherwise expressly provided by Act of Congress, any civil action brought in a State court of which the district courts of the United States have *original jurisdiction*, may be *removed by the defendant* or the defendants, to the district court of the United States for the district and division embracing the place where such action is pending. For purposes of removal under this chapter, the citizenship of defendants sued under fictitious names shall be disregarded.

(b) Any civil action of which the district courts have original jurisdiction founded on a claim or right arising under the Constitution, treaties or laws of the United States shall be removable without regard to the citizenship or residence of the parties. Any other such action shall be removable *only if none* of the parties in interest properly joined and served as *defendants is a citizen of the State in which such action is brought*.

(c) Whenever a separate and independent claim or cause of action within the jurisdiction conferred by section 1331 of this title [federal question jurisdiction], is joined with one or more otherwise nonremovable claims or causes of action, *the entire case may be removed* and the district court may determine all issues therein, or, in its discretion, may remand all matters not otherwise within its original jurisdiction.

Section 1446: Procedure for Removal

(a) A defendant or defendants desiring to remove any civil action or criminal prosecution from a State court shall file in the district court of the United States for the district and division within which such action is pending a notice of removal signed pursuant to Rule 11 of the Federal Rules of Civil Procedure and containing a short and plain statement of the grounds for removal, together with a copy of all process, pleadings, and orders served upon such defendant or defendants in such action.

(b) The notice of removal of a civil action or proceeding shall be filed within *30 days* after receipt by the defendant, through service or otherwise, of a copy of the initial pleading setting forth the claim for relief upon which such action or proceeding is based, or within *30 days* after the service of summons upon the defendant if such initial pleading has been filed in court and is not required to be served on the defendant, whichever period is shorter.

If the case stated by the initial pleading is not removable, a notice of removal may be filed within *30 days* after receipt by the defendant, through service or otherwise, of a copy of an amended pleading, motion, order, or other paper from which it may first be ascertained that the case is one which is or has become removable, except that a case may *not* be removed on the basis of jurisdiction conferred by section 1332 of this title *more than 1 year after commencement of the action*.

Section 1447: Procedure After Removal Generally

(c) If at any time before final judgment it appears that the district court lacks subject matter jurisdiction, the case shall be *remanded*. An order remanding the case may require payment of just costs and any actual expenses, including attorney fees, incurred as a result of the removal. . . .

(d) An order remanding a case to the State court from which it was removed is not reviewable on appeal or otherwise. . . .

A. ORIGINAL JURISDICTION NECESSARY
Under section 1441(a), a defendant can only remove an action that could have originally been brought by the plaintiff in the federal courts.

1. When
The prevailing rule is that removal is tested only as of the date of removal. Some courts held under the statute as it existed before 1989 that original jurisdiction must have existed both at the time the suit was instituted in the state court and at the time of removal. [*In re* Carter, 618 F.2d 1093 (5th Cir. 1980)]

2. Federal Defense Insufficient
A defendant cannot remove on the ground that she has a defense grounded in federal law, since the existence of a federal defense is insufficient to confer original federal question jurisdiction under section 1331.

3. State Court Need Not Have Had Jurisdiction
By statute, the federal court *may* hear and decide a claim in a removed civil action even where the state court had no jurisdiction because the action is exclusively federal. [28 U.S.C. §1441(e)] Formerly, the federal court was required to dismiss.

B. ONLY DEFENDANT MAY REMOVE; ALL MUST SEEK REMOVAL
Only defendants can exercise the right of removal. Thus, a plaintiff cannot remove on the ground that a counterclaim against him could have been brought independently in a federal court.

If there is more than one defendant, ***all defendants*** must join in the removal. Thus, if some defendants are precluded under section 1446(b) from removing because of delay, or refuse to join in the removal, removal is not authorized.

C. VENUE

Venue for an action removed under section 1441(a) lies in the federal district court "embracing the place where such [state] action is pending." Note that in removal cases section 1441(a) determines proper venue, not section 1391(a). Thus, in a properly removed case, venue is proper in the federal court of the state where the case was pending, even if venue would have been improper had the plaintiff originally filed the action in the federal district court of that state.

Example: Linda, a citizen of State A, sues Jim, a citizen of State B, in the state court in State Z in the amount of $2 million for negligent acts Jim committed in State B. Jim may remove the case to the federal district court of State Z because the court has diversity jurisdiction and Jim is not a citizen of State Z. Although under section 1391(a) venue would have been improper if Linda had filed her case in the State Z federal district court, under section 1441(a) venue is proper in the federal district court of State Z because it "embraces the place" where the state court action was pending.

D. LIMITATIONS ON REMOVAL IN DIVERSITY OF CITIZENSHIP CASES

1. Defendant Citizen of Forum State

When the jurisdiction of the federal court is based on diversity and one of the defendants is a citizen of the state in which the state action was brought, the action is not removable.

Example: Jones, a citizen of State A, sues Brown, a citizen of State B, and Smith, a citizen of State C, in the state court in State B. Although diversity jurisdiction would have existed originally (assuming the jurisdictional amount had been met), Brown and Smith cannot remove. Had Jones brought the action in the state court in State A, Brown and Smith could remove. [28 U.S.C. §1441(b)]

When the original jurisdiction of the district court would have been based on a federal question, the defendants can remove without regard to the citizenship of the parties.

2. One Year Rule

A case may not be removed on the basis of diversity of citizenship jurisdiction more than one year after it was commenced in state court. [28 U.S.C. §1446(b)] Note, however, that a case must be removed no later than 30 days after the defendant discovers, through service of an amended pleading, order, etc., that the case has become removable (*see* G.2., *infra*). Because most cases will be removable, if at all, at commencement of the action, the one-year deadline generally will not be difficult to meet. The provision may be important, however, if the case is not removable at the outset, but becomes removable later. The one-year rule does not apply to removals based upon federal question jurisdiction.

Examples: 1) A (a citizen of State A) sues B (a citizen of State B) in state court in State A, seeking damages of $100,000. The case is removable at its commencement, since the case meets the requirements of diversity of citizenship jurisdiction and no defendant is a citizen of the forum. B must remove the case within 30 days of being served with process.

2) P (a citizen of State A) sues D1 (a citizen of State B) and D2 (a citizen of State A) in state court in State C, seeking damages of $250,000. The case is not removable at its commencement, since it does not satisfy the complete diversity rule for diversity of citizenship jurisdiction. However, if P later voluntarily dismisses the claim against D2, the case becomes removable. D1 must then remove within 30 days. But if more than a year has passed since the state case was commenced, D1 cannot remove on the basis of diversity of citizenship. This rule has been criticized, since it permits P to join a defendant who destroys diversity jurisdiction, wait a year and a day, dismiss the claim against that defendant, and thus thwart the diverse defendant's ability to remove the case to federal court.

E. DISMISSAL OF NONDIVERSE PARTY ALLOWS REMOVAL

If no federal question is involved and diversity does not exist because a party is a co-citizen of an opposing party, removal will be permitted if the nondiverse parties are thereafter dismissed from the action and there is complete diversity between the remaining parties. The removal must be made within 30 days after the defendant discovers, through service of an amended pleading, order, etc., that the case has become removable, and not more than one year after the action was commenced. (*See* G.2., *infra.*)

Example: Brown, a citizen of State B, sues Jones, a citizen of State A, and Smith, a citizen of State B, in the state court in State B. No removal is possible because complete diversity does not exist. However, if Smith is dismissed from the state action, Jones can remove to the federal court (assuming time limits are met) because all parties remaining are diverse.

F.   DEFENDANT MAY REMOVE SEPARATE AND INDEPENDENT FEDERAL QUESTION CLAIM

If there are multiple claims or multiple parties, under 28 U.S.C. section 1441(c), a defendant may remove a *whole case* if it contains "a separate and independent claim or cause of action" within federal question jurisdiction. The federal district court may then retain the whole case, or sever and remand the matters not within its original jurisdiction.

G.   PROCEDURE FOR REMOVAL

1.   Notice of Removal

A defendant seeking removal must file a notice of removal—containing a short and plain statement of the grounds for removal and signed under Rule 11—in the federal district court in the district and division within which the action is pending. A copy of the notice should be sent to the other parties *and* to the state court. Once this is done, the state court can no longer deal with the case. If the state court attempts to do so, the federal court can enjoin the state court's action.

2.   Time

A defendant must file a notice of removal within 30 days "after receipt by the defendant, through service or otherwise, of a copy of the initial pleading." [28 U.S.C. §1446(b)] The "through service or otherwise" language is intended to address different state approaches to the order of filing a case and serving process. For instance, in some states, the defendant is served with a summons but not a copy of the complaint. For such defendants, the 30-day removal period would start to run upon formal receipt of the complaint.

Example: P files an action against B in state court. P faxes a "courtesy copy" of the complaint to B, but does not have formal process (a summons and complaint) served for two weeks. D removes the case within 30 days after being served with process, but more than 30 days after receiving the faxed copy of the complaint. Was removal timely? Yes. The 30 days ran from service of process on the defendant. [Murphy Brothers v. Michetti Pipe Stringing, Inc., 526 U.S. 344 (1999)]

3.   Procedure After Removal

After removal, the case proceeds according to the federal rules of procedure. Repleading is not necessary unless the court so orders. If the defendant has not answered, she must answer or present the other defenses or objections available to her under the Federal Rules within 20 days after being served, or within five days after filing the petition for removal, whichever period is longer. Amendments may be made to pleadings filed before removal.

4.   Right to Jury Trial

a.   Demand for Jury Trial

The right to a jury trial in a case removed to a federal court may be waived unless a timely demand for a jury trial is filed. If, at the time of removal, all necessary pleadings have been served, a trial by jury will be granted to a party so entitled. The removing party must file a demand for jury trial within 10 days after the notice of removal is filed. The nonremoving party must file for jury trial within 10 days after service on her of the notice of filing for removal.

b.   Demand Not Required

A party who, *prior to removal*, has made an express demand for trial by jury in accordance with state law, need not make a demand after removal. In addition, if *state law* applicable in the court from which the case is removed does not require the parties to make an express demand in order to claim trial by jury, they need not make such demand after removal unless the court directs they do so.

5. Remand

A plaintiff can file a motion to have the case remanded (sent back) to the state court. If the plaintiff bases this motion on a defect other than subject matter jurisdiction (*e.g.,* a defect in removal procedures), it must be brought within 30 days of removal. The court must remand, however, whenever it is shown that there was no federal subject matter jurisdiction. If the court erroneously fails to remand, but the subject matter defect is cured before trial begins, failure to remand does not require that the federal judgment be vacated. [Caterpillar Inc. v. Lewis, 519 U.S. 61 (1996)] The federal court has discretion to remand a case to state court once all federal claims have been resolved, leaving only state claims over which there would be no diversity jurisdiction. [Carnegie-Mellon University v. Cohill, 484 U.S. 343 (1988)] Appellate review of remand orders is generally barred [28 U.S.C. §1447(d)]; however, appeal is allowed where a case involving civil rights is remanded to state court. Remand orders can also be reviewed by means of a mandamus if the remand represented a refusal to exercise plainly proper jurisdiction. [Thermtron v. Hermansdorfer, 423 U.S. 336 (1976)]

a. Subject Matter Jurisdiction Generally Considered First

Ordinarily, a federal court will determine whether it has subject matter jurisdiction before it considers the merits of the case. [Steel Co. v. Citizens for Better Environment, 523 U.S. 83 (1998)] However, the Supreme Court has held that a federal court could address the issue of personal jurisdiction before assessing subject matter jurisdiction. The circumstances of the case were unusual, however, in that the defendant removed on a novel theory attempting to invoke a rarely used basis of subject matter jurisdiction, and whether that basis was met would have been an issue of first impression. On the other hand, the personal jurisdiction issue was relatively uncomplicated and presented no difficult issue of state law. In these circumstances, the court did not abuse its discretion by addressing personal jurisdiction first. [Ruhrgas AG v. Marathon Oil Co., 526 U.S. 574 (1999)]

H. SPECIFIC TYPES OF ACTIONS

1. Removable

Statutes allow removal of certain actions against *federal officers* when they were allegedly acting under color of law [28 U.S.C. §1442] and *federal employees* for torts by motor vehicle committed in the scope of employment [28 U.S.C. §2679(d)]; actions involving *international banking*; and criminal or civil actions where the defendant will be denied a right protected under federal *civil rights* statutes [28 U.S.C. §1443], but only if the denial is inevitable under state law [Georgia v. Rachel, 384 U.S. 780 (1966)]. Not all of these special types of cases could have been brought originally in the federal courts.

2. Nonremovable

Actions under the Federal Employers Liability Act ("FELA") and the Jones Act are not removable; nor are actions for less than $10,000 against carriers for losses to certain shipments in interstate commerce, workers' compensation proceedings [28 U.S.C. §1445], or actions under the Fair Labor Standards Act. The plaintiff thus has the option to bring these cases in state court.

a. All Writs Act Not a Basis for Removal

Some courts permitted removal of a case under the All Writs Act, 28 U.S.C. section 1651 (permitting federal courts to "issue all writs necessary or appropriate in aid of their respective jurisdictions and agreeable to the usages and principles of law"), even if the case did not invoke federal subject matter jurisdiction. However, the Supreme Court held that the All Writs Act does not provide an independent basis for removal jurisdiction; a case thus must satisfy some independent basis of subject matter jurisdiction, such as diversity of citizenship or federal question jurisdiction. [Syngenta Crop Protection, Inc. v. Henson, 537 U.S. 28 (2002)]

VI. CONFLICT OF JURISDICTION BETWEEN STATE AND FEDERAL COURTS

A. INJUNCTIONS AGAINST PENDING STATE PROCEEDINGS

A federal court is prohibited from enjoining *pending* state court proceedings unless *expressly* authorized by statute (*e.g.,* the interpleader provision expressly authorizes injunctions against state court proceedings), or "where necessary in aid of its jurisdiction, or to protect or effectuate its judgments." [28 U.S.C. §2283]

B.   INJUNCTIONS AGAINST THREATENED STATE CRIMINAL PROSECUTIONS
Threatened state criminal prosecutions (*i.e.,* where state court proceedings have not already been instituted) will be enjoined only when necessary *to prevent irreparable harm* which is clear and imminent *and* where *appellate remedies in the criminal case are clearly inadequate to provide relief.* Such injunctions are almost invariably denied, except where a federal right of free speech or assembly or a federally protected civil right is threatened by the state criminal proceeding, and it is shown that the prosecution is in bad faith or is for the purpose of harassment. Relief by declaratory judgment will ordinarily be denied if an injunction would be denied.

C.   INJUNCTIONS AGAINST STATE TAX PROCEDURES
28 U.S.C. section 1341 prohibits injunctions against the assessment, levy, or collection of state taxes "where there is a plain, speedy and efficient remedy . . . in the courts of such State." [*See* Rosewell v. LaSalle National Bank, 450 U.S. 503 (1980)]

D.   THE DOCTRINE OF ABSTENTION

1.   **Policy of Abstention**
Under certain circumstances the federal courts will retain jurisdiction over a suit involving *a challenge to the constitutionality of a state law* but abstain from deciding the question until a decision has been made by the state courts on the meaning of the state law. A determinative interpretation of the state law may obviate the federal constitutional question. The considerations that have led federal courts to refrain from deciding a challenge to the constitutionality of a state law include:

(i)   Possible unnecessary friction with the state, particularly when a state regulatory plan based on predominantly local factors is in issue;

(ii)   Possible error in the construction of an unclear state law; and

(iii) Reluctance to decide constitutional questions unnecessarily (where the state court might construe the state statute in such a way that it would be constitutional).

Note that in cases where abstention would be proper, the federal courts ordinarily should stay the federal action rather than dismiss it.

2.   **Federal Intervention in Certain Cases**
If the challenged state statute is "flagrantly and patently violative of express constitutional prohibitions in every clause, sentence and paragraph, and in whatever manner and against whomever an effort might be made to apply it" [Huffman v. Pursue, Ltd., 420 U.S. 592 (1975)], then "the federal court need not stay its hand in the face of pending state proceedings" [Moore v. Sims, 442 U.S. 415 (1979)].

Federal intervention on constitutional grounds may occur if the federal plaintiff can demonstrate:

a.   Great and immediate irreparable injury;

b.   Bad faith in the prosecution of the state action; or

c.   Harassment or other unusual circumstances calling for federal equitable relief.

VII.   THE FEDERAL RULES OF CIVIL PROCEDURE

A.   COMMENCEMENT OF THE ACTION
Rule 3 provides that an action is commenced by *filing a complaint* with the court. Federal courts may adopt local rules to permit filing by fax or other electronic means. Filing a complaint before the statute of limitations has run will satisfy the statute of limitations in federal question cases and in diversity cases where the state rule is similar. However, the Supreme Court has held that a state rule that an action is commenced for purposes of the statute of limitations *only upon service of process* must be applied in diversity cases. [Walker v. Armco Steel Corp., 446 U.S. 740 (1980)]

B. SERVICE OF PROCESS

1. Who May Serve
Rule 4 authorizes any person not a party to the action who is at least 18 years old to serve process (summons and complaint). In certain limited situations (*e.g.,* where the United States or an officer or agency of the United States is plaintiff), a party may request that service be made by a United States marshal, or by another person appointed by the court for that purpose.

2. How Service Is Made
Generally, Rule 4 provides that personal service or service left at the defendant's usual place of abode with one of suitable age and discretion residing therein, or service upon an authorized agent of the defendant, is valid. Alternatively, service may be made under state rules or, under the waiver of service provision of Rule 4(d), by mail.

a. Service Under State Rules
Rule 4(e) provides that service may alternatively be made as provided by the rules of the state in which the federal court sits or the state in which service is to be effected, regardless of whether the action is founded on diversity of citizenship jurisdiction. Hence, federal courts can use state long arm provisions.

b. Waiver of Service (Service by Mail)
Alternatively, plaintiff may mail to defendant (by first class mail) a copy of the complaint with a request to waive formal service of summons. The waiver is effected by defendant's return of a waiver form included in the mailing. Defendant has 30 days from the date the request is sent in which to return the waiver. The waiver of service does not waive defendant's right to object to venue or jurisdiction. Failure of defendant to waive formal service requires plaintiff to effect service by some other proper method, and defendant shall be liable for the cost of this service. A defendant who waives formal service obtains an advantage in addition to avoiding the costs of alternative service: she must answer not later than *60 days* after the date on which the request for waiver was mailed to her, as compared to *20 days* if the plaintiff is required to effect formal service of the summons and complaint.

3. Parties Served Outside State
The court will acquire personal jurisdiction over parties served outside the state:

(i) Under statute and rules for extraterritorial service of the state in which the federal court sits (domiciliaries, long arm jurisdiction, and in rem jurisdiction);

(ii) If they are third-party defendants [Fed. R. Civ. P. 14] or required to be joined for just adjudication [Fed. R. Civ. P. 19], if served within 100 miles from the place where the action is pending (but within the United States); and

(iii) If out-of-state service is permitted by federal statute (*e.g.,* interpleader).

As to a federal question claim, the court can exercise personal jurisdiction over a defendant who is not subject to the jurisdiction of a particular state, as long as the defendant's contacts with the United States would satisfy the constitutional standard for exercise of jurisdiction and jurisdiction is not precluded by statute.

4. Immunity from Process
The federal courts recognize the immunity from service of process of parties, witnesses, and attorneys who enter a state to appear in another action. In addition, if a party was induced by the plaintiff's fraud or deceit to enter a state so that he could be served, the service is invalid and the court does not acquire personal jurisdiction.

C. EXTENSION OF TIME PERIODS
Rule 6(b) gives the district court power to extend the period within which actions under the Federal Rules must be performed. However, certain time periods may never be extended. The following motions must be filed, with no extensions, *within 10 days after entry of judgment*: renewed motion for judgment as a matter of law, motion to amend judgment, motion for new trial, motion to amend findings of fact in nonjury case, and grant of new trial on court's initiative.

D. INTERLOCUTORY INJUNCTIONS
An interlocutory injunction is an equitable remedy by which a person is ordered to act or to

refrain from acting in a specified manner. Interlocutory injunctions are granted to maintain the status quo until a trial on the merits may be held.

1. **Preliminary Injunction**
A preliminary injunction is sought by a party prior to a trial on the merits of the complaint. A preliminary injunction may not be issued without notice to the adverse party. [Fed. R. Civ. P. 65(a)]

2. **Temporary Restraining Order**
A temporary restraining order ("TRO") is granted by a court when it is necessary to prevent irreparable injury to a party, and the injury will result before a preliminary injunction hearing can be held.

   a. **Requirements for Ex Parte Temporary Restraining Orders**
   Generally, notice must be given before a TRO is issued. However, a court may grant a TRO *without notice to the adverse party* if three requirements are met [Fed. R. Civ. P. 65(b), (c)]:

      1) **Specific Facts Showing Immediate and Irreparable Injury**
      The moving party must give specific facts in an affidavit or in the verified complaint to establish that immediate and irreparable injury will result to the moving party before the adverse party can be heard in opposition.

      2) **Efforts to Give Notice**
      The moving party must certify in writing all efforts she made to give notice to the adverse party and the reasons why notice should not be required.

      3) **Security**
      The moving party must provide some security, the amount of which is determined by the court, to pay for any costs and damages incurred by the adverse party if he was wrongfully enjoined or restrained.

   b. **Discretion of Court**
   Even if the above requirements are met, the court still has discretion whether to issue the TRO. The court may look at the likelihood that the plaintiff will prevail on the merits of the complaint. Also, the court may weigh the injury anticipated by the moving party against the harm caused by issuing the TRO.

   c. **Ten Day Limit**
   The TRO will expire within 10 days unless the restrained party consents to an extension or good cause is shown for an extension.

E. **PLEADINGS**
Pleadings serve the function of giving *notice* to the opposing parties.

1. **Complaint**
Each claim for relief should contain:

   a. A short statement of the grounds for the court's jurisdiction;

   b. A short statement of the claim showing that the pleader is entitled to relief; and

   c. A demand for judgment for relief, which may be in the alternative.

2. **Pre-Answer Motions**

   a. **Rule 12(b)**
   Prior to filing an answer, the defendant may, if he chooses, file a motion and raise any or all of the following defenses:

      (i) Lack of subject matter jurisdiction;

      (ii) Lack of personal jurisdiction;

      (iii) Improper venue;

      (iv) Insufficiency of process;

(v)   Insufficiency of service of process;

(vi) Failure to state a claim upon which relief can be granted (*i.e.,* even if plaintiff's allegations are taken as true, relief could not be granted); or

(vii) Failure to join a party needed for a just adjudication (includes necessary and indispensable parties).

The first defense may be raised at any time—even for the first time *on appeal*. The defendant must raise defenses (ii) through (v) *at the time he files a motion or his answer*—whichever is first. If he does not, the defendant waives these defenses. The last two defenses (if limited to failure to join an "indispensable party") can be made *at any time prior to trial or "at trial."* The defendant may choose not to file a motion and instead raise these defenses in his answer.

b.   **Motion for More Definite Statement**
A party may move for a more definite statement before responding (by filing an answer or reply) to a pleading (a complaint) that is so vague or ambiguous that a responsive pleading cannot reasonably be framed. The opposing party has 10 days after notice of an order to obey unless the court fixes a different time. If not obeyed, the court may strike the pleading. [Fed. R. Civ. P. 12(e)]

c.   **Motion to Strike**
Before responding to a pleading or, if no responsive pleading is permitted, within 20 days after service of the pleading, a party may move to have stricken any insufficient defense, or any redundant, immaterial, impertinent, or scandalous matter. Such motion may also be made upon the court's initiative at any time. [Fed. R. Civ. P. 12(f)]

And note: An objection of failure to state a legal defense to a claim is not waived merely because a Rule 12(f) motion is not made. Such a defense can be made by motion for judgment on the pleadings, or at the trial. [Fed. R. Civ. P. 12(h)]

3.   **Answer**

a.   **Must Contain Denials or Admissions and Any Affirmative Defenses**
The answer must contain a *specific* denial or admission of each averment of the complaint, or a *general* denial with specific admissions to certain averments. Where the defendant is without knowledge or information sufficient to form a belief, a statement to that effect constitutes a denial. A *failure to deny* constitutes an **admission.** The answer must also state any *affirmative defenses* the defendant may have, such as statute of limitations, Statute of Frauds, res judicata, etc.

b.   **Time**
If no Rule 12 motion is made, a defendant who was formally served with a summons and complaint must present an answer within *20 days* after service; a defendant to whom the complaint was mailed and who waives formal service must answer within *60 days* after the request for waiver was mailed to her. If a Rule 12 motion is made and the court does not fix another time, the responsive pleading is to be served within *10 days* of the court's denial or postponement of the motion. The answer is due within *10 days* of service of a more definite statement if the court grants a Rule 12(e) motion.

c.   **Counterclaims**
Claims that the defendant may have against the plaintiff may be pleaded in the answer as counterclaims. If a counterclaim arises out of the *same transaction or occurrence* as one of the plaintiff's claims, it is a *compulsory* counterclaim and must be pleaded or it will be barred. Any other counterclaim is permissive and may be asserted even though there is no connection at all between it and the plaintiff's claim.

4.   **Inconsistent Claims or Defenses**
A party may set out as many alternative claims or defenses as he may have regardless of consistency.

5.   **Special Pleading**
The general rule of pleading is for short and plain statements, but there are certain rules for special circumstances. Note that in some of these situations (notably concerning fraud,

mistake, and special damages), the Federal Rules require a party to state more detail than simply a short and plain statement. These situations requiring greater specificity are narrow, however, and the Supreme Court has emphasized that courts have no power to impose such rigorous pleading requirements outside the areas addressed by Federal Rule or statute. [Swierkiewicz v. Sorema N.A., 534 U.S. 506 (2002)—lower court erred by requiring detailed pleading of employment discrimination claim; Leatherman v. Tarrant County, 507 U.S. 163 (1993)—lower court erred by requiring detailed pleading of civil rights case against municipality]

a. Capacity
Capacity or authority to sue or be sued *need not be alleged*. A person wishing to challenge a party's capacity has the duty to raise the issue by specific negative averment, including such particulars as are within his knowledge.

b. Fraud or Mistake
Circumstances that establish fraud or mistake must be stated with *particularity*. [Fed. R. Civ. P. 9(b)] By statute (the Private Securities Litigation Reform Act), plaintiffs in federal securities fraud cases must plead with particularity facts relating to the defendant's acting with the required scienter.

c. Conditions of the Mind
Malice, intent, knowledge, or other conditions of the mind may be averred *generally*.

d. Conditions Precedent
The performance of conditions precedent may be alleged *generally*. Denial of performance or occurrence must be made specifically and with particularity.

e. Official Document or Act
When dealing with an official document or act, it is *sufficient* to aver that it was issued or the act was *done in compliance with the law*.

f. Judgment
It is *not necessary to aver jurisdiction* when a domestic or foreign court or a board or officer renders a judgment or decision.

g. Timing
Time and place averments are *material* for the purpose of testing the sufficiency of a pleading.

h. Special Damages
Elements of special damages must be *specifically* stated. [Fed. R. Civ. P. 9(g)]

6. Reply
A reply *by the plaintiff* is required *only* where the defendant's answer contains a counterclaim denominated as such. The reply must be served within 20 days after service of the answer or, if the reply is ordered by the court, within 20 days of the court order. A plaintiff need not reply to an affirmative defense; he is deemed to deny or avoid the allegation of the defense.

7. Amendment and Supplemental Pleadings

a. Amendment
As a matter of course, a pleading may be amended *once* before a responsive pleading is served, or if no responsive pleading is required, within 20 days of service of the pleading. Thereafter, a pleading may be amended only by the written consent of the adverse party or by leave of the court upon motion. Leave of the court is "freely given when justice so requires."

1) Relation Back
Amendments relate back to the date that the original pleading was filed if the conduct, transaction, or occurrence set forth in the amendment was set forth or attempted to be set forth in the original pleading. Amendments also relate back if relation back is permitted by the law that provides the statute of limitations applicable to the action.

2) Changing Party

An amendment changing the party or the naming of the party against whom a claim is asserted relates back if the amendment concerns the same conduct, transaction, or occurrence as the original pleading *and* if, within 120 days after filing the complaint (and such additional time as the court may order upon showing of good cause) the party to be brought in by amendment:

a) Has received such notice of the action that she will not be prejudiced in maintaining her defense on the merits; and

b) Knew or should have known that, but for a mistake concerning the proper party's identity, the action would have been brought against her.

3) Conform to Evidence

A pleading may be amended during or after trial or even after judgment to conform to the evidence, reflect an issue actually tried by the express or implied consent of the parties, or permit raising new issues at trial. However, a party may not raise a new claim or defense for which the opposing party had no opportunity to prepare and which would result in prejudice in maintaining his action or defense. [Fed. R. Civ. P. 15(b)]

4) Due Process Limitation

Amendments to pleadings must satisfy due process. For example, in *Nelson v. Adams U.S.A. Inc.*, 529 U.S. 460 (2000), the trial court permitted a post-verdict amendment to add a defendant, and simultaneously entered judgment against that new defendant. The Supreme Court held that this procedure violated the new defendant's due process rights. The Federal Rules are meant to provide an opportunity for an added defendant to respond to a claim, and do not permit such "swift passage from pleading to judgment in the pleader's favor."

b. Supplemental Pleadings

Supplemental pleadings relate to matters *occurring after* the date of the original pleading. The permission of the court, upon motion, is required. Permission may be granted even though the original pleading is defective in its statement of a claim for relief or a defense. [Fed. R. Civ. P. 15(d)]

8. Rule 11

a. Certification upon Presenting Paper to Court

In federal civil cases, the attorney (or unrepresented party), by presenting to the court a pleading, written motion, or other paper, certifies that to the best of her knowledge, information, and belief formed after an inquiry reasonable under the circumstances:

(i) The paper is not presented for any *improper purpose* (harassment, delay, etc.);

(ii) The legal contentions therein are *warranted by existing law* or a nonfrivolous argument for the *modification of existing law* or the establishment of a new law;

(iii) The allegations and factual contentions either have, or upon further investigation or discovery are likely to have, *evidentiary support*; and

(iv) Denials of factual contentions are *warranted on the evidence* or, where specified, are reasonably based on a lack of information and belief.

The certification applies anew each time an attorney or unrepresented party "later advocates" a position contained in a pleading, motion, etc. Thus, a paper that was not sanctionable when first presented may become sanctionable if the attorney or party later advocating a position contained in the paper has since learned that the position no longer has merit.

b. Sanctions

The court has discretion to impose sanctions, "limited to what is sufficient to deter repetition of such conduct," against a party who presents a paper to the court in violation of the above requirements, either on the court's own initiative or on motion of the opposing party.

Where appropriate, sanctions may be imposed against parties, attorneys, or law firms, and may consist of nonmonetary directives or monetary penalties including payment of expenses and attorneys' fees incurred because of the improper paper.

1) Court's Initiative
A court on its own initiative may enter an order describing the matter that appears to violate Rule 11 and direct the proponent to show cause why sanctions should not be imposed.

2) Party's Motion
A party who believes that his opponent has presented a paper in violation of Rule 11 may serve a motion for sanctions on the party. If the party does not withdraw or correct the matter within 21 days, the moving party may then file the motion for sanctions with the court.

F. JOINDER

1. Joinder of Parties

a. Capacity
An individual's capacity to sue or be sued is determined by the law of her domicile; the capacity of an organization (*e.g.,* an association or partnership) is determined by the law of the state where the federal court sits, except that a partnership or unincorporated association always has capacity where a substantive federal right is asserted by or against it.

b. Compulsory Joinder—Persons Needed for Just Adjudication
Under Rule 19, a party is "needed for just adjudication" if: (i) complete relief cannot be given to existing parties in her absence; (ii) disposition in her absence may impair her ability to protect her interest in the controversy; *or* (iii) her absence would expose existing parties to a substantial risk of double or inconsistent obligations. *But note:* The Supreme Court has held that a joint tortfeasor subject to joint and several liability is not a person needed for just adjudication. [Temple v. Synthes Corp., 498 U.S. 5 (1990)]

1) Must Be Joined If Possible
If a party needed for just adjudication is amenable to process *and* her joinder will not destroy diversity or venue, she must be joined.

2) Where Joinder Is Impossible
If joinder is not feasible (*i.e.,* the party is not subject to process, objects to venue, or would destroy diversity jurisdiction), the court must decide whether the action can proceed in the party's absence or must be dismissed. The court must consider these four factors:

(i) Whether the judgment in the party's absence would prejudice her or the existing parties;

(ii) Whether the prejudice can be reduced in shaping the judgment;

(iii) Whether a judgment in the party's absence would be adequate; and

(iv) Whether the plaintiff will be deprived of an adequate remedy if the action is dismissed.

The cases have shown a preference for dismissal if there is a state forum where all the parties may be joined in practice as well as in theory.

c. Permissive Joinder

1) Requirements
Parties may join as plaintiffs or be joined as defendants whenever:

(i) Some claim is made by each plaintiff and against each defendant relating to or arising out of the *same series of occurrences or transactions; and*

(ii) There is a *question of fact or law common* to all the parties.

> *Example:* It is very common for all persons injured in an automobile accident to join as plaintiffs. The common issue is the defendant's negligence; the other issues of contributory negligence and damages are tried individually for each plaintiff.

The court is given wide discretion to order separate trials where joinder would be unfair to a party not sufficiently involved in all the claims.

2) Jurisdiction

The rule permitting broad joinder does not alter the requirements of jurisdiction: There must be **complete diversity**, and each claim must satisfy the **jurisdictional amount**, except that plaintiffs with a common undivided interest in a claim exceeding $75,000 may join in asserting it, even if their individual share in the interest is less than $75,000.

2. Joinder of Claims

The policy of the Federal Rules is to permit the adjudication of all claims between the parties and all claims arising out of a single transaction. A plaintiff can join any number and type of claims against a defendant; where multiple plaintiffs or multiple defendants are involved, it is essential only that at least one of the claims arise out of a transaction in which all were involved.

a. Successive Claims

Rule 18(b) permits the plaintiff to join two claims when success on the first is a prerequisite to the second, such as a claim for money damages and a suit to set aside a conveyance that was fraudulent because of the debt asserted in the first claim.

b. Jurisdiction

When jurisdiction is based on the diversity of citizenship between the plaintiff and defendant, the plaintiff may aggregate all claims she has against the defendant to satisfy the jurisdictional amount. Where jurisdiction is based on a "federal question" claim, a nonfederal claim can be joined only if it is regarded as part of the same case or controversy as the federal claim, *i.e.,* the "pendent" jurisdiction test of state and federal claims arising from a "common nucleus of operative fact."

> *Example:* Plaintiffs claimed that the defendant appropriated plaintiffs' literary work in such a way as to (i) infringe federal law copyright, and (ii) constitute state law unfair competition. There was federal pendent jurisdiction over the state claim. [Hurn v. Oursler, 289 U.S. 238 (1933)]

c. Class Actions

1) Prerequisites

Rule 23 takes a functional approach to the class action device. Named representatives will be permitted to sue on behalf of a class if:

a) The class is so **numerous** that joinder of all members is **impracticable**;

b) There are **questions of law or fact** common to the class;

c) The **named parties' interests are typical** of the class;

d) The named representatives will ensure the **fair and adequate representation** of the interests of absent members of the class [Rule 23(a)]; and

e) The action meets **any** of the following requirements of Rule 23(b):

(1) Separate actions by class members would create a **risk of inconsistent results** or, as a practical matter, would impair the interests of other absent members of the class; or

(2) A defendant has acted or refused to act on grounds applicable to the class and **injunctive or declaratory relief is appropriate** for the class as a whole (*e.g.,* most civil rights actions); or

(3) There are **questions of fact or law common to members** of the class that **predominate** over individual issues and a class action is superior to the alternative methods of adjudication.

2) Consideration in Treating Case as a Class Action
The court should determine at an early practicable time whether the action may be maintained as a class action, *i.e.,* whether to "certify" a class, but may determine at any time thereafter that the action is not an appropriate one for class action treatment. In determining whether to treat the case as a class action, the court should consider, inter alia, the following factors: (i) the interest of individual control, (ii) the extent and nature of litigation elsewhere on the same subject, (iii) the desirability of having the whole package in this court, and (iv) the difficulties in managing the class action.

a) Court Must Define Class Claims, Issues, or Defenses
The court, in certifying a class, must "define the class and the class claims, issues, or defenses."

b) Appointment of Class Counsel
The court must appoint class counsel for every certified class and expressly mandates that the attorney must fairly and adequately represent the interests of the class. [Rule 23(g)(1)]

3) Effect of Judgment
All members of a class will be *bound* by the judgment rendered in a class action *except* those in a "common question" class action [Fed. R. Civ. P. 23(b)(3); *see* (3), *supra*] who notify the court that they do not wish to be bound ("opting out"). Members of Rule 23(b)(1) and 23(b)(2) classes cannot opt out. Note, however, that if the substantive claim of the individual representing the class is mooted, this *does not* render the class action moot. [United States Parole Commission v. Geraghty, 445 U.S. 388 (1980)—release from prison of named plaintiff in class action suit challenging parole procedure did not moot entire class action suit]

a) Personal Jurisdiction Over Absent Class Members Not Required
The due process/minimum contacts requirements that must be met for the assertion of personal jurisdiction need not be satisfied to bind absent members of the plaintiff class in a Rule 23(b)(3) ("common question") suit who chose not to opt out. [Phillips Petroleum Co. v. Shutts, 472 U.S. 797 (1985)] This allows a state or federal court to bind persons to a class action judgment under Rule 23(b)(3) even though they have no contact at all with the state.

4) Notice

a) Notice Required in Common Question Suits
Notice to all members of the class of the pendency of the class action *of the pendency* of the class action is required under Rule 23 only in *"common question" suits* [Fed. R. Civ. P. 23(b)(3)], so that class members can opt out. The notice must state (i) the nature of the action, (ii) the definition of the class, (iii) the class claims, issues, or defenses, and (iv) the binding effect of a class judgment.

b) Notice Discretionary in Other Types of Class Action Suits
Notice to members of the class of the pendency of the class action in other class suits is discretionary with the court. [*See* Eisen v. Carlisle & Jacquelin, 417 U.S. 156 (1974); Oppenheimer v. Sanders, 437 U.S. 340 (1978)]

Note: Notice of *dismissal or compromise* is a separate notice. It must be given to class members of all types of class actions if the case is dismissed or settled. (*See* 6), *infra.*)

5) Jurisdiction

a) Diversity Action
In class actions founded on diversity, only the *citizenship of the named representatives* of the class is taken into account to establish diversity. The *amount* in controversy may be *aggregated* only in the rare situation where the *claims* of the parties are *"joint" or "common."* In the more common situation, in which class members are not asserting joint or common claims, the Supreme Court has held that the claim of *each class member* (not merely

the representatives) must meet the jurisdictional minimum in a diversity of citizenship case. [Zahn v. International Paper Co., 414 U.S. 291 (1967)]

(1) Does the Supplemental Jurisdiction Statute Overrule *Zahn*?
Six of the United States Courts of Appeals—the Fourth, Fifth, Sixth, Seventh, Ninth, and Eleventh Circuits—have held that the supplemental jurisdiction statute (*see* II.A.5., *supra*) overrules *Zahn* and requires only that the claim of the class representative exceed $75,000. [*See* Allapattah Services, Inc. v. Exxon Corp., 333 F.3d 1248 (11th Cir. 2003); Rosmer v. Pfizer, Inc., 263 F.3d 110 (4th Cir. 2001); Gibson v. Chrysler Corp., 261 F.3d 927 (9th Cir. 2001); Free v. Abbott Laboratories, 51 F.3d 524 (5th Cir. 1995); Stromberg Metal Works, Inc. v. Press Mechanical, Inc., 77 F.3d 928 (7th Cir. 1996); Olden v. LaFarge Corp., 383 F.3d 495 (6th Cir. 2004)] On the other hand, four other Courts of Appeals (the First, Third, Eighth, and Tenth Circuits) have rejected this argument and continue to require that each class member's claim meet the jurisdictional minimum. [*See* Rosario Ortega v. Star-Kist Foods, Inc., 370 F. 3d 124 (1st Cir. 2004); Trimble v. Asarco, Inc., 232 F.3d 946 (8th Cir. 2000); Meritcare, Inc. v. St. Paul Mercury Insurance Co., 166 F.3d 214 (3d Cir. 1999); Leonhardt v. Western Sugar Co., 160 F.3d 631 (10th Cir. 1998)] The unfortunate split of authority on this issue remains.

b) Federal Question Action
If the class asserts a claim arising under federal law, it can invoke federal question jurisdiction. In that sort of case, of course, the citizenship of the parties and the amount in controversy are irrelevant. (*See* III. above.)

6) Court Approval
The court must approve the dismissal or settlement of a class action. The class must satisfy the requirements for certification under Rule 23(a) and (b) before a court can approve a class settlement (*see* 1), above). [Amchem Products, Inc. v. Windsor, 521 U.S. 591 (1997)]

a) Notice of Dismissal or Settlement
Moreover, notice of the proposed dismissal or settlement must be given to all members of the class in a manner as directed by the court. [Fed. R. Civ. P. 23(e)] This notice is required in all types of class actions, unless the judgment will not bind the class. The purpose of notice to class members is to allow them to object to the proposed dismissal or settlement when the court holds a "fairness hearing" to determine whether to approve the dismissal or settlement. (*See* below.)

b) Procedures for Settlements of Class Action Suits
Rule 23(e) requires a settlement hearing (usually called a "fairness hearing") if the judgment will bind the class and permits settlement only if the court finds the terms to be fair, reasonable, and adequate. The court must make a finding supporting its conclusion that the settlement meets that standard. Parties seeking approval of a settlement must inform the court of any collateral agreements made in connection with the class settlement.

(1) "Opt Out" Provision
The court may refuse to approve a settlement of a Rule 23(b)(3) class action if members are not provided a new opportunity to opt out. Thus, members who received notice of the pendency of the class action (*see* 4), above) but refused to opt out may be permitted a second opportunity to opt out, essentially to reject the terms of the settlement and proceed on their own.

c) Appeal of Approval of Settlement
A class member who objects to the approval of settlement may bring an appeal of the approval of settlement. [Devlin v. Scardelletti, 536 U.S. 1 (2002)]

7) Appeal of Class Action Certification Decision
Although a court's order granting or denying the certification of a class is not a final judgment in the case, a party may seek review of the decision in the court of appeals under Rule 23(f). (*See* VIII.C.5., *infra*.)

d. Shareholder Derivative Suits

1) Minority Shareholder Allegations

Under Rule 23.1, a minority shareholder, suing on behalf of other minority shareholders to enforce some right of the corporation which the corporation refuses to assert, *must allege* in a *verified* complaint:

a) That she made *demand on the directors* and, if required by state law, on the shareholders (or some adequate excuse for failure to make the demand);

b) That she was a *shareholder at the time* of the transaction complained of (or received her shares thereafter by operation of law); *and*

c) That she can adequately and *fairly represent the interests* of the shareholders.

2) Corporation Named as Defendant

The corporation must be named as a defendant if those who control the corporation are antagonistic to the action sought by the plaintiffs. If not so named, the court will align the corporation as a defendant to reflect the antagonism.

3) Jurisdictional Amount and Venue

The judgment runs to the corporation; therefore, the jurisdictional amount looks to the damages allegedly suffered by the corporation. By statute, venue is proper wherever the corporation could have sued the same defendants (*i.e.,* usually in the state of its incorporation). [28 U.S.C. §1401]

4) Court Approval

The court must approve the dismissal or settlement of a derivative suit.

e. Interpleader

1) Purpose Is to Avoid Double Liability

Interpleader permits a person in the position of a stakeholder to require two or more claimants to litigate among themselves to determine which, if any, has the valid claim where separate actions might result in double liability on a single obligation. Interpleader is available under Rule 22 and under the Federal Interpleader Statute. [28 U.S.C. §1335]

2) Rights of Plaintiff Stakeholder

The plaintiff stakeholder does not have to admit liability to any claimant and the claims do not have to have common origin. Once the court has allowed interpleader, a trial by jury is available to determine the issues of fact.

3) Jurisdiction

a) **Rule 22 Interpleader**

If Rule 22 interpleader is relied on, the normal rules as to subject matter jurisdiction apply. Therefore, there must be either a federal question claim, or complete diversity between the stakeholder and the claimants and more than $75,000 in controversy.

b) **Federal Interpleader Statute**

Under the Federal Interpleader Statute, on the other hand, the jurisdictional requirements are less restrictive. The federal statute permits jurisdiction where the amount in controversy is $500 or more and where there is diversity between *any two* contending claimants. Venue lies where any claimant resides, and process may be served anywhere in the United States under the statute (but not under Rule 22). The plaintiff stakeholder must deposit the amount in controversy (or a bond) with the court.

f. Intervention

Intervention may be granted to a party of right or permissively.

1) Intervention of Right

Intervention of right is available whenever the applicant claims an interest in the property or transaction that is the subject matter of the action, and the disposition of the action without her may impair her ability to protect that interest (unless her interest is already represented). The possible *stare decisis* effect of a judgment may be sufficient "interest" to authorize intervention of right. Traditionally, intervention of right invoked ancillary jurisdiction, so that no independent basis of subject matter jurisdiction was required over claims by or against the intervenor of right. Under the supplemental jurisdiction statute, however, it appears that there is *no* supplemental (ancillary) jurisdiction over claims by or against one seeking to intervene in a diversity action. The United States has a right of intervention in all cases where the constitutionality of a United States statute is raised.

2) Permissive Intervention
Permissive intervention is available when the applicant's claim or defense and the main action have a question of fact or law in common; no direct personal or pecuniary interest is required. A claim in permissive intervention must not destroy complete diversity (if it does, intervention will be denied), and *must be supported by its own jurisdictional ground*.

3) Caveat
In all cases of intervention, the application must be timely, a matter within the court's discretion.

g. Third-Party Practice (Impleader)

1) Claims for Indemnity
A defending party may implead a nonparty who is or may be liable to her for any part of a judgment that the plaintiff may recover against her, *i.e.*, claims based on indemnity. If the indemnity claim by the defending party against the third-party defendant does not meet the requirements for diversity of citizenship or federal question jurisdiction, it will invoke supplemental (ancillary) jurisdiction, because such claims will meet *the "same transaction or occurrence" requirement of supplemental (ancillary) jurisdiction* and are asserted by a party other than the plaintiff. (*See* II.A.5., 6.e., *supra*.) Thus, the defending party may assert an indemnity claim in federal court even if there is no diversity between the defending party and the third-party defendant and the third-party claim is based on state law. Furthermore, *venue need not be proper* for the third-party defendant.

2) Non-Indemnity Claims
As part of the third-party complaint, the third-party plaintiff (*i.e.*, the original defending party) may join *other* (non-indemnity) claims she may have against the third-party defendant. *If these other claims cannot invoke diversity of citizenship or federal question jurisdiction, they would also need to invoke supplemental (ancillary) jurisdiction* (*see* II.A.5., 6.e., *supra*), although it is less likely that the "same transaction or occurrence" requirement could be met.

3) Severance of Third-Party Claims
In any event, *even if jurisdiction exists*, the court *may sever any third-party claim* to be tried separately *if it is just to do so* (*e.g.*, if addition of those claims would lead to unfair prejudice to one of the parties).

4) Response of Impleaded Party
After he is joined by the third-party complaint, the third-party defendant may assert defenses to the plaintiff's original claim, as well as defenses to the third-party liability asserted against him.

5) Impleading Insurance Companies
In some states, a defendant may not implead its own insurance company, but if the insurance company denies coverage and refuses to defend, then the defendant may implead the company and have that issue decided in the same case.

h. Cross-Claims
Co-parties may assert claims against each other that arise out of the same transaction or occurrence as the main action by filing cross-claims. Since a cross-claim is, by definition, transactionally related to the existing action, it is commonly considered to come within the court's ancillary (supplemental) jurisdiction at least if the claim is by a defendant against a co-defendant.

G. DUTY OF DISCLOSURE; DISCOVERY

1. Disclosure Requirements

Rule 26 requires parties to disclose certain information to other parties without waiting for a discovery request. However, Rule 26 also has provisions allowing stipulation of the parties or court order to modify some disclosure requirements.

a. Types of Disclosure Required

Before making her disclosures, a party has an obligation to make a reasonable inquiry into the facts of the case. Rule 26 requires parties to disclose all information "then reasonably available" (and not privileged or protected as work product). A party is not relieved from her obligation to disclose merely because she has failed to complete her investigation or because another party has not made his disclosures or has made inadequate disclosures.

Rule 26 requires three types of disclosure: *initial* disclosures, disclosure of *expert testimony*, and *pretrial* disclosures.

1) Initial Disclosures

Without waiting for a discovery request, a party must provide to other parties (unless stipulation or court order provides otherwise):

(i) The names, addresses, and telephone numbers of individuals likely to have discoverable information that the disclosing party may use to support its claims or defenses, unless solely for impeachment;

(ii) Copies or descriptions of documents or things in the disclosing party's possession or control that the disclosing party may use to support its claims or defenses, unless solely for impeachment;

(iii) A computation of damages claimed by the disclosing party and copies of materials upon which the computation is based; and

(iv) Copies of insurance agreements under which an insurer might be liable for all or part of any judgment that might be entered.

These disclosures must be made *within 14 days* after the meeting of the parties required by Rule 26(f) (discussed at H.1., *infra*) unless a different time is set by court order or by stipulation.

a) Exemptions from Initial Disclosure Requirement

Initial disclosures are not required in particular types of cases, such as actions to review an administrative record, actions to enforce an arbitration award, pro se litigation brought by prisoners, actions to quash or enforce subpoenas, or habeas corpus petitions. [Fed. R. Civ. P. 26(a)(1)(E)]

2) Disclosure of Expert Testimony

A party must also disclose to other parties the identities of expert witnesses expected to be used at trial. This disclosure must be accompanied by a report prepared and signed by each expert witness stating her qualifications, the opinions to be expressed, and the basis for those opinions. This disclosure must be made at the time directed by the court or, in the absence of any directions or any stipulations among the parties, at least 90 days before trial; if the evidence is intended solely to rebut another party's disclosure of expert testimony, it must be made within 30 days after disclosure of the evidence being rebutted.

3) Pretrial Disclosures

At least 30 days before trial, a party must disclose to the other parties and file with the court a list of the witnesses she expects to call at trial, the witnesses she will call if the need arises, the witnesses whose testimony will be presented by means of a deposition and a transcript of pertinent portions of the deposition, and a list of documents or exhibits she expects to offer or might offer if needed. Within 14 days after this disclosure, a party may serve objections to use of the depositions at trial and to the admissibility of disclosed documents and exhibits. Such objections are waived if not made at this point, except for objections that the evidence is irrelevant, prejudicial, or confusing under Federal Rules of Evidence 402 and 403.

2. Scope of Disclosure and Discovery

a. In General

Discovery may be had of *any matter not privileged that is* "*relevant* to the claim or defense of any party," including the identity of persons having knowledge of relevant facts. As long as the information sought is reasonably calculated to lead to the discovery of admissible evidence on a claim or defense in the case, it is not required that the information itself be admissible at trial. [Fed. R. Civ. P. 26(b)(1)]

Note: The requirement that the information sought be relevant to a claim or defense became effective December 1, 2000, and is narrower than the previous provision that the information be "relevant to the subject matter involved in the pending action." Henceforth, this broader scope is appropriate only if the court so orders, for good cause shown.

b. Trial Preparation Materials

Work product of lawyers and others *in anticipation of litigation* is discoverable only upon showing *"substantial need"* and to avoid *"undue hardship"* in obtaining materials in an alternative way, but the court must secure against disclosure of mental impressions, opinions, and conclusions. [*See* Hickman v. Taylor, 329 U.S. 495 (1947)] However, a party may obtain, without showing need and hardship, a copy of any statement previously made by *that party*. [Fed. R. Civ. P. 26(b)(3)]

c. Experts

A party may depose experts who are expected to be called at trial (*testifying experts*). The opinions of experts who are retained in anticipation of litigation but who are not expected to testify at trial (*consulting experts*) may be discovered only upon a showing of exceptional circumstances under which it is impracticable to obtain facts or opinions by other means. [Fed. R. Civ. P. 26(b)(4)]

d. Protective Orders

Protective orders may be obtained under Rule 26(c) to limit the nature and scope of examination or to terminate examination if discovery is abused.

e. Supplementation of Disclosures and Discovery Responses

A party has a duty to supplement required disclosures if she learns that the information disclosed was materially incomplete or incorrect and the new information has not been made known to the other party in discovery or in writing. The duty to supplement also applies to an expert's reports and information from any deposition of an expert. [Fed. R. Civ. P. 26(e)(1)] In addition, a party is under a duty seasonably to amend prior responses to interrogatories, requests for production, and requests for admission if the party learns that a prior response is materially incorrect or incomplete, and the new information has not been made known to the other party in discovery or in writing. [Fed. R. Civ. P. 26(e)(2)]

3. Types of Discovery

a. Pre-Action Discovery

A person may, by deposition, *perpetuate* her own testimony or that of another in regard to any matter that may be cognizable in any United States court by filing a verified petition and serving a copy of the petition and a notice of application for an order for pre-action discovery on each person named as an expected adverse witness at least 20 days before the date of hearing. (The petition must show, among other things, that the petitioner expects to be a party to an action cognizable in a court of the United States but is *presently unable* to bring it or cause it to be brought.) Depositions may also be used in this manner to perpetuate the testimony of witnesses while an appeal is pending. [Fed. R. Civ. P. 27]

b. Discovery of Documents and Things; Orders for Physical and Mental Examinations

1) Oral Deposition of a Witness, Including a Party-Witness

A common form of discovery is the oral deposition under Rule 30. If the deponent is not available at trial, it may be used in lieu of her appearance as a witness. The deposition may be recorded by sound, sound and visual, or stenographic means.

Depositions may be taken by telephone or through other remote electronic devices. All parties may pose questions to the deponent. A party may not take more than *10 depositions,* nor may she depose the same person more than once, without leave of court or stipulation of the parties. A deposition may not exceed "one day of seven hours" absent court order or stipulation to the contrary.

2) Deposition of Witnesses upon Written Questions
Rule 31 provides for written questions to witnesses and is designed to facilitate the depositions of witnesses living a great distance from the parties. All parties can pose questions to the deponent. A party may not take more than *10 depositions,* nor may she depose the same person more than once, without leave of court or stipulation of the parties.

3) Interrogatories to the Parties
Rule 33 provides for written interrogatories to other parties and written answers by the party to whom the interrogatories are directed. The party must respond not only with facts which she herself knows, but also with facts that are available to her. The party may also be asked to give opinions, even on the application of law to facts. Initially, the requesting party may not serve more than *25 interrogatories including subparts* without court order or stipulation, and leave may be granted to serve additional ones.

4) Production of Physical Material; Inspection
Rule 34 provides (i) for the production by a *party* (or, if accompanied by a subpoena, a nonparty) of physical material, including documents, relevant to the pending action; and (ii) that a party be required to permit entry onto land for relevant testing.

5) Physical and Mental Examinations

a) Order for Examination
Rule 35 provides for an independent physical or mental examination of a party when that party's physical or mental condition is in controversy. Such exam is available only if ordered by the court, on showing of good cause. Traditionally, this rule has allowed exams only by "physicians." Now, however, it allows exams by a "suitably licensed or certified examiner," which would include, for example, doctors, dentists, occupational therapists, and any others required to be licensed and qualified to comment on a physical or mental condition.

b) Report of Findings
The person examined may request a copy of the examiner's report, but if that person so requests or takes a deposition of the examiner, she waives any privilege and must produce, upon demand, copies of her own doctor's reports of any other examinations of the same condition.

6) Requests for Admission
Any party may serve on any other party a written request for admission as to the truth or genuineness of any matter or document described in the request. The matters will be considered admitted unless the party upon whom the request was served returns a sworn statement denying the truth of the matters set forth in the request, or explaining why she cannot admit or deny them. Alternatively, the party upon whom the request was served can file written objections to those requests that she has a legal basis for not answering. A party may be asked to admit matters that are genuine issues for trial. [Fed. R. Civ. P. 36] An admission under Rule 36 is for the purpose of the pending action only and may not be used against the party in any other proceeding.

4. Enforcing Disclosure and Discovery

a. Motion to Compel and Sanctions for Violation of Order to Compel

1) Motion to Compel Disclosures and Discovery
If a party fails to provide discovery or provides incomplete discovery (including disclosures and answers to interrogatories and deposition questions), the other

party may move to compel discovery. A motion to compel must certify that the moving party has made a good faith attempt to obtain the discovery.

2) Sanctions for Violation of Order to Compel
If a party fails to comply with an order to provide discovery, the court may: (i) order the matters to be treated as admitted; (ii) prohibit the party from supporting or opposing designated claims or defenses; (iii) strike pleadings, stay or dismiss the action, or render a default judgment; or (iv) hold the delinquent party or witness in contempt (but the contempt sanction may not be used for refusal to submit to a physical or mental examination). The court may also assess reasonable expenses incurred because of the refusal, including attorneys' fees. [Fed. R. Civ. P. 37(b)]

b. Immediate Sanction
If a party fails to attend his own deposition or fails to provide *any* answers to interrogatories, a party may move for *immediate sanctions* (as opposed to moving to compel discovery). The motion must certify that the moving party has made a good faith attempt to obtain the answers. In response to a motion for immediate sanctions, the court may make such orders in regard to the failure as are "just," including: (i) ordering the matters to be treated as admitted; (ii) prohibiting the party from supporting or opposing designated claims or defenses; and (iii) striking pleadings, staying or dismissing the action, or rendering a default judgment. [Fed. R. Civ. P. 37(d)]

c. Automatic Sanction
The rules also provide for an *automatic sanction* against a party who "without substantial justification" fails to disclose information as required under Rule 26, or who fails to supplement or amend discovery responses under Rule 26(e)(1) or (2) (*see* 2.e., *supra*). Rule 37 provides that the party who fails to make required disclosures will not be permitted to use the information withheld as evidence at trial, at a hearing, or on a motion, unless such failure was "harmless." The court may impose other appropriate sanctions including: (i) ordering the matters to be treated as admitted; (ii) prohibiting the party from supporting or opposing designated claims or defenses; (iii) striking pleadings, staying or dismissing the action, or rendering a default judgment; and (iv) informing the jury of the failure to make the disclosure. [Fed. R. Civ. P. 37(c)]

Note: Apparently, the failure to make required disclosures under Rule 26 may result in either a motion to compel or automatic sanctions.

5. Use of Depositions at Trial or Hearing
Subject to the rules of evidence, a deposition may be used against any party who was present at the deposition or had notice of it:

a. *To impeach* the testimony of the deponent as a witness;

b. For any purpose if the court finds that the deponent (including a party-deponent) is *dead,* at a distance greater than *100 miles* from the place of trial (unless the absence was procured by the party offering the deposition), or *unable to testify* because of age, sickness, etc.; or

c. For any purpose if the *deponent is an adverse party*.

6. Errors and Irregularities in Depositions

a. As to Notice
Errors and irregularities relating to the notice of deposition are waived unless written objection is promptly served on the party giving notice.

b. As to Manner of Taking
Errors of any kind which could have been obviated if promptly presented are waived unless *seasonable* objection is made at the time of taking the deposition (applies to form of questions, oath, conduct of parties, etc.).

c. As to Completion and Return
Errors and irregularities as to the completion and return of the deposition are waived unless a motion to suppress is made with reasonable promptness after the error was or should have been discovered (applies to signing, sealing, certification, and transmittal).

d. As to Form of Written Questions
Objections to the form of written questions are waived unless served on the party propounding them within the time for serving succeeding questions and within five days after service of the last questions authorized.

H. PRETRIAL CONFERENCES

1. Rule 26(f) Conference of Parties—Planning for Discovery
As soon as practicable, and in any event at least 21 days before a scheduling conference is held or the scheduling order required by Rule 16(b) is due (*see* below), the parties must confer to consider their *claims and defenses,* the *possibility of settlement, initial disclosures,* and a *discovery plan.* The parties must submit to the court a proposed discovery plan within 14 days after the conference addressing the timing and form of required disclosures, the subjects on which discovery may be needed, the timing of and limitations on discovery, and relevant orders that may be required of the court.

2. Rule 16(b) Scheduling Conference
The court must (except in classes of cases exempted by local rule) hold a scheduling conference among the parties or counsel. The conference may be held by telephone, mail, or other suitable means. The court must, within 90 days after the appearance of a defendant and within 120 days after the complaint has been served on a defendant, enter a scheduling order limiting the time for *joinder*, *motions*, and *discovery*. The order may also include dates for *pretrial conferences*, *a trial date*, and *any other appropriate matters*. This schedule cannot be modified except by leave of court upon a showing of good cause. [Fed. R. Civ. P. 16(b)]

3. Pretrial Conferences
The court may also hold pretrial conferences as necessary to expedite trial and foster settlement. A *final pretrial conference*, if any, is held as close to the time of trial as reasonable, and is for the purpose of formulating a plan for the trial, including a program for admission of evidence. This conference is to be attended by at least one of the lawyers for each side who will actually be conducting the trial, and by any unrepresented parties. After a pretrial conference, an order must be entered that *controls the subsequent course of events* in the case. Thus, the final pretrial conference order is a blueprint for the trial, usually listing witnesses to be called, evidence to be presented, factual and legal issues needing resolution, and like matters. It is thus said to supersede the pleadings, and may be modified "only to prevent manifest injustice."

4. Sanctions
A party or counsel may be sanctioned for failure to attend a conference or obey an order entered pursuant to a conference, for being substantially unprepared to participate in a conference, or for acting in bad faith. The court has a broad range of available sanctions including contempt, striking pleadings, and prohibiting the introduction of evidence. In addition, the court shall require the disobedient party or counsel to pay expenses incurred (including attorneys' fees) by other parties, unless the court finds that circumstances make such an award unjust.

I. TRIAL

1. Jury Trial Problems
Rule 38 requires a party who desires a jury trial (on some or all fact issues) to file a written demand with the court and serve it on the parties. (Such demand may be indorsed upon a pleading of the party.) Failure to make such a demand within 10 days after the filing of the pleading in which the jury-triable issue arose constitutes a *waiver* by that party of any right to trial by jury. A court may, within its discretion, order a trial by jury if the plaintiff's waiver was not intentional. In the absence of compelling reasons to the contrary, a court should grant relief from waiver if the issue is one normally tried by a jury. [Cox v. Masland & Sons, Inc., 607 F.2d 138 (5th Cir. 1979)]

a. Right to Jury Trial
The Seventh Amendment preserves the right to a jury trial in federal courts of facts in all "suits of common law" where the amount in controversy exceeds $20. The distinction is historical and turns initially on whether the claim or relief was available at law or in equity in 1791. The Supreme Court has demonstrated a clear *preference for jury trial* in doubtful cases by holding that:

1) If legal and equitable claims are joined in one action involving common fact issues, the **legal claim should be tried first to the jury** and then the equitable claim to the court (the jury's finding on fact issues will bind the court in the equitable claim);

2) If a procedure formerly available only in equity, such as a class suit, interpleader, or derivative action, is now permitted under the Federal Rules for determining a "legal" claim, a **jury should try the fact issues**;

3) If damages are claimed as part of an action seeking an injunction, the defendant **cannot be denied a jury on the damages issues** on the ground that they are "incidental" to the equitable relief; and

4) If a new claim is created that did not exist at common law, a right to a jury trial will exist if the claim is similar to a claim for common law rights and remedies, unless the statute creating the right provides otherwise. [*See, e.g.,* Feltner v. Columbia Pictures Television, Inc., 523 U.S. 340 (1998)—statutory damages under Copyright Act to be tried to jury]

b. Jury Trials in Diversity Cases

1) Right to a Jury Trial
The federal court **must permit a jury trial** in any diversity "suit at common law" even though the state court would deny a jury (the Seventh Amendment prevails over *Erie*); and a federal court will generally **follow the federal practice** of submitting issues of fact to the jury even though the state law assigns the issue to the court. [Byrd v. Blue Ridge Rural Electric Cooperative, Inc., II.C.2.b., *supra*] If the state rule requires submission of a fact issue to the jury, the federal court may nonetheless direct a verdict under the usual standards or otherwise follow a federal practice that calls for the court to be the trier of fact. Likewise, state law is disregarded in determining the sufficiency of the evidence to create a jury issue; *i.e.*, the directed verdict standards are always federal.

2) Motion for New Trial Based on Excessiveness of Verdict
The Supreme Court has required federal trial courts to apply a state standard when considering a motion for a new trial based on excessiveness of the verdict. [Gasperini v. Center for Humanities, Inc., II.C.3., *supra*] Under the Seventh Amendment, federal appellate review of whether a trial court properly denied a motion to set aside a verdict as excessive is limited to whether the trial court abused its discretion in denying the motion. In contrast, a jury's determination of the amount of a punitive damage award is reviewed de novo on appeal. [Cooper Industries, Inc. v. Leatherman Tool Group, Inc., 532 U.S. 424 (2001)]

c. Jury Size and Composition
In federal civil cases, a jury must have at least six and not more than 12 jurors. There is no provision for alternate jurors. A juror may be excused for good cause (*e.g.*, illness) without causing a mistrial, so long as at least six jurors participate in reaching the verdict. The verdict must be unanimous unless the parties agree to the contrary. A race-neutral reason is required in exercising peremptory strikes of potential jury members from the panel. [Edmonson v. Leesville Concrete Co., 500 U.S. 614 (1991)] In cases in which the government is a litigant, peremptory challenges must be used for a gender-neutral reason. [J.E.B. v. Alabama, 511 U.S. 127 (1994)] Because striking potential jurors significantly involves the state, this holding will undoubtedly be extended to litigation completely between private parties.

d. Jury Instructions
At the close of the evidence, or sooner at the court's direction, a party may file proposed instructions. **Objections** to giving or failing to give instructions must be made **before** the **jury retires** to consider a verdict. [Fed. R. Civ. P. 51]

2. Consolidation and Separate Trials
Rule 42(a) allows the court to consolidate actions then before it when the actions have a common question of law or fact. Rule 42(b) allows the court to order separate trials of any claim, cross-claim, counterclaim, or other issues when such separation will foster judicial economy.

3. **Voluntary Dismissal by Plaintiff**

A plaintiff may dismiss his action *without prejudice* as a matter of right only before the defendant files an answer or a summary judgment motion, or by stipulation of all parties. Otherwise, a dismissal without prejudice can be taken only with leave of the court. [Fed. R. Civ. P. 41(a)] Whether to allow such a dismissal is in the court's discretion.

4. **Motion for Judgment as a Matter of Law (Formerly Directed Verdict)**

Historically, a judge could direct a particular verdict whenever the evidence—viewed in the light most favorable to the party against whom the verdict was directed (including legitimate inferences in that party's favor) and without considering the credibility of witnesses—was such that reasonable persons could come to only one conclusion. Today, this can be done pursuant to a party's *motion for judgment as a matter of law*. The motion may be made by any party anytime before submission of the case to the jury, and the moving party must specify the judgment sought and the law and facts on which it is entitled to judgment. The motion may be granted only after the nonmoving party "has been fully heard" and regarding issues or claims as to which "there is no legally sufficient evidentiary basis for a reasonable jury" to conclude in favor of the nonmoving party. [Fed. R. Civ. P. 50(a)]

5. **Renewed Motion for Judgment as a Matter of Law (Formerly Judgment Notwithstanding the Verdict ("JNOV"))**

Historically, a party against whom judgment was entered could move for JNOV if the judgment was based upon a verdict that reasonable persons could not have reached and if the moving party had sought a directed verdict at the close of all the evidence. Now, the motion for JNOV is called a *renewed motion for judgment as a matter of law*. It must be filed no later than 10 days after entry of judgment. The *moving party must have moved for judgment as a matter of law* at the close of all evidence to preserve the right to have the court consider a renewed motion for judgment as a matter of law. The standard is the same as for the motion for judgment as a matter of law. [Fed. R. Civ. P. 50(b)]

6. **Motion for New Trial**

A motion for a new trial must be filed no later than 10 days after judgment is entered. Within that period, the court may order a new trial on its own motion.

   a. **Reasons for Granting New Trial**

   The court may grant a new trial because of an error during the trial (usually going to the admissibility of evidence or the propriety of the instructions), because the verdict is against the weight of the evidence (limited to cases where the judge finds the verdict seriously erroneous), or because the verdict is excessive. [Fed. R. Civ. P. 60(b)]

      1) **Remittitur**

      If the trial judge feels that the jury's compensatory damages award is so excessive as to "shock the conscience" (or in a diversity case if the award meets the state standard for excessiveness), the judge may order a new trial or may offer the alternative of remittitur. When offered remittitur, the plaintiff is given the choice between accepting an award less than that given her by the jury or submitting to a new trial. Note that the court cannot simply lower the award given by the jury. It must offer the plaintiff the alternative of a lower award or a new trial. [Hetzel v. Prince Williams County, 523 U.S. 208 (1998)]

   b. **Renewed Motion for Judgment as a Matter of Law with Motion for New Trial**

   When a renewed motion for judgment as a matter of law and a motion for a new trial are made *in the alternative* and the renewed motion is granted, the court must rule hypothetically on the new trial motion so that no remand is required if the judgment on the merits ruling is subsequently reversed on appeal.

7. **Judgment on Partial Findings**

In a nonjury trial, the judge may enter judgment as a matter of law against a party on any issue whenever there are sufficient facts to resolve the issue, provided that the party has been fully heard on the issue. If the issue is dispositive of a claim or defense, the judge may enter judgment as a matter of law against a party on that claim or defense. The judge may also wait until the close of all evidence to render judgment. Because the judge is acting as the trier of fact, she decides issues of disputed facts, and she may consider the credibility of witnesses. The judgment must be supported by findings of fact and conclusions of law. [Fed. R. Civ. P. 52]

8. Summary Judgment

a. Standard
Summary judgment must be granted if, from the pleadings, affidavits, and discovery materials, it appears that there is *no genuine issue of material fact* and the moving party is entitled to judgment as a matter of law. [Fed. R. Civ. P. 56] The court may not decide disputed fact issues on a motion for summary judgment; if there is a disputed material fact, the case must go to trial.

b. Applicable to All Civil Actions
Rule 56 applies to all parties and civil actions that are subject to the Federal Rules including actions by and against the United States, and to all types of claims that appear in a civil action (counterclaim, cross-claim, declaratory judgment, injunction, and interpleader).

c. Time
The *claimant* may move for summary judgment at any time after *20 days* from commencement of the action or after service of a motion for summary judgment by an adverse party. A *defending party* may move at *any time*. Both claimant and defendant, however, must move within such time so as not to delay the trial.

Note that the motion must be served at least 10 days before the time fixed for the hearing, but the adverse party may serve opposing affidavits on the day prior to the day of the hearing.

d. Partial
The judgment may be partial as well as complete. A summary judgment may be rendered on the issue of liability alone although there is a genuine issue as to the amount of damages.

e. Support
The motion may be supported or opposed with affidavits, depositions, pleadings, admissions, and answers to interrogatories.

f. Affidavits

1) Affidavits must be made on personal knowledge, shall set forth such facts as would be admissible in evidence, and shall show the affiant is competent to testify. If the affidavit refers to outside documents, sworn or certified copies of those documents (or the relevant parts of the documents) must be attached.

2) When a motion for summary judgment is supported by affidavits, etc., an adverse party may not rest upon mere pleading allegations or denials. His response must be shown by affidavits or otherwise and must set forth specific facts showing there is a genuine issue for trial. If he does not so respond, summary judgment, if appropriate, will be entered against him.

3) When *affidavits are unavailable* to the party opposing the motion, he may, by affidavit, state the reasons for their unavailability. The court may then deny the motion, order a continuance to permit affidavits to be obtained or depositions to be taken, or make such other order as is just.

4) When affidavits are made in *bad faith*, the court may:

   a) Order the party using them to reimburse the other party for those expenses that the affidavits caused him, including attorneys' fees.

   b) Adjudge in contempt the offending party or attorney.

g. Nonappealability
The denial of a motion for summary judgment is generally not appealable.

h. Relationship to Motion to Dismiss and Motion for Judgment on the Pleadings
A motion pursuant to Rule 12(b)(6) to dismiss a complaint for failure to state a claim upon which relief can be granted differs from a motion for summary judgment in that the former is addressed only to the *legal sufficiency of the complaint*.

Similarly, a motion for judgment on the pleadings presents the moving party's contention that on the *face of the pleadings*, he is entitled to judgment. Theoretically, matters outside the pleadings are irrelevant to a decision on either of these motions. However, a party making such a motion and accompanying it with an affidavit or other matters outside the pleadings may in reality be making a motion for summary judgment, putting the wrong label on the motion. The court is expressly authorized to treat such a motion as one for summary judgment and to conduct subsequent proceedings thereon in accordance with the rule on summary judgment, giving the parties full opportunity to present material made relevant by that rule.

VIII.   FINAL JUDGMENT AND APPELLATE REVIEW

A.   JUDGMENT

1.   Relief that May Be Given
Except in default cases, the court is not limited to the demand for relief in the pleadings and may give *any relief* that is appropriate based on the evidence. Thus, damages may exceed the plaintiff's demand and an injunction may be entered although not requested. Interest on a money judgment is awarded at the rate provided under state law from the date of judgment.

2.   Judgment on Multiple Claims or Parties
When multiple claims or multiple parties are involved in an action, the court may enter a final judgment as to fewer than all of the claims or parties only upon (i) an express determination that there is no just reason for delay, and (ii) an express direction for the entry of judgment. *Unless* the trial judge makes such an *express determination*, the order determining the merits of fewer than all of the claims or dismissing fewer than all of the parties is *not a final judgment and is not appealable*. This is in accord with the traditional policy against piecemeal appeals. [Fed. R. Civ. P. 54(b)]

B.   TIME FOR APPEALS
Under Rules 3 and 4 of the Federal Rules of Appellate Procedure, an appeal may be taken by filing a notice of appeal with the district court *within 30 days* from the entry of the judgment appealed from (60 days where the United States is a party to the action). However, if a *timely* renewed motion for judgment as a matter of law (formerly a motion for JNOV) or motion for new trial is made, or if a motion to set aside or amend the judgment is made within 10 days of judgment, the running of the 30 days is terminated. Upon the entry of an order based on such post-trial motions, a new 30-day period begins to run. However, a notice of appeal filed during the pendency of such a post-trial motion will become effective on final disposition of the motion by the trial court. Upon a showing of excusable neglect, made within 30 days after the time to appeal has expired, the district court may extend the time for filing a notice of appeal by 30 days from the time it would otherwise have run, or 10 days from the date of the order granting the extension, whichever is later.

C.   REVIEWABLE ORDER
Generally, *only final orders* are reviewable. A final order is one that disposes of the whole case on its merits, by rendering final judgment not only as to all the parties but as to all causes of action involved. [Cunningham v. Hamilton County, 527 U.S. 198 (1999)—order imposing sanctions on attorney is not a final order even when the attorney no longer represents a party to the case] However, certain interlocutory orders are *also reviewable*:

1.   Interlocutory Orders as of Right

a.   Injunction
A party may appeal as of right any order granting, continuing, modifying, refusing, dissolving, or refusing to dissolve or modify an injunction.

b.   Receivers
A party may appeal as of right any order appointing a receiver, or refusing to wind up or take steps to accomplish purposes of receiverships (*e.g.,* directing sales or other disposals of property).

c.   Admiralty
An order finding liability but leaving damages to be assessed later in admiralty cases may be appealed.

d. Patent Infringement
A patent infringement order where only an accounting is wanting may be appealed.

e. Property Possession
A party may appeal as of right any order whereby possession of property is changed or affected, such as orders dissolving writs of attachment and the like.

2. Interlocutory Appeals Act
Review under the Interlocutory Appeals Act is *discretionary* and may be available when: (i) the trial judge certifies that the interlocutory order involves a controlling question of law, as to which there is substantial ground for difference of opinion, and immediate appeal from the order may materially advance the ultimate termination of the litigation; and (ii) the court of appeals then agrees to allow the appeal. A party obtaining such a certificate from the trial judge must, within *10 days,* apply to the court of appeals, where two out of three judges must agree with the trial judge.

3. Fewer than All Claims or Parties
(*See* A.2., *supra.*)

4. Collateral Order Rule
If the claim or issue is separable from and collateral to the main suit and is too important to require deferring appellate review, it may be classified as a judgment in a separate ("collateral") proceeding and thus be appealable. [Puerto Rico Aqueduct & Sewer Authority v. Metcalf & Eddy, Inc., 506 U.S. 139 (1993)—governmental entity's claim of Eleventh Amendment immunity from suit denied; issue appealable immediately under collateral order rule because failure to permit interlocutory appeal would effectively eviscerate Eleventh Amendment immunity from suit in federal court by requiring entity to litigate to final judgment before appealing]

5. Orders Made Appealable (or Nonappealable) by Writ
In exceptional cases, nearly all jurisdictions allow some circumvention of the final judgment rule through the appellate writs of mandamus and prohibition. Mandamus commands a trial judge to act, and prohibition commands the judge to refrain from acting. The writs are available only if an appeal will be insufficient to correct a problem and the trial court's actions constitute a serious abuse of power that must be immediately corrected.

6. Certification of Class Actions
A district court's order granting or denying certification of a class action can be appealed within 10 days of entry of the order. [Fed. R. Civ. P. 23(f)] The court of appeals has complete discretion in deciding whether to hear the appeal. If the court decides to hear the appeal, proceedings are *not stayed* at the district court unless the district court or court of appeals so orders.

D. STAY PENDING APPEAL

1. Execution
No execution on judgments is allowed for 10 days after entry except injunctions or receiverships, which are not held up unless otherwise ordered by a court.

2. Enforceability
Judgments are *enforceable during pendency of post-trial motions unless* a court otherwise orders in its discretion and on such conditions for the security of the adverse party as are proper.

3. Bond
A supersedeas bond is required in sufficient size to satisfy the judgment, costs, interest, and damages for delay, should the appeal be dismissed or affirmed. Upon filing such a bond, an appellant has a stay pending appeal—unless the order was for an injunction or receivership.

4. Injunction Order

a. Power of Trial Court
When appeal is taken from an interlocutory or final judgment granting, dissolving, or denying an injunction, the court may suspend, modify, restore, or grant an injunction during the pendency of the appeal upon such bond as it considers proper for the security of the adverse party.

b. Power of Appellate Court
An appellate court has similar power to grant a stay or injunction pending appeal, or to vacate one granted by the trial court, or to make any order appropriate to preserve the status quo or the effectiveness of the judgment subsequently to be entered. Ordinarily such a stay or injunction pending appeal must be sought in the trial court before the appellate court will entertain it.

E. SUPREME COURT JURISDICTION
The Supreme Court has direct appeal jurisdiction from any order granting or denying an injunction in any proceeding required to be heard by a three-judge court. [28 U.S.C. §1253]

1. Court of Appeals Cases
Cases in the courts of appeals may be reviewed by the Supreme Court:

(i) *By certiorari* granted upon petition of any party to any civil or criminal case, before or after rendition of judgment or decree; or

(ii) *By certification* by the court of appeals of any question of law in any civil or criminal case as to which it desires instructions. Upon such certification, the Supreme Court may give binding instructions or may require the entire record to be sent to it for decision of the entire case.

[28 U.S.C. §1254]

2. Cases from Highest State Court
Final judgments rendered by the highest court of a state in which decision could be had may be reviewed by the Supreme Court *by certiorari* in the following circumstances:

(i) Where the validity of a *treaty or federal statute* is drawn into question; or

(ii) Where the validity of a *state statute* is drawn into question on the ground that it is repugnant to the federal Constitution or to a treaty or federal statute; or

(iii) Where any *title*, *right*, *privilege*, *or immunity* is claimed under the federal Constitution or treaty or federal statute.

[28 U.S.C. §1257]

IX. EFFECTS OF JUDGMENT ON FUTURE CASES

A. RES JUDICATA (CLAIM PRECLUSION)

1. Definition
Once a *final* judgment *on the merits* has been rendered on a particular cause of action, the claimant is barred by res judicata (also called claim preclusion) from asserting the *same cause* of action in a later lawsuit.

2. Terminology Used to Describe Effect—"Merger" and "Bar"
When the *claimant wins* the earlier lawsuit, the cause of action is said to have been "*merged*" into the judgment. When the *defendant wins,* the claimant is said to be "*barred*" by the earlier adverse judgment. Both terms simply mean that the *claimant cannot sue again* on the same cause.

3. Requirements for "Merger" and "Bar"
Before merger or bar apply, it must be shown that (i) the earlier judgment is a valid, final judgment "*on the merits*"; (ii) the cases are brought by the *same claimant* against the *same defendant*; and (iii) the *same "cause of action"* (or "claim") is involved in the later lawsuit.

4. Valid, Final Judgment "On the Merits"
Res judicata (claim preclusion) flows from the entry in an earlier case of a valid, final judgment "on the merits." A judgment is valid as long as it is not void (*e.g.*, for lack of subject matter jurisdiction). Whether a judgment is final for these purposes is generally the same as whether it is final for purposes of taking an appeal. (*See* VIII.C., *supra.*) Usually, the more difficult issue is whether the valid, final judgment is considered "on the merits" for

res judicata purposes. Often, a judgment will be based on actual litigation between the parties, but it can also be a default judgment entered as a penalty against a party (such as a dismissal for willful violation of discovery orders) or an involuntary dismissal closely related to the merits (such as for failure to state a claim upon which relief may be granted). In contrast, other involuntary dismissals not involving the merits (such as those based on lack of jurisdiction, improper venue, or failure to join an indispensable party) are not a judgment on the merits and do not have claim preclusive effect. Although Federal Rule 41(b) indicates that all dismissals are to operate "as an adjudication on the merits" unless based on jurisdiction, improper venue, or failure to join an indispensable party, the Supreme Court has held that Rule 41(b) does **not** govern whether the judgment is "on the merits" for res judicata purposes. [Semtek, Inc. v. Lockheed Martin Corp., 531 U.S. 497 (2001)] Thus, jurisdictions may take different views of whether a particular dismissal—*e.g.*, dismissal because the statute of limitations has run—is deemed "on the merits" for res judicata purposes.

5. **Same Claimant Versus Same Defendant**
Res judicata applies only if the earlier case and the latter case are brought by the same claimant against the same defendant. It is not enough that the same litigants were also parties in the previous case; they must have been in the same configuration of one asserting a claim against the other.

Examples: 1) In Case One, A sues Z to recover damages for personal injuries suffered in an automobile collision between the two. A valid, final judgment on the merits is entered. Now A sues Z again, this time to recover damages for property damage inflicted in the same wreck. Assuming that both cases involve the same "cause of action" (discussed immediately below), res judicata would apply, because both cases were brought by A against Z.

2) In Case One, A sues Z to recover damages for personal injuries suffered in an automobile collision between the two. A valid, final judgment on the merits is entered. Now Z sues A to recover for her personal injuries suffered in the same wreck. Res judicata **does not apply.** Here, the second case is brought **by Z against A, while the first case was brought by A against Z.** *Note:* Z may be barred from asserting her claim because of the compulsory counterclaim rule, but not because of res judicata. The compulsory counterclaim rule requires a defending party to assert against the claimant **in the pending case** any claims arising from the same transaction or occurrence as the claimant's claim. (*See* VII.E.3.c., *supra.*)

6. **"Cause of Action"**
While various tests have been used to define "cause of action," the modern approach is to require assertion of all claims arising out of the same transaction or occurrence that is the subject matter of a claim asserted by the claimant.

a. **Common Examples**

1) **Accidents**
The claimant seeks to recover separate damages from the same accident in separate actions. The claimant may not seek damages for neck injuries in one action and leg injuries in another. Likewise, most courts would not permit the claimant to sue for personal injuries and property damage in separate actions. However, if the claimant is insured for property damage and, after payment of the claim, the claimant assigns her cause of action for property damage to the insurance company, most courts would consider the property damage claim and personal injury claim as two separate causes of action.

2) **Installment Obligations**
In the situation of a series of obligations, such as installment payments on a debt or lease, the claimant is required to sue on all installments due at the time of suit, but not later installments. But if the contract has an acceleration clause that makes all installments due if earlier ones are not paid, the claimant must sue for all installments (unless the acceleration clause is optional and the claimant elects not to exercise the option). This rule does not apply if the installment obligations are represented by separate notes; in such cases, suit as each note comes due represents suit on a separate cause of action.

B. COLLATERAL ESTOPPEL (ISSUE PRECLUSION)

1. Definition
A judgment binds the plaintiff or defendant (or their privies) in subsequent actions on different causes of action between them (or their privies) as to *issues actually litigated* and *essential to the judgment* in the first action. This conclusive effect of the first judgment is called collateral estoppel, or issue preclusion. Note that collateral estoppel is narrower than res judicata. Res judicata focuses on something relatively large—the scope of a *"cause of action."* If it applies, the result is usually to bar the claimant from asserting a second case. Collateral estoppel, in contrast, focuses on something relatively narrow—*an issue* that was litigated and determined in the first case, and that is relevant in a second case. With collateral estoppel, the issue is deemed established in the second case without need to proffer evidence on it.

2. Requirements

a. First Case Ended in a Valid, Final Judgment on the Merits
This requirement is the same as was just discussed above regarding res judicata. (*See* IX.A.4., *supra.*)

b. Issue Actually Litigated and Determined
The issue on which collateral estoppel applies must actually have been litigated and determined in the previous case. Thus, if a *default* or *consent* judgment is entered, there is generally no collateral estoppel as to the fact issues that would have been tried had the case gone forward.

c. Issue Was Essential to the Judgment

1) It must be clear exactly how the issue was decided by the trier of fact.
   Example: P sues for personal injuries based on D's negligence. D pleads contributory negligence as a defense. If the jury renders a general verdict for D, the decision will have no collateral estoppel effect in a subsequent case involving either P or D's negligence, since there is no way of knowing whether the jury found that D was not negligent or that P was contributorily negligent, or both.

   Compare: However, if the jury found for P for the full amount of his injuries, it clearly had to decide that D was negligent and P was not. Thus, both issues could have collateral estoppel effect in a later case.

2) The judgment must depend on the issue of fact decided.
   Example: If, in a personal injury action, the jury specially finds that neither P nor D was negligent—thereby rendering a verdict for D—the finding that P was not negligent was *not* essential to judgment and will have no collateral estoppel effect in a later suit.

3) Note that the "essential fact" rule tends to reduce the number of cases in which collateral estoppel can be applied, thus eliminating some of the burden from the first suit.

d. Due Process and Mutuality Considerations

1) *Against* Whom Is Collateral Estoppel Used?
   Collateral estoppel may be asserted *only against* someone who was a party (or in privity with a party) to the previous case (the case in which the issue was actually litigated and determined). This requirement is imposed by due process, and thus is the rule in every jurisdiction.

2) *By* Whom Is Collateral Estoppel Used?
   Under the traditional "mutuality" rule, only someone who was a party (or in privity with a party) in the previous case can use collateral estoppel. This requirement is not imposed by due process, however, and has been subject to modification in certain circumstances to allow nonparties to take advantage of a prior judgment, as discussed in D., below.

C. RES JUDICATA AND COLLATERAL ESTOPPEL IN SPECIAL SITUATIONS

1. Judgments for Specific Performance
Rules of bar and collateral estoppel apply in actions brought for specific performance and the like. However, *merger does not apply* because such a judgment, unlike one for money, cannot be enforced by bringing a suit on the judgment. Thus, if the defendant fails to obey the first judgment, the claimant may sue again.

2. In Rem Judgments
If a court exercises in rem jurisdiction over some property or status within its control, and if proper notice has been given to all interested persons, the judgment as to title or status is *binding on all persons*.

3. Quasi In Rem Judgments
A quasi in rem judgment determines the rights of the parties only in the specific property before the court. *No personal judgment* is granted against anyone, and *no other property is affected*.

D. WHICH PERSONS ARE BOUND BY A JUDGMENT?

1. Parties Are Bound
Parties are persons named as parties who have the power to control the action or who, if they lack capacity, are represented by guardians. *Nonparties* normally are *not bound*. Even where the lawsuit raises an issue as to performance or rights, nonparties normally are not bound by the judgment; *e.g.,* an assignor who has no control over the suit and no interest in the outcome, or an employee who allegedly was negligent, where the suit is filed only against the employer.

2. Privies to Parties Are Bound
Persons who control the litigation and who will be affected by the outcome are bound by collateral estoppel as to *all issues litigated*. For example, if the owner of a patent assumes control of an infringement suit brought by her licensee against a competitor, and the court holds the patent invalid, the owner is barred on that issue should she sue the same competitor. The owner has had her day in court.

Persons whose interests are represented are bound. *Beneficiaries* are bound by an action brought or defended on their behalf by the fiduciary, provided the fiduciary is operating within her authority. *Holders of future interests* are bound. *Unborn or unascertained* persons having future interests in property are bound by judgments as to the property if their interests are identical to those of parties to the action, or if a special representative is appointed for them. This rule reflects public policy favoring free marketability of property. *Members of a class* are bound by a valid class action judgment. *Successors in interest* are bound. *Transferees of property* are in privity with prior owners and thus are bound by a prior judgment concerning the property. This rule protects the public as to security of titles.

Note, however, that one is not barred from asserting a claim simply because she is asserting the same claim that a previous claimant has already litigated.
Example: Citizen A sues to challenge a tax as unconstitutional and loses. Citizen B is not barred from suing to challenge the same tax on the same basis unless Citizen A and Citizen B are in privity or Citizen A represented Citizen B in bringing the first suit. [Richards v. Jefferson County, 517 U.S. 793 (1996)]

In *vicarious liability* situations (master-servant, principal-agent, insurer-insured) a judgment exonerating either generally is held to preclude an action on the same claim against the other.
Example: P sues Principal claiming injuries as a result of Agent's negligence. P alleges Agent was acting in the course and scope of agency at the time of harm. A judgment in favor of Principal on the ground that Agent was not negligent would in some jurisdictions preclude suing Agent thereafter on the theory that Agent was negligent in causing the harm. If P first sued Agent and Agent was found not negligent, P should thereafter be barred from suing Principal for the negligence of Agent causing the harm.

3. Strangers May Take Advantage of Collateral Estoppel in Certain Circumstances
While persons who are neither parties nor privies cannot be bound by a judgment, such persons may be able to take advantage of, or to assert, collateral estoppel (issue preclusion).

a. **Traditional "Mutuality" Rules**
Since a judgment cannot be used *against* a person who was not a party (because such use would violate due process rights), that person has traditionally been barred from *taking advantage* of the judgment—even though this may make little sense in a specific case, and even though this is not required by due process.

b. **Exceptions to Mutuality When Judgment Used as a Shield**
When a nonparty wishes to utilize a prior judgment *to avoid liability* in a subsequent suit, there are often compelling reasons for allowing her to do so. For example, if P unsuccessfully sues a person primarily liable (*e.g.,* a servant), P's later suit against a person secondarily liable (*e.g.,* against the master for the servant's acts) will be barred by collateral estoppel in virtually all courts. Similarly, if P unsuccessfully sues a person secondarily liable, there is little reason why the person primarily liable should be subjected to a separate suit, and most courts so hold.

Note: This rule does not apply if the first suit was or could have been decided solely on the ground that the defendant was *not* secondarily liable (*e.g.,* where the defendant claims no master-servant relationship exists).

c. **Exceptions to Mutuality When Judgment Used as a Sword**

1) **Collateral Estoppel Generally Unavailable to Nonparty Plaintiffs**
Courts have been very reluctant to permit a nonparty to use a judgment to aid him (as a plaintiff) to obtain relief. For example, suppose one of many passengers in a public vehicle successfully sues the driver for injuries received in an accident, and other passengers wish to utilize the judgment to establish liability. While a few courts have permitted such use, others refuse. They fear a situation in which 10 plaintiffs each sue and lose, and the 11th plaintiff wins, and all other potential plaintiffs seek to ignore the first 10 suits and rely solely on the 11th; application of collateral estoppel in such a situation is considered unfair and demeaning to the legal system.

2) **Courts Should Consider Fairness to Defendant**
The United States Supreme Court, in *Parklane Hosiery Co. v. Shore,* 439 U.S. 322 (1979), upheld the use of collateral estoppel as a sword. In the first action, brought by the Securities and Exchange Commission, the defendant was held to have violated the federal securities laws. The second suit, brought by a private plaintiff against the same defendant, alleged damages resulting from the same violation established in the first action. The Court allowed the latter plaintiff to rely on collateral estoppel to establish the existence of the violation since under all the circumstances it was fair to the defendant to do so.

d. **Present Status of Mutuality**
In jurisdictions where the mutuality principle has been eroded, a *four-part test* is usually applied to determine whether a stranger may rely on a prior judgment:

(i) Was the issue decided in the first case *identical* to that in the second?

(ii) Was there a final judgment on the *merits*?

(iii) Did the party against whom the judgment is to be used have a *fair opportunity to be heard* on the critical issue?

(iv) Is the posture of the case such that it would *not* be *unfair or inequitable* to a party to apply collateral estoppel?

If *all* these questions are answered affirmatively, collateral estoppel will normally be upheld. A court may find, however, that a party has not had a fair opportunity to be heard if the first case was insignificant (*e.g.,* brought for $200), while the second is more substantial (*e.g.,* brought for $200,000).

E. **WHICH CHOICE OF LAW RULES APPLY TO PRECLUSION QUESTIONS?**
Preclusion questions—whether claim preclusion or issue preclusion—always involve at least two cases. One case has gone to a valid, final judgment on the merits. Preclusion law determines whether that judgment (in "case one") precludes litigation of any matters in a pending case ("case two"). (By the way, note that "case one" was not necessarily filed first; it is "case one" because it

went to judgment first.) Although rarely tested on bar exams, a choice of law issue arises when case two is brought in a different jurisdiction than case one; *i.e.,* what law does the court in case two use to determine whether the judgment in case one is entitled to claim or issue preclusion?

1. **Case One Decided in State Court**

   When case one has been decided in state court, the court in case two (whether state or federal) generally will apply the claim or issue preclusion law of the jurisdiction that decided case one.

   Example: Judgment is entered in a case in Kansas. A second case is brought in Missouri. To decide whether that case is subject to claim or issue preclusion, the judge in Missouri should generally apply Kansas law on claim or issue preclusion.

2. **Case One Decided in Federal Court Under Diversity Jurisdiction**

   What if case one was decided in a federal court under diversity jurisdiction? Here, the Supreme Court held that the court in case two should apply federal law (because a federal court decided case one). However, it also held that usually the federal law in such an instance would be the state law of the state in which the federal court sat.

   Example: After plaintiff files suit in a California state court, defendant removes the case to federal court based on diversity jurisdiction. Plaintiff's federal court case is then dismissed under Rule 41(b) (involuntary dismissal) because it is barred by California's statute of limitations. Plaintiff files the same claims in state court in Maryland (which has a longer statute of limitations). In determining whether to dismiss the case under claim preclusion, the Maryland state court should look to federal law. But federal law would adopt the California law (unless "state law is incompatible with federal interests"). Because California law would allow the plaintiff to file in a jurisdiction with a longer statute of limitations, the Maryland court should not dismiss under claim preclusion. [Semtek, Inc. v. Lockheed Martin Corp., A.4., *supra*]

BAR REVIEW

Leases

celebrating over
35 YEARS
*of preparing
law students
for the bar exam*

LEASES—MASSACHUSETTS

TABLE OF CONTENTS

I. INTRODUCTION

Because the application of Uniform Commercial Code ("U.C.C.") Article 2 (Sales) to leases was unclear, the drafters of the U.C.C. wrote Article 2A to govern leases, and Massachusetts has adopted Article 2A. Article 2A generally follows Article 2 by substituting the term "lease" for the term "sale," but there are a few new or different rules in Article 2A, which are noted below.

II. SCOPE OF ARTICLE 2A

A. LEASE DEFINED

The definition of "lease" in Article 2A restricts its coverage to a *lease of goods*. A "lease" is "a transfer of a right to possession and use of goods for a term in return for consideration." [U.C.C. §2A-103(1)(j)] "Goods" is defined in the same way it is defined in Article 2: "all things that are movable at the time of identification to the lease contract." [U.C.C. §2A-103(1)(h)]

1. Sublease Included
The definition of a "lease" includes a sublease. [U.C.C. §2A-103(1)(w)]

B. LEASE VS. DISGUISED SALE ON CREDIT

Article 2A applies only to *true leases*. If the so-called lease is really a sale of goods on credit, Article 2A does not apply. Instead, the "lessor" is really a seller of goods (so that Article 2 governs the transaction) and is also an Article 9 *secured party* and should take the steps Article 9 requires for perfection of the seller's security interest in the goods. If the lessor fails to do this, the lessor risks losing the goods to other claimants. (*See* Secured Transactions outline.)

1. Test for Telling a Lease from a Disguised Sale
Under U.C.C. section 1-201(37)(a) - (e), a contract is a disguised sale on credit (secured transaction) rather than a true lease if:

(i) The "lessee" has *no right to terminate his obligation to pay* during the lease term (an attribute of a sale on credit is that the buyer generally cannot use purchased goods and later decide to stop making payments and return the goods); *and*

(ii) One of the following is present:

  i. The lease (including any mandatory renewals) *is for the entire economic life* of the goods or gives the "lessee" an *option to renew* for the rest of the economic life *for nominal or no additional consideration*; *or*

  ii. The lease provides that the *"lessee" will become the owner* of the goods or has an *option to purchase* the goods *for nominal or no additional consideration*.

  Example: Sally agrees to sell a tractor to Bob on credit. However, for tax reasons the parties decide to disguise the sale as a lease. They then draw up a "lease" with Sally as the "lessor" and Bob as the "lessee." The so-called lease will run for 10 years, the entire useful life of the tractor. The lease is not terminable by Bob, but Sally reserves the right to repossess the tractor in the event of Bob's nonpayment. The lease also provides that at the end of the lease period, the goods become Bob's property on the payment of $1. Under the above test, this is not a true lease, but a disguised sale on credit. The obligation to pay is not terminable by Bob, the "lease" lasts the entire economic life of the tractor, and Bob has the option to purchase the tractor at the end of the lease for nominal consideration. Therefore, Sally is an Article 2 seller of goods, and because she reserves the right to repossess in the event of nonpayment, Sally also is an Article 9 secured party. Consequently, the transaction creates a security interest in the goods, and Articles 2 and 9, rather than Article 2A, will govern the transaction.

2. Factors that by Themselves Do Not Indicate a Disguised Sale
In other situations, the nature of the transaction must be determined by the facts of the case. A transaction is not necessarily a disguised sale merely because (i) the lessee pays consideration equal to or even greater than the fair market value of the leased goods (as long as the lease does not cover the total economic life of the goods), or (ii) the lessee assumes major duties (*e.g.,* paying taxes, assuming the risk of loss, etc.) as to the goods.

3. Protective Article 9 Filing

In situations that are doubtful one way or another, the careful attorney advises the lessor-client to make a protective filing under Article 9. Section 9-505 permits the filing of a financing statement using the terms "lessor" and "lessee" instead of the usual Article 9 terms "secured party" and "debtor." If the alleged lease is subsequently judged to be a secured transaction, this filing will protect the seller from other creditors without in any way being a legal admission that anything other than a true lease has occurred.

III. ARTICLE 2 RULES COPIED

A. IN GENERAL

As stated above, with minor exceptions throughout, Article 2A slavishly copies the rules of Article 2 set out in your Multistate Sales outline. Only the important differences are noted below.

B. STATUTE OF FRAUDS

A lease must be in writing if the total of payments under the lease will be *$1,000 or more*, and the writing must be signed, describe the leased goods and the lease term, and indicate that a lease contract has been made between the parties. As in Article 2, the writing must specify the *quantity* of the leased goods. [U.C.C. §2A-201]

C. NO "BATTLE OF THE FORMS" PROVISION

Recognizing the wisdom of avoiding all the trouble caused by the original, Article 2A has no "battle of the forms" section at all.

D. CONSUMER PROTECTION

If the lessee is a consumer, a consumer lease arises. [U.C.C. §2A-103(1)(e)] Article 2A contains various rules protecting the consumer. Among these are the following:

1. Option to Accelerate at Will

If the lease contains a term allowing acceleration of the entire lease obligation at the will of the lessor, the term is enforceable only if the lessor exercises it in *good faith*, which the lessor has the burden of proving. [U.C.C. §2A-109(2)]

2. Unconscionability

Article 2A contains an unconscionability section modeled after U.C.C. section 2-302, but goes a bit further. Like its predecessor, section 2A-108 does not define unconscionability, but does have the following rules:

a. Substantive Unconscionability Not Required

Article 2A's rules on unconscionability do *not* require both procedural *and* substantive unconscionability. If a consumer lease has been induced by unconscionable conduct, the court may award appropriate relief even though the lease is otherwise fair. The same rule applies if the lessor engages in unconscionable conduct in the collection of a claim arising from the lease (such as using force or violence). [U.C.C. §2A-108(2)]

b. Attorneys' Fees

In consumer lease litigation, the successful consumer is permitted to recover attorneys' fees. The amount of the fees is not limited by the amount of the recovery. If the consumer loses the lawsuit and the court finds that the consumer brought an action that the consumer knew to be groundless, the consumer must pay attorneys' fees to the lessor. [U.C.C. §2A-108(4)(a), (b)]

IV. WARRANTIES

A. IN GENERAL

In an Article 2A lease, the lessor makes all the usual warranties that are made by a seller in Article 2. There is one major exception: the finance lease.

B. FINANCE LEASE

1. Defined

In a "finance lease," the lessee, instead of buying goods and financing the sale, has the lessor buy the goods from a seller (called a *supplier* in Article 2A) and then lease them to the lessee. [U.C.C. §2A-103(1)(g)]

Example: Waldo picked out the car of his dreams from Facade Motors, but for tax reasons did not want to buy the car and instead wished to lease it. Waldo went to Last National Bank ("LNB") and asked LNB if it would buy the car from Facade Motors and then lease the car to Waldo for three years. LNB did this. This transaction is called a finance lease. LNB is the lessor, Waldo is the lessee, and Facade Motors is the supplier.

a. Lessee Must Select Goods
If the lessor is in the business of selecting or manufacturing or selling the kinds of goods involved, no finance lease occurs. The lessor must be a true financer, and the *lessee* must be the entity that selects the goods or approves their purchase.

2. Finance Lease Warranties
In a finance lease, the lessor makes no implied warranties, but instead any warranties, express or implied, made by the supplier to the lessor are passed on to the lessee, who has a direct cause of action on them against the *supplier* to the extent of the lessee's interest in the goods, regardless of the lack of privity between the lessee and the supplier. [U.C.C. §2A-209]

3. The "Hell or High Water" Clause
A finance lease imposes an *absolute obligation* on the lessee to make payments to the lessor no matter how badly the leased goods perform or break down. The lessee is supposed to deal with the supplier to work out problems, and must keep making the lease payments in the meanwhile. This is called a "hell or high water" clause, and, whether or not specifically provided for in the lease, is the law. [U.C.C. §2A-407] The rule kicks into effect as soon as the lessee "accepts" the goods. [U.C.C. §§2A-407(a), 2A-515] Note, however, that the rule *does not apply to consumer leases.*

V. REMEDIES

A. DEFAULT BY LESSOR
Default by the lessor gives the lessee the same rights and remedies the lessee would have had if the transaction had been a sale and Article 2 applied. [U.C.C. §§2A-508 through 2A-522] Thus, the lessee may accept the goods and recover damages for breach of warranty, or may reject the goods and cover or seek the market price-lease differential. [U.C.C. §2A-519] Revocation of acceptance is permitted under rules similar to Article 2, except that in a finance lease, revocation of acceptance is not permitted for quality problems first arising after acceptance, but only for substantial breaches of the lease agreement between the lessor and the lessee. [U.C.C. §2A-517]

B. DEFAULT BY LESSEE
Default by the lessee invokes remedies similar to those given a seller in Article 2. [U.C.C. §§2A-523 through 2A-532] The lessor may cancel the lease only if the lessee's default substantially impairs the value of the lease contract. For breaches that do not substantially impair the value of the lease contract, the lessor is relegated to an action for damages. [U.C.C. §2A-523(3)(b), and Official Comment] The lessor is given the right to repossess the goods without a court proceeding if repossession can be done *without a breach of the peace.* [U.C.C. §2A-525(c)]

1. What Constitutes Substantial Impairment?
A substantial impairment will arise if a lessee: (i) wrongfully rejects or revokes acceptance of goods; (ii) fails to make payment when due; or (iii) repudiates with respect to any goods involved. [U.C.C. §2A-523(1)]

2. Limitation of Damages After Repossession
At common law and as a matter of contract, lessors frequently repossessed and then sued the lessee for the entire amount of rent called for in the lease. Article 2A does not allow the lessor to get a windfall of this magnitude, but relegates the lessor to the actual damages suffered, which the lessor must prove. [U.C.C. §2A-528] If the lessor repossesses and then relets the goods to someone else, the new lease is a mitigating factor and must be taken into account in computing damages. [U.C.C. §2A-527]

3. Action for Rent
If there is a substantial default by the lessee, the lessor may sue for the entire future rent

only if the goods were *neither repossessed nor tendered* by the lessee (because, for example, they have been destroyed or have ceased to have any value). An action for the rent also lies where the lessor proves that the return of the goods was in no way a mitigating factor, as, for example, where the lessor proves to have an inventory of leased goods that would cover any number of rentals, so that the lessor has *lost volume* by the refusal of the lessee to go through with the deal. [U.C.C. §2A-529, Official Comment 2]

VI. PRIORITY DISPUTES

A. ABILITY TO SUBLEASE
In spite of an agreement otherwise, section 2A-303 clearly allows subleasing (or any transfer of the lease). This is done in the interest of commerce.

1. Sublease as Material Violation of Prime Lease
Although subleasing is permissible, Article 2A also provides that a transfer of the lease in *material* violation of the terms of the prime lease is a ground for default and gives rise to an action for damages, or allows a court "to grant other appropriate relief, including cancellation of the lease contract or an injunction against the transfer." [U.C.C. §2A-303(5)(b)]

2. Meaning of "Material"
The statute does not define "material," but the parties may set standards to determine its meaning. [U.C.C. §2A-303, Official Comment 2]

3. Assignment of Right of Payment Allowed
When the lessor has no remaining significant affirmative duties (called in the trade a *"non-operating lease"*), a transfer of a right to payment arising out of a lease is not a material transfer and is allowed despite agreement otherwise. On the other hand, where the lessor does have significant remaining duties, such as maintenance of the leased property (a so-called *"operating lease"*), a transfer of a right to payment without the agreement of the lessee would be a ground for default. [U.C.C. §2A-303(4), and Official Comment]

4. Security Interest in Lessor's Rights Allowed
Section 2A-303(3) permits the lessor to grant a security interest in the lessor's interests under the lease despite agreement otherwise, and does not allow the lessee to claim that doing so is a breach of the lease agreement.

B. RIGHTS OF SUBLESSEE
Generally, a sublessee is subject to the terms of the prime lease and gets no better rights in the leased goods than the sublessor had. [U.C.C. §2A-305] Thus, a sublessee faces the prospect that a default by the sublessor on the prime lease could result in repossession of the leased goods from the sublessee. One major exception is based on the entrusting rule of U.C.C. section 2-403 in Article 2 (*see* Sales outline), adapted to leases in sections 2A-304 and 2A-305. If anyone entrusts goods to a merchant who deals in goods of that kind, a buyer or lessee in the ordinary course takes free of the claims of the entruster. This means that if the sublessor is someone who regularly leases goods to others, the sublessee in the ordinary course of business would prevail over the prime lessor's rights in the leased goods.

C. CREDITORS' RIGHTS
Generally, creditors of either party to the lease get no better rights than their debtors have in the leased property. Thus, creditors of the lessor cannot levy on the leased property in the hands of the lessee, and creditors of the lessee cannot seize the leased property and appropriate it to pay the debt owed by the lessee to the creditors. [U.C.C. §2A-307] There are, however, exceptions.

1. Not a True Lease
Repeating what was said above (*see* II.B., *supra*), if the so-called lease is not a true lease but is instead a sale on credit, the "lessor" is really an unpaid seller. If the "lessor" has not taken the steps required by Article 9 to perfect a security interest in the leased goods, the creditors of the lessee will prevail. [U.C.C. §9-322]

2. Statutory Lienholders
In a rule similar to the one found in U.C.C. section 9-333, section 2A-306 gives a valid lien to artisans who perform work on the leased property, and this lien prevails over all other claims as long as the artisan maintains possession. Thus, if the lessee takes the leased goods

to a repair shop for servicing, the repair shop would obtain an artisan's lien on the goods for the value of the repairs, and as long as the repair shop did not surrender possession of the goods, its lien would prevail over the rights of all other parties.

3. **Lessor's Preexisting Creditors**

A creditor of the lessor whose lien or security interest attaches to the leased goods *after* the lease was in effect cannot realize on the leased property to the prejudice of the lessee. However, a creditor of the lessor whose lien or security interest attached *prior* to the lease may repossess unless the lessor leased the goods in the ordinary course of the lessor's business to a lessee who gave value and was unaware that the lease was in violation of the rights of the creditor. [U.C.C. §2A-307]

BAR REVIEW

Mortgages

celebrating over
35 YEARS
of preparing
law students
for the bar exam

MORTGAGES—MASSACHUSETTS

TABLE OF CONTENTS

I. GENERAL NATURE

A. GENERAL DEFINITION

A mortgage is the conveyance of title to real property by the mortgagor to the mortgagee for purposes of securing an obligation owed the mortgagee.

B. MORTGAGE AS CONVEYANCE

1. Title Theory State

Massachusetts is a common law "title theory" state with respect to mortgages. This means that a mortgage deed *passes legal title* to the real property to the mortgagee. *Compare:* The majority of states follow the "lien theory," which provides that a mortgage constitutes only a lien on the premises and does not actually pass title.

2. Mortgagor Holds Equity of Redemption

Since the mortgagor parts with legal title upon executing the mortgage, he is left with only the "equity of redemption," which is the right to have title revested in him when he duly pays or performs the obligations secured by the mortgage. As holder of the equity of redemption, however, the mortgagor, until such time as there is a default under the mortgage, has the right to treat the mortgaged premises as his own, including the right to possess them, take rents and profits from them, and freely convey them subject to the mortgage. [Mass. Gen. L. ch. 183, §26] The mortgaged premises are part of the mortgagor's estate if he dies and are subject to the claims of the mortgagor's creditors. Thus, as a practical matter, although legal title technically passes to the mortgagee, the mortgagee's status is much more that of a lienholder, as opposed to a titleholder.

3. Mortgage Must Be in Writing

Because a mortgage is a conveyance of real estate, it must be in writing to satisfy the Statute of Frauds and be enforceable. Any partial release or discharge of the mortgage must likewise be in writing. [Mass. Gen. L. ch. 259, §1] (*See* II., *infra,* with respect to the more detailed formalities of the creation of a mortgage.)

4. Mortgage May Effect Severance of Joint Tenancy

Note that because a mortgage conveys legal title, it can effect a severance of a joint tenancy if one joint tenant mortgages his interest and the other does not. In such case, the joint tenant mortgaging his interest would become a tenant in common vis-a-vis his co-tenant(s). Note that a tenant by the *entirety* may mortgage her interest without destroying the tenancy. In so doing, however, the mortgagee takes only the interest the mortgagor has to give—*i.e.,* an interest in the land defeasible at the mortgagor's death. [Corracio v. Lowell Five Cent Savings Bank, 425 Mass. 145 (1993)]

Example: Husband and Wife hold Blackacre as tenants by the entirety. Husband grants Happy Bank a mortgage on his interest in Blackacre to secure a $10,000 note. On Husband's death, Happy Bank immediately begins foreclosure proceedings. Since the surviving holder of a joint tenancy or tenancy by the entirety takes free of the deceased's interest, Wife now has full title to Blackacre. Thus, while Happy Bank may attempt to collect the $10,000 due on the note from Husband's estate, it has *no interest* in Blackacre and may not foreclose.

C. PROPERTY SUBJECT TO MORTGAGE

The real estate described in the mortgage and property later affixed to the real estate, such as buildings, structures, and other installations in the nature of fixtures, constitute the property subject to the mortgage.

Caveat: The security interest in fixtures created by a mortgage is subject to the Massachusetts Uniform Commercial Code, which provides that a security interest attaching *before* goods are affixed to the real estate takes priority over existing mortgages. Thus, a fixture filing is good against subsequent real estate interests, but a prior real estate interest will prevail over a subsequent secured party. Subsequent advances made by the holder of an existing mortgage will not be subject to a security interest attaching before goods are affixed to the real estate if the advances are made without knowledge of the security interest and before it is perfected.

D. MORTGAGE AS SECURITY FOR OBLIGATION

As noted in the above definition, a mortgage is a conveyance of real property for purposes of securing an obligation owed the mortgagee. This obligation is most frequently the repayment of a debt, but it can also be an obligation to perform some act or service, as long as the obligation can be reduced to a money equivalent to be satisfied out of the proceeds of a foreclosure sale.

1. **Obligation Should Be Expressed in Separate Instrument**
   Generally, the obligation secured by the mortgage should be expressed in a separate written instrument, such as a note or contract, that governs the terms of the obligation. The provisions of the mortgage itself typically regulate the mortgagor's use, operation, and maintenance of the real property as the security for the underlying obligation.

2. **Mortgage Can Secure Existing Obligations**
   A mortgage can secure existing obligations, including antecedent debts. (*See* E., below.) For example, mortgages are commonly created to secure an obligation to repay money loaned to the mortgagor at the time the mortgage is granted.

3. **Mortgage Can Secure Future Advances**
   A mortgage can also be created to secure money to be loaned to the mortgagor in the future. Examples include the following:

   a. **Construction Mortgages**
      Typically, construction loans involve mortgages that provide that they will secure specified dollar amounts that will be loaned to the mortgagor over a future period as the construction progresses. These future advances will have the same priority as the mortgage securing them, provided that the lender is under an obligation to make them. This priority applies notwithstanding intervening liens between the time the construction mortgage is recorded and the time the future advance is made.

   b. **Open-Ended Mortgages**
      While construction mortgages generally stipulate the face amount of the construction loan and so have a specified limit of coverage, "open-ended" mortgages are also recognized as valid in Massachusetts. Open-ended mortgages have "dragnet clauses" written to cover "all future indebtedness of the mortgagor to the mortgagee, regardless of specified amount." [Everett Credit Union v. Allied Ambulance Service, Inc., 12 Mass. App. Ct. 343 (1981)] Sums lent by the mortgagee to the mortgagor after the recording of such a mortgage are equally secured and have the same priority with respect to principal, interest thereon, and other charges and fees as the sums disbursed at the time of the recording of the mortgage. [Mass. Gen. L. ch. 183, §28B] However, regarding mortgages recorded after the effective date of section 28B (August 6, 1986), priority applies *only* to the amount of the principal sum that is specified in the mortgage as the maximum sum intended to be secured.

   c. **Advances For Upkeep, Taxes, Etc.**
      By statute, sums advanced by a mortgagee for taxes and other like charges and assessments, for repairs, improvements, or replacements to the mortgaged premises, and for fuel will be secured by and have equal priority with the mortgage up to the original amount secured by it. [Mass. Gen. L. ch. 183, §28A] This statute benefits the mortgagee only if the original principal amount of the mortgage loan has been sufficiently paid down so that the sums advanced by the mortgagee can be added to the mortgage within the limits of this principal amount.
      Example: Owner has granted Mortgagee a $10,000 mortgage. After five years, the unpaid balance of the mortgage loan is $5,000. Owner then fails to pay his real estate taxes, which total $6,000. Mortgagee pays them. $5,000 of Mortgagee's payment is within the limits of the face amount of the mortgage and so would be secured by and have the same priority as the mortgage. The additional $1,000 would not.

E. **CONTRACT DISTINGUISHED**
   A mortgage is a conveyance, not a contract; thus, a mortgage *need not* be supported by separate consideration. This being the case, a mortgage can secure:

   (i) An *antecedent debt*; or

   (ii) The *debt of a third party*; *e.g.,* A can give B a mortgage to secure the repayment of money loaned by B to C.

Although the mortgage itself need not be supported by separate consideration, the underlying obligation it secures must be supported by consideration. A mortgage is unenforceable if the debt the mortgage secures is unenforceable. Thus, if the mortgagor can offer a defense to the debt, he can prevent the mortgagee from foreclosing. Note also that contracts for the sale of land or contracts that merely give the obligor the option of selling the property do not create mortgages. A mortgage must be created by a mortgage deed (*see* II.A.1., *infra*).

Examples: 1) Don runs up $10,000 in gambling debts to Freddie. Mary agrees to secure the debt by giving Freddie a mortgage on Blackacre. Later Don fails to pay, and Freddie attempts to foreclose. Mary may offer the defense that the debt is unenforceable because gambling is against public policy. If Mary is successful, Freddie may not foreclose, since there is no valid debt to be satisfied from the sale of the property.

2) Creditor loans Debtor $10,000. Debtor agrees to repay the funds in one year and, if she fails to do so, agrees to either sell her business to raise the funds *or* convey Blackacre to Creditor. The contract is not a mortgage. Creditor does not receive any present interest in Blackacre since Debtor retains the option of selling her business. Whether Creditor can force Debtor to specifically perform her agreement to convey Blackacre is purely a question of contract law.

F. DISCRIMINATION PROHIBITED

1. Persons
Persons engaged in the business of granting mortgage loans may not discriminate against any person in the granting of a loan or the interest rate, term, or duration of the loan because of race, color, religious creed, national origin, sex, sexual orientation, ancestry, or, subject to certain exceptions, age of such person. [Mass. Gen. L. ch. 151B, §4]

2. Location of Property
Where owner-occupied property of four or fewer units is involved, mortgagees may not practice "red-lining," *i.e.,* discriminate in lending against an applicant on the basis that the property is located in a specific neighborhood or geographical area. [Mass. Gen. L. ch. 183, §64]

II. CREATION OF MORTGAGES

A. GENERAL PREREQUISITES

1. Mortgage Deed
A mortgage is created by a written mortgage deed, which must contain at least:

a. The name of the grantor/mortgagor;

b. Words of grant or conveyance;

c. The name of the grantee/mortgagee;

d. A property description sufficient to identify the mortgaged premises;

e. The mortgagor's signature; and

f. An acknowledgment sufficient for recordation.

2. Delivery
To be effective and binding, a mortgage must be delivered.

B. EQUITABLE MORTGAGES
A mortgage deed (*see* typical form described in C., *infra*) should recite that the grant is being made as security for an obligation. The problem of equitable mortgages arises when the deed given is absolute on its face; *i.e.,* it does not recite that it is being delivered to secure an obligation, when in fact the intention of the parties is that it be a mortgage. In such situations, the mortgagor must prove this intention to the court in an equitable proceeding to either compel reformation of the absolute deed into a mortgage deed or, if the mortgagor has duly paid or performed the obligation secured by the equitable mortgage, to compel a reconveyance of the property to him. Parol evidence is admissible for purposes of proof of intention. [Fales v. Glass, 9 Mass. App. Ct. 570 (1980)] The parties' intention at the time the deed is executed is determinative. Courts usually look to the circumstances surrounding the negotiation and execution of the deed, but the parties' intention may be inferred from subsequent conduct.

C. FORM OF MORTGAGE
A standard Massachusetts form of mortgage is as follows:

> Owner, of Boston, Suffolk County, Massachusetts, for consideration paid, grants to Mortgagee, of said Boston, with Mortgage Covenants, to secure the payment of $20,000 in twenty-five years with ten percent interest per annum, payable monthly, as provided in a note of even date, the land in (here put a description of the land and encumbrances, if any).
>
> This mortgage is upon the Statutory Condition, for any breach of which the mortgagee shall have the Statutory Power of Sale.
>
> Witness my hand and seal this twentieth day of June, 2001.
>
> (acknowledgment added here)　　　/s/　　　Owner

[Mass. Gen. L. ch. 183, §18; ch. 183, Appendix 5] This mortgage form is basically as prescribed by statute, but it is not mandatory and may be modified. [Mass. Gen. L. ch. 183, §8] However, it does contain certain important words that have statutorily defined meanings. These words are discussed immediately below.

D. "MORTGAGE COVENANTS"
By statutory definition the mortgage covenants are:

(i)　The mortgagor is *lawfully seised* in fee simple of the mortgaged premises;

(ii)　The mortgaged premises are *free from encumbrances* except as noted;

(iii)　The mortgagor has good *right to sell* and convey;

(iv)　The mortgagor will *warrant and defend the title* against the claims of others; and

(v)　Upon sale made under the power of sale, the mortgagor will execute and deliver to the purchaser at foreclosure sale a *deed of release* confirming the sale and a full transfer of all insurance policies.

[Mass. Gen. L. ch. 183, §19] *Note:* Because of the warranty covenants contained in the mortgage covenants, the doctrine of estoppel by deed applies. (*See* Real Property outline.) Also, these mortgage covenants facilitate transfer of insurance policies at foreclosure.

E. "STATUTORY CONDITION"
The Statutory Condition requires the mortgagor to:

(i)　Pay the *principal and interest* secured by the mortgage when it is due and perform the obligations set forth in the note, mortgage, or other instruments;

(ii)　Perform the conditions of *prior mortgages*;

(iii)　Pay the *taxes, charges, and assessments* on the mortgaged premises or on the debt or obligation;

(iv)　Keep the buildings *insured* against fire in an amount not less than the amount secured by the mortgage for the benefit of the mortgagee, and at least two days before policy expiration deliver new policies to the mortgagee;

(v)　Not commit or allow *waste* or stripping of the premises; and

(vi)　Not breach *covenants* of prior mortgages.

[Mass. Gen. L. ch. 183, §20] The Statutory Condition also provides that the mortgage deed becomes void once the mortgagor has satisfied the debt. Failure to give a discharge after the underlying debt has been satisfied subjects the recalcitrant mortgagee to liability in tort. [Mass. Gen. L. ch. 183, §55; Maglione v. BancBoston Mortgage Corp., 29 Mass. App. Ct. 88 (1990)]

F. "STATUTORY POWER OF SALE"
The inclusion by reference in the mortgage of the Statutory Power of Sale permits the mortgagee, upon default of the Statutory Condition or any of the other conditions set forth in the mortgage,

to sell the mortgaged premises (or any portion thereof as shall remain subject to the mortgage after a partial release) at *public auction*. The auction must be held on or near the mortgaged premises or, if there are several parcels of land subject to the mortgage, on or near one of the parcels. The sale must comply with the terms of the mortgage and all statutes dealing with foreclosure of mortgages by the exercise of the power of sale. Such a properly conducted foreclosure sale will bar the equity of redemption absolutely, so the mortgagor will have no further right or interest in the mortgaged premises. [Mass. Gen. L. ch. 183, §21]

If reference is not made in the mortgage to the Statutory Power of Sale, the mortgagee is generally relegated to foreclosing by entry, which takes three years to perfect. (*See* discussion in V.C.2., *infra*.)

G.   FURTHER PROTECTION FOR MORTGAGEE
In addition to the statutorily defined words just described, the mortgage may include other provisions designed to afford further protection to the mortgagee. These typically include:

1.   A requirement that the *mortgagor* periodically *deposit in escrow* with the mortgagee sums necessary to pay *real estate taxes* and assessments as they become due;

2.   A requirement that the *mortgagor obtain insurance* coverage in addition to that required by the Statutory Condition, such as extended coverage insurance. However, a commercial mortgagee may not require casualty insurance exceeding the replacement cost of the buildings on the premises [Mass. Gen. L. ch. 183, §66];

3.   A provision allowing the *mortgagee to collect insurance proceeds* in the event of a loss and to apply them against the mortgage debt rather than to reconstruction of the mortgaged premises;

4.   A requirement that the *mortgagor maintain the premises* in good repair and condition— otherwise under the Statutory Condition the mortgagor's only obligation is the very limited one of not committing voluntary waste;

5.   A provision giving the *mortgagee the right to enter the premises* to inspect them and make repairs—otherwise the mortgagee would not have such rights unless and until the mortgage is in default; and

6.   A provision giving the *mortgagee the right to accelerate the entire indebtedness* secured by the mortgage in the event of a failure to pay a single installment or other default— otherwise the mortgagee would not be able to foreclose for purposes of collecting the entire loan amount, but rather only the installment that was then due, but unpaid. Note that once a mortgagee exercises such a right of acceleration of the debt, the mortgagee may initiate and continue foreclosure proceedings notwithstanding the mortgagor's paying of all arrearages, since such payments are treated only as payments on account of the full accelerated debt and are not sufficient to cure the breach once acceleration has occurred.

H.   REVERSE MORTGAGE LOANS
Massachusetts statutory law provides that reverse mortgage loans may be granted to homeowners who are at least 60 years of age and who occupy the mortgaged real estate. In a reverse mortgage loan, the proceeds are advanced to the mortgagor, either directly or indirectly, in installments at agreed-upon times, and the lien increases with each installment. Massachusetts prohibits a bank from making a reverse mortgage loan unless the borrower has first completed a home equity conversion counseling program approved by the Executive Office of Elder Affairs. [Mass. Gen. L. ch. 167E, §2; ch. 183, §67]

I.   RIGHT TO RESCIND CERTAIN MORTGAGES ON DWELLING
A consumer has a limited right to rescind certain types of mortgages. A consumer who gives a *nonpurchase money* mortgage (*e.g.*, a second mortgage) on or other nonpurchase money security interest in her *principal dwelling* has a right to rescind the transaction at no cost for *three business days*. The creditor must apprise the consumer of this right and must disclose all finance charges. Failure to do this results in the consumer's having *four years* to rescind the transaction. [*See* Mayo v. Key Financial Services, Inc., 424 Mass. 862 (1997)—misstatement totaling $28 led to rescission] Note that this right of rescission *does not* apply to transactions involving the *purchase or construction* of a primary dwelling.

III. TRANSFER OF MORTGAGES, TRANSFER OF EQUITY OF REDEMPTION, AND ACCELERATION CLAUSES

A. TRANSFER OF MORTGAGES

1. Necessity of Writing

To be effective, a transfer of a mortgage must be in writing.

2. Rights of Transferee

    a. Transferee of Note and Mortgage

    The transferee of a note and mortgage generally has all the rights of the original transferring mortgagee.

    b. Transferee of Note Only

    If the transferring mortgagee transfers the note but not the mortgage, the transferee has the right to the *transfer of the mortgage,* which is deemed to be held in trust for him by the transferring mortgagee.

    c. Transferee of Mortgage Only

    If the mortgage is transferred without the note, the transferee has the right to a *transfer of the note* even if it has already been transferred to a third party (unless the third party is a holder in due course, in which case the holder would have a right to the mortgage).

3. Obligations of Mortgagor

The mortgagor remains obligated in the event of a transfer of the note and mortgage, and if the note was negotiable, the transferee need not give the mortgagor notice of the assignment. If the mortgagor then makes payments to the prior holder of the mortgage, she does so at her peril and is still liable to pay the transferee.

B. TRANSFER OF EQUITY OF REDEMPTION (THE PROPERTY)

As already noted, as holder of the equity of redemption the mortgagor has the right to transfer the property. Such transfers may take different forms depending on the degree of responsibility the transferee assumes in connection with the mortgage and the extent to which the mortgagor/transferor is relieved of his duties under the mortgage.

1. Transfer Subject to Mortgage

    a. Transferee Does Not Agree to Obligation

    The transferee may take title to the property subject to the mortgage, but not agree with any party to pay or perform the obligation it secures. In such case, if the transferee fails to make payments to the mortgagee when due, the mortgagee may not sue him but may *foreclose* the mortgage.

    b. Mortgagor Becomes Quasi-Surety

    The mortgagor in this case remains personally liable to the mortgagee, but his position is one of a quasi-surety with the following consequences:

    1) If the mortgagor pays the note, he is entitled to be subrogated to the mortgage so he can foreclose it.

    2) The land constitutes the "primary fund" to satisfy the obligation, and if the land is released from the mortgage, the mortgagor is no longer liable. The mortgagor can force the mortgagee to proceed first against the land by foreclosure before going against the mortgagor on the note.

    3) Also, if an extension for payment of the mortgage is granted by the mortgagee to the transferee without the mortgagor's consent, it appears that the mortgagor will be released from liability to the extent of the loss of value of the property during the extension. *Note:* There is even some authority that such an extension may effect a total release of the mortgagor's liability.

2. Transfer Subject to Mortgage with Transferee Assuming Obligation

The general rule is that when property is transferred subject to a mortgage, the grantee does not, by merely accepting the deed, undertake to pay the mortgage debt. However, the deed may expressly indicate that the grantee agrees to become personally liable.

a. **Mortgagee and Mortgagor May Enforce Obligation**
If the transferee agrees with the transferring mortgagor to assume and pay the mortgage debt or other obligation secured by the mortgage, the mortgagor has the right to sue the transferee if the transferee fails to duly pay the obligation. The mortgagee also may be able to enforce such an agreement between the transferee and the transferring mortgagor as a third-party beneficiary.

b. **Mortgagor Becomes True Surety**
Once again the mortgagor remains personally liable to the mortgagee, but the cases indicate that his status becomes one of a true surety (not "quasi" surety), so that any release of the mortgaged premises by the mortgagee or any extension of the time for performance granted by the mortgagee to the transferee extinguishes the mortgagor's continuing liability.

3. **Novation**
In this situation, the transferee takes subject to and assumes the mortgage and enters into an agreement with the mortgagee to perform the mortgagor's obligations, with the mortgagor being correspondingly released from his obligations by the mortgagee. Such an agreement releasing the mortgagor from liability *must be in writing* to be effective. Here the mortgagor is released from liability, and the mortgagee has a direct contractual relationship with the transferee.

4. **Transfer of Equity of Redemption upon Death of Mortgagor**
When property subject to a mortgage passes to a devisee, the property continues to be subject to the mortgage, but the personal representative is not responsible for satisfaction of the mortgage and the devisee or heir is not personally liable. The testator may, by will, impose on her estate the burden of satisfying the mortgage, but must do so expressly. The devisee receives only the equity of redemption.

C. **ACCELERATION CLAUSES**
Acceleration clauses make the entire sum on the note due and payable when some condition of the mortgage is breached. Particularly when the mortgagee is a bank, one condition of the mortgage is generally the regular monthly payment of the amount due on the note. Failure to observe the condition generally gives the mortgagee the right to accelerate, making the entire sum on the note due and payable immediately. Since mortgagors who are incapable of making monthly payments are rarely able to pay the full amount due in one lump sum, foreclosure generally follows. Absent some defense to the mortgage as a whole (such as fraud, mistake, or duress), acceleration clauses are enforceable on their terms. Where the borrower pays the note in full after acceleration, such a payment is not a "prepayment," and the lender may not invoke any prepayment penalty. [Ferreira v. Yared, 32 Mass. App. Ct. 328 (1992)]

1. **"Due on Sale" Clauses**
A due on sale clause in a home mortgage is a device used in real property security transactions to provide, at the lender's option, for acceleration of the maturity of a loan (*i.e.,* entire amount becomes due) upon the transfer of the real property security.
Example: Seller wanted to transfer his mortgage to Buyer when Seller sold his home. The mortgage contained a due on sale clause, which Bank waited to enforce until three months after Seller's attempt to alienate the mortgage. The court held that Bank had a reasonable time in which to elect to accelerate and declare the debt due. It concluded such clauses are reasonable restraints on the transfer of property and enforceable by nature. [Dunham v. Ware Savings Bank, 384 Mass. 63 (1981); Kornatowski v. Family Mutual Savings Bank, 388 Mass. 1011 (1983)]

Note: By statute, a transfer from one spouse to the other, under a separation agreement or pursuant to a court order in a divorce proceeding, does not render a due on sale clause operative. [Mass. Gen. L. ch. 208, §34A]

2. **"Due on Encumbrance" Clauses**
Due on encumbrance clauses provide, at the lender's option, for acceleration of maturity of the loan upon the subsequent placement of a mortgage or lien on the property. The Massachusetts Appeals Court, relying on *Dunham, supra,* has upheld the use of due on encumbrance clauses in Massachusetts. [Egbert v. Freedom Federal Savings & Loan Association, 14 Mass. App. Ct. 383 (1982)] However, the Appeals Court also ruled that it would apply traditional rules of equity in litigation concerning the effect of the clause in the case.

a. Not Cured by Satisfaction of Encumbrance

A due on encumbrance clause may be enforced even if the mortgagor later procures a discharge of the subsequent mortgage or lien. The rationale is that the mortgagee has bargained for the right to have the security unimpaired, and this right was breached once the mortgagor granted a second mortgage or permitted a lien to attach. The initial breach is *not* cured simply by removing the subsequent encumbrance.

Example: Smith takes out a mortgage from Happy Bank with a due on encumbrance clause. Smith later gives a second mortgage to his cousin, Jones. Happy Bank accelerates the debt, notifying Smith that the entire amount of the loan is now due. Even if Smith removes the encumbrance by procuring a discharge from Jones, Smith has nevertheless breached his agreement. Happy Bank may therefore demand the entire sum due and may foreclose if it is not paid. [*See* Egbert v. Freedom Federal Savings & Loan Association, *supra*]

IV. RIGHTS AND OBLIGATIONS OF MORTGAGEE AND MORTGAGOR WITH RESPECT TO LAND

A. PRIOR TO DEFAULT

1. Mortgagor

As noted *supra* (I.B.2.), failing a specific agreement to the contrary, the mortgagor, as holder of the equity of redemption, has the right until default to possess and use the premises and collect the rents and profits therefrom. If the mortgage simply refers to the Statutory Condition as described *supra* (II.E.), the mortgagor may not suffer or commit voluntary waste, but she is not obligated to make repairs or improvements. [Mass. Gen. L. ch. 183, §26]

2. Mortgagee

Until default, the mortgagee has no right to possess the premises or to collect the rents and profits therefrom, and concomitantly has no obligations with respect to the premises. Fundamentally, his legal position is one of a lienholder, as opposed to a titleholder.

a. Entitled to Damages for Permanent Injury to Land

The mortgagee is, in general, entitled to damages for injuries permanently affecting the value of the land. Thus, where the mortgaged land is taken by eminent domain, both the mortgagor and mortgagee may join in the petition for award of damages, and the judgment on the petition apportions the damages according to each party's interests. [Mass. Gen. L. ch. 79, §§32, 33]

b. May Add Taxes Paid by Mortgagee to Mortgage Debt

If the mortgagor fails to pay taxes, the mortgagee may do so and add the amount paid to the mortgage debt. [Mass. Gen. L. ch. 60, §58] If separate assessments are made, and either the mortgagor or the mortgagee fails to pay, the other may do so, and the amount will be added to or deducted from the mortgage debt.

c. Late Payment Penalty Restriction

A mortgagee of a dwelling house with four or fewer separate households or of a condominium unit occupied by the mortgagor cannot require the mortgagor to pay a late charge or penalty for any payment made within 15 days of the due date. [Mass. Gen. L. ch. 183, §59]

3. Variation by Agreement

Note that the above rights and obligations may be varied by agreement of the parties. For example, the mortgage or other related agreements (*e.g.*, a construction loan agreement) may require that the mortgagor maintain the premises in good order and condition and/or erect certain improvements on them and permit the mortgagee to enter upon the premises to inspect them or make repairs. Also, mortgages may provide that if the mortgagor transfers the premises without the mortgagee's consent, the transfer will operate as an event of default. Note that a later modification of a mortgage agreement by a senior mortgagee may not prejudice the rights or impair the security of a junior mortgagee without the consent of the latter. [Shane v. Winter Hill Federal Savings & Loan Association, 397 Mass. 479 (1986)]

4.   **Future Advances**
A mortgage may be written to cover future advances and will be binding as to third parties if
it is recorded and the mortgagee is under obligation to make the advances. Sums loaned for
repairs, fuel, or taxes may also have the same priority as long as the original amount secured
is not exceeded. (*See* I.D.3.c., *supra.*)

B.   AFTER DEFAULT

1.   **Mortgagee May Take Possession or Foreclose**
Upon default, the mortgagee has the right, if he can do so *openly and peaceably*, to take
possession of the premises as mortgagee in possession. As mortgagee in possession he may
operate the premises and collect the rents and profits therefrom as described below. The
mortgagee is not, however, under any obligation to so take possession, even if the premises
are abandoned, and may proceed to foreclose his mortgage without actually becoming a
mortgagee in possession.

2.   **Mortgagor May Remain in Possession**
If the mortgagee does not take possession of the premises, the mortgagor may remain in
possession and receive the rents and profits from them with no liability to account to the
mortgagee on account thereof.

3.   **Mortgagee in Possession Must Account for Rents and Profits**
As a mortgagee in possession, the mortgagee may collect the rents and profits from the
premises and may repair and improve them. By statute, a mortgagee in possession must
account for the rents and profits he receives, but he is entitled to deduct amounts expended
for *reasonable* repairs and improvements and for taxes and assessments and other necessary
expenses of care and management. [Mass. Gen. L. ch. 244, §20] Note that courts have held
a charge equal to 5% of the rents to be reasonable for care and management. The mortgagee
is required to apply any rents and profits in excess of these deductions to a reduction of the
mortgage debt.

4.   **Mortgagee in Possession Must Use Reasonable Care**
By becoming a mortgagee in possession, the mortgagee imposes upon himself the duty of a
provident owner; he must use reasonable care and diligence to maintain the property and
collect the rents therefrom. As a result, many mortgagees, as a practical matter, do not wish
to take possession and thereby assume such responsibilities.

V.   FORECLOSURE

A.   CUTS OFF EQUITY OF REDEMPTION
In the event of a default by the mortgagor, the mortgagee may act to cut off the mortgagor's
equity of redemption. The process by which this is accomplished is called foreclosure. However,
a mortgagee is under no affirmative obligation to a junior mortgagee as attaching creditor to
promptly commence foreclosure as soon as his mortgage is in default, even if a delay diminishes
the value of the junior interests. The procedures for foreclosure of mortgages are discussed
below.

B.   SOLDIERS AND SAILORS CIVIL RELIEF ACT PROCEDURES
The Soldiers and Sailors Civil Relief Act provides that foreclosures of a military person's property during the period of his service and within three months thereafter are invalid. [50 U.S.C.
appendix §§501 *et seq.*]

1.   **Procedure**
To ensure that no person interested in the premises to be foreclosed possesses rights under
this Act, a judicial procedure is mandated by statute. This procedure involves filing a petition with either the land court or the superior court naming all persons interested in the
equity of redemption, including all mortgagees and lienholders. The court then issues notice
to be sent by registered mail to each defendant, published in a newspaper designated by the
court, and recorded at the Registry of Deeds. If no one establishes entitlement to the protection of the Act, the court issues an order authorizing foreclosure. The order should be recorded and is conclusive evidence of compliance.

2.   **Failure to Follow Procedure Creates Title Defect**
A title defect arises if these procedures are not complied with, since the foreclosure sale

could be rescinded by one entitled to the Act's protection. However, only a person entitled to the protection of the Act can raise such a challenge to the validity of the sale.

C. TYPES OF FORECLOSURE
There are basically three proceedings by which foreclosure may be effected:

(i)   A bill in equity to foreclose;

(ii) Foreclosure by entry; or

(iii) Foreclosure under a power of sale provision in the mortgage.

[Mass. Gen. L. ch. 244, §§1 *et seq.*] The first procedure is generally not available for use, while the second two procedures are frequently used concurrently.

1. Foreclosure by Bill in Equity
Foreclosure by bill in equity involves an equity proceeding in which the mortgagee petitions the court to establish a performance date for the obligation and if there is no performance by the stipulated date, the equity of redemption is extinguished. This procedure lies only where there is ***no adequate remedy at law***, and therefore is, as a practical matter, unavailable.

2. Foreclosure by Entry

a. Requirements

1) Entry and Possession for Three Years
Under this procedure, the mortgagee makes entry on the premises, if he can do so openly and peaceably, and then continues "in possession" for three years. At the end of the three-year period, the equity of redemption is extinguished and the mortgagee obtains title in fee simple. [Mass. Gen. L. ch. 244, §1]

2) Memorandum of Entry
The requirement of possession for three years is more fictional than actual, since all that is required is that the mortgagee step onto the land openly and peaceably, recite that he has entered for purposes of foreclosing the mortgage, and then record either (i) a memorandum of entry noted on the mortgage or (ii) a certificate of entry made under oath by two competent witnesses proving the entry. After the procedures are followed, the mortgagee need not reenter upon the premises again, and in three years the equity of redemption will be cut off. The three-year period is measured from the date of the recording of the memorandum or certificate. [Mass. Gen. L. ch. 244, §2]

If the mortgagee cannot make the entry by open and peaceable means, he can nevertheless obtain legal possession for purposes of foreclosure by means of a statutory action for possession.

Note: If the mortgagee in fact takes physical possession of the premises during the three-year period as a mortgagee in possession, the principles discussed in IV.B.3., 4., *supra,* apply.

b. Statutory Right of Redemption
The mortgagor has the right to redeem the property during the three-year period it takes to extinguish her equity of redemption.

1) Statutory Right of Redemption vs. Equity of Redemption
The right of redemption must be distinguished from an equity of redemption. The right of redemption does not arise until ***after foreclosure*** and is primarily for the benefit of the mortgagor. The right is statutory and is to be enforced as the statute provides. [*See* Mass. Gen. L. ch. 244, §18] The equity of redemption rests upon principles of equity and involves the mortgagor's rights ***before foreclosure***. (*See* I.B.2., *supra.*)

2) Who May Redeem?
Any person who may have acquired any interest in the premises, legal or equitable, by operation of law or otherwise, in privity of title with the mortgagor, may redeem and protect the interest.

a) Possible Redeemers

Among those who may redeem under this rule, in addition to the mortgagor (as long as she is living and has not completely divested herself of all interest) are: purchasers of the equity from the mortgagor; an heir or devisee; any other person who succeeds to the mortgagor's interest in the mortgaged property; an owner of a limited interest such as a tenant for life or years, a remainderman or reversioner, or one who has dower, or the holder of an easement; joint tenants; junior lienors; and trustees, to whom legal title to mortgaged property is conveyed by trust deed.

b) Priority Among Redeemers

Among several persons who may be entitled to redeem, the one whose interest is superior has priority; *i.e.,* a second mortgagee comes ahead of a third mortgagee.

3) Procedure for Redemption

To redeem, the person entitled to redeem must pay or tender to the mortgagee the whole amount then due and payable on the mortgage and perform or tender performance of every other condition contained in the mortgage. If there has been any action to recover the land, the redeemer must also pay or tender the costs of the action. Alternatively, the redeemer may commence suit for redemption, offering to pay the amount as shall be found due from him or to perform such other conditions as the case may require. [Mass. Gen. L. ch. 244, §§19, 21-34]

4) Mortgagee Does Not Accept Redemption

If the person entitled to redeem makes the above tender and the mortgagee does not accept it, the mortgagor may, within one year after the tender, commence suit for redemption, then paying to the clerk of the court the amount tendered. [Mass. Gen. L. ch. 244, §21]

5) Mortgagee's Accounting

If the mortgagee has had possession, he must account for rents and profits, and must be allowed all amounts expended in reasonable repairs and improvements, all lawful taxes and assessments paid, and all other necessary expenses in the care and management of the land. [Mass. Gen. L. ch. 244, §20]

c. Mortgage Debt Extinguished to Extent of Property Value

With foreclosure by entry, the mortgage debt is automatically extinguished at the end of the three-year period to the extent of the value of the property at that time. Thus, if the value of the property at the time of this extinguishment is less than the mortgage debt, there is a deficiency. If so, a suit to collect the deficiency must be commenced within two years after the end of the three-year entry period or it will be barred. Recovery of a deficiency judgment reopens the period of redemption for a period of one year.

d. Must Use Entry If No Power of Sale Provision

The procedure of foreclosure by entry must be used if a power of sale provision was not included in the mortgage. Even if there is foreclosure under a power of sale, foreclosure by entry is frequently used concurrently with it so that if the foreclosure sale is defective, the foreclosure will nevertheless be perfected by the entry after three years.

3. Foreclosure Under Power of Sale

A foreclosure under power of sale is a procedure that is available only if a provision for it is included in the mortgage. It is the most frequently used procedure because it is the fastest way to cut off the equity of redemption. The sale can be effected either by judicial action or by nonjudicial sale. [Mass. Gen. L. ch. 244, §14]

a. Judicial Action

The judicial action is rarely used. It involves obtaining a conditional judgment for the amount due on the debt. The mortgagor then has two months to pay or the court may order a sale upon such instructions as it stipulates. After the sale, the mortgagee files with the court a report on oath of the sale, and the court may then confirm the sale or set it aside and order a resale. [*See* Mass. Gen. L. ch. 244, §5]

b. Nonjudicial Sale

To effect a sale, the following statutorily prescribed formalities must be complied with:

1) **Notice**
Notice must be published once a week for three successive weeks in a newspaper published in the town (or if none in the town, in the county) where the land lies, with the first publication of notice to be at least 21 days before the sale. Notice must also be sent 14 days before the sale, by registered mail, to: (i) the owner or owners of the equity of redemption (owners determined as of 30 days before sale), and (ii) all persons of record who hold an interest in the property junior to the mortgage being foreclosed (although junior interest holders of record as of 30 days before the sale may waive the requirement of notice). [Hull v. Attleboro Savings Bank, 402 Mass. 1102 (1988), *cert. denied,* 488 U.S. 856 (1989); Mass. Gen. L. ch. 244, §14]

2) **Compliance with Power of Sale and Statute**
The sale must be conducted in accordance with the power of sale contained in the mortgage and in accordance with the applicable statutory requirements. (*See* II.F., *supra.*) However, it is proper to sell to the second highest bidder after the highest bidder defaults if the procedure was announced orally at the sale, even though not mentioned in the published notice of sale. [Dundas Corp. v. Chemical Bank, 400 Mass. 588 (1987)]

3) **Notice and Affidavit Must Be Recorded**
Within 90 days after the sale, the mortgagee must record a copy of the notice of sale and an affidavit stating his acts with the Registry of Deeds. If the affidavit shows compliance with the power of sale and statute, it is admissible as evidence of due execution of the power of sale. [Mass. Gen. L. ch. 244, §15]

4) **Good Faith and Diligence Required**
When conducting the sale, the mortgagee must comply with the requirements of the statute and the power of sale contained in the mortgage. The mortgagee also must exercise good faith and reasonable diligence with due regard for the interests of the mortgagor. However, a disparity in the fair market value of the property and the price obtained at sale does not alone establish lack of good faith and reasonable diligence in the conduct of the sale. [Katz v. Winokur, 386 Mass. 1102 (1982)]

5) **Mortgagee May Purchase at Sale**
Unless the mortgage prohibits it, the mortgagee may purchase at the foreclosure sale. In the absence of bad faith, there is no legal objection to the auctioneer making a bid for the mortgagee or purchaser. The fact that the mortgagee, through an agent, is the only bidder and is not personally present to bid will not invalidate a sale.

6) **Notice to Co-Signers Required**
Where the note secured by a mortgage is co-signed by another party, the co-signer has an equitable right to notice of the foreclosure. This is so even if the co-signer of the note has no legal interest in the property that serves as the note's security. [Seronik v. Levy, 26 Mass. App. Ct. 367 (1988)] The burden of giving notice rests on the maker of the note, whose right to contribution may be destroyed if she does not inform her co-signers. The purpose of the rule is to protect the co-signer, who may become liable for any deficiency, by giving the co-signer the opportunity to bid on the property at a foreclosure sale. (*See* E., *infra.*)

7) **Mortgagor Can Enjoin Irregular Sale**
If the sale does not comply with the statutory power of sale requirements or is otherwise irregularly held, the mortgagor can sue to have it enjoined or, if already held, set aside. Also, the mortgagor may sue the mortgagee in tort for damages and may be entitled to recover for mental suffering.

8) **Postponement of Sale Permitted**
Reasonable postponement of a foreclosure sale is allowed, and if the postponement is announced at the published time of sale, the sale need not be readvertised.

4. **Deed in Lieu of Foreclosure**
The mortgagor may also tender to the mortgagee a deed in lieu of foreclosure. In effect, the mortgagor simply turns over her equity of redemption to the mortgagee. Acceptance of a deed in lieu of foreclosure permits the mortgagee to take immediate possession without the

formalities of a foreclosure sale. The mortgagee, however, *may not* then sue for any deficiency on the note. Mortgagors cannot be compelled to tender such a deed, and mortgagees have the right to refuse the deed and proceed to foreclosure.

D. DISTRIBUTION OF PROCEEDS OF SALE
The proceeds of sale are distributed first to the foreclosing mortgagee to cover the mortgage debt, interest due, and costs of foreclosure. Any proceeds remaining are then distributed to junior lienors according to their priority, and then to the mortgagor. [Mass. Gen. L. ch. 183, §27]

E. DEFICIENCIES AFTER SALE

1. Deficiency Notice
If the mortgagee wishes to sue for a deficiency in case the sale proceeds turn out to be less than the amount owed him, he must notify the defendant by registered mail at least 21 days before the date of sale. The notice must indicate the mortgagee's intent to foreclose and warn of the liability for a deficiency. [Mass. Gen. L. ch. 244, §17B; Wornat Development Corp. v. Vakalis, 403 Mass. 340 (1988)] Note that a maker seeking to enforce contribution against a co-maker has an equitable obligation to forward the statutory notice to the co-maker. [Seronick v. Levy, C.3.b.6), *supra*]

2. Commencement of Suit
Suit on the deficiency must be commenced within *two years* after the date of the sale or it will be barred. [Mass. Gen. L. ch. 244, §17A]

F. EFFECT OF FORECLOSURE SALE

1. Purchaser Takes Subject to Senior Interests
Title to the premises is vested in the purchaser subject to all restrictions, easements, improvements, outstanding tax titles, municipal or other public taxes, assessments, liens, and existing encumbrances of record created *prior* to the mortgage (*i.e.,* senior to the mortgage).

2. Junior Interests Are Cut Off
The foreclosure cuts off all interests, including mortgages, *junior* to the mortgage being foreclosed. The junior mortgagees may still sue the mortgagor personally on their notes, however, if not adequately compensated as a result of the foreclosure sale.
Example: Blackacre is subject to three mortgages to Alice, Becky, and Carl, respectively. Becky, as second mortgagee, forecloses and sells to Tim. Tim takes title subject to the first mortgage to Alice, while the third mortgage to Carl is cut off.

3. Leasehold Tenants
Like other tenants, leasehold tenants on foreclosed property may be evicted only through summary process. This applies to holdover tenants as well as to tenants with enforceable leases. [Attorney General v. Dime Savings Bank, 413 Mass. 284 (1992)]

VI. PRIORITIES

A. GENERAL RULE
"First in time of recording, first in right"—as a general matter the first mortgage recorded as reflected by the date and time shown on the recorded instrument has the prior right.

B. EXCEPTIONS

1. No Notice
Since Massachusetts is a *notice-type recording jurisdiction,* under some circumstances the first mortgage to be recorded may not be the first in right.
Example: Owner owns Blackacre.

Day 1: Owner sells Blackacre to Adam, who mortgages it to First Bank. Adam fails to promptly record his deed and the mortgage.

Day 3: Owner sells Blackacre again, this time to Bonnie, who mortgages it to Second Bank.

Day 4: Adam records his deed and First Bank's mortgage and soon thereafter, Bonnie records her deed and Second Bank's mortgage.

The result is that Second Bank's mortgage has priority because when it was granted, Second Bank did not have notice of Adam's and First Bank's interest, because Adam and First Bank had failed to record before Owner's conveyance to Bonnie and Bonnie's mortgage to Second Bank. However, this result applies only if Second Bank did not have **actual knowledge** of First Bank's mortgage, making Second Bank a purchaser in good faith without knowledge. If a mortgagee has actual (not constructive) notice of a prior unrecorded mortgage, his mortgage will be subject to it.

2. Municipal Liens and Taxes
Municipal liens for taxes and water and sewer use charges have priority over all mortgages.

3. Condominium Charges
When the mortgage is on a condominium, unpaid common area assessments ("condo fees") may take priority over a first mortgage. However, the priority amount may equal only up to six months' unpaid assessments, plus reasonable collection costs and attorney's fees. To obtain priority for costs and fees, the condominium owners' association must give the mortgagee two written notices of arrearage: the first after fees have been delinquent for 60 days, and the second notice 30 days before commencing suit for the delinquency. Failure to give such notice removes the priority for costs and fees, but not for the six-month arrearage itself. A mortgagee may restore its priority position by paying the delinquent fees itself, and then bringing an action against the mortgagor. [Mass. Gen. L. ch. 183A, §6]

C. SPECIAL PROBLEMS

1. Extension of Mortgages
Generally, extensions of time for payment of a mortgage can be made without a loss of priority.

2. Future Advances
(*See* I.D.3., *supra*.)

3. Judicial Lien Creditors
A creditor who has reduced his claim to judgment may attempt to attach property that is already subject to a mortgage. Under the principle of "first in time, first in right," such a creditor normally takes his interest in the property **subject to** a properly recorded mortgage. Consequently, while the attaching creditor can force the sale of the property, the proceeds of the sale first go to any prior mortgagees.

a. Sham Mortgages
To discourage creditors from seeking attachments, a property owner might collude with a third person to arrange and record a "mortgage" that secures no debt. Such mortgages are void as to all creditors.

b. Mortgages Fraudulently Induced
A creditor or junior mortgagee has standing to challenge the validity of a mortgage on the grounds that it was induced by fraud, duress, or undue influence. Thus, if the mortgagor lacked capacity to enter into a valid mortgage (*e.g.,* because of insanity) the attaching creditor may move to have the mortgage set aside. [Kirk v. MacDonald, 21 Mass. App. Ct. 832 (1985)]

4. Statutory Lien Creditors
A contractor who makes improvements to the mortgaged property acquires, by operation of law, a lien against the value of the improvements. [Mass. Gen. L. ch. 254, §2] The lien does not take priority over any previously recorded mortgage, but does take priority over any subsequent mortgage. To fix this priority, however, the statutory lien creditor must record a notice of contract with the Registry of Deeds. [Mass. Gen. L. ch. 254, §2]

5. Deed in Lieu of Foreclosure
When a mortgagee takes by a deed in lieu of foreclosure, the mortgagee is a "purchaser" for purposes of figuring priority even though the mortgagee, in theory, already had legal title to the land.

Example: Mortgagor hires Contractor to build the foundations for a subdivision. Contractor performs the work. Later, Mortgagor, effectively bankrupt, tenders a deed in lieu of foreclosure to the mortgagee, Bank. Bank happily accepts. Two days later, Contractor files his notice of contract at the Registry of Deeds. Although Bank, the mortgagee, had legal title to the land both at the time the work was performed and at the time the lien was filed, Bank takes free of Contractor's lien, since the lien was not recorded prior to the conveyance of the mortgagor's equity of redemption. [J & W Wall Systems, Inc. v. Shawmut First Bank & Trust Co., 413 Mass. 42 (1992)]

D. SUBORDINATION
A mortgagee may voluntarily make his mortgage subject to a junior encumbrance by executing and recording a written subordination agreement.

E. UNRECORDED MORTGAGES
An unrecorded mortgage is valid as between the parties to it, but it does not have priority over subsequent recorded mortgages unless the subsequent mortgagee(s) had *actual knowledge* of its existence.

F. MORTGAGE ON REGISTERED LAND
A mortgage on registered land is registered by filing the deed and entering a memorandum on the owner's duplicate certificate. [Mass. Gen. L. ch. 185, §§67, 68] Discharge and foreclosure are effectuated similarly to those procedures for unregistered land. [Mass. Gen. L. ch. 185, §§69, 70] A mortgagee who fails to ensure that the appropriate notation is made on the mortgagor's duplicate certificate of title risks losing priority to a subsequent purchaser of the land who takes for value without notice. If a purchaser of registered land takes with actual knowledge of the encumbrance, however, the purchaser takes subject to it. [Wild v. Constantine, 415 Mass. 663 (1993)]

G. MORTGAGES HELD BY SEVERAL PARTIES
A single mortgage may be taken by several parties, in which case the mortgagees may hold legal title as tenants in common or as joint tenants, depending on the intent of the parties. As a practical matter, the question tends to arise only when there is some dispute as to how the proceeds of the note should be divided.

Example: Amy, Bob, and Carol hold Blackacre as joint tenants. They sell Blackacre to Dee and take back a mortgage. Later, Carol dies. Since Amy, Bob, and Carol held Blackacre as joint tenants, the court will presume that they held the mortgage as joint tenants as well. Thus, Amy and Bob will now hold the mortgage free of Carol's interest, and Carol's estate will not be entitled to share in any payments that Dee makes. [Bertolami v. Corsi, 27 Mass. App. Ct. 1132 (1989)] If Amy, Bob, and Carol held the mortgage as tenants in common, Carol's heirs would be entitled to one-third of the proceeds because Carol could pass her interest to them by descent or devise.

VII. DEFENSES AND EXTINGUISHMENT

A. DEFENSES

1. Defenses to Underlying Obligation
Since a mortgage is granted to secure an obligation, if the obligation is unenforceable, so is the mortgage. Therefore, defenses in an action on the underlying obligation are defenses against an action on the mortgage, including:

a. Failure of consideration;

b. Duress;

c. Mistake; or

d. Fraud.

2. Statute of Limitations—Fifty Years
There is a 50-year statute of limitations which renders a mortgage unenforceable after 50 years *from the date of its recording*, unless an extension of mortgage or an affidavit that the mortgage is not satisfied is recorded within the last 10 years of the 50-year period. [Mass. Gen. L. ch. 260, §33]

3. Possession After Mortgage Due
By statute, a mortgagor or the holder of the equity of redemption may petition the court to discharge a mortgage if the mortgagor and those having his estate in the premises have been in uninterrupted possession thereof for any period of *20 years* after the expiration of the time for performance of the mortgage. [Mass. Gen. L. ch. 240, §15]

B. EXTINGUISHMENT

1. Satisfaction of Debt

Upon the satisfaction of the debt or other obligation secured by the mortgage, it is no longer enforceable and the mortgagor has the statutory right to a discharge to clear title to the property. If the mortgagee fails to give such a discharge within seven days after request, he is liable in tort for all damages caused by his refusal. [Mass. Gen. L. ch. 183, §55]

2. Deed of Release or Acknowledgment

A mortgage is discharged by a deed of release or by a written acknowledgment of payment or satisfaction of the debt recorded by the mortgagee or one or more of several joint mortgagees. [Mass. Gen. L. ch. 183, §54] The recordation of a duly executed and acknowledged deed of release or written acknowledgment of payment or satisfaction is conclusive evidence that the mortgage has been discharged, notwithstanding the fact that the party signing the instrument may have assigned the note or other evidence of debt to another party, unless such assignment has been duly recorded prior to the instrument discharging the mortgage.

3. Partial Releases

A mortgagee may partially release his mortgage.

BAR REVIEW

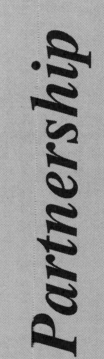

Partnership

PARTNERSHIP

TABLE OF CONTENTS

I. NATURE OF A PARTNERSHIP

A. IN GENERAL

1. "Partnership" Defined

The Uniform Partnership Act ("U.P.A.") defines a partnership as an association of two or more competent persons to carry on as co-owners a business for profit. [U.P.A. §6(1)] The law of partnership is based on the law of contracts and agency.

a. "Person" Defined

The U.P.A. defines a person to include an individual, partnership, corporation, or other association. [U.P.A. §2]

2. Joint Venture Is a Partnership

Courts sometimes seek to distinguish a joint venture (*i.e.*, a single or limited enterprise or venture) from a partnership. However, a joint venture is a partnership, and the legal consequences of a joint venture are almost identical to those of a partnership.

B. PARTNERSHIP NOT A LEGAL ENTITY

A partnership is unlike a corporation in that it lacks some of the entity characteristics of a corporation. For example, the debts of the partnership are the debts of the individual partners, and any one partner may be held liable for the partnership's entire indebtedness. However, in some cases, the partnership, at least in form, is treated as an entity.

1. Title to Land

Title to land may be taken in the partnership name.

2. Lawsuits

Whether a partnership may sue or be sued in the partnership name depends on the procedural rules in each state.

a. Entity Theory States

In those states that view the partnership as an entity, a partnership may sue or be sued in the partnership name or in the names of the individual partners, or both.

b. Aggregate Theory States

In those states that do not view the partnership as an entity, suits by and against the partnership must name the individual partners.

II. FORMATION OF A PARTNERSHIP

A. APPLICABILITY OF CONTRACT RULES

Because a partnership is the result of an agreement, it is necessarily governed by the general rules applicable to contracts. In jurisdictions that have adopted the U.P.A., the provisions of the U.P.A. will apply only if the particular issue is *not addressed* by a partnership agreement; however, in a few cases, *e.g.,* those involving partners' fiduciary duties, the principles of the U.P.A. may not be changed by agreement.

1. Capacity

a. Who May Be a Partner

The basic rule is the same as respects a principal in agency: Anyone may be a partner who is capable of entering into a binding contract.

b. Liability Where No Capacity

If a would-be partner lacks capacity, she is *not personally liable* for the obligations of the partnership or for breaches of the partnership agreement. She is, however, bound to the extent of her contribution of capital to the partnership.
Example: A, age 17, and B, age 21, form a partnership. Each contributes $1,000. The partnership incurs a debt of $2,000 to T. The $1,000 contributed by A is subject to claim by T.

2. Formalities

a. General Rule—No Formalities

No particular formalities are essential to the validity of a contract of partnership. In the absence of a controlling statute, the partnership agreement may be either express or implied (*i.e.,* established solely from the conduct of the parties). It is normally not necessary for the partnership agreement to be in writing.

b.   When Writing Necessary

   1)   Statute of Frauds
   Partnership agreements that cannot be performed within one year must be in writing to satisfy the Statute of Frauds.

   2)   When Statute of Frauds Violated
   If parties act upon an oral partnership agreement that must be in writing to satisfy the Statute of Frauds, they will be treated as partners at will. Such a partnership may be terminated at any time.

3.   Legality of Purpose
The purpose for which the partnership was formed or is to be formed must be legal. The illegality of the enterprise will make the partnership void. Where a partnership has been formed for an illegal purpose, the court will not compel an accounting or a settlement of the partnership affairs.
Example: A and B formed a partnership for the purpose of making wagers on horses. This was contrary to state law. The money secured by the operation of the partnership was deposited in A's name. In an action by B to secure an accounting of the partnership funds held by A, the court will refuse to grant the accounting on the ground of illegality of the partnership.

4.   Consent
Unless the agreement provides otherwise, no one can become a partner in a partnership without the express or implied consent of ***all partners.*** [U.P.A. §18(g)]

B.   PROOF OF PARTNERSHIP EXISTENCE

1.   Rules for Determining Existence
Generally, the courts look to the intent of the parties to determine the existence of a partnership. This is not difficult where the parties have an express contract, but where their intention is unexpressed, a problem may arise. To make a determination in the latter case, the courts and section 7 of the U.P.A. have provided certain tests to be applied to the acts of the parties. Should the problem arise on the bar examination, you should consider the following:

   a.   Title to Property
   Joint or common tenancies of any type do ***not*** establish, by themselves, the existence of a partnership, even if the co-owners share profits from the use of the property. [U.P.A. §7(2)]

   b.   Designation of Entity by Parties
   The designation by the parties of their entity as a "partnership" or some other business entity form is important as indicative of intent, but is ***not conclusive.***

   c.   Amount of Activity Involved
   The amount of activity involved in the enterprise undertaken by the parties will be considered a relevant factor in determining whether a partnership exists.
   Examples: 1) A and B each contribute $5,000 and purchase Blackacre.

              2) A and B each contribute $5,000 and purchase Blackacre. Thereafter, they develop the land by building apartments and proceed to manage the development.

   The second example, because of the degree of activity, is much more likely to be held a partnership than the first example.

   d.   Sharing of Gross Returns
   The sharing of gross returns does ***not*** by itself establish a partnership, irrespective of whether the persons sharing them have a joint or common interest in any property from which the returns are derived. [U.P.A. §7(3)]

    e.   **Sharing of Profits**

        1) **General Rule—Prima Facie Evidence of Partnership**
The receipt by a person of a share of the profits of a business is *prima facie evidence* that he is a partner in the business.

        2) **Exceptions to Inference of Partnership**
No such inference of partnership will be drawn if the profits were received in payment as:

           (i) *A debt,* by installment or otherwise [U.P.A. §7(4)(a)];

          (ii) *Wages* of an employee [U.P.A. §7(4)(b)];

         (iii) *Rent* to a landlord [U.P.A. §7(4)(b)];

         (iv) *Annuities to a surviving spouse* or representative of a deceased partner [U.P.A. §7(4)(c)];

          (v) *Interest* on a loan even though the amount varies with the profits of the business [U.P.A. §7(4)(d)]; or

         (vi) *Consideration for the sale of goodwill* of a business, by installments or otherwise [U.P.A. §7(4)(e)].

           Example: A owns a piece of land. B desires to rent it and to build and operate a hotel thereon. A leases the land to B, who agrees to pay A 10% of the net profits earned from the operation of the hotel. X, who delivers goods to B for the hotel, seeks to hold A liable for the goods as B's partner when B fails to pay for the goods. X cannot recover from A. The 10% payments are rent.

        3) **Subpartnership**
A subpartner who shares with a partner of a principal partnership profits derived from that partnership is not thereby deemed a partner of the principal partnership.
          Example: A and B enter into a written partnership agreement that provides that they will share profits of the business equally. B then enters into an agreement with C that provides that B and C will share the profits received by B from the A/B partnership. In this example, C is not a partner in the A/B partnership even though he will, in effect, be receiving a share of the A/B profits. At most, he is a member of the B/C partnership.

    f.   **Sharing of Losses**
While there is no statutory requirement that sharing losses is necessary to create a partnership, the *absence* of an agreement to share losses is evidence that the parties did *not* intend to form a partnership.

C. PARTNERSHIP BY ESTOPPEL

The discussion above considered a true partnership, *i.e.,* one where there is an agreement, express or implied, between the parties. In certain situations, however, even though there is no agreement and the parties as between themselves are not partners, they may nevertheless be held *liable to third parties* as if they were partners. This "partnership by estoppel" issue is most likely to arise in the following situations:

1.   Liability of Person Who Is Held Out as Partner
When a person, by words or conduct, represents herself or permits another to represent her as a partner, she will be liable to third parties who extend credit to the actual or apparent partnership on the faith of (*i.e.,* in reliance on) the representation. [U.P.A. §16(1)]

2.   Liability of Person Who Holds Another Out as Partner
When a person, by words or conduct, holds another person out to be her partner, she thereby makes the alleged partner her agent with the *power to bind* her to third parties as if the other were, in fact, a partner. [U.P.A. §16(2)] Note that if the person making the representation is in fact a member of an already existing partnership and the representation is to the effect that the would-be partner is a member of this partnership, only those partners who made or consented to the representation will be bound.

Example: A, B, and C are partners in a textile manufacturing concern. To obtain financing for herself, D, with the knowledge of B and C, represents herself to be a member of the ABC partnership. In fact, D is not a partner. On the strength of this representation, S lends money to D, believing it to be for the ABC partnership. Upon a later default, S may hold B, C, and D liable. Neither A nor the ABC partnership is liable.

III. PROPERTY OF A PARTNERSHIP

A. IN GENERAL

In addition to testing whether a partnership exists, partnership questions often focus on the rights and liabilities as between partners and third parties—both in the ongoing conduct of the partnership and in any eventual dissolution. In analyzing such issues, it may be important to distinguish which property belongs to the partnership and which belongs to the individual partners. If the property belongs to the partnership, how should it be characterized and what are the rights of the individual partners in that property?

B. CLASSIFICATIONS OF PROPERTY

1. Partnership Capital

Partnership capital consists of the *property or money contributed* by each of the partners for the purpose of carrying on the partnership's business.

2. Partnership Property

Partnership property, in its broadest sense, embraces everything that the partnership owns, consisting both of the capital contributed by its members *and* the properties subsequently acquired in partnership transactions.

Example: A and B form a partnership, each contributing $500. During the first year of operation, the partnership earns a profit of $20,000. A and B each take a $7,500 draw. Partnership capital is still $1,000. Partnership property is now $6,000.

C. WHAT IS INCLUDABLE IN PARTNERSHIP PROPERTY

Absent an agreement, there is no restriction as to what may be included in partnership property. The controlling factor in determining what comprises partnership property is the *partner's intent to devote the property to partnership purposes*. The following criteria are usually applied in making this determination. However, no factor by itself will be conclusive.

1. Acquisition with Partnership Funds

Unless a contrary intention appears, property acquired with partnership funds is usually partnership property. [U.P.A. §8(2)]

2. Use of Property

The use of the property by the partnership in conducting its business is evidence that the partnership intended it to be partnership property.

3. Improvement of Property by Partnership

If the property that was acquired has been improved by the partnership, it is more likely than not to be partnership property.

4. Relation of Property to Business

If the acquired property is closely related in character to the business operations of the partnership, it is likely that the property was meant to be partnership property.

5. Title to Property

If the property has been acquired in the partnership name, it is partnership property.

6. Entry in Partnership Books

If the property has been listed as an asset on the partnership books, particularly where all the partners are aware of this fact, it is likely the property will be considered partnership property.

7. Maintenance and Expenses

If the partnership has paid the taxes, insurance, maintenance costs, and other expenses associated with the property, this is evidence that the property is partnership property.

D.   PARTNER'S RIGHTS IN PARTNERSHIP PROPERTY—TENANCY IN PARTNERSHIP
A partner's ownership interest in any *specific item* of partnership property is not that of an outright owner, joint tenant, or tenant in common, but rather is that of a *tenant in partnership.* The incidents of this tenancy are:

1.   **Possession**
Each partner has an *equal right* with copartners to possess partnership property for partnership purposes, but has no right to possess it for any other purpose without the consent of his copartners. [U.P.A. §25(2)(a)]

2.   **Assignability**
A partner's right in specific partnership property is *not assignable* to nonpartners except in connection with the assignment of the rights of all the partners in the property. If, therefore, a partner attempts to assign his interest in specific partnership property to someone who is not already a partner, the attempted assignment will convey no right, title, or interest in the specific property. [U.P.A. §25(2)(b)]
Example: A, B, and C are partners. The partnership owns a building on which a fire insurance policy was issued in the partnership name. A thereafter assigned his interest in the building to X. The building is then destroyed by fire. The assignment made by A did not pass any interest in the building to X because A's right in the building was only to use it for partnership purposes. Therefore, the insurance company's defense that there was an unauthorized transfer of title is invalid.

Compare: An assignment or sale of the partner's interest in specific partnership property to one or more of his *copartners* passes title to the property.

3.   **Mortgage**
An attempted mortgage of one of the partners' interest in specific partnership property has no effect upon the passing of title to the property. The mortgagee will have no rights against the property.
Example: A and B are partners. The partnership owns Blackacre. A borrowed money from X and gave as security therefor a mortgage on his interest in Blackacre. The attempted mortgage given by A passed no interest in Blackacre to X. Therefore, X cannot foreclose on Blackacre if A does not repay the money he borrowed from X.

4.   **Death**
Upon the death of a partner, his right in specific partnership property vests in the surviving partner(s). Upon the death of the last surviving partner, his right in the partnership property vests in his legal representative. [U.P.A. §25(2)(d)] The surviving partner(s) or the legal representative of the last surviving partner has no right to possess partnership property for any but a partnership purpose.

5.   **Dower**
A partner's right in specific partnership property is not subject to dower, curtesy, or allowances to a surviving spouse, heirs, or next of kin. [U.P.A. §25(2)(e)]

6.   **Attachment of Specific Property**
A partner's interest in specific partnership property is not subject to attachment or execution at the instance of his individual creditors. It is subject to attachment or execution only on a claim against the partnership. [U.P.A. §25(2)(c)]

7.   **Homestead**
None of the partners may assert any claim to specific partnership property under the homestead or exemption laws. [U.P.A. §25(2)(c)]

E.   COMPARE—PARTNER'S INTEREST IN THE PARTNERSHIP

1.   **Interest Is Personal Property**
Each partner has an interest in the partnership itself, which consists of a share of the *profits and surplus* and is treated as personal property. [U.P.A. §26] There is a legal presumption that interests of partners in profits and surplus are equal, in the absence of evidence of an agreement to the contrary.

2. Assignment of Interest

Because a partner's interest in the partnership is personalty and consists only of his share of the profits and surplus, it *may be assigned* by him at any time. Such a conveyance does not dissolve the partnership. [U.P.A. §27(1)] This right to assign profits and surplus should not be confused with the limitation upon the right to assign an *interest* in *specific* partnership property (*see* D.2., above).

a. Method of Assignment

The usual rules for transfer of personal property are applicable, including the requirements of delivery and acceptance. Under some circumstances, it has been held that a partner's purported transfer or sale of specific partnership property (although obviously ineffective to transfer an interest in the specific property) is an effective assignment of the partner's partnership interest.

b. Assignee's Rights

1) In Partnership

As against the other partners, in the absence of an agreement, an assignment of a partner's partnership interest does not entitle the assignee to interfere in the management or administration of the partnership business or affairs, to require any information or account of the partnership transactions, or to inspect the partnership books. Rather, an assignment merely entitles the assignee to receive, in accordance with his contract, *profits* to which the assigning partner would otherwise be entitled. [U.P.A. §27(1)]

2) At Dissolution

In the case of a dissolution of the partnership, the assignee is entitled to receive his assignor's interest and may require an accounting only from the date of the last accounting agreed to by all the partners. [U.P.A. §27(2)]

Example: A and B are partners. B assigns his interest in the partnership to X. X cannot interfere in the management of the partnership business; he has none of the rights of a partner nor any of the obligations. X is entitled only to the profits that are due to B. If the partnership is dissolved on May 1, 2003, and the last accounting was held on July 1, 2000, X is entitled to an accounting from July 1, 2000, up to the time of dissolution.

3. Charge of Interest (Attachment)

A judgment creditor of a partner, on application to the court that entered the judgment or other competent court, may charge the interest of the debtor partner with payment of the unsatisfied amount of the judgment debt with interest thereon. The court may then or later appoint a receiver of the debtor partner's share of the profits, and of any other money due or to become due to him in respect of the partnership. [U.P.A. §28(1)]

Example: A and B are partners in a partnership that carries an account at X Bank. P, a creditor of A, secures a judgment against A individually. Upon execution of the judgment, the partnership account at X Bank was attached. In an action by B to set aside the attachment, the court held that the partnership property could not be attached to satisfy an individual creditor of one of the partners. The appropriate remedy is for the creditor to secure a charging order from the court that would attach the interest of A in the partnership.

IV. RELATIONS BETWEEN PARTNERS

A. FIDUCIARY DUTY

Each partner owes a fiduciary duty to the partnership. As such, each partner is bound to use the partnership property and exercise her partnership powers for the benefit of the partnership and not for herself alone. Profits made in the course of the partnership *belong to the partnership,* and a partner who personally profits from any transaction connected with the partnership, at the expense of the partnership and without the consent of the other partners, must hold those profits as trustee for the partnership. [U.P.A. §21(1)]

B. RIGHT TO PARTICIPATE IN MANAGEMENT

Absent an agreement to the contrary, all partners have equal rights in the management of the partnership business.

Example: Cambodian Holidays Company is a partnership; Jackson has a 40% interest in the profits, Maxwell 25%, Morgan 25%, and Ryan 10%. Each of the partners is entitled to one vote in determining the management policies, unless the partnership agreement provides otherwise.

C. RIGHT TO DISTRIBUTIONS

Absent an agreement to the contrary, each partner *shares equally in the profits and surplus* remaining after all liabilities, including those to partners, are satisfied. Each partner must contribute to the losses, whether capital or otherwise, sustained by the partnership according to her share in the profits. Furthermore, unless the partners agree otherwise, each partner is to be repaid her contribution, whether by way of capital or advances to the partnership property. Any payment or advance made by a partner to or on behalf of the partnership beyond her agreed-upon contribution constitutes a loan to the partnership which must be repaid with interest. [U.P.A. §18(a), (c)]

D. REMUNERATION

1. General Rule—No Remuneration Except for Extraordinary Services

A partner is not entitled to any remuneration for services rendered to the partnership unless the agreement provides to the contrary. [U.P.A. §18(f)] This is true even in cases where one partner is forced to assume more work than he had anticipated and the other partner does nothing to further the affairs of the partnership. However, where partners do not have an equal interest, are not equally liable, and are not equally responsible for the conduct of the partnership business, it is possible to imply an agreement to compensate a partner for extraordinary services.

2. Exception—Winding Up by Surviving Partner

A surviving partner is entitled to reasonable compensation for his services in winding up the partnership affairs. [U.P.A. §18(f)]

3. Breach of Agreement to Work for Partnership

Unless the circumstances indicate otherwise, it is implied that each partner will devote his entire time and energies to the business of the partnership. Where a partner has impliedly or expressly promised to devote time to the partnership business and he fails to do so, he may be charged in an accounting for *damages* caused to the partnership. This includes the amount expended by the partnership to replace the services he should have performed as well as any other loss caused by his breach of contract.

E. INDEMNIFICATION

The partnership must indemnify every partner in respect of payments made and personal liabilities reasonably incurred by him in the ordinary and proper conduct of its business, or for the preservation of its business or property. [U.P.A. §18(b)]

F. CONTRIBUTION

Where one partner is compelled to pay or satisfy the whole or more than her share of a partnership debt, she may require (usually in an action in equity) the other partners to contribute their *pro rata shares*. [U.P.A. §18(a)]

G. BOOKS AND INFORMATION

The partnership books must be kept, subject to an agreement to the contrary, at the partnership's principal place of business, and every partner has the *right to inspect and copy* them. [U.P.A. §19] Each partner, upon demand of another partner (or his legal representative), must "render true and full information of all things affecting the partnership." [U.P.A. §20]

H. LEGAL ACTIONS BETWEEN PARTNERS

1. General Rule—No Action at Law

As a general rule, a partner cannot sue or be sued by the partnership (in an action at law), nor may one partner sue another partner on matters related to the partnership business.

Example: A is a member of the partnership of A, B, and C. A maintains a separate business of his own. A sells certain goods to the partnership. A cannot maintain an action to recover for the goods sold and delivered because, in effect, he would be suing himself as a party defendant.

a. Rationale

1) Plaintiff on Both Sides of Suit
Because a partner is personally liable for all debts and obligations of the partnership, he will, in effect, be partially suing himself if he sues the partnership.

2) Accounting Is Necessary
There is a general policy against having piecemeal litigation, and settlement of a partner's claim without a complete accounting and settlement of all the partnership affairs could lead to violation of this policy. An accounting is necessary because:

a) Partnership Assets Applied
Claims by one partner arising out of partnership business must first be satisfied out of partnership assets. Thus, it is possible that even though the plaintiff partner's claim is valid, he will—because of other transactions—owe money to the partnership.

b) Creditors' Priority
The result of litigation between partners is not binding on third-party creditors. Hence, without an accounting, the losing partner might have double liability—*i.e.,* to the prevailing partner and then to an unpaid partnership creditor who decides to seek relief against the losing partner.

b. Exceptions
One partner may sue the other at law when *no complex accounting* is required or when the subject matter of the suit is *independent* of the partnership.

2. Actions for an Accounting
An accounting is an equitable proceeding that considers all transactions between partners in connection with the partnership. It is usually held in connection with a *final settlement* of the partnership affairs. The liabilities between each partner and the partnership are thereby converted into liabilities between the partners individually, and an action lies to recover the balance due any partner.

Example: A and B were partners. A final accounting was held upon dissolution of the partnership in which it was found that A owed B the sum of $500. A is liable to B for this sum.

There are a few situations in which an accounting may be had *other* than in connection with a final settlement and dissolution.

a. Wrongful Exclusion
A partner is entitled to an accounting if he has been wrongfully excluded from participation in the partnership business or from joint possession of the partnership property. [U.P.A. §22(a)]

b. Agreement
An accounting can always be obtained in accordance with the partnership agreement. [U.P.A. §22(b)]

c. Secret Profits
Where one partner has improperly obtained secret profits in violation of his fiduciary duty to the partnership, an action for an accounting may be maintained against him. [U.P.A. §22(c)]

d. Other Circumstances
An accounting may be had whenever the court feels it is "just and reasonable." [U.P.A. §22(d)]

3. Separate Actions at Law
There are a few situations in which an action at law may be maintained separate and apart from an accounting.

a. Segregated Transactions
Where the partnership has dealt with one partner as if he were a third person and it is clear that the transaction is not to be reflected in the general partnership account, an action may be maintained.

Example: A, B, and C form a partnership, ABC Bank. A opens a savings account at ABC Bank and deposits money therein. A is entitled to all of the rights of an ordinary depositor.

b. Tort Claims

1) Negligent Partner
Where one partner negligently injures the person or property of another, the injured partner may maintain an action against the tortfeasor partner.

2) Negligent Employee
Where injury to a partner is caused by the negligence of an employee of the partnership, the traditional rule has been that the negligence of the employee would be imputed to the partnership and partners, thus barring suit. However, the modern trend is to *permit the partner to sue.* [*See, e.g.,* Smith v. Hensley, 354 S.W.2d 744 (Ky. 1961)]

V. RELATIONS OF PARTNERS TO THIRD PARTIES

A. IN GENERAL—APPLICATION OF THE LAW OF AGENCY
The authority of a partner to bind the partnership when dealing with third parties is governed by the law of agency. Under agency principles, every partner is an agent of the partnership for the purpose of its business. The act of every partner "for apparently carrying on in the usual way the business of the partnership" (within the scope of the partnership business) will bind the partnership and thereby bind the other partners. The partnership's liability for the act of a partner may be in *contract, in tort, or for breach of trust.*

B. ACTUAL AUTHORITY
A partner has whatever authority the partner reasonably believes he has based on the communications between the partnership and the partner. Actual authority can be granted either in the partnership agreement or by the consent of the partners.

1. Authorized in Agreement
The partnership agreement may authorize a partner to act, in which case no further partnership action is required for the partner to act.
Example: The partnership agreement of ABC states that B shall have exclusive authority to make all decisions regarding the purchase and sale of commodity futures. A purchase by B of commodity futures will be binding on the partnership.

2. Majority Vote
If the acting partner is not specifically authorized by the partnership agreement to do the particular act, then a majority vote of the partners is required. The majority vote can, of course, authorize a partner to act in certain classes of transactions without further consultations with the other partners.

3. Unanimous Vote
Unanimous consent of all partners is required in several situations.

a. Statutory Provisions
Unless the partnership agreement provides otherwise, *unanimous consent is required* to authorize any of the following acts:

1) Arbitration
A partner may not bind the partnership, nor her copartners individually, to a submission to arbitration. [U.P.A. §9(3)(e)]

2) Assignment for Benefit of Creditors
A partner cannot bind her copartners by an assignment of partnership property for the benefit of creditors. [U.P.A. §9(3)(a)]

3) Confession of Judgment
A partner has *no implied power* to confess a judgment or give a warrant of attorney to confess a judgment against the partnership, although she has the power to compromise a debt in good faith and without fraud or collusion. [U.P.A. §9(3)(d)]

4) Goodwill

A partner has no implied power to dispose of the goodwill of the business. [U.P.A. §9(3)(b)]

5) Interference with Ordinary Partnership Business

No partner may do any other act that would make it impossible to carry on the ordinary business of the partnership. [U.P.A. §9(3)(c)]

b. Agreement

If the partnership agreement specifically provides for other than a majority vote, then it, of course, governs. It is generally held that unanimous consent is needed to engage in business other than that contemplated by the agreement.

Example: A, B, and C enter into a partnership to operate a retail dry cleaning establishment. B uses partnership funds to buy, in the partnership name, a retail grocery store. This action is not binding on the partnership and, subject to the rights of innocent third persons, the partnership may rescind the transaction.

C. APPARENT AUTHORITY

Even where a partner lacks actual authority, he can—under general agency principles—bind the partnership because of his apparent authority (*i.e.,* authority arising from a reasonable belief in the mind of a third party that the partner has authority to contract based on the partnership's actions; *see* Agency outline). There are specific rules regarding the disposition of property that are helpful in analyzing problems in this area.

1. Real Property

The U.P.A. sets out the following rules regarding the apparent authority of a partner to convey real property of the partnership.

a. Title in Partnership Name

1) Conveyance in Partnership Name

If title is held in the partnership name, title may be conveyed in the partnership name by any one partner. However, if the partner lacked actual or apparent authority to convey title, the partnership may recover the property from the transferee unless the transferee has conveyed the property to a bona fide purchaser. [U.P.A. §10(1)] A bona fide purchaser is one who takes for value and without knowledge that the partner exceeded his authority.

2) Conveyance in Individual Partner's Name

If title is held in the name of the partnership but a conveyance is made in an individual partner's name, the conveyance will pass the equitable interest of the partnership in the property only if the conveyance was authorized. If the conveyance was not authorized by the partnership, no interest passes. [U.P.A. §10(2)]

b. Title in Name of Fewer than All Partners

1) Conveyance in Name of Titleholders

If title is held in the name of fewer than all of the partners, and the record does not show the right of the partnership, conveyance by the titleholders in their own names is effective. However, if they lacked actual or apparent authority to convey title, the partnership may recover the property from the transferee unless the transferee, or his assignee, is a bona fide purchaser. [U.P.A. §10(3)]

2) Conveyance in Name of Partnership or Fewer than All Titleholders

Where title is held in the name of one or more partners, conveyance in the name of the partnership or fewer than all titleholders passes the equitable interest of the partnership if the conveyance was authorized. Otherwise, no interest will pass. [U.P.A. §10(4)]

c. Title in Name of All Partners

If title is in the name of all of the partners, only a conveyance by all the partners passes the equitable interest in the property as well as legal title. [U.P.A. §10(5)]

2. Other Transfers of Interest in Real Property

a. Mortgages
The same rules regarding transfers of title are generally applicable.

b. Leases
Ordinary contract rules govern. To the extent that the lease is within the scope of partnership business, one partner has the apparent authority to execute the lease on behalf of the partnership.

3. Personal Property
Ordinary contract rules govern both the sale and pledge of personal property.

D. NOTICE AND KNOWLEDGE
For bar exam purposes, it is sometimes important to determine when information possessed by or notice given to a partner (or agent) is to be imputed to the partnership (or principal).

1. When Notice Effective

a. "Notice" Defined
"Notice" is a communication by a third person about a matter relating to partnership business that is transmitted to one or more partners with the intent that the partnership be informed of the message communicated.
Example: T notifies A, who is a partner of ABC partnership, that he, T, is exercising his right to renew his lease of space from the partnership for an additional two years. T has given ABC effective notice of the exercise of his right.

b. How Delivered

1) Oral-Direct
Unless otherwise required to be in writing, notice may be delivered orally by a third person to a partner. [U.P.A. §3(2)(a)]

2) Written
Notice may be given by delivering a written statement to a partner or to a *proper* person at the partner's office or residence. [U.P.A. §3(2)(b)]

2. When Knowledge Imputed

a. "Knowledge" Defined
"Knowledge" refers to information that is or reasonably should be known by an individual partner. When asking whether a partner "knows" something, you are concerned with what was actually in the partner's mind, although it will be necessary to resort to external objective criteria to make the determination. Furthermore, a person is deemed to know something when "he has knowledge of such other facts as in the circumstances shows bad faith." [U.P.A. §3(1)]

b. Whose Knowledge
In determining whether the partnership is to be charged with the knowledge of a partner regarding a particular transaction, it is necessary to distinguish between knowledge of a partner who is participating in the transaction and a partner who is not so participating.

1) Participant
To determine when a participating partner's knowledge will be imputed to the partnership, it is necessary to determine *when* the partner acquired the knowledge.

a) Acquired When Partner
If the knowledge was acquired by the partner while he was a member of the partnership, his knowledge will be *imputed* to the partnership.

b) Acquired When Not a Partner
If the knowledge was acquired when the partner was not a member of the partnership, then his knowledge will be *imputed* to the partnership *only if* the information is "present to his mind" at the time he is acting for the partnership. [U.P.A. §12]

2) Nonparticipant

Information possessed by a partner who is not participating in a transaction will be imputed to the partnership *if,* under the circumstances, the partner "reasonably could and should have communicated it" to the participating partner. Fraud is an exception to this rule (*see* below). [U.P.A. §12]

E. FRAUD

The partnership is liable for any wrongful act or omission by a partner "acting in the ordinary course of the business of the partnership or with authority of his copartners." [U.P.A. §13]

1. Fraud on Third Party

a. Within the Scope of Partnership Business

Where one partner, acting within the scope of partnership business, defrauds a third party, the partnership will be held liable.

Example: P, a partner in a brokerage firm, accepts securities from a customer of the firm and, without knowledge of the other partners, endorses the securities, converts them to cash, and deposits the cash in his own bank account. The partnership is liable.

b. Outside the Scope of Partnership Business

In this category, it is often difficult to determine whether the partner is defrauding a third party, the partnership, or both. Generally, if the fraudulent act involves a transaction outside the scope of partnership business, the partnership will *not* be held liable.

Example: P, a partner in a law firm, tells T, a client of the firm, that the firm is making investments for clients. T gives P a check for $3,000 made out to the firm. P has the check deposited in the firm account. He then draws a firm check payable to and signed by himself, and deposits it in his own account. Is the firm liable to T? No, because P had no authority to accept the check, the investment business was outside the scope of partnership business, and P was acting for his own benefit. P's knowledge will not be imputed to the firm.

2. Fraud on Partnership

If a partner seeks to defraud the partnership as part of a transaction with a third party and that party is aware of the fraud, the partnership is not liable to the third party.

Example: P is a partner in a manufacturing business. He contracts to sell $5 million worth of widgets to T for $1 million, with the understanding that T will pay him a kickback of $1 million. T cannot enforce the contract against the partnership.

F. BREACH OF TRUST

The partnership is liable if one partner misapplies money or property of a third person received by him *within the scope of his apparent authority.* [U.P.A. §14(a)] The partnership is also liable if money or property received in the *ordinary course of business* is misapplied by a partner while in the custody of the partnership. [U.P.A. §14(b)]

G. LIABILITY OF PARTNERS

1. Civil Liability

a. Types of Civil Liability

1) Contract Liability

Partners will be liable on contracts made by a partner in the scope of the partnership business and on any other contracts expressly authorized by the partners.

2) Tort Liability

Partners will be liable for any torts committed by a partner or by an employee of the partnership *in the course of partnership business.* [U.P.A. §13] Note that this liability will be extended to cover frauds committed by a copartner in the course of partnership business, even though the other partners have no connection with, knowledge of, or participation in the fraud.

Example: A, B, and C are partners and members of a stock brokerage firm.

The firm has received certain securities belonging to X. A, one of the partners, fraudulently converts the securities to his own use. In an action by X against the partnership, C defends on the ground that she did not participate in or have knowledge of the conversion. C is liable because the conversion took place while she was a partner.

Compare: C would not be liable if the partnership business was totally unrelated to securities. In that case, A would not have had authority to receive securities.

b. Nature of Partner's Liability

1) In General
Under the U.P.A., all partners are *jointly and severally* liable for a partner's wrongful acts and breaches of trust (misapplication of money or property received from third persons). The partners are *jointly* liable for all other debts and obligations of the partnership. [U.P.A. §15] However, many jurisdictions have modified the U.P.A. to provide that all partnership liability is joint and several.

2) Parties

a) Joint and Several
Where there is joint and several liability, an action may be brought against any one or more of the partners or the partnership. However, a judgment is not personally binding on a partner unless she has been served.

b) Joint
Where there is simply joint liability, *all* partners must be served. They are indispensable parties, and the action cannot be maintained without service on all unless the partner who is not served is outside the jurisdiction of the court or is bankrupt.

c. Extent of Partner's Liability
Each partner is *personally and individually liable* for the entire amount of all partnership obligations, whether arising in contract or tort. Where one partner is thus compelled to pay or satisfy the whole of a partnership obligation, he is entitled to indemnification from the partnership. He also may require the other partners to *contribute their pro rata shares* of the payment if the partnership is unable to indemnify.

d. Change of Partnership Membership as Affects Partners' Liability

1) Liability of Incoming Partner
A person admitted as a partner into an existing partnership is liable for all the obligations of the partnership arising before his admission as though he had been a partner when such obligations were incurred. However, his liability may be satisfied *only* out of *partnership property*. [U.P.A. §17]

Note: He may make himself personally liable for the existing obligations (beyond his interest in the partnership property) by novation or by promising to pay existing obligations.

2) Liability of Retiring Partner
A retiring partner remains liable on all obligations incurred by the partnership while a member of the partnership, unless there has been payment, release, or novation. In general, he is liable for acts done until he has not only withdrawn from the partnership, but has also given *notice of his withdrawal*. (*See* VI.B., *infra*.)

2. Criminal Liability
The mutual agency of partners is not sufficient to make other partners criminally responsible for the crime of a partner committed within the scope of the partnership business, unless the other partners participated in the commission of the crime either as principals or accessories.

VI. DISSOLUTION AND TERMINATION OF A PARTNERSHIP

A. METHODS OF DISSOLUTION

Dissolution is the "change in the relationship of the partners caused by any partner ceasing to be associated in the carrying on as distinguished from the winding up of the business." [U.P.A. §29] It is important to note that a dissolution is simply a change in legal relationship. It does not mean that the business has been ended or that any assets have been distributed to partners. Dissolution may be caused in three ways: (i) by an act of the partners, (ii) by the operation of law, or (iii) by a court decree.

1. Act of the Partners

a. Per Agreement

A partnership contract may set a definite term to the partnership relationship, or it may set achievement of a particular undertaking as a purpose of the partnership. When that term has elapsed or the undertaking is accomplished, the partnership automatically terminates or dissolves. [U.P.A. §31(1)(a)] *Note:* Even where partners covenant with each other that the partnership shall continue for a fixed period, any partner may dissolve it by her express will at any time [U.P.A. §31(2)], although she may subject herself to an action for damages for the breach of the partnership agreement.

b. Mutual Assent

A partnership may be brought to an end at any time by the mutual assent of all partners who have not assigned their interests or suffered them to be charged for their separate debts. [U.P.A. §31(1)(c)]

c. Expulsion of Partner

If any partner is expelled from the business in accordance with a power to do so conferred by the agreement between the partners, this will result in dissolution. [U.P.A. §31(1)(d)]

d. Partnership at Will

Dissolution may be caused without liability by the express will of any partner when no definite term or particular undertaking is specified. [U.P.A. §31(1)(b)]

Example: A and B enter into an oral partnership agreement to continue for five years. A notifies B of her intention to dissolve the partnership before the expiration of the five years. Because the oral agreement is unenforceable under the Statute of Frauds, the partnership is treated as a partnership at will, and therefore may be dissolved by either partner without liability at any time.

2. Operation of Law

a. Partnership Activity Unlawful

Any event that makes it unlawful for the partnership business to be carried on will dissolve the partnership. [U.P.A. §31(3)]

Example: A and B are copartners in the business of selling liquor when the state in which the business is carried on passes a prohibition law making such business illegal. The partnership is thereby dissolved.

b. Death of a Partner

The death of a partner will dissolve the partnership unless the partnership agreement provides to the contrary. [U.P.A. §31(4)]

c. Bankruptcy

The bankruptcy of any partner or the partnership will dissolve the partnership. [U.P.A. §31(5)]

3. Decree of Court of Equity

Upon the application of one or more of the partners, a court of equity may, for sufficient reason, decree the dissolution of a partnership. The following are sufficient reasons for a decree of dissolution:

a. Breach of Agreement

A partner commits willful or persistent breaches of the partnership agreement or otherwise conducts herself so that it is not reasonably practicable to carry on the business in partnership with her [U.P.A. §32(1)(d)];

b. Unprofitability
The business can only be carried on at a loss [U.P.A. §32(1)(e)];

c. Misconduct
A partner is guilty of such conduct as tends to "affect prejudicially the carrying on of the business" [U.P.A. §32(1)(c)];

d. Incompetence
A partner has been declared mentally ill or incompetent in a judicial proceeding or is shown to be of unsound mind [U.P.A. §32(1)(a)];

e. Incapability
A partner is shown to be incapable of performing her part of the partnership contract [U.P.A. §32(1)(b)]; and

f. Other Circumstances
The court determines that other circumstances would render a dissolution equitable [U.P.A. §32(1)(f)].

B. NOTICE OF DISSOLUTION (TERMINATION OF APPARENT AUTHORITY)

1. "Proper" Notice
Third parties who have had "dealings" with the partnership (except those who have extended credit (*see* below)) and those who have simply known of the partnership prior to dissolution are entitled to proper notice published in newspapers of general circulation in the area in which the partnership carries on its business. Failure to furnish this information to such third parties will bind members of the former partnership to such third parties who, while unaware of the dissolution, extend credit to the partnership.

2. Personal Notice
Those who were *creditors at the time of dissolution* or who had *extended credit to the partnership prior to dissolution* are entitled to *personal notice*. It does not matter whether a creditor has advanced a large or small amount or if there were only one or two transactions between the partnership and the creditor. Note that a third party who has dealt with the partnership only on a cash basis and has never been a partnership creditor is entitled only to the notice that is given the general public.

3. Liability of "Invisible Partners"
The liability of a partner for postdissolution transactions when notice was not given is *limited to partnership assets* if the partner was so inactive in partnership affairs that credit to the partnership was not based on her personal credit and the creditor in fact did not know she was a partner.

C. AUTHORITY OF PARTNERS TO TRANSACT BUSINESS AFTER DISSOLUTION

1. General Rule
As a general rule, the dissolution of a partnership *terminates the authority* of any partner to act as an agent for either the partnership or the other partners, except for the purpose of winding up the partnership affairs. However, if the partnership agreement provides that the business is to be continued by one or more of the partners, the agreement controls and the business will be continued by the new partners without any winding up.

2. Winding Up
After dissolution, absent an agreement to the contrary, the partnership must be wound up. A partner has authority to carry out the necessary acts to wind up the partnership. However, generally *only transactions* designed to *terminate*, rather than to carry on, the business are within the scope of the partner's actual authority. In short, "old business" can be wrapped up; if "new business" is entered into, the partner who continues to carry on business on behalf of the partnership with knowledge of the dissolution assumes sole liability for her actions (unless partnership liability arises from failure to give notice as described above). If losses result, she alone will bear them.

a. **"Old Business" vs. "New Business"**
After dissolution but *before termination*, the liquidating partners can bind the partnership in transactions *winding up old business*, but not in transactions constituting new business.

1) **Old Business**
The following are old business:

a) Assigning claims;

b) Selling partnership assets;

c) Performing contracts made prior to dissolution;

d) Collecting debts due;

e) Compromising claims;

f) Paying off creditors (*see* D., below); and

g) Distributing remainder of business (*see* D., below).

2) **New Business**
The following are new business:

a) Extending time on a debt;

b) Entering into new contracts; and

c) Increasing any obligation of the partnership, even by one cent—*except necessary contracts* such as hiring an accountant to help wind up the business.

b. **Who May Wind Up**

1) **All Partners**
If all partners agree to a dissolution of the partnership or the partnership term expires, then all the partners have the right to wind up the affairs of the partnership.

2) **Remaining Partners**
If a partner dissolves the partnership by bankruptcy, then the remaining partner(s) have the right to wind up the partnership's affairs.

3) **Surviving Partners**
If a partnership is dissolved by the death of a partner, then the surviving partner(s) have the right to wind up partnership affairs.

4) **Executor**
If the partnership affairs have not been wound up when the last surviving partner dies, then the executor or administrator of such last survivor's estate has the right to wind up the partnership's affairs. [U.P.A. §37]

5) **Partner Wrongfully Dissolving Partnership—Cannot Wind Up**
A partner who wrongfully dissolves a partnership is not entitled to wind up the affairs of the partnership.

D. DISTRIBUTION OF ASSETS—FINAL ACCOUNTING

1. **Order of Distribution**
When a solvent partnership is dissolved and its assets are reduced to cash, the cash must be used to pay the partnership's liabilities in the following order, as prescribed by U.P.A. section 40:

a. **Outside Creditors**
Creditors who are *not partners* must be paid before the partners themselves receive any payments.

b. Partners

1) Advances
When a partner advances *more* than the capital provided for in the agreement, such advances (and any interest due) must be returned to him before the surplus can be divided among the partners.

2) Contributions to Capital
After payments of advances or loans, payments are to be made to partners on account of agreed contributions to capital.

3) Surplus or Profits
Whatever cash remains after the above payments are made is distributed among the partners.

Example: Alex and Becky form a partnership. Alex contributes $1,000 in cash and Becky contributes her full-time efforts. The partnership agreement is silent as to how profits and losses are to be split (and thus, an equal split is presumed). On dissolution, the partnership liquidates all of its assets and has $6,500 in cash. The partnership owes creditors $5,000. How will the cash be distributed? The creditors will first receive their $5,000, leaving $1,500. Alex is entitled to the return of his $1,000 contribution; only $500 is profit—to be divided equally. Thus, Alex is entitled to $1,250 and Becky is entitled to $250.

2. Specific Situations

a. Partnership Assets Insufficient to Pay Liabilities
If the partnership assets are insufficient to pay partnership liabilities, the shortfall is a *loss* that must be divided among the partners.

Example: If, in the above example, the partnership had only $5,700 after liquidating its assets, there would be a $300 shortfall ($5,000 owed to creditors plus $1,000 contribution that has not been repaid). Each partner would have a $150 loss. Thus, Alex would be entitled to a return of his $1,000 contribution minus his $150 loss (*i.e.*, $850) and Becky would have to pay in $150 to cover her loss.

b. One Partner Pays More than His Share of Debt
When a partner is forced to pay more than his share of the partnership's debt, he is entitled to *contribution* from the others to equalize it.

c. Insolvency—Conflict Between Partnership Creditors and Partner's Separate Creditors
When the partnership and a partner are both insolvent, it is important to stress the significance of ranking or priority of creditors. The rule under U.P.A. section 40 is one of *dual priority.* Specifically, partnership creditors enjoy priority in partnership assets, and the separate creditors of the partner have a corresponding priority with respect to the partner's individual assets. Note, however, that the *Bankruptcy Code* rejects the dual priority rule and accords partnership creditors *parity* with respect to the *individual assets* of insolvent partners, as well as *priority* with respect to *partnership assets*. [11 U.S.C. §723(c)] The federal rule controls in all bankruptcy proceedings.

VII. CONTINUANCE OF BUSINESS AFTER DISSOLUTION

A. RIGHT TO CONTINUE
Unless otherwise agreed, dissolution gives to each partner the right, subject to limited exception, to have the business liquidated and his share of the surplus paid in cash. This can result in the sacrifice of going concern values. Thus, under various circumstances, the remaining partners have the right to continue the partnership business.

1. Dissolution Contrary to Terms of Agreement
If a partner dissolves a partnership in contravention of the partnership agreement, the remaining partners have the right to continue the partnership. They need only pay the dissolving partner the fair value of his share, offsetting damages suffered by them for breach of the partnership agreement.

Example: A, B, and C enter into a partnership agreement for five years. After three years, B wishes to dissolve the partnership. A and C may continue the partnership, paying B the fair value of his share less damages for his breach.

2. Expulsion of Partner
If a partner is expelled according to the terms of the partnership agreement, the other partners may elect to continue the partnership. Once again, they must pay the expelled partner the fair value of his share.

3. By Agreement
The partners may agree to continue the partnership after dissolution. This provision may be contained in the original partnership agreement or may be arrived at subsequently. If a right to continue is set forth in the partnership agreement, the withdrawing partner's rights against the partnership are defined by the agreement.

4. Continuation Without Settlement
When a partner dies or withdraws under any of the above circumstances and the business is continued without settlement of his share, the withdrawn partner or estate representative has the option of receiving the value of his share plus either (i) interest on his share from the date of dissolution to the date of settlement, or (ii) in lieu of interest, a share of the profits attributable to the use of his property in the partnership for that period.

B. RIGHTS OF PARTNERS IN THE PARTNERSHIP
When a partnership for a fixed term or particular undertaking is continued after the termination of the term or particular undertaking without any express agreement, the rights and duties of the partners remain the same as they were at the termination, as far as is consistent with a *partnership at will*.

C. RIGHTS OF CREDITORS
Section 41 of the U.P.A. is designed to protect a partnership's creditors. When a partnership is dissolved by a change in personnel, or when the partnership property is transferred nonfraudulently to some of the existing partners or to existing partners and others who continue the business without liquidation, creditors of the existing partnership *retain their rights* as creditors of the partnership continuing the business.

Examples: 1) A, B, and C are equal copartners in the ABC partnership. C assigns all his right, title, and interest in the partnership to A and B who are to continue the business under the partnership name of A & B. The new partnership does not agree to pay the former partnership creditors. M and N are creditors of the ABC partnership. Under section 41(1), M and N are expressly made partnership creditors of the new partnership A & B.

                   2) Same facts, but assume further that X and Y become creditors of the partnership A & B. If A and B dissolve the new partnership, M and N would have equal rights with the new partnership creditors, X and Y. Thus, M, N, X, and Y would share in the distribution of the assets of the new partnership A & B. This does not in any way change the liabilities of the individual partners. C, of course, is liable to M and N because C was a partner when the liabilities were incurred. However, if M and N knew of the dissolution, it may be inferred from their behavior that they agreed to the release of C and agreed to look solely to A & B. [U.P.A. §36(2)]

VIII. LIMITED LIABILITY PARTNERSHIPS

A. INTRODUCTION
Nearly all states allow the creation of limited liability partnerships ("L.L.P.s"). An L.L.P. is essentially a general partnership and subject to the U.P.A.; however, the partners in an L.L.P. are *not personally liable* for some or all of the partnership debts and obligations.

B. FORMATION
Although state statutes vary, most states require an L.L.P. to register with the state and adopt a business name that indicates the partnership's limited liability status (*e.g.*, by including the words "limited liability partnership" or the abbreviation "L.L.P." in the partnership name). Some states limit the formation of L.L.P.s to professional partnerships such as those comprised of attorneys, doctors, or accountants. Some states also require an L.L.P. to carry insurance against acts protected by the L.L.P. statute, usually in an amount between $100,000 and $1 million.

C. LIABILITY

Once an L.L.P. has registered with the state, most state statutes provide that a partner in an L.L.P. is **not personally liable** for the debts and obligations of the partnership arising from the negligence, wrongful acts, or similar misconduct (*i.e.*, torts) of her co-partners. Many states go further and shield a partner from personal liability for any partnership debts and obligations, whether arising in contract, tort, or otherwise. Note though that in most states, even if a partner in an L.L.P. is not liable for some or all partnership debts and obligations, the partner remains personally liable for her **own wrongful acts** and for those committed by someone whom she directly supervises.

IX. LIMITED PARTNERSHIPS

A. INTRODUCTION

A limited partnership is composed of one or more general partners and one or more limited partners. It differs from a general partnership in two basic ways: (i) a limited partnership is unknown at common law and is created **under specific statutory authority;** and (ii) the liability of a limited partner for partnership debts is generally **limited** to the capital that she contributes to the partnership.

B. APPLICABLE LAW

The law of limited partnership is governed in nearly all states by the Revised Uniform Limited Partnership Act of 1976 ("R.U.L.P.A."). Most states have also adopted a number of amendments to the R.U.L.P.A. which were proposed in 1985 by the Commissioners on Uniform State Laws and subsequently made part of the R.U.L.P.A. This state has adopted the R.U.L.P.A. as amended.

Note: The R.U.L.P.A. will govern all issues dealing with limited partnership. However, where the R.U.L.P.A. does not provide an applicable rule, the courts will look to the U.P.A. [R.U.L.P.A. §1105]

C. FORMATION

1. Certificate of Limited Partnership
A certificate of limited partnership must be filed with the secretary of state, and must set forth, among other things: (i) the partnership name, (ii) the name and address of the agent for service of process, (iii) the name and business address of each **general** partner (the limited partners' names need not be included), and (iv) the latest date upon which the limited partnership is to dissolve. [R.U.L.P.A. §201] The certificate must be signed by all general partners. [R.U.L.P.A. §204]

2. Records Office
A limited partnership must also maintain in its state of organization an office with such records as the certificate of limited partnership, any partnership agreements, the limited partnership's tax returns for the three most current years, the names and addresses of the partners (both limited and general), etc. Either the partnership agreement or some other record must contain: (i) the amount and a description of each partner's contribution, (ii) times or events that trigger additional contributions from the partners, (iii) special rights of the partners regarding distributions, and (iv) a description of the events that will trigger dissolution of the partnership. [R.U.L.P.A. §105]

3. Agent for Service of Process
Each limited partnership must continuously maintain an agent in the state to receive service of process. [R.U.L.P.A. §104]

D. NAME OF PARTNERSHIP

The partnership name may **not** contain the name of a limited partner unless it is also the name of a general partner, or the partnership business had been carried on under that name before the admission of that limited partner. The name of each limited partnership must contain the words "Limited Partnership." The name may not be the same as, or deceptively similar to, the name of another limited partnership or corporation organized in the same state. [R.U.L.P.A. §102]

E. ADMISSION OF ADDITIONAL GENERAL AND LIMITED PARTNERS

A person may be admitted as a general or limited partner as provided in the partnership agreement. If the partnership agreement does not so provide, a person may be admitted as a general or limited partner on the **written consent of all partners**. [R.U.L.P.A. §§301, 401]

F. NATURE OF PARTNER'S CONTRIBUTION

    1. Cash, Property, or Services
    A partner's contribution may be in cash, property, *or services* rendered, or may be a *promise* to contribute cash or property, or to render services. [R.U.L.P.A. §501]

    2. Liability for Contribution
    Unless the partnership agreement provides otherwise, a partner is obligated to perform any promise to contribute cash or property or to perform services, even if the partner is unable to perform because of death, disability, or other reason. If a partner does not make a promised contribution of property or services, the partnership may hold the partner liable for the cash equivalent of the promised contribution. [R.U.L.P.A. §502(b)]

    Note: A promise by a *limited partner* to contribute to the limited partnership is not enforceable unless it is set out in a writing signed by the limited partner.

    3. Compromise of Liability
    Unless otherwise provided in the partnership agreement, a partner's obligation to make a contribution may be compromised only by the consent of *all* of the partners. Even if the other partners consent to a compromise regarding contribution, a previous creditor (*i.e.*, one who extends credit before the compromise) may enforce the original obligation. [R.U.L.P.A. §502(c)]

    4. Liability for Return of Contribution
    If a partner properly receives the return of any part of her contribution, she remains liable to the partnership for one year thereafter, but only to the extent necessary to discharge the partnership's liabilities to creditors who extended credit to the partnership during the period the contribution was held by the partnership. If the return was improper under either the partnership agreement or the R.U.L.P.A., the partner remains liable for six years for the entire amount of the contribution returned. [R.U.L.P.A. §608]

G. LIABILITY OF PARTNERS

    1. Liability of General Partner
    Except as provided by statute or in the partnership agreement, a general partner of a limited partnership is subject to all of the liabilities of a partner in a regular partnership. [R.U.L.P.A. §403] Thus, a general partner is personally liable for the limited partnership's obligations.

    2. Liability of Limited Partner

        a. General Rule—Not Liable for Partnership Obligations Beyond Contribution
        As a general rule, a limited partner is not liable beyond her contribution for obligations of the limited partnership. [R.U.L.P.A. §303(a)] Therefore, in an action by or against the limited partnership, only the *general* partners are necessary parties.

        b. Exceptions
        There are three exceptions to the general rule:

            1) Is also a General Partner
            A limited partner is liable to any creditor of the limited partnership if the limited partner is also a general partner. [R.U.L.P.A. §303(a)]

            2) Participates in Control of Business
            A limited partner is liable as a general partner if she participates in the control of the business *and* the person dealing with the limited partnership *reasonably believes*, based on the limited partner's conduct, that the limited partner is a general partner. [R.U.L.P.A. §303(a)]

                a) "Control" Defined
                The R.U.L.P.A. has a "safe harbor" provision that allows a limited partner to participate in the partnership without risk of being found to have participated in control of the partnership. Most of these "safe harbors" involve providing services for the partnership (*e.g.,* as an employee, consultant to a general partner, surety, etc.) or taking part in extraordinary partnership affairs (*e.g.,* bringing a derivative action, participating in dissolution, voting for a sale of a

substantial part of the partnership assets or a change in the nature of the partnership business, etc.). [R.U.L.P.A. §303(b)]

3) Permits Name to Be Used in Name of Partnership
A limited partner who knowingly permits her name to be used improperly (*see* D., *supra*) in the name of the limited partnership is liable to creditors who are *without actual knowledge* that she is not a general partner. [R.U.L.P.A. §303(d)]

H. RIGHTS OF PARTNERS

1. Rights of Both General and Limited Partners

a. Right to Share of Profits and Losses
A partner is entitled to his share of the profits and losses specified in the partnership agreement. If the partnership agreement is silent on this, profits and losses are allocated on the basis of the value of the contributions. [R.U.L.P.A. §503] Note that this is contrary to the presumption under the U.P.A. that profits and losses be shared equally.

b. Right to Assign Partnership Interest
A partner has an interest in the partnership that may be assigned, but upon the partner's assignment of her entire partnership interest, she ceases to be a partner. [R.U.L.P.A. §702] A partner's assignment of her partnership interest does not entitle the assignee to exercise the rights of a partner. The assignment only entitles the assignee to receive distributions to which the assignor would be entitled.

1) Partnership Interest May Be Charged by Judgment Creditors
A partner's interest in the partnership may be charged by her judgment creditors upon application to a proper court. To the extent so charged, the creditor has only the rights of an assignee of the partnership interest. [R.U.L.P.A. §703]

2) Assignee's Right to Become Limited Partner
An assignee (including an assignee of a general partner) may become a limited partner *only to the extent* that: (i) the assignor had authority in the partnership agreement to convey that right (and did so accordingly), *or* (ii) all other partners consent. If an assignee becomes a limited partner, the assignor is *not* released from liability for her partnership contribution. [R.U.L.P.A. §704]

c. Right to Transact Business with the Partnership
A partner may lend money to and transact other business with the limited partnership, and generally has the same rights and obligations with respect to the transaction as a person who is not a partner. [R.U.L.P.A. §107]

d. Right to Withdraw

1) General Partner
A general partner may withdraw from the partnership at any time by providing written notice to the other partners, but if the withdrawal is in violation of the partnership agreement, the partner will be liable to the partnership for damages caused by his breach of the agreement. [R.U.L.P.A. §602]

2) Limited Partner
A limited partner may withdraw in accordance with the provisions of the partnership agreement. If the agreement does not provide for withdrawal, the limited partner must give six months' prior written notice of withdrawal to each general partner. [R.U.L.P.A. §603]

3) Distributions
Upon withdrawal, a partner has the right to receive any distribution to which she is entitled under the partnership agreement. Also, unless otherwise provided in the partnership agreement, the partner is entitled to receive, within a reasonable time after withdrawal, the fair value of her partnership interest as of the date of withdrawal based on her right to share in partnership distributions. [R.U.L.P.A. §604] However, a partner may not receive a distribution to the extent that, after giving effect to the distribution, all liabilities of the partnership, other than liabilities to partners on account of their partnership interests, exceed the fair value of the partnership assets. [R.U.L.P.A. §607]

e. **Right to Dissolve**
Any partner may apply for a decree of dissolution of the limited partnership whenever it is not reasonably practicable to carry on the business in conformity with the partnership agreement. [R.U.L.P.A. §802]

2. **Rights Specific to General Partners**
Except as provided by statute or in the partnership agreement, a general partner of a limited partnership also has all of the rights of a partner in a regular partnership, including the right to manage the limited partnership. [R.U.L.P.A. §403]

3. **Rights Specific to Limited Partners**

a. **Right to Vote**
A limited partner may vote on *specific matters,* but may not participate in the control of the business. [R.U.L.P.A. §303(b); *see* G.2.b.2)a), *supra*]

b. **Right to Information**
Each limited partner has the right to: (i) inspect and copy any partnership records required to be maintained; and (ii) obtain from the general partners, upon reasonable demand, full information regarding the state of the business and financial condition of the limited partnership, its income tax returns, and other information regarding the affairs of the limited partnership as is reasonable. [R.U.L.P.A. §305]

c. **Right to Bring Derivative Action**
A limited partner may bring an action in the right of the limited partnership to recover a judgment in its favor *if* the general partners refuse to do so, *or* if an effort to cause those partners to do so is not likely to succeed. [R.U.L.P.A. §1001]

I. ONE WHO ERRONEOUSLY BELIEVES HERSELF TO BE A LIMITED PARTNER

1. **General Rule—Not Bound as a General Partner**
A person who makes a contribution to a business enterprise and erroneously, but in good faith, believes that she has thereby become a limited partner rather than a general partner can avoid being held liable as a general partner if, on ascertaining the mistake, she:

(i) Files an appropriate certificate of limited partnership or certificate of amendment with the secretary of state; or

(ii) Withdraws from future equity participation in the enterprise by filing with the secretary of state a certificate declaring withdrawal.

[R.U.L.P.A. §304(a)]

2. **Exceptions**
Notwithstanding the above rule, a person who erroneously believes that she is a limited partner will be bound as a general partner to any third party who actually believed in good faith that the partner was a general partner and transacted business with the enterprise:

(i) Before the partner withdraws and an appropriate certificate is filed to show the withdrawal; or

(ii) Before an appropriate certificate is filed to show that she is not a general partner.

[R.U.L.P.A. §304(b)]

J. DISSOLUTION AND DISTRIBUTION

1. **Dissolution**
A limited partnership will be dissolved by any of the following:

(i) The occurrence of the time stated in the certificate of limited partnership;

(ii) The occurrence of the time or event specified in the partnership agreement;

(iii) Written consent of all partners;

(iv) Withdrawal of a general partner unless: (a) at the time there is at least one other general partner and the partnership agreement permits the partnership to be carried on, or (b) within 90 days after the withdrawal, all the partners agree in writing to continue the limited partnership and to the appointment of any necessary or desired general partners; or

(v) Entry of a decree of judicial dissolution (*see* H.1.e., *supra*).

[R.U.L.P.A. §801]

2. Distribution of Assets

Upon the winding up of a limited partnership, the assets are distributed as follows:

(i) To creditors, including general and limited partners who are creditors, in satisfaction of liabilities of the limited partnership other than liabilities for distributions to partners upon withdrawal (*see* H.1.d.3), *supra*) or for interim distributions (*e.g.,* periodic distributions provided for in the partnership agreement);

(ii) Except as provided in the partnership agreement, to general and limited partners and former partners in satisfaction of liabilities for interim distributions and to former partners to satisfy distributions owing upon the partners' withdrawal; and

(iii) Except as provided in the partnership agreement, to general and limited partners *first* for the return of their contributions and *second* for partnership profits and property in the proportions in which the partners share in distributions.

[R.U.L.P.A. §804]

BAR REVIEW

Professional Responsibility

celebrating over
35 *YEARS*
*of preparing
law students
for the bar exam*

PROFESSIONAL RESPONSIBILITY—MASSACHUSETTS

TABLE OF CONTENTS

I. REGULATORY CONTROLS OVER ATTORNEYS AND UNAUTHORIZED PRACTICE

A. GENERAL SOURCES OF REGULATION

Practice in state courts is regulated by the courts, legislature, and bar of each state. Practice in the federal courts is regulated by the rules of each district court and circuit court of appeals, rules promulgated by the Supreme Court of the United States, and rules passed by Congress.

1. State Regulation

a. Supreme Court and Legislature

The Massachusetts Supreme Judicial Court has the exclusive authority to regulate admission to the bar and the practice of law. [*In re* Opinion of the Justices, 289 Mass. 607 (1935)] The Massachusetts legislature, however, is empowered to enact statutes to aid the Supreme Judicial Court in fulfilling its duties. [*In re* Keenan, 310 Mass. 166 (1941)]

b. State Bar Association

Two general classes of state bar associations can be distinguished: integrated bar associations and voluntary bar associations. Integrated bar associations *require all attorneys* within the state to *join* and thereby subject themselves to the rules promulgated by the association. Voluntary bar associations do not encompass the entire community of practicing lawyers within a state unless they all voluntarily join. Still, these voluntary associations have often been in the forefront of proposing ethical standards and attempting to regulate the unauthorized practice of law. Massachusetts has a voluntary bar association.

2. Federal Regulation

a. Federal Courts

Each federal district and appellate court promulgates its own rules independent of those that exist for the state courts in the jurisdiction where the federal court sits.

1) Requirements for Admission

Most federal courts require only that the attorney seeking admission be a member of the bar of the state in which the court sits and make formal application for admission to the federal bar.

2) Interstate Federal Practice

Under limited circumstances, an attorney who is a member of the bar in one state and admitted to practice before a federal court in that state may be permitted to appear in a federal court in another state.

a) "Pro Hac Vice" Appearances

An attorney who is a member of the bar in one state may be allowed to appear "pro hac vice" in federal court in another state to argue or try a particular case. In such instances, the state in which the federal court sits cannot limit the attorney's rights.

Example: An attorney who specializes in antitrust law and is a member of the bar in State A appears in federal court in State B on a complex antitrust matter. State B cannot limit the attorney's right to practice in federal court on the ground that he is not licensed to practice in State B.

b) Continuous Federal Practice

A different result is reached when an attorney attempts to conduct a full-time federal practice within a state in which he has not been admitted to the bar. Under such circumstances the state is fully within its rights in limiting the attorney's access to the courts even though he has limited himself exclusively to federal matters.

b. Federal Administrative Agencies

In most instances, the only requirement for practice before a federal administrative agency is that the attorney be a member of the bar of the state in which the agency sits.

Certain specialized agencies, such as the United States Patent Office, also require that the attorney pass a special examination to test his expertise. In addition, it has been recognized that federal law may totally preempt an area in such a manner so as to allow anyone who meets specific qualifications to practice law in that field regardless of whether he is admitted to practice in a particular jurisdiction.

Example: An attorney or nonlawyer "agent" may be admitted to practice law before the Patent Office provided he has passed a special examination. A state cannot prohibit a qualified patent agent from practicing patent law in that state on the basis that he is not admitted to that state's bar and is thereby engaged in the unauthorized practice of law. [Sperry v. Florida, 373 U.S. 379 (1963)]

Most federal administrative agencies have a procedure whereby an attorney may be suspended or disbarred from practice before the agency.

c. Federal Government Attorneys
A federal government attorney is subject to state *ethics* laws and rules (as well as local federal court rules) governing attorney conduct in each state in which the attorney engages in her duties. [28 U.S.C. §530B(a); 28 C.F.R. §§77.2, .3]

3. American Bar Association
The American Bar Association ("ABA") is a voluntary national organization which, since its inception, has performed many important advisory functions relating to the regulation of the legal profession.

a. Model Rules of Professional Conduct
In August 1983, the ABA approved its standards for professional responsibility, the Model Rules of Professional Conduct. Massachusetts has adopted a modified version of the Model Rules. The Massachusetts Rules of Professional Conduct ("RPC") became effective on January 1, 1998.

B. ADMISSION TO THE LEGAL PROFESSION
In regulating admission to practice, each jurisdiction has formulated certain prerequisites. While the details of satisfying these will vary by state and federal district, the applicant normally must meet educational requirements, pass (except where waived if from another jurisdiction) a bar examination, and show that she is a person of good moral character. To satisfy constitutional standards of equal protection of the laws, any prerequisite to admission must bear a *rational relationship* to the applicant's fitness or capacity. [Schware v. Board of Bar Examiners of New Mexico, 353 U.S. 232 (1957)]

1. Educational Requirements
Massachusetts requires that applicants for the bar have: (i) graduated from high school or its equivalent, (ii) completed the work acceptable for a bachelor's degree at a college or university or its equivalent, and (iii) graduated from an ABA-accredited law school or one that is authorized by state statute to grant a degree of bachelor of laws or juris doctor. [Supreme Judicial Court Rule ("Rule") 3:01, §3]

2. Bar Examination
Massachusetts requires applicants to pass a bar examination administered by the Board of Bar Examiners, as well as the Multistate Professional Responsibility Examination ("MPRE"). However, an attorney who has been admitted to practice law in another state for at least five years and has practiced or taught law since the prior admission may be admitted without examination if she: (i) meets the Massachusetts educational requirements (*see* above), (ii) provides three letters of recommendation, and (iii) passes (or has previously passed) the MPRE. [Rule 3:01, §§2, 3, 6]

3. Citizenship Requirements
A state may not require that an applicant be a citizen of the United States. [*In re* Griffiths, 413 U.S. 717 (1973)]

4. Residency Requirements
The United States Supreme Court, in *Supreme Court of New Hampshire v. Piper,* 470 U.S. 274 (1985), ruled that state residency requirements for bar admission violate the Privileges and Immunities Clause of the United States Constitution. The Court found the right to

practice law to be "fundamental," and declared that states may discriminate against nonresidents only where their reasons are **substantial** and the difference in treatment bears a close or **substantial relation** to those reasons. The Court found the reasons advanced by New Hampshire to be insubstantial.

a. Admission on Motion

A state residency requirement for admission to the state's bar without examination (on motion) is unconstitutional. Requiring nonresidents to sit for a bar examination while residents may be admitted on motion violates the Privileges and Immunities Clause. [Supreme Court of Virginia v. Friedman, 487 U.S. 59 (1988)]

b. Residency for Federal Court Practice

The Supreme Court has also struck down a local rule of a federal district court that required, in addition to bar membership in the state in which the court sits, that applicants to the court's bar also live or maintain an office in that state. The Court found this requirement unnecessary and irrational. [Frazier v. Heebe, 482 U.S. 641 (1987)]

5. Character Requirements

Every jurisdiction, including Massachusetts, places on each applicant the burden of showing that he possesses "good moral character." [Rule 3:01, §5]

a. Applicant's Procedure

Each applicant is required to answer a detailed background questionnaire and to furnish references to the Board of Bar Examiners. The refusal to furnish such information is grounds for rejection of the applicant.

Example: An applicant who refuses to answer questions concerning his possible membership in the Communist Party may be rejected because such inquiries are merely a prelude to an investigation into his moral character. [Konigsberg v. State Bar of California, 366 U.S. 36 (1961)]

b. Procedural Protections

An applicant is entitled to procedural due process with regard to actions taken by the Board in reviewing his application. This includes the right to a *hearing* before the Board and *confrontation of adverse witnesses,* as well as the right to *judicial review* of the denial of an application based on bad moral character. [Willner v. Committee on Character and Fitness, 373 U.S. 96 (1963)]

c. Conduct Failing the "Good Moral Character" Test

The purpose of the Board's investigation into the background of an applicant is to determine if there is anything in his past that reflects adversely upon his honesty and integrity. The general benchmark used to measure this is whether any of the applicant's past conduct involved "moral turpitude," *i.e.,* acts that involve intentional dishonesty or are repugnant to accepted moral standards. Any conduct or charges against the applicant involving such crimes as bribery, perjury, theft, murder, rape, etc., would fall within the definition of "moral turpitude," but a variety of illegal acts, such as draft evasion and possession of marijuana for personal use, may or may not be acts involving "moral turpitude," depending upon the nature of the offense and the intent of the individual.

Example: An applicant who had used aliases to hide his Jewish background from employers and who had been arrested along with other discontented laborers was found not to have committed an act of "moral turpitude." [Schware v. Board of Bar Examiners of New Mexico, *supra*]

d. Constitutional Limitations on Regulatory Authorities

Although a state regulatory agency may establish criteria that must be met by persons seeking admission to practice law within the state, there must be a *nexus* between the requirements for admission and an applicant's fitness to practice law. For instance, the state regulatory authority may not reject an applicant solely because of *membership in a political organization,* as opposed to active and knowing participation in the organization with the intent to advance specific goals.

Nor may rejection be based on the *personal beliefs* of an applicant where those beliefs are not translated into an illegal advocacy to action. In this context, the Supreme Court rulings in bar admission proceedings have tracked the development of standards for the invocation of free speech and associational rights under the First Amendment.

Example: An applicant may not be rejected merely on the basis of his membership in the Communist Party where there is no showing that he ever engaged in, or even advocated, actions to overthrow the government by force or violence. [Schware v. Board of Bar Examiners of New Mexico, *supra*]

e.   **Attorney's Duty to Cooperate with Character Investigations**
An *applicant* for admission to the bar, or a *lawyer* in connection with a bar admission application or in connection with a disciplinary matter, must not: (i) knowingly make a false statement of material fact; or (ii) fail to disclose a fact necessary to correct a misapprehension known by the person to have arisen in the matter, or knowingly fail to respond to a lawful demand for information from an admissions or disciplinary authority. This rule does not require disclosure of information otherwise protected by RPC 1.6 (relating to confidentiality). [RPC 8.1]

C.   DISCIPLINARY PROCESS

1.   **General Substantive Standards**
The Massachusetts Rules list general prohibitions, the violation of which may, as do violations of the specific prohibitions in the Rules, lead to disciplinary measures. Under these prohibitions, a lawyer may not:

(i)   Violate or attempt to violate the Rules of Professional Conduct, knowingly assist or induce another to do so, or do so through the acts of another;

(ii)   Commit a criminal act that reflects adversely on the lawyer's honesty, trustworthiness, or fitness as a lawyer in other respects;

(iii)   State or imply an ability to improperly influence a government agency or official;

(iv)   Knowingly assist a judge or judicial officer in conduct that violates applicable rules of judicial conduct or other law;

(v)   Fail without good cause to cooperate with Bar Counsel or the Board of Bar Overseers;

(vi)   Engage in conduct involving dishonesty, fraud, deceit, or misrepresentation;

(vii)   Engage in conduct prejudicial to the administration of justice; or

(viii)   Engage in any other conduct that adversely reflects on her fitness to practice law.

[RPC 8.4]

2.   **Disciplinary Procedure**
The Massachusetts Supreme Judicial Court appoints a Board of Bar Overseers ("Board") to investigate and dispose of all matters relating to the misconduct of attorneys. [Rule 4:01, §5]

a.   **Complaint**
The disciplinary proceeding is initiated by the filing of a grievance or complaint to the Board, which may be filed by a dissatisfied client, member of the bar, or any other interested party. The filing of a complaint is generally considered a *privileged communication* and the complainant is usually protected from subsequent action by the attorney for defamation or malicious prosecution as a matter of public policy.

b.   **Screening and Hearing**
The Board appoints a chief Bar Counsel to make a preliminary investigation into all matters involving alleged attorney misconduct. [Rule 4:01, §§5, 7, 8] Bar Counsel may recommend to the Board that:

(i)   A formal complaint be dismissed;

(ii)   An attorney be administered an admonition;

(iii)   Formal proceedings be instituted; or

(iv)   Formal discipline be imposed by agreement.

A designated Board member may approve, reject, or modify Bar Counsel's recommended action. [Rule 4:01, §8]

1) Commencement of Hearing
If the Board decides to pursue a formal proceeding, a hearing will be held before the Board or a panel of the Board, or before a special hearing officer or hearing committee appointed by the Board, after notice to the attorney under investigation. The special hearing officer, hearing committee, or panel of the Board must report promptly to the Board any findings and recommendations, together with a record of the proceedings. [Rule 4:01, §8]

2) Procedural Protections
The Due Process Clauses of the Fourteenth Amendment and relevant state constitutions are applicable to state disciplinary proceedings. Thus, while the specific procedures vary by jurisdiction, a lawyer subject to a disciplinary hearing retains the basic *rights to counsel and to cross-examination of witnesses* at the hearing. [*In re* Ruffalo, 390 U.S. 544 (1968)] He also has the absolute right to invoke, without penalty, the Fifth Amendment *protection against self-incrimination* under the Supreme Court's ruling in *Spevack v. Klein,* 385 U.S. 511 (1967).

3. Forms of Disciplinary Sanction
The penalties for engaging in unethical or unprofessional conduct are:

a. *Disbarment* (permanent revocation of an attorney's license);

b. *Suspension* (temporary revocation of an attorney's right to practice);

c. *Public reprimand* by the Board; and

d. *Admonition* by Bar Counsel.

4. Effect of Disciplinary Action on Other Court Systems
Each state and federal court system is considered a separate, autonomous unit for discipline as well as admission of attorneys. Thus, disciplinary proceedings by the state courts located within the federal district have no binding effect on the attorney's ability to practice before the federal courts in that district. Similarly, foreign state courts must make their own independent evaluation of an attorney's conduct when he has been disciplined in a sister state. However, most states give some effect to the sister state's determination during their own proceedings on the basis of "full faith and credit" or "comity."

5. Practice in Multiple States
A lawyer admitted to practice in Massachusetts is subject to the disciplinary authority of Massachusetts, regardless of where the lawyer's conduct occurs. A lawyer may be subject to the disciplinary authority of both Massachusetts and another jurisdiction where the lawyer is admitted for the same conduct. [RPC 8.5(a)]

D. UNAUTHORIZED PRACTICE OF LAW
In addition to regulating the admission and discipline of lawyers, Massachusetts has sought to prevent the unauthorized practice of law. This prohibition is predicated upon the public's need for integrity and competence of those persons purporting to render "legal" services. It is not unauthorized practice, however, for a layperson to represent herself.

1. Definition of Unauthorized Practice
The Rules do not attempt to set forth a single definition of those activities that constitute the unauthorized practice of law. They adopt instead a functional definition. The Rules do, however, prohibit a lawyer from (i) practicing law in a jurisdiction where doing so violates the regulation of the legal profession in that jurisdiction, and (ii) assisting a person who is not a member of the bar in the performance of an activity that constitutes the unauthorized practice of law. [RPC 5.5]

2. Limited Exception Where Professional Judgment Not Required
Where the professional judgment of a lawyer is not involved, nonlawyers such as court clerks, abstracters, and many government officials are authorized to engage in occupations even if they require a special knowledge of law in certain areas.

3. Definition Applied to Specific Activities
The actual determination of what constitutes unauthorized practice has been left to the

Massachusetts Supreme Judicial Court. Some states have attempted to define the practice of law in connection with specific activities, but in large measure the distinctions between such practice and proper lay activities are based on the particular circumstances of each case.

a. Preparation of Documents

1) Real Estate Brokers
Real estate brokers may not draft contracts but may fill in the blanks on standard contracts as long as separate fees are not charged for such services.

2) Title Insurance and Escrow Companies
Title insurance and escrow companies are permitted to fill in standardized mortgage and deed forms in certain jurisdictions but are restrained from doing so in others.

3) Lay Tax Advisers
In theory, lay tax advisers may not counsel individuals as to the legal implications of their conduct but may, if qualified (*i.e.*, by accountancy training), prepare tax returns for clients.

Example: Client goes to see his tax accountant to consult with him concerning tax shelters for his large income. The accountant may not give advice to Client on tax shelters because such advice requires the professional judgment of a lawyer as to the legality of specific action under the tax laws.

4) Estate Planners
Estate planners may not draft wills or prepare plans for specific individuals but may disseminate general information to the public through commercial or noncommercial means.

Example: An estate planner published a book entitled *How to Avoid Probate*, which was in effect a "do-it-yourself" probate kit. He was subsequently charged with practicing law without a license. The court ruled that he was merely disseminating information to the public to enable individuals to represent themselves. [New York County Lawyers' Association v. Dacey, 287 N.Y.S.2d 422 (1967)]

b. Representation of Clients

1) Corporations
Corporations, other than nonprofit legal service groups or recognized professional corporations, generally may not represent a client directly in judicial proceedings or provide representation through their attorney-employees.

2) Collection Agencies
Collection agencies in a number of jurisdictions may not bring suit directly to enforce a debt assigned to them for collection. However, a state statute defining debt collection as the practice of law, thus limiting debt collection activities to members of that state's bar, was held to be an unconstitutional imposition on interstate commerce. [National Revenue Corp. v. Violet, 807 F.2d 285 (1st Cir. 1986)]

3) Representation "In Propria Persona"
Individuals (not corporations) have the right to represent themselves even if they are not attorneys.

4. Practicing Across Jurisdictional Boundaries
A lawyer engages in unauthorized practice by practicing law in a jurisdiction where he is not admitted. There are several caveats to this principle:

a. "Pro Hac Vice" Appearances
Lawyers are routinely admitted "pro hac vice" to appear in individual proceedings on behalf of a client. However, a lawyer must be a member in good standing of at least one bar before he can be admitted "pro hac vice." Note that there is no right of federal origin that permits out-of-state lawyers to appear in state courts without meeting that state's bar admission requirements. [Leis v. Flynt, 439 U.S. 438 (1979)]

b. **Clients Involved in Multistate Business**
Since the business of a single client may involve legal problems in several states, the RPC do not contain regulations specifically imposing territorial limits upon a lawyer's right to handle the affairs of a client.

c. **Multistate Law Partnerships**
Multistate law partnerships are acceptable as long as the individual lawyers practice in the jurisdiction(s) in which they are admitted and the firm letterhead so indicates.

d. **Practice Before Federal Administrative Agencies**
A state may not prevent a person licensed by a federal agency, such as the Patent Office, from carrying on activities related to his work before that agency. (*See* A.2.b., *supra*.)

5. **Judges and Court Officers**
Full-time judges and court officers (including clerks) may not practice law, nor may law students represent clients except where authorized to do so under the supervision of a licensed attorney. [Rules 3:03, 3:09, 3:12]

6. **Attorneys Aiding Lay Practitioners**
A lawyer may not practice law in association with, or otherwise share fees with, a layperson and may be disciplined for aiding a nonlawyer in the unauthorized practice of law.

7. **Law Firms and Nonlawyers**
Law firms, whether in the form of professional corporations or associations, may not be set up in such a way that a nonlawyer owns an interest therein (except for a fiduciary representative during the administration of an estate), a nonlawyer is a corporate officer or director thereof, or a nonlawyer has the right to direct or control a lawyer's professional judgment.

E. **LAW-RELATED (ANCILLARY) SERVICES**
Lawyers are permitted to provide law-related services to clients. Law-related services (often referred to as ancillary services) are services that might reasonably be performed in conjunction with (and are related to) the provision of legal services and that are not prohibited as unauthorized practice of law when provided by a nonlawyer. Examples of law-related services include financial planning, accounting, trust services, real estate counseling, and tax return preparation. A lawyer is subject to the Rules of Professional Conduct with respect to the provision of law-related services if she provides those services under circumstances that are not distinct from her provision of legal services to clients. [RPC 5.7(a)(1)]

1. **Services Provided by Entity Controlled by Lawyer**
When the law-related services are provided by a separate entity controlled in whole or in part by a lawyer, the lawyer is subject to the Rules of Professional Conduct with respect to those services unless she takes reasonable measures to ensure that the recipient of the services knows that the services provided by the entity are not legal services and that the protections of the lawyer-client relationship do not apply. [RPC 5.7(a)(2)]

II. ESTABLISHING A LEGAL PRACTICE

A. **FORMS OF PRACTICE**
Lawyers have the opportunity to practice law in myriad ways. The most prevalent of these various forms are sole practitioners; law firms; lawyers involved in the executive, legislative, and judicial aspects of government; legal services organizations; and counsel to special interest groups and business enterprises, most notably corporations, banks, and insurance companies.

1. **The Law Firm**

a. **Relationship of Attorneys Within the Firm**
Law firms range in size from two to over 1,000 lawyers, and their activities encompass the entire ambit of legal services. Three categories of practitioners generally are distinguished within the firm framework: partners, associates, and attorneys of counsel.

1) **Partners**
Partners are those lawyers who share responsibility and liability for the activities of the firm. In many jurisdictions, a firm may not be designated as a partnership

unless the "partners" share in the profits as well as the expenses of the firm. Expense-sharing associations are not considered partnerships and may not be held out to the public as such.

2) Associates
Associates do not share full responsibility or liability for the firm's work and are often limited in their contact with clients due to the organizational characteristics of the firm.

3) "Of Counsel"
"Of counsel" denotes an attorney who has a continuing relationship with a law firm, other than as a partner or associate. The ABA has determined that while a lawyer conceivably could be "of counsel" to two law firms or lawyers, the nature of the relationship is such that one cannot simultaneously have more than two "of counsel" relationships.

b. Designation of "General Counsel"
"General counsel" or a similar professional reference may be used by a law firm that devotes a substantial amount of professional time to the representation of a client.

c. Protecting Client's Interests
Whatever the structure of the firm, a lawyer in practice must ensure that the interests of the client are paramount to the interests of the firm and that the client's problems are handled with competence and care.

d. Naming the Law Firm
A lawyer must not use a firm name, letterhead, or other professional designation that is false or misleading. A private practitioner may use a trade name that does not imply a connection with a government agency or with a legal services organization. [RPC 7.5]

1) Firm Members in Public Service
The name of a lawyer holding a public office must not be used in the name of a law firm, or in communications on its behalf, during any substantial period in which the lawyer is not actively and regularly practicing with the firm.

2) Offices in Other Jurisdictions
A law firm with offices in more than one jurisdiction may use the same firm name in each jurisdiction. However, when identifying its lawyers, the firm must list the jurisdictional limitations of those lawyers not licensed to practice in that jurisdiction. [RPC 7.5]

2. Lawyers in Association with Nonlawyers

a. Partnerships with Laypersons that Involve Legal Practice
A lawyer may not be a partner with a nonlawyer if any of the partnership activities consists of the practice of law. [RPC 5.4]

b. No Sharing of Legal Fees
A lawyer or law firm must not share legal fees with a nonlawyer, except that: (i) an agreement by a lawyer with the lawyer's firm, partner, or associate may provide for the payment of money, over a reasonable period of time after the lawyer's death, to the lawyer's estate, or to one or more specified persons; (ii) a lawyer who purchases the practice of a deceased, disabled, or disappeared lawyer may pay to the estate or other representative of that lawyer the agreed-upon purchase price (*see* E., *infra,* for sale of a law practice discussion); and (iii) a lawyer or law firm may include nonlawyer employees in a compensation or retirement plan, even though the plan is based in whole or in part on a profit-sharing arrangement. [RPC 5.4]

c. Lawyer Must Exercise Independent Judgment
A lawyer must not permit a person who recommends, employs, or pays the lawyer to render legal services for another to direct or regulate the lawyer's professional judgment in rendering such legal services. [RPC 5.4]

3. The Legal Corporation
Due to favorable tax treatment for corporate pension and profit-sharing plans, all 50 states

and the District of Columbia allow lawyers to incorporate into highly regulated special business structures known by various titles, such as professional corporations and professional associations.

a. Cannot Limit Liability
The liability of the lawyer to the client may not be limited in a legal corporation.

b. Nonlawyer May Not Have an Interest
A lawyer may not practice in a legal corporation if a nonlawyer has an interest in the corporation as a shareholder, officer, or director. However, a fiduciary representative of the estate of a lawyer may hold the stock or interest of the lawyer for a reasonable time during administration. Also, a lawyer may not participate in such a practice if her professional judgment is subject to the direction or control of a nonlawyer.

4. Legal Services Organizations

a. Legal Aid and Public Defenders
Legal aid offices and public defender services provide legal assistance for the poor. They are usually operated or sponsored by an accredited law school, a nonprofit community organization, a government agency, or a bar association representative.

b. Military Legal Assistance Offices
Military legal assistance offices provide legal services to military personnel and their families.

c. Lawyer Referral Services
Lawyer referral services maintain lists of lawyers who are willing to accept new clients. The individual seeking help is referred by the service to an attorney for an initial consultation at a prearranged low fee. Further arrangements are left to the attorney and the client. If the client is unhappy with the attorney, he may return to the service for another referral.

d. Group Legal Service Plans
Group legal service plans are plans designed to provide various legal services to members of a specific group. Such groups may consist of union members, members of an association, and participants in prepaid legal insurance programs.

e. Advertising by Legal Service Plans
The preceding legal service plans may advertise their availability to the public. This is simply another means of providing access to legal services and is not considered to constitute solicitation of business.

f. Membership in Legal Services Organizations
A lawyer may serve as a director, officer, or member of a legal services organization, other than the law firm with which the lawyer practices, notwithstanding that the organization serves persons having interests adverse to a client of the lawyer. However, the lawyer must not knowingly participate in a decision or action of the organization:

(i) If participating in the decision would be incompatible with the lawyer's obligations to a client under RPC 1.7 (relating to conflicts of interest); or

(ii) Where the decision could have a material adverse effect on the representation of a client of the organization whose interests are adverse to a client of the lawyer.

[RPC 6.3]

B. RESPONSIBILITIES OF A PARTNER OR SUPERVISORY LAWYER

1. Law Firm Must Ensure Member Lawyers Conform to Rules
A partner in a law firm must make reasonable efforts to ensure that the firm has in effect measures giving reasonable assurance that all lawyers in the firm conform to the Rules of Professional Conduct. [RPC 5.1]

2. Supervisory Attorneys Have Comparable Responsibility
A lawyer having direct supervisory authority over another lawyer must make reasonable efforts to ensure that the other lawyer conforms to the Rules of Professional Conduct. A

lawyer having direct supervisory authority over a nonlawyer must make reasonable efforts to ensure that the person's conduct is compatible with the professional obligations of the lawyer. [RPC 5.1, 5.3]

3.   When Lawyer Responsible for Another Lawyer's Violation of the Rules
A lawyer will be responsible for another lawyer's violation of the Rules of Professional Conduct if: (i) the lawyer *orders or ratifies the conduct* involved; or (ii) the lawyer is a partner in the law firm in which the other lawyer practices, or has *direct supervisory authority* over the other lawyer, *and knows of the conduct* at a time when its consequences can be avoided or mitigated but fails to take reasonable remedial action. Similar rules apply with respect to a lawyer's responsibility for a nonlawyer's violation of the Rules of Professional Conduct. [RPC 5.1, 5.3]

C.   RESPONSIBILITIES OF A SUBORDINATE LAWYER
A lawyer is bound by the Rules of Professional Conduct notwithstanding that the lawyer acted at the direction of another person. A subordinate lawyer does not violate the Rules of Professional Conduct if he acts in accordance with a supervisory lawyer's reasonable resolution of an arguable question of professional duty. [RPC 5.2]

D.   RESTRICTIONS ON RIGHT TO PRACTICE
A lawyer must not participate in offering or making: (i) a partnership or employment agreement that restricts the rights of a lawyer to practice after termination of the relationship, except an agreement concerning benefits upon retirement; or (ii) an agreement in which a restriction on the lawyer's right to practice is part of the settlement of a controversy. [RPC 5.6] This rule does not apply to prohibit restrictions included in the terms of the sale of a law practice pursuant to RPC 1.17 (*see* below).

E.   SALE AND PURCHASE OF A LAW PRACTICE
The Rules of Professional Conduct permit the sale of a law practice, including goodwill, if *written notice* is given to each of the seller's clients regarding: (i) the proposed sale, (ii) the terms of any proposed change in fee arrangement, (iii) the clients' right to retain other counsel or to take possession of their files, and (iv) the fact that consent will be presumed if a client fails to take action within 90 days. If notice cannot be given to a client, a court order is required to authorize the transfer of the representation of the client to the purchaser. Clients' fees may not be increased because of the sale. However, the purchaser may refuse to represent a client unless the client consents to pay a fee at a rate not exceeding that charged by the purchaser for substantially similar services prior to initiation of purchase negotiations. [RPC 1.17]

III.   INFORMATION ABOUT LEGAL SERVICES

A.   BACKGROUND OF ADVERTISING AND SOLICITATION RULES
"Advertising" generally refers to a lawyer's communication with the public at large or a segment of the public. In contrast, "solicitation" generally refers to individual contact with a layperson, initiated by a lawyer (or lawyer's agent), that is designed to entice the layperson to hire the lawyer. A blatant form of solicitation is "ambulance chasing," in which a lawyer (or lawyer's agent) seeks out injured people and urges them to hire the lawyer to represent them.

1.   Supreme Court Cases on Advertising and Solicitation
The United States Supreme Court has recognized lawyer advertising as commercial speech protected by the First and Fourteenth Amendments, holding that a state may adopt reasonable regulations to insure that lawyer advertising is not false or misleading, but may not flatly prohibit all lawyer advertising. [Bates v. State Bar of Arizona, 433 U.S. 350 (1977)]
Examples: 1)   The Missouri Supreme Court Rules prohibited deviations from a precise listing of areas of practice, prohibited a lawyer from identifying the jurisdictions in which he is licensed to practice, and prohibited mailing of cards announcing the opening of an office to persons other than lawyers, clients, former clients, personal friends, and relatives. The United States Supreme Court held these provisions unconstitutional absent a showing that the advertising was misleading, or that mailings and handbills would thereby be more difficult to supervise. [*In re* R.M.J., 455 U.S. 191 (1982)]

2)   An attorney had placed two newspaper ads, one offering to represent "drunk drivers" and return the legal fees if the driver is convicted, and the other offering to represent women who were injured through use of the

Dalkon Shield, with no legal fees to the client absent a recovery. The latter ad also included an illustration of the shield. The state reprimanded the attorney for improperly soliciting business involving a specific legal problem. On review, the United States Supreme Court held that states can impose disclosure requirements but cannot ban the use of illustrations merely because they are undignified or ban ads merely because they are aimed at specific potential plaintiffs. [Zauderer v. Office of Disciplinary Counsel of the Supreme Court of Ohio, 471 U.S. 626 (1985)]

3) The Kentucky Supreme Court Rules prohibited attorneys from sending letters to potential clients faced with particular legal problems. An attorney who planned to mail letters to potential clients who had foreclosure suits filed against them challenged the validity of the rule. The United States Supreme Court found that a state may not prohibit attorneys from sending truthful and nondeceptive letters to potential clients known to face particular legal problems. [Shapero v. Kentucky Bar Association, 486 U.S. 466 (1988)]

a. **False and Misleading Ads and In-Person Solicitation May Be Banned**
A state may flatly prohibit lawyer advertising that is false or misleading. [*In re* R.M.J., *supra*] Similarly, a state may adopt prophylactic rules to forbid in-person solicitation for profit in circumstances that are likely to result in overreaching or misleading a layperson. [Ohralik v. Ohio State Bar Association, 436 U.S. 447 (1978)]

b. **When Regulation of Truthful, Nondeceptive Advertising Permitted**
Since attorney advertising is commercial speech, regulation of it is subject to only intermediate, rather than strict, scrutiny. [Florida Bar v. Went For It, Inc., 515 U.S. 618 (1995)] Thus, this type of commercial speech may be regulated if the government satisfies a three-prong test:

(i) The government must assert a *substantial interest* in support of its regulation;

(ii) The government must demonstrate that the restriction on commercial speech *directly and materially advances the interest;* and

(iii) The regulation must be *narrowly drawn.*

[Florida Bar v. Went For It, Inc., *supra, citing* Central Hudson Gas & Electric Corp. v. Public Service Commission of New York, 447 U.S. 557 (1980)]

Example: After conducting a two-year study on the effect of lawyer advertising on public opinion, which included surveys and hearings, the Florida Bar adopted a rule prohibiting lawyers from sending *any* targeted direct-mail solicitations to victims and their relatives for 30 days following an accident or disaster. The United States Supreme Court upheld the regulation, finding that it met the three-prong test above. The Court found that: (i) the state bar has a substantial interest in protecting the privacy and tranquility of its citizens as well as in protecting the reputation of the legal profession; (ii) the studies show that the public was offended by these solicitations and that the 30-day ban directly advances the state bar's interests; and (iii) the regulation is narrowly tailored to achieve the desired results. [Florida Bar v. Went For It, Inc., *supra*]

B. ADVERTISING

1. **Basic Rule—Communications Must Be True and Not Misleading**
A lawyer is subject to discipline for *any type* of communication about the lawyer or the lawyer's services that is *false or misleading.* [RPC 7.1] This rule applies to all kinds of communications, including advertisements, personal communications, office signs, professional cards, professional announcements, letterheads, brochures, letters sent by mail, and recorded telephone messages.

2. **Definition of "False or Misleading"**
The RPC list three types of false or misleading communications:

a. **Misstating or Failing to State Material Information**
A lawyer must not make a *material misstatement* of fact or law or make a statement that *omits* a fact necessary to make the statement, considered as a whole, *not materially misleading.* [RPC 7.1(a)]

> *Example:*   Lawyer L put a short advertisement in the classified section of the local newspaper: "Divorce—$300. Credit can be arranged. Telephone 477-4949." L does charge only $300 for a simple, uncontested divorce where the couple has no significant assets to divide and no children. However, for anything more complex than that, L charges $75 per hour, and most divorces she handles cost more than $300. L's ad is materially misleading.

b. Creating Unjustified Expectations

A lawyer must not create unjustified expectations about the results the lawyer can achieve. This rule ordinarily precludes statements about the results obtained for a particular client, statements about the lawyer's "track record" in obtaining favorable verdicts, and statements containing client endorsements. Further, a lawyer must not imply that she can obtain results by means that would violate the law or a disciplinary rule. [RPC 7.1(b)]

c. Making Unverifiable Comparisons

A lawyer must not compare her services with services offered by other lawyers, unless the comparison can be factually substantiated. [RPC 7.1(c)]

> *Example:*   Attorney A advertises that she charges the "Lowest Fees in Oakvale." If A cannot prove by hard statistics that her fees are the lowest in Oakvale, she is subject to discipline.

3. Limits on Advertising

Lawyers have broad latitude in advertising their services. For example, they may advertise via radio or television, periodicals, phone books, legal directories, billboards, circulars, brochures, recorded telephone messages, and even in letters mailed to persons who have been identified as having a particular legal problem. All statements made in advertisements must be true and not misleading, as explained above. [RPC 7.2] In addition, all advertisements are subject to the following restrictions:

a. Fields of Practice

Communications about the fields of law in which the lawyer practices must comply with Rule 7.4 (*see* D., *infra*).

b. Consent of Named Clients

If a lawyer wishes to identify some regular clients in an advertisement, the lawyer should first obtain the clients' consent. [RPC 7.2, comment]

c. Identification of Advertiser

Every advertisement must include the name of at least one lawyer who is responsible for its content. [RPC 7.2(d)]

d. Copies and Recordings of Advertisements

The lawyer must keep a copy or recording of all advertisements and an accurate record of when and where the advertisement was used. These copies, recordings, and records must be kept for at least two years after the advertisement is last disseminated. [RPC 7.2(b)] The purpose is to assist disciplinary authorities in policing false or misleading advertisements.

e. Payments for Recommending a Lawyer's Services

Except in connection with the sale of a law practice, a lawyer must not give anything of value to a person for recommending the lawyer's services. [RPC 7.2(c)] This rule does not prohibit a lawyer from paying the reasonable cost of advertising, nor does it prohibit a lawyer from paying someone to prepare the advertising. Further, the rule does not prohibit the payment of referral fees permitted by Rule 1.5(e), *see* IV.E.5., *infra*, nor does it prohibit an organization (such as a legal aid office or a group legal service plan) from advertising the services offered by the organization. Finally, it does not prevent a lawyer from paying the usual fee charged by a nonprofit lawyer referral service.

> *Example:*   The A, B & C firm seeks to increase its client base. The firm may hire and pay a media consultant to design some newspaper advertisements, and it may pay the newspaper for the advertising space. The firm may also participate in a prepaid legal service plan that advertises to obtain new members. Further, some of the lawyers in the firm are listed with

the nonprofit lawyer referral service run by the local county bar association; when those lawyers obtain clients through the referral service, they may pay the referral fee charged by the service.

C. SOLICITATION

The basic rule is this: A lawyer must not seek fee-paying work by initiating a personal or live telephone contact with a prospective client. [*See* RPC 7.3] In Massachusetts, prospective clients include a lawyer's friends, relatives, and former clients. Thus, an attorney who hangs around in the hallway of the courthouse, offering legal services for a fee to criminal defendants who are not represented by counsel is subject to discipline. Likewise, a lawyer who hears on the radio that a person was badly injured in an accident and promptly telephones that person's spouse offering legal services for a fee is subject to discipline. [*See also* 49 U.S.C. §1136(g)(2)—federal law prohibits lawyers from communicating with victims of an airplane accident, or their families, until 45 days after the accident]

1. Use of Agents to Solicit

A lawyer is prohibited from using an agent to do that which the lawyer must not do, *e.g.,* violate a law or disciplinary rule. Thus, a lawyer must not use an agent (sometimes called a "runner" or "capper") to contact prospective clients in a manner that would violate Rule 7.3.

Examples: 1) Lawyer L hired R to be a "claims investigator." R's work involved checking accident and crime reports at the local police station and then personally contacting those involved to "advise them of their legal rights." L furnishes R with copies of her standard form retainer agreement and instructs R to sign up clients when possible. L is subject to discipline.

2) Attorney A has an arrangement with a "debt consolidation" company. Employees of the company interview debtors and advise them about loans and ways to get out of debt. If it appears that a debtor needs legal assistance, the company employee refers the debtor to A. A is subject to discipline.

2. Offers of Free Legal Service

The basic rule prohibiting solicitation applies only "when a significant motive" for the lawyer's solicitation "is the lawyer's pecuniary gain." [*See In re* Primus, 436 U.S. 412 (1978)—lawyer could not be disciplined for offering free legal services of the ACLU] Thus, a lawyer who volunteers to represent someone without a fee, and without other hope of pecuniary gain, is not subject to discipline for solicitation.

Example: When lawyer L learned that the police arrested 65 persons in an animal rights protest, she went to the police station, spoke with the leader of the group, and volunteered to represent the arrested persons without a fee. L realized that the case might receive wide press coverage, and that the publicity might lure fee-paying clients in other matters, but this was not a substantial motive for her offer. L is not subject to discipline for solicitation.

3. Targeted Direct-Mail Solicitations

Absent actual knowledge that the prospective client does not wish to receive communications from the lawyer, a lawyer is not prohibited from sending truthful, nondeceptive letters to any person, including one known to face a specific legal problem. [RPC 7.3]

4. Communications Against Client's Wishes or Involving Coercion

A lawyer may not contact or send a written communication to a prospective client for the purpose of obtaining professional employment if: (i) the lawyer knows or reasonably should know that the physical, mental, or emotional state of the person is such that he could not exercise reasonable judgment in employing a lawyer; (ii) the person has made known to the lawyer a desire not to receive communications from the lawyer; or (iii) the communication involves coercion or harassment. [RPC 7.3(a), (b)]

Example: Lawyer L obtained a mailing list of all persons who used a certain prescription drug that allegedly caused grave side effects. L sent personal letters to each person, offering to represent them for a fee in litigation against the drug manufacturer. C, one of the recipients of L's letters, telephoned L's office and told her that she did not want to sue anyone and did not want to hear further from L. Nonetheless, L sent C a series of follow-up letters, each urging C to join in litigation against the drug manufacturer. L is subject to discipline.

5. Labeling Solicitations as Advertising

A written or recorded communication must be clearly labeled "Advertising" on its face and on any envelope or container. The lawyer must retain a copy of the communication for two years. [RPC 7.3(c)]

6. **Referrals and Lawyer Referral Services**
A lawyer is prohibited from paying any person or organization to solicit professional employment on his behalf from a prospective client. However, this rule does not prohibit a lawyer from requesting referrals from a lawyer referral service operated, sponsored, or approved by a bar association or from cooperating with any qualified legal assistance organization. [RPC 7.3(e)]

D. COMMUNICATION OF FIELDS OF PRACTICE
A lawyer may publicly hold himself out as a specialist in particular services, fields, and areas of law if the holding out is not deceptive. A lawyer holds himself out if he:

(i) *Makes a statement* that he concentrates in, specializes in, is certified in, has experience in, or limits his practice to a particular service, field, or area of law;

(ii) *Appears in a directory listing* by a particular service, field, or area of law; or

(iii) *In any other way associates his name* with a particular service, field, or area of law.

[RPC 7.4(a)]

1. **"Certified" Lawyers**
A lawyer who holds himself out as "certified" in a particular service, field, or area of law must name the certifying organization. If the certifying organization is a private organization the lawyer must state that the organization is "a private organization, whose standards for certification are not regulated by the Commonwealth of Massachusetts." If the certifying organization is a governmental body, the lawyer must name the governmental body. [RPC 7.4(b)]

2. **Standard of Performance**
Lawyers who associate their names with a particular service, field, or area of law imply an expertise and will be held to the standard of performance of a specialist in that particular service, field, or area. Lawyers may limit their responsibility with respect to a particular service, field, or area of law to the standard of an ordinary lawyer by holding themselves out in a fashion that does not imply expertise (*e.g.,* by advertising that they "handle" or "welcome" cases "but are not specialist in" a particular service, field, or area of law). [RPC 7.4(c)]

IV. ENTERING INTO THE ATTORNEY-CLIENT RELATIONSHIP

A. LAW REFORM ACTIVITIES AFFECTING CLIENT INTERESTS
A lawyer may participate in law reform activities even if such reform may affect the interests of any of her clients. However, when the lawyer knows that a client's interests may materially benefit due to a decision in which the lawyer participates, the lawyer must disclose that fact to the reform organization (but need not identify the client). [RPC 6.4]

B. ACCEPTING APPOINTMENTS
A lawyer must not seek to avoid appointment by a tribunal to represent a person except for good cause, such as: (i) representing the client is likely to result in a violation of the RPC or other law; (ii) representing the client is likely to result in an unreasonable financial burden on the lawyer; or (iii) the client or the cause is so repugnant to the lawyer as to be likely to impair the client-lawyer relationship or the lawyer's ability to represent the client. [RPC 6.2]

C. CLIENT UNDER A DISABILITY
When a client's ability to make adequately considered decisions in connection with the representation is impaired, whether because of minority, mental disability, or some other reason, the lawyer must, as far as reasonably possible, maintain a normal client-lawyer relationship with the client. If a lawyer reasonably believes that a client has become incompetent and is at risk of substantial harm (whether physical, mental, or financial), the lawyer may: (i) consult with family members, adult protective agencies, or other individuals that have authority to protect the client; and (ii) if reasonably necessary, seek the appointment of a guardian or conservator. The lawyer may disclose confidential information of the client only to the extent necessary to protect the client's interests. [RPC 1.14]

D. AVOIDING CONFLICTS OF INTEREST

A lawyer must be careful not to enter into a relationship where there is a potential conflict of interest that is likely to adversely affect his ability to exercise independent and professional judgment. After accepting employment, a lawyer should carefully refrain from acquiring a property right or assuming a position that would tend to make his judgment less protective of the interests of his client unless the client consents.

1. Representation of Client Adverse to Interests of Another Client

A lawyer must not represent a client if the representation of that client will be directly adverse to another client unless: (i) the lawyer reasonably believes that representation will not adversely affect the relationship with the other client; *and* (ii) each client consents after consultation. [RPC 1.7]

2. Conflict of Interest with Other Responsibilities of Lawyer

A lawyer must not represent a client if the representation of that client may be materially limited by the lawyer's responsibilities to another client or to a third person or by the lawyer's own interests, unless:

(i)   The lawyer *reasonably believes* the representation will not be adversely affected; and

(ii) The client *consents* after consultation. When representation of multiple clients in a single matter is undertaken, the consultation must include explanation of the implications of the common representation and the advantages and risks involved.

[RPC 1.7]

3. Prohibited Transactions

a. Ownership or Financial Interest Adverse to Client

A lawyer must not enter into a business transaction with a client or knowingly acquire an ownership or other pecuniary interest adverse to a client unless:

(i)   The transaction and terms in which the lawyer acquires the interest are fair and reasonable to the client and are fully disclosed and transmitted in writing to the client in a manner that can be reasonably understood by the client;

(ii) The client is given a reasonable opportunity to seek the advice of independent counsel on the transaction; and

(iii) The client consents in writing thereto.

[RPC 1.8(a)]

b. Improper Use of Information Adverse to Client

A lawyer must not use information relating to representation of a client to the disadvantage of the client or for the advantage of the lawyer or a third person, unless the client consents after consultation, except as permitted or required by RPC 1.6 (relating to confidentiality of information) or RPC 3.3 (relating to candor toward the tribunal). [RPC 1.8(b)]

c. Designating Oneself as a Beneficiary

A lawyer must not prepare an instrument giving the lawyer or a person related to the lawyer as parent, child, sibling, or spouse any substantial gift from a client, including a testamentary gift, except where the client is related to the donee. [RPC 1.8(c)]

d. Literary or Media Rights Based on Representation

Prior to the conclusion of representation of a client, a lawyer must not make or negotiate an agreement giving the lawyer literary or media rights to a portrayal or account based, in substantial part, on information relating to the representation. [RPC 1.8(d)]

e. Financial Assistance to Client

A lawyer must not provide financial assistance to a client in connection with pending or contemplated litigation, except that: (i) a lawyer may advance court costs and expenses of litigation, the repayment of which may be contingent on the outcome of the matter; and (ii) a lawyer representing an indigent client may pay court costs and expenses of litigation on behalf of the client. [RPC 1.8(e)]

f. Compensation from Party Other than Client
A lawyer must not accept compensation for representing a client from someone other than the client unless: (i) the client consents after consultation; (ii) there is no interference with the lawyer's independence of professional judgment or with the client-lawyer relationship; and (iii) information relating to representation of a client is protected as required by RPC 1.6 (relating to confidentiality of information). [RPC 1.8(f)]

g. Aggregate Settlement or Agreement in Multiple Representation
A lawyer who represents two or more clients must not participate in making an aggregate settlement of the claims of or against the clients, or in a criminal case an aggregate agreement as to guilty or no contest pleas, unless each client consents after consultation, including disclosure of the existence and nature of all the claims or pleas involved and of the participation of each person in the settlement or agreement. [RPC 1.8(g)]

h. Limiting Liability for Malpractice
A lawyer must not make an agreement prospectively limiting the lawyer's liability to a client for malpractice unless permitted by law and the client is independently represented in making the agreement. [RPC 1.8(h)]

i. Settling Claim with Unrepresented or Former Client
A lawyer must not settle a claim for malpractice liability with an unrepresented client or former client without first advising that person in writing that independent representation is appropriate in connection therewith. [RPC 1.8(h)]

j. Lawyer's Relationship to Another Lawyer
Where two lawyers are related to one another as parent, child, sibling, or spouse, they must not represent clients whose interests are "directly adverse" without first getting the consent of the respective clients after consultation. [RPC 1.8(i)] This type of conflict is *not* imputed to other lawyers within a law firm.

k. Proprietary Interest in the Cause of Action
A lawyer must not acquire a proprietary interest in the cause of action or subject matter of litigation the lawyer is conducting for a client, except that the lawyer may: (i) acquire a lien granted by law to secure the lawyer's fee or expenses; and (ii) contract with a client for a reasonable contingent fee in a civil case. [RPC 1.8(j)]

4. Conflict of Interest Regarding Former Client
A lawyer who formerly represented a client in a matter may not thereafter represent another person in the same or a substantially related matter if that person's interests are materially adverse to those of the former client, unless the former client consents after consultation. [RPC 1.9(a)] Also, a lawyer is prohibited from knowingly representing a person in the same or a substantially related matter in which a firm with which the lawyer formerly was associated had previously represented a client: (i) whose interests are materially adverse to that person; and (ii) about whom the lawyer had acquired information protected by RPC 1.6 (relating to confidentiality of information) and RPC 1.9(c) (relating to using or revealing information) that is material to the matter, unless the former client consents after consultation. [RPC 1.9(b)]

a. Using or Revealing Information
A lawyer who has formerly represented a client in a matter or whose present or former firm has done so may not thereafter: (i) use information relating to the representation to the disadvantage of the former client or for the advantage of the lawyer or a third person, except as permitted or required by RPC 1.6 (relating to confidentiality of information), RPC 3.3 (relating to candor toward the tribunal), or RPC 4.1 (relating to truthfulness in statements to others); or (ii) reveal information relating to the representation except as permitted or required by RPC 1.6 or 3.3 with respect to a client. [RPC 1.9(c)]

5. Problems with Testifying for Client
An attorney ordinarily may not represent a client in litigation where the attorney is likely to be a necessary witness. (*Note:* An attorney *may* act as advocate in a trial in which another attorney in the attorney's firm is likely to be called as a witness unless precluded from doing so by the rules relating to conflict of interest.) If an attorney is likely to be a necessary witness, the attorney should refuse employment or, if he has already been retained, should withdraw from the case. Clearly, if there is a question as to whether he will be called upon as a

witness, all doubts should be resolved in favor of withdrawing from the case. There are *three recognized exceptions* to this prohibition noted below. [RPC 3.7]

a. **Uncontested Matter**
   If the attorney's testimony will relate solely to an uncontested matter, representation is not prohibited.
   Example: In a proceeding concerning an uncontested will, an attorney may testify as to the testamentary capacity of the decedent.

b. **Nature and Value of Legal Services**
   If the attorney's testimony will concern only the nature and value of legal services rendered to the client, the attorney will not be prohibited from representing the client.
   Example: B's suit against C includes a legitimate cause of action for attorneys' fees. Attorney X may testify as to the value of the services that he has rendered to B.

c. **Substantial Hardship**
   If the withdrawal of the attorney for the purpose of testifying would result in substantial hardship to the client because of the *distinctive value* of the attorney or firm to the case, the attorney may continue to represent the client.
   Example: X represents B in a highly complex case that is in the middle of trial. Defendant C attempts to bribe X. X's testimony becomes highly relevant to the case at this point, but he cannot withdraw from the case because B would not be able to secure adequate replacement representation on such notice. X should be permitted to testify and to continue to represent B.

6. **Conflicts in Corporate Representation**
   A special problem of multiple representation occurs when a lawyer is asked to represent both an entity such as a corporation and its labor force or a corporation and its governing components (*i.e.*, its directors and officers). [RPC 1.13]

   a. **Lawyer Represents Organization**
      A lawyer employed or retained to represent an organization represents the organization acting through its duly authorized constituents.

   b. **Lawyer Must Act in Best Interest of Organization**
      If a lawyer for an organization knows that an officer, employee, or other person associated with the organization is engaged in action, intends to act, or refuses to act in a matter related to the representation that is a violation of a legal obligation to the organization, or a violation of law that reasonably might be imputed to the organization, and is likely to result in substantial injury to the organization, the lawyer must proceed as is reasonably necessary in the best interest of the organization.

   c. **Factors Lawyer Must Consider in Representing Organization**
      In determining how to proceed, the lawyer must give due consideration to the seriousness of the violation and its consequences, the scope and nature of the lawyer's representation, the responsibility in the organization and the apparent motive of the person involved, the policies of the organization concerning such matters, and any other relevant considerations. Any measures taken must be designed to minimize disruption of the organization and the risk of revealing information relating to the representation to persons outside the organization. Such measures may include, for example:

      1) Asking for *reconsideration* of the matter;

      2) Advising that a *separate legal opinion* on the matter be sought for presentation to the appropriate authority in the organization; and

      3) Referring the matter to a *higher authority* in the organization, including, if warranted by the seriousness of the matter, referral to the highest authority that can act on behalf of the organization as determined by applicable law.

   d. **Lawyer's Responsibility Based on Action of Organization's Highest Authority**
      When the organization's highest authority insists upon action, or inaction, that is

clearly a violation of law and is likely to result in *substantial injury to the organization,* the lawyer may resign in accordance with Rule 1.16 (relating to termination of representation) and make such disclosures as are consistent with Rules 1.6 (relating to confidentiality), 3.3 (relating to candor toward the tribunal), and 4.1 (relating to truthfulness in statements to others).

e. **Disclosing Identity of Client**
In dealing with an organization's directors, officers, employees, members, shareholders, or other constituents, a lawyer must explain the identity of the client when it is apparent that the organization's interests are adverse to those of the constituents with whom the lawyer is dealing.

f. **Multiple Representation Permissible**
A lawyer representing an organization may also represent any of its directors, officers, employees, members, shareholders, or other constituents, subject to the provisions of RPC 1.7 (relating to conflict of interest—disclosure and consent requirements). If the organization's consent to the dual representation is required, the consent must be given by an appropriate official of the organization other than the individual who is to be represented, or by the shareholders.

7. **Imputed Disqualification**

a. **Representation by One Lawyer Imputed to Entire Firm**
When lawyers are associated in a firm, none of them may knowingly represent a client when any one of them practicing alone would be prohibited from doing so by other RPC provisions relating to conflict of interest. [RPC 1.10]

b. **Effect of Lawyer's Termination with Firm**
When a lawyer has terminated an association with a firm, the firm is not prohibited from thereafter representing a person with interests materially adverse to those of a client represented by the formerly associated lawyer and not currently represented by the firm, *unless*: (i) the matter is the same or substantially related to that in which the formerly associated lawyer represented the client; and (ii) any lawyer remaining in the firm has information protected by RPC 1.6 (relating to confidentiality) and RPC 1.9(c) (relating to using or revealing information pertaining to the representation) that is material to the matter. [RPC 1.10]

c. **Effect of Lawyer's Representation of Former Client**
When a lawyer becomes associated with a firm, the firm may not knowingly undertake or continue to represent a person in the same or a substantially related matter in which that lawyer, or a firm with which the lawyer was associated, had previously represented a client whose interests are materially adverse to that person *unless*:

(i) The disqualified lawyer *has no information* protected by Rule 1.6 (relating to confidentiality) or Rule 1.9 (relating to using or revealing information pertaining to the representation) that is material to the matter; or

(ii) The disqualified lawyer *had neither substantial involvement nor substantial material information* relevant to the matter, *is screened* from participation in the matter, and is apportioned no part of the fee therefrom.

[RPC 1.10(d)]

d. **Waiver of Imputed Disqualification**
A disqualification may be waived by the affected client. [RPC 1.10]

8. **Successive Government and Private Employment**

a. **Prior Public Legal Employment Creates Conflict of Interest**
Except as otherwise expressly permitted by law, a lawyer must not represent a private client in connection with a matter in which the lawyer participated personally and substantially as a public officer or employee, unless the appropriate government agency consents after consultation. [RPC 1.11]

b. **Lawyer's Conflict of Interest Not Necessarily Imputed to Firm**
No lawyer in a firm with which that lawyer is associated may knowingly undertake or

continue representation in a matter in which the lawyer participated personally and substantially as a public officer or employee unless:

(i) The disqualified lawyer is *screened* from any participation in the matter and is apportioned no part of the fee therefrom; and

(ii) *Written notice* is promptly given to the appropriate government agency to enable it to ascertain compliance with the provisions of this rule.

[RPC 1.11]

c. **Conflict of Interest May Arise If Lawyer Has Confidential Information**
Except as law may otherwise expressly permit, a lawyer having information that the lawyer knows is confidential government information about a person, acquired when the lawyer was a public officer or employee, may not represent a private client whose interests are adverse to that person in a matter in which the information could be used to the material disadvantage of that person. A firm with which that lawyer is associated may undertake or continue representation in the matter only if the disqualified lawyer is screened from any participation in the matter and is apportioned no part of the fee therefrom. [RPC 1.11]

d. **Prohibited Actions of Public Law Officer or Employee**
Except as otherwise expressly permitted by law, a lawyer serving as a public officer or employee may not: (i) participate in a matter in which the lawyer participated person-ally and substantially while in private practice or nongovernmental employment, unless under applicable law no one is, or by lawful delegation may be, authorized to act in the lawyer's stead in the matter; or (ii) negotiate for private employment with any person who is involved as a party or as attorney for a party in a matter in which the lawyer is participating personally and substantially, except that a lawyer serving as a law clerk to a judge or arbitrator may negotiate for private employment after so notify-ing the judge or arbitrator. [RPC 1.11]

9. **Former Judge, Arbitrator, Mediator, or Law Clerk**
A lawyer must not represent anyone in connection with a matter in which the lawyer par-ticipated personally and substantially as a judge or other adjudicative officer, arbitrator, mediator, or law clerk to such a person, unless all parties to the proceeding consent after disclosure. However, an arbitrator selected as a partisan of a party in a multimember arbitra-tion panel is not prohibited from subsequently representing that party. [RPC 1.12] If a lawyer is disqualified pursuant to this rule, no lawyer in a firm with which that lawyer is associated may knowingly undertake or continue representation in the matter unless: (i) the disqualified lawyer is screened from any participation in the matter and is apportioned no part of the fee therefrom; and (ii) written notice is promptly given to the appropriate tribunal to enable it to ascertain compliance with this rule.

10. **Screening Procedure**
For the purposes of Rules 1.10, 1.11, and 1.12 (*see* above), a disqualified lawyer will be deemed to have been *screened* from participation in a matter if:

(i) All material information which the disqualified lawyer has is isolated from the firm;

(ii) The disqualified lawyer is isolated from all contact with the client relating to the matter, and any witness for or against the client;

(iii) The disqualified lawyer and the firm are precluded from discussing the matter with each other;

(iv) The former client of the disqualified lawyer or firm which the lawyer was associated with receives notice of the conflict and an affidavit from the lawyer and firm describ-ing the procedures used to screen the lawyer and attesting that: (i) the lawyer will not participate in the matter and will not discuss the matter, (ii) no material information was transmitted by the lawyer before the screening procedure and notice to the former client, and (iii) the participating lawyers and employees know that the disqualified lawyer is screened from participation; and

(v) The disqualified lawyer and the firm reasonably believe that the steps taken to accomplish the screening are likely to be effective in preventing the disclosure of material information.

[RPC 1.10(e)]

E. ESTABLISHING COMPENSATION FOR LEGAL SERVICES
The fee arrangement for representation of a client is a matter left for the individual attorney and client. There are, however, certain principles governing the setting of fees and the forms of compensation.

1. Duty to Avoid Fee Misunderstandings
When the lawyer has not regularly represented the client, the basis or rate of the fee must be communicated to the client, preferably in writing, before or within a reasonable time after commencing the representation. [RPC 1.5]

2. Fee Must Not Be Excessive
A lawyer must not enter into an agreement for, charge, or collect an illegal or clearly excessive fee. Among the factors to be considered in determining the excessiveness of a fee are:

(i) The time and labor required;

(ii) The novelty and difficulty of the questions involved;

(iii) The skill required to perform the legal service;

(iv) The interference with other employment of the lawyer to the extent the likelihood of interference is apparent to the client;

(v) The customary fee within the locality for similar work;

(vi) The amount involved and the result obtained;

(vii) The nature and length of the relationship between the parties;

(viii) The experience, ability, and reputation of the attorney;

(ix) The time limitations imposed by the client or the circumstances; and

(x) Whether the fee is fixed or contingent.

[RPC 1.5(a)]

3. Minimum and Maximum Fee Schedules

a. Minimum Fees Violate Antitrust Laws
In *Goldfarb v. Virginia State Bar,* 421 U.S. 773 (1975), the United States Supreme Court declared that the imposition of minimum fee schedules by state bar associations was a violation of the federal antitrust laws.

b. Regulation of Maximum Fees
Maximum fees for certain types of legal work have been imposed in a number of jurisdictions either by statute, court rules, or court decisions. Areas affected by such regulation include workers' compensation claims, claims by soldiers against the government, probate and guardianship matters, Social Security claims, representation of indigents in criminal proceedings, and contingent fee arrangements. Such maximums are strictly enforced, although procedures may exist for additional compensation in unusual cases. Under the reasoning of the Court in *Arizona v. Maricopa County Medical Society,* 457 U.S. 332 (1982), an agreement by members of a bar association to follow a schedule of maximum fees would probably violate the antitrust laws.

4. Contingent Fees
A contingent fee is a fee that is dependent on the successful resolution of a client's case and payable from the judgment proceeds. Usually, such fees take the form of a set percentage of the recovery, the fee being zero if there is no recovery. The RPC approve of contingent fees within certain limits.

a. **Disclosure Requirements**

Except for contingent fee arrangements concerning the collection of commercial accounts and insurance company subrogation claims, a contingent fee agreement must be *in writing and signed in duplicate* by both the lawyer and the client within a reasonable time after making the agreement. The lawyer must retain a copy of the agreement (and proof that the duplicate copy was delivered or mailed to the client) for seven years after the conclusion of the contingent fee matter. The writing must state:

(i) *The name and address of each client and lawyer* to be retained;

(ii) *The nature of the claim or controversy* and other matters with reference to which services are to be performed;

(iii) *The contingency upon which compensation is to be paid*, and whether and to what extent the client will be liable to pay compensation other than from amounts collected for him by the lawyer;

(iv) *The method by which the fee is to be determined*, including the percentage(s) that will accrue to the lawyer out of amounts collected; and

(v) *The method by which litigation and other expenses are to be deducted* from the recovery and whether such expenses are to be deducted before or after the contingent fee is calculated.

Upon the conclusion of a contingent fee matter, the lawyer must provide the client with a written statement of the outcome of the matter. Such statement must also show any remittance to the client and the method of its determination. [RPC 1.5(c)]

b. **Offer of Other Fee Arrangement**

If there is any doubt as to whether a contingent fee is consistent with the client's best interest, the lawyer should offer the client alternative bases for the fee and explain their implications. [RPC 1.5, comment; *and see* ABA Formal Op. 94-389 (1994)] A contingent fee does not become improper simply because the client can afford to pay on some other basis or the case is a clear winner, but in those situations the lawyer should give the client a chance to make an informed choice as to the fee arrangement. [*See* ABA Formal Op. 94-389 (1994)]

c. **When Contingent Fee Is Prohibited**

A lawyer must not enter into an agreement for, charge, or collect:

(i) Any fee in a *domestic relations matter*, the payment or amount of which is contingent upon the securing of a divorce or upon the amount of alimony or support, or property settlement in lieu thereof; or

(ii) A contingent fee for representing a defendant in a *criminal case.*

[RPC 1.5] Subject to these limitations, contingent fees are generally permitted in civil cases.

d. **Discharge of a Lawyer on Contingency**

A client retains the authority to discharge an attorney hired on a contingency basis at any stage of the proceedings. Usually, but not always, the lawyer will be entitled to the reasonable value of the services performed up to the time of the discharge.

5. **Referral Fees Are Unethical**

"Referral fees," whereby the primary attorney pays a portion of his fee to a second attorney who suggested him to the client, are clearly unethical. A lawyer may ethically divide fees with an outside attorney only if the client consents and the total fee is reasonable. A lawyer is not required to disclose to the client the share of the fee each lawyer is to receive unless the client so requests. [RPC 1.5, comment] Rule 1.5 does not prohibit payment to a former partner or associate pursuant to a separation or retirement agreement.

Note: The rule does not require that a division of fees be in proportion to the services performed by each lawyer unless, with the client's written consent, each lawyer assumes joint responsibility for the representation. [RPC 1.5, comment]

V. THE LAWYER'S RESPONSIBILITIES TO THE CLIENT

A. THE BASIC OBLIGATIONS OF COMPETENCE AND CARE

Once having entered into an attorney-client relationship, a lawyer must act competently and with care in handling legal matters for that client. There are several facets to these related obligations.

1. Competent Representation

Competent representation requires the legal knowledge, skill, thoroughness, and preparation reasonably necessary for the representation. [RPC 1.1]

a. Knowledge and Skill

In determining whether a lawyer employs the requisite knowledge and skill in a particular matter, relevant factors include the relative complexity and specialized nature of the matter, the lawyer's general experience, the lawyer's training and experience in the field in question, the preparation and study the lawyer is able to give the matter, and whether it is feasible to refer the matter to, or associate or consult with, a lawyer of established competence in the field in question. In many instances, the required proficiency is that of a general practitioner. Expertise in a particular field of law may be required in some circumstances.

b. Thoroughness and Preparation

Adequate preparation is determined in part by what is at stake. Major litigation and complex transactions ordinarily require more elaborate treatment than matters of lesser consequence.

2. Diligence

A lawyer must act with reasonable diligence and promptness in representing a client and should represent a client zealously within the bounds of the law. [RPC 1.3]

3. Communication

A lawyer must keep a client reasonably informed about the status of a matter and promptly comply with reasonable requests for information. A lawyer must explain a matter to the extent reasonably necessary to permit the client to make informed decisions regarding the representation. [RPC 1.4]

B. THE DUTY TO PRESERVE CONFIDENTIALITY OF INFORMATION

1. Attorney-Client Privilege

Generally, the attorney-client privilege allows a client to refuse to testify and prevent his lawyer from testifying in court about communications between the two. It applies to confidential communications made by an individual to an attorney who is sought out for the purpose of obtaining legal advice. The theory behind the rule is to promote full disclosure between the client and the lawyer so that the lawyer can most capably represent the client. A client is a person or entity seeking legal services from a lawyer.

a. Corporate Client—Attorney-Employee Communications

When the client is a corporation, the privilege covers confidential communications between the lawyer and a high-ranking corporate official. It also covers communications between the lawyer and other corporate employees if:

(i) The employee communicates with the lawyer *at the direction of the employee's superior*;

(ii) The *employee knows* that the communication is to help the corporation get legal advice; and

(iii) The communication concerns a *subject within the scope of the employee's duties* for the corporation.

[Upjohn Co. v. United States, 449 U.S. 383 (1981)]

b. Privilege Limited to Communications Between Parties

The attorney-client privilege is limited to communications between the parties; the privilege does not apply to anything the attorney discovers on her own. If the substance of the communication is revealed to another who is not a party to the privileged relationship, the privilege is destroyed. However, an *exception* is made for those individuals, such as law clerks and secretaries, who are necessary to enable the lawyer to properly perform her duties. In such situations, the privilege extends to communications made in the presence of such essential third parties.

c.   Duration of Privilege
The attorney-client privilege continues indefinitely. Termination of the attorney-client *relationship* does not terminate the privilege. The privilege even survives the death of the client. *Rationale:* Knowing that communications will remain confidential even after death encourages the client to communicate fully and frankly with his attorney. [Swidler & Berlin v. United States, 524 U.S. 399 (1998)]

2.   Duty of Confidentiality
Except as noted below, a lawyer must not reveal confidential information relating to the representation of a client. [RPC 1.6] The duty of confidentiality applies to *all information* about a client "relating to the representation," regardless of when or where it was acquired, regardless of whether the client asked for it to be kept in confidence, and regardless of whether revealing it might harm or embarrass the client. The duty of confidentiality continues to apply even after the attorney-client relationship has terminated.

a.   Exceptions to Duty

1)   **Client Consent**
A lawyer may reveal information relating to the representation of a client if the client consents after consultation, or if such disclosure is impliedly authorized in order to carry out the representation. [RPC 1.6]

2)   **Prevention of Certain Criminal Acts**
A lawyer may reveal such information to the extent she reasonably believes necessary to prevent: (i) the client from committing a criminal or fraudulent act that the lawyer believes is likely to result in *death, substantial bodily harm, or substantial injury to the financial interests or property of another*; or (ii) *the wrongful execution or incarceration of another*. [RPC 1.6]

3)   **Required by Court, Ethics Rules, or Law**
A lawyer must comply with the *final* orders of a court or tribunal of competent jurisdiction requiring the lawyer to give information about a client. There are also circumstances under which the ethical rules permit or require the lawyer to disclose information relating to representation (*e.g.*, when false evidence introduced in court). Lastly, there may be statutes requiring the lawyer to reveal information in certain circumstances.

4)   **Need to Collect a Fee or Protect Reputation**
A lawyer may reveal such information to the extent the lawyer reasonably believes necessary to establish a claim or defense on behalf of the lawyer in a controversy between the lawyer and the client, to establish a defense to a criminal charge or civil claim against the lawyer based upon conduct in which the client was involved, or to respond to allegations in any proceeding concerning the lawyer's representation of the client. [RPC 1.6]

5)   **Rectify Client Fraud**
A lawyer may reveal such information to the extent the lawyer reasonably believes necessary to rectify client fraud in which the lawyer's services have been used, subject to Rule 3.3 (relating to candor toward the tribunal), *see* VI.E., *infra*. [RPC 1.6]

3.   Evaluation for Use by Third Persons
A lawyer may undertake an evaluation of a matter affecting a client for use by someone other than the client if:

(i)   The lawyer reasonably believes that making the evaluation is compatible with other aspects of the lawyer's relationship with the client; and

(ii)   The client consents after consultation.

[RPC 2.3] Such evaluation may include, for example, an opinion concerning the title of property rendered at the behest of a vendor for the information of a prospective purchaser, or at the behest of a borrower for the information of a prospective lender. In some situations, the evaluation may be required by a government agency.

Except as disclosure is required in connection with a report of an evaluation, information relating to the evaluation is otherwise protected by the confidentiality of information rules.

C. THE DUTY TO PROTECT A CLIENT'S PROPERTY

1. Separation of Funds
A lawyer must hold property of clients or third persons that is in the lawyer's possession in connection with a representation separate from the lawyer's own property. Funds must be kept in a separate account maintained in the state where the lawyer's office is situated, or elsewhere with the consent of the client or third person. Other property must be identified as such and appropriately safeguarded. [RPC 1.15]

a. Trust Accounts
A lawyer or law firm must hold all client funds, other than advances for costs and expenses, in an identifiable trust account. The lawyer must deposit nominal funds or funds to be held for a short time in a pooled ("IOLTA") account. The interest from this account is paid to the Massachusetts Legal Assistance Corporation and other charities designated by the Supreme Judicial Court. All other funds must be deposited in an individual account with interest payable to the client. [RPC 1.15(e)]

The only funds belonging to the lawyer or law firm that may be deposited in a trust account are: (i) funds reasonably sufficient to pay bank service charges, and (ii) funds belonging in part to the client and in part to the lawyer or firm and the lawyer's or firm's interest in that portion has not become fixed. If a client disputes any portion of a fee due a lawyer or firm, the disputed portion must remain in the trust account pending resolution of the controversy. [RPC 1.15(d)]

2. Recordkeeping Requirements
Complete records of the receipt, maintenance, and disposition of account funds and other property must be kept by the lawyer from the time of receipt to the time of final distribution and preserved for six years after termination of the representation. [RPC 1.15]

3. Lawyer's Duty to Keep Client Informed
Upon receiving funds or other property in which a client or third person has an interest, a lawyer must promptly notify the client or third person. [RPC 1.15]

4. Remittance of Funds and Property
Except as stated in RPC 1.15, or otherwise permitted by law or by agreement with the client, a lawyer must promptly deliver to the client or third person any funds or other property that the client or third person is entitled to receive and, upon request by the client or third person, must promptly render a full accounting regarding such property. [RPC 1.15]

5. Property Claimed by Lawyer and Other Person
When in the course of representation a lawyer is in possession of property in which both she and another person claim interests, such property must be kept separate by the lawyer until there is an accounting and severance of their interests. If a dispute arises concerning their respective interests, the disputed portion must be kept separate by the lawyer until resolution of the dispute. [RPC 1.15]

VI. THE DUTIES AND BOUNDS OF A LAWYER'S REPRESENTATION

A. DUTY AS ADVISER
In representing a client, a lawyer must exercise independent professional judgment and render candid advice. In rendering advice, a lawyer may refer not only to law, but to other considerations such as moral, economic, social, and political factors that may be relevant to the client's situation. [RPC 2.1]

B. SCOPE OF REPRESENTATION
Both the lawyer and the client are responsible for determining the scope of the representation that

the lawyer will engage in on behalf of the client. While the client has the ultimate authority to determine the scope of the lawyer's representation, the lawyer is responsible for informing the client of, and operating within, the limitations imposed by the RPC and applicable laws. Within these limits, the client has the right to discuss with the lawyer the means that will be employed to pursue a particular matter. However, this does not mean that the lawyer is required to pursue objectives or means simply because it is the client's wish, particularly if the lawyer finds the means or objectives repugnant to his beliefs. Further, a lawyer does not violate his obligations to the client by acceding to the reasonable requests of opposing counsel, by being punctual in fulfilling all professional commitments, by avoiding offensive tactics, or by treating all persons involved in the legal process with courtesy and consideration. [RPC 1.2]

1. **Means and Objectives**
   A lawyer is to exercise independent professional judgment at all stages of the relationship with a client. However, the ultimate control of a matter is in the hands of the client, and she has broad authority as to the course of action to be taken. This indicates that the lawyer may not take independent action on behalf of the client without consultation. A lawyer must seek the lawful objectives of his client through reasonable means permitted by law and the Rules.

   a. **Decisions to Be Made by Client**
      Decisions that will affect the merits of the case or substantially prejudice the client's rights may be made only by the client. Examples of decisions to be made by the client in a *civil case* include the decision to *accept a settlement* offer or to *waive an affirmative defense*. In a *criminal case*, it is the client's decision, after consultation with the attorney, as to what *plea* to enter, whether to waive a *jury trial*, whether the *client will testify*, and whether to *appeal* a conviction. [RPC 1.2(a)]

   b. **Decisions to Be Made by Lawyer**
      Those decisions left to the lawyer are not spelled out in the Rules. Generally, they are recognized to encompass the *procedural details* of litigation (often referred to as "tactics"), such as the choice of motions, the scope of discovery, nonsubstantive stipulations, which witnesses to call, and the nature of direct and cross-examination.

2. **Limiting the Scope of the Representation**
   When a lawyer represents a client, the representation does not imply that the lawyer endorses the client's political, economic, social, or moral positions. [RPC 1.2(b)] Nevertheless, lawyers sometimes feel a distinct lack of sympathy, or even antipathy, for their clients' positions or objectives. Where that is true, a lawyer may *limit* the objectives of a representation, provided that the client consents after consultation. [RPC 1.2(c)]

3. **Assisting the Client in Criminal or Fraudulent Conduct**
   A lawyer must not counsel or assist a client in conduct that the lawyer knows is criminal or fraudulent. [RPC 1.2(d)]

   a. **Discussing Proposed Conduct**
      A lawyer may discuss a proposed course of conduct with a client, and explain to the client that the conduct would be unlawful. [RPC 1.2(d)] If the client later uses the lawyer's advice to carry out a crime or fraud, that does not make the lawyer a party to the illegal conduct. However, the lawyer must *not* recommend the illegal conduct, nor instruct the client how to break the law and get away with it. [RPC 1.2, comment]

   b. **Withdrawal May Be Required**
      When a lawyer discovers that a client expects assistance that violates a law or a rule of professional conduct, the lawyer must tell the client why the lawyer cannot provide such assistance. [RPC 1.2(e)] If the client insists on illegal or unethical assistance, the lawyer must withdraw. [RPC 1.16(a)(1)]

   c. **Discovering Illegal Conduct**
      When a lawyer originally believes that a client is engaged in lawful conduct, but then discovers that the client is using the lawyer's services to commit a crime or fraud, the lawyer must withdraw. [RPC 1.16(a)(1); 1.2, comment]

   d. **Testing the Law**
      A lawyer may counsel and assist a client to make a good faith effort to determine the validity, scope, meaning, or application of a law. [RPC 1.2(d)] This is proper, even if it requires the client or the lawyer to disobey the law.

Example: The school board passed a rule prohibiting public school students from wearing certain articles of religious significance while attending school. A group of concerned citizens asked Attorney how to challenge the constitutionality of the rule. Attorney may advise them of the several ways to gain legal standing, including disobedience of the rule.

C. TRANSACTIONS WITH THIRD PERSONS

1. Communication with Adverse Parties and Third Persons

a. Communication with Represented Person Impermissible
In the representation of a client, a lawyer must not communicate about the subject of the representation with a person he knows to be represented by counsel in the matter unless the other counsel has granted permission or he is otherwise authorized by law to make such direct communication. [RPC 4.2] This rule applies to communications with *any person,* even if not a party to a formal adjudicative proceeding, contract, or negotiation, who is represented by counsel concerning the matter to which the communication relates.

1) Exception—Lawyer Does Not Have Actual Knowledge of Representation
The prohibition on communications with a represented person applies only if the lawyer knows that the person is represented in the matter to be discussed. This requires *actual knowledge* of the representation. However, knowledge may be inferred from the circumstances when there is substantial reason to believe that the person with whom communication is sought is represented in the matter to be discussed.

2) Exception—Communication Authorized by Law
A lawyer is not prohibited from communicating with a represented person if the communication is authorized by law. Communications authorized by law include, for example, the right of a party to a controversy with a government agency to speak with government officials about the matter. Such authorized communications also include constitutionally permissible investigative activities of lawyers representing governmental entities (directly or through investigative agents), prior to commencement of criminal or civil enforcement proceedings. For such investigative activities to be authorized, there must be judicial precedent that has either: (i) found such activities permissible under RPC 4.2; or (ii) found the rule inapplicable.

3) Exception—Matters Outside the Representation
Note that RPC 4.2 does not prohibit communications with a represented person, or an employee or agent of such person, concerning matters outside the representation. Also, parties to a matter may communicate directly with each other and a lawyer having independent justification for communicating with a represented person is permitted to do so.

b. Application of Rule to Organizations
Corporations and other organizations are "persons" for the purposes of this rule. Thus, a lawyer must get the consent of the organization's counsel before communicating with:

(i) A person who has present *managerial responsibility* for the organization;

(ii) A person whose conduct may be *imputed* to the organization for purposes of criminal or civil liability; or

(iii) A person whose statements may constitute an *admission* by the organization.

[RPC 4.2, comment] However, consent is usually *not* needed before talking with a *former employee*, unless the former employee has extensive knowledge of the organization's relevant privileged information. [*See, e.g.,* ABA Formal Op. 91-359 (1991); Camden v. Maryland, 910 F. Supp. 1115 (D. Md. 1996)]

c. Communication with Unrepresented Person Permissible
When a person does not have counsel of his own, a lawyer representing a client may communicate with such person directly. However, when dealing with the unrepresented person, the lawyer must not state or imply that she is disinterested. When the lawyer knows or reasonably should know that the unrepresented person misunderstands the

lawyer's role in the matter, the lawyer must make reasonable efforts to correct the misunderstanding. [RPC 4.3]

Note: During the course of a client's representation, a lawyer must not give advice to an unrepresented person, other than to secure counsel, if the interests of such person are or have a reasonable possibility of being in conflict with the client's interests.

2. **Respect for Rights of Third Persons**
   In representing a client, a lawyer must not use means that have no substantial purpose other than to embarrass, delay, or burden a third person; or use methods of obtaining evidence that violate the legal rights of such a person. [RPC 4.4]

3. **Truthfulness in Statements to Others**
   In representing a client, a lawyer must not knowingly: (i) make a false statement of material fact or law to a third person; or (ii) fail to disclose a material fact to a third person when disclosure is necessary to avoid assisting a criminal or fraudulent act by a client, unless disclosure is prohibited by RPC 1.6 (relating to confidentiality of information). [RPC 4.1]

D. THE CONDUCT OF LITIGATION

The general precepts governing a lawyer's professional responsibility obviously remain in effect during the course of an actual trial, whether judicial or administrative in nature. The RPC also set out certain specific principles governing the lawyer's zealous representation during the conduct of litigation.

1. **Meritorious Claims and Contentions**
   A lawyer must not bring or defend a proceeding, nor assert or controvert an issue therein, unless there is a basis for doing so that is not frivolous (*e.g.*, a good faith argument for an extension, modification, or reversal of existing law). A lawyer for the defendant in a criminal proceeding, or the respondent in a proceeding that could result in incarceration, may nevertheless defend a proceeding so as to require that every element of the case be established. [RPC 3.1]

2. **Expediting Litigation**
   A lawyer must make reasonable efforts to expedite litigation consistent with the interests of the client. [RPC 3.2] Delay should not be indulged merely for the convenience of the advocates or for the purpose of frustrating an opposing party's attempts to obtain rightful redress.

E. CANDOR TOWARD THE TRIBUNAL

A lawyer must not knowingly:

(i) Make a false statement of material fact or law to a tribunal;

(ii) Fail to disclose a material fact to a tribunal when disclosure is necessary to avoid assisting a criminal or fraudulent act by the client, except as provided in Rule 3.3(e), *see* 1.a.2), below;

(iii) Fail to disclose to the tribunal legal authority in the controlling jurisdiction known to the lawyer to be directly adverse to the position of the client and not disclosed by opposing counsel; or

(iv) Offer evidence that the lawyer knows to be false, except as provided in Rule 3.3(e), *see* 1.a.2), below. If a lawyer has offered, or the lawyer's testifying client or witnesses have given, material evidence and the lawyer comes to know of its falsity, he must take reasonable remedial measures.

The duties apply until the conclusion of the proceeding, which includes appeals, even if compliance requires disclosure of information otherwise protected by the rules on confidentiality. [RPC 3.3]

1. **False Evidence**
   A lawyer *must* refuse to offer evidence that the lawyer *knows* is false regardless of the client's wishes. A lawyer *may* refuse to offer evidence that the lawyer *reasonably believes* to be false even if the client instructs him to use it. [RPC 3.3(a), (c)]

   a. **False Testimonial Evidence (Witness Perjury)**

      1) **Nonclient Witnesses**
         Under the above rule, a lawyer generally cannot call a witness he believes will

testify falsely, and if he discovers a witness has done so, he must reveal it to the court.

2) Criminal Clients

Unlike in civil cases where the lawyer can refuse to call his perjurious client as a witness (*see* 3), *infra*), application of the rule is trickier when the client is a criminal defendant. In criminal cases, it is the client (not the lawyer) who decides whether the client will testify (*see* B.1.a., *supra*); furthermore, a criminal defendant has a constitutional right to testify. The Rules require a lawyer to take a certain course of action regarding a client's false testimony or intention to testify falsely depending on when the lawyer discovers the false testimony or intention to testify falsely.

a) Discovers Intention Before Representation

If a lawyer discovers a defendant's intention to testify falsely before accepting representation of the defendant, the lawyer must attempt to persuade the defendant not to testify falsely. If persuasion fails, the lawyer must not accept representation. [RPC 3.3(e)]

b) Discovers Intention After Representation but Before Trial

If a lawyer discovers the intention of his client to testify falsely after representation but before trial, the lawyer must attempt to persuade his client not to testify falsely. If persuasion fails, the lawyer must seek to withdraw. If disclosure of privileged or prejudicial information is necessary to withdrawal, the lawyer must request withdrawal by making an application ex parte before a judge other than the judge who will preside at trial. If the lawyer is unable to withdraw, the lawyer may not prevent the client from testifying. [RPC 3.3(e)]

c) Discovers Intention During Trial

If a lawyer discovers the intention of his client to testify falsely while the trial is ongoing, the lawyer must attempt to persuade his client not to testify falsely. If persuasion fails, the lawyer may seek to withdraw, but he has no obligation to withdraw if he reasonably believes that to do so would prejudice the client. As noted above, the lawyer may not prevent the client from testifying. [RPC 3.3(e)]

d) Discovers False Testimony During Trial

If during the client's testimony or after the client has testified, the lawyer knows that the client has testified falsely, the lawyer must attempt to persuade the client to rectify the false testimony. If the client refuses or is unable to do so, the lawyer is prohibited from revealing the false testimony to the tribunal. [RPC 3.3(e)]

e) Lawyer May Not Assist Client in Presenting False Testimony

If in any of the above circumstances the lawyer cannot convince his client to testify truthfully or recant if she has testified falsely, the lawyer may not examine his client in such a manner to elicit false testimony, nor argue the probative value of the false testimony in closing argument or on appeal. [RPC 3.3(e)]

3) Civil Clients

If a lawyer knows that his client in a civil case intends to lie on the stand, the lawyer can and *must* refuse to call the client as a witness. If the lawyer learns after the fact that the client has perjured herself, the lawyer should: (i) attempt to persuade the client to recant; (ii) if persuasion fails, seek to withdraw; and (iii) if withdrawal will not remedy the situation or is impossible, disclose the matter to the court, even if doing so will result in a mistrial. [RPC 3.3 and comments]

b. Duration of Obligation to Remedy False Evidence

The obligation to reveal false evidence ends at the conclusion of the proceeding, including all appeals. Thus, if the lawyer learns of the perjury *after* the proceeding and any appeal, he has no duty to reveal it to anyone.

2. Required Disclosures in Ex Parte Proceeding

In an ex parte proceeding, a lawyer must inform the tribunal of all material facts known to the lawyer that will enable the tribunal to make an informed decision, whether or not the facts are adverse to his client. [RPC 3.3]

F.   FAIRNESS TO OPPOSING PARTY AND COUNSEL

A lawyer must not:

(i)   Unlawfully *obstruct* another party's *access to evidence* or unlawfully alter, destroy, or conceal a document or other material having potential evidentiary value, or counsel or assist another person to do any such act;

(ii)   *Falsify evidence*, counsel or assist a witness to testify falsely, or offer an inducement to a witness that is prohibited by law;

(iii)   *Knowingly disobey an obligation* under the rules of a tribunal except for an open refusal based on an assertion that no valid obligation exists;

(iv)   In pretrial procedure, *make frivolous discovery requests* or fail to make reasonably diligent efforts to comply with legally proper discovery requests by an opposing party;

(v)   In trial, *allude to any matter* that the lawyer does not reasonably believe is relevant or that will *not* be *supported by admissible evidence,* assert personal knowledge of facts in issue except when testifying as a witness, or state a personal opinion as to the justness of a cause, the credibility of a witness, the culpability of a civil litigant, or the guilt or innocence of an accused;

(vi)   *Request a person* other than a client *to refrain from voluntarily giving relevant information* to another party unless: (i) the person is a relative or an employee or other agent of a client; and (ii) the lawyer reasonably believes that the person's interests will not be adversely affected by refraining from giving such information;

(vii)   *Pay, offer to pay, or acquiesce in the payment of compensation* to a witness contingent on the content of her testimony or the outcome of the case. But a lawyer may advance, guarantee, or acquiesce in the payment of: (i) expenses reasonably incurred by a witness in attending or testifying; (ii) reasonable compensation to a witness for loss of time in attending or testifying; and (iii) reasonable compensation for the services of an expert;

(viii)   *Present, participate in presenting, or threaten to present criminal or disciplinary charges* solely to obtain an advantage in a civil matter; or

(ix)   In appearing in a professional capacity before a tribunal, *engage in conduct manifesting bias or prejudice* based on race, sex, religion, national origin, disability, age, or sexual orientation against a party, witness, counsel, or other person.

[RPC 3.4]

G.   AVOIDING IMPROPER CONTACT WITH JURORS AND THE COURT

Based on its concern with the integrity of legal proceedings and the importance of the appearance of fairness to our legal system, the RPC forbid improper contact with jurors and the court, whether it be a judicial or administrative tribunal. Specifically, a lawyer *must not:* (i) *seek to influence* a judge, juror, prospective juror, or other official by means prohibited by law; (ii) *communicate ex parte* with such a person except as permitted by law; (iii) engage in conduct intended to *disrupt* a tribunal; or (iv) *initiate communication* with a juror after the discharge of the jury, except by leave of court granted for good cause. [RPC 3.5]

Note: If a juror initiates contact with a lawyer, the lawyer must not ask questions or make comments intended to harass or embarrass the juror or to influence her actions in future jury service. Under no circumstances may a lawyer inquire of a juror concerning the jury's deliberation process.

H.   ADVOCATE IN NONADJUDICATIVE PROCEEDINGS

A lawyer representing a client before a legislative or administrative tribunal in a nonadjudicative proceeding must disclose that the appearance is in a representative capacity. [RPC 3.9]

I.   TRIAL PUBLICITY

To maintain the dignity of the profession and ensure against prejudicial publicity, the RPC provide restraints on public statements by lawyers on either side with regard to the matter at issue in a civil or criminal trial.

1. **Basic Test**

   A lawyer who is participating or has participated in the investigation or litigation of a matter must not make an extrajudicial statement that a reasonable person would expect to be disseminated by means of public communication if the lawyer knows or reasonably should know that it will have a substantial likelihood of materially prejudicing an adjudicative proceeding in the matter. This prohibition also applies to any such lawyer's associates in a firm or government agency. [RPC 3.6(a)]

2. **Permitted References**

   A lawyer may state:

   (i)   The *claim, offense, or defense* involved and, except when prohibited by law, the *identity* of the persons involved;

   (ii) The *information contained in a public record;*

   (iii) That an *investigation* of a matter is in progress;

   (iv) The *scheduling or result* of any step in litigation;

   (v)   A *request for assistance in obtaining evidence* and information necessary thereto;

   (vi) A *warning of danger* concerning the behavior of a person involved when there is reason to believe that there exists the likelihood of substantial harm to an individual or to the public interest; and

   (vii) In a criminal case, in addition to the above, (i) the identity, residence, occupation, and family status of the accused; (ii) if the accused has not been apprehended, *information necessary to aid in apprehension* of that person; (iii) the fact, time, and place of arrest; and (iv) the identity of investigating and arresting officers or agencies and the length of the investigation.

   [RPC 3.6(b)]

3. **Areas Likely to Have Prejudicial Effect**

   There are certain subjects that are more likely than not to have a material prejudicial effect on a proceeding, particularly when they refer to a civil matter triable by a jury, a criminal matter, or any other proceeding that could result in incarceration. These subjects relate to:

   (i)   The *character, credibility, reputation, or criminal record* of a party, suspect in a criminal investigation, or witness; the *identity of a witness*; or the *expected testimony* of a party or witness;

   (ii) In a criminal case or proceeding that could result in incarceration, the *possibility of a guilty plea* to the offense or the existence or contents of any *confession,* admission, or statement given by a defendant or suspect or that person's refusal or failure to make a statement;

   (iii) The performance or *results of any examination* or test or the refusal or failure of a person to submit to an examination or test, or the identity or nature of physical evidence expected to be presented;

   (iv) Any *opinion as to the guilt or innocence* of a defendant or suspect in a criminal case or proceeding that could result in incarceration;

   (v)   *Information* the lawyer knows or reasonably should know is likely to be *inadmissible as evidence* in a trial and would, if disclosed, create a substantial risk of prejudicing an impartial trial; or

   (vi) The fact that a defendant has been *charged with a crime,* unless there is included therein a statement explaining that the charge is merely an accusation and that the defendant is presumed innocent until and unless proved guilty.

   Another relevant factor in determining prejudice is the *nature of the proceeding*. Thus, criminal jury trials are most sensitive to extrajudicial speech, while civil trials may be less sensitive. Nonjury hearings and arbitration proceedings may be even less affected. [*See* RPC 3.6, comment]

4. Right of Reply

A lawyer is permitted to make a statement that a reasonable lawyer would believe is required to protect a client from the substantial undue prejudicial effect of recent publicity not initiated by the lawyer or her client. Any statement made pursuant to this rule must be limited to information that is necessary to mitigate the recent adverse publicity. [RPC 3.6(c)] A lawyer also is permitted to reply to charges publicly made against her and to participate in proceedings of a legislative, administrative, or other investigative body.

VII. TERMINATION OF THE ATTORNEY-CLIENT RELATIONSHIP

A. IN GENERAL

Just as the Rules of Professional Conduct regulate the formation of attorney-client relationships, they also spell out the proper procedures for withdrawal from the representation of a client. The Rules distinguish between situations where the attorney must terminate employment (mandatory withdrawal) and situations where she is permitted to terminate employment (permissive withdrawal).

B. MANDATORY WITHDRAWAL

Withdrawal is mandatory (after obtaining permission from the tribunal if required by its rules), or representation should be declined if:

(i) The representation will result in *violation of the Rules of Professional Conduct* or other law;

(ii) The lawyer's *physical or mental condition materially impairs* the lawyer's ability to represent the client; or

(iii) The lawyer is *discharged.*

[RPC 1.16]

C. PERMISSIVE WITHDRAWAL

A lawyer may withdraw from representing a client if withdrawal can be accomplished without material adverse effect on the interests of the client, or if:

(i) The *client persists* in a course of action involving the lawyer's services that the lawyer reasonably believes is *criminal or fraudulent*;

(ii) The *client has used the lawyer's services to perpetrate a crime or fraud*;

(iii) A client insists upon pursuing an objective that the lawyer considers *repugnant or imprudent*;

(iv) The *client fails substantially to fulfill an obligation to the lawyer* regarding the lawyer's services and has been given reasonable warning that the lawyer will withdraw unless the obligation is fulfilled;

(v) The representation will result in an *unreasonable financial burden* on the lawyer or has been rendered unreasonably difficult by the client; or

(vi) Other *good cause* for withdrawal exists.

[RPC 1.16]

D. WHEN LAWYER MUST CONTINUE REPRESENTATION

If permission for withdrawal from employment is required by the rules of a tribunal, a lawyer must continue representation until the tribunal consents to withdrawal. [RPC 1.16(c)]

E. PROTECTION OF CLIENT'S INTERESTS ON TERMINATION

Upon termination of representation, a lawyer must take steps to the extent reasonably practicable to protect a client's interests, such as giving reasonable notice to the client, allowing time for employment of other counsel, surrendering papers and property to which the client is entitled, and refunding any advance payment of fee that has not been earned. [RPC 1.16]

F. MATERIALS THAT MUST BE MADE AVAILABLE TO CLIENT

A lawyer must make available to a former client, within a reasonable time following the client's request for his file, the following:

(i) *All papers, documents, and other materials* the client supplied to the lawyer;

(ii) *All pleadings and other papers* filed with or by the court or served by or upon any party;

(iii) *All investigatory or discovery documents* for which the client has paid the lawyer's out-of-pocket costs, including but not limited to medical records, photographs, tapes, disks, investigative reports, expert reports, depositions, and demonstrative evidence;

(iv) If the lawyer and client *entered into a contingent fee agreement*, the lawyer must provide *copies of the lawyer's work product* (*i.e.,* documents and tangible things prepared in the course of representation by the lawyer or someone at the lawyer's direction, such as legal research, records of witness interviews, and correspondence); and

(v) If the lawyer and client *did not enter into a contingent fee agreement*, the lawyer must provide the client with *that portion of the work product for which the client has paid*.

[RPC 1.16(e)] The lawyer may at his own expense retain copies of any materials contained in (i) or (iii) above. The client may be required to pay any copying charge consistent with the lawyer's actual cost for the materials contained in (ii) and (iv) above, unless the client has already paid for such materials. A lawyer may not refuse, on the grounds of nonpayment, to make available materials in the client's file when retention would unfairly prejudice the client.

VIII. THE LAWYER'S RESPONSIBILITIES TO THE LEGAL PROFESSION

A. IN GENERAL
Given the unique nature of the legal profession in society, every lawyer bears the burden of assisting in the improvement of the legal system and ensuring that the profession itself is not brought into disrepute. Many of the RPC provisions discussed so far attempt to accomplish this by regulating relationships with a client and need not be restated here. However, there are other provisions of the Rules, as well as some general principles, that give further substance to the lawyer's obligations to the legal system and profession. These are set forth below.

B. LAWYER'S CONDUCT WHILE NOT IN PRACTICE
Lawyers acting in their private business or personal capacities are still bound by professional standards of conduct and can be disciplined for conduct violating such standards.

C. GENERAL GUIDELINES FOR A LAWYER'S CONDUCT
When explicit ethical guidelines do not exist to control a lawyer's conduct, he should determine his conduct by acting in a manner that promotes public confidence in the integrity and efficiency of the legal system and profession.

D. JUDICIAL AND LEGAL OFFICIALS
A lawyer must not make a statement that the lawyer knows to be false or with reckless disregard as to its truth or falsity concerning the qualifications or integrity of a judge or magistrate, or of a candidate for appointment to judicial or legal office. A lawyer who is a candidate for judicial office must comply with the applicable provisions of the Code of Judicial Conduct. [RPC 8.2]

E. THE SPECIAL ROLE OF THE PUBLIC PROSECUTOR
The prosecutor in a criminal case must:

(i) Refrain from prosecuting a charge that the prosecutor knows is not supported by *probable cause*;

(ii) Make reasonable efforts to ensure that the *accused has been advised of the right to, and the procedure for obtaining, counsel* and has been given reasonable opportunity to obtain counsel;

(iii) *Not seek* to obtain from an unrepresented accused a *waiver* of important pretrial rights such as the right to a preliminary hearing, unless a court first has obtained from the accused a knowing and intelligent written waiver;

(iv) Make *timely disclosure* to the defense of all evidence or information known to the prosecutor that tends to negate the guilt of the accused or mitigate the offense, and in connection with sentencing, disclose to the defense and to the tribunal all unprivileged mitigating information known to the prosecutor, except when the prosecutor is relieved of this responsibility by a protective order of the tribunal;

(v) Exercise *reasonable care to prevent* investigators, law enforcement personnel, employees, or other persons assisting or associated with the prosecutor in a criminal case from making an *extrajudicial statement* that the prosecutor would be prohibited from making under RPC 3.6 (relating to trial publicity);

(vi) *Not subpoena a lawyer in a criminal proceeding* to present evidence about a client unless the prosecutor reasonably believes: (i) the information is not protected by privilege; (ii) the evidence is essential to an ongoing investigation or prosecution; and (iii) there is no feasible alternative to obtain the information;

(vii) Refrain from making *extrajudicial comments* that have a substantial likelihood of heightening public condemnation of the accused (except for statements that are necessary to inform the public of the nature and extent of the prosecutor's action and that serve a legitimate law enforcement purpose);

(viii) *Not assert personal knowledge* of facts in issue, except when testifying as a witness; and

(ix) *Not assert a personal opinion* as to the justness of a cause, the credibility of a witness, the culpability of a civil litigant, or the guilt or innocence of an accused.

[RPC 3.8]

F. REPORTING PROFESSIONAL MISCONDUCT

A lawyer having knowledge that another lawyer has committed a violation of the Rules that raises a *substantial question* as to that lawyer's honesty, trustworthiness, or fitness as a lawyer in other respects, should inform the Bar Counsel's office. A lawyer having knowledge that a judge has committed a violation of applicable rules of judicial conduct that raises a substantial question as to the judge's fitness for office likewise should inform the Commission on Judicial Conduct. This rule does not require disclosure of information otherwise protected by RPC 1.6 (relating to confidentiality of information). [RPC 8.3]

BAR REVIEW

SECURED TRANSACTIONS

TABLE OF CONTENTS

I. INTRODUCTION

A. OVERVIEW OF STATUTORY SCHEME

The hardest part of secured transactions is understanding how the major concepts fit together. This general overview introduces you to the statutory scheme and terminology of Article 9, which governs secured transactions. Secured transactions questions generally involve credit transactions. Typically one party (the *debtor*) buys something from another (the *creditor or secured party*) but does not pay immediately. The creditor wants to be able to rely on something other than the debtor's promise to ensure payment. A security interest is that something. A security interest is a limited right in specific personal property (the *collateral*) of the debtor that allows the creditor to take the property if the debtor fails to fulfill the credit obligation. A security interest is effective between the parties when certain steps are taken to *attach* the interest. Once the interest attaches, as between the parties, if the debtor defaults, the creditor has some right to take the collateral to satisfy the obligation. However, attachment generally does not provide the creditor with rights against third parties who might also have an interest in the same collateral. To gain rights over such third parties, the creditor must take additional steps to *perfect* the security interest. Perfection basically serves as a form of notice that the creditor has a security interest in the collateral, and because of this notice, the creditor has rights in the collateral superior to certain third parties who might also have an interest in the same collateral (there are rules of *priority* to determine whose rights are superior).

B. SCOPE OF ARTICLE 9

1. In General

Article 9, with the exceptions listed in C., below, applies to all kinds of contractual security interests in personal property and fixtures (*i.e.,* personal property that is firmly affixed to real property; *see* IV.B.3.f.1), *infra*). [U.C.C. §9-109(a)(1)] A *security interest* is an interest in personal property or fixtures that secures payment or performance of an obligation. [U.C.C. §1-201(37)]

a. Sales of Receivables

Outright *sales* of accounts, chattel paper, payment intangibles, and promissory notes are also treated as security interests and are covered by Article 9. [U.C.C. §§1-201(37), 9-109(a)(3)] (For definitions of these terms, *see* E.2., *infra*.)

Example: Becky's Interiors, Inc. does home remodeling under oral contracts in which her customers promise to pay her in the future for her services rather than paying her immediately (these promises constitute "accounts"). Becky's is in need of cash and sells its outstanding accounts to Alex Finance Co., which immediately pays Becky's. Even though this is an outright sale of the accounts, Article 9 is triggered and Alex Finance must comply with Article 9 to protect its interest against competing third parties.

b. Consignments

In a typical consignment, the consignor (*i.e.,* the owner of goods, such as a manufacturer or wholesaler) retains title to goods and delivers them to the consignee (*e.g.,* a retailer) for sale to the public. If the goods are not sold, the consignee may return them to the consignor. In cases where a creditor of the consignee would have difficulty distinguishing inventory that a consignee is selling on consignment from inventory that the consignee actually owns, Article 9 considers the consignment to be a security interest and requires the consignor to comply with its provisions to give notice to the consignee's creditors. A consignor *must comply with Article 9* to protect its interest in consigned goods against creditors of the consignee if:

(i) The consigned goods are worth a total of *$1,000 or more;*

(ii) The consignor did *not* use the goods for personal, family, or household purposes (*e.g.,* a person's consignment of his old clothes would not be covered by Article 9); and

(iii) The consignee is a person who:

    i. Deals in *goods of that kind* under a name *other than the consignor's;*

    ii. Is *not an auctioneer*; and

   iii. Is *not generally known* by her creditors to be substantially engaged in *selling the goods of others* (*i.e.,* the goods are not being sold at a "consignment store").

[U.C.C. §9-102(a)(20)]
Example: Johnny, a music promoter, delivers compact discs ("CDs") worth $1,500 by the band No Tolerance to CD Barn to be sold on consignment. If CD Barn is not a consignment store, Johnny must comply with the provisions of Article 9 to protect his interest in the CDs against CD Barn's creditors.

 c. Agricultural Liens
  Article 9 also covers agricultural liens, *i.e.,* nonpossessory liens on farm products (crops, livestock, etc.; *see* E.1.a.2), *infra*) that are created by state statute in favor of a person providing goods, services, or rental land to a farmer. While the statutes creating the liens govern their creation and enforcement, Article 9 governs their *perfection and priority*. [U.C.C. §9-109(a)(2)] The rules for perfection and priority of agricultural liens generally are the same as those for security interests.
  Example: Farmer Brown hires Laborer to grow crops on his farm in State X. Under state statute, Laborer has a lien on the crops he grows if Farmer Brown fails to pay him. Although Laborer can enforce his lien against Farmer Brown under the provisions of the State X statute, because his lien is an "agricultural lien" under Article 9, Laborer must comply with Article 9's perfection requirements to protect his interest from other creditors who also have interests in the crops.

2. Lease-Purchase Agreements
Certain types of transactions that the parties attempt to characterize as legal arrangements other than security interests may be governed by Article 9 if the transactions are, in fact, intended to have effect as security. The most common of these are lease-purchase agreements intended for security, rather than as "true" leases. Whether a lease of goods is intended as security is determined on a case-by-case basis. However, a transaction will be deemed to create a *security interest* rather than a lease if the rental obligation is *not terminable* by the lessee *and either*: (i) the lease term is equal to or greater than the remaining economic life of the goods; (ii) the lessee is bound to purchase the goods at the end of the lease or to renew the lease for the remaining economic life of the goods; or (iii) at the end of the lease, the lessee has an option to purchase the goods or renew the lease for the remaining economic life of the goods for no or nominal consideration. [U.C.C. §1-201(37)]

C. EXCEPTIONS
Article 9 does *not* apply to certain transactions, including:

(i) Transactions governed by other federal, state, or foreign laws;

(ii) Most transactions involving interests in or liens on *land* (except transactions involving fixtures);

(iii) Assignments of *tort claims* (other than *commercial tort claims, i.e.,* claims filed by organizations or claims filed by individuals that arose out of the individuals' business and that do not involve personal injury), except with respect to proceeds of the tort claims and priority in those proceeds;

(iv) Assignments of *deposit accounts* in *consumer transactions* (*i.e.,* transactions in which an individual creates a security interest in property bought or used for *personal, family, or household purposes*), except with respect to consumer deposit accounts that are proceeds of collateral, and priorities in those proceeds;

(v) State statutory or common law liens (other than agricultural liens) *given for services or materials,* such as mechanics' liens, except with respect to priorities in the personal property covered by the liens; and

(vi) Assignments of claims for *wages.*

[U.C.C. §9-109]

D. SECURITY INTERESTS

Security interests generally relate to financing. There are three major types of financing: consumer, business, and agricultural. Article 9 contains rules that apply generally to all three methods of financing and special rules that relate to each specific type.

1. Typical Security Interest

In a typical Article 9 security interest, one party (the **creditor**) gives another party (the **debtor**) something of value in exchange for the debtor's giving the creditor an interest in the debtor's personal property or fixtures (the **collateral**). The creditor's interest in the collateral is not a full ownership interest, but rather is the right to keep or sell the collateral if the debtor defaults on his obligation to the creditor.

2. Purchase Money Security Interests

A purchase money security interest ("PMSI") is a special type of security interest in goods that has priority over all other security interests in the same goods if certain requirements are met (*see* IV.B.3.d., *infra*). A PMSI arises when:

(i) A creditor **sells the goods** to the debtor on credit, retaining a security interest in the goods for all or part of the purchase price (creditor and seller are the same person); or

(ii) A creditor **advances funds** that are used by the debtor to purchase the goods (creditor and seller are different persons).

[U.C.C. §9-103]

Examples: 1) Matt purchases a $1,000 stereo on credit from Radio Hut and signs a security agreement giving Radio Hut a security interest in the stereo. Radio Hut has a PMSI in the stereo since in reality its credit enabled Matt to purchase the stereo.

2) Susan goes to Bank and asks Bank for $1,000 to purchase a stereo. Bank gives Susan the money, Susan signs a security agreement giving Bank a security interest in the stereo, and Susan purchases the stereo from Radio Hut using that $1,000. Bank has a PMSI in the stereo since it advanced the money that was used to purchase the stereo.

3) Alice goes to Bank and asks Bank for $1,000 to purchase a stereo. Bank gives Alice the money, and Alice signs a security agreement giving Bank a security interest in the stereo to be purchased. Alice gambles away the $1,000. Alice then goes to Radio Hut, buys a $1,000 stereo on credit from the store, and signs a security agreement giving Radio Hut a security interest in the stereo. Radio Hut has the PMSI and not Bank since Radio Hut advanced the funds that were used to pay for the stereo.

4) Brian wants to borrow $1,000 from Bank. Bank agrees to give Brian the money if he will give Bank a security interest in a stereo that he already owns. Although Bank may have a security interest, it will not have a PMSI in the stereo since Brian already owned the stereo (and so Bank did not advance funds that were used to purchase the stereo).

Note: A good rule of thumb is this: A PMSI exists if (i) credit was advanced or a loan was made for the **purpose** of enabling the debtor to **acquire** the collateral, and (ii) the credit or loan proceeds were **actually used** to acquire the collateral. The importance of whether a security interest is a PMSI will be discussed later.

a. PMSI in Software

If a creditor acquires a security interest that qualifies as a PMSI in a computer, the PMSI extends to any **software** that is also covered by the creditor's security interest if the software was purchased in a related transaction for use on the purchased computer.

Example: William buys a computer and some accompanying software on credit from Computer Hut and signs a security agreement giving Computer Hut a security interest in the computer and software. Computer Hut has a PMSI in both the computer and software as long as the software was bought for use on the purchased computer.

b. Dual Status Rule

A security interest in **nonconsumer goods** (*i.e.,* goods that are not used or bought for personal, family, or household purposes; *see* E.1.a.1), *infra*) **does not lose its status as a PMSI** if:

(i)   The purchase money collateral also secures an obligation that is not a purchase money obligation (*e.g.,* a lender lends the debtor money to purchase a widget machine and takes a security interest in the machine, and three months later lends the debtor additional funds secured by the formerly purchased machine);

(ii) Nonpurchase money collateral also secures the purchase money obligation (*e.g.,* a loan is secured both by collateral to be purchased by the debtor using the loan proceeds and by collateral already owned by the debtor); or

(iii) The purchase money obligation has been renewed, refinanced, consolidated, or restructured.

[U.C.C. §9-103(f)] This rule, often referred to as the *"dual status" rule*, applies only to nonconsumer goods. If the goods are *consumer goods*, the Code requires that the *courts* determine the appropriate rules. [U.C.C. §9-103(h)]

E.   COLLATERAL

As indicated above, collateral is the property subject to a security interest. Under Article 9, there are various types of collateral that may be divided into three broad classifications: tangible collateral or goods, intangible or semi-intangible collateral, and proceeds. It is important to know the collateral's type because certain rules (*e.g.,* rules for how to perfect and priority rules) depend on the type of collateral involved.

1.   Tangible Collateral or Goods

"Tangible" collateral or "goods" includes all things movable at the time the security interest attaches (including timber to be cut, unborn animals, and growing crops, but excluding money and intangibles) and fixtures.

a.   Types

There are four types of tangible collateral:

1)   Consumer Goods

Goods used or bought for personal, family, or household purposes (*e.g.,* a tractor used to mow the grass at home) are consumer goods. [U.C.C. §9-102(a)(23)]

2)   Farm Products

Crops, livestock, unmanufactured products of livestock (*e.g.,* eggs), and supplies used or produced in farming operations are farm products *if* they are in the possession of or used by a farmer. [U.C.C. §9-102(a)(34)]

3)   Inventory

Goods that are leased or that are held for sale or lease (*e.g.,* a tractor at a farm implement store), goods that are furnished or to be furnished under a contract of service, supplies that are used in manufacturing, materials that are used up quickly or consumed in a business (*e.g.,* fuel used to run a factory), and work in progress (*e.g.,* a partially built tractor) are inventory. [U.C.C. §9-102(a)(48)]

4)   Equipment

Goods that are not consumer goods, farm products, or inventory are equipment (*e.g.,* durable goods used in a business, such as machinery used in a factory or a painting on an office wall). [U.C.C. §9-102(a)(33)]

b.   Determining Type

The category into which tangible collateral is placed does not depend on the nature of the collateral, but rather on the *primary use* to which the debtor puts the collateral *at the time the security interest attaches*.

Example: If a debtor maintains an electric razor in his office to keep himself trim for business purposes, it is equipment. If he keeps the razor at home, it is consumer goods. If he opens a store and puts the razor in stock to sell, it is inventory.

2.   Intangible or Semi-Intangible Collateral

There are eight types of intangible or semi-intangible collateral:

a.   Instruments

Instruments are pieces of paper that represent the right to be paid *money*. They include promissory notes, drafts (*e.g.,* checks), and certificates of deposit, and are sometimes divided into negotiable and nonnegotiable instruments. [U.C.C. §9-102(a)(47)]

b. Documents

Documents are pieces of paper that represent the right to receive *goods*. They include bills of lading and warehouse receipts, and are sometimes divided into negotiable and nonnegotiable documents. [U.C.C. §9-102(a)(30)]

c. Chattel Paper

Chattel paper is a record or records evidencing *both* (i) a monetary obligation and (ii) a security interest in or a lease of specific goods, excluding the charter of vessels. A *"record"* is information that is stored in either a tangible medium (*e.g.,* written on paper) or an intangible medium (*e.g.,* electronically stored) and retrievable in perceivable form. Chattel paper that is stored in an electronic medium is also called *"electronic chattel paper,"* and chattel paper that is stored in a tangible medium is also called *"tangible chattel paper."* [U.C.C. §9-102(a)(11), (31), (78)]

Example: Buyer purchases a stereo from Radio Hut ("RH") on credit, giving a written promissory note and a written security agreement in exchange for the stereo. RH borrows money from Radio Sellers Bank ("RSB"). As security for the loan to RH, RSB takes Buyer's promissory note and security agreement. The note and security agreement constitute chattel paper collateral. Note that because the promissory note and security agreement are written, they are records and they are also considered to be *tangible* chattel paper collateral.

d. Accounts

An account is any right to payment for goods, services, real property, use of a credit card, or lottery winnings that is *not* evidenced by an instrument or chattel paper (*e.g.,* the money owed to a doctor after she sees a patient). This term *does not include* deposit accounts (*see* below), investment property (*see* below), commercial tort claims (*see* below), or rights to payment for funds that are advanced or sold (*e.g.,* a bank's right to payment for a loan). [U.C.C. §9-102(a)(2)]

e. Deposit Accounts

Deposit accounts are accounts maintained with a bank, such as savings or passbook accounts. [U.C.C. §9-102(a)(29)] Recall that Article 9 only applies to nonconsumer deposit accounts and deposit accounts that are claimed as proceeds of other collateral (*see* I.C., *supra*).

f. Investment Property

Investment property includes items such as stocks, bonds, mutual funds, and brokerage accounts. [U.C.C. §9-102(a)(49)]

g. Commercial Tort Claims

Tort claims that are filed by *organizations* (*e.g.,* partnerships and corporations) are commercial tort claims. Tort claims that are filed by *individuals* that arose out of the individuals' business and that *do not involve personal injury* are also commercial tort claims. [U.C.C. §9-102(a)(13)]

h. General Intangibles

General intangibles include any intangible not coming within the scope of the definitions of the other types of intangibles—*e.g.,* software, patent and trademark rights, copyrights, and goodwill. [U.C.C. §9-102(a)(42)] A general intangible in which the principal obligation of one of the parties is the *payment of money* is also called a *payment intangible*. [U.C.C. §9-102(a)(61)]

3. Proceeds

Proceeds include whatever is received upon the sale, lease, exchange, license, collection, or other disposition of collateral or proceeds. [U.C.C. §9-102(a)(64)] Proceeds differ from the other types of collateral in that they constitute any collateral that has *changed in form* from a previous category. For instance, if a farmer borrows money from a creditor and gives the creditor a security interest in the wool from the farmer's sheep, the wool is collateral of the farm product type. If the farmer exchanges the wool for a tractor or money, the tractor or money now becomes a proceed of the wool. In addition, the tractor can also be classified as equipment. Proceeds are sometimes divided into cash and noncash proceeds because of the application of certain rules to each. Money, checks, deposit accounts, and the like are *cash proceeds*. All other proceeds are noncash proceeds.

a. "Proceeds" Include Second Generation Proceeds

Proceeds can go through several transformations and still retain their character as proceeds.

Examples: 1) Bank has a security interest in Debtor's car. Debtor trades the car for a pickup truck. The pickup truck is a proceed. Debtor decides that he is not really a "pickup" person and trades the pickup truck for a bass boat. The bass boat is still a proceed of the original collateral (*i.e.*, the car).

2) Finance Company has a security interest in the inventory of Dealer. Dealer sells a car to Consumer and receives a note and security agreement (chattel paper). The chattel paper is a proceed. Consumer sends Dealer a check for her monthly payment on her note. The check is a proceed. Dealer deposits the check in its bank account. The money attributable to the check remains a proceed while it is in the account.

b. Insurance Payments and Claims for Damage Are "Proceeds"

If the collateral is insured and money is received from the insurance company on account of loss or damage to the collateral, the money is a proceed of the collateral (up to the value of the collateral) unless it is payable to someone other than the debtor or the secured party claiming it. Furthermore, any claims arising out of the loss of, defects in, or damage to collateral are proceeds of the collateral up to the value of the collateral.

Examples: 1) Debtor One's insurance policy has an endorsement providing that if the collateral is destroyed, payment will be made to the secured party. The collateral is destroyed. The insurance money is a proceed.

2) Debtor Two's insurance policy has no special endorsement. When the collateral is stolen, the insurance money is paid to the debtor. The insurance money is still a proceed.

3) Secured Party A and Secured Party B both have security interests in the same item of collateral. The insurance policy covering the collateral has an endorsement providing that if the item is damaged, the insurance money is payable to Secured Party B. The insurance money is a proceed as to Secured Party B, but not as to Secured Party A.

4) Creditor advances money to Debtor to purchase goods from Seller, and in return Creditor takes a security interest in the goods. When Debtor receives the goods, she discovers that they are defective. Any claim that Debtor has against Seller is a proceed of the goods.

II. CREATION (ATTACHMENT) OF SECURITY INTEREST

A. INTRODUCTION

Article 9 concerns the secured party's rights against both the debtor and third parties who may have an interest in the debtor's property. The former involves a process called attachment and the latter involves a process called perfection. This section covers attachment. A security interest is not enforceable (*i.e.*, the creditor may not repossess the collateral) unless it has attached.

B. REQUISITES FOR ATTACHMENT

There are three requirements for attachment of a security interest: (i) the parties must have an *agreement* that the security interest attach; (ii) *value* must be given by the secured party; and (iii) the debtor must have *rights* in the collateral. [U.C.C. §9-203(b)]

1. Parties' Agreement

The parties must *agree* to create the security interest (*i.e.*, they must enter into a *security agreement*). This agreement must be *evidenced* in one of the following ways:

a. Authenticated Security Agreement

The parties' security agreement may be evidenced by a *record* (*i.e.*, written or electronically stored information; *see* I.E.2.c., *supra*) *authenticated by the debtor* that *describes the collateral* and, if the collateral is timber to be cut, *describes the land* concerned. [U.C.C. §9-203(b)(3)(A)] A record is *authenticated* if it is *signed or marked electronically* with the present intent to identify the authenticating person and adopt the agreement. [U.C.C. §9-102(a)(7)]

1) Description of Collateral

The description of the collateral in the authenticated security agreement is sufficient if it *reasonably identifies* the collateral. Description of the collateral may be *specific* (*e.g.,* by serial number or by identifying it as "the debtor's tractor" if the debtor only has one tractor), or it may be by *category, type* (*e.g.,* "all of debtor's equipment"), *quantity, computational formula, or any other method* in which the identity of the collateral *is objectively determinable.* However, a *supergeneric* description of collateral, such as "all the debtor's assets" or "all the debtor's personal property," is *not* sufficient. [U.C.C. §9-108(a) - (c)]

a) **Exception—Collateral that Cannot Be Described by Type Alone**
    The following collateral cannot be described by type alone: (i) commercial tort claims, (ii) consumer goods, and (iii) consumer securities accounts. Such collateral must be described more specifically to be covered by the authenticated security agreement (*e.g.,* the description, "the tort claim arising out of the December 13, 2001, explosion of debtor's factory," is sufficient, but the description, "all of debtor's commercial tort claims," is not sufficient). [U.C.C. §9-108]

b. **Possession**
The security agreement may be evidenced by the *creditor's possession* of the collateral. [U.C.C. §9-203(b)(3)(B)]

1) **Rights and Duties of Secured Party in Possession**
    When a secured party has possession of the collateral for purposes of attachment or perfection (*see* III.C., *infra*), or upon the debtor's default (*see* V.B.1.d., *infra*), the secured party has certain rights and duties regarding the collateral:

    a) **Duty of Reasonable Care**
        The secured party must use reasonable care in storing and preserving the collateral. [U.C.C. §9-207(a)]

    b) **Right to Reimbursement for Expenses**
        The secured party may charge the debtor for any reasonable expenses incurred in preservation of the collateral, including the cost of insurance. [U.C.C. §9-207(b)(1)]

    c) **Risk of Loss**
        Risk of accidental loss or damage is on the debtor to the extent of any insurance coverage deficiency. [U.C.C. §9-207(b)(2)]

    d) **Accounting for Profits**
        The secured party may hold as additional security any increase in value of or profits from the collateral except money. Money received from the collateral must be either given to the debtor or applied against the secured obligation. [U.C.C. §9-207(c)(1) - (2)]

    e) **Right to Repledge**
        The secured party may repledge the collateral (*i.e.,* the secured party may use the collateral as collateral for an obligation under which the secured party is a debtor). [U.C.C. §9-207(c)(3)]

c. **Control**
If the collateral is a *nonconsumer deposit account, electronic chattel paper, or investment property,* the security agreement may be evidenced by control. [U.C.C. §9-203(b)(3)(D)] The method by which control may be obtained depends on the type of collateral involved.

1) **Nonconsumer Deposit Accounts**
    The *bank* in which a nonconsumer deposit account is maintained *automatically* has control over the deposit account. If the secured party is *not* such a bank, it may obtain control over a nonconsumer deposit account by either: (i) putting the deposit account in the secured party's name, or (ii) agreeing in an authenticated record with the debtor and the bank in which the deposit account is maintained that the *bank will comply with the secured party's orders* regarding the deposit account without requiring the debtor's consent. [U.C.C. §9-104]

2) **Electronic Chattel Paper**
    Control of electronic chattel paper is the functional equivalent of possession of tangible chattel paper. To obtain control over electronic chattel paper, the secured party must have the *authoritative copy* of the record or records constituting the

electronic chattel paper (*e.g.*, a computer file) that identifies the secured party as the assignee of record of the chattel paper. Any other copy of the record or records that is not the authoritative copy must be marked as such. [U.C.C. §9-105]

3) Investment Property

Basically, a secured party (or other purchaser) has control of an item of investment property when the secured party has taken whatever steps are necessary to be able to have the investment property sold without further action from the owner. [U.C.C. §§8-106 and comment 1; 9-106(a)]

a) Stocks and Bonds

Generally, a secured party will have control over a certificated stock or bond if the secured party takes possession of the stock or bond. If the stock or bond is not in "bearer" form (*i.e.*, if the certificate says it is payable only to a specific person rather than to "bearer"), the secured party must also have the specific person indorse the certificate over to him.

Example: Alex borrows $10,000 from Becky and agrees to give her a security interest in his 200 shares of Levco stock. The stock is certificated and payable to "bearer." Becky has control of the stock when she takes possession of the share certificates.

b) Securities Accounts

Relatively few people actually physically possess the stocks or bonds they own; instead they instruct brokers or mutual fund companies to purchase stocks, bonds, or mutual fund shares on their behalf and hold them in a securities account. A creditor can take a security interest in such an account. A secured party will have control over a securities account if the owner of the account contacts the broker or mutual fund company (called a "securities intermediary") and instructs the intermediary either that the secured party now has whatever right in the account that the owner has or that the intermediary is to comply with the secured party's orders without further consent of the owner.

Example: Alex borrows $100,000 from Bank. As security, Bank requires Alex to give it a security interest in his Squabb brokerage account, which has a current market value of $200,000. Bank can attach this interest through control by having Alex instruct Squabb to follow Bank's orders regarding the account.

4) Rights and Duties of Secured Party in Control

A secured party in control must *account for profits* of the collateral. She may also *repledge the collateral*. [U.C.C. §9-207(c)]

5) Duties of Secured Party in Control When There Is No Outstanding Obligation

If there is no outstanding obligation of the debtor and no commitment on the part of the secured party to make further advances, the secured party must do the following *within 10 days after demand* by the debtor:

(i) If the secured party has control of a nonconsumer *deposit account* due to an *agreement with the debtor and bank* (*see* 1), *supra*), or has control of a *securities account* due to an *agreement with the debtor and the securities intermediary* (*see* 3)b), *supra*), the secured party must send the bank or intermediary an authenticated record *releasing* the bank or intermediary from its obligation to comply with the secured party's orders.

(ii) If the secured party obtained control of a nonconsumer *deposit account* by putting the account *in its name* (*see* 1), *supra*), the secured party must *pay* the debtor the balance of the deposit account or transfer the balance into a deposit account in the debtor's name.

(iii) If the secured party has control over *electronic chattel paper* (*see* 2), *supra*), the secured party must either *return the authoritative copy* of the electronic chattel paper to the debtor or, if the electronic chattel paper is in the possession of a custodian, instruct the custodian in an authenticated record to only follow the *debtor's orders* regarding the electronic chattel paper.

[U.C.C. §9-208]

2. **Value**

 Value must be given by the secured party (or on his behalf) before a security agreement will be effective to create a security interest. Any consideration sufficient to support a simple contract is value. There is no requirement that the consideration actually have been performed; it is sufficient if the secured party is under a binding obligation to perform. In addition, *a preexisting debt is considered to be value given* (even though it does not constitute consideration) *if* the security interest is intended as security for the preexisting debt. [U.C.C. §1-204]

3. **Rights in Collateral**

 The debtor must have *rights in the collateral* to create a security interest. An ownership interest in or the right to obtain possession of the collateral qualifies as "rights in the collateral." (For a discussion of the attachment of a security interest to property acquired after the security agreement is entered into, *see* C., below.)

4. **Coexistence Required**

 The three above requirements may occur in any order, but they *must coexist* before the security interest attaches.

 Example: On August 1, Sara fills out a loan application from Bank to borrow $1,000 to buy a stereo and signs a security agreement giving Bank a security interest in the stereo. Bank tells Sara that it will take five days to process the loan, so if approved Sara can pick up the money on August 6. On August 6, Sara obtains the money from Bank. On August 7, Sara buys the stereo. The security interest attaches on August 7 because that is the earliest date on which all three requirements for attachment were met—the agreement was authenticated on August 1, value was given on August 6, and Sara obtained rights in the stereo on August 7.

C. **PROPERTY IN WHICH DEBTOR ACQUIRES INTEREST IN FUTURE (AFTER-ACQUIRED PROPERTY); FUTURE ADVANCES**

 1. **After-Acquired Property**

 A secured party will sometimes want to obtain a security interest not only in a debtor's present property, but also in property that the debtor will obtain in the future. This is permissible.

 a. **General Rule—Security Interest May Attach to After-Acquired Property**

 A valid security agreement may create a security interest in property to be acquired in the future that will attach to the property *as soon as the debtor acquires an interest in the property*. Such an interest generally may be created only by specifically including in the security agreement an after-acquired property clause (*e.g.*, "this security agreement is secured by debtor's equipment now owned or acquired in the future"). [U.C.C. §9-204(a)]

 1) **Proceeds and Floating Liens**

 A security interest attaches to identifiable proceeds of collateral whether or not the security agreement specifically so provides. The security agreement need not even mention proceeds. [U.C.C. §§9-203(f), 9-315] Similarly, a security interest in an aggregation of individual items that are expected to be disposed of and replaced (*i.e.*, a so-called floating lien on collateral such as inventory, accounts, stock, etc.) automatically attaches to the new individual items as they replace individual items that have been disposed of.

 Examples: 1) Bank has a security interest in Debtor's car. Debtor trades the car for a pickup truck. Bank's security interest attaches to the pickup truck whether or not the security agreement specifically reserves a security interest in proceeds.

 2) Bank has a security interest in Debtor's inventory of televisions. At the time Bank obtained its security interest, Debtor's inventory included 20 Brand A televisions. Ten Brand A televisions have been sold and Debtor has restocked with 12 Brand B televisions. Bank's security interest extends to the 12 new Brand B televisions.

 b. **Exception—Consumer Goods and Commercial Tort Claims**

 An after-acquired property clause is ineffective as to *consumer goods* other than accessions (*i.e.,* goods that are physically attached to other goods; *see* IV.B.3.f.2), *infra*) when given as additional security, unless the debtor acquires rights in the goods **within 10 days** after the creditor gives value. In addition, an after-acquired property clause is ineffective as to **commercial tort claims**. [U.C.C. §9-204(b)]

Examples:	1) On March 1, Debtor purchases a stereo from Radio Hut ("RH") on credit. To secure repayment, Debtor signs a security agreement giving RH a security interest in "all of Debtor's home televisions, now owned or hereafter acquired" (recall that consumer goods must be described specifically in an authenticated security agreement). On March 3, Debtor purchases for cash a new television for his home. On March 25, Debtor purchases for cash a second new television for his home. Because of the after-acquired property clause, RH's security interest attaches to the first television, but not to the second television, which was purchased more than 10 days after RH gave value (*i.e.*, the stereo).

2) Widgetco signs a security agreement giving Bank a security interest in "all of Widgetco's present and future commercial tort claims arising out of the June 3 factory explosion" (recall that commercial tort claims also must be described specifically in an authenticated security agreement). While the security agreement is effective as to Widgetco's present commercial tort claims arising out of the explosion, it is ineffective as to Widgetco's future commercial tort claims.

2. Future Advances

Sometimes, a secured party contemplates making future loans to the debtor and wants to secure these future advances in the present security agreement (*e.g.*, a line of credit arrangement). This is permissible. The security agreement may cover future advances on present collateral or collateral to be acquired in the future, regardless of whether the secured party is obligated to make such advances. If the security agreement contains such a "future advance" clause, a **new security agreement is not needed** when a future loan is made. [U.C.C. §9-204(c)]

Example:	On March 1, First Finance loans Pizza Parlor $10,000 and takes a security interest in Pizza Parlor's equipment. The security agreement provides that the equipment is to be collateral not only for this loan, but also for any future loans made by First Finance to Pizza Parlor. On May 1, First Finance makes another loan to Pizza Parlor. It will be secured by Pizza Parlor's equipment under the March 1 security agreement.

III. PERFECTION OF SECURITY INTEREST

A. IN GENERAL

As noted above, attachment establishes the secured party's rights to the collateral vis-a-vis the debtor. However, other parties may also have rights in the collateral (*e.g.*, subsequent purchasers of the collateral, unsecured creditors, and other secured creditors). To acquire the maximum priority in the collateral over most such third parties, it is not enough that the security interest has attached; the secured party must also "perfect." There are five methods of perfection: (i) filing; (ii) taking possession of the collateral; (iii) control; (iv) automatic perfection; and (v) temporary perfection.

1. Timing of Perfection

A security interest is not enforceable against *any* party until it has attached to the collateral. Thus, perfection of a security interest cannot be completed until it has attached. In some circumstances, however, a party may complete all of the other steps necessary for perfection (*e.g.*, filing) before the security interest has attached (*e.g.*, where an after-acquired property clause is used). In such a case, the security interest will become perfected at the time that it attaches (*i.e.*, as soon as the debtor obtains an interest in the collateral).

Example:	On August 1, Charlie fills out a loan application from Bank to borrow $1,000 to buy a stereo and signs a security agreement giving Bank a security interest in the stereo. Bank tells Charlie that it will take five days to process the loan, so if approved Charlie can pick up the money on August 6. On August 2, Bank files a financing statement covering the stereo that Charlie will purchase. On August 6, Charlie obtains the money from Bank. On August 7, Charlie buys the stereo. Perfection occurs here on August 7 because that is when the security interest attached. (*See* II.B.4., *supra*.)

2. **Effect of Perfection Limited**

Despite perfection, a nonpossessory security interest may nevertheless be subordinated to some types of adverse third-party claims (*e.g.*, to ordinary course buyers of inventory, to holders in due course of negotiable instruments). (*See* IV., *infra.*)

B. PERFECTION BY FILING

A security interest may be perfected by filing (either in writing or electronically) as to all kinds of collateral *except deposit accounts and money*. [U.C.C. §§9-310, 9-312(b)] *Note:* If deposit accounts or money are claimed as *proceeds* of other collateral (*e.g.*, if money is a proceed of sold equipment), a filed security interest in the original collateral perfects a security interest in the deposit accounts or money as proceeds of the original collateral.

1. **Records to Be Filed (the Financing Statement)**

The Code simply requires "notice" filing. It does not require that a copy or abstract of the security agreement be filed. Notice filing contemplates that once a third party discovers that a debtor's property is covered by a financing statement, she will make further inquiry about the particular security agreement covering the property. "Notice" is given by the filing of a *"financing statement,"* which contains the following elements:

(i) The *name and mailing address of the debtor*;

(ii) The *name and mailing address of the secured party*;

(iii) An *indication of the collateral* covered by the financing statement; and

(iv) If the financing statement covers *real-property-related collateral* (*i.e.*, minerals, timber to be cut, or fixtures), the financing statement must also provide a *description of the real property* to which the collateral is related.

[U.C.C. §9-502]

a. **Debtor's and Secured Party's Names**

Financing statements are indexed under the debtor's name. Although minor errors in the debtor's name will not invalidate the financing statement, the statement must not contain any *seriously misleading* errors. If the debtor is a *registered organization* (*e.g.*, a corporation, limited partnership, or limited liability company), the debtor's name is seriously misleading if it does not match the name under which the debtor was organized. Use of the debtor's *trade name* also is insufficient. However, under a "safe harbor" provision, if the financing statement *would be discovered in a filing office search* under the debtor's correct name, the incorrect name is not seriously misleading. [U.C.C. §§9-503, 9-506] Because financing statements generally are not indexed under the secured party's name, errors in the secured party's name will *not* make the financing statement seriously misleading. [U.C.C. §9-506, comment 2]

Example: A debtor's name is listed in its filed articles of incorporation as "World Travel, Inc." Creditor takes a security interest in World Travel, Inc.'s equipment and files a financing statement naming the debtor as "World Travel." Although leaving "Inc." out of the debtor's name is technically seriously misleading because the financing statement does not match the name listed on the debtor's articles of incorporation, the "safe harbor" provision may make the financing statement effective if a filing office search under "World Travel" would reveal "World Travel, Inc."

1) **Debtor Name Change**

If the debtor changes its name *after* a financing statement has been filed and the new name is seriously misleading (*see supra*), the financing statement is effective only against collateral acquired by the debtor *before* the name change and within *four months* after the change. The secured party must refile using the debtor's new name to perfect a security interest in collateral acquired after the four-month period.

b. **Debtor's and Secured Party's Addresses**

If a financing statement that does not contain the debtor's or secured party's mailing address is *accepted* by the filing office, the financing statement is *effective* despite the lack of the address. [U.C.C. §§9-516(b), 9-520(a)]

    c.   **Indication of Collateral**

A financing statement will sufficiently indicate the collateral if it identifies it specifically or identifies it by category, type, quantity, computational formula, or any other method in which the identity of the collateral is objectively determinable. In addition, unlike descriptions of collateral in authenticated security agreements, the financing statement also may indicate that it covers *"all assets"* or *"all personal property."* [U.C.C. §9-504]

    d.   **Description of Related Real Property**

If the financing statement covers collateral related to real property (*e.g.*, fixtures), the property to which the collateral is related must also be described, although generally a full legal description is not required. [U.C.C. §9-502]

    e.   **Debtor Must "Authorize" Filing of Financing Statement**

For a financing statement to be effective, the debtor must *authorize it in an authenticated record* (*i.e.,* the authorization cannot be oral). The debtor may authorize the financing statement *after* it is filed, as long as the debtor eventually authorizes it. The debtor authorizes the financing statement if she *authenticates the financing statement* or *authenticates a security agreement* covering the same collateral as the financing statement. *Note:* A financing statement covering only an *agricultural lien* is effective even if the debtor does not authorize it. [U.C.C. §9-509]

    f.   **After-Acquired Property**

The financing statement need *not* mention after-acquired property in order to perfect a security interest in such property if the description in the financing statement is broad enough to cover the after-acquired property. [U.C.C. §9-502, comment 2] *Rationale:* Perfection is intended merely to put a party on notice that there *may be* a security interest in the collateral and further investigation may be necessary to disclose the full state of affairs.

    Example: On March 1, Printco purchases a printing press from Manuco on credit. To secure the purchase price, Printco gives Manuco a security interest "in all of Printco's equipment, now owned or hereafter acquired." Manuco files a financing statement describing the collateral merely as "equipment." On March 21, Printco purchases a new collating machine for cash. Manuco's security interest extends to the collating machine by virtue of the after-acquired property clause, and the security interest is perfected because the description in the financing statement ("equipment") is broad enough to cover the new machine.

2.   **Authenticated Security Agreement Itself May Be Filed**

The authenticated security agreement itself may be filed as the financing statement if the parties so desire. If it is filed, it must contain all the elements described above. Similarly, a recorded real property mortgage that lists the fixtures and contains all of the above elements is effective as a financing statement for perfecting a security interest in the fixtures.

    a.   **Compare—Financing Statement as Authenticated Security Agreement**

A financing statement, unlike an authenticated security agreement, does not need to be authenticated by the debtor to be effective. However, if the debtor does authenticate the financing statement, the U.C.C. is silent as to whether an authenticated financing statement can be used as an authenticated security agreement. The traditional rule is that a financing statement cannot serve as a security agreement because a security agreement must create the security interest, and to create the security interest, courts have held, there must be words of grant. [*See, e.g.,* American Card Co. v. H.M.H. Co., 196 A.2d 150 (R.I. 1963)] A financing statement usually does not contain words of grant, and so, under the traditional rule, cannot qualify as a security agreement. Some courts, however, do not require words of grant and allow the financing statement to serve as a security agreement. In any case, if the financing statement is authenticated and contains words of grant, it can serve as a security agreement.

3.   **Place of Filing**

    a.   **General Rule—File Centrally**

Generally, filing must be done *centrally* with the *secretary of state*. [U.C.C. §9-501(a)(2)]

    b.   **Exception—Timber to Be Cut, Minerals, and Fixtures**

If the collateral is timber to be cut or minerals, or if the collateral is or is to become a fixture and the filing is a fixture filing, filing is in the office where a *lien on real property* would be filed *("locally")*. Often, the secured party will not be certain whether particular collateral is a fixture. In such a case, the only safe procedure is to file *both* in the *real property records* and with the *secretary of state*. [U.C.C. §9-501(a)(1)]

1)   Transmitting Utilities—File Centrally
A creditor of a transmitting utility, such as a telephone or electric company, can perfect a security interest on the utility's poles and towers by a central filing with the secretary of state, even though the collateral could be considered to be fixtures. [U.C.C. §9-501(b)]

4.   Period for Which Filing Is Effective

a.   Original Filing
A financing statement is effective for *five years*. [U.C.C. §9-515(a)]

1)   Exceptions—Utilities and Some Fixtures
Filings for transmitting utilities continue until terminated, and a recorded real property mortgage covering fixtures continues until the mortgage is released or satisfied. [U.C.C. §9-515(f) - (g)]

2)   Exception—Manufactured Home and Public Finance Transactions
A financing statement filed in connection with a manufactured home transaction or a public finance transaction is effective for a period of *30 years*. [U.C.C. §9-515(b)]

b.   Continuation Statement
Continuation statements may be filed during the last six months of the effective period of a prior filing and will continue the effectiveness of the filing for *five more years*. The debtor need not authorize the continuation statement; only the secured party needs to authorize it. [U.C.C. §§9-509(d), 9-515(c) - (e)]

c.   Termination of Financing Statements
Generally, a secured party is not obligated to terminate a financing statement. *Exceptions:* If there is no outstanding obligation of the debtor and no commitment on the part of the secured party to make further advances, or if the debtor did not authorize the filing of the initial financing statement, the secured party must, *on demand* of the debtor, within 20 days, file a termination statement or provide one to the debtor. In the case of *consumer goods*, the secured party must *file* the termination statement within one month after there is no obligation or commitment, or if the debtor demands it, within 20 days of the demand. [U.C.C. §9-513]

Note: If no termination statement is filed, a filing remains effective for the whole five years, *even if the original obligation for which it was filed has been satisfied*.
Example: On January 1, Debtor borrows $10,000 from Bank and gives Bank a security interest in Debtor's equipment. Bank immediately files a financing statement covering the equipment. On March 1, Debtor repays Bank. On January 1 of the following year, Debtor borrows another $10,000 from Bank and gives Bank a security interest in Debtor's equipment. Bank does not have to make a new filing to perfect; the original filing is still effective.

5.   Filing as to Motor Vehicles for Which Certificates of Title Are Issued

a.   Users
Under the state's certificate of title law, security interests in motor vehicles required to be titled (except security interests created by dealers who hold the motor vehicles for sale or lease) are perfected by *notation on the certificate of title* issued by the state. Filing or possession under Article 9 is neither required nor effective. [U.C.C. §9-311]

b.   Dealers
Security interests created by dealers in leased motor vehicles or motor vehicles held in *inventory* for sale or lease are *perfected by filing* under the ordinary Code rules, even though a certificate of title covering the vehicle is outstanding. [U.C.C. §9-311]

      c.   Aircraft and Railroad Rolling Stock
         Security interests in domestic aircraft and railroad rolling stock are perfected by filing with the appropriate federal agencies. [U.C.C. §9-311]

C. PERFECTION BY TAKING POSSESSION (PLEDGE)

A secured party may perfect a security interest in most types of collateral simply by taking possession of the collateral. [U.C.C. §9-313]

  1. Collateral that Cannot Be Pledged
     A security interest in *accounts, certificate of title goods, deposit accounts, nonnegotiable documents, electronic chattel paper, or general intangibles cannot* be perfected by possession, even if tangibly represented; perfection by another means is required. [U.C.C. §9-313]

  2. Time of Perfection
     The time when perfection by possession occurs depends on whether the secured party has actual possession of the collateral or whether the collateral is in the hands of a bailee.

     a. Actual Possession
        Where the secured party takes actual possession of the collateral, the security interest is perfected from the moment of possession, and continues as long as possession is retained. [U.C.C. §9-313]

     b. Collateral in Hands of Bailee
        Where the collateral (other than certificated securities and goods covered by a document) is in the hands of a bailee, the secured party is deemed to be in possession from the moment the bailee *authenticates a record* acknowledging that it is holding the collateral for the secured party's benefit. [U.C.C. §9-313(c)]

  3. Relation to Other Methods of Perfection
     The security interest may be perfected either *before or after* possession by any other applicable method.

  4. Rights and Duties of Secured Party in Possession
     Recall that a secured party with possession of collateral has certain rights and duties regarding the collateral (*see* II.B.1.b.1), *supra*).

D. PERFECTION BY CONTROL

Security interests in investment property, nonconsumer deposit accounts, and electronic chattel paper may be perfected by "control." (*See* II.B.1.c., *supra*, regarding methods for obtaining control and rights and duties of a secured party with control.)

E. AUTOMATIC PERFECTION

In some transactions, the Code provides that the security interest is perfected simply by the attachment of the security interest, without taking any additional steps. This is referred to as "automatic" perfection. Perfection is automatic in the following circumstances:

  1. PMSI in Consumer Goods
     A PMSI in consumer goods is perfected as soon as it *attaches*. [U.C.C. §9-309(1)] (Recall that a PMSI arises where the creditor (i) sells goods to the debtor on credit and reserves a security interest or (ii) advances the funds used to purchase goods and reserves a security interest, *see* I.D.2., *supra*; and a PMSI in goods generally will attach when the debtor receives the goods, *see* II.B.4., *supra*.)

     *Note: **The only type of PMSI that is automatically perfected is a PMSI in consumer goods.** A PMSI in inventory or equipment must be filed to be valid.*

     a. Limitation—Motor Vehicles
        Recall that a security interest in noninventory motor vehicles generally can be perfected only by notation on the vehicle's certificate of title; there is no automatic perfection even for a motor vehicle that constitutes consumer goods.

     b. Partial Limitation—Fixtures
        If the consumer goods collateral is or is to become a fixture (*i.e.*, something firmly affixed to real property), a fixture filing is necessary to obtain priority over an encumbrancer of the real property. (*See* IV.B.3.f.1), *infra*.)

2. **Small-Scale Assignments of Accounts or Payment Intangibles**
The security interest is perfected automatically in the case of assignments of accounts or payment intangibles that do not alone, or in conjunction with other assignments to the same assignee, transfer a significant part of the outstanding accounts or payment intangibles of the assignor. [U.C.C. §9-309(2)]

3. **Sales of Payment Intangibles or Promissory Notes**
The sale of a payment intangible or a promissory note is automatically perfected. [U.C.C. §9-309(3) - (4)]

4. **Beneficial Interest in a Decedent's Estate**
A security interest created by an assignment of a beneficial interest in a decedent's estate is automatically perfected. [U.C.C. §9-309(13)]

5. **Investment Property**
A security interest in investment property is automatically perfected in the following cases:

(i) The debtor is a *securities intermediary* (*e.g.,* a securities intermediary borrows money from a bank and grants the bank a security interest in securities identified on a list provided to the bank on a daily basis);

(ii) If the *debtor purchased the asset through a securities intermediary and has not paid the price*, the intermediary has an automatically perfected security interest to secure the purchase price;

(iii) If *one who deals in securities* or similar financial assets purchases a certificated security *from another such dealer* under an agreement calling for *delivery against payment*, the person delivering the asset has an automatically perfected security interest in the security to secure payment of the price.

[U.C.C. §§9-206, 9-309]

F.   TEMPORARY PERFECTION

1. **Twenty-Day Period for Proceeds**
A security interest in proceeds from original collateral is continuously perfected for 20 days from the debtor's receipt of the proceeds. [U.C.C. §9-315(d)] This security interest becomes unperfected on the 21st day after the debtor's receipt of the proceeds unless the statutory requirements are complied with. (*See* G., *infra.*) In many cases the requirements are automatically met.

2. **Twenty-Day Period for Instruments, Negotiable Documents, and Certificated Securities**

a. **New Value Given**
As to instruments, negotiable documents, or certificated securities, a secured party who advances new value under an authenticated security agreement obtains a 20-day perfection period from the time of attachment, even though the secured party does not file a financing statement or take possession of the collateral. [U.C.C. §9-312(e)]
Example: Debtor has a promissory note (an instrument). He grants Bank a security interest in it, and Bank loans him $2,000. If there is an authenticated security agreement, Bank's security interest is perfected for 20 days. If by the end of the 20 days Bank has not filed or taken possession, its security interest becomes unperfected.

b. **Delivery of Collateral to Debtor for Disposition**
Where the creditor has a possessory security interest in an instrument, negotiable document, certificated security, or goods not covered by a negotiable document in possession of a bailee, and makes any of the above available to the debtor on a temporary basis (*e.g.,* for sale, exchange, or presentation), perfection continues for *20 days,* after which time the creditor must reperfect by filing or taking possession or lose his perfection. [U.C.C. §9-312(f) - (g)]
Example: George makes a loan to Chuck, and Chuck gives his promissory note to George in exchange for the loan. George pledges the note to Bank to secure a loan made to him by Bank. When it is time for Chuck to pay on

the note, Bank redelivers the note to George so that he may present it to Chuck for payment. Bank's security interest remains perfected for 20 days.

3. Interstate Shipments

When collateral or the debtor moves from one state to another, and the location of the collateral or debtor determines which state's law governs perfection, a security interest in the collateral that was perfected in the original state will often remain temporarily perfected in the new state. (*See* VI., *infra*, for a detailed explanation.)

G. CONTINUATION OF PERFECTION OF INTEREST IN PROCEEDS

As stated above, if a secured party has a perfected security interest in collateral and the debtor sells, exchanges, or otherwise disposes of the collateral, the secured party has a temporarily (20-day) perfected security interest in whatever proceeds the debtor receives in exchange for the collateral. The security interest in proceeds will continue to be perfected *beyond* the 20 days if:

(i) The security interest in the original collateral was *perfected by filing* a financing statement, a security interest in the type of collateral constituting the proceeds would be *filed in the same place* as the financing statement for the original collateral, and the proceeds were not purchased with cash proceeds of the collateral (this is sometimes called the "same office" rule);

(ii) The *proceeds are identifiable cash proceeds* (this is sometimes called the "cash proceeds" rule); or

(iii) The security interest in the proceeds is *perfected within the 20-day period*.

[U.C.C. §9-315]

Examples: 1) Debtor grants Secured Party a security interest in inventory. Secured Party properly perfects by filing a financing statement listing the collateral as "inventory" in the secretary of state's office. Debtor sells an item of inventory on credit and thereby generates an account. Secured Party's security interest attaches to the account because it is a proceed of the original collateral. Moreover, the security interest in the account remains perfected beyond the 20-day period because perfection of a security interest in accounts is achieved by filing with the secretary of state. (*See* B.3.a., *supra.*) This is an application of the "same office" rule.

2) Same facts as in 1), except Debtor sells the item of inventory for cash. Secured Party's security interest in the cash remains perfected beyond the 20-day period as long as it remains an identifiable proceed of the inventory. This is an application of the "cash proceeds" rule.

3) Secured Party takes a security interest in Debtor's equipment and inventory and files a financing statement describing the collateral as "all of Debtor's assets." Buyer purchases an item of Debtor's inventory for cash, and Debtor uses the cash to purchase a new cash register (which is equipment). Secured Party's security interest attaches to the new cash register because it is a proceed of the inventory, and the security interest remains perfected beyond the 20-day period because Secured Party's interest in the proceeds was perfected within the 20-day period (the original security agreement and financing statement cover the cash register as equipment and thus perfect Secured Party's interest in the cash register). Note that the "same office" rule does not apply here because the cash register was purchased with cash proceeds of the inventory.

IV. PRIORITIES

A. INTRODUCTION

The heart of Article 9 is its allocation of rights or priorities between conflicting interests. In resolving a priority question, it is important to note the type of collateral involved and the types of parties involved. Conflicts can arise between (i) a secured party and another secured party, (ii) a secured party and a buyer or other transferee of the collateral, (iii) a secured party and a lien creditor (usually a trustee in bankruptcy) or a holder of a possessory lien, and (iv) a secured party and an Article 2 claimant.

Note: Although Article 9 provides rules for priority, parties entitled to priority under Article 9 may *contractually subordinate* their rights to other parties. [U.C.C. §9-339]

B. SECURED PARTY VS. SECURED PARTY

1. Priority Between Unperfected Secured Parties
If both security interests are unperfected, the *first to attach* has priority. [U.C.C. §9-322(a)(3)] This rule has little practical application because either secured party can easily get priority by perfecting.

2. Priority Between Unperfected and Perfected Secured Parties
Generally, a perfected security interest prevails over an unperfected security interest, even if the perfected secured party takes her security interest with knowledge of the earlier unperfected security interest. [U.C.C. §9-322(a)(2)]

3. Priority Between Perfected Secured Parties

a. General Rule—First to File or Perfect
When there are conflicting perfected security interests in the same collateral, priority goes to whichever party was the *first to either file or perfect*—whichever is earlier—provided that there is no period thereafter when there is neither filing nor perfection. [U.C.C. §9-322(a)(1)] Thus, if both parties perfected by filing, the one who filed first has priority—even if perfection was not complete upon filing (*see* III.A.1., *supra*). If one party perfected by filing and the other party perfected by some other method (*e.g.,* taking possession), the party who filed will have priority if he filed before the other party perfected. And if neither party perfected by filing, the one who completed perfection first will have priority.

Example: On June 1, Debtor applies for a $10,000 loan from Bank A. Debtor signs a financing statement and a security agreement granting a security interest in Debtor's equipment. On June 2, after checking the files and finding no competing interests, Bank A *files* the financing statement. On June 3, Debtor borrows $20,000 from Bank B, giving Bank B a security interest in the same equipment. Bank B loans the money and immediately *files* a financing statement covering the equipment. On June 10, Bank A loans Debtor $10,000. Bank A has priority to the equipment under the "first to file or perfect" rule since it was first to file, even though Bank B perfected its security interest before Bank A perfected its security interest.

b. Special Priority Rules for Investment Property
Generally, the first to file or perfect rule governs priority questions regarding investment property. However, a security interest *perfected by control has priority* over a security interest perfected by any other method (*i.e.,* by filing or automatic perfection).

c. PMSI Superpriority
PMSIs enjoy a *superpriority*—they are superior to prior perfected security interests in the same goods if certain conditions (discussed below) are met. *Rationale:* The PMSI superpriority does not really harm the competing security interest since, but for the PMSI creditor, the debtor would not have the goods. (Recall that a PMSI arises only where the seller sells goods to the debtor on credit and reserves a security interest in the goods or where the creditor advances funds used by the debtor to purchase goods; *see* I.D.2., *supra*.)

1) PMSI in Inventory
A PMSI in inventory has priority over a conflicting security interest in the *inventory itself*, proceeds that are *chattel paper* (or proceeds of that chattel paper), proceeds that are *instruments*, and any identifiable *cash* proceeds that are received on or before delivery to a buyer if:

(i)   The PMSI in inventory is *perfected* at the time the debtor gets *possession* of the inventory (the filing must take place before the inventory is delivered to the debtor); and

(ii) Any secured party who has filed her security interest in the same inventory receives an *authenticated notification* of the PMSI before the debtor receives possession of the inventory, and the notification states that the purchase money party has or expects to take a PMSI in inventory of the debtor described by kind or type. The notification is effective for deliveries of the same type of collateral for *five years*.

[U.C.C. §9-324(b) - (c)] *Note:* A PMSI in *livestock* generally follows the same rules.

Examples: 1) On March 1, First Bank loans Acme Feed Store money and takes a security interest in Acme's existing inventory and all after-acquired inventory. A financing statement is filed. On April 1, Second Bank promises to loan Acme $10,000 to purchase flour. Second Bank immediately files a financing statement and notifies First Bank in a signed writing of the impending loan and its purchase money interest. The loan is then made to Acme, which indorses the Second Bank check over to the flour distributor in exchange for the flour. Second Bank's PMSI in the flour has priority over First Bank's after-acquired property interest.

2) If in the above example Acme sold some of its newly purchased flour to Customer in exchange for a promissory note (an instrument), Second Bank would have PMSI superpriority in the promissory note as a proceed of the inventory.

a) Consignor Has PMSI in Inventory

Under Article 9, a consignor's interest in the consigned goods is considered to be a PMSI in inventory. Therefore, a consignor can acquire PMSI superpriority in consigned goods if she complies with the above requirements for gaining PMSI superpriority in inventory.

Example: Joe delivers his new line of hats to Department Store to be sold on consignment. As long as Joe perfects his interest in the hats before he delivers them to Department Store and properly notifies any secured parties with conflicting security interests in Department Store's inventory, Joe will have PMSI superpriority.

2) PMSI in Goods Other than Inventory and Livestock

A PMSI in goods other than inventory or livestock has priority over conflicting security interests in the same goods and their identifiable proceeds only if the interest is perfected before or within *20 days* after the debtor receives possession of the goods. There is no requirement that the secured party notify other holders of security interests. [U.C.C. §9-324(a)]

Examples: 1) As of January 2, Bank holds a perfected security interest in all of Debtor's equipment and after-acquired equipment. On July 16, Dealer sells and delivers to Debtor a piece of equipment, retaining a security interest in the equipment. On July 25, Dealer files a financing statement perfecting a security interest in the equipment. Even though Dealer knew of Bank's after-acquired property security interest, Dealer has priority as to the piece of equipment.

2) On July 16, Dealer sells and delivers to Debtor a piece of equipment, retaining a security interest in the equipment. On July 20, Bank loans Debtor $10,000, taking a security interest in all of Debtor's equipment as collateral, and files a financing statement covering the equipment. On July 25, Dealer files a financing statement perfecting a security interest in the piece of equipment. Dealer has priority to the equipment, because Dealer filed within the statutory period.

3) PMSI in Software

Recall that a PMSI in software arises if there is a PMSI covering both the software and the computer in which the software is to be used (*see* I.D.2.a., *supra*). This PMSI in software and its identifiable proceeds has the same priority as the security interest in the computer in which the software is used. Therefore, if the computer is inventory, the PMSI in software has superpriority if the PMSI in the computer has superpriority under the applicable rules for inventory. Likewise, if the computer is not inventory (*e.g.,* it is equipment), the PMSI in the software has superpriority if the PMSI in the computer has superpriority under the applicable rules for noninventory goods. [U.C.C §9-324(f)]

4) Conflicting PMSIs

If more than one party has PMSI superpriority in collateral, the following rules apply:

(i)   A secured party who has a PMSI in collateral *as a seller* has priority over a secured party who has a PMSI in the same collateral as a lender.

(ii)   Otherwise, the *first* secured party to file or perfect prevails.

[U.C.C. §9-324(g)]

Example: Johnny wants to purchase a new home entertainment system. Bank loans Johnny $1,000 for the purpose of allowing Johnny to purchase the home entertainment system and takes a security interest in the system to be purchased. Bank then perfects its security interest by filing. Johnny goes to Megastore to purchase the system, but discovers it costs $1,500. Johnny pays for part of the system using the money loaned to him by Bank. He pays for the remainder of the system by signing a credit agreement with Megastore covering the system for $500. (Recall that Megastore's PMSI is automatically perfected.) Megastore as the seller of the collateral has priority over Bank as the lender.

d.   "Purchasers" of Chattel Paper and Instruments

Article 9 contains special rules for *"purchasers"* of (who include parties taking a *security interest* in) chattel paper and instruments.

1)   Chattel Paper Purchasers

If a purchaser of chattel paper in *good faith* gives *new value* and takes *possession* of the chattel paper in the ordinary course of business (or takes *control* of electronic chattel paper), the purchaser will have priority over:

(i)   A security interest in chattel paper that arises merely as *proceeds of inventory,* as long as the chattel paper does not indicate that it has been assigned to anyone other than the purchaser; and

(ii)   *Any other security interest* in the chattel paper, as long as the chattel paper purchaser acquired its interest *without knowledge that its purchase violated the rights of the secured party.* Any notation on the chattel paper stating that the chattel paper has been assigned to a secured party is sufficient to give the purchaser knowledge that the purchase violates the rights of the secured party.

[U.C.C. §9-330(b), (f)]

Examples: 1) Friendly Sam ("Sam"), a used car dealer, borrows $100,000 from First State Bank ("FSB") to finance the purchase of Sam's used car inventory, and gives FSB a security interest in all of his present and after-acquired inventory. FSB perfects its security interest by filing. Sam sells five cars out of his inventory in exchange for chattel paper. (Under the rules discussed above, FSB's security interest in the proceeds is perfected and dates from the filing for the original collateral because a security interest in chattel paper is filed in the same office as a security interest in inventory.) Sam then obtains a $50,000 loan from Car Seller's Bank ("CSB"). To secure the loan, CSB in good faith perfects a security interest in Sam's chattel paper by taking possession of it. There is no notation on the chattel paper of FSB's interest. Sam defaults on both loans. CSB has priority in the chattel paper even though it perfected after FSB, because FSB's interest in the chattel paper is merely as proceeds of Sam's inventory.

2) In the above example, if FSB had taken a security interest in Sam's present and after-acquired chattel paper, rather than inventory, CSB would still have priority, as long as it took possession of the chattel paper without knowledge that the purchase violated the rights of FSB.

Note: A chattel paper purchaser also has priority in the *proceeds* of the chattel paper if either (i) she would have had priority under the *general priority rules* (*i.e.,* the purchaser was the first party to file perfect), or (ii) the proceeds are the *specific goods covered by the chattel paper or cash proceeds of the specific goods.* [U.C.C. §9-330(c)]

2) Instrument Purchasers

A purchaser of an instrument has priority over a perfected security interest in the instrument if the purchaser gives *value* and takes *possession* of the instrument in *good faith* and *without knowledge that the purchase violates the rights of the secured party.* Any notation on the instrument stating that the instrument has been assigned to a secured party is sufficient to give the purchaser knowledge that the purchase violates the rights of the secured party. Notice that, unlike the above rules for chattel paper, the purchaser does not have to give "new" value or take possession "in the ordinary course of business." [U.C.C. §9-330(d), (f)]

Example: Big Bank secures Debtor's outstanding debt worth $10,000 by taking a security interest in all of Debtor's presently owned and after-acquired instruments. Big Bank then immediately files a financing statement covering Debtor's instruments. Subsequently, Debtor sells its instruments to Purchaser for $10,000 and gives Purchaser possession of the instruments. As long as Purchaser bought the instruments without knowledge that the purchase violated the rights of Big Bank, Purchaser has priority in the instruments.

e. Priority in Proceeds

For purposes of determining the priority of security interests in proceeds, the Code divides collateral into "filing collateral" and "non-filing collateral." *Filing collateral* is collateral in which a secured party would normally achieve priority by filing a financing statement (*i.e.,* goods, accounts, commercial tort claims, general intangibles, and nonnegotiable documents); *non-filing collateral* is collateral in which a secured party would normally achieve priority by possession or control, rather than filing (*e.g.,* cash, chattel paper, nonconsumer deposit accounts, negotiable documents, instruments, and investment property).

1) General Rule

Generally, under the "first to file or perfect" rule, a perfected security interest in proceeds will have the *same date of priority* as the perfected security interest in the original collateral, as long as the perfection of the security interest in the proceeds extends beyond the 20-day temporary perfection period (*see* III.F.1., *supra*). Recall that there are also special superpriority rules for proceeds of collateral subject to PMSIs (*see* c., *supra*). [U.C.C. §9-322(a)]

Example: On January 1, ABC Co. borrows $10,000 from Bank 1 and grants Bank 1 a security interest in all of its present and after-acquired inventory. Bank 1 perfects immediately by filing a financing statement. On March 1, Bank 2 loans ABC Co. $5,000 and takes a security interest in ABC Co.'s present and after-acquired accounts. Bank 2 perfects immediately by filing a financing statement. On July 1, ABC Co. sells an item of inventory on credit to a customer, creating an account. Bank 1 has priority in the account because its priority in the account as a proceed of inventory dates back to January 1.

2) Special Rule for Certain Proceeds of Non-Filing Collateral

Because the rules governing priority in non-filing collateral contain many exceptions to the "first to file or perfect" rule (*e.g.,* a party with control over a deposit account has priority over a party without control, regardless of when control was obtained), the Code contains a special priority rule for certain proceeds of that collateral. A secured party has priority in the proceeds of non-filing collateral if: (i) she has *priority* in the original collateral, (ii) her security interest in the proceeds is *perfected*, and (iii) the proceeds are *cash proceeds or proceeds of the same type as the original collateral.* If the proceeds are proceeds of proceeds, all *intervening proceeds* must either be cash proceeds, proceeds of the same type as the original collateral, or accounts relating to the collateral. [U.C.C. §9-322(c)]

Example: First Bank loans Debtor $1,000 and perfects a security interest in Debtor's investment property by filing. Subsequently, Second Bank loans Debtor $1,000 and perfects a security interest in Debtor's certificated securities by obtaining control and by filing against investment property. Debtor then receives proceeds of the certificated securities consisting of stock dividends. Second Bank has priority in the stock dividends because: (i) it had priority in the original collateral through control, (ii) its security interest in the stock dividends was perfected by the filing of the financing statement covering investment property, and (iii) the proceeds were of the same type as the original collateral.

a) **Exception—Filing Collateral as Proceeds of Non-Filing Collateral**
If a security interest in *original collateral* that is *non-filing collateral* is perfected by a method *other than filing*, and the *proceeds* of the original collateral are *filing collateral*, the first secured party to *file* a financing statement covering the proceeds has priority in the proceeds. [U.C.C. §9-322(d) - (e)]

Example: On January 1, East Bank loans XYZ, Inc. $20,000 and perfects a security interest in XYZ, Inc.'s deposit account by obtaining control. On July 1, West Bank loans XYZ, Inc. $10,000 and perfects a security interest in XYZ, Inc.'s present and after-acquired equipment by filing a financing statement. On December 1, XYZ, Inc. takes money out of its deposit account and uses it to buy a new piece of equipment. West Bank has priority in the new equipment because: (i) East Bank's original security interest was in non-filing collateral (the deposit account) and was perfected by control, rather than filing, (ii) the proceeds of the deposit account were filing collateral (the new equipment), and (iii) West Bank was the first party to file a financing statement.

f. **Security Interests in Fixtures, Accessions, and Crops**
The Code provides special rules concerning (i) the priority of a security interest in a fixture over a security interest in the real estate to which the fixture is attached, (ii) the priority of a security interest in an accession over a security interest in the goods to which it is attached, and (iii) the priority of a security interest in crops over a security interest in the real property on which the crops are growing. [U.C.C. §§9-334 to 9-335]

1) **Fixtures—General Rule**
Fixtures are goods that become so attached or otherwise related to real property that an interest in them arises under real property law (*e.g.,* a built-in oven). [U.C.C. §9-102(a)(41)] However, ordinary building materials (*e.g.,* bricks) are not considered to be fixtures. Generally, in a contest between a holder of a security interest in a fixture and a holder of an interest in the real property to which the fixture is attached, the *first party to file a fixture filing or record its real property interest prevails*. [U.C.C. §9-334]

Example: Gino owns an Italian ristorante and pizzeria. Bank holds a mortgage on the building and property and has since January 1, but failed to ever record the mortgage. Gino borrows $10,000 to use in his business on January 3, and gives Finance Co. a security interest in the new woodburning oven at his pizzeria. Finance Co. properly files its fixture filing on January 30. Finance Co. will prevail over Bank.

a) **"Fixture Filing" Required**
To gain priority over a holder of an interest in real property, a party with a security interest in a fixture must perfect by making a "fixture filing." A fixture filing is accomplished by filing a financing statement in the office where a mortgage on the *real property* would be recorded. In addition to the usual requirements for a financing statement, a fixture filing financing statement must contain a *description of the real property* to which the fixture is attached. [U.C.C. §9-502]

b) **Exceptions to General Rule**
The following are exceptions to the general rule:

(1) **PMSIs**
A PMSI secured party who makes a fixture filing within *20 days* after affixation will prevail over a real property interest in the same fixture that was recorded prior to affixation.

(a) **Exception to PMSI Exception—Construction Mortgages**
This exception does not apply to a prior *construction mortgage* (*i.e.,* a mortgage securing an obligation incurred for the construction of an improvement on land). A construction mortgage has priority over a PMSI in a fixture that was filed within the 20-day grace period if the construction mortgage was *recorded before the goods became fixtures* and if the goods became fixtures *before the completion of construction*. [U.C.C. §9-334(h)]

Example: Bank finances the building of Sam's new store and takes out a construction mortgage on the store. Subsequently, while the store is being built, CoolCo sells a central air conditioner to Sam's builder and makes a fixture filing one day after the air conditioner is affixed to Sam's store. Even though CoolCo filed within the 20-day grace period for PMSIs in fixtures, Bank's construction mortgage has priority.

(2) No Fixture Filing Required
In some situations, a party with a security interest in a fixture does not need to perfect by making a fixture filing to gain priority over the holder of the real property interest. Rather, the security interest can be perfected in any manner authorized by the Code (*e.g.,* automatic perfection).

(a) Readily Removable Collateral
A security interest perfected in *any manner* authorized by the Code *before affixation* will prevail over a real property interest if:

(i) The collateral is a *readily removable office or factory machine*;

(ii) The collateral is *readily removable equipment* that is not primarily used or leased for use in the operation of real property; or

(iii) The collateral is a *readily removable replacement of a domestic appliance that is a consumer good*.

[U.C.C. §9-334(e)(2)]

(b) Later-Acquired Liens
A security interest in fixtures perfected in *any manner* authorized by the Code will prevail over a *later-acquired lien* on the real property (*see* D.1., *infra*). [U.C.C. §9-334(e)(3)]

(3) Real Property Encumbrancer Consents
A security interest in fixtures (perfected or unperfected) will prevail over a prior real property interest if the real property encumbrancer or owner, in an *authenticated record*, either *consents* to the security interest or *disclaims* its interest. [U.C.C. §9-334(f)(1)]

(4) Debtor Has Right to Remove Fixtures
If the debtor has a right to remove the fixtures as against the real property owner, the attached security interest has priority. [U.C.C. §9-334(f)(2)]
Example: A tenant has a right to remove trade fixtures. An attached security interest in the trade fixtures has priority over the mortgage holder or owner of the building.

2) Accessions—General Rule
Accessions are goods that are physically united with other goods in such a manner that the identity of the original goods is not lost (*e.g.,* new pedals on a bike). [U.C.C. §9-102(a)(1)] Usually, the general rules for priority (*e.g.,* first to file or perfect, PMSI superpriority) apply to accessions.
Example: On January 1, State Bank loans Stella $5,000 and takes a security interest in all of Stella's presently owned and thereafter acquired equipment. State Bank then perfects its security interest by filing. At the time State Bank's security interest was created, Stella owned a computer that she used for business purposes. On July 1, Computer Bob sells a hard drive to Stella on credit and takes a security interest in the hard drive. Stella plans to install the hard drive in her business computer, so Computer Bob perfects his interest by filing a financing statement two days after Stella receives the hard drive. Stella then defaults on her payments to both State Bank and Computer Bob. Computer Bob has priority in the

hard drive because he has a PMSI in the hard drive that was perfected within 20 days after Stella received the hard drive.

a) Exception

However, if the accession (*e.g.,* a new motor) becomes a part of a whole that is subject to a security interest perfected by **notation on a certificate of title** (*e.g.,* a car), the security interest in the whole (the car) has priority over the security interest in the accession (the new motor). [U.C.C. §9-335(d)]

Example: On January 1, State Bank loans Florence $5,000 and takes a security interest in Florence's car by putting a notation on the certificate of title. Several months later, the car needs a new transmission, and Florence brings the car to Lemon-Aid Auto Repair. Lemon-Aid sells her the new transmission on credit, takes a security interest in the transmission, and perfects on the day of sale by filing a financing statement. Florence then defaults in her payments to both State Bank and Lemon-Aid. In spite of Lemon-Aid's perfected PMSI, State Bank has priority in the transmission because it perfected its security interest in the car by making a notation on the certificate of title.

3) Effect of Fixture or Accession Interest with Priority

When the security interest in the fixture or accession has priority over all interests in the real property or goods, the holder of the security interest in the fixture or accession may, upon default, remove the fixture or accession from the real property or goods. Note that if the debtor does not own the property from which the collateral is removed, the creditor must reimburse the owner of the property for the cost of any repairs of damage to the property caused by removal, but not for any other diminution in value. [U.C.C. §§9-335(e) - (f), 9-604]

4) Crops

A perfected security interest in crops has priority over a conflicting interest in the real property on which the crops are growing, regardless of the time of filing or perfection. [U.C.C. §9-334(i)]

C. SECURED PARTY VS. BUYER OR OTHER TRANSFEREE

1. Unperfected Secured Party vs. Buyer

a. General Rule—Buyer Prevails

A buyer of collateral (or a *lessee* of goods) takes free of a security interest covering the collateral if she both *gives value and receives delivery* of the collateral *without knowledge* of the security interest *before it is perfected*. [U.C.C. §9-317(b) - (c)]

Example: On February 1, Manufacturer borrows money from Bank, giving a security interest in a piece of equipment as collateral. On February 2, Manufacturer makes a contract to sell the equipment to X, who pays the full price. On February 3, Bank properly files a financing statement. On February 4, X takes delivery of the equipment. Bank prevails over X, because even though X paid before Bank perfected by filing, he did not take possession before that time.

Note: If the collateral is an account, electronic chattel paper, a general intangible, or investment property other than a certificated security, there is *no delivery requirement* because there is nothing tangible to deliver. [U.C.C. §9-317(d)]

b. Exceptions

1) Buyers of Receivables

Recall that sales of certain receivables (*i.e.,* accounts, chattel paper, payment intangibles, and promissory notes) are treated by Article 9 as being creations of security interests in the receivables being sold (*see* I.B.1.a., *supra*) and, therefore, the purchaser is not considered a "buyer" as the term is used in this section. Rights between such purchasers of receivables and other holders of security interests in the same accounts are governed by the rules applicable between conflicting security interests. (*See* B.3., *supra.*)

2) PMSI Grace Period

If a secured party *attaches a PMSI* in the debtor's collateral *before* the buyer or lessee without knowledge pays value and receives delivery (if required), the secured party will have *priority* over the buyer or lessee if she *files within 20 days* after the *debtor* receives the collateral.

Example: On March 1, Seller sells equipment to Buyer on credit and takes a PMSI in the equipment. Buyer receives the equipment on March 5. Buyer then sells the equipment for $1,000 to Retailer, who receives the equipment without knowledge of Seller's PMSI on March 13. Seller then files a financing statement covering the equipment on March 15. Even though Seller's PMSI was not perfected before Retailer gave value and received the equipment, Seller has priority over Retailer because Seller filed within 20 days after Buyer received the equipment.

2. Perfected Secured Party vs. Buyer

Generally, a perfected security interest in goods is good against subsequent buyers. There are, however, some cases in which the buyer will defeat even a perfected prior security interest.

a. Secured Party Consents to Sale

If the secured party consents to a sale, lease, or other transfer of the collateral free of the security interest, the transferee will take free of the secured party's perfected security interest. [U.C.C. §9-315(a)]

b. Buyer in the Ordinary Course of Business

A buyer who buys goods in the ordinary course of business from a seller who is engaged in the business of selling goods of the kind purchased generally *takes free of a nonpossessory perfected security interest* in the inventory even if the buyer knows of it, unless the buyer also knows that the sale is in violation of the terms of the security agreement. [U.C.C. §9-320(a)]

Example: Bank has a perfected security interest in the inventory of Mariner Sam's Boat Sales, Inc. Customer buys a boat from Mariner Sam's. Customer will take free of Bank's security interest.

Note: This rule also applies to *lessees of goods* and *nonexclusive licensees of general intangibles* in the ordinary course of business. [U.C.C. §9-321]

1) Seller Must Be in Business of Selling Goods of the Kind

A buyer will not qualify as a buyer in the ordinary course ("BIOC") unless the seller is in the business of selling goods of the kind that the buyer buys.

Example: Honest John is in the business of buying and selling used cars. When Honest John sells a car to Customer, Customer is a BIOC because Honest John is in the business of selling cars. However, when Honest John *buys* a car from Customer, Honest John is *not* a BIOC because Customer is not in the business of selling cars.

Note: The sale must be in the seller's ordinary course of business, but there is no restriction on the use to which the buyer puts the goods. Thus, in the example above, Customer can qualify as a BIOC even if he purchased the car for use in his business.

2) Buyer Takes Free Only of Interests Created by His Seller

To qualify under the BIOC rule, the security interest must have been *created by the buyer's seller*; if the security interest was created by someone else, the BIOC rule does not apply.

Example: Bank has a perfected security interest in Sally's diamond ring. Sally sells the ring to Jeweler. As discussed above, Jeweler cannot qualify as a BIOC because Sally is not in the business of selling jewelry, and thus, Jeweler takes the ring subject to Bank's perfected security interest. Jeweler then sells the ring to Becky. Even though Becky purchased the ring from a seller in the business of selling rings, Becky is subject to Bank's perfected security interest because that interest was not created by Becky's seller.

3) Knowledge

Note that a buyer may still qualify under the BIOC rule even if the buyer knows that the inventory is subject to a security interest, *unless* the buyer also knows that the sale violates the security agreement.

Example: Ajax Appliance Store has given Bank a security interest in its inventory of refrigerators to secure a loan. Ajax sells one of these refrigerators to Buyer. Buyer knows that Bank has a security interest in Ajax's inventory of refrigerators. Even so, Buyer takes free of Bank's interest since he is entitled to assume that the agreement between Bank and Ajax permits such sales. If, however, Buyer knows that Bank requires Ajax to get a specific release for each refrigerator sold and that Ajax did not do so in this case, Buyer would take subject to Bank's security interest.

c. PMSI in Consumer Goods

It has already been pointed out that PMSIs in consumer goods are perfected automatically without filing. However, in such a case, if the buyer of the consumer goods in turn resells them to another consumer (*i.e.,* a buyer who buys for his own personal, household, or family use), the second buyer takes free of the security interest if he buys without knowledge of it for value and before a financing statement covering the goods has been filed. This is often called the "garage sale" rule. Therefore, while a holder of a PMSI in the goods just described is perfected as against lien creditors and other security interests without filing, she loses to consumer buyers unless she files. [U.C.C. §9-320(b)]

Example: Computertown sold Tom a computer on credit, retaining a purchase money security interest in the computer. The computer was purchased for Tom's household purposes, but after only a few months' use, he tired of it. Tom then sold the computer to his next door neighbor, Jeff, for Jeff's personal use. Jeff takes the computer free from Computertown's security interest unless he knows about the security interest, or unless Computertown filed a financing statement before Jeff purchased the computer from Tom.

d. Future Advances

Generally, if a creditor makes a future advance (*i.e.,* advances value secured by an earlier security agreement under which there was an advance of value), the time of perfection of the future advance relates back to the time of perfection of the *original advance*. However, a buyer (or lessee) *not in the ordinary course of business* can gain priority over a secured party who makes a future advance on collateral after the buyer purchases the collateral. Such a buyer has priority over a future advance made (i) after the secured party *learned* of the purchase, or (ii) more than *45 days* after the purchase. [U.C.C. §9-323]

Example: On August 12, Alex sells a valuable oil painting that adorns his law office wall to Becky, a client who admires it. Unbeknownst to Becky, all of Alex's equipment (including the oil painting) is covered by a perfected security interest in favor of CindiCo Finance. On August 15 and October 15, CindiCo loans Alex $5,000 pursuant to a future advance clause. Becky takes free of the security interest in the painting to the extent of the October 15 loan (because it was made more than 45 days after Alex sold the painting to Becky). Whether Becky takes free of the security interest of the August 15 loan depends on whether CindiCo knew of the sale when it made that loan.

1) Exception

Even if a secured party makes an advance after it learned of the purchase or more than 45 days after the purchase, if the future advance was made *pursuant to a commitment* made without knowledge of the purchase and before expiration of the 45-day period, the future advance has priority. [U.C.C. §9-323]

3. Secured Party vs. Holder in Due Course or the Like

A holder in due course ("HDC") of a negotiable instrument (or a holder to whom a negotiable document of title has been negotiated, or a protected purchaser of a security) takes priority over any security interest in the negotiable instrument. [U.C.C. §9-331]

Example: On August 1, Fred borrows $500 from Ethel in exchange for his $500 negotiable promissory note. On August 3, Ethel borrows $400 from Bank and gives Bank a security interest in the note. Bank allows Ethel to retain possession of the note. (Bank's security interest is temporarily perfected; *see* III.F.2., *supra*.) On August 5, Ethel sells the note to Lucy, who qualifies as an HDC. Lucy takes the note free of Bank's security interest because she is an HDC.

4. **Secured Party vs. Transferee of Money or Deposit Account Funds**
If a debtor transfers money or deposit account funds (*e.g.,* by writing a check or making an electronic funds transfer) to a person, that person *takes free of any security interest in the money or funds,* unless the transferee acts in collusion with the debtor in violating the rights of the secured party. If deposit account funds are in the form of a check, the holder of the check may also have priority as a holder in due course (*see supra*). [U.C.C. §9-332]
Example: Creditor takes a perfected security interest in all of Debtor's accounts. Debtor deposits money received from these accounts into a deposit account containing only money received from the accounts. Creditor has a perfected security interest in the deposit account funds as proceeds of Debtor's accounts. Debtor then writes a check drawn on the deposit account for $1,000 and gives it to Transferee. Transferee takes the check free of Creditor's perfected security interest, unless Transferee was acting in collusion with Debtor.

D. **SECURED PARTY VS. JUDICIAL LIEN CREDITOR OR HOLDER OF POSSESSORY LIEN**

1. **Unperfected Secured Party vs. Judicial Lien Creditor**
A judicial lien creditor (*i.e.,* a person who has acquired a lien on the collateral through judicial attachment, levy, or the like) prevails over the holder of a security interest in collateral if the lien creditor becomes such *before* the security interest is *perfected*. [U.C.C. §9-317(a)]

   a. **Trustee in Bankruptcy**
   Judicial "lien creditor" includes a trustee in bankruptcy, who is said to be a hypothetical judicial lien creditor in all of the debtor's property beginning on the date the bankruptcy petition is filed. [U.C.C. §9-102(52)]

   b. **PMSI Grace Period Exception**
   A secured party who *attaches a PMSI* in the debtor's collateral *before* a judicial lien creditor acquires an interest in the collateral will have *priority* over the judicial lien creditor if it *files within 20 days* after the debtor receives the collateral. [U.C.C. §9-317(e)]
   Example: On October 1, Bank loans money so that Debtor can buy new equipment and the value advanced is used for that purpose. Debtor signs a security agreement giving Bank a PMSI in the purchased equipment. On October 2, D purchases and takes possession of the equipment. On October 4, Judgment Creditor has the sheriff levy on the new equipment, acquiring judicial lien creditor status. On October 8, Bank files a financing statement perfecting its PMSI in the equipment. Under the grace period exception, Bank acquires priority over the lien creditor even though Bank's interest was not perfected on October 4, at the time the judicial lien creditor acquired her status.

2. **Perfected Secured Party vs. Judicial Lien Creditor**

   a. **General Rule—Lien Subject to Prior Perfected Interest**
   A prior perfected security interest in the collateral has priority over a judicial lien creditor's interest in the same collateral (*see* 1., *supra*). [U.C.C. §9-317(a)(2)]

      1) **Prior Filed Security Interest May Also Have Priority**
      If a secured party files a security interest but does not attach (and therefore does not perfect) before a judicial lien creditor's interest arises, the secured party has priority over the judicial lien creditor as long as the secured party (i) evidences its security agreement with an authenticated security agreement, possession, or control, and (ii) eventually attaches and perfects its security interest. [U.C.C. §9-317(a)(2), and comment 4]
      Example: On September 1, Mae agrees to lend Tom $1,000 in return for a security interest in Tom's equipment. Tom signs a security agreement and Mae files a financing statement on the same day, but Mae does not yet loan Tom the money. On September 5, Sarah causes a lien to attach to Tom's business computer. On September 30, Mae gives

Tom the $1,000. Even though Mae's security interest was unperfected at the time Sarah's lien attached, Mae has priority in the business computer (equipment) because she authenticated a security agreement and filed a financing statement before Sarah's lien attached, and Mae eventually attached and perfected.

b. Exception—Lien Has Priority Over Some Future Advances
A judicial lien creditor's interest can gain priority over certain future advances that would otherwise have priority under the above general rule; *i.e.,* under the general rule, the future advances would have priority if they were made pursuant to a perfected security interest that was filed or perfected before the lien arose. Under this exception, the judicial lien creditor will have priority if the future advance was made *more than 45 days* after the lien arose, *unless* the future advance was made (i) *without knowledge* of the lien, or (ii) *pursuant to a commitment made without knowledge* of the lien. [U.C.C. §9-323(b)]

Example: Bank perfects a security interest in Debtor's equipment. The security agreement provides that the collateral will also secure future advances and obligates Bank to make loans for one year, as long as Debtor makes regular repayments on the loan balance. Pursuant to its commitment, Bank loans Debtor $10,000 every month, starting in February. On April 1, the equipment is seized by the sheriff on behalf of a lien creditor. All of Bank's loans, including those made more than 45 days after April 1, have priority over the judicial lien creditor's interest in the equipment, because these future advances were made pursuant to the commitment.

3. Holders of Possessory Liens Arising by Operation of Law
By statute or common law, most states grant people who supply goods or services a lien on goods in their possession to secure payment for the goods or services provided (*e.g.*, so-called mechanics' liens or artisans' liens). Generally, Article 9 does not govern such liens (other than agricultural liens) except with regard to priority. Article 9 provides that such possessory liens have priority over any security interests in the collateral as long as the goods or services were provided in the ordinary course of business and the collateral remains in the lienholder's possession, unless the lien is created by a statute that provides otherwise. [U.C.C. §9-333]

Example: Becky purchased a used car on credit from Honest Al's used car lot and gave Al a security interest in the car to secure the purchase price. Al perfected by notation on the car's certificate of title. The car soon developed a knock, and Becky took the car to Ms. Mary's Motor Repair ("MMMR"). Mary did not look at the car for several weeks, and repairs took a few more weeks because Mary had to wait for parts. In the interim, Becky lost her job and was unable to pay MMMR or make any payments to Honest Al. If state law gives MMMR an artisans' lien, MMMR's lien is superior to Al's perfected security interest as long as MMMR retains possession of the car.

E. SECURED PARTY VS. ARTICLE 2 CLAIMANT
Article 2 sometimes grants a buyer or seller a possessory security interest or a right similar to a security interest in goods (*e.g.,* if the buyer rightfully rejects or revokes acceptance of goods, or if the seller rightfully stops delivery of goods in transit). (*See* Sales outline for further discussion.) If a secured party also has a security interest in the goods, the Article 2 claimant will have priority over the secured party as long as the Article 2 claimant retains *possession* of the goods. [U.C.C. §9-110]

F. PRIORITIES IN A NUTSHELL
When a debtor defaults and a number of persons have an interest in the same item of collateral, remember the following hierarchy: the person with the highest priority has first rights in the collateral; if any part of the collateral or its proceeds is left, the next person can recover, etc. Excluding investment property and nonconsumer deposit accounts, in which the party with *control* generally has priority, the ranking is as follows:

1. *Buyers in the ordinary course of business* who do not know the sale is in violation of the security interest.

2. *Holders in due course* and the like of negotiable instruments (*i.e.,* commercial paper, documents of title, securities).

3. *Transferees of funds from deposit accounts*.

4. Certain *purchasers of chattel paper or instruments* who have possession or control.

5. *Possessory lienholders*.

6. *Article 2 claimants* with *possession* of goods.

7. *PMSIs* (except a consumer purchaser from a consumer—such as a neighbor buying from a neighbor—has priority over an *automatically perfected* PMSI in the consumer goods). Recall that only a PMSI in consumer goods is perfected automatically. Other PMSIs must be perfected through some other method (generally by filing), but there is a 20-day grace period for PMSIs in goods other than inventory and livestock.

8. *Perfected security interests* and *liens that have attached* to the collateral (including *trustees in bankruptcy* as of the date the bankruptcy petition is filed).

   a. As between perfected security interests in the same collateral, the *first to file or perfect* has priority.

   b. As between a perfected security interest and a lien, the lien has priority if it was created *before* the security interest was *filed or perfected*. Otherwise, the perfected security interest has priority.

9. *Purchasers* of collateral who *buy for value and receive delivery without notice* of any *unperfected* security interest.

10. *Unperfected security interests* (rank in priority according to order of attachment).

11. The *debtor*.

V. RIGHTS ON DEFAULT

A. DETERMINING WHEN DEFAULT HAS OCCURRED
Article 9 does not define the events that will trigger a default; rather, the security agreement will usually provide that upon certain events (*e.g.*, failure to make timely payment, failure to keep the collateral insured, unauthorized transfer of the collateral, etc.) the secured party may exercise default remedies. Default on an agricultural lien is determined by the lien statute. [U.C.C. §§9-601, comment 3, 9-606]

B. RIGHT TO TAKE POSSESSION OF AND SELL COLLATERAL
The right to take possession of and sell the collateral on default is the most important and most used of the rights on default.

1. **Taking Possession**

   a. **Self-Help**
      The secured party may take possession by self-help without judicial process if she can do so *without a breach of the peace*. [U.C.C. §9-609] Without removal, the secured party may also make equipment unusable and dispose of it on the debtor's property if she can do so without a breach of the peace. This latter right is directed toward the problem of taking possession of heavy, bulky equipment that is not easily movable.

      1) **"Breach of the Peace"**
         A repossession made over any protest by the debtor constitutes a "breach of the peace," even though no violence or significant disturbance occurs. Constructive force or actions that contain implied threats are not peaceful. Thus, the secured party breaches the peace by carrying a weapon or dressing as a law enforcement officer. Breaking and entering is probably a breach of the peace, but simple trespass is not. Thus, for example, a repossessor may hot wire a car sitting on a driveway, but not one sitting in a closed garage.

      2) **Consequences of Breach of the Peace**
         When a secured party breaches the peace, he loses the Code's authorization to

repossess and may be sued for conversion and is liable for actual (and frequently punitive) damages.

b. **Collection Rights of Secured Party**
With non-goods collateral such as accounts and instruments, if the debtor who gave a security interest in the collateral defaults, the secured party can notify the person owing money to the debtor (*i.e.,* the account debtor) to make payment to the secured party, rather than to the debtor. Upon notification, the account debtor must pay the *secured party* rather than the debtor. [U.C.C. §§9-406, 9-607]
Example: Dr. Bones gets a loan from Bank to remodel his office. To secure the loan, Dr. Bones gives Bank a security interest in all of his then-owned and after-acquired accounts (*i.e.,* accounts receivable owed by patients). Dr. Bones then defaults on the Bank loan. Bank can notify all of Dr. Bones's patients to pay Bank instead of Dr. Bones.

c. **Replevy Action**
The secured party may always take possession by replevying the collateral pursuant to judicial process.

d. **Rights and Duties of Secured Party in Possession**
A secured party with possession of collateral after default has the same rights and duties regarding the collateral that she had before default (*see* II.B.1.b.1), *supra*). [U.C.C. §9-601(b)]

2. **Sale**
The secured party, after default, may sell, lease, or license collateral either in its condition when taken or after commercially reasonable preparation or processing. Disposition may be by either *public* (auction) or *private sale*, and by one or more contracts. [U.C.C. §9-610(a) - (b)]

a. **Commercial Reasonableness**
The general test as to validity of the sale is *commercial reasonableness* of the method, manner, time, place, and terms. The mere fact that a better price could have been obtained from a sale at a different time or in a different manner is not sufficient to establish that the sale was not commercially reasonable. A sale is made in a commercially reasonable manner if it is done in the usual manner in a recognized market or at the market price in such a market at the time of sale. A sale is also commercially reasonable if it conforms with reasonable commercial standards among dealers in the kind of goods sold. [U.C.C. §§9-610(b), 9-627(a) - (b)]

b. **Notice**
Unless the collateral is perishable or threatens to decline rapidly in value or is of a kind ordinarily sold in a recognized market, reasonable notice that is *authenticated* by the secured party (*i.e.,* the notice cannot be oral) must be given to the debtor and any sureties on the debt. However, *after default*, the debtor or surety may, in an authenticated agreement, *waive* the right to notice of the sale. Except in the case of consumer goods, the same notice must be given to any other secured parties who have given an authenticated notification to the secured party in possession of their interests, and any secured parties who have perfected by filing a financing statement or making a notation on a certificate of title. [U.C.C. §§9-611, 9-624(a)]

1) **Timeliness of Notice**
Notice must be sent within a *reasonable time* before the sale. What constitutes a reasonable time is a *question of fact.* However, in a *nonconsumer transaction*, notice is deemed to be sent within a reasonable time if it is sent *10 days or more* before the time of sale. [U.C.C. §9-612]

2) **Contents of Notice**

a) **Collateral Other than Consumer Goods**
In a sale of collateral *other than consumer goods,* the notice *should* contain the following:

(i) A *description of the debtor and the secured party;*

(ii) A *description of the collateral;*

        (iii) The *method of sale* (*i.e.,* public or private);

        (iv) A *statement that the debtor is entitled to an accounting* for the unpaid indebtedness and the *charge* for performing the accounting; and

        (v) The *time and place of public sale or the time after which a private sale will be made.*

If the notice contains all of the above information, it is *per se sufficient*; if it lacks any of the above information, its sufficiency will be a *question of fact.* [U.C.C. §9-613]

b) Consumer Goods Collateral

In a sale of *consumer goods,* the notice *must* contain all of the information listed in a), above, to be sufficient. In addition, it must contain a description of the recipient's *liability for a deficiency,* a *telephone number* from which the recipient can discover the *cost of redeeming* the collateral, and a *telephone number or mailing address* from which the recipient can get *additional information* concerning the sale. [U.C.C. §9-614]

3) Explanation of Deficiency or Surplus

If the debtor is a *consumer*, after the sale, the secured party must send the debtor an *explanation* of the calculation of any debt still owed (the deficiency) or money the debtor will receive (the surplus).

c. Purchase by Secured Party

Generally, the secured party may purchase the collateral at a *public sale*. The secured party may purchase at a *private sale* if the collateral is of a type customarily sold in a recognized market or is of a type on which there are widely distributed price quotations. [U.C.C. §9-610(c)]

d. Effect of Sale

Absent bad faith on the part of the purchaser, the purchaser of the collateral generally takes all of the debtor's rights in the collateral. The sale also discharges the security interest under which the sale is being made and all subordinate security interests and liens. However, the purchaser is still subject to superior security interests. [U.C.C. §9-617]

e. Proceeds

Upon sale, the proceeds go first to the expenses of the repossession and sale; then to the satisfaction of the debt; then to the satisfaction of subordinate third-party security interest debts and interests of consignors, in the order of their priority (if an authenticated demand is received); and finally any surplus goes to the debtor. If the collateral when sold does not bring enough to pay the expenses of sale and the debt, the secured party may recover any deficiency from the debtor. *Note:* If the secured party, a person related to the secured party, or a surety on the debt purchases the collateral for an amount *significantly below* the expected price, the deficiency will be calculated according to what the amount *would have been* if a disinterested party had purchased the collateral. [U.C.C. §9-615(f)]

3. Retention of Collateral in Full or Partial Satisfaction of Debt ("Strict Foreclosure")

a. General Rule

After default, the foreclosing secured party may keep the collateral to fully or partially satisfy the debt (*i.e.,* the creditor may make a full or partial *strict foreclosure*) if:

    (i) The *debtor consents* to the strict foreclosure by either:

        i. *Agreeing* to the strict foreclosure in an *authenticated record* after default; or

        ii. In the case of a *full* strict foreclosure, *failing to make an authenticated objection* within *20 days* after the secured party sent notice (a debtor cannot consent to a partial strict foreclosure in this manner);

    (ii) The secured party sends an *authenticated notice* of intent to keep the collateral in satisfaction of the debt to:

   i. The *debtor*;

   ii. Any *other secured party* from whom the foreclosing party has received notice of a claim to the collateral; and

   iii. Any other secured party who has perfected a security interest in the collateral *by filing a financing statement or making a notation on a certificate of title*; and

  (iii) *None of the notified parties objects* within 20 days after the notice is sent (if a notified party objects, the collateral must be disposed of by sale).

[U.C.C. §§9-620 - 9-621] Note that these requirements *cannot be waived*, even after default. [U.C.C. §9-602(10)]

 b. Exceptions

  1) No Partial Strict Foreclosure in Consumer Transactions
   In a *consumer transaction*, a secured party may *not* keep the collateral in partial satisfaction of the debt and seek a deficiency judgment. The secured party may keep the collateral *only* in full satisfaction of the debt.

  2) Consumer Goods Sixty Percent Rule
   In *consumer goods* cases where the debtor has paid at least 60% of the *cash price* in the case of a PMSI or 60% of the *loan* in other cases, the secured party must sell the collateral *within 90 days* after repossession, unless, *after default*, she gets an authenticated agreement from the debtor waiving this right or extending the time in which the collateral may be sold. If the debtor has paid less than 60%, the general rules, above, apply. [U.C.C. §9-620(e) - (f)]

4. Right to Redeem Collateral
Until the secured party has sold the collateral or has discharged the debt by retention of the collateral, a debtor, a surety, or any other secured party or lienholder, unless he has otherwise agreed *after default*, may redeem the collateral by paying all obligations secured by the collateral plus the reasonable expenses incurred by the secured party in relation to the repossession, including reasonable attorneys' fees. [U.C.C. §9-623]

5. Secured Party's Liability for Failure to Comply with Code Requirements
A secured party is liable for the *actual damages* caused by failure to follow *any* of the Code's rules.

6. Secured Party's Liability for Failure to Comply with Code Default Rules

 a. Minimum Recovery for Consumer Goods
  If the collateral is consumer goods and the secured party violates Code default rules (*i.e.,* the rules in section V. of this outline), the debtor is entitled to a minimum of 10% of the cash price of the goods plus an amount equal to all the interest charges to be paid over the life of the loan. [U.C.C. §9-625]

 b. Possible Loss of Deficiency Judgment
  A secured party who violates the default rules also may lose her right to a deficiency judgment. In *nonconsumer transactions,* the *"rebuttable presumption rule"* applies— *i.e.,* the value of the collateral is presumed to equal the amount of the debt unless the secured party proves otherwise. [U.C.C. §9-626] *The Code does not provide a rule for consumer transactions,* and leaves the determination of a rule to the courts. Courts have generally taken three approaches. They either:

  1) Follow the above *rebuttable presumption rule;*

  2) Deny the secured party a deficiency regardless of whether the secured party can prove that the collateral is worth less than the debt (the *"absolute bar rule"*); or

  3) Allow the secured party to recover the deficiency minus any actual damages that the debtor can prove (the *"setoff rule"*).

C. OTHER RIGHTS OF SECURED PARTY ON DEFAULT
Instead of taking possession and selling the collateral under Article 9, the secured party on

default may bring an ordinary judicial action for the amounts due and levy on the collateral after judgment. The secured party may begin her judicial action and seize the property at the same time. However, an extremely long delay after the property is seized and before judgment is rendered might result in the secured party's liability for failure to act in a commercially reasonable manner.

D. REMEDIES ARE CUMULATIVE

All rights and remedies under Article 9 are cumulative. This allows the secured creditor to pursue any remedy (foreclosure by sale, strict foreclosure, or a judgment) until the debt obligation is paid in full, although, of course, the creditor is entitled to only one satisfaction.

VI. JURISDICTIONAL RULES

A. WHICH STATE'S LAW GOVERNS PERFECTION?

The question of which state's law governs the perfection of a security interest is especially important when a security interest is perfected by filing, because filing must occur in the proper state.

Example: Bank wishes to file a financing statement to perfect its security interest in Debtor's equipment. Bank must file in the *proper state.* If Bank files in the wrong state, its security interest will not be perfected.

1. General Rule—Law of State Where Debtor Is Located Governs Perfection

The law of the *state where the debtor is located* generally governs perfection of the security interest. [U.C.C. §9-301(1)]

a. Location of Debtor

If the debtor is an *individual,* she is located in the state of her *principal residence.* If the debtor is a *registered organization* (*e.g.,* a corporation, limited liability company, or limited partnership), the debtor is located in the state under whose laws it is *organized* (*i.e.,* where its articles of incorporation are filed). If the debtor is an *unregistered organization* (*e.g.,* a general partnership), it is located at its *place of business* if it only has one place of business or at its *chief executive office* if it has more than one place of business. [U.C.C. §9-307]

Examples: 1) XYZ, Inc. grants Bank a security interest in equipment located in State A. XYZ, Inc. has places of business in several states, its chief executive office is in State B, and its articles of incorporation are filed in State C. The law of State C governs perfection of the security interest because XYZ, Inc. was organized under the laws of State C. Therefore, if Bank wishes to file a financing statement to perfect its security interest in the equipment, it must file its financing statement in State C.

2) Same facts as above, except that XYZ is an unregistered partnership (and thus articles of incorporation were not filed). XYZ is located in State B because it has more than one place of business and its chief executive office is in State B. Therefore, if Bank wishes to file a financing statement to perfect its security interest in the equipment, it must file its financing statement in State B.

2. Exceptions

a. Possessory Security Interests and Security Interests in Fixtures and Timber to Be Cut

The perfection of possessory security interests, as well as security interests in fixtures and timber to be cut, is governed by the law of the *state in which the collateral is located.* [U.C.C. §9-301(2) - (3)]

b. Goods Covered by Certificate of Title

If goods are covered by a certificate of title, the law of the *state issuing the most recent certificate of title* governs perfection. [U.C.C. §9-303]

c. Deposit Accounts

If the collateral is a deposit account, unless the debtor's agreements with the bank provide *otherwise,* the law of the *state in which the bank has its chief executive office* governs perfection. [U.C.C. §9-304]

d. **Investment Property**
If the collateral is a *certificated security,* the law of the *state where the certificated security is located* governs perfection. If the collateral is an *uncertificated security,* unless the debtor's agreements with the issuer provide otherwise, the law of the *state where the issuer was organized* governs perfection. If the collateral is a *securities account,* unless the debtor's agreements with the securities intermediary provide otherwise, the law of the *state where the securities intermediary's chief executive office is located* governs perfection. [U.C.C. §9-305]

1) **Exception—Perfection by Filing or Automatic Perfection**
If a security interest in investment property *is perfected by filing*, or if it is *automatically perfected* by a securities intermediary, the law of the *state where the debtor is located* governs perfection. [U.C.C. §9-305]

e. **Agricultural Liens**
The perfection of an agricultural lien is governed by the law of the *state in which the farm product covered by the lien is located.* [U.C.C. §9-302]

B. **MOVEMENT OF DEBTOR OR COLLATERAL FROM ONE STATE TO ANOTHER**
If the perfection of a security interest in collateral is governed by the law of the state where a person or collateral is located and that person or collateral moves to another state, the security interest generally remains temporarily perfected. If the secured party does not perfect in the *new state* before the temporary perfection period lapses, the security interest will become *unperfected* and thus *lose its time of priority.* The rules for temporary perfection in the new state are as follows.

1. **General Rule**
If the perfection of a security interest is governed by the law of the state in which the *debtor is located,* and the debtor moves from one state to another, the security interest will remain perfected without any further action until *four months* after the debtor moves or until perfection in the first state *lapses*, whichever occurs earlier. If the collateral is *transferred to a new debtor located in a different state*, the security interest will remain perfected without any further action until *one year* after the sale of the collateral or until perfection in the first state *lapses,* whichever occurs earlier. [U.C.C. §9-316(a)]

2. **Exceptions**

a. **Security Interest Perfected by Possession**
If a perfected security interest is a *possessory* security interest (which is governed by the law of the state in which the *collateral is located*), and the collateral is moved from one state to another, the security interest will remain perfected without any further action as long as the security interest is also perfected by possession under the laws of the *new* state. [U.C.C. §9-316(c)]

b. **Certificate of Title Property (Automobiles and Other Vehicles)**
All states require security interests in vehicles to be perfected by notation on a certificate of title. If a vehicle is moved from one state to another, and is covered by a certificate of title issued by the new state, a security interest in the vehicle that was properly perfected in the original state *lasts as long as it would have if the vehicle had not been covered by the new certificate of title*. [U.C.C. §9-316(d)]

1) **Exception—Purchasers for Value**
If a vehicle subject to a perfected security interest in one state is moved to a new state and is covered by a certificate of title issued by the new state, the security interest in the original state is perfected as against a *purchaser for value* of the vehicle only until the *earlier* of:

(i) The time when the security interest would have become *unperfected* in the original state if the vehicle had not been covered by the new certificate of title (same rule as the general rule); *or*

(ii) *Four months* after the vehicle is covered by the new certificate of title.

[U.C.C. §9-316(e)]

2) Exception—Clean Certificate of Title Issued in New State
If the certificate of title issued in the new state *does not note the secured party's interest* in the vehicle, the following parties have priority over the secured party:

(i) A *buyer* of the vehicle who is not in the business of selling vehicles who purchases for *value* and receives *delivery* of the vehicle *without knowledge* of the security interest; and

(ii) A *secured party* who *perfects* a security interest in the vehicle *without knowledge* of the other security interest *after* the clean certificate of title is issued in the new state.

[U.C.C. §9-337]

c. Deposit Accounts, Uncertificated Securities, and Securities Accounts
Recall that if collateral is a deposit account, an uncertificated security, or a securities account, perfection is governed by the law of the state where the bank, issuer, or securities intermediary is located (*see* A.1., *supra*). If the bank, issuer, or securities intermediary moves to a new state, perfection of an interest in the deposit account, uncertificated security, or securities account *continues until the earlier* of:

(i) The time when the security interest would have become *unperfected* in the original state if the bank, issuer, or securities intermediary had not moved to the new state; *or*

(ii) *Four months* after the bank, issuer, or securities intermediary moves to the new state.

[U.C.C. §9-316(f)]

BAR REVIEW

Trusts

TRUSTS—MASSACHUSETTS

TABLE OF CONTENTS

I. INTRODUCTION

A. TRUST DEFINED

A trust is a fiduciary relationship in which a trustee holds *legal title* to specific property under a fiduciary duty to manage, invest, safeguard, and administer the trust assets and income for the benefit of designated beneficiaries, who hold *equitable title*. If a person wants to make a lifetime gift to her son, she can give the property outright to him, or she can create an inter vivos trust for his benefit. If a person wants to leave property to his daughter by will, he can bequeath the property outright to her, or he can create a testamentary trust for the daughter's benefit. A gift in trust rather than an outright gift might be advantageous if the beneficiary is a minor, is incapacitated, or is inexperienced in handling money. Inter vivos and testamentary trusts are often created for tax reasons.

B. TYPES OF TRUSTS

Trusts are classified according to the method of their creation: (i) *express* trusts, which arise from the expressed intention of the owner of property to create the relationship with respect to the property; (ii) *resulting* trusts, which arise from the presumed intention of the owner of property; and (iii) *constructive* trusts, which do not depend on intention but rather constitute a useful equitable remedy in cases involving fraud and unjust enrichment.

II. FORMAL REQUISITES OF EXPRESS TRUSTS

A. IN GENERAL

An express trust arises from the expressed intention of the owner of property to create a trust with respect to the property. To have a trust, there must be a *settlor* who *delivers* the trust *res* (property) to a *trustee* with the *intention to create a trust*, whereupon the trustee holds, manages, and administers the res for the benefit of designated *beneficiaries*. The trust must be for a *lawful purpose*. No writing is required for the creation of a trust unless an interest in land is involved. Consideration is not required for the creation of a trust. In fact, most trusts are created gratuitously. Express trusts fall into two categories: private trusts and charitable trusts.

1. Private Trusts

A private ("noncharitable") trust has one or more ascertainable persons as beneficiaries, *e.g.,* a trust to pay the income to the settlor's wife for life and at her death to distribute the corpus to the settlor's descendants then living.

2. Charitable Trusts

A charitable trust is one for a purpose that is classified as charitable (*e.g.,* the advancement of religion, science, or education, or the promotion of health) and cannot be for the benefit of identifiable individuals. A basic distinction between private and charitable trusts lies in the application of the Rule Against Perpetuities. A charitable trust *can be perpetual*; it is not subject to the Rule. A private trust, on the other hand, is subject to the Rule Against Perpetuities. For a private trust, it must be shown that all interests in the trust must vest, if at all, within the common law period of lives in being plus 21 years, or that under Massachusetts's Uniform Statutory Rule Against Perpetuities, all interests actually vest or fail within the alternate vesting period of 90 years.

3. Jurisdiction—Probate Court

The probate court has exclusive jurisdiction over all proceedings concerning private and charitable trusts, whether created during the testator's lifetime ("inter vivos trust") or by will ("testamentary trust").

B. SETTLOR

A settlor is a property owner with legal capacity (*i.e.,* of legal age and sound mind, with capacity to convey title to the trustee) who intends to create a trust, and who makes an appropriate transfer of assets to the trustee.

C. DELIVERY

1. Delivery Requirement for Inter Vivos Trusts Naming Third Person as Trustee

To create a valid trust under which someone other than the settlor is to serve as trustee, there must be a delivery of assets to the trustee with the intention to create a trust. The mere expression of an intention to create a trust, without delivery of assets to the trustee, has no legal consequences.

Example: S told his broker that he intended to set up a trust for his daughter D, consisting of 100 shares of IBM stock that were in the broker's custody, and that he intended to name X Bank as trustee. S instructed the broker to transfer title to the securities to the bank as trustee. Before the transfer was made, S died. Under agency law, his death automatically revoked his broker's authority. The gift fails and no trust is created. Even though S clearly indicated his intent that a trust be created, he did not effectuate that intent during his lifetime.

2. No Requirement of Delivery for Declaration of Trust or Testamentary Trust
The delivery requirement does not apply to a declaration of trust, where the settlor declares himself trustee for the benefit of another person, or for the benefit of himself and another person. Also, no delivery is required for a testamentary trust.

D. TRUSTEE
An individual who is named as trustee must be of legal age, must be competent, and must have capacity to enter into contracts. As for corporations, only a bank or trust company that is given trustee powers in its charter can serve as trustee of a trust.

1. Nonresident Trustee Must Appoint Resident Agent
A nonresident can serve as a trustee, but *must designate a resident agent for service of process*. [Mass. Gen. L. ch. 195, §8]

2. Settlor Can Be Trustee
The settlor can be a co-trustee. He can also be the sole trustee, provided that he is not the sole beneficiary of the trust.

3. If Sole Trustee Is Also Sole Beneficiary—No Trust
A trust beneficiary can serve as trustee. However, if the sole trustee of a trust is also the sole beneficiary, there is no trust. The legal and equitable titles merge, and the person holds title free of any trust. The underlying rationale is that the trust relationship presupposes enforceable fiduciary duties. There must be someone who can hold the trustee accountable (suing, if necessary) to carry out the terms of the trust, and the same person cannot owe duties to himself as trustee.

Examples: 1) Mother transfers property to Sonny as trustee: "The trustee shall pay the trust income to Sonny until he attains age 40, at which time the trustee shall distribute the trust property to Sonny free of any trust." No trust arises, because the sole trustee is also the sole beneficiary.

    2) Settlor names herself as trustee in a revocable self-declaration of trust (*see* III.C., *infra*): "The trustee shall pay trust income to Settlor for life. On Settlor's death, Mary Smith shall become successor trustee, and Mary, as trustee, shall distribute the trust property to Bobby Smith if he is then living, otherwise to my heirs at law." This is a valid trust even though Settlor is the sole trustee and the only income beneficiary during her lifetime, because Settlor is not the sole trust beneficiary. Bobby Smith is also a trust beneficiary, and is recognized as such even though his interest is a contingent remainder (contingent on his surviving Settlor) and is subject to being defeated if Settlor revokes the trust. [*See* Sullivan v. Burkin, 390 Mass. 864 (1984)]

4. Acceptance by Trustee

a. No One Can Be Compelled to Serve as Trustee
If the person named as trustee chooses not to accept the appointment, she incurs no liability with respect to the trust. The reason for this rule is that no one can be forced to take on the duties, responsibilities, and potential liabilities of a fiduciary.

b. What Constitutes Acceptance by Trustee
The signature of the person named as trustee on the trust instrument or on a separate written acceptance is conclusive that she accepted the appointment. If the person named as trustee exercises powers or performs duties under the trust, she is presumed to have accepted the trust by her conduct.

5. Co-Trustees Hold Title in Joint Tenancy
Co-trustees hold title to trust property in joint tenancy with right of survivorship. Thus,

where one of two or more trustees dies, title to the trust property vests in the surviving trustee or trustees (absent contrary provision). [Feeney v. Feeney, 335 Mass. 534 (1956)]

6. **No Trust Fails for Lack of Trustee**
This is a basic rule of trust law. If the named trustee dies, resigns, or is removed for misfeasance, and the settlor has not provided for designation of a successor trustee, the court will appoint someone to serve as trustee. [Mass. Gen. L. ch. 203, §5] Similarly, if a testator's will devises property in trust but fails to name a trustee, the court will appoint a trustee. [Mass. Gen. L. ch. 203, §4] *Rationale:* The settlor's primary intention was to create a trust to carry out the specified objectives; the naming of the specific trustee was incidental to this primary purpose. The mere fact that the named trustee cannot serve or continue to serve is no reason to defeat the settlor's primary intention, so the court will appoint someone else to carry out the trust.

   a. **Exception If Powers Intended to Be Personal to Named Trustee**
   The rule stated above is subject to an exception. If the court finds that the trust powers were intended to be personal to this trustee, and that the settlor would not intend for the trust to continue if the named trustee could not serve, then the trust will be terminated. This exception is rarely invoked, however. Invariably, the court will find that the settlor's primary intent was to accomplish the stated trust purposes and not that the particular person serve as trustee.

7. **Trustee Holds Legal Title, Not Beneficial Interest**
A trustee's creditors cannot satisfy their claims from trust assets. [Shamrock, Inc. v. F.D.I.C., 36 Mass. App. Ct. 162 (1994)] Also, on the death of the sole surviving trustee, the trust assets do not pass to her estate nor are they subject to her spouse's elective share rights. Unless the settlor has named a successor trustee, title to the trust estate vests in the court, which will name a suitable successor trustee to carry out the terms of the trust. [Mass. Gen. L. ch. 203, §5]

8. **Removal of Trustee**

   a. **Grounds for Removal**
   Upon petition of a beneficiary, the court may remove a trustee if it finds that removal is in the best interest of the beneficiaries, or if the trustee has become incapacitated or is otherwise incapable or unsuitable. [Mass. Gen. L. ch. 203, §12] Grounds for removal include: commission of a breach of trust, refusal to give an accounting, and commingling trust funds with personal funds. It is not necessary to show that the trustee acted from dishonest or selfish motives. [Cooney v. Montana, 347 Mass. 29 (1964)]

      1) **Hostility Between Trustee and Beneficiaries**
      Mere hostility between the trustee and the beneficiaries is not sufficient grounds for removal unless the hostility affects the proper administration of the trust. [Symmons v. O'Keeffe, 419 Mass. 288 (1995)] To carry out the settlor's intent that this particular person or bank serve as trustee, the trustee should be allowed to serve as long as she is faithfully performing her duties. [Hardiman v. Hardiman, 11 Mass. App. Ct. 626 (1981)] Only if the hostility *precludes the trustee from exercising prudence and judgment* in the management of the trust is this a sufficient ground for removal. [Gorman v. Stein, 1 Mass. App. Ct. 244 (1973)]

      2) **Discretionary Trust—Hostility May Warrant Removal**
      In the case of a discretionary trust, where the amount of income to be distributed to the beneficiary is in the trustee's discretion, it may be appropriate to remove the trustee on grounds of hostility even if the hostility is not the fault of the trustee. A trustee "cannot reasonably be expected to exercise his [discretionary] power with desirable perspective and detachment when his motives and integrity are constantly impugned by the beneficiaries and the parties have been mired for years in litigation." [Shear v. Gabovitch, 43 Mass. App. 650 (1997)]

      3) **Potential Conflicts of Interest Known to Settlor**
      The court will not ordinarily remove a trustee named by the settlor on the basis of potential conflicts of interest existing at the time of his appointment, and in spite of which the settlor appointed him. [Symmons v. O'Keeffe, *supra*—"[t]he settlor of the trusts knew, at the time he created the trusts, that O'Keeffe held and would hold these various positions"]

b. Beneficiaries Cannot Compel Removal of Trustee Without Grounds

Without grounds, the beneficiaries cannot compel the removal of a trustee, unless this power is granted to them by the trust instrument. The power to remove a trustee without grounds also may be reserved by the settlor.

9. Disclaimer or Resignation by Trustee

A trustee who has not accepted the trust, either expressly or by implication or by contracting in advance to do so, can disclaim and refuse appointment arbitrarily and without giving any reasons whatever. She cannot, however, accept a trust in part and disclaim it in part. Moreover, once having accepted the trust, she cannot thereafter resign without permission of the court, unless authorized to do so by the terms of the trust or unless consent is given by all of the beneficiaries, all of whom must have capacity to give this consent. The acceptance of a trustee's resignation is within the discretion of the court.

E. INTENTION TO CREATE A TRUST

Typically, if a trust instrument is drafted by an attorney, there is no question that a trust was intended. However, the question can arise in deeds or wills drafted by a nonattorney where language is used in an ambiguous manner. Sometimes the language merely recites the motivation for the devise or gift, and the courts generally prefer to construe the language as not creating a trust or an enforceable obligation.

1. Precatory Language—No Trust or Enforceable Gift Created

What should a court do with language like this: "I give the residue of my estate to my brother John, but I would like him to give our sister Mary the 10-acre spread north of Hopkinton"? Did the settlor intend to create an *enforceable obligation*, meaning that John is under a duty to convey the 10 acres to Mary? Or was this just precatory language, meaning that John takes the entire residue with a suggestion or supplication from the testator that John consider giving the 10 acres to Mary? There are no hard and fast rules in this area; the cases turn on the particular language viewed in the total context of the will or trust instrument.

a. Ambiguous Language Usually Held Not to Create Enforceable Duty

Language such as "I desire," "it is my wish that," "I would like," etc., ordinarily does not impose a mandatory obligation; rather, such language is *precatory* and thus creates no enforceable obligation. In the foregoing example, most courts would likely rule that John does not have an enforceable obligation to give the 10 acres to Mary. However, the fact that such language has been used does not preclude a court from finding that an enforceable obligation was intended. The central question: *What was the testator's probable intent?*

Example: T's will left her estate to her husband for life, and further provided that on his death "it is my wish that the remaining estate shall pass to my cousins in Dedham." The court concluded that, based on the context and T's definite and precise directions, although T said, "I wish," what she really meant was "I direct" and "I want." [Frederick v. Frederick, 355 Mass. 662 (1969)]

b. Directions Addressed to Fiduciary

If directions are addressed by a decedent to his *executor or administrator*, or to one who otherwise occupies the position of a fiduciary under the will, this suggests that the testator's language was intended to be mandatory and to impose a trust.

c. Expression of Motive for Gift Does Not Create Enforceable Duty

The settlor must intend to impose an enforceable obligation on the transferee. Thus, a transfer "to my sister Sarah so she will have sufficient funds to be able to take care of Dad" merely expresses the motive for the gift, and does not impose a duty on Sarah to use the funds for Dad's support or maintenance.

2. Use of the Word "Trust" Not Required

No particular words are required to express an intent to create a trust. But the intent cannot be a secret one; it must be expressed by some words or conduct. The use of the words "trust" or "trustee" is not necessary. Moreover, the fact that the words "trust" or "trustee" were used does not compel a finding that a trust was created. The expression of intent must be sufficiently definite that a court can enforce it, particularly the description of the trust property, the beneficiaries, and their interests.

Examples: 1) A deed conveying certain realty to a named person (who was then a director of the School for the Blind) "for the use and benefit of the Lowell School for the Blind" creates a charitable trust in light of the circumstances, even though the words "as trustee" or "in trust" were not used.

2) Mother conveyed land to her son "Michael Scheltz, Trustee." No trust powers or terms were set out in the deed or in any other document. *Held:* Despite the use of the word "trustee," no trust was created; Michael holds on a resulting trust for the beneficiaries under Mother's will (Mother having since died). To show that an express trust has been created: (i) the words of the settlor must be construed as imperative and thus imposing an obligation on the trustee (the mandatory versus precatory distinction); (ii) the subject to which the trust obligation relates must be certain (the res requirement); and (iii) the person intended to be the trust beneficiary must be identified. Here there is no indication that any trust duties were imposed, and there is no indication of who the beneficiaries were supposed to be. The missing terms of an express trust may not be established by parol evidence.

3. **Trustee of Real Property Must Have Active Duties to Perform**
Under the Statute of Uses (1539), if legal title to land was transferred to a "trustee," but the trustee had no active duties to perform, the trust was "executed." The trust was not recognized; instead, the beneficiary held legal title free of any trust. Massachusetts has enacted its version of the Statute of Uses. If legal title is transferred to a trustee but it is a *passive trust* because the nominal trustee has no active duties, no trust arises. The person entitled to actual possession of the land (the "beneficiary") holds legal title.

4. **Promise to Create Trust Unenforceable Unless Supported by Consideration**
Once a trust is created either by declaration or transfer, it is enforceable by the beneficiary even though no consideration was given. If, however, instead of presently creating the trust, a person promises to create a trust in the *future*, he incurs no enforceable liability to the beneficiary unless the promise was supported by consideration. While a promise to create a trust in the future is unenforceable as a trust, it may be valid as a contract if supported by consideration.

An attempt to create a present trust that fails for lack of one of the necessary elements (*e.g.,* identifiable trust res) will, if supported by consideration, be enforced as a promise to create a trust when the deficiency is overcome.

Examples: 1) In writing, S declares himself trustee, for the benefit of B, of all of his profits from stock trading for the next year. No trust is created because there is no trust res. There are no "profits from stock trading" in existence at the time S's declaration of trust was made. If (but only if) consideration was given for the promise, S's declaration of trust will be construed as a promise to create a trust, which will be enforceable when S receives the profits from stock trading.

2) A pays S $1,000 for S's written promise to hold in trust for B any land that he acquires in the next five years. The promise is enforceable and if S acquires any land within the stipulated period, B may secure specific performance.

5. **Trust Distinguished from Agency Relationship**
Unlike a trustee, an agent does not hold legal title to assets, but only has the authority to deal with them on behalf of the principal. An agency relationship involves the continuing supervision of the agent by the principal, whereas the settlor of a trust ordinarily has no power to supervise the trustee. (When establishing a trust, the settlor can reserve the power to revoke or amend it. If the power is not expressly reserved, the trust is irrevocable and cannot be amended.)

6. **Trust Distinguished from Debtor-Creditor Relationship**
A debtor-creditor relationship involves only a personal claim against the debtor's general estate, whereas the beneficiary of a trust has "equitable ownership" of specific, identifiable property in the hands of his trustee. One test of whether a transfer of property was intended to create a trust is to determine whether the transferee was privileged to commingle it with his own assets, using it for his own purposes (indicates debt or gift), or was obliged to segregate it from his other assets, preserving it as an identifiable fund (indicates trust).

F.   RES

"Res" is the *property* subject to the trust. It is also called "corpus" or "principal."

1.   Basis of Res Requirement

Because a trust involves the transfer of title to specific property, there must be specific assets to which the trust duties relate. The trustee's fiduciary obligation to manage assets for the benefit of a beneficiary must exist with respect to specific assets, so that the beneficiary who is dissatisfied with the trustee's performance can say, "You are not fulfilling your fiduciary duty with respect to *these assets*."

a.   Debtor Cannot Hold Own Debt in Trust

A debtor cannot hold his own debt in trust. For example, if A owes B $10,000 and A declares herself trustee of the debt for B's benefit, no trust is created. The debt is a *general claim* against the debtor's estate and there is no specific property subject to the trust. (For this reason, a person cannot hold her own promissory note or check in trust.) Thus, the relationship between A and B remains that of debtor-creditor, not trustee-beneficiary. (*Note:* This might be important if: (i) the issue arises as to whether the statute of limitations against the debt has run; (ii) the debtor declares bankruptcy; or (iii) A dies, and the question is whether B made a timely filing of his claim, which he must do if he is a creditor.)

b.   Creditor Can Hold Debt of Another in Trust

A chose in action is an intangible property interest and *can* be the subject of a trust. Thus, an enforceable promissory note or other obligation running to a person may be the res of a trust created by that person.

Examples: 1) A owes B $10,000. B declares himself trustee of A's debt for the benefit of C. A valid trust is created.

2) A declares herself trustee for the benefit of B of her savings account in X Bank. Since A has a chose in action against the bank, a valid trust is created.

2.   Any Property that Settlor Has Power to Convey Can Be Subject of Trust

The trust res must be existing property that the settlor has the power to convey. The res *need not be tangible* property, but the settlor must have an assignable interest. Thus a promissory note, a contract, a patent or royalty interest, and a future interest can be the subject matter of a trust.

3.   Expectancy Is Not "Property" and Cannot Be Subject of Trust

Property that the settlor expects to own in the future but has no present right to transfer cannot be the subject matter of a present trust.

Examples: 1) A is his mother's only expectant heir and is the sole beneficiary named in his mother's will. A cannot gratuitously transfer his expected inheritance or interest under the will while his mother is alive. (But if A transfers his expectancy *for consideration* and later acquires the interest under his mother's will or by inheritance, A's transfer of the expectant interest will be enforced on a contract theory.)

2) A cannot create a present trust in his stock trading profits for the coming year or in whatever land he may acquire in the next five years, although he could declare a trust of existing stock holdings to pay the income to a beneficiary for a period of time. (The basic distinction here is between "interests" and "expectancies.")

4.   Trust Property Must Be Adequately and Specifically Described

The creation of a trust with respect to "most of my stock," or a "generous portion of my land," is obviously an insufficient description. Such a description does not indicate what assets are to be subject to the trust. However, a *fractional interest* in specific property is sufficient (*e.g.,* "a one-third undivided interest in my lot on Jefferson Avenue").

The designation of "all my property" or "all the rest, residue, and remainder of my estate," in setting up a testamentary trust, is sufficient. The specific property that will be the subject of the trust can be ascertained from the facts known at the time the trust is created on the testator's death.

G.   BENEFICIARIES

1. **No Notice to Beneficiaries Required**
   A trust may be validly created without notice to the beneficiaries.

2. **Acceptance by Beneficiary Presumed**
   To have a valid gift, there must be donative intent, delivery of the subject matter of the gift, *and* acceptance of the gift by the donee. No one can be compelled to be a donee against his will. (Human nature being what it is, there are very few cases invoking the "acceptance" requirement!) As with outright gifts, a gift in trust requires acceptance by the donee. However, acceptance by a beneficiary of his interest in a trust is presumed, unless the beneficiary affirmatively disclaims the interest.

3. **Beneficiaries Must Be Ascertainable**
   A private express trust must be for ascertainable beneficiaries, for there must be someone who can enforce the trust. If the beneficiary designation does not specifically describe an individual or a group of persons, the trust fails.
   Example: A trust for the benefit of "my relations" or "my son's family" is valid, with the identity of the beneficiaries determined by reference to the intestate succession laws in defining "family" or "relations." However, a trust "to pay the income to my best friends" is too indefinite to establish a valid trust.

   a. **Class Gifts**
   There is no difficulty with the designation of a definite class of beneficiaries, *e.g.,* "my descendants," "my heirs." Determination of who constitutes the group of takers, in such a class gift, is made by reference to the rules applicable to class gifts generally. As long as the individual members are readily ascertainable, the trust beneficiaries may be a large group (*e.g.,* all the employees of a large company).

   b. **Unborn Beneficiaries**
   Subject only to the Rule Against Perpetuities, an unborn person may be a beneficiary of a trust. Thus, if A conveys to T in trust for B for life, remainder to B's "children," the beneficiaries are "definite" even though B has no children at the time the trust is established. It is sufficient that the beneficiaries will be identifiable at the time their interests come into enjoyment (here, at B's death).

   c. **"Ascertainable Beneficiaries" Rule Does Not Apply to Charitable Trusts**
   A charitable trust *cannot* be for the benefit of identifiable private individuals. (*See* IV.C., *infra.*)

4. **Settlor as Beneficiary**
   The settlor can be a beneficiary of the trust. He can even be the only beneficiary—as long as he is not also the only trustee.
   Example: A revocable inter vivos trust under which trust income is paid to the settlor during his lifetime is a commonly encountered example of a trust in which the settlor is also a beneficiary.

H. TRUST PURPOSES
A trust may be created or established for any purpose that is not illegal or contrary to public policy. A trust whose terms require the trustee to commit a criminal or tortious act or an act that is against public policy will fail. A trust will also fail if it was created to defeat the settlor's creditors, or if it was based on illegal consideration.

1. **Restraints on Marriage and Conditions that Encourage Divorce Are Void**
   A restraint on marriage is void, and the beneficiary takes the interest free of the restriction, *provided* that the condition is intended to compel the beneficiary to remain single and *serves no reasonable purpose*. Similarly, a condition whose purpose is to encourage divorce or separation is void as contrary to public policy (*e.g.,* "the trust income shall be paid to my son John until he divorces his present wife, at which time the principal shall be paid to him"—the condition is void and John takes the fee simple free of any trust).
   Example: A trust provides that the trustee shall pay trust income to the settlor's unmarried daughter "provided that she does not marry." The condition is void because its sole purpose is to impose an economic compulsion that the daughter remain single. The daughter is entitled to trust income for life even if she marries. However, a testamentary trust provision "to pay the income to my widow for life or until she remarries," at which time the income is to be paid to the couple's children, is invariably upheld on the ground that it was reasonable for the testator to provide for his wife during her widowhood, but

that he could expect a second husband to provide for her support thereafter. [Knight v. Mahoney, 152 Mass. 523 (1890)]

a. Partial Restraints on Marriage Are Valid

While a condition tied to a total restraint on marriage is invalid, the courts will give effect to a partial restraint.

Example: T's will creates a trust for his children, but provides that if any child "shall marry a person not born of the Hebrew faith," his interest in the trust shall terminate. *Held:* This is a valid condition. The limitation did not operate as a total restraint on marriage, but merely narrowed the beneficiary's range of choices for a spouse. Nor was this a denial of religious freedom, as the beneficiary was free to reject the gift by marrying outside the faith. [Gordon v. Gordon, 332 Mass. 197 (1955)]

Compare: T's will devised property to his niece "provided that she marries a member of the Society of Friends." *Held:* Condition is void because there were only five or six unmarried male Friends in the county. In view of the small number of eligible bachelors in the community, the condition operated as a virtual prohibition against marriage and thus was an unreasonable restraint. [Maddox v. Maddox, 52 Va. 804 (1854)]

2. Provision Calling for Destruction of Property Is Void

A provision in a will or trust calling for the destruction of property is void as against public policy, since it would result in destruction of an asset for no discernible purpose. "Although a person may wish to deal capriciously with his property while he is alive, his self-restraint will usually prevent him from doing so. After his death there is no such restraint." [Will of Pace, 93 Misc. 2d 969 (N.Y. Sur. Ct. 1977)]

I. FORMALITIES OF CREATION

No particular formalities are required for the creation of a trust; a trust need not be in writing unless an interest in land is involved.

1. Trusts for Real Property Must Be in Writing

If the subject matter of an inter vivos trust is land, whether the trust is created by a declaration of trust or by a transfer to another to hold in trust, a written instrument is required to make the trust effective. [Mass. Gen. L. ch. 203, §1] The writing must be signed by the person entitled to impress the trust upon the property (*i.e.,* the settlor). In Massachusetts, it is not necessary that the deed of the real property actually contain the terms of the trust. It is sufficient that another writing executed contemporaneously with the deed contain the trust terms. Thus, a deed, absolute on its face, may nevertheless be held to create a trust with the transferee as trustee, if at the same time the deed is executed, the intent and terms of the trust are set out in a separate writing (*e.g.,* a letter) that satisfies the Statute of Frauds. [*See* Bellamy v. Bellamy, 342 Mass. 534 (1961)]

2. Testamentary Trusts Must Comply with Statute of Wills

A trust created by will must comply with the Statute of Wills. (*See* Wills outline.)

3. Oral Trusts of Tangible or Intangible Personal Property Are Valid

Oral trusts of personal property are valid. However, the personal property must be in existence at the time of the transaction that is alleged to give rise to the trust. Of course, cases in which an oral trust is alleged invariably raise problems of proof, and in most instances are handled under a constructive trust analysis because the "trustee" insists that the assets were transferred to her as beneficial owner free of any trust, and the "beneficiaries" contend that she is unjustly hiding the ball.

4. Trust Need Not Be Supported by Consideration

Since a trust is a donative transfer, no consideration for the trust is required. All that is required is the delivery of the subject matter of the trust with the intention to create a trust. However, a promise to create a trust in the *future*, if not supported by consideration, is unenforceable.

III. VARIOUS TYPES OF TRUSTS; WILL SUBSTITUTES

A. INTER VIVOS AND TESTAMENTARY TRUSTS

A trust may be created during the settlor's lifetime (inter vivos trust) or by her will (testamentary trust).

B. REVOCABLE TRUSTS

A revocable inter vivos trust is not a will because the interest in the property passes to the beneficiary *during the settlor's lifetime*; it merely becomes *possessory* on the settlor's death. A revocable trust has a number of advantages over a will: (i) it does not have to comply with the formalities of the Statute of Wills, (ii) it avoids the costs and delays of probate, and (iii) the interest can be revoked or divested during the settlor's life.

1. Trusts Are Irrevocable by Settlor Unless Expressly Made Revocable

In Massachusetts (as in nearly all states), a trust is irrevocable and cannot be amended by the settlor unless the power to revoke or amend is expressly retained in the trust instrument.

2. Use of Revocable Trusts in Estate Planning

Revocable trusts are often used in Massachusetts and other states for a variety of planning reasons.

a. Management of Assets

Harold and his wife, Wanda, have retired, and they do a lot of vacation traveling, especially during the winter months. This makes management and supervision of their investments rather inconvenient, so they transfer their investment assets to Shawmut Bank as trustee of a revocable trust: to pay the income to Harold and Wanda jointly for life, then to the survivor for life, then to distribute the principal to their descendants per stirpes. This arrangement provides for effective management of their assets by a bank with investment expertise, and provides the other benefits described below.

b. Planning for Incapacity—Avoidance of Guardianship

Suppose that Harold, in the above example, has a stroke and is incapacitated. If Harold had not established the revocable trust (and if Harold had not given Wanda or some other family member a "durable" power of attorney), it would be necessary to have Harold adjudicated as incapacitated and a guardian or conservator appointed to manage his assets. But because Harold and Wanda transferred legal title in their investment assets to the bank as trustee, the trust continues to operate for Harold's benefit without the necessity of a guardianship administration.

c. Avoidance of Probate

Assets held in trust are not subject to probate administration. Suppose Harold dies, survived by Wanda and their children. Since legal title to Harold's investment assets is held by the bank as trustee, the assets are not subject to probate administration. The assets continue to be held for the benefit of Wanda (and the children) without the expenses and delays of a probate administration. The trust operates to transfer beneficial interests at the settlor's death even though the trust was not executed with the formalities required for a will (*i.e.,* no attesting witnesses). This is because trust law, not wills law, governs the trust's creation and amendment. [National Shawmut Bank v. Joy, 315 Mass. 457 (1944)] This is true even if the trust was created shortly before the settlor's death for the avowed purpose of avoiding the need for a will. [Ascher v. Cohen, 333 Mass. 397 (1956)]

3. Validity of Revocable Trusts in Massachusetts

In Massachusetts, an inter vivos trust is valid even though the settlor retains any one or more of the following powers: (i) the power to *revoke, alter, amend, or modify* the trust instrument; (ii) the power to *appoint the income or principal* of the trust by deed or will; (iii) the power to *add to or withdraw property from* the trust; (iv) the power to *remove trustees* and appoint new ones including the settlor; and (v) the *right to the income* of the trust. [National Shawmut Bank v. Joy, *supra*]

4. "Pour-Over" from Will to Inter Vivos Trust

Suppose that C has created a revocable trust that will continue after her death for the benefit of her nephews and nieces. By her will, C wants to bequeath her residuary estate in trust for the same nephews and nieces. One approach might be for C's will to create a testamentary trust. However, this would result in two trusts for the same beneficiaries, two sets of trustee's commissions, and added complications. Instead, C's will might provide: "I bequeath my residuary estate to First National Bank, trustee under an instrument of trust executed by me on May 11, 2000, to be added to and administered in accordance with the trust terms, including any amendments thereto." Such a gift to an inter vivos trust (called a *pour-over* gift in practice) is valid under Massachusetts's version of the Uniform Testamentary Additions to Trusts Act. [Mass. Gen. L. ch. 203, §3B] The statute thus permits the integrated disposition of testamentary assets with a trust created during the settlor's lifetime. Because trust law (and not wills law) applies, the trust (and any amendments thereto) need not be executed and attested with the formalities required for a will.

a. Trust Need Not Be in Existence When Will Executed
In many states, a pour-over gift from a will to an inter vivos trust is not valid unless the trust was executed prior to, or contemporaneously with, the will. Massachusetts has no such requirement. "A devise or bequest may be made to the trustee of a trust established *or to be established* by the settlor." [Mass. Gen. L. ch. 203, §3B]

b. Trust May Be Amendable and Revocable
A pour-over gift by will is valid even though the inter vivos trust is amendable and revocable. The gift is to the trust as it exists at the testator's death, including amendments to the trust made after the will was executed.

c. Gift Is Valid Even Though Trust Unfunded During Settlor's Lifetime
The statute authorizes pour-over gifts to a trust that is not funded with any assets during the settlor's lifetime and whose sole purpose is to receive such a testamentary gift. The statute eliminates any basis for challenging the gift on the ground that no valid trust was created during the settlor's lifetime because the trust had no res. Such a devise is valid even though the only res of the trust is the possibility of receiving a devise under a will. "The statute is not conditioned upon the existence of a trust but upon the existence of a trust *instrument*." [Clymer v. Mayo, 393 Mass. 754 (1985)] Another statute authorizes the payment of life insurance proceeds, employee death benefits, and similar benefits to an unfunded trust whose sole purpose is to receive such benefits on the settlor's death.

5. Surviving Spouse's Elective Share
Until 1984, a revocable trust could be used to defeat the elective share entitlement of the settlor's spouse. This is no longer the case. Assets in a revocable trust that was created or amended *on or after January 23, 1984*, are subject to the surviving spouse's elective share. (*See* Wills outline.)

6. Settlor's Creditors Can Reach Assets in Revocable Trust
Where the settlor retains the power to revoke the trust, his creditors can reach the trust assets during his lifetime to satisfy their claims. If the settlor declares bankruptcy, the trustee in bankruptcy can exercise the power to revoke and bring the trust assets into the bankruptcy estate. On the settlor's death, assets in the revocable trust can be reached by creditors of the estate, but only after the probate estate has been exhausted by the payment of expenses and claims. [State Street Bank & Trust Co. v. Reiser, 7 Mass. App. Ct. 633 (1979)]

C. DECLARATION OF TRUST
A declaration of trust, in which the settlor declares herself trustee for the benefit of other persons (or for the benefit of herself and other persons), is valid in Massachusetts. The settlor can reserve the power to revoke the trust, and can also be a beneficiary as long as she is not the sole beneficiary. Where there is a declaration of trust, no delivery is required because the settlor is the trustee and already has the assets in her possession. But if the settlor retains the property, a trust by parol declaration must be created by acts and words of a clear and unequivocal character; the nature and extent of the beneficiaries' interest must be made certain through evidence found in surrounding circumstances and the subsequent conduct of the parties.

D. LIFE INSURANCE PROCEEDS AS TRUST ASSET

1. Unfunded Revocable Life Insurance Trusts Valid
(*See* B.4.c., above.)

2. Testamentary Trustee May Be Beneficiary of Insurance Proceeds and Death Benefits
Early decisions invalidated a life insurance beneficiary designation of "the trustee named in my will." The courts reasoned that the insured did not create a valid trust during her lifetime because the trust did not come into existence until after the insured's death. Also, the beneficiary designation was not effective as a testamentary gift because it was not executed with testamentary formalities. [Frost v. Frost, 202 Mass. 100 (1909)] Massachusetts is one of a number of states that have eliminated this problem by a statute expressly authorizing designation of a testamentary trustee as the beneficiary of life insurance proceeds and the proceeds of employee death benefits. [Mass. Gen. L. ch. 203, §3B]

a.   **Payment of Proceeds If No Trustee Qualifies Within One Year**
Under such a beneficiary designation, if no qualified trustee makes claim to the proceeds within one year after the insured's or employee's death, the proceeds are paid to the contingent beneficiary named in the policy or (if there is none) to the insured's estate.

b.   **Spendthrift Protection Retained**
The statute also provides that the proceeds so paid to the testamentary trustee are not subject to the claims of creditors of the testator's estate. A standard provision in life insurance contracts gives spendthrift protection against claims of the insured's creditors unless the proceeds are payable to the insured's executor or estate. Thus the statute makes it clear that, for purposes of creditors' rights, a payment of the proceeds to a testamentary trustee is *not* to be considered a payment to the insured's executor or estate.

E.   TOTTEN TRUST BANK ACCOUNTS

"Totten trust" is the name given to an "A, trustee for B" bank account. Under such a bank account, A, the depositor, retains the passbook and continues to make deposits and withdrawals during her lifetime. B has no beneficial interest in the account during A's lifetime, but succeeds to whatever is on deposit at A's death. It is called a Totten trust because it was first recognized in *Matter of Totten*, 179 N.Y. 112 (1904).

1.   **Trustee-Depositor Has Full Rights During Lifetime**
A Totten trust is not really a trust because no separation of legal and equitable title is involved. The depositor remains the owner of all funds on deposit during her lifetime and can withdraw them at any time. [Mass. Gen. L. ch. 167D, §6]

2.   **Revocation by Other Lifetime Act**
While Totten trusts are revoked by withdrawals, they can also be revoked by any lifetime act that manifests an intent to revoke.
Example: A delivered to her attorney a document expressly revoking "all of my 'in-trust-for' accounts." This is a valid revocation, even though the revoking instrument was not delivered to the various banks. Thus, the funds passed under A's will rather than to the designated Totten trust beneficiaries. The fact that A did not comply with the method for changing beneficiaries set out in the bank signature card was irrelevant; that agreement was solely for the protection of the bank and did not limit A's right to revoke.

3.   **Revocation by Will**
If A leaves a will that says, "I bequeath all funds on deposit in my 'in-trust-for' savings accounts to my friend C," this is a valid disposition. C, and not the beneficiaries named in A's Totten trusts, is entitled to the funds on deposit. By contrast, a joint bank account with survivorship provisions *cannot* be given by will.

4.   **Gift upon Delivery of Passbook**
Most states hold that if depositor A delivers the passbook to beneficiary B, this constitutes a valid gift to B of the amount on deposit. (The issue has not arisen in Massachusetts.)

5.   **Subject to Creditors' Claims and Elective Share**
Since the depositor has complete control over the deposit during his lifetime, he is treated as the owner insofar as his creditors are concerned. His creditors can reach the deposit while he is living, and can reach it as part of his estate on death. A Totten trust bank account also is subject to a surviving spouse's elective share entitlement because the depositor can revoke the account by withdrawing the amounts on deposit. [Bongaards v. Millen, 440 Mass. 10 (2003)] (*See* Wills outline.)

6.   **Terminates If Beneficiary Predeceases Depositor**
If beneficiary B predeceases depositor A, the trust automatically terminates. The funds on deposit belong to A absolutely and do not pass to B's estate. (You have to survive the depositor-trustee in order to succeed to the amount on deposit under a Totten trust account.)

F.   JOINT AND SURVIVOR BANK ACCOUNTS

A deposit made in a bank account in the name of the depositor and another person, to be paid to either or the survivor of them, creates a valid survivorship account. [Mass. Gen. L. ch. 167D, §5] Either co-owner may withdraw the entire account.

1.   **Revocation by Will**
As stated above, generally, a joint and survivor bank account cannot be given by will.
Example: A deposits funds in a savings account, the signature card for which (signed by A and B) provides that A and B hold "as joint tenants with right of survivorship." A leaves a will that purports to bequeath all of her interest in the bank account to C. The will gift is ineffective since on A's death the fund passed by right of survivorship to B.

However, it may be shown by attendant facts and circumstances that the deceased did not intend to make a present completed gift of a joint interest in the account or that the joint account was created only as a matter of convenience and did not constitute a completed gift. [Astravas v. Petronis, 361 Mass. 366 (1971)]

G.   **UNIFORM TRANSFERS TO MINORS ACT**
Massachusetts has enacted the Uniform Transfers to Minors Act ("UTMA"). [Mass. Gen. L. ch. 201A] The UTMA provides a convenient means of making gifts to minors that: (i) avoids the need for appointment of a guardian for the minor, and (ii) qualifies for a $10,000 present interest exclusion under the federal gift tax.

1.   **Gift to Custodian for Minor**
A custodial gift is made by transferring property to (or having title taken in the name of) "[name of custodian] as custodian for [name of minor] under the Massachusetts Uniform Transfers to Minors Act." This automatically gives the custodian statutory powers to: (i) manage and invest the property; (ii) pay to or for the minor's benefit so much or all of the property as the custodian deems advisable for the minor's support, maintenance, education, and benefit; (iii) pay over the property (to the extent not expended) when the minor attains age 21 (or to the minor's estate if the minor dies before age 21); (iv) invest under a prudent person standard; and (v) sell, exchange, convert, vote securities, etc., without court order or approval.

a.   **Tax Purpose—Qualify for Gift Tax Annual Exclusion**
The federal gift tax allows a $11,000 per donee annual exclusion for gifts of present interest but not for gifts of future interests. Recognizing that many people want to make gifts to minor children, but not outright gifts because of the guardianship concern, the Internal Revenue Code makes an exception to the "future interest" rule for gifts to minors: No gift to an individual shall be considered a gift of a future interest if the property and the income therefrom may be expended by, or for the benefit of, the donee before his attaining the age of 21, and will, to the extent not so expended:

(i)   Pass to the donee on or before his attaining the age of 21, and

(ii)   In the event the donee dies before attaining the age of 21, be payable to the estate of the donee or as he may appoint under a general power of appointment.

The provisions of the UTMA satisfy this test; thus, a custodial gift qualifies for the annual exclusion.

2.   **Any Property Can Be Subject of Custodial Gift**
Any property—securities, life insurance policies, etc.,—can be given under the UTMA.

3.   **Single Custodianship**
A transfer may benefit only one minor and only one person may act as custodian. All property held for a minor by a custodian is considered part of a single custodianship regardless of when the transfers occurred.

H.   **"TRANSFER ON DEATH" REGISTRATION OF SECURITIES**
Massachusetts has enacted the Uniform Transfer on Death Securities Registration Act. [Mass. Gen. L. ch. 201E, §101] The Act authorizes the registration of securities in various forms that will allow title to the securities to pass on the owner's (or a beneficiary's) death as valid nonprobate transfers.
Examples: 1) Alan purchases AT&T stock, and causes the stock certificate to be registered in the name of "Alan Smith and Betty Smith JT TEN TOD Sam Smith LDPS." (JT TEN stands for "joint tenancy," TOD stands for "transfer on death," and LDPS stands for "lineal descendants per stirpes.") On Alan's death, title to the securities

will pass to Betty by right of survivorship. On Betty's death, title will pass to Sam Smith or, if Sam has died, to his lineal descendants per stirpes.

2) Suppose, instead, that Alan registers the securities in the name of "Alan Smith POD Betty Smith SUB BENE Sam Smith." (POD stands for "pay on death," and SUB BENE stands for "substitute beneficiary.") On Alan's death, title to the securities will pass to Betty or, if she has died, to Sam as substitute beneficiary.

I.   DURABLE POWER OF ATTORNEY

1.   Durable Power of Attorney May Survive Disability of Principal
A power of attorney is an instrument executed by a party (the "principal") that gives another party (the "attorney-in-fact") agency authority to act on the principal's behalf. In Massachusetts, a power of attorney does not terminate on the disability or incapacity of the principal if the instrument states that "this power of attorney shall not be affected by disability of the principal" or contains words of like effect. [Mass. Gen. L. ch. 201B, §1] This provision, borrowed from the Uniform Probate Code, makes the power of attorney far more useful in handling the affairs of elderly persons. In many instances, the existence of a durable power of attorney will eliminate the need to appoint a guardian for a person who later becomes incapacitated. Absent this statute, the power, being an agency power, would automatically terminate on the principal's incapacity, a consequence that would make third parties extremely reluctant to deal with someone acting under the authority of the power of attorney.

2.   Effect of Principal's Death or Incapacity
A durable power of attorney is revocable by the principal. Also, being an agency power, the power of attorney *automatically terminates* on the principal's death. If a guardian or conservator for the principal is appointed, the agent is accountable to the guardian or conservator, who has the same right to revoke or amend the power of attorney as the principal would have if not disabled or incapacitated. [Mass. Gen. L. ch. 201B, §3] However, a third party who acts in good faith reliance on a power of attorney, without knowledge that it has been revoked, is protected. [Mass. Gen. L. ch. 201B, §5]

J.   NOMINEE TRUSTS
Massachusetts is among the very few states that recognizes the nominee trust as a form of real estate ownership. A nominee trust is an entity created for the purpose of holding legal title to real estate, with the trustee having only nominal duties. Unlike a genuine trust, the trustee (frequently a clerical employee of the beneficiary) has no power to act with respect to the trust property, but may act only at the direction of the beneficiary. Nominee trusts are often used to hold title to real estate so that the identity of the true owner may remain undisclosed.

1.   Trust Form Respected in Contract Actions Only
As to contracts, the court will generally respect the trust form of a nominee trust. Thus, a creditor who fails to obtain the personal guarantee of the beneficiary may enforce the contract only against the assets of the "trust." In all other respects, however, and particularly with regard to torts, the court will ignore the trust form and treat the beneficiary as the true owner. Note that statutory provisions limiting the liability of a trustee or beneficiary do not apply to nominee trusts. [Morrison v. Lennett, 415 Mass. 857 (1993)]

IV.   CHARITABLE AND HONORARY TRUSTS

A.   DISTINCTIVE RULES APPLY TO CHARITABLE TRUSTS
Charitable trusts, because of their substantial benefit to society, are granted some special exemptions from the rules that apply to private trusts. In general, charitable trusts are liberally construed. The rules governing charitable trusts differ from those applicable to private express trusts in three important particulars.

1.   Must Have Indefinite Beneficiaries
To be sustained as a charitable trust, the trust, if not for a specified charitable agency, must be in favor of a reasonably large class of indefinite beneficiaries and cannot be for the benefit of identifiable individuals. By contrast, a private trust must be for definite and ascertainable beneficiaries.

2.   Cy Pres Doctrine Applicable
If the charitable purpose is accomplished or the designated charity goes out of existence, the

court may redirect the trust to a purpose "as near as possible" to the charitable endeavor initially designated by the settlor.

3. May Be Perpetual
A charitable trust may last forever; it is not subject to the Rule Against Perpetuities. [Mass. Gen. L. ch. 184A] By contrast, all interests in a private trust must "vest" within the period of the Rule Against Perpetuities or, under the alternate vesting period of the Uniform Statutory Rule Against Perpetuities, within 90 years.

B. TRUST MUST BE FOR CHARITABLE PURPOSES
The purposes of a charitable trust must be strictly limited to those considered to *benefit the public*, including the relief of poverty, the advancement of religion or education, the promotion of health, and the accomplishment of governmental purposes (*e.g.,* parks, museums, playgrounds). A trust to use the income "for charitable purposes" is a valid charitable trust even though no specific charitable purpose has been indicated. [Sullivan v. Roman Catholic Archbishop of Boston, 368 Mass. 253 (1975)] A purpose that limits the benefits of the trust to a particular class of the public (*e.g.,* Springfield orphans) may be charitable, but the class may not be so narrowly defined that it designates only a few individuals upon whom the settlor wishes to confer private benefits. However, if the purpose of a trust is charitable, the mere fact that the settlor requested that preference be given to certain relatives or friends and their descendants, who are within the object of the trust, does not make it invalid as a charitable trust. A trust for the dissemination of ideas may be charitable even though the ultimate purpose may be to accomplish a change in present law, *e.g.,* a trust to promote the abolition of discrimination against women, tariffs, or capital punishment.

Examples: 1) A trust for the benefit of the descendants of the settlor who are poor is not charitable.

2) A trust for the expense of Masses for the repose of the souls of the testator, her deceased parents, and other relations has repeatedly been upheld as a trust for charitable or religious purposes.

1. Mixed Trusts
Where the purposes of a single trust are both charitable and noncharitable, the trust is a "mixed trust," and the special rules for charitable trusts do not apply. However, if there is some indication as to how much of the corpus the settlor intended to be applied for charitable purposes, two separate trusts will be found.

Example: T bequeaths $100,000 to trustees to distribute the income "to such educational institutions and worthy individuals as the trustees should select." This is a mixed trust and is not exempt from the Rule Against Perpetuities as charitable trusts are (*see* below). It is void because the trustees' discretionary power to distribute income to worthy individuals can be exercised beyond the perpetuity period. (*See* Real Property outline on Rule Against Perpetuities applied to powers of appointment.)

C. INDEFINITE BENEFICIARIES
Since the purpose of a charitable trust is to benefit the community, the courts consider the community at large the beneficiary of a charitable trust rather than the particular individuals who happen to receive benefits from it.

1. Settlor and Potential Beneficiaries Have No Standing to Sue Charitable Trustee
The settlor of a charitable trust is deemed to have no greater interest in the performance of a charitable trust than any other member of the community, and therefore may not maintain an action for its enforcement. Nor may any potential recipients of the charitable largess maintain such an action. "While the plaintiff's relationship with the [public charity] is indeed different from a member of the public who is not a member of the [public charity], . . . membership in a public charity, alone, is [not] sufficient to give standing to pursue claims that a charitable organization has been mismanaged or that its officials have acted ultra vires." [Weaver v. Wood, 425 Mass. 270 (1997)]

Example: S creates a trust to provide scholarships for Spanish-speaking residents of Boston. S has no standing to bring suit against the trustee concerning administration of the trust, nor does Juanita Hernandez, who lives in Boston and claims that she has been discriminated against in not receiving a scholarship from the trust.

2.   **Charitable Trusts Enforceable by Massachusetts Attorney General**
The duty to enforce charitable trusts is placed upon the Massachusetts Attorney General. [Mass. Gen. L. ch. 12, §8] Thus, in the above example, the settlor or Juanita Hernandez would have to persuade the attorney general to look into the matter.

D.   **RULE AGAINST PERPETUITIES**
Charitable trusts may be perpetual. The Rule Against Perpetuities does not apply to charitable trusts. Also, under the "charity to charity" exception to the Rule, the Rule Against Perpetuities does not apply to transfers where a limitation is used to shift the beneficial interest from one charity to another on the happening of a remote condition. Note carefully, however, that the Rule *will apply to a limitation shifting the interest* from a private use to a charitable use or from a charitable use to a private use.

Examples: 1) "To the Lexington YMCA for so long as the premises are used for YMCA purposes, and if the premises shall ever cease to be so used, then to the Lexington United Fund." The gift is valid under the charity to charity exception.

2) "To the Lexington YMCA, its successors, and assigns: provided, however, that if the premises ever cease to be used for YMCA purposes, then over to Joan Smith, her heirs, successors, and assigns." The gift over violates the Rule; the invalid interest is stricken, and the Lexington YMCA has a fee simple absolute.

3) "To Joan Smith, her heirs, successors, and assigns for so long as the land is used for residential purposes, and if the land ever ceases to be used for residential purposes, then over to the Lexington YMCA." The gift over violates the Rule; Joan Smith has a fee simple determinable and the grantor has a possibility of reverter.

E.   **CY PRES**
Since a trust for charitable purposes may be perpetual, it often happens that the specific charitable purpose indicated by the settlor is accomplished (*e.g.,* a trust to combat yellow fever) or becomes impractical. In such a case, where the settlor had a general charitable purpose, the court will direct that the trust property be applied to another charitable purpose as close as possible to the original one, rather than permit the trust to fail and become a resulting trust. [Boston Seaman's Friend Society v. Attorney General, 379 Mass. 414 (1980)]

1.   **Rationale**
The idea underlying cy pres (translated, it means "as near as possible") is this: The settlor had a general charitable intent as reflected by the trust (such as the curing of disease, the dissemination of knowledge by providing scholarships, or the promulgation of a particular religious faith). To carry out her general charitable objective, she selected this particular agency as trustee or as the beneficiary. But her general charitable intent should not be frustrated because this secondary intent (that the named trustee or charitable beneficiary be the agency for carrying out these objectives) can no longer be accomplished. Instead, the court will select another trustee or beneficiary whose work will most closely approximate the general objectives sought by the settlor. [Hillman v. Roman Catholic Bishop of Fall River, 24 Mass. App. Ct. 241 (1987)]

2.   **Massachusetts Requires Application of Cy Pres**
Where the specified charitable use is no longer possible or practical, in most states the court must decide whether the settlor intended the trust to fail or would have wished the property devoted to a similar use. No such problem arises in Massachusetts. By statute, a court *must* apply cy pres to reform a charitable trust that has become impossible or impractical to carry out under its original terms unless "the instrument creating the trust [explicitly] provides to the contrary." [Mass. Gen. L. ch. 12, §8K]

Examples: 1) T's will establishes a testamentary trust, "to expend the income to provide medical care for indigent patients at the Suffolk County General Hospital." Thirty years later, Suffolk County General Hospital ceases to operate. Since T's primary intent was to provide funds for medical care for indigent persons in Suffolk County, the court should direct the trustee to pay trust income to another hospital (or hospitals) in the county that treats indigent patients.

2) T's will bequeaths her residuary estate "to the Brockton Home for Crippled Children." The Brockton Home disbands during T's lifetime, but T does not revise her will. Cy pres will be applied, and the court should direct the executor to distribute the residuary estate to another children's home in

the Brockton area. (Cy pres can be applied to outright gifts to charity as well as charitable trusts.)

3. Selecting a Purpose "As Near As Possible"
In formulating an alternative use for the trust property, the court must determine the settlor's primary purpose, although her other purposes should be taken into account.

Example: Where funds were given to a church to build a memorial hospital for tuberculosis patients, in formulating an alternative use it must be decided which of the settlor's purposes she considered most important: the church as recipient, the memorial nature of the building, or the medical nature of the gift.

F. LIMITED LIABILITY FOR CHARITABLE TRUSTEES
By statute, Massachusetts provides that the trustee of a charitable trust is not personally liable "for any acts or omissions relating solely to the performance of his duties." The immunity conferred, however, does not extend to acts "intentionally designed to harm or to any grossly negligent acts or omissions." [Mass. Gen. L. ch. 231, §85W] Thus, the trustee of a charitable trust may generally be sued only in his representative capacity. Furthermore, Massachusetts places a $20,000 limit on recovery against the trust itself. [Mass. Gen. L. ch. 231, §85K]

G. HONORARY TRUSTS
An "honorary" trust is a gift in trust that is *not for charitable purposes* and has *no private beneficiaries*. Suppose that Grant's will bequeaths $25,000 to his friend Fred as trustee, "to use the trust income to care for my beloved cat, Sylvester," or "to use the trust income to upgrade and maintain my rose garden." The disposition *is not a legally enforceable trust* because it is not for a charitable purpose (meaning that it does not benefit the public) and there are *no beneficiaries who can enforce the trust*. To have a valid trust, the trustee must owe enforceable fiduciary duties to someone, and cats (or rose gardens) cannot file lawsuits. Although the disposition is not enforceable as a trust, it is not wholly invalid. The arrangement will be upheld in the sense that although Fred cannot be compelled to perform, the courts will permit him to carry out the specified purpose if he is willing to do so. This type of gift is sometimes called an *honorary trust*, because the named person is on his honor in carrying out the testator's directive. It must be understood, however, that an honorary trust is *not actually a trust*. If the person refuses to carry out the specified purpose, a *resulting trust* arises in favor of the testator's estate.

1. Honorary Trust Void If It May Continue Beyond Perpetuities Period
Most courts hold that an honorary trust is void if it may continue beyond lives in being plus 21 years. This creates a problem for, *e.g.,* a trust for the testator's pet cat. Since the "measuring lives" that can be used for Rule Against Perpetuities purposes must be human lives (cannot use cats, turtles, or elephants), absent special drafting to avoid the problem, a trust for the care of the settlor's pet cat may be held invalid. Under the "what might happen" remote possibilities test of the Rule Against Perpetuities, the cat *might* outlive anyone now alive by more than 21 years. Since the named trustee cannot be compelled to carry out the terms of the trust, he is treated as having a power of appointment, which might be exercisable beyond the period of the Rule Against Perpetuities.

2. Massachusetts—Honorary Trust Valid for Ninety Years
Under Massachusetts's Uniform Statutory Rule Against Perpetuities, an honorary trust is valid for 90 years.

3. Massachusetts Exception for Burial Places
The Rule Against Perpetuities is applicable in most jurisdictions for all honorary trusts. In Massachusetts, however, an honorary trust for the maintenance or care of any public or private burial ground, churchyard, or other place of burial is exempted from the application of the Rule Against Perpetuities in the same manner that charitable trusts are exempted.

V. RESULTING AND CONSTRUCTIVE TRUSTS

A. RESULTING AND CONSTRUCTIVE TRUSTS ARE NOT TRUE TRUSTS
In an express trust, the trustee holds and administers assets for the benefit of beneficiaries over a period of time. By contrast, once a resulting or constructive trust is implied, title "shoots out of" the trustee to the beneficiary, who holds legal and equitable title and can demand an immediate conveyance of the assets.

The Statute of Frauds does not apply to resulting and constructive trusts because they are not really trusts. Resulting and constructive trusts, even with respect to land, can be established by parol testimony.

B. RESULTING TRUSTS

The term "resulting trust" describes a situation in which the courts imply a trust based on the presumed intent of the settlor and declare the settlor or his heirs to be the beneficiary of the resulting trust. A resulting trust arises when: (i) an express trust fails in whole or in part, (ii) the settlor makes an incomplete disposition of trust property, or (iii) A pays the purchase price for property and places title in B's name.

1. Resulting Trust Implied from Failure of Express Trust

On failure of an express trust, if the settlor has not declared her intent, the beneficial interest in the trust property is in the settlor or, if she is dead, it passes to her successors.

Example: S transfers property to T as trustee, "to pay the income to my best friends." The trust fails for want of identifiable beneficiaries. T holds on a resulting trust for S, which simply means that S can compel a reconveyance of the property at any time.

2. Resulting Trust by Reversion—Implied from Excess Corpus

A resulting trust in favor of the settlor or his successors also arises when the trust purpose is fully satisfied and some trust property remains. There could be a resulting trust of part of the corpus even where the trust is not completely terminated if it is clear that the trust property is in excess of the amount needed to carry out the trust purpose. As used in this context, the term "resulting trust" is another name for "reversion," for it covers the situation where the settlor or testator has made an *incomplete disposition of assets* transferred in an express trust.

Example: S establishes a trust under which income is payable to her son B for life, and on B's death the corpus is to be distributed to B's issue then living per stirpes. B is not survived by issue. There is a resulting trust in favor of S or her estate.

3. Purchase Money Resulting Trust

If A pays the purchase price for property and causes title to be taken in B's name, and if A and B are not related (reducing the likelihood that a gift was intended), a presumption arises that B holds on a resulting trust for A, meaning that A can compel a reconveyance of the property at any time. [Nessralla v. Peck, 403 Mass. 757 (1989)] A purchase money resulting trust ("PMRT") arises by virtue of the presumed intent that A did not contemplate making a gift, but had some other reason for taking title in this manner. [Crowell v. Stefani, 12 Mass. App. Ct. 966 (1981)]

a. Transactions Between Spouses—Presumption of Gift

Where one spouse purchases land and takes title in the other spouse's name, the presumption is that a gift (and not a PMRT) was intended. Clear and convincing evidence is needed to rebut the presumption of gift. If one spouse purchases land and takes title in both spouses' names, the presumption is that a gift of a one-half interest in the property was intended. [Ross v. Ross, 2 Mass. App. Ct. 52 (1974)]

C. CONSTRUCTIVE TRUSTS

A constructive trust is not really a trust at all. Rather, "constructive trust" is the name given to a *flexible remedy* imposed by a court of equity to prevent an unjust enrichment of one person at the expense of another as the result of fraud, undue influence, abuse of confidence, or mistake in the transaction that originates the problem. [Superior Glass Co. v. First Bristol County National Bank, 380 Mass. 829 (1979)] Constructive trusts are distinguished from express and resulting trusts in that they do not arise by virtue of agreement or intention, but *by operation of law*. The constructive trustee's *only* duty is to convey the property to the person who would have owned it but for the wrongful conduct. This permits the wronged party to receive the very property of which he was deprived, and not just money damages. This remedy is especially important where property has increased in value since it was wrongfully acquired.

Proof of the facts necessary to establish a constructive trust must be by *clear and convincing evidence*.

1. Key to Analysis—Wrongful Conduct Resulting in Unjust Enrichment

One of the advantages of the constructive trust remedy is its flexibility. It can be adapted to meet any situation in which a party would be unjustly enriched as a result of wrongful conduct.

2. Transfer Procured by Fraudulent Misrepresentation, Mistake, Undue Influence, or Duress

A transfer procured by fraudulent misrepresentation, mistake, undue influence, or duress is commonly undone by imposing a constructive trust.

Example: In the leading case of *Latham v. Father Divine,* 299 N.Y. 22 (1949), T's will, as drafted, gave her entire estate to Father Divine. Allegations were made that T had a new will prepared making gifts to others, but by reason of fraudulent misrepresentations, then undue influence, and finally, the murder of T in a contrived surgical operation, T was prevented from revoking the old will and executing the new one. *Held:* As far as wills law is concerned, the new will cannot be admitted to probate because it was not executed. The old will must be probated because it was not revoked. *But* if the allegations are proven, the takers under the old will hold on a constructive trust for those who would have taken but for the fraudulent misrepresentations and undue influence.

3. Imposed to Disgorge Unjust Enrichment Even If Another Committed Wrongful Conduct

The Massachusetts courts have imposed constructive trusts against parties who were innocent of wrongful conduct, if the parties would be unjustly enriched by the wrongful conduct of another person.

Example: In a property settlement agreement attendant to a divorce, H agreed to keep a $25,000 life insurance policy in force, with the couple's child C as beneficiary. H later named his sister S as beneficiary of the policy. *Held:* Constructive trust impressed on the insurance proceeds for the benefit of C. While S was innocent of any wrongdoing, she would be unjustly enriched by H's wrongful conduct. Since S was not a bona fide purchaser for value, her rights as a gratuitous donee are inferior to the equitable rights of C.

4. Acquisition of Property in Violation of Fiduciary Duty

A constructive trust may be imposed if a person in a fiduciary relationship acquires or retains property in violation of his fiduciary duty. This rule is not limited to trustees, executors, and guardians, but applies to other fiduciary relationships as well (*e.g.,* attorneys, partners, and directors or officers of a corporation). [Meehan v. Shaughnessy, 404 Mass. 419 (1989)—law partners] The rule can be invoked in a variety of fact settings, including the sale of a person's individual assets to himself as fiduciary, purchase by the fiduciary of property he should have purchased for the beneficiary, and the use of confidential information for personal benefit. Imposition of a constructive trust enables the injured party to recover the very property involved. If the property has increased in value, this remedy is more advantageous than an action for money damages.

Examples: 1) O, an officer of an oil drilling company, gains access to confidential information that oil has been discovered in an area in which the company was exploring for oil and gas leases. O buys the lease for himself. O has breached his fiduciary duty as a corporate officer, and holds the leases under a constructive trust for the benefit of the company.

2) E, executor of an estate, needs to sell estate assets in order to raise cash to pay taxes. E sells estate assets to himself, which constitutes self-dealing. E holds the assets on a constructive trust for the estate's beneficiaries, who can recover the assets if it is in their interest to do so (*i.e.,* if the assets go up in value after E's purchase).

3) M, managing partner of a partnership, sells land to C for a modest profit, which M shares with his partners. However, C has secretly agreed to convey the land back to M. Shortly thereafter, M sells the land at nearly double the price of the first sale. Because M breached his fiduciary duty to his partners, M holds the profits from the second sale on a constructive trust for the benefit of his partners.

5. Oral Trusts of Land—Lifetime Transfers

The Statute of Frauds requires trusts of land to be in writing and signed by the grantor. What happens when there is an outright conveyance of land, but it is alleged that the grantee agreed to hold the land in trust for purposes communicated to her by the grantor? In certain well-defined situations, a constructive trust may be imposed.

a.   **Generally No Constructive Trust Imposed If Deed Absolute on Its Face**
Where a deed is absolute on its face but an oral agreement to hold in trust is alleged,
the general rule (which, as we shall see, is rarely invoked) is that the grantee gets to
keep the land free from trust. An oral trust also may not be proven in order to show that
the grantee was not intended to take any beneficial interest and will be unjustly enriched if allowed to keep the land. The Statute of Frauds bars oral proof of the trust.
The grantee may choose to perform her moral obligation, but she cannot be compelled
to do so.

b.   **Exceptions to General Rule**

1)   **Fraud in the Inception—Constructive Trust Imposed**
If it is shown that the grantee agreed to hold in trust and *at the time she agreed*
she had no intention of carrying out the trust, a constructive trust will be imposed
in favor of the intended beneficiaries. (Note the induced reliance factor here.) The
grantee's promise must be proven by *clear and convincing evidence*. But where
the grantee determines to avoid the trust only *after* agreeing, the courts deny any
remedy on the theory that the Statute of Frauds permits refusal to fulfill an oral
trust of land and therefore the grantee has done nothing not expressly permitted by
law.

2)   **Duress or Undue Influence—Constructive Trust Imposed**
An oral agreement to hold land in trust may be shown where the transfer was
obtained by duress or undue influence. The grantee would hold in trust for the
intended beneficiaries.

3)   **Confidential Relationship—Constructive Trust Imposed**
Where the grantee who orally promises to hold land in trust is in a confidential
relationship with the grantor (attorney-client, business partners, etc.), the transfer
is constructively fraudulent and the agreement to hold in trust may be shown for
the purpose of imposing a constructive trust for the benefit of the intended beneficiaries. The grantee's promise must be proved by *clear and convincing evidence*.

This is the big loophole in the Statute of Frauds. Such a confidential relationship
exists not only where there is a fiduciary relationship such as attorney-client, but
also where the transferor, because of family relationships or otherwise, is accus-
tomed to being guided by the judgment of the transferee. However, a confidential
or fiduciary relationship does not arise solely by virtue of close familial or business ties. [Schleifstein v. Greenstein, 9 Mass. App. Ct. 344 (1980)]

4)   **Promise to Sell Land and Hold Sale Proceeds in Trust**
Suppose that A transfers land to B on the basis of B's promise to sell the land and
hold the sale proceeds in trust for the benefit of C. If B actually sells the land, the
trust is enforceable by C. *Rationale:* The sale proceeds are personal property, and
thus are not subject to the Statute of Frauds. Oral trusts of personal property are
valid.

6.   **Oral Trusts—Testamentary Transfers**

a.   **Absolute Gift But Trust Intended (Secret Trust)—Trust May Be Enforced**
In the case of a secret trust, the will makes a gift, absolute on its face, to a named
beneficiary. In reality, however, the gift was made in reliance upon the beneficiary's
promise to hold the gift property in trust for another. To prevent the unjust enrichment
of the named beneficiary (secret trustee), courts will allow the intended trust beneficiary to present *extrinsic evidence* of the agreement. If the agreement can be proved by
clear and convincing evidence, a constructive trust will be imposed on the named
beneficiary. The *Statute of Frauds* is not a bar because the suit is not to compel enforcement of the trust, but rather to impose a constructive trust to prevent unjust enrichment. The *Statute of Wills* is not a bar because the constructive trust does not
operate on the will itself, but rather on the property, once it comes into the hands of the
named beneficiary. [Ham v. Twombly, 181 Mass. 170 (1902)]
Example: T left 14 colleges $1.6 million. Concerned about a statutory restriction
on gifts to charities, T executed a codicil giving the residue of his estate
to R. The will gave no indication of a trust, or that R was not to have

beneficial ownership. On T's death, the gift to the colleges failed and passed to R through the residuary clause. Evidence was offered that R had promised to hold the residuary in trust for the colleges. *Held:* To prevent unjust enrichment, a constructive trust will be imposed upon clear and convincing evidence that R agreed to hold the gift in trust. [Trustees of Amherst College v. Ritch, 151 N.Y. 282 (1897)]

1) **Promise Enforceable Whether Made Before or After Will's Execution**
Unlike the rule applicable to lifetime conveyances (fraud in the inception, above), in the case of wills, relief is given whether the agreement to hold in trust is made before or after the will is executed. In either situation there is *induced reliance*—if the promise is made after the will's execution, the testator is induced not to change her will. Also, it does not matter whether the person intended to perform the agreement at the time he made his promise. All that matters is that the testator executed her will in reliance on the promise.

2) **Compare—Attempted Modification of Gift Outside the Will**
If a testator executes a will making an absolute devise, then writes a note (opened after the testator's death) telling the legatee that she wants the legatee to hold the property in trust for certain enumerated purposes, the Statute of Wills prevents enforcement of the trust. No constructive trust is raised because there is no induced reliance and no unconscionable conduct on the part of the legatee. He cannot be compelled to execute the trust because no trust was created by the will.

b. **Gift "In Trust" Without Beneficiary (Semi-Secret Trust)—No Trust Created**
In the case of a semi-secret trust, the will makes a gift to a person "in trust," but *does not name the beneficiary*. The testator may have communicated the terms to the "trustee." Following the majority rule, the Massachusetts courts have taken the position that the trust is unenforceable because of the Statute of Wills. The will does not identify the intended beneficiary, and it would be violative of the policy of the wills statute to permit their identification by parol testimony. The gift fails for want of identification of the beneficiary. The named trustee holds the property on a resulting trust for the testator's heirs.

Example: T's will bequeaths her residuary estate to C, "to be disposed of by her as I have previously instructed her." The gift fails (and the residuary estate passes by intestate succession) even if C is willing to identify the intended beneficiaries and carry out T's oral instructions. Identification of the beneficiaries by parol testimony would be violative of the statutory requirement that wills must be in writing. [Olliffe v. Wells, 130 Mass. 221 (1881)]

c. **Different Result in "Secret Trust" and "Semi-Secret Trust" Cases Explained**
Why is it that in the secret trust cases (will purports to make absolute disposition) the trust can be proved, but in the semi-secret trust cases it cannot? The answer lies in who the litigants are in the two cases. In the secret trust case, the issue is between the legatee and the beneficiaries of the alleged oral promise; to prohibit proof of the legatee's promise would lead to unjust enrichment. But in the semi-secret situation, the one thing that is clear is that the legatee himself was not intended to take beneficial enjoyment; the disposition to him was "in trust." Thus, the dispute is between the intended but unidentified beneficiaries and the heirs; the "induced reliance-unjust enrichment" element is not present.

VI. TRANSFERABILITY OF BENEFICIARY'S INTEREST; CREDITORS' RIGHTS

A. **VOLUNTARY ASSIGNMENT PERMITTED IF NO SPENDTHRIFT CLAUSE**
The equitable interest of a beneficiary of a trust is as freely transferable by him as the corresponding legal interest would be. Thus, in the absence of a spendthrift clause, the beneficiary may voluntarily assign his right to trust income or principal, and these interests are subject to the claims of his creditors.

B. **SPENDTHRIFT CLAUSES IN TRUSTS ARE VALID AND GIVEN FULL EFFECT**
A spendthrift trust is one in which, by statute or more often by virtue of the terms of the trust, the beneficiary is *unable voluntarily or involuntarily to transfer his interest* in the trust. In other

words, he cannot sell or give away his right to future income or capital, and his creditors are unable to collect or attach such rights. This type of trust is usually created to provide a fund for the maintenance of the beneficiary which will be secure against his own improvidence. Like most jurisdictions, Massachusetts gives full effect to spendthrift clauses.

Example: A trust provides: "The trustee shall pay the income to A for life and on A's death shall distribute the trust principal to B." The trust contains a spendthrift clause: "No interest of any beneficiary in the income or principal of this trust shall be transferable by the beneficiary, nor shall such interest be subject to the claims of the beneficiary's creditors by garnishment, attachment, or other legal process." The spendthrift clause is valid, and A's creditors cannot reach his income interest in the trust.

1. Spendthrift Clauses as to Trust Principal Are Valid
Massachusetts follows the majority rule in holding that spendthrift clauses are enforceable with respect to a beneficiary's interest in trust principal as well as income interests.

Example: In the example given above, B's creditors cannot attach or garnish B's remainder interest in the trust because the spendthrift clause expressly applies to interests in trust principal.

2. Income or Principal Loses Spendthrift Protection After Distribution from Trust
Once income (or principal) is distributed to the beneficiary by the trustee, it loses its trust character and is no longer protected by the spendthrift clause. The beneficiary's creditors can reach the income—if they move fast enough. But the effect of the spendthrift rule is that the creditors' most efficient remedies (garnishment and attachment) are not available.

C. EXCEPTIONS TO THE SPENDTHRIFT RULE

1. Creditors Who Furnish Necessaries
Where a trust provides for the mandatory payment of trust income (*e.g.*, "the trustee *shall* pay all trust income to B"), a creditor who furnishes necessaries (food, clothing, shelter, medical services, etc.) can reach the beneficiary's income interest by appropriate judicial process even though the trust contains a spendthrift clause. *Rationale:* This exception to the spendthrift rule actually works to the advantage of the beneficiary. If a creditor who furnishes necessaries could not reach a spendthrift trust, a beneficiary whose primary source of income is a trust might have difficulty obtaining necessaries.

2. Alimony and Child Support
In Massachusetts (as in most states), a spendthrift trust can always be reached by writ of garnishment or attachment to satisfy an alimony or child support obligation. [Wolfe v. Wolfe, 21 Mass. App. Ct. 254 (1985)]

3. Claims by Federal and State Governments
The interest of a beneficiary of a spendthrift trust can be reached to satisfy a claim of the United States government (*e.g.*, federal tax liens) or of a state.

D. SPENDTHRIFT CLAUSE INVALID AS TO SETTLOR'S RETAINED INTEREST
In all jurisdictions that recognize spendthrift clauses, a property owner cannot use a spendthrift trust to insulate his own assets from the reach of present or future creditors. Thus, spendthrift clauses are invalid as applied to the interest of a beneficiary who is also the settlor of the trust. His interest in the trust can be reached by his creditors under the generally applicable rules. [Merchants National Bank v. Morrisey, 329 Mass. 601 (1953)]

1. Settlor-Beneficiary Can Assign Interest
Under the same reasoning, a settlor-beneficiary can transfer his interest even if the trust that he created contains a spendthrift clause that purports to prohibit the transfer. The spendthrift rules simply have no application to the settlor-beneficiary's interest.

2. Revocable Trust Is Reachable by Settlor's Creditors and by Trustee in Bankruptcy
Where a settlor reserves a right of revocation over the trust estate, he remains the absolute owner of the property as far as the rights of his creditors are concerned. Since a trustee in bankruptcy can exercise any power the bankrupt could exercise for his own benefit, she can exercise the bankrupt's power to revoke a trust and pay claims to the estate from trust assets. [11 U.S.C. §541] On the settlor's death, his creditors can reach the revocable trust assets to the extent that their claims are not satisfied from the settlor's probate estate. [State Street Bank & Trust Co. v. Reiser, 7 Mass. App. Ct. 633 (1979)]

3. Creditors Can Reach Only Settlor's Retained Interest
If the trust is irrevocable and the settlor retains some but not all of the beneficial interest in the trust (*e.g.,* income to settlor for life, remainder to others), his creditors can reach the full amount of the interest retained by the settlor, but no more. To the extent that he has irrevocably given the property to others (the remainder interest), his creditors have no claim.

a. Exception—Fraudulent Conveyance
If creation of the trust was a "fraudulent conveyance" under creditors' rights law, the creditors can reach the entire trust property that was transferred with an intent to defraud creditors.

E. DISCRETIONARY AND SUPPORT TRUSTS

1. Discretionary Trusts
A discretionary trust is one in which the trustee is given discretion to decide whether to distribute or to withhold payments of income or principal to a beneficiary. This discretion relates to more than just the time and manner of payment, but actually limits the extent of the rights of the beneficiary to the amounts the trustee decides to give him, with the rest eventually going over to others.

a. Creditors' Rights

1) Before Trustee Exercises Discretion—Interest Cannot Be Reached
Before the trustee exercises his discretion to make payments to the beneficiary, the beneficiary's interest is not assignable and cannot be reached by his creditors. The theory is that, because the beneficiary has no right to payments that he can enforce against the trustee, there is nothing substantial enough for the creditors to reach. That is, the creditors' rights cannot rise above those of the beneficiary.

2) After Trustee Exercises Discretion—Interest Can Be Reached
Once the trustee exercises his discretion and elects to make payments to the beneficiary, if he has notice of an assignment or attachment by the creditors, the trustee must make those payments not to the beneficiary but to his creditors or assignees, *unless the beneficiary's interest is also protected by a spendthrift restriction*.
Example: T bequeaths a sum in trust to pay the income and principal to A in the trustee's uncontrolled discretion. A's creditors cannot require the trustee to pay the income or principal to them. However, by giving notice of assignment or attachment to the trustee, they can prevent the trustee from paying A until they are paid first. If there is a spendthrift clause, they cannot reach A's interest in any way and the trustee can pay A if he chooses to do so.

3) Creditors May Reach Discretionary Interest Created for Settlor
Where a discretionary interest is created for the settlor herself, her creditors can usually reach the retained interest.

b. Beneficiary's Rights
The beneficiary cannot interfere with the exercise of the trustee's discretion unless the trustee abuses his power. What constitutes abuse depends upon the extent of discretion conferred upon the trustee. If the trust is a "support trust," there is more room for a court's interference because the trust has a specific purpose, but even if the settlor says the trustee's discretion is uncontrolled, the court will interfere if the trustee acts in bad faith or dishonestly.

2. Support Trusts
A support trust is one in which the trustee is required to pay or apply *only so much* of the income or principal as is necessary for the support of the beneficiary.

a. All Income for Support—Not Support Trust
A trust to "pay all the income to A for his support" is *not* a support trust. When the whole of the income is to be paid to A for his support, the words "for his support" merely state the motive for the transfer. The beneficiary is not limited to what is necessary for his support.

b. Not Assignable

Even without a spendthrift clause, the character of a beneficiary's interest in a support trust is such that no one but the beneficiary can enjoy it; his interest is not assignable by definition. His creditors (except those that have provided support) cannot reach it. This would defeat the purpose of the trust.

c. Effect of Other Resources Available to Beneficiary

Suppose the beneficiary of a support trust has other income or resources that can be used for his support. Is the beneficiary entitled to support out of the trust fund without taking into account such other resources? This is a question of the *settlor's intention* and the cases are fairly evenly divided between inferring that the beneficiary receive his support from the trust regardless of other resources, and inferring that the beneficiary's other resources be considered.

Example: T bequeaths a fund in trust to pay such income to A as is necessary to support A. A requires $25,000 a year for support. A has $5,000 income from other sources. The cases are split as to whether A gets $25,000 from the trust or only $20,000.

VII. MODIFICATION AND TERMINATION OF TRUSTS

A. MODIFICATION OF ADMINISTRATIVE PROVISIONS—CHANGED CIRCUMSTANCES

Suppose that, due to changed circumstances not known to the settlor or anticipated by him, compliance with the trust's administrative provisions would defeat or substantially impair a material purpose of the trust. Upon petition of the settlor, the trustee, or a beneficiary, the court may order that the trust terms be modified. Most of the cases involve restrictions on the sale of a trust asset. However, it takes a strong case—frustration of a material trust purpose—to justify modification of the trust's terms as established by the settlor. The mere fact that a sale or a different investment would be beneficial to the trust is not, in itself, a basis for permitting a modification.

Example: T directed the trustee to continue to publish his newspaper, the *New York World,* and prohibited sale of the publishing company's stock so long as the trust was in existence. Trust income was to be paid to his wife, then children, then grandchildren. Losses incurred in publishing the paper threatened to eliminate the profits from other assets of the trust. Thus, little or no trust income was available for the family. On petition, the court authorized the trustees to sell the newspaper. The court used the "primary intent, secondary intent" analysis we have seen in other contexts (cy pres, appointment of successor trustee where primary trustee dies, etc.). The primary purpose of the trust was to provide income to T's family; retention of newspaper stock was incidental to that. To carry out the specific direction that the stock not be sold would frustrate the primary purpose of the trust. [Matter of Pulitzer, 139 Misc. 575 (N.Y. 1931)]

1. Reformation to Correct Scrivener's Error

The court can modify or reform a trust instrument that fails to embody the settlor's intentions due to a scrivener's error. A scrivener's error is typically a failure by a lawyer to draft an instrument that clearly reflects the settlor's intention. Reformation, however, is available only on full, clear, and decisive proof of error or inadvertence by the drafter. [Loeser v. Talbot, 412 Mass. 361 (1992)]

2. Reformation for Tax Purposes

The Massachusetts courts have been very generous in approving reformations that put trusts in a better tax posture. [*See, e.g.*, Fleet Bank v. Fleet Bank, 429 Mass. 1003 (1999)—after settlor and her husband had both died, court found that settlor did not intend to give her husband a taxable general power of appointment] "A testator who wishes to make a gift to his State and country can do so directly, and he should not be presumed to have intended such a gift by indirect means." [Putnam v. Putnam, 366 Mass. 261 (1974)]

B. TERMINATION ACCORDING TO TRUST'S TERMS

A trust will terminate automatically at the expiration of the time specified in the instrument. If there is no direction that the corpus be paid out to designated persons, the trustee holds on a resulting trust for the settlor or his successors.

Examples: 1) O conveys assets in a trust under which the income is to be paid to A for life, then to B until he attains the age of 30, at which time the principal is to be distributed to B. A dies; thereafter, B attains the age of 30. The trust ends according to its terms; B is entitled to a distribution of the principal free of the trust.

2) T devises the residue of his estate in trust: "The trustee shall pay the income to my son John for life, and on John's death shall distribute the trust principal to John's descendants then living per stirpes." Some years later John dies; he is not survived by descendants. Since T's will made no provision for the contingency that has occurred, the trust terminates and there is a reversion. Since the incomplete gift was in the residuary clause, it passes to T's heirs. The trustee holds on resulting trust for T's heirs (or their successors, if T's heirs have died).

After termination, the trustee may continue to exercise trust powers for the reasonable time required to wind up the affairs of the trust and to make distribution to the beneficiaries.

C. TERMINATION OF TRUST BY SETTLOR

1. Revocable Trust Can Be Terminated by Settlor at Any Time
If a trust, by its terms, is revocable, it may be terminated by the settlor at any time. But remember that all trusts (except Totten trust bank accounts) are irrevocable by the settlor unless the power to revoke is expressly reserved.

2. Irrevocable Trust Can Be Terminated by Settlor If All Beneficiaries Consent
If the settlor and all beneficiaries consent, a trust can be terminated even though it is a discretionary trust or spendthrift trust. The reason for this rule is that if all the interested parties agree that the trust should not continue any longer, there is no real point in continuing it. The trustee's consent to the termination is not required. She is not deemed to have an interest in the trust for this purpose.

a. All Beneficiaries Must Be Sui Juris
Consent of *all* beneficiaries is required. If any beneficiary (whether of a vested or contingent interest) is incompetent or is a minor, the trust cannot be terminated because the incompetent's conservator or the minor's guardian cannot give the necessary consent.

D. TERMINATION OF TRUST BY BENEFICIARIES
Suppose the settlor is dead. Can all the beneficiaries, if they are sui juris (*i.e.*, not under any legal disability), agree to terminate the trust, and have the assets distributed to them free of the trust?

1. Only If All Beneficiaries Consent and No Further Trust Purpose to Be Served
A trust *cannot be terminated* even if all the beneficiaries consent, *if the termination would be contrary to the material purposes of the settlor*. [West v. Third National Bank, 11 Mass. App. 577 (1981)] This is known as the Claflin doctrine, named after the leading case of *Claflin v. Claflin,* 149 Mass. 19 (1889). A trust cannot be terminated where its continuance is necessary to carry out a material purpose of the trust.

2. Trust for Fixed Period of Time Cannot Be Terminated Before that Time
Where there is a clear and unambiguous provision in a trust instrument as to the duration of the trust (*e.g.,* 10 years), the trust may not be terminated before that time. If the settlor has decided, for whatever reason, to postpone distribution of the trust corpus for a fixed period of time, the courts have no authority to interfere with that decision. This is based on a fundamental principle of the law of trusts and estates: As long as no illegality is involved, anyone may do with his property as he wishes.
Example: T creates a trust to pay the income to A *until he is 30 years old*, and then to distribute the remainder to him. Even though A is the sole beneficiary of the trust, A should not be allowed to terminate the trust. The primary purpose of the trust was to keep the trust principal out of A's hands until he reached the designated age. To permit an early termination of the trust would defeat a material purpose of the settlor.

3. Spendthrift Trusts Cannot Be Terminated
Suppose a trust is created to pay the income to A for life, remainder to B. The trust contains a spendthrift clause prohibiting A's transfer of his income interest. A and B are both adults and they want to terminate the trust. Can they do so? The answer is no. The courts reason that a material purpose of the settlor was to give A an income interest that would last for his lifetime, protecting A against his own indiscretions and securing the interest from the reach

of A's creditors. This material purpose of the settlor would be defeated if the trust were terminated before the date set for its termination. Spendthrift trusts are sometimes referred to as "indestructible," since they cannot be terminated by the beneficiaries.

E. TERMINATION OF TRUST BY COURT

1. **Trust Purposes Have Been Accomplished or Have Become Illegal or Impossible**
   Upon petition, the court may order termination of a trust prior to the time fixed for its termination if it finds that the trust purposes have been accomplished or the trust purposes have become illegal or impossible to carry out. [Mass. Gen. L. ch. 203, §25]

2. **Uneconomical Trust**
   Upon petition, the court may order termination of a trust (or consolidation of the trust with another trust), even if it is a spendthrift trust, if the court finds that the costs of administration make the trust uneconomical or would defeat or substantially impair the purposes of the trust. [Mass. Gen. L. ch. 203, §25]

VIII. TRUST ADMINISTRATION—TRUSTEE POWERS AND DUTIES

A. INTRODUCTION
A trustee has legal title to the trust assets and is charged with the duty of effectively managing and administering the trust estate. There are three basic categories of trust administration problems: (i) the powers and duties of the trustee in handling trust affairs; (ii) the duty of fairness to both income beneficiary and remainderman in investment decisions and in apportioning receipts and expenses among the income and principal accounts; and (iii) the rules prohibiting self-dealing by the trustee. Additionally, there are the two related problem areas involving trustee liability for improper conduct and the liability of third persons who deal with the trust.

B. POWERS AND DUTIES OF TRUSTEE

1. **Powers**
   As holder of legal title to the trust property, the trustee has the power to manage and control the trust property similar to an individual owner. In general, she has all those powers that are necessary to the proper administration of the trust and any additional powers granted to her in the trust instrument. She may sell personal property in the trust without court order, but to sell real estate—unless a power of sale is included in the trust instrument—the trustee must obtain a license from the court. Note that a trustee's powers may be increased if the trust instrument incorporates by reference the statute that provides for "statutory optional fiduciary powers." [Mass. Gen. L. ch. 184B]

2. **Sale or Mortgage of Real Property Requires Court Approval**
   Unless the governing instrument grants an express power of sale of real property, a sale requires court approval upon petition of the trustee or an interested person. The court can direct that the property be sold at either a public sale (*i.e.*, an auction) or a private sale. The court can authorize the trustee to purchase the real property if after full disclosure the court determines that such a purchase would not be prejudicial to the trust. [Mass. Gen. L. ch. 203, §16] The mortgage of real property also requires court approval unless an express power to mortgage is granted in the trust instrument. [Mass. Gen. L. ch. 203, §23] Note, however, that routine sales of personal property for purposes of investment and reinvestment do not require court approval. [Mass. Gen. L. ch. 203, §19]

3. **Duties**
   In addition to her duties to refrain from self-dealing, to be fair to all beneficiaries, and to make the trust property productive, each of which is discussed separately below, a trustee has the following duties:

   a. **Duty to Take Possession of Trust Property**
      Not only must the trustee take possession of trust property, but she must ordinarily take title to it as well. There is one exception. By statute, a trustee is permitted to take title to stock in nominee form. This means that the record ownership of the stock is not in the trustee but is in her nominee. This facilitates transfer of the stock. However, the trustee is personally liable for any improper acts of her nominee.

b. **Duty Not to Delegate Fiduciary Responsibilities**
A trustee may not delegate her duties other than acts that it would be unreasonable to require her to perform personally (*e.g.*, typing and mailing letters). Thus, it is a breach of trust if the trustee delegates decisions regarding the distribution of trust property. However, a trustee may employ agents such as attorneys and accountants. She may take their advice into account, but may not act without independent examination of their advice. Note, however, that a trustee *can* delegate investment and management functions (*see* C.5., *infra*).

c. **Duty to Make Periodic Accountings**
The duty to keep and render accounts, and to furnish information to the beneficiary or his agent at the beneficiary's request is one way of insuring that the trustee is meeting her obligation of loyalty. Statutory law requires a yearly accounting from a trustee who is required to give bond. [Mass. Gen. L. ch. 206, §1]

d. **Duty to Keep Trust Property Separate—No Commingling**
Absent a contrary provision in the trust instrument, a trustee must keep the assets of the trust separate from her own individual assets and separate from the assets of other trusts. There is one exception: By statute, a trustee may invest in common trust funds. These funds are created by banks so that the assets of several smaller trusts can be combined for the purpose of investment. This permits greater diversification and economies of scale.

e. **Discretionary Support Trust—Duty to Inquire into Beneficiary's Resources**
A trust that gives the trustee a discretionary power to pay out the principal for the "comfortable support and maintenance" of the beneficiary imposes a duty on the trustee to inquire into the financial resources of the beneficiary so as to recognize his needs. The appropriate remedy for failure to make inquiry, thus depriving the beneficiary of such funds, is to impress a constructive trust on the amounts that should have been distributed to the beneficiary but were not because of the trustee's error. [Marsman v. Nasca, 30 Mass. App. Ct. 789 (1991)]

C. INVESTMENT POWERS
Massachusetts has enacted the Prudent Investor Act, which is based on the *modern portfolio theory* of investments. Under the Act, the trustee is held to a standard of prudence; *i.e.*, he must use reasonable care, skill, and caution in investing and managing the trust assets as a prudent investor would, taking into account the purposes and terms of the trust. [Mass Gen. L. ch. 203C, §3(a)] The standard of prudence is applied in view of the entire investment portfolio, and not to particular investments viewed in isolation. [Mass. Gen. L. ch. 203C, §3(b)]

Examples: 1) To achieve a balanced investment portfolio, as part of the overall investment strategy it may be appropriate to invest in securities of different industries (*e.g.*, computers, utilities, transportation, pharmaceuticals), even though some of these industries may decline in value whereas others may achieve considerable growth.

2) It may be prudent to invest in an asset that is not income-producing but has growth potential, if the overall portfolio is invested so as to meet appropriate income objectives.

1. **Prudent Investor Act Looks to Conduct, Not Outcome or Performance**
Whether the fiduciary has complied with the Act is determined in light of the facts and circumstances at the time the investment decision is made, and not in hindsight. [Mass. Gen. L. ch. 203C, §9] A fiduciary who acts in substantial compliance with the prudent investor rule is not liable to the beneficiaries, even if the trust estate declines in value or produces less income than anticipated.

2. **Trustee Must Establish and Pursue Overall Investment Strategy**
The Prudent Investor Act requires that the trustee establish a custom-tailored strategy for the particular trust and that he invest and manage the trust assets as a prudent investor would, considering the purposes, terms, and other circumstances of the trust. [Mass. Gen. L. ch. 203C, §3(a)] Within a reasonable time after accepting the trusteeship or receiving trust assets, the trustee must review the trust assets and make and implement decisions concerning their retention and disposition, taking the following factors into account:

(i) General economic conditions;

(ii) The possible effect of inflation or deflation;

(iii) The expected tax consequences of investment decisions or strategies;

(iv) The role that each investment plays within the overall trust portfolio;

(v) The expected total return from income and appreciation of capital;

(vi) Needs for liquidity;

(vii) An asset's special relationship or value to the purposes of the trust or to one of the beneficiaries; and

(viii)Any differing interests of the income beneficiaries and the remaindermen.

[Mass. Gen. L. ch. 203C, §§3(c), 5, 7]

3. **Any Type of Investment Is Permitted**
The Prudent Investor Act permits a fiduciary to invest in any kind of property or any type of investment "consistent with the standards of this chapter." [Mass. Gen. L. ch. 203C, §3(e)]

4. **Diversification of Investments**
A trustee must reasonably diversify the investments of the trust unless under the circumstances it is prudent not to do so. [Mass. Gen. L. ch. 203C, §4]

5. **Delegation of Investment Function Permitted**
A trustee may delegate investment and management functions. [Mass. Gen. L. ch. 203C, §10] This provision recognizes that the trustee (especially an individual trustee) may have limited investment expertise, and that even an experienced investor may have limited expertise in sophisticated investment vehicles. The trustee must exercise *reasonable care in selecting* an agent and *in periodically reviewing* the agent's performance. The agent has the duty to exercise reasonable care in complying with the terms of the delegation.

6. **Fiduciaries with Special Skills Held to Higher Standard**
A bank, trust company, or professional investment advisor that has, or represents that it has, special skills or expertise must exercise such skills or expertise. [Mass. Gen. L. ch. 203C, §3(f)]

7. **Above Rules Apply Absent Contrary Provision**
Remember that the Prudent Investor Act is "default legislation" that can be superseded by the governing instrument or court order. In establishing a trust, the settlor can "write her own ticket," and can expand or limit any of the trustee's powers, including investment powers. [Mass. Gen. L. ch. 203C, §2(b)]

D. ALLOCATION OF RECEIPTS AND EXPENSES

1. **Income and Principal Rules**
Suppose the trust provides: "The trustee shall pay the income to A, and on A's death shall distribute the trust principal to B." When the trustee receives a distribution from some source, does he pay it out to A as income, or does he add it to the corpus of the trust for eventual distribution to B?

   a. **Interest, Rents, Etc.—Income**
   Interest on bonds, bank accounts, loans, and payments for the rental of trust property are all income.

   b. **Proceeds of Sale, Etc.—Principal**
   All money and other consideration received: (i) upon sale or exchange of an asset or upon the granting of an option, (ii) upon liquidation of a corporation whose securities were held as a trust asset, (iii) as compensation from eminent domain proceedings, or (iv) as proceeds of insurance on lost or damaged property are principal.

   c. **Capital Gains—Principal**
   Suppose that the trustee buys 100 shares of AT&T common stock at $50, and later sells the shares at $60, thus making a $1,000 "profit." The entire proceeds of sale, including the capital gain, are principal—the proceeds of sale of a trust asset.

2. **Corporate Distributions**

   a. **Cash Dividends—Income**
   Cash dividends are distributable to the income beneficiary as income.

b. Stock Dividends, Stock Splits, and Other Distributions—Principal

Suppose X Corporation declares a 5% cash dividend and a 5% stock dividend. The cash dividend is distributable to the income beneficiaries as income, but the stock dividend is added to corpus. Also added to corpus are stock subscription rights, stock purchase options, and new shares resulting from a merger, consolidation, or reorganization.

1) Exceptions

Where the trustee has the *option* of receiving a dividend either in cash or in shares, it is considered a cash dividend and thus income. Also, if a stock dividend is the distribution of *shares in another corporation* (*i.e.,* some corporation other than the one declaring the dividend), it is income, *unless* the trustee determines that the distribution is essentially a distribution of principal. [Mass. Gen. L. ch. 203, §21A]

3. Bonds Purchased at Discount or Premium

Suppose a trustee purchases a corporate bond at a discount because the bond's stated interest rate is low in relation to the market. Only the interest paid on the bond is income. On redemption, the entire bond proceeds are allocated to principal. If a bond is purchased at a premium because it pays interest at higher than market rates, the interest is allocated to income without amortization *unless* the premium exceeds 6% of the bond's maturity value. [Mass. Gen. L. ch. 203, §21B] On redemption only the face amount is allocated to principal.

Examples: 1) Trustee purchases a $1,000 Acme Company 6% bond for $890. The trustee holds the bond to maturity, when it is redeemed for $1,000. The interest of $60 per year is income. On redemption, the full $1,000 (including the $110 profit) is allocated to principal.

2) Trustee purchases a $1,000 Zircon Company 9% bond for $1,050. Each year's interest of $90 is income. The $1,000 received on redemption of the bond is allocated to principal. There is no amortization against income for the bond's decrease in value from its purchase to its redemption, because the premium was less than 6% of the bond's maturity value.

a. Exception—Bonds and Other Obligations Bearing No Stated Interest

If a bond or other obligation bears no stated interest and is redeemable at maturity for a specified amount, the difference between the purchase price and the redemption price is income. For example, a U.S. Series EE bond has no stated interest rate. Instead, the interest is built in as an increase in value. The same rule applies to Treasury bills, which are issued at a redemption amount, with the purchase price determined by prevailing market interest rates. If a $10,000 T-bill is purchased for $9,200, on redemption the $800 increase in value is allocated to income.

Example: Trustee purchases a Series EE bond for $750. The bond is redeemable in a specified number of years for $1,000. Upon redemption, $250 is allocated to income, and the $750 purchase price is allocated to principal.

4. Business and Farming Operations—Generally Accepted Accounting Principles

If a trustee uses any part of the principal to continue a business in which the settlor was a sole proprietor or a partner, the net profits of the business, determined in accordance with generally accepted accounting principles ("GAAP"), are income. GAAP are also used to determine the income from a farming operation.

5. Trustees' Commissions—Apportioned

At one time, the trustee's compensation was charged entirely against income. When this created a hardship on income beneficiaries during the Great Depression, the law was changed to provide that absent contrary provision in the governing instrument, trustees' commissions and attorneys' fees are to be apportioned between the principal and income accounts "*as the court may determine*." [Mass. Gen. L. ch. 206, §16; Old Colony Trust Co. v. Townsend, 234 Mass. 298 (1949)]

6. Other Expenses

Ordinary expenses incurred in the administration of a productive trust are usually charged against income, while extraordinary and unusual expenses, including costs of litigation, are ordinarily charged to principal. [Trustees of Dartmouth College v. Quincy, 331 Mass. 219 (1954)] Brokers' commissions and other costs incurred in the sale, exchange, or purchase of trust assets, and expenses incurred in proceedings to appoint or remove a trustee, are charged to principal. [Mass. Gen. L. ch. 203, §22]

E. PROHIBITED TRANSACTIONS—NO SELF-DEALING

1. In General

Absent a contrary trust provision or court approval, a trustee cannot enter into any transaction in which he is dealing with the trust in his individual capacity. A trustee cannot "wear two hats," representing both his personal interest and the interests of the trust estate in the same transaction. The concern of the self-dealing rules is not that the trustee might act improperly or take advantage of the situation; rather, the concern is that the trustee's personal interest might affect his judgment as to whether, for example, the price is a fair one or whether the asset should be sold at all. The possible effect of self-interest on the trustee's judgment as to the wisdom of the action is what makes the self-dealing transaction improper. A trustee owes a *duty of undivided loyalty* to the trust and its beneficiaries, and that loyalty might be tainted by his personal interest. The self-dealing rules apply to all fiduciaries, including guardians, custodians, and personal representatives of decedents' estates.

a. Cannot Buy or Sell Trust Assets

A trustee may not purchase any property owned by the trust even if he pays full value, and may not sell assets to the trust even if the price is a fair one.

Example: The trust's assets include 2,000 shares of IBM common stock. Determining that there is a need to diversify the trust's investments, the trustee purchases 1,000 shares of IBM stock from the trust, paying the market value as determined by the New York Stock Exchange quotes on the day of purchase. This is improper self-dealing. If the IBM stock later goes up in value, the trust beneficiaries can demand that the trustee return the IBM stock to the trust and take back his purchase price without interest. (If the IBM stock later goes down in value, the beneficiaries would ratify the transaction and waive the breach of trust, in effect telling the trustee, "thanks for getting rid of that lousy investment.")

b. Cannot Borrow Trust Funds or Make Loans to Trust

A trustee may not borrow trust funds, no matter how fair the interest rate and how well-secured the loan. A trustee may not loan his personal funds to the trust, and any interest paid on such a loan must be returned to the trust.

c. Cannot Use Trust Assets to Secure Personal Loan

A trustee may not use trust assets to secure a personal loan, and the lender does not obtain a valid security interest if she knew or had reason to know that the assets belonged to a trust.

d. Cannot Personally Gain Through Position as Trustee

A trustee cannot gain any personal advantage from his position (other than compensation for serving as trustee). For example, the trustee cannot receive a commission on the sale of a trust asset. The trustee is accountable for any profit arising out of administration of the trust, even if the profit did not result from a breach of trust.

e. Indirect Self-Dealing—Transactions with Relatives, Business Associates, and Corporation

The above self-dealing rules apply to sales or loans to a trustee's relatives, business associates, and to a corporation of which the trustee is a director, officer, or principal shareholder.

f. Corporate Trustee Cannot Invest in Its Own Stock

A corporate trustee cannot invest in its own stock as a trust investment. It can, however, *retain* its own stock if the stock was a part of the original trust res when the trust was established, provided that retention of the stock meets the prudent investor standard.

2. Settlor or Court Can Authorize Self-Dealing

The self-dealing rules apply absent a contrary provision in the trust instrument. The settlor can dispose of her property as she chooses, and the self-dealing rules can be relaxed by appropriate language in the trust instrument. However, provisions that authorize self-dealing are strictly construed, and any transaction involving self-dealing must be closely scrutinized to determine whether the trustee's actions may have involved fraud, bad faith, or overreaching.

Upon petition, the court can authorize a self-dealing transaction, but only if all relevant facts are disclosed to the court and it is shown that the transaction is in the trust beneficiaries' interest.

3. "No Further Inquiry" Rule—No Defense to Self-Dealing Transaction

A self-dealing transaction not authorized by the settlor or approved by the court triggers the *"no further inquiry" rule*. Under this rule, all the beneficiary has to show is that the trustee engaged in self-dealing—no further inquiry is made. Self-dealing is an automatic wrong. There is no defense; the only issue is damages. As in any breach of trust, the beneficiaries may either ratify the transaction and waive the breach of trust (as they would do if the trust benefited from the breach) or they may sue the trustee for damages (as they would do if the breach was detrimental to the trust).

Example: T, as trustee, sells trust assets worth $10,000 to itself for an equivalent amount of cash. If the trust assets later decline in value, the trust beneficiaries will ratify the breach of trust and in effect say, "Boy, we are sure glad that you own those assets and not the trust." But if the assets increase in value, the beneficiaries will sue to have the assets returned to the trust.

F. TRUSTEE LIABILITY

1. General Test of Liability

The general test of a trustee's liability for losses is whether he has exercised that degree of care and diligence with respect to the trust that a person of ordinary prudence would exercise in the management of his own affairs. If the trustee has special skills or is named trustee on the basis of representations of special skills or expertise, he is under a duty to use those skills. Whether the requisite care has been exercised should be determined from the facts of the particular case, but if there is no bad faith and nothing willful, the court will favor the trustee.

2. Liability for Breach of Trust

Surcharge is the name of the action brought by a beneficiary who seeks to show that the trustee has committed a breach of trust, as by engaging in self-dealing, exercising a power that he did not have, making an imprudent investment, or failing to safeguard and preserve trust assets. In addition to seeking removal of the trustee, the beneficiary may seek to recover the full amount of loss to the trust estate because of the improper conduct.

a. More than One Breach of Trust—Gains Cannot Offset Losses

Where a trustee is liable for losses resulting from one breach of trust, he cannot reduce the amount of this liability by offsetting against it a gain resulting from *another* breach of trust.

Example: Trustee is required by the trust instrument to invest in bonds. He invests one-half the corpus ($50,000) in Green stock and one-half ($50,000) in Purple stock. Both investments are improper because Trustee was directed to invest in bonds, not common stock. Purple stock becomes worthless, but Green stock doubles in value; so there is no net loss. Even so, the gain in Green stock *cannot* be set off against the loss in Purple stock. Therefore, Trustee is personally liable for the $50,000 loss in Purple stock.

3. Statute of Limitations

The statute of limitations does not begin to run on any action against a trust unless: (i) the trustee *repudiates the trust* (the buzz words used by the courts) by denying the existence of a trust with respect to the property, (ii) the trustee gives an accounting that reports the conduct giving rise to the action, or (iii) the trust relationship between the parties comes to an end (*e.g.,* if the trustee resigns or dies, or if the trust terminates according to its terms).

a. Action Based on Fraud—Discovery Rule

Where the beneficiary's action is based on fraud, the statute of limitations does not begin to run until the plaintiff discovers the fraud or could have discovered it with reasonable diligence.

4. Beneficiary's Remedies

Where the trustee has committed a breach of trust, in addition to petitioning for removal of the trustee, the beneficiary may: (i) *ratify* the transaction if it is in her interest to do so, or (ii) *recover damages* for the resulting loss.

Example: The trustee purchases 1,000 shares of stock in Alchemy, Inc., a company that claims to have developed a formula for turning lead into gold (clearly too speculative an investment). If the stock goes up in value, the beneficiary would ratify the transaction even though the stock does not satisfy the prudent investment standard: "Thanks for doing a good job of investing!" If the stock goes down in value, the beneficiary would exercise her other remedy (*i.e.*, recovery of damages) by bringing an action to hold the trustee personally liable for the amount lost (plus interest).

a. Standing

In the case of a noncharitable trust, only a named beneficiary, or one suing on her behalf, can maintain an action to enforce the trust. [Collector of Taxes of Lowell v. Slafsky, 332 Mass. 700 (1955)]

5. Trustee's Liability for Acts of Others

a. Agents

A trustee is *not liable* to the beneficiaries for the acts of her agents *unless* the trustee:

1) Directs, permits, or acquiesces in the act of the agent or conceals the act, or negligently fails to compel the agent to redress his wrong;

2) Fails to exercise reasonable supervision over the agent;

3) Permits the agent to perform duties the trustee was not entitled to delegate; or

4) Fails to use reasonable care in the selection or retention of the agent.

b. Co-Trustees

A trustee is *not liable* to the beneficiary for a breach of trust committed by a co-trustee *unless* the trustee:

1) Improperly delegated his authority to the co-trustee (one trustee cannot delegate to a co-trustee power to manage the property);

2) Participated, approved, or acquiesced in the breach by the co-trustee; or

3) Concealed the breach or failed to take proper steps to compel redress of it by the co-trustee.

c. Successor Trustees

A trustee is *not liable* to the beneficiary for breaches of trust committed by a predecessor trustee *unless* he:

1) Knew or should have known of the breach and failed to take proper steps to prevent further breach or to compel redress of a prior breach; or

2) Negligently failed to determine the amount of property that should have been turned over to him, or otherwise neglected to obtain delivery of the full trust property from the predecessor.

6. Effect of Exculpatory Clauses

An exculpatory clause is one that attempts to relieve a trustee of liability for ordinary negligence, errors of judgment, or acts and omissions. Such clauses are valid, although the courts construe them strictly and narrowly. However, an exculpatory clause that purports to remove liability for *gross negligence, willful misconduct, or bad faith* is against public policy and is void.

Example: The trust agreement authorizes Trustee to continue the settlor's business and provides that the trustee shall not be personally liable for negligence. The front steps of the business develop a large hole. Trustee is aware of this and does nothing about it for an unreasonable period. Z falls into the hole and is injured. Trustee is liable since his conduct was not simply negligent but was reckless.

7. Trustee's Liability to Third Parties

a. Trustee Not Liable on Contracts

A trustee is not personally liable on contracts properly entered into in his fiduciary capacity in the course of trust administration unless the contract provides otherwise, or unless the trustee fails to reveal his representative capacity and identify the trust in the contract. [Mass. Gen. L. ch. 203, §14A]

b. Trustee Not Liable on Torts Unless Personally At Fault
A trustee is personally liable for torts committed in the course of administration, only if he was personally at fault. [Mass. Gen. L. ch. 203, §14A]

c. Trustee Is Proper Defendant
Claims based on contract, tort, or any other obligation are asserted by bringing an action against the trustee, whether or not the trustee is personally liable therefor. [Mass. Gen. L. ch. 203, §14A]

8. Consent of Beneficiary; Estoppel
A beneficiary who gives his consent to the trustee's act or omission is estopped from holding the trustee liable for breach of trust. Thus, a trustee who makes an improper investment with the knowledge, assent, and acquiescence of the beneficiary cannot be held to make good a loss if one occurs. However, other beneficiaries who did not give their consent or acquiescence are not estopped from suing the trustee.

G. LIABILITY OF THIRD PARTIES TO THE TRUST

1. Transfer to Bona Fide Purchaser Cuts Off Beneficiaries' Interests
A third party who acquires the legal title to trust property *for value and without notice of the trust* takes the property free of the equitable interests of the beneficiaries. The existence of trust powers and their proper exercise by the trustee may be assumed without inquiry. A third person, without actual knowledge that the trustee is exceeding his powers or improperly exercising them, is fully protected in dealing with the trustee, as if the trustee possessed and properly exercised the power he purports to exercise.

2. Participation in Breach of Trust
A third party who *knowingly* participates in a breach of trust by the trustee is liable for the resulting loss to the trust estate. One who *innocently participates* in a breach of trust is generally not liable to the beneficiaries, except to the extent he is obligated to return property transferred to him when not protected as a bona fide purchaser.

3. Beneficiary Usually Cannot Sue Third Party Directly
The beneficiaries of a trust cannot, with certain exceptions noted below, bring an action in law or in equity against a third party who damages the trust property or is liable to the trustee on a contract. The trustee is the proper person to sue the third party.

a. Exceptions

1) Trustee Participates in Breach
If the third party participates with the trustee in a breach, the beneficiaries can sue the third party directly. *Rationale:* The third party has directly wronged the beneficiaries by inducing the trustee to commit a breach of trust.

2) Trustee Fails to Sue
If the trustee fails to sue a third party liable in tort or contract, the beneficiaries can bring a suit in equity to compel him to perform his duty. To prevent multiplicity of actions, the third party can be joined in this suit.

3) Trustee Abandons Office
If the trustee has abandoned his office or has left the jurisdiction and a successor trustee has not been appointed, the beneficiaries can sue the third party in equity without joining the trustee.

H. LIABILITY OF TRUSTEE'S ATTORNEY

1. Attorney's Duty of Care Runs to Trustee Only; Beneficiaries Cannot Sue for Negligence
An attorney's duty of care runs only to the trustee who retained her, and no attorney-client relationship exists between the attorney and the trust's beneficiaries. While it is generally true that an attorney owes a duty to nonclients whom the attorney knows will rely on her services, such a duty cannot be imposed where the attorney is also under an independent

and potentially conflicting duty to a client. If a trustee's attorney owed a duty not only to the trustee but also to the trust beneficiaries, conflicting loyalties could impermissibly interfere with the attorney's task of advising the trustee. Consequently, the beneficiaries cannot sue the trustee's attorney for negligence. [Spinner v. Nutt, 417 Mass. 549 (1994)]

a. **Beneficiaries' Remedy Is to Bring Action Against Trustee**
   If the beneficiaries have been damaged by the trustee's improper conduct based on bad legal advice, their remedy is to bring an action against the trustee. The trustee, in turn, may move to join the attorney in the action, or may bring a direct action against the attorney, if appropriate. [Spinner v. Nutt, *supra*]

BAR REVIEW

Wills

celebrating over
35 *YEARS*
of preparing law students for the bar exam

WILLS—MASSACHUSETTS

TABLE OF CONTENTS

I. INTESTATE DESCENT AND DISTRIBUTION

A. TERMINOLOGY

1. Probate
Probate refers to the proceeding in which an instrument is judicially established as the duly executed last will of the decedent, or if there is no will, the proceeding in which the decedent's heirs are judicially determined. In the probate proceeding, the probate court issues "letters" to the *personal representative* (called an *executor* if named in the will or an *administrator* if appointed by the court), who administers the estate. The *letters testamentary* (if a will) or *letters of administration* (if no will) show the personal representative's authority to act on behalf of the estate.

2. Heirs
Persons who inherit property by intestate succession are called *heirs*. Persons who take property under a will are called *beneficiaries* (or legatees or devisees).

3. Issue
The Massachusetts intestacy and wills statutes use the term "issue" rather than "descendants." These terms are synonymous. A person's issue are her lineal descendants in whatever degree (children, grandchildren, great-grandchildren, etc.), and include adopted offspring.

B. WHEN INTESTATE SUCCESSION RULES APPLY
The rules governing intestate succession [Mass. Gen. L. ch. 190, §§1-8] apply when: (i) the decedent left *no will*; (ii) the decedent's *will is denied probate* (*e.g.,* will was not properly executed, or will was successfully contested by the decedent's heirs); (iii) the decedent's *will does not make a complete disposition* of the estate (resulting in a "partial intestacy"); or (iv) the testator *married after execution of the will*, in which case the will is revoked by operation of law. (*See* IV.B.1., *infra*.) The intestacy rules also apply in cases invoking the *omitted child statute*. (*See* IV.B.3., *infra*.)

C. INTESTATE SHARE OF SURVIVING SPOUSE
If a decedent was survived by a spouse, the amount of the spouse's intestate share depends on which other relatives also survived the decedent. [Mass. Gen. L. ch. 190, §1]

1. Survived by Issue—One-Half of the Estate
If the decedent was survived by issue, whether of this marriage or an earlier marriage, the surviving spouse takes one-half of the estate. The other one-half passes to the decedent's issue.

2. Survived by Kindred But Not Issue—First $200,000 Plus One-Half of Balance
If the decedent was survived by a spouse and kindred (*i.e.*, parents, brothers, sisters, or *any relative by blood or adoption*), the spouse inherits the first $200,000 off the top, plus one-half of the balance of the estate. The other one-half passes to the decedent's kindred under the rules described below. The purpose of this rule is to insure that, in small estates, the entire estate passes to the spouse if the decedent is not survived by issue.

a. The $200,000 Is Satisfied from Personal Property
The $200,000 is satisfied first out of personal property in the estate, to the extent available. If the personal property is insufficient, real property may be sold or mortgaged to raise any deficiency.

3. Not Survived by Issue or Kindred—Entire Estate
If the decedent was survived by a spouse but not by issue or kindred, the spouse inherits the decedent's entire estate. This rule is rarely invoked because, as is noted below, there is no limit on the degree of relationship needed to take as an heir. If the decedent left any relatives by blood or adoption, no matter how remotely related, the "first $200,000 plus one-half of the balance" rule applies.

4. Gift to "Heirs" Presumptively Includes Spouse
Because the statutes make the spouse an heir, a gift by will or trust to a person's "heirs" presumptively includes the person's spouse. The spouse's share of the gift is determined by reference to the intestacy statutes as though the person had died intestate. [Gustafson v. Svenson, 373 Mass. 273 (1977)] However, a gift to a person's "next of kin" presumptively includes only relatives by blood or adoption, and not the person's spouse. [First Safe Deposit National Bank v. Westgate, 346 Mass. 444 (1963)]

Example: T's will creates a trust: "Income to my son, John, until he attains age 40, at which time the trust principal shall be distributed to him. If John dies before attaining age 40, the trust principal shall be distributed to his heirs at law." John dies at age 35, survived by his wife and one child. The trust principal is distributable one-half to the wife and one-half to the child, as these are the shares the wife and child would have taken had John died intestate. [Waltham Bank & Trust Co. v. Miller, 325 Mass. 330 (1950)]

D. INTESTATE SHARES OF OTHER HEIRS

1. Issue Take Per Capita with Representation

The share of the estate that does not pass to the surviving spouse (or the entire estate if the decedent left no surviving spouse) passes to the decedent's issue, who take per capita with representation ("first per capita, then by representation"). Under this pattern of distribution, the property is divided into equal shares at the first generational level at which there are living takers. Each living person at that level takes a share, and the share of each deceased person at that level passes to his issue by right of representation. [Mass. Gen. L. ch. 190, §§3, 8]

Examples: 1) D, a widow, dies intestate survived by: (i) child A, who has a son, W; (ii) X and Y, grandchildren by D's deceased child B; and (iii) Z, the daughter of D's deceased child C.

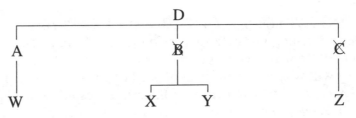

Since there is a living heir at the first generational level, D's estate is divided into three equal shares at that level. A takes one-third. The one-third that B would have inherited had he survived D passes by right of representation to his children, X and Y (one-sixth each). Similarly, Z takes a one-third share. W takes nothing, even though he is D's issue, because his mother A is alive to inherit.

2) Same family tree as above, except that A also predeceased D. Since there are no living takers at the first generational level, the shares are determined at the second generational level. Each grandchild takes per capita (here, a one-fourth share).

2. Not Survived by Issue—To Parents or Surviving Parent

If the intestate decedent is not survived by issue, the share of the estate that does not pass to the surviving spouse (or the entire estate if the decedent left no spouse) passes to the decedent's parents (one-half each) or surviving parent (who takes all). Collateral kin never inherit if the decedent was survived by a parent.

3. Not Survived by Issue or Parents—To Issue of Parents

If no issue or parents survive the decedent, the share of the estate that does not pass to the surviving spouse (or the entire estate if the decedent left no spouse) passes to the decedent's brothers or sisters (and the issue of deceased brothers and sisters, who take by representation).

4. Not Survived by Issue of Parents—To Next of Kin in Equal Degree

If the decedent is not survived by parents or by issue of parents, the share of the estate that does not pass to the surviving spouse (or the entire estate if the decedent left no spouse) passes in equal shares to the decedent's next of kin (*i.e.*, relatives in the nearest degree of kinship to the decedent). If there are two or more kindred in equal degree claiming through different ancestors, those claiming through the nearest ancestor take to the exclusion of those claiming through a more remote ancestor. [Mass. Gen. L. ch. 90, §3]

5. Not Survived by Spouse or Kindred—Escheat to Commonwealth

The Uniform Probate Code and several states have enacted so-called laughing heir statutes that eliminate inheritance by persons so remotely related to the decedent that they suffer no sense of loss—only gain—at the news of her death. Massachusetts has not enacted such a statute. Only if the decedent was not survived by any living relative does the estate *escheat* to the Commonwealth.

E. SPECIAL CASES

1. Adopted Child

a. As to Adopting Family—Treated Same as Natural Child
The effect of an adoption is to transplant completely an adopted child into the adopting family. The adopted child and his issue inherit from and through the adopting parents (and the adopting parents and their kin inherit from and through the child) as though he were a natural child. [Mass. Gen. L. ch. 210, §7]

b. As to Natural Parents—Termination of Parental Rights Also Terminates Inheritance Rights
Termination of the parent-child relationship between a minor child and his parents is a predicate to the child's being adopted by a new family. The permanent termination of parental rights concerning a minor child ends kinship between the child and the parent whose rights are terminated. The child has no inheritance rights from his parent whose rights were terminated (or the parent's kin), and vice versa. [Mass. Gen. L. ch. 210, §7]

c. Adoption by Spouse of Natural Parent After Death of Other Natural Parent
Adoption by the spouse of a natural parent who remarried after the death of the other natural parent has no effect on the relationship between the child and the family of the deceased natural parent.
Example: Frank and Wanda have a child, Clyde. Frank dies; Wanda marries Harold, and Harold adopts Clyde. Clyde has inheritance rights from and through his mother, Wanda, his adoptive father, Harold, *and* the family of his deceased natural father, Frank. Thus, if Frank's mother were to die intestate, Clyde would inherit.

2. Stepchild and Foster Child—No Inheritance Rights
A stepchild or foster child who is not adopted has no inheritance rights from her stepparent or foster parent.

a. Exception—Adoption by Estoppel
Under the doctrine of adoption by estoppel (sometimes called "equitable adoption"), if the stepparent or foster parent obtained custody of a child based on *an agreement to adopt* the child, and the stepparent or foster parent does not perform his agreement, under estoppel principles the child is entitled to inherit as though she were adopted.
Examples: 1) M, a teenager, gives birth to a child (C) out of wedlock. M relinquishes possession of the child to F and his wife, G, based on an agreement that, if given custody, they will adopt C. F and G do not perform their agreement. Some years later, F dies intestate. *Held:* Just as F would be estopped to deny his promise to adopt, so also are F's heirs who claim through him. C is entitled to the intestate share she would have taken were she adopted. (Same result if the facts and circumstances warrant an inference of an agreement to adopt.)

2) Same facts as above, except that it is C who dies intestate and unmarried. Neither F nor G has inheritance rights in C's estate. Since equitable adoption is based on estoppel principles, this is a one-way street rule. C never did anything to give rise to an estoppel against her estate.

3. Nonmarital Child

a. As to Mother—Full Inheritance Rights
A nonmarital child (and his kin) has full inheritance rights from his mother and the mother's kin (and vice versa). [Mass. Gen. L. ch. 190, §5]

b. As to Natural Father
Until 1980, a nonmarital child could inherit from and through the natural father only if the parents married after the child's birth *and* the man either acknowledged the child as his own or was adjudged to be the father in a paternity suit. This statute was held unconstitutional as violative of the Equal Rights Amendment to the Massachusetts Constitution. [Lowell v. Kowalski, 380 Mass. 663 (1980)] The statute was amended that same year. Under the current statute, a nonmarital child inherits from the father and the father's kin if:

(i) The parents *married* after the child's birth *and* the father either *acknowledged* the child as his child or was *adjudged* the father in a paternity suit (the former exclusive test for inheritance);

(ii) The man *acknowledged* the child as his child [Higgins v. Ripley, 16 Mass. App. Ct. 928 (1983)—oral testimony of mother, pediatrician, and friend that man had acknowledged paternity];

(iii) The man was *adjudged* to be the father in a *paternity action*; or

(iv) After the man's *death*, he is *adjudged* to be the father in the probate proceeding *if* the action is filed within one year after the man's death.

[Mass. Gen. L. ch. 190, §7] *Note:* The Massachusetts Appellate Court has held that the one-year statute of limitations under (iv) is constitutional. [Hunter v. Porter, 57 Mass. App. 233 (2003)]

c. **Inheritance from Nonmarital Child**
If a nonmarital child dies intestate, his mother and her kindred have full inheritance rights in all cases. The child's father and his kindred can inherit only if the child could have inherited from the father under the rules set out above. [Mass. Gen. L. ch. 190, §6]

4. **Child Conceived Following Artificial Insemination**
A child conceived by the artificial insemination of a married woman with the consent of her husband is the husband's legitimate child for inheritance purposes. [Mass. Gen. L. ch. 46, §4B]

a. **Posthumously Conceived Child Can Inherit**
A child conceived after the sperm donor's death can inherit from the decedent's estate *if* it is affirmatively shown that (i) the decedent *consented to posthumous conception*, (ii) the decedent *consented to support any resulting child*, and (iii) *prompt and orderly administration* of the estate is not compromised. (*Note*: The one-year statute of limitations for paternity actions does not apply.) [Woodward v. Commissioner of Social Security, 435 Mass. 536 (2002)] In *Woodward*, twins born two years after the sperm donor-husband's death were entitled to Social Security benefits if they were entitled to inherit under Massachusetts law. No guidance was given as to how much of a time span would compromise the prompt and orderly administration of an estate, as the government's attorneys had advised the court that this was not relevant to the issue of entitlement to Social Security benefits.

5. **Posthumous Child Takes as Heir**
Generally, one claiming as an heir must be alive at the decedent's death. An exception is made for a child (or other heir) who was conceived and in gestation before the decedent's death and is born thereafter. The posthumous child (or other heir) takes as if born during the decedent's lifetime, both for purposes of intestate succession and for purposes of the decedent's will. [Mass. Gen. L. ch. 190, §8] However, a fetus, not born alive, is not an heir. [Harding v. DeAngelis, 39 Mass. App. Ct. 455 (1995)]

6. **No Distinction Between Collateral Kin of the Half Blood and Whole Blood**
At common law and in many states today, brothers and sisters of the half blood (*i.e.*, only one common parent) inherit half as much as siblings of the whole blood. Massachusetts has abolished this distinction. Kindred of the half blood are treated the same as kindred of the whole blood. [Mass. Gen. L. ch. 190, §4]
Example: D dies intestate survived by his brother B and his half sister S as his nearest kin. B and S each inherit one-half of D's estate.

7. **Will Provision Attempting to Disinherit Is Ineffective**
If a testator wants to disinherit someone, he must make a complete disposition of his estate by his will. If any portion of the estate passes by intestate succession, the intestacy statute and not the will governs the distribution. *Rationale:* Unless the decedent's will makes another disposition of his property, the property passes to the heirs, not by force of the will, but by force of the laws governing inheritance.
Example: Bill was survived by two sisters as his nearest kin. He left a will that provided:

"I give, devise, and bequeath my entire estate to my sister Stella. I do not want my sister Cora to receive or take any part or share of my estate." Stella predeceased Bill leaving no descendants, and the devise to her lapsed. (*See* VII.A., *infra*.) Cora inherits Bill's entire estate.

II. SUCCESSION PROBLEMS COMMON TO INTESTACY AND WILLS

A. SIMULTANEOUS DEATHS

1. Uniform Simultaneous Death Act—Property Passes as Though Owner Survived
Massachusetts has enacted the Uniform Simultaneous Death Act ("USDA"). When the title to property or its devolution depends on priority of death, and there is no sufficient evidence that the persons have died other than simultaneously, the property of each person is distributed as if he had survived. [Mass. Gen. L. ch. 190A, §1] The purpose of the USDA is to prevent the property of one person from passing to a second person (and then to the second person's beneficiaries), resulting in double administration of the same assets in quick succession, even though the second person did not survive long enough to enjoy ownership of the property.

2. USDA Applies to All Types of Transfers
The USDA applies to distributions of property by any means (intestacy, will, joint tenancy with right of survivorship, life insurance contract, etc.).

Examples: 1) Alice is the insured under a life insurance policy that names Alice's brother, Ben, "if he survives the insured," as the primary beneficiary and Carol as the contingent beneficiary. Alice has a will that devises Blackacre to Ben and her residuary estate to the Red Cross. Ben has no will. Alice and Ben die simultaneously in a plane crash. The life insurance proceeds are distributed as though Alice, the insured, survived Ben, the beneficiary. Thus, the proceeds are paid to Carol. For purposes of construing Alice's will, Alice, the testator, is deemed to have survived Ben, the beneficiary. Thus, the devise to Ben lapses, and Blackacre passes under the residuary clause as undisposed-of property. For purposes of distributing Ben's intestate estate, Ben, the property owner, is deemed to have survived Alice.

2) H and W own real estate as joint tenants with right of survivorship. H and W die simultaneously in an automobile accident. The property is distributed as though it were held as a tenancy in common. Thus, one-half passes through W's estate as though W survived H, and the other half passes through H's estate as though H survived W. (The point: There is no evidence to trigger the right of survivorship.)

3. USDA Applies Unless Instrument Provides Otherwise
No one is compelled to have the statute's presumption apply to her estate. The statute applies only if there is no provision in the will, trust agreement, deed, contract of insurance, or other governing instrument making a distribution different from the provisions of the USDA.

4. Evidence of Simultaneous Death
The USDA applies only if there is "no sufficient evidence" of survival. Suppose that Sue has a will that devises her entire estate "to my sister Mary if she survives me; otherwise to my brother Bill." Mary has a will that devises her estate to her husband Horace. Sue and Mary are in a terrible automobile accident. Sue is pronounced dead at the scene of the accident. Mary, alive but unconscious, is taken to a local hospital where she dies two hours later. Here, there is sufficient evidence that Mary survived Sue. Thus, Sue's entire estate passes under her will to Mary, and then passes under Mary's will to Horace.

a. Uniform Probate Code's 120-Hour Rule Not Adopted in Massachusetts
To cover the above situation, the Uniform Probate Code ("UPC") provides that a person must survive the decedent by 120 hours to take as a will beneficiary, intestate heir, life insurance beneficiary, or surviving joint tenant (absent a contrary provision). However, Massachusetts did not adopt the UPC's 120-hour rule.

b. Time-of-Survival Clause

In drafting wills, the technique most commonly used to cover the contingency of simultaneous deaths, or deaths in quick succession, is to make all bequests contingent on surviving the testator by, *e.g.,* 30 days.

B. DISCLAIMERS

1. Disclaimed Interest Passes as Though Disclaimant Predeceased Decedent

The Massachusetts disclaimer statute [Mass. Gen. L. ch. 191A, §1] recognizes that no one can be compelled to be a beneficiary of a gift or an intestate heir against his will. A beneficiary or heir may disclaim (*i.e.,* refuse to accept) an interest that otherwise would pass to the person from the decedent's estate, with the result that the disclaimed interest passes as though the disclaiming party predeceased the decedent. If a party disclaims a lifetime gift (*e.g.,* as beneficiary of an irrevocable inter vivos trust), the situation is treated as though the disclaimant had died at the time the transfer was made. Disclaimers are made primarily for tax reasons.

Example: Mary dies leaving a will that devises her substantial estate to her descendants by right of representation. Mary is survived by her daughter Donna and her son Stan, each of whom has several children in college. Donna, a partner in a Boston law firm, is independently wealthy and has a substantial income. The effect of the inheritance will be to aggravate her own income tax and estate planning problems. If Donna accepts the inheritance and then makes gifts to her children, there will be gift tax consequences. Thus, Donna disclaims all or a part of her inheritance. (Partial disclaimers are valid under both the Massachusetts statute and federal tax law.) The result is that the disclaimed interest passes directly from the decedent to Donna's children by representation, with no gift tax consequences.

In contrast, Stan is a law professor whose only source of outside income is from fees for giving bar review lectures. Under these circumstances, the thought of disclaiming his inheritance does not even cross his mind.

2. Interests that Can Be Disclaimed

Any interest in property can be disclaimed in whole or in part, including interests passing by intestate succession, lifetime or testamentary gifts, life insurance proceeds, death benefits under an employee retirement plan, and interests passing by the exercise or nonexercise of a power of appointment. A surviving joint tenant or tenant by the entirety can disclaim, but only to the extent that the decedent furnished the consideration for the property's acquisition. [Mass. Gen. L. ch. 191A, §2]

3. Procedure for Disclaimer

a. In Writing and Signed

To be valid, a disclaimer must be in writing, must describe the property or interest being disclaimed, and must be signed by the disclaimant. [Mass. Gen. L. ch. 191A, §3]

b. Real Property—Must Be Acknowledged and Recorded

If an interest in real property is disclaimed, the instrument of disclaimer must be acknowledged before a notary public in the manner provided for deeds of real property, and a copy of the disclaimer must be recorded in the office of the register of deeds in the county in which the land is located. [Mass. Gen. L. ch. 191A, §5]

c. Must Be Filed Within Nine Months

To be valid, the disclaimer must be filed with the court in which the decedent's estate is being administered within nine months after the decedent's death. If the disclaimer is of an interest in a lifetime transfer, the instrument must be delivered to the trustee, or other person having title to or possession of the property, within nine months after the transfer. [Mass. Gen. L. ch. 191A, §3]

d. Disclaimer Is Irrevocable

Once a disclaimer has been filed and recorded, it is binding on the disclaimant and cannot be revoked. [Mass. Gen. L. ch. 191A, §7]

4. Disclaimer Can Be Made on Behalf of Infant, Incompetent, or Decedent with Court Approval

A disclaimer may be made by the guardian or conservator of a person under a legal disability, and by the personal representative (*i.e.,* executor or administrator) of a deceased person, but only if the probate court finds that a disclaimer is in the best interests of the beneficiary or her estate. [Mass. Gen. L. ch. 191A, §2]

Example: H dies leaving a will that devises all of his property to his wife, W. W survives H, but dies four months later. Because of the unlimited marital deduction under the federal estate tax, the property is not taxed in H's estate, but the entire property is taxed in W's estate with no marital deduction available. To avoid this result, W's executor could disclaim, on behalf of W's estate, one-half of the bequest from H, thus eliminating the estate tax on that one-half in W's estate.

5. Disclaimer Not Valid Against Creditors

In many states, a disclaimer can be used to defeat the claims of the beneficiary's or heir's creditors. This is not so in Massachusetts. A disclaimer cannot be made by a beneficiary or heir who is insolvent, and the attempted disclaimer is subject to the fraudulent transfer rules of the Massachusetts statute [Mass. Gen. L. ch. 109A, §§1-13], as if the disclaimer were a conveyance. [Mass. Gen. L. ch. 191A, §8(2)]

6. When Right to Disclaim Is Barred

The right to disclaim is barred if the beneficiary or heir accepts the property or any of its benefits, enters into a contract for the property's sale, assigns or mortgages the interest, or signs a written waiver of the right to disclaim. [Mass. Gen. L. ch. 191A, §8]

a. Spendthrift Clause Does Not Prevent Disclaimer

The right to disclaim exists irrespective of any limitation on the interest in the nature of a spendthrift clause or other restriction in the instrument of transfer. [Mass. Gen. L. ch. 191A, §9] *Rationale:* The spendthrift restriction does not attach unless and until the beneficiary accepts the interest.

C. DECEDENT'S DEATH CAUSED BY HEIR OR BENEFICIARY

Many states have so-called slayer statutes, under which a person who wrongfully brings about the death of the decedent (*i.e.,* by murder or manslaughter) forfeits all interests in the decedent's estate (including an interest in life insurance proceeds). The estate is distributed as though the killer predeceased the victim. Massachusetts does not have such a statute, but reaches the same result through the imposition of a ***constructive trust,*** under the equitable principle that one should not be permitted to be unjustly enriched by reason of his wrongful conduct. (*See* Trusts outline.)

D. ADVANCEMENTS OF INTESTATE SHARE

An advancement is a lifetime gift made to an heir with the intent that the gift be applied against any share the heir inherits from the donor's estate.

1. Common Law—Lifetime Gift to Heir Presumptively Advancement

At common law, it was presumed that a parent would intend to treat all of his children equally. Consequently, when a parent made a substantial gift to one child (and not to others) and then died without a will, the gift was presumed to be an "advancement" (*i.e.,* an advance payment) of the child's intestate share upon the parent's death.

2. Massachusetts—Proof of Advancement Must Be in Writing

By statute in Massachusetts, proof of an advancement must be evidenced by a writing. No gift is to be considered an advancement unless the intention to have it so treated is declared in a writing by the donor or acknowledged in writing as an advancement by the donee heir. [Mass. Gen. L. ch. 196, §5]

3. Procedure If Advancement Found

Once it has been determined that an advancement was made, the amount advanced is added to the net value of the estate for purposes of computing the intestate shares. (This does not mean that the heir has to give back the property, only that its value is brought in for computational purposes.) Thus, if an heir who has received an advancement wants to share in the intestate distribution of the decedent's estate, his share is reduced by the amount of the advancement. However, if the advancement is greater than the heir's intestate share, he is not responsible for returning the excess.

Examples: 1) In a state that applies the common law doctrine of advancements, Hortense, a widow, gives land worth $50,000 to her son Seth, and tells Seth that the gift is to be considered as part of his share of Hortense's estate. Several years later, Hortense dies intestate survived by Seth and her daughter, Debbie, as her nearest kin. Hortense leaves an estate valued at $200,000. The land given to Seth is worth $80,000 at Hortense's death. The gift to Seth is treated as an advancement; *i.e.,* a partial satisfaction of Seth's share of his mother's estate. If Seth wishes to take a share of the estate as heir, he must allow the *date of gift value* to be considered part of the estate for intestate distribution purposes:

$200,000	actual intestate estate
+50,000	date of gift value of advancement
$250,000	

Seth's share of the estate is $125,000, of which he is deemed already to have received $50,000. Thus, Seth takes $75,000 of Hortense's estate, and Debbie takes $125,000.

2) Same facts, except that Massachusetts law applies. The gift is *not treated as an advancement* unless Hortense so indicated in a writing, or unless Seth made a written declaration that he understood that the gift was intended as an advancement. If there is no such writing, the gift to Seth is ignored, and the $200,000 estate is divided equally between Seth and Debbie.

4. **Effect on Advancee's Next of Kin**
   If the donee of an advancement fails to survive the decedent, the gift to the donee is binding on his issue, who take by representation. [Mass. Gen. L. ch. 196, §7]

5. **Advancement Doctrine Applies Only in Cases of Intestacy**
   The doctrine of advancements applies only in cases of intestacy. If a person without a will makes a gift intended as an advancement and later makes a will that bequeaths property to the same donee, the will is presumed to have been made with full knowledge of the earlier gift. Unless the will provides otherwise, the testamentary bequest is *not* reduced by the earlier gift. [Old Colony Trust Co. v. Underwood, 297 Mass. 320 (1937)]

E. **SATISFACTION OF LEGACIES**
   Related to the advancements doctrine is the doctrine of satisfaction of legacies. Suppose that a testator executes a will that makes various bequests, and thereafter the testator makes a gift to one of the will beneficiaries. Should the lifetime gift be deemed to have been in partial (or total) satisfaction of the bequest made by the will?

1. **Common Law—Lifetime Gift Presumptively in Satisfaction of Legacy**
   At common law, a lifetime gift to a beneficiary was presumptively in satisfaction of the legacy to the extent of the gift. The burden of proof was on the beneficiary to show that the gift was not intended to reduce the legacy.

2. **Massachusetts—No Satisfaction Unless Proven by Writing**
   By statute in Massachusetts, a lifetime gift to a will beneficiary is not treated as a partial or total satisfaction of a legacy unless: (i) the testator declares in a *contemporaneous* writing that the gift is intended to be in satisfaction of the legacy; (ii) the beneficiary *acknowledges in writing* that the gift is in satisfaction; or (iii) *the will expressly states* that legacies are to be reduced by such lifetime gifts. [Mass. Gen. L. ch. 197, §25A] Note that the beneficiary's written acknowledgment can be made at any time (before or after the gift), but the testator's written declaration must be contemporaneous with the gift. The statute provides the exclusive means of proof, and other evidence of the testator's intent (no matter how compelling) is not admissible to prove a satisfaction of the legacy by lifetime gift.

   Example: Terry executes a will that includes a bequest of "$25,000 to my grandson Gregory." Two years later, Terry gives $25,000 to Gregory, telling Gregory (in the presence of witnesses) that "I don't want you to wait until I die to enjoy your inheritance." When Terry dies, his will is admitted to probate. At common law, the gift would be held to have been in total satisfaction of Gregory's legacy, and Gregory would take nothing under the will. Under the Massachusetts statute, however, Gregory takes the $25,000 bequest because there was no writing by the testator or the donee, and the will did not contain a provision that legacies were to be reduced by lifetime gifts.

F. **CONFLICT OF LAWS**

1. **Real Property**
   The formal or intrinsic validity, effect, interpretation, revocation, or alteration of a *testamentary disposition of real property*, and the manner in which such property descends *when not disposed of by will*, are determined by the law of the jurisdiction in which the *land is situated*.

2. **Personal Property**
   The intrinsic validity, effect, revocation, or alteration of a *testamentary disposition of personal property*, and the manner in which such property devolves when *not disposed of by will*, are determined by the law of the jurisdiction in which the *decedent was domiciled* at death. [Mass. Gen. L. ch. 199, §1]

III. EXECUTION OF WILLS

A. GENERAL REQUIREMENTS

1. **Must Be Eighteen Years Old and of Sound Mind**
   In Massachusetts (as in nearly all states), a person who has attained the age of 18 has the right and power to make a will. [Mass. Gen. L. ch. 191, §1] If a 16-year-old executes a will and dies 20 years later, the will is not valid because the testator did not have capacity at the time the will was executed. In addition, the testator must be of sound mind. The requirements for establishing testamentary capacity are discussed in Chapter IX., Will Contests.

2. **Testamentary Instrument**
   A will is an instrument executed with certain formalities that is testamentary in character, revocable during the lifetime of the maker, and operative at the testator's death. Thus, an instrument that is operative during the maker's lifetime (as by presently transferring an interest in property) *cannot be a will.*

   a. **Codicil**
      A codicil is a *supplement* to a will that alters, amends, or modifies the will.

   b. **Instrument Need Not Dispose of Property to Be a Will**
      Although many laypersons believe that an instrument cannot be a will unless it disposes of property at death, this is not a legal requisite of a will. The term "will" includes an instrument that merely appoints a personal representative or revokes or revises an earlier will.

   c. **Will Has No Legal Effect Until Testator's Death**
      A will takes effect only upon the death of the testator. Until that time, the will may be revoked or amended, and the beneficiaries have only an *expectancy* (*i.e.,* they acquire no property rights under the will until the testator's death). Because of the ambulatory nature of a will, it operates upon circumstances and properties as they exist at the time of the testator's death ("a will speaks at the time of death"). In construing the will, however, the circumstances that existed at the time the will was executed are considered to discern what the testator meant by the words she used.

3. **Testamentary Intent**
   For a will to be valid, the testator must intend that the particular instrument operate as her will. In the case of a well-drafted will, this issue is rarely in doubt. Testamentary intent is established by the document itself (*e.g.,* "I, Hobie Gates, do hereby declare this instrument to be my Last Will"). The problem cases have involved instruments that contain no such recital and are ambiguous as to whether they were intended to be testamentary in effect.

   a. **Present Intent Required**
      The intention required is a present testamentary intent. A signed and witnessed statement of an intent to make a will in the future (*e.g.,* "I am going to make a will leaving all my property to you") is not a will, for it shows that the instrument itself was not intended to be a will.

   b. **Sham Wills**
      An instrument containing a recital that "this is my Last Will" raises a presumption of testamentary intent, but the presumption is rebuttable. Evidence is admissible to show, for example, that a person made a will naming his girlfriend as beneficiary to induce

her to sleep with him [Fleming v. Morrison, 187 Mass. 120 (1904)], or that the instrument was executed as part of a ceremonial initiation into a secret order [Vickery v. Vickery, 170 So. 745 (Fla. 1936)].

c. Ineffective Deed Cannot Be a Will
If a deed fails as an inter vivos conveyance (*e.g.,* for want of delivery), it cannot be probated as a will even though it was signed and attested by the required number of witnesses. If the grantor intended the deed to be operative during his lifetime, it cannot be a will.

4. Conditional Wills
A conditional will is one that expressly provides that it shall be operative only if some condition stated in the will is satisfied. However, language that reads like a condition may be interpreted by the court as merely expressing the *motive* or *inducement* for making the will.

a. Condition Must Be Expressed in Will
Parol evidence is not admissible to show that a will absolute on its face was intended to be conditional. Parol evidence may be admitted to show that the instrument was not meant to have any effect at all (*e.g.,* a sham will), but not to show conditions.

b. Condition vs. Motive
Suppose Mary signs a duly attested instrument that reads, "I am going on a safari to Africa. If anything happens to me on the trip, here is how I want my property disposed of . . . ." Mary returned safely from the trip and died five years later. Should her will be admitted to probate? This question has no clear answer, and in your answer you should *argue both ways*. Many courts have held that this language merely reflects that Mary was thinking generally about the possibility of death and the need for a will, which at that moment took the specific shape of not returning from Africa. [Evans v. Brown, 193 U.S. 411 (1904)] However, on very similar facts, a number of cases have held the will to be conditional on not returning from the particular trip, and have denied probate. [Pascal's Estate, 2 Misc. 2d 337 (N.Y. 1956)] The following factors have been cited by the courts in favor of holding that the will was unconditional:

1) Intestacy Avoided
The fact that the testator executed a will is an indication that she *did not intend to die intestate*.

2) Preservation of Will
The fact that the testator *preserved the document* after returning from the trip is another indication that the will's operation was not intended to be limited.

B. FORMAL REQUISITES
In Massachusetts, there are four formal requirements that must be satisfied in order to validly execute a will or codicil: (i) the will or codicil must be *signed by the testator* (or by another person in his presence and by his direction); (ii) the instrument must be *attested by two witnesses*; (iii) the testator must *sign the will* (or acknowledge his earlier signature) *in each witness's presence*; and (iv) *each witness must sign in the testator's presence*. [Mass. Gen. L. ch. 191, §1]

1. Testator's Signature
Any mark affixed by the testator, with the intent that it operate as the testator's mark or signature, satisfies the signature requirement. "Aunt Margaret," "J.R.," or the "X" of an illiterate person are all valid signatures. [*See, e.g.,* Plakas v. Plakas, 11 Mass. App. Ct. 922 (1981)]

a. Testator May Be Assisted in Signing Will
Suppose that the testator, because of physical infirmity, is too weak to sign his name. He asks his attorney to guide his hand; the attorney does so as the testator feebly scrawls his name on the will. This is a valid signature. Even though the testator needed assistance, the act of signing was his volitional act.

b. Proxy Signature
As is true in most states, the Massachusetts statute permits the testator's signature to be made by another person at the testator's direction and in the testator's presence. If the person also signs her own name, her signature can be counted as one of the two necessary witnesses' signatures. [Steele v. Marble, 221 Mass. 485 (1915)]

c. Order of Signing

Suppose that T asks two friends to witness his will. The two friends sign as witnesses and then T, realizing that he forgot to sign, adds his signature about 30 seconds after the witnesses signed. Two early Massachusetts cases held that in this situation the will should be denied probate. What the witnesses attest to is the testator's signature, which must be on the will when the witnesses sign. [Marshall v. Mason, 176 Mass. 216 (1900); Barnes v. Chase, 208 Mass. 490 (1911)] Modernly, most cases in other jurisdictions have allowed such wills into probate. These cases have held that the exact order of signing is not critical as long as the will signing ceremony is a single, *contemporaneous transaction*. Because recent Massachusetts cases have given a liberal interpretation to the will execution statute in other contexts, it is possible that the "contemporaneous transaction" doctrine might be applied if this question were to arise today.

2. Testator Must Either Sign or Acknowledge Earlier Signature in Presence of Each Witness

The testator must either sign the will or acknowledge his earlier signature in each witness's presence. The two witnesses do not have to be present at the same time (although this is commonly done). For example, the testator might sign the will in the presence of one witness, and then acknowledge his earlier signature in the presence of the other witness. "Acknowledging" his signature means that the testator must bring to the witness's attention that he has already signed the will, as by proffering the will with his signature showing. However, the Massachusetts cases have given a decidedly liberal interpretation to this requirement. Several cases have upheld probate where the will was unintentionally folded over so that the testator's signature was not showing; it was held to be sufficient if the testator exhibited the will to the witness, stating that it was his will, and requested the witness to sign. [Estate of Dunham, 334 Mass. 282 (1956); LeBlanc v. Coombs, 325 Mass. 431 (1950)]

3. Two Attesting Witnesses

While there is *no minimum age requirement* for serving as an attesting witness, the two witnesses must be "competent," and must have "sufficient understanding" of what it means to be an attesting witness. [Mass. Gen. L. ch. 191, §2] If a witness is competent at the time of her attestation, her subsequent incompetency does not affect the will's validity. [Mass. Gen. L. ch. 191, §3]

4. Each Witness Must Sign in Testator's Presence

While the witnesses do not have to sign in each other's presence, each witness must sign the will in the testator's presence.

5. What Constitutes Presence—Line of Sight Test

As noted above, the testator must sign the will (or acknowledge his earlier signature) in the presence of each witness, *and* each witness must sign the will in the testator's presence. As for what constitutes "presence," the Massachusetts courts have adopted the *line of sight* (scope of vision) test. While the testator does not have to actually see the witness, the witness must be in the testator's line of sight, *with no physical impediment to eye contact*.

Examples: 1) T, who was ill, was lying in a bed two feet from an entry hall. The witnesses took the will to a table at the end of the entry hall, nine feet away. T did not see the witnesses sign because he was lying on his back, staring at the ceiling. *Held:* Will validly executed. T could have seen the witnesses if he had sat up in bed and looked down the entry hall. Therefore, the witnesses were in T's line of sight. [Raymond v. Wagner, 178 Mass. 315 (1901)]

2) Same facts, except that the witnesses signed the will in an adjoining room, on a table around the corner from the entry hall. *Held:* Will denied probate. Although T knew where the witnesses were and what they were doing, they were not in T's line of sight because of the wall. [Mendell v. Dunbar, 169 Mass. 74 (1897)]

6. Massachusetts Requirements Differ from Those of Other States

Several states impose additional will execution requirements that are not required in Massachusetts. If a question presents any of these facts, a strong answer would point out that, "While this would be a problem under the Probate Codes of some states, Massachusetts does not require . . . ."

a. **No Requirement that Testator Sign at End of Will**
In some states, the testator must sign the will "at the foot or end thereof." In Massachusetts, the testator's signature can appear anywhere on the will, as long as the testator intended it as his signature. [Porter v. Ballou, 303 Mass. 234 (1939)]
Example: A handwritten, witnessed will that began with "Be it remembered that I, Sarah J. Armstrong, being of sound mind . . . ," followed by written bequests, was not signed at the end. The court concluded that the testator's writing her name at the beginning of the instrument was with the intent that it be her signature. [Meads v. Earle, 205 Mass. 553 (1910)]

b. **No Publication Requirement**
Some states require that a testator "publish" his will, so that the witnesses know they are attesting a will as distinguished from some other legal document. Massachusetts has no such requirement, and the witnesses have validly attested even if they thought they were witnessing a deed or a power of attorney. [Genovese v. Genovese, 338 Mass. 50 (1958)]

c. **Witnesses Need Not Sign in Each Other's Presence**
Unlike the law of some states, the attesting witnesses do not have to sign in each other's presence, as long as each witness signed in the testator's presence. [Ela v. Edwards, 82 Mass. 91 (1860)]

d. **Will Need Not Be Dated**
In Massachusetts, it is not necessary that a will bear the date of its execution. The time of execution can be shown by extrinsic evidence.

7. **Will Executed in Another Jurisdiction**
Under Massachusetts's version of the Uniform Execution of Foreign Wills Act, a will is admissible to probate in Massachusetts if it is in writing and was validly executed in accordance with: (i) Massachusetts law, (ii) the law of the state where it was executed (regardless of the testator's domicile), or (iii) the law of the state where the testator was domiciled. [Mass. Gen. L. ch. 191, §5] Under this statute, even a holographic will (*i.e.,* a handwritten and signed but unwitnessed will), which generally is not valid in Massachusetts, would be admissible to probate if it was written in a state (*e.g.*, California or Texas) that recognizes holographic wills.

C. INTERESTED WITNESSES
At common law, an attesting witness who was also a beneficiary under the will was not a competent witness, and was barred from testifying as to the will's execution. If one of the two necessary attesting witnesses was a beneficiary, the will was denied probate. This harsh rule has been abolished in every state.

1. **Will Valid But Bequest to Witness or Witness's Spouse Void**
The fact that the will makes a beneficial gift to an attesting witness *never* affects the validity of the will. The only consequence is that the witness-beneficiary may lose his legacy. [Mass. Gen. L. ch. 191, §2] This type of interested witness statute is called a "purging" statute. The statute eliminates the problem of interest by purging the witness's legacy, thereby making him a disinterested witness. The Massachusetts statute also operates to void a beneficial gift to the spouse of an attesting witness. The voided gift passes as though the beneficiary predeceased the testator.

2. **Exception—Supernumerary Rule**
The bequest is not voided if the will was also witnessed by two disinterested witnesses. In this situation, the beneficiary was a "supernumerary" witness who was not needed for the will's due execution. But if two out of three attesting witnesses are beneficiaries, neither is a supernumerary witness, and both lose their bequests.

3. **What Constitutes Beneficial Gift for Purposes of Statute**

a. **Gift Must Be Vested (Not Contingent) Pecuniary Interest**
Only the gift of a vested pecuniary interest triggers the interested witness statute.
Example: Thad's will devises Blackacre "to my sister Sarah if she survives me; otherwise, to my nephew Norman." Norman is one of the two attesting witnesses to the will. Sarah predeceases Thad. The interested witness statute does not apply, and Norman takes Blackacre under the will.
Rationale: The gift to Norman was contingent, and who would attempt

to overreach by serving as an attesting witness just to take a contingent interest? [Rockland Trust Co. v. Bixby, 247 Mass. 449 (1924)]

b. **Gift Must Be Direct (Not Indirect) Benefit**
A bequest to a church or lodge is not void merely because a member of the church or lodge witnessed the will. [Rockland Trust Co. v. Bixby, *supra*] But if the member-witness had guaranteed a note on behalf of the church or lodge, the interested witness statute would apply, because the gift would reduce the witness's liability as a guarantor. [Crowell v. Tuttle, 218 Mass. 445 (1914)]

c. **Executor's Compensation Not a Beneficial Gift**
Suppose that a will names Edward as executor (or testamentary trustee), and Edward is an attesting witness to the will. The interested witness statute does not apply even though Edward will be paid from the estate for serving as executor (or trustee). An executor's commission is compensation for services rendered, not a beneficial gift. [Lord v. Miller, 277 Mass. 276 (1931)]

D. SPECIAL TYPES OF WILLS

1. **Holographic Wills Not Valid**
About one-half of the states and the Uniform Probate Code recognize holographic wills, *i.e.*, wills that are handwritten and signed, but unwitnessed. Massachusetts does not recognize holographic wills. Except for oral wills (allowed under very limited circumstances), all wills must be in writing, signed by the testator, *and* witnessed by two attesting witnesses.

2. **Oral Wills—Recognized Only for Armed Forces and Mariners at Sea**
A soldier in actual military service or a mariner at sea may dispose of his personal property (but not any real property) by an oral ("nuncupative") will. [Mass. Gen. L. ch. 191, §6]

3. **Statutory Will**
To enable persons of modest circumstances to write a will without the assistance of an attorney, Massachusetts has enacted the Uniform Statutory Will Act. [Mass. Gen. L. ch. 191B, §1] The Act contains a Statutory Will Form that includes various printed provisions and has blanks for insertion of the names of beneficiaries, a personal representative, and a guardian of minor children. The form also contains various definitions and instructions on how the will should be executed.

E. PROOF OF WILLS IN PROBATE

1. **Will Has No Effect Unless Admitted to Probate**
No will is effective to pass any property, or to prove title and ownership unless it has been duly proved and allowed in the probate court. [Mass. Gen. L. ch. 191, §7]

2. **Burden of Proof on Will Proponent**
The person offering a will for probate has the burden of proving that it was duly executed, with testamentary intent, and free from fraud, undue influence, etc. However, once the proponent proves that the will was executed in compliance with the execution statute in one of the ways listed below, it is presumed to have been executed with testamentary intent and free from undue influence, etc.

3. **Method of Proving Wills**

a. **Testimony of One Attesting Witness If Will Not Contested**
If probate of the will is not contested, the will may be admitted to probate on the testimony of one of the attesting witnesses. The witness must testify that the requirements of due execution were complied with. [Mass. Gen. L. ch. 192, §2] If, however, probate of the will is objected to by an interested party, both attesting witnesses must testify as to due execution. [Finer v. Steuer, 225 Mass. 611 (1926)]

b. **Witness with Bad Memory—Not a Problem**
Probate of a will does not turn on the memory of the attesting witnesses. Failure by the witnesses to recall the detailed circumstances of the will's execution is not fatal if they identify the signatures as their own. [Pebler v. Pebler, 332 Mass. 297 (1955)] Upon proof of all of the signatures, a presumption arises that the will was properly executed—even if the living witness cannot recollect the circumstances, and even if the will does not contain an attestation clause reciting the elements of proper execution. [Goodwin v. Riordan, 337 Mass. 317 (1956)]

    c.   **Witness Has Died, Is Out of State, or Cannot Be Located—Proof of Signature**
If an attesting witness has died, resides outside the state, or cannot be located, it suffices to prove the witness's signature, either by someone who is familiar with the witness's writing or by a handwriting expert. [Sheinkopf v. Eskin, 4 Mass. App. Ct. 826 (1976)]

    d.   **Special Situations Where Testimony Not Required**

        1)   **Surviving Spouse and Next of Kin Agree in Writing**
A will is admissible to probate without the need of any testimony if probate is assented to in writing by the surviving spouse and the decedent's heirs at law and next of kin. [Mass. Gen. L. ch. 192, §2(iv)]

        2)   **Self-Proving Affidavit If Probate Not Contested**
Massachusetts is one of many states that have a self-proving affidavit procedure, which recognizes that most probates are harmonious, nonlitigious affairs in which no one contests the validity of the decedent's will. During the same ceremony at which the will is signed and attested, the testator and witnesses sign a sworn affidavit before a notary public. The affidavit recites all of the elements the witnesses would testify to in open court: (i) that the testator requested the witnesses to sign her will; (ii) that they signed the will in the testator's presence; and (iii) that the testator was over the age of 18 and of sound mind. The affidavit serves the same function as a deposition or interrogatory, and is a substitute for the witnesses' live testimony in open court. If, however, probate is objected to by an interested party, the self-proving affidavit cannot be used, and both attesting witnesses must be called to testify. [Mass. Gen. L. ch. 192, §2(ii)]

IV. REVOCATION OF WILLS

A. IN GENERAL

1.   **Must Have Capacity to Revoke Will**
A person who has testamentary capacity (is of sound mind and has the capacity to know the nature of the act he is doing, etc.) may revoke his will at any time prior to death.

2.   **Burden of Proof on Party Contending Will Was Revoked**
The burden of proof is on the party contending that a will has been revoked. [First National Bank of Adams v. Briggs, 329 Mass. 320 (1952)]

3.   **Contractual Will May Be Revoked**
Even a testator who has validly contracted not to revoke a will may do so, and the will must be denied probate. In this case, however, there may be an action for breach of contract against the decedent's estate, and the remedy may be the imposition of a constructive trust upon the beneficiaries under the will. (*See* VI., *infra.*)

4.   **Methods of Revocation**
Once validly executed, a will may be revoked only by the methods prescribed by statute. These methods include revocation by operation of law, by a subsequent testamentary instrument, and by physical act.

B. REVOCATION BY OPERATION OF LAW
In Massachusetts and many other states, a will may be partially or totally revoked by operation of law in the event of subsequent marriage, divorce, or birth or adoption of children. The theory of the rules providing such revocation is that it is assumed the testator would not want the will (or the will provision) to operate in view of the changed family situation.

1.   **Marriage After Will's Execution—Entire Will Revoked**
By statute in many states, if a person marries after executing a will and the spouse survives the testator, the spouse takes an intestate share of the testator's estate (subject to certain exceptions). After the "pretermitted" spouse's share is set aside, the will applies to any remaining assets. The Massachusetts statute operates very differently. In Massachusetts, marriage following execution of a will revokes the will in its entirety *unless* it appears from the will (*i.e.,* no extrinsic evidence) that the will was made in contemplation of the marriage. [Mass. Gen. L. ch. 191, §9] The result is an intestate distribution of the testator's estate.

a. **Exception—Will Exercises Power of Appointment**
    If the will exercised a power of appointment and the takers in default of appointment were persons other than the testator's heirs, then so much of the will as exercises the power of appointment is *not* revoked by the marriage.
    Example: Peter's mother created a trust: "income to Peter for life, remainder to such persons as Peter appoints by will; in default of appointment (*i.e.,* if Peter does not exercise the power), to Tufts University." Peter executed a will that: (i) exercised the power of appointment in favor of Peter's niece Nellie; and (ii) left his residuary estate to his nephew Nosh. Peter subsequently married Peggy and died without having changed his will. The marriage operated to revoke Peter's will, and Peter's estate passes by intestate succession. However, the marriage did *not* revoke Peter's will insofar as it exercised the power of appointment in favor of Nellie.

b. **Statute Does Not Apply to Statutory Will**
    The "marriage revokes" rule does not apply to a statutory will unless the will provides otherwise. [Mass. Gen. L. ch. 191, §9]

2. **Divorce or Annulment Revokes All Provisions and Fiduciary Appointments in Favor of Former Spouse**
    If the testator is divorced or his marriage is annulled after making a will, all gifts to the former spouse, and all appointments of the spouse as executor, guardian, or trustee under the will, are revoked. The will takes effect as though the former spouse had predeceased the testator. [Mass. Gen. L. ch. 191, §9]

    a. **Read Will as Though Former Spouse Predeceased Testator**
        When provisions in favor of a former spouse are revoked, the rest of the will remains valid and is read as though the ex-spouse predeceased the testator.
        Example: Mary's will provides: "I leave all my property to my husband, Horace, if he survives me; and if Horace does not survive me, I leave it all to my sister, Sue. I name my husband, Horace, as executor if he survives me; otherwise, I name my brother, Bill, executor." Thereafter, Mary divorces Horace; then Mary dies without having changed her will. Even though Horace survived Mary, the statute revokes the provisions in his favor. Sue takes Mary's estate under the will, and Bill is appointed as executor.

    b. **Does Not Apply to Decree of Separation**
        The statute does not apply to a decree of separation that did not terminate the status of husband and wife.

    c. **Does Not Apply If Parties Remarry**
        If the parties reconcile and remarry, all provisions in favor of the former spouse are revived. The statute operates to revoke provisions in favor of the former spouse only if the parties are divorced (or the marriage annulled) at death.

    d. **Statute Does Not Apply to Life Insurance Policies, Other Nonprobate Transfers**
        The "divorce revokes" rule applies only to wills. It does not apply to life insurance policies or other nonprobate transfers (with the exception of certain unfunded revocable trusts, discussed below).
        Example: Mary is the insured under a $100,000 life insurance policy that names "the insured's husband, Harold Brown" as beneficiary. Thereafter, Mary divorces Harold; then Mary dies without having changed the beneficiary on the policy. Harold takes the $100,000, the divorce notwithstanding. The statute that automatically revokes gifts upon divorce applies only to wills. The courts have rejected the argument that the reference to "the insured's *husband*, Harold Brown" made being her husband a condition to the gift. The reference to "husband" was merely descriptive, *i.e.,* to identify the Harold Brown to whom she was referring.

    e. **Statute *Does* Apply to *Unfunded* Revocable Trust Tied to Pour-Over Gift from Will**
        The "divorce revokes" rule applies to *unfunded* revocable trusts tied to pour-over gifts from the decedent's will. In *Clymer v. Mayo,* 393 Mass. 754 (1985), W signed a revocable trust instrument as settlor, but did not transfer any assets to the trust. She then executed a will that made a "pour-over" gift to the unfunded trust (*see* Trusts outline), and named the trustee of that trust as beneficiary of a life insurance policy on her life and death benefits under a retirement plan. The trust, which was not to be funded until

W's death, made provisions for her husband, H. Thereafter, W divorced H; then W died without changing the will, the trust, or the life insurance and retirement plan beneficiary designations. The court held that the "divorce revokes" rule applied to the trust, including the life insurance and retirement benefits payable thereto as well as the assets passing to the trust under the will. The court noted that since the trust was unfunded, it had no independent significance during W's lifetime. "Decedent's will and trust were integrally related components of a single testamentary scheme. For all practical purposes the trust, like the will, 'spoke' only at the decedent's death." It would be different, said the court, if the trust had been substantially funded with assets during W's lifetime. In that case, the "divorce revokes" rule would revoke *only* provisions in favor of H passing under the will's pour-over gift, but *not* the assets already in the trust or the life insurance proceeds and retirement benefits payable thereto.

f. Statute Applies Only to Divorce by Testator
The only divorce relevant under the statute is the testator's.
Example: T's will bequeaths property "to my brother's wife, Louise Ellstrom." Thereafter, T's brother divorces Louise, and Louise changes her name back to Smith, her maiden name. Louise takes the gift under T's will. The designation of "my brother's wife" was not a condition to the gift, but was merely descriptive of which Louise T had in mind.

g. Does Not Revoke Bequests to Kin of Divorced Spouse
The statute does not operate to revoke gifts to blood relatives of the divorced spouse. Nothing in the statute indicates that the legislature presumed to know that divorce would affect a testator's relations with the former spouse's family members. [Clymer v. Mayo, *supra*—bequests to nephews and nieces of former spouse upheld]

h. Does Not Apply to Statutory Will
The "divorce revokes" rule does not apply to a statutory will unless the will provides otherwise. [Mass. Gen. L. ch. 191, §9]

3. Omitted Child Takes Intestate Share
In most states, the "pretermitted child" statutes give protection only to children born to or adopted by the testator *after* the will's execution. In Massachusetts, the "omitted child" statute applies to *all children, including those alive when the will was executed.* If a testator does not provide for or mention any of his children (or the issue of any deceased children), whether born before or after the testator's death, the omitted child takes the same share of the estate she would have taken had the testator died intestate. [Mass. Gen. L. ch. 191, §20] There is no requirement that the testator bequeath anything to her children (not even the proverbial $1). However, this statute makes it strongly advisable for the testator to at least mention all of her children in her will.

Note: The omitted child statute does *not* revoke the testator's will, and does not result in an intestate distribution of the remaining assets. The intestacy rules are resorted to solely for the purpose of determining the amount of the omitted child's share. The will applies to the remaining assets.

a. Exception—Omission Was Intentional
The omitted child takes nothing if omission from the will was intentional and not occasioned by accident or mistake. Evidence that the omission was intentional can be established by the will itself or from any other appropriate evidence, including oral testimony. [Jones v. Jones, 297 Mass. 198 (1937)] The burden of proof is on the party contending that the omission was intentional. The "accident or mistake" that would permit a child to take means a mistake in the expression of the will or its transcription (*e.g.,* a will clause was accidentally left out), and *not* a mistaken understanding of the facts. [White v. White, 322 Mass. 30 (1948)] For example, a provision in a codicil revoking a gift to a child based on his mother's erroneous belief that the child was dead is *not* the kind of accident or mistake that entitles the child to a share. [Draper v. Draper, 267 Mass. 528 (1929)]

b. Exception—Child Provided for by Testator in His Lifetime
The omitted child takes nothing if the child was "provided for by the testator in his lifetime." Curiously, there are no cases interpreting this provision. Some cases are easy (*e.g.,* a substantial lifetime gift or trust for the child's benefit). But how would the court treat life insurance proceeds, or a joint bank account that is paid on the testator's death;

are these provisions by the testator *in his lifetime*? Cases in other states have answered this question in the affirmative (and the child takes nothing). Although the payment does not occur until after the testator's death, provision was made during the testator's lifetime when he named the child as policy beneficiary, or opened the joint and survivor bank account.

c. **Real Property—Claim Must Be Filed Within One Year**
No child (or issue of a deceased child) shall take any real property as an omitted child unless a claim is filed on behalf of the child within one year after the date on which the executor's bond was approved.

d. **Statute Does Not Apply to Nonprobate Assets**
The omitted child's share is determined by reference to the value of assets in the testator's probate estate. It does not apply to nonprobate assets, such as life insurance proceeds, revocable trusts, or assets over which the testator held a testamentary power of appointment. [White v. Massachusetts Institute of Technology, 171 Mass. 84 (1898)]

e. **Does Statute Apply to Nonmarital Children?**
In *Hanson v. Markham,* 371 Mass. 262 (1976), the court held that the omitted child statute did not apply to a nonmarital child unless the child had been legitimated by the parents' marriage. Since that decision, the intestacy statute then in force was held unconstitutional as applied to nonmarital children, and the rights of such children have been expanded. It is believed that the courts would now rule that a nonmarital child is entitled to protection as an omitted child.

f. **Assets from Which Share Satisfied—All Testamentary Gifts Abate Pro Rata**
The amount necessary to satisfy an omitted child's share is taken proportionately from all beneficiaries under the will (*i.e.,* all gifts are reduced pro rata). However, if the obvious intention of the testator as to some particular provision would be defeated by a pro rata reduction, the particular gift may be exempted from apportionment and a different apportionment adopted, in the discretion of the court. [Mass. Gen. L. ch. 191, §25]

C. REVOCATION BY WRITTEN INSTRUMENT

1. **Instrument of Revocation Must Be Executed with Testamentary Formalities**
A will may be revoked in whole or in part by a later will, codicil, or other writing declaring such revocation, as long as the instrument is executed with the same formalities as are required for the execution of a will. [Mass. Gen. L. ch. 191, §8]
Example: Revocation can be by a writing that says nothing more than "I revoke my will," provided such writing is signed and witnessed with proper formalities. However, the usual method of revoking a will is to execute a new will that states: "This is my last will and testament, and I hereby revoke all earlier wills and codicils."

2. **Revocation by Implication—Inconsistent Provisions**
Suppose that a testator executes a second testamentary instrument that does not contain any express language of revocation of an earlier will, and does not even refer to the earlier will. To the extent possible, the two instruments are read together; *i.e.,* the second instrument is treated as a codicil to the will. The second instrument revokes the first only to the extent of any inconsistent provisions. [Currier Gallery of Art v. Packard, 23 Mass. App. Ct. 988 (1987)]
Examples: 1) T executes a will that leaves all her property to John. Two years later, T executes a second will that leaves all her property to Dolly but does not contain an express clause revoking the earlier will. When T dies, Dolly takes T's entire estate, the first will having been revoked completely by the inconsistent provision of the second will.

2) By his first will, Ned bequeaths his stamp collection to Art and his residuary estate to Ruth. By a later instrument executed with proper formalities, Ned bequeaths his stamp collection to Jack, his Chevy convertible to Susan, and $5,000 to Tom. This second instrument contains no words of revocation. The second instrument is treated as a codicil, and revokes the first will only to the extent of inconsistent provisions. Thus, Jack (not Art) takes the stamp collection, Susan takes the Chevy, Tom takes $5,000, and Ruth takes Ned's residuary estate.

D. REVOCATION BY PHYSICAL ACT

1. Requires Physical Act and Intent to Revoke

A will or codicil can be revoked in whole or in part by burning, tearing, canceling, or obliterating it with the intent, and for the purpose, of revocation. [Mass. Gen. L. ch. 191, §8] Questions sometimes arise as to the sufficiency of a particular physical act of revocation.

Examples: 1) T writes "Void. Isadore Berman" at the bottom of each page of a three-page will, not intersecting or coming into contact with any portion of the will. *Held:* The will was not revoked: (i) it is not a revocation by subsequent instrument because Isadore's writing was not signed by attesting witnesses; and (ii) it is not a revocation by physical act because none of the words of the will were canceled, defaced, or obliterated. [Yont v. Eads, 317 Mass. 232 (1944)]

2) T's act of writing "Not Valid" across the *face* of each page of a three-page will constitutes a sufficient canceling and obliterating to revoke the will. Cancellation of a will is effected by the defacement or mutilation of the words of the will. [Putnam v. Neubrand, 329 Mass. 453 (1953)]

3) T cuts her signature off the will with scissors, or crosses out her signature. *Held:* Valid revocation by physical act, as this act of canceling or defacing shows a clear intent to revoke the will in its entirety. [Sanderson v. Norcross, 242 Mass. 43 (1922)]

a. Intent to Revoke Must Be Concurrent with Physical Act

The intention to revoke must be present at the time of the physical act for revocation to be effective.

Example: Tom's house is badly damaged by a fire. When advised that his will was among the items destroyed by the fire, Tom states: "That's all right; I wanted to revoke it anyhow." The will has not been revoked since the intent to revoke did not accompany the physical act of destruction.

b. Revocation by Proxy Permitted

As is true of most states, Massachusetts permits a will to be revoked by physical act by another person, provided that the revocation is: (i) at testator's direction, and (ii) in testator's presence. [Mass. Gen. L. ch. 191, §8]

2. Partial Revocation by Physical Act

Massachusetts, like most states, permits partial revocations by a physical act of the testator, as by crossing out one clause in the will. The rest of the will remains in full force.

Example: Clause 9 of T's will devises land near Concord to Fred. Thereafter, T crosses out Clause 9 with a felt-tip pen with the intent to revoke the gift. The partial revocation is valid. [Walter v. Walter, 301 Mass. 289 (1938)]

3. Presumptions as to Revocation

a. Will Not Found After Testator's Death

When a will that was last seen in the testator's possession or control cannot be found after the testator's death, a presumption arises that the will was revoked; *i.e.,* the reason the will cannot be located is that the testator destroyed it with the intent to revoke. [Gannon v. McDonald, 361 Mass. 851 (1972)] Declarations of the testator are admissible to rebut the presumption of revocation.

However, no presumption of revocation arises if the will was last seen in the possession of a person adversely affected by its contents (*e.g.,* an heir, or a legatee under an earlier will).

b. Will Found After Death in Mutilated Condition

When a will last seen in the testator's possession or control is found after his death in a mutilated condition (*e.g.,* torn in two, or crossed out with a felt-tip pen), a presumption arises that the testator did the mutilating with the intent to revoke the will.

4. Effect of Revocation on Other Testamentary Instruments

a. Wills Executed in Duplicate

When a will has been executed in duplicate (both original and duplicate are signed and witnessed), an act of revocation performed by the testator upon *either* copy revokes the will. Both signed copies of the will are of the same legal stature. Revocation occurs even though the other signed copy is found in good condition. [Irwin v. Miniter, 338 Mass. 8 (1954)]

However, the destruction of an *unexecuted* copy (*e.g.*, a *photocopy*) of the will, accompanied by an intent to revoke, does *not revoke* the will. The act of obliteration, destruction, etc., must be done on the will itself.

b.   Revocation of Will Revokes All Codicils
The revocation of a will revokes all codicils to that will.

c.   Effect of Revoking Codicil
The revocation of a codicil to a will does not revoke the will, and in the absence of evidence to the contrary, it is presumed that in revoking the codicil the testator intended to reinstate the will provisions changed by the codicil as though the codicil had never been executed.
Example: T executed a will, and later executed three separate codicils to the will. Thereafter, T revoked the third and then the second codicil; then T died. *Held:* Read the will and first codicil as though the second and third codicils had never been made.

d.   Revival of Revoked Wills—Testator's Intent Controls
The issue of revival arises on the following facts: Toby executes a will. Toby later executes a new will, "hereby revoking all wills heretofore made by me." However, Toby does not destroy the first will. Toby then revokes the second will by physical act. Did Toby's destruction of the second will (and its language of revocation) automatically restore or "revive" the first will? In Massachusetts, the first will is not revived *unless* it is evident from the circumstances of the revocation of the second will or from the testator's contemporary or subsequent declarations that he intended the first will to take effect as executed. [Aldrich v. Aldrich, 215 Mass. 164 (1913)] Under the Massachusetts rule, *the exception is the most important part of the rule*. Any evidence that the testator intended to revive the first will is sufficient to reinstate that will.

5.   Proof of Lost, Destroyed, or Suppressed Will
Suppose that a will is accidentally destroyed in a fire, or that the will cannot be located after the testator's death, but the presumption of revocation that is raised by such facts is overcome by proof that the testator did not intend to revoke the will. As in all states, Massachusetts permits probate of a lost or destroyed will. The policy underlying this rule is obvious. Otherwise, probate could be frustrated by the accidental—or intentional—destruction of the will. Due execution of the will must be proved, but the contents of the will can be established by secondary evidence (*e.g.*, a copy of the will, or testimony of someone who read the will). It is not necessary that the witness be able to reconstruct the exact language of the will. It is sufficient if the substance of the will's provisions are established. [Gannon v. McDonald, *supra*] However, proof of an alleged lost will by oral testimony must be "strong, positive, and free from doubt." [Coghlin v. White, 273 Mass. 53 (1930)]

E.   ALTERATIONS ON FACE OF WILL
Any addition, alteration, or interlineation made after the will has been signed and attested is ineffective to change the will, unless the will is reexecuted with proper formalities. Only the words present at the time the will was executed constitute the decedent's will. Any writings added thereafter are disregarded as unattested words. [Flynn v. Barrington, 342 Mass. 189 (1961)] Where a will offered for probate shows that it has been changed by alterations or interlineations, the burden of proof is on the proponent to show that the changes were made and known to the testator before he signed the will. [O'Connell v. Dow, 182 Mass. 541 (1903)]
Examples: 1) T executes a will that includes a bequest of "$2,000 to my niece Nellie." Thereafter, T crosses out the "$2,000" and writes in "$5,000" above the crossout, and initials and dates the margin. The attempt to increase the gift to Nellie is ineffective as an unattested writing. (Nellie takes the original $2,000, even though it was revoked by the crossout, under the doctrine of dependent relative revocation. *See* below.)

2) Same facts as above, except that the evidence shows that the change was made immediately before T and the attesting witnesses signed the will. The change is valid and Nellie takes the $5,000, because the gift to Nellie as modified was part of the will at the time it was signed and witnessed.

F. DEPENDENT RELATIVE REVOCATION

1. Mistake of Law as to Validity of Another Disposition

Dependent relative revocation ("DRR") has nothing to do with dependent relatives! DRR is an equity-type doctrine under which a ***court may disregard the revocation*** of a will if it determines that the act of revocation was premised on a ***mistake of law as to the validity of another disposition***, and would not have occurred but for the mistaken belief that the other disposition was valid. If the other disposition is ineffective for some reason, the revocation accompanying the attempted disposition also fails, and the will remains in force. If, however, the testator revokes her will with a general intent to make a new will at some future time, but no new will is made, DRR does ***not*** apply.

Examples: 1) Tillie validly executes a will that devises her entire estate to her sister Ann. Several years later, Tillie executes a second instrument that bequeaths $10,000 to her friend Fred and the remainder of her estate to Ann. However, the instrument is signed by only one attesting witness. Tillie, erroneously believing that the second instrument has been validly executed, tears up her first will. Tillie dies, survived by her sister Ann and her brother Bob as her nearest kin. The second instrument is not admitted to probate because it was not properly attested. On these facts, DRR would be applied so as to disregard the revocation of the first will, which would be admitted to probate upon compliance with the rules governing proof of lost wills. *Rationale:* Although Tillie revoked the first will by physical act, her act of revocation was based on her mistaken assumption that the second instrument was a valid will. Had Tillie known that the second will was invalid, she would not have revoked the earlier will. (Of course, if Tillie had known the true situation, she would have properly executed the second will! However, it's too late for that now.) Since sister Ann was the principal beneficiary under both instruments, disregarding the revocation of the first will comes closer to what Tillie tried (but failed) to do than would an intestate distribution under which brother Bob would take one-half of Tillie's estate. [*See* Putnam v. Neubrand, 329 Mass. 453 (1952)]

2) Tim's validly executed will includes a bequest of "$2,000 to my niece Nellie." Thereafter, Tim crosses out the "$2,000" and writes in "$5,000" above it, intending thereby to revoke the gift of $2,000 and replace it with a gift of $5,000. The attempt to increase the gift to Nellie is ineffective as an unattested writing. Although Tim's striking of "$2,000" was an effective partial revocation by physical act, DRR will be applied so as to disregard the revocation. Tim would not have revoked the $2,000 bequest but for the erroneous belief that the $5,000 bequest was valid. [Schneider v. Harrington, 320 Mass. 723 (1947)] (But if Tim had attempted to reduce the $2,000 bequest to $500, DRR would not be applied. In this situation, by striking the $2,000, Tim in effect said, "I do not want Nellie to take $2,000." It cannot be assumed that Tim would prefer Nellie to take $2,000 rather than zero.)

2. Doctrine Should Not Be Applied to Defeat Intent

For DRR to be applied, the disposition that results from disregarding the revocation must come closer to effectuating what the testator tried (but failed) to do than would occur if the revocation is given effect.

Example: Same facts as in Example 2), except that Tim strikes the entire "$2,000 to my niece Nellie," and writes above it "$5,000 to my sister Sue." Here, DRR should not be applied. Tim's revocation of the gift to Nellie (in effect, "I do not want Nellie to take anything") would be ***independent*** of his ineffective attempt to make a gift to Sue. To disregard the revocation would defeat Tim's intent. On these facts, the conventional rules would be applied, and the bequest to Nellie would be revoked.

V. COMPONENTS OF A WILL

A. INTEGRATION

A will often consists of several sheets of paper, yet the testator and the witnesses sign and attest on only one sheet: the last page of the will. The rarely litigated doctrine of "integration" concerns the following question: What sheets were present at the time the will was executed and thus comprise the decedent's last will? If an integration question is raised, the will proponent must show that the pages were present when the will was executed and were intended by the testator to be a part of the will. The requirements of intent and presence are presumed when there is a physical connection of the pages (staple, paper clip, etc.), or when there is an internal coherence by provisions running from one page to the next. [Ela v. Edwards, 82 Mass. 91 (1860)]

Example: A will was prepared in haste for T, who was hospitalized. By oversight, page 4 (which named an executor) of the five-page will was left out when the will was stapled. Thus, only pages 1 through 3 and 5 (which contained the dispositive provisions) were part of the will that was signed and witnessed. On these facts, pages 1 through 3 and 5 should be admitted to probate. Page 4 cannot be admitted to probate because it was not part of the duly executed will. However, the other four pages should be admitted if they embrace the substance of T's dispositive plan.

B. CODICIL

A codicil is a later testamentary instrument that amends, alters, or modifies a previously executed will. A codicil must be executed with the same testamentary formalities as a will.

1. Republication by Codicil

In some cases, it may be important to establish the date on which a will is deemed to have been executed. Under the doctrine of republication by codicil, a will is treated as having been executed on the date of the last validly executed codicil thereto.

Example: Fran executes a will that bequeaths $25,000 to her friend Grace Daniels, her residuary estate to her sister Sue, and names First Bank as executor. The will is witnessed by Grace Daniels and Paul Smart as attesting witnesses. (If the story stopped here, the bequest to Grace would be purged under the interested witness statute. *See* III.C., *supra.*) Later, Fran executes a codicil to her will that names Second Bank instead of First Bank as executor, makes no other changes, and notes "and I hereby reaffirm and republish my first will." The codicil is witnessed by Harold Ross and Paul Smart (and ***not*** by Grace Daniels) as attesting witnesses. Under the doctrine of republication by codicil, the will is deemed to have been republished and executed on the date of the codicil. On Fran's death, the bequest to Grace is ***not purged*** by the interested witness statute. *Rationale:* When Fran executed the codicil, she is presumed to have reaffirmed her wishes in the will, and this time Grace was not an attesting witness.

C. PROPERTY ACQUIRED AFTER EXECUTION OF WILL

A will is construed to pass all property the testator owns at death, including property acquired after execution of the will.

D. INCORPORATION BY REFERENCE

In Massachusetts and most states, an extrinsic document (not present at the time the will was executed and thus not part of the will under the doctrine of integration) may be incorporated into the will by reference so that it is considered a part of the will.

1. Requirements

To incorporate a document by reference, three requirements must be met:

(i) The document must be ***in existence*** at the time the will is executed;

(ii) It must be ***clearly identifiable*** from the will; and

(iii) The ***intent to incorporate*** the document must be shown.

[Bemis v. Fletcher, 251 Mass. 178 (1925)]

Example: In 2001, James, who is single, executes a will that bequeaths $10,000 to his niece, Nellie, $5,000 to his nephew, Norman, and his residuary estate to his mother, Mary. Two years later, James marries Julie. The marriage operates to revoke James's will. (*See* IV.B.1., *supra.*) If this were the end of the matter, on James's death his estate would pass by intestate succession: Julie would inherit $200,000 plus one-half the balance of the estate, and the remaining one-half would pass to James's kindred. (*See* I.C.2., *supra.*) However, in 2004, James executes what he calls "a codicil to the will that I executed on May 11, 2001." (James is unaware that his 2001 will was revoked by operation of law.) The "codicil," which is properly signed and witnessed, makes only one change: It increases the bequest to nephew Norman from $5,000 to $10,000, "and I hereby reaffirm and republish my 2001 will." The 2001 instrument is incorporated by reference by the 2004 instrument, because: (i) it was in existence when the 2004 instrument was executed; (ii) the 2004 instrument shows an intent to validate the terms of the 2001 instrument; and (iii) it is clearly identifiable. Nellie and Norman each take $10,000, and James's residuary estate passes to his mother.

Note: This case does **not** involve the doctrine of republication by codicil, discussed above. To have a codicil, there must be an underlying will, and the 2001 will was revoked by operation of law. As a result, the "codicil" was actually James's last will. Also, the doctrine of republication by codicil concerns when a **valid** will is deemed to have been executed. After James's marriage, the 2001 instrument was no longer a valid will—until it was incorporated by reference in the 2004 will.

2. Document Must Be in Existence at Time of Execution of Will

The requirement for incorporation most strictly adhered to by courts is that the document must be in existence at the time the will is executed. The courts are fearful that if this requirement is not adhered to, a testator could incorporate "a paper to be written which will be placed in my desk drawer," and could thereafter change his will by an unattested writing.

Examples: 1) If the will provides "$1,000 to each of the persons named in a letter that I have written and dated March 1, 2004, which will be found in my safe deposit box at the Acme Bank," and if the letter was in existence at the time the will was executed, the letter is incorporated by reference and the gifts are valid.

2) If the will provides "$1,000 to each of the persons named in a letter that will be found in my safe deposit box at the Acme Bank," but it can be shown that the letter was written **after the will's execution,** the letter is **not** incorporated by reference and the intended gifts will fail.

3. Exception for List Disposing of Items of Tangible Personal Property

Some clients seem more concerned about making gifts of personal items of sentimental value (crystal bowls, Winchester rifles, etc.) than about disposing of their intangible wealth or real estate holdings. Also, division of personal and household effects among the surviving family members can lead to arguments unless the testator has given clear directions as to how these items are to be divided. To provide a convenient mechanism for making gifts of such items, the Massachusetts courts have carved out an exception to the general rule that, to be incorporated by reference, the document must be in existence and cannot be changed after the will is executed. A will may refer to a written statement or list to dispose of items of **tangible personal property** not otherwise specifically disposed of by the will, **other than money or intangible property**. While the writing **must be in existence** when the will is executed and must be referred to in the will, the contents of the list **can be altered at any time** without having to reexecute the will. [Clark v. Greenhalge, 411 Mass. 410 (1991)]

4. Oral Instructions Not Incorporated by Reference

Because of the requirement that all wills must be in writing, oral instructions cannot be incorporated in a will by reference, and in such cases extrinsic evidence is not admissible to show the testator's intent. In the absence of fraud, the person designated to take under the will is entitled to the property absolutely and free of the restrictions contained in the testator's oral instructions. However, if the testator makes a specific provision only after the person designated as beneficiary has assured him that he will dispose of the property as the testator has instructed, then parol evidence is admissible to show fraud in the inducement, and a constructive trust arises in favor of the intended objects of the testator's bounty. (*See* Trusts outline.)

E. ACTS OF INDEPENDENT SIGNIFICANCE

Under the "acts of independent significance" doctrine (sometimes called the doctrine of "nontestamentary acts"), a will may dispose of property by reference to acts and events that have significance apart from their effect on the dispositions made by the will. Even though the identification of a beneficiary or the amount of a bequest will be determined by some future unattested act, the bequest is nonetheless valid if the act has some lifetime significance or motive other than providing for the testamentary gift.

1. **Identification of Beneficiaries**

    The future act may relate to the identification of the beneficiaries.

    Example: T's will provides "a legacy of $1,000 to each person who is in my employ at the time of my death." Thereafter, T hires three new employees and fires two long-time employees. Under this doctrine, it is assumed that T would not make employment decisions simply to make or unmake legacies in her will. The act of employment has independent significance apart from its effect on T's will. The gifts are valid.

2. **Identification of Property**

    This doctrine also permits identification of the property that is to be the subject matter of a bequest.

    Example: T's will bequeaths "my house and its contents to my sister Sarah." Thereafter, T buys new furniture and several valuable paintings, totally redecorating the house. The gift is valid, and includes all items of furniture and furnishings that are in T's house at her death. The gift ***does not include title documents***—assets whose title is evidenced by a writing. Thus, the gift does not include T's farm even though a deed to the farm was in the house, and the gift does not include stock certificates and bank account passbooks that are in the house.

F. NONPROBATE ASSETS CANNOT BE DISPOSED OF BY WILL

Only property owned by the decedent at death can be disposed of by will. A will cannot make a gift of "nonprobate assets"—interests that pass at death other than by will or intestacy. Also, nonprobate assets are not subject to the personal representative's possession for purposes of administering the decedent's estate. There are three principal categories of nonprobate assets.

1. **Property Passing by Contract—Life Insurance Proceeds and Employee Benefits**

    Life insurance proceeds (and death benefits under an employee retirement plan) are payable to the beneficiary designated by the insured (or employee) in his contract with the life insurance company (or retirement plan carrier).

    Example: Tom is the insured under a $50,000 Prudential life insurance policy that names Mary as primary beneficiary. Tom dies leaving a will that provides: "I direct that the $50,000 proceeds under my Prudential life insurance policy be paid to my brother Bill rather than to Mary." This will provision is ineffective. Payment of the insurance proceeds is governed by the contract between Tom and Prudential, and the beneficiary could be changed only by complying with the terms of the policy governing beneficiary designations. Mary takes the $50,000 proceeds.

2. **Property Passing by Right of Survivorship**

    Property held by the decedent and another person as joint tenants with right of survivorship, and property held by the decedent and his spouse as tenants by the entirety, pass directly to the survivor outside of the probate process.

    Example: John and his sister, Mary, own Greenacre as joint tenants with right of survivorship. John dies leaving a will that devises "all of my interest in Greenacre to my wife, Joan." The devise is ineffective. On John's death, title passed to Mary by right of survivorship, as John had no interest in Greenacre that he could devise by will.

3. **Property Held in Trust**

    When an inter vivos trust is established, legal title to the settlor's assets is transferred to the trustee and, if the trust continues in operation after the settlor's death, the trust's terms govern the disposition of the property.

    Example: Sam establishes a revocable self-declaration of trust that names himself as trustee. The trust provides that all income is to be paid to Sam for life. Upon Sam's death or incapacity, Cambridge Trust Co. is to become successor trustee. After Sam's death, all trust income is to be paid to Sam's wife, Wilma, for life. On the death of the survivor of Sam and Wilma, the trust principal is to be distributed to Sam's descendants. Sam dies; the trust continues in operation free of the probate process.

G. POWERS OF APPOINTMENT

A power of appointment is an authority created in or reserved by a person, enabling that person (called the ***donee*** of the power) to designate, within the limits prescribed by the creator of the power (called the *donor*), the persons who shall take the property and the manner in which they shall take it. When a person reserves a power in herself, she is both the donor and donee of the power. The *takers in default of appointment* are the persons designated to take the property if the donee fails to effectively exercise the power of appointment.

1. **General vs. Special Power**
   While the distinction between general and special powers derives from the common law, the only definition of importance today is the one set forth in section 2041 of the Internal Revenue Code, which applies the federal estate tax to property over which the decedent held a general power, but not to property over which she held a special power.

   a. **General Power of Appointment**
      A general power of appointment is a power exercisable in favor of the donee herself, her estate, her creditors, *or* the creditors of her estate.

   b. **Special Power of Appointment**
      A special power of appointment is one that is exercisable in favor of a limited class of persons, which class does *not* include the donee, her estate, her creditors, or the creditors of her estate.

2. **Inter Vivos vs. Testamentary Power**
   An inter vivos power of appointment (sometimes called a presently exercisable power) is one that is exercisable by the donee during his lifetime. A testamentary power is one that is exercisable only by the donee's will.
   Examples: 1) T's will devises property "to A for life, and on A's death to such persons as A shall appoint by will; in default of appointment, to B." T is the donor of the power of appointment. A is the donee of a *general testamentary power*. It is a general power because A is not limited as to the persons to whom he can appoint. A could appoint to his creditors or to the creditors of his estate. B is the taker in default of appointment.

   2) T's will devises property "to A for life, and on A's death to such one or more of A's descendants as A shall appoint by will; in default of appointment, to A's descendants then living, per stirpes." A is the donee of a *special testamentary power*. It is a special power because A is limited in appointing among his descendants. "A's descendants then living" are takers in default of appointment.

3. **General Language in Donee's Will Does Not Exercise Power of Appointment**
   A residuary clause or other general language in the donee's will does not operate to exercise any power of appointment held by the donee, *unless* reference is made to powers of appointment, or there is some other indication of an intent to exercise the power. [Mass. Gen. L. ch. 191, §1A(4)] Furthermore, a donor may call for the exercise of a power of appointment by a specific reference to the power.
   Examples: 1) Tammy's will gives her husband, Alan, a life estate in a trust and a general power to appoint trust principal "to such persons, including Alan's estate, as Alan appoints by a will that specifically refers to this power of appointment." Alan's will leaves "all my property, including all property over which I have a power of appointment, to my daughter Mary." Alan's will does not exercise the power because, although his will made reference to powers of appointment, it did not make specific reference to *this* power of appointment. [National Shawmut Bank v. Joy, 315 Mass. 457 (1944)]

   2) Same facts, except that Alan's will leaves "all my property, including all property over which I have any power of appointment *given to me by my wife, Tammy*, to my daughter Mary." This was held to be a sufficient specific reference to the power of appointment, and Mary takes the property. [Shine v. Monahan, 354 Mass. 680 (1968)]

4. **Exercise by Implication**
   A power of appointment may be exercised by implication when the donee purports to dispose of the property as though it were her own, meaning that the disposition can be given effect only if it is treated as an exercise of the power.
   Example: Betty holds a life estate and a general testamentary power over a group of assets that includes Greenacre. Betty dies, leaving a will that provides: "I

devise Greenacre to my husband, Robert." Betty's general power is exercised with respect to Greenacre, for this is the only way the disposition in Betty's will can be given effect.

5. **Creditors Can Reach Assets Subject to General Power Only If Donee Exercises Power**
When a person has an inter vivos or testamentary general power of appointment and exercises that power, the property so appointed is considered part of his assets and can be reached by his creditors. [State Street Trust Co. v. Kissel, 302 Mass. 328 (1939)] If, however, the donee does not exercise the general power of appointment, his creditors cannot reach the property.

VI. CONTRACTS RELATING TO WILLS; JOINT WILLS

A. DEFINITIONS

1. **Joint Will**
A joint will is the will of two or more persons executed on the same piece of paper.
Example: The will of Mary and her husband, John, reads: "This is our last will and testament, and we and each of us hereby give all of our property, real and personal, to the survivor of us, to be used, possessed, and enjoyed by said survivor during his or her lifetime; and on the death of the survivor of us, all of said property shall pass one-half to Mary's daughter Dawn and one-half to John's son Samuel."

   a. **Joint Will Admissible to Probate on Death of Each Testator**
   A joint will is admissible to probate on the death of each of the joint testators just as if there were separate pieces of paper. If one of the joint testators revokes her joint will, the instrument would still serve and be admissible to probate as the will of the other.

2. **Mutual Wills**
Mutual wills are two separate wills containing reciprocal ("mirror") provisions.
Example: Horace's will devises all of his property to his wife, Wilma, if she survives him, otherwise one-half to Horace's brother Bob and one-half to Wilma's sister Sue; the will names Wilma as executor. Wilma's will, executed at the same time, devises all of her property to Horace if he survives her, otherwise one-half to Wilma's sister Sue and one-half to Horace's brother Bob; the will names Horace as executor.

3. **Revocability**
Joint wills or mutual wills are revocable by a testator in the same manner as any other will. [Tweedie v. Sibley, 402 Mass. 1104 (1988)] This is true even though the wills are executed pursuant to a contract under which the parties agree that neither party will revoke the will and make a new will without notice to the other party. It is the contract to make a joint and mutual will, not the will itself, that is irrevocable by the survivor after the death of one of the parties to the contract. Since, however, revocation of the will is in breach of the contract, the beneficiaries under the new will hold on a constructive trust for the beneficiaries of the contractual will. (*See* Trusts outline.)

B. STATUTE OF FRAUDS APPLIES TO ALL CONTRACTS RELATING TO WILLS
Massachusetts law requires that all contracts to make a will or not to revoke a will must be evidenced by a writing, signed by the obligor, that satisfies the Statute of Frauds. The mere existence of a joint will, or of mutual wills containing reciprocal provisions, is not sufficient to establish the existence of a contractual obligation.
Example: An alleged oral promise made by the testator to his former wife, that he would bequeath two-thirds of his estate to the couple's children, was unenforceable. [Ryan v. Ryan, 419 Mass. 86 (1994)]

1. **Procedure If Will Contractual**
If a will is found to be contractual, the second will is probated, and a constructive trust is imposed for the beneficiaries of the first (contractual) will.
Example: H and W execute a joint will that expressly provides that the will is contractual, and that the survivor cannot revoke it after the first party's death. H dies; W probates the will and accepts its benefits. W then executes a new will that revokes the first will and devises her estate to other beneficiaries. After W's death, both wills are offered for probate.

The first will cannot be probated because W revoked it by a later will. The second will is admissible to probate because it was W's last will and it was validly executed. (Wills law controls until this point.) However, the beneficiaries of the first will can now bring an action to impress a constructive trust against the beneficiaries of the second will, since execution of that will was in breach of W's contract with H.

VII. CHANGES IN BENEFICIARIES AND PROPERTY AFTER THE WILL'S EXECUTION

A. LAPSED GIFTS AND THE MASSACHUSETTS ANTI-LAPSE STATUTE

1. Beneficiary Predeceases Testator—Gift Lapses

If a will beneficiary dies during the testator's lifetime, the gift lapses; *i.e.,* it fails. A will cannot make a gift to a dead person. If a devise other than a residuary devise fails for any reason, it becomes a part of the residue. [Franklin Square House v. Siskind, 322 Mass. 556 (1948)]

Example: T's will provides: "I bequeath all of my IBM stock to my brother-in-law, Jim Brown; and I bequeath my residuary estate to my sister, Sarah Goode." Jim Brown predeceases T. Although Jim Brown left two children who survived T, the Massachusetts anti-lapse statute (discussed below) does not apply because Jim Brown was not related to T by blood or adoption. [Horton v. Earle, 162 Mass. 448 (1894)] The gift to Jim Brown lapses, and the IBM stock falls into the residuary estate as undisposed-of property.

2. Massachusetts Anti-Lapse Statute

Nearly all states have anti-lapse statutes that operate to save the gift if the predeceasing beneficiary was in a specified degree of relationship to the testator *and* left issue (*i.e.,* lineal descendants), who survived the testator. The beneficiary's issue take by substitution under the anti-lapse statute. In several states (*e.g.,* Illinois), the statute applies only when the predeceasing beneficiary was a child or other descendant of the testator. In Massachusetts, however, the scope of the anti-lapse statute is very broad. It covers predeceasing beneficiaries who were *the children of the testator or were otherwise related to the testator by blood or adoption*. [Mass. Gen. L. ch. 191, §22]

Examples: 1) T's will provides: "I devise Blackacre to my brother, William Baxter; and I devise my residuary estate to my husband, John." William predeceases T, leaving a will that bequeaths "all my property" to his wife, Wanda; William is survived by Wanda and by a child, Billy, both of whom survive T. Since brother William was a blood relative of T, the Massachusetts anti-lapse statute applies. Billy takes Blackacre by substitution under the statute.

Note: Blackacre does *not* pass to Wanda under William's will. The anti-lapse statute does not save the gift for the predeceasing beneficiary's estate. Instead, it provides substitute takers—here, William's descendant Billy. William, having predeceased T, had no interest in T's estate that he could devise by will.

2) Same facts, except that William was not survived by any descendants. Although William (T's brother) was within the scope of the anti-lapse statute, the statute does not apply because William left no issue. The gift of Blackacre lapses; Blackacre falls into the residuary estate and passes to T's husband, John.

a. Anti-Lapse Statute Does Not Apply If Contrary Provision in Will

The anti-lapse statute applies unless a contrary intention appears in the will.

Example: T's will provides: "I bequeath $25,000 to my daughter Mary *if she survives me*." Mary dies during T's lifetime, leaving a child (Monica) who survives T. The anti-lapse statute does *not* operate in Monica's favor because the will shows a contrary intention. The gift to Mary was, by its terms, contingent on Mary's surviving T. Since Mary predeceased T, the condition to the gift was not satisfied. The gift fails according to its own terms.

b.   Anti-Lapse Statute Applies Only to Gifts by Will
The Massachusetts anti-lapse statute applies only to testamentary gifts. It does not apply to inter vivos trusts, life insurance beneficiary designations, or other nonprobate transfers.

c.   Anti-Lapse Statute Applies to Gifts by Exercise of Testamentary Power of Appointment
The Massachusetts courts have held that the anti-lapse statute applies to gifts made by the exercise of a testamentary power of appointment. [Pitman v. Pitman, 314 Mass. 465 (1943)]

Example: Roger died leaving a will that created a trust: "Income to my son Cedric for life, and on his death principal to such of Cedric's descendants as he appoints by his last will." Cedric then executed a will that exercised the power of appointment in favor of his daughter Donna. Donna died leaving two children (Dick and Derek). Cedric then dies, and his will is admitted to probate. Because Donna predeceased Cedric, the anti-lapse statute applies in favor of her issue. Dick and Derek take the trust property.

3.   Lapse in the Residuary Gift

a.   Surviving Residuary Beneficiaries Take
Suppose the beneficiary who predeceases the testator is one of the legatees named in the will's residuary clause. Under the common law (and in Massachusetts until 1978), any lapsed residuary gift "fell out of the will" and passed under the intestacy statutes to the testator's heirs. By statute, Massachusetts has replaced this "no residue of a residue" rule with a rule under which the residuary beneficiaries who survive the testator take the deceased beneficiary's share of the residuary estate. If the residue is devised to two or more persons and the share of one of them fails for any reason, absent a contrary will provision, his share passes to the other residuary beneficiaries in proportion to their interests in the residue. [Mass. Gen. L. ch. 191, §1A(5)] One of the consequences of this rule is that it tends to avoid partial intestacies. There will be a partial intestacy only if all of the residuary beneficiaries predecease the testator (and the anti-lapse statute does not apply).

Example: T's will devises "all the rest, residue, and remainder of my estate in equal shares to my friend Alan Adams, my Uncle Bill, and my sister Carrie." Alan Adams predeceases T, leaving a child (Alice) who survives T. Since Alan was not related to T, the anti-lapse statute does not apply. Under the "surviving residuary beneficiaries rule," the one-third share devised to Alan passes to the other residuary devisees. Bill and Carrie each take one-half of the residuary estate.

b.   Exception If Anti-Lapse Statute Applies
If the predeceasing residuary beneficiary was within the scope of the anti-lapse statute and left descendants, the anti-lapse statute takes precedence over the rule that the surviving residuary beneficiaries take.

Example: Suppose in the previous example that Uncle Bill predeceased T, leaving a child (Willette) who survives T. Since Bill was a blood relative of the testator, the anti-lapse statute applies, and Willette takes the one-third share of the residuary estate that was devised to Bill. The "surviving residuary beneficiaries rule" gives way to the anti-lapse statute when the predeceasing residuary beneficiary is within the scope of the statute *and* leaves issue who survive the testator.

4.   Class Gifts

a.   Class Gift Rule—Class Members Who Survive Testator Take the Gift
If a will makes a gift to a class of persons ("children," "brothers and sisters," etc.) and a class member dies during the testator's lifetime, those class members who survive the testator take the gift (absent a contrary will provision). [Ashley v. Lester, 281 Mass. 261 (1933)] The rationale for the class gift rule is that the testator did not want anyone other than members of the designated class to share in the gift. Another explanation for the rule is that the will is read and the takers are determined as of the testator's death, and only those who meet the class description at that time share in the gift. The best way to understand the class gift rule is to contrast it with the courts' treatment of gifts to individually named beneficiaries.

Examples: 1) Tammy's will devises Blackacre "in equal shares to my good friends, Al Anson, Bill Bryce, and Carol Carter," and bequeaths her residuary estate to her husband, Fred. Al Anson dies leaving two children; then Tammy dies. The anti-lapse statute does not apply because Al Anson was not related to Tammy. Since this was a gift of one-third shares to the three individually named beneficiaries, the class gift rule does not apply. [Best v. Berry, 189 Mass. 510 (1905)] The share devised to Al Anson lapses and falls into the residuary estate. Tammy's husband, Fred, owns one-third of Blackacre along with Bill Bryce and Carol Carter.

2) Tom's will bequeaths 600 shares of Xerox stock "to the children of my good friend, Homer Hanson," and devises his residuary estate to his sister. At the time the will is executed, Homer has three children: Dan, Fran, and Stan. Dan predeceases Tom, leaving two children who survive Tom. The anti-lapse statute does not apply because Dan was not related to Tom. Since the bequest of the Xerox stock was made to a class, Dan's share of the gift does not fall into the residuary estate. Instead, the class gift rule applies, and the class members who survived the testator share the gift. Thus, Fran and Stan each take 300 shares of Xerox stock.

b. Exception If Anti-Lapse Statute Applies
As with the "surviving residuary beneficiaries rule," the "class gift rule" gives way to the anti-lapse statute when the predeceasing class member was within the scope of that statute *and* left issue who survive the testator.

Example: Consider the same facts as in the previous example, except that the gift of Xerox stock was "to the children of my *son*, Homer Hanson." Again, Dan predeceases Tom, leaving two children who survive Tom. The Massachusetts anti-lapse statute applies to "a devise or legacy under a class gift whether the death occurred before or after the execution of the will." [Mass. Gen. L. ch. 191, §22] Since Dan was related to Tom by blood or adoption, his two children take by substitution under the anti-lapse statute. They take 100 shares each; Fran and Stan take 200 shares each.

c. Adopted Children Presumptively Included
A gift in a will or trust to someone's "children," "grandchildren," "descendants," "issue," or "heirs" presumptively includes an adopted child unless a contrary intent plainly appears in the terms of the instrument. [Mass. Gen. L. ch. 210, §8] In a gift to "children of the body" of a person, however, the clear reference to the biological process shows an intent to exclude adopted children. [Schroeder v. Danielson, 37 Mass. App. Ct. 450 (1994)]

d. Nonmarital Children Presumptively Included
A gift in a will or trust to a person's "children," "issue," "descendants," etc., presumptively includes nonmarital children *if the transfer was made on or after April 17, 1987*. [Powers v. Wilkinson, 399 Mass. 650 (1987)—overruling prior decisions, but changing law prospectively only]

e. Gift to Issue or Descendants
A gift in a will or trust to a person's "issue" or "descendants" implies that the descendants shall take per stirpes, *i.e.*, by right of representation. Thus, such a gift does not include the children of living descendants unless that is the clear intention of the testator. [Theopold v. Sears, 357 Mass. 460 (1970); Prince v. Prince, 354 Mass. 588 (1968)]

f. Gift to Heirs
A gift in a will or trust to a person's "heirs" is to the parties who would take if the person died intestate.

Example: T's will devised property to her brother B if he survives T, otherwise to B's "heirs." B predeceased T, survived by his wife but no descendants. B's wife (T's sister-in-law) took the property, as she was B's sole heir. [Gustafson v. Svenson, 373 Mass. 273 (1977)]

5. Beneficiary Dead When Will Executed—Gift Void But Same Rules Apply
If a will makes a gift to a beneficiary who was dead at the time the will was executed, the

gift is void. In Massachusetts, the rules that apply to lapsed gifts (anti-lapse statute; "surviving residuary beneficiaries rule") also apply to void gifts.

B. ADEMPTION BY EXTINCTION

Under the doctrine of ademption (sometimes called "ademption by extinction"), when specifically bequeathed property is not owned by the testator at death (*e.g.,* it was destroyed, sold, given away, or lost during the testator's lifetime), the bequest is adeemed (*i.e.,* it fails). Ademption applies because the property that was to have satisfied the bequest is not in the estate. Unlike several states and the Uniform Probate Code, Massachusetts has no statutes altering the common law doctrine. Ademption applies *regardless of the testator's probable intent*. [Walsh v. Gillespie, 338 Mass. 278 (1959)]

1. Applies to Specific Devises and Bequests

The doctrine of ademption applies *only* to specific devises and bequests—*i.e.,* a gift of property that is particularly designated and is to be satisfied only by the receipt of the particular property described.

Examples: 1) T's will bequeaths "my Rolex watch to my sister Sue." After the will is executed, T sells her Rolex watch and uses the sale proceeds to purchase a Seiko watch. Ademption operates since the testamentary disposition was of a Rolex watch, not a Seiko, and T did not own a Rolex watch at her death. Sue takes nothing.

2) T's will devises Blackacre to her brother Bill. Thereafter, T sells Blackacre for $30,000 and deposits the sale proceeds in a savings account. Ademption applies, and Bill takes nothing. Neither the proceeds of the sold item nor similar items purchased with the proceeds go to the beneficiary. [Baybank Harvard Trust Co. v. Grant, 23 Mass. App. Ct. 653 (1987)]

a. Does Not Apply to Gift of Sale Proceeds

Suppose, in the second example above, that T's will provides: "I direct that my executor sell Blackacre and distribute the sale proceeds to my brother Bill." Ademption does not apply, and Bill takes the sale proceeds—to the extent that they can be traced. *Rationale:* Since the gift was of the proceeds from the sale, it should not matter whether Blackacre was sold by T during her lifetime or by the executor after T's death. T's intent can still be effectuated by giving the sale proceeds to Bill. (But if the sale proceeds cannot be traced—if, *e.g.,* T has spent the proceeds—ademption applies.)

b. May Not Apply to Gift of Testator's Interest in Property

If the bequest is of the testator's interest in the property, rather than of the property itself, the gift may not be adeemed.

Example: T's will devises "all of my right, title, and interest in Blackacre to my brother Bill." T sells Blackacre on an installment contract, under which the vendee promises to pay T $10,000 per year for 10 years. The contract gives T a vendor's lien. Since the gift was not of Blackacre itself but of T's *interest* in Blackacre, Bill takes T's interest as it exists at T's death. Bill takes the remaining installment payments and T's security interest (the vendor's lien).

c. Applies If Testator Entered into Contract for Sale of Real Property

If a testator enters into a contract for the sale of specifically devised real property but dies before the contract is fully performed, ademption applies and the beneficiary takes nothing. To hold otherwise would be contrary to legislative intent, as the probate court has authority to compel specific performance of the sale if the testator dies after entering into a written agreement for the conveyance of real property. [Mass. Gen. L. ch. 204, §1; Kelley v. Neilson, 433 Mass. 706 (2001)]

d. Applies to Specific Gift Made by Revocable Trust that Is Part of Testamentary Plan

The doctrine of ademption by extinction applies to a specific gift contained in a revocable trust, at least where the trust is part of a comprehensive testamentary plan.

Example: In 1982, D created a revocable trust naming herself as trustee, and conveyed various assets (including an apartment building in Waltham) to the trust. On D's death, Cohen, as successor trustee, was to distribute the apartment building to Wasserman, and various other assets to other beneficiaries. D had sold the apartment building for $575,000 in 1988, but did not add the sale proceeds to the trust. The court held that since the trust was part of D's comprehensive estate plan and disposed of many of D's assets at her death, the trust should be construed according to the same rules as are traditionally applied to wills. The gift of the apartment building was adeemed, and Wasserman took nothing. [Wasserman v. Cohen, 414 Mass. 172 (1993)]

e. Partial Ademption

Partial ademption applies when, for example, the testator devises a large tract of land, then sells a portion of the tract. Ademption applies to the portion of the property not in the estate, but the remaining portion in the estate at death passes to the beneficiary.

2. Exception—Sale of Specifically Devised Property by Guardian or Conservator

The Uniform Probate Code and statutes in several states have engrafted a number of exceptions to the ademption doctrine. Massachusetts has not enacted any such statute, but the courts have carved out an exception to the ademption doctrine where the testator writes a will and is later adjudged an incapacitated person. If the testator's guardian or conservator sells specifically bequeathed property, the beneficiary is entitled to receive the sale proceeds—but only to the extent that the proceeds can be traced to the sale and have not been expended for the testator's care. [Walsh v. Gillespie, 338 Mass. 278 (1959)] *Rationale:* Otherwise, the guardian or conservator could effectively change the testator's will by deciding which assets to sell. Also, the testator did not have the capacity to change his will so as to adjust to the fact that the property had been sold.

3. Ademption Does Not Apply to General or Demonstrative Legacies

a. General Legacy

A general legacy is a bequest of a dollar amount that is payable out of the general assets of the estate without a claim on any particular source of payment.

Example: "I bequeath the sum of $5,000 to my nephew Ringo." At T's death, there is not that much cash in his estate. It does not matter. Ademption does not apply to general legacies. Other property in T's estate must be sold, if necessary, to satisfy Ringo's general legacy. Alternatively, the personal representative could make a "distribution in kind" (*i.e.,* a distribution of assets worth $5,000) in satisfaction of the legacy.

b. Demonstrative Legacy

A demonstrative legacy is a gift of money that identifies a particular asset as the primary source of payment. The distinction between demonstrative and specific legacies is that in the former the primary intention is that the legacy be paid in any event, even though the designated source fails, while in the latter the main intention is that the legacy be paid by the delivery of the identified thing, and that thing only.

Example: "I bequeath $10,000 to my niece Nancy, to be paid out of the proceeds of sale of my IBM stock." Before his death, T sells all of his IBM stock, and there is no such stock in his estate at his death. The $10,000 legacy is not adeemed; the $10,000 must be raised by the sale of other property in T's estate. Ademption does not apply to demonstrative legacies.

c. Bequests of Securities—Special Rules Apply

The courts (in Massachusetts as elsewhere) will construe a bequest of securities as a general legacy, if it is possible to do so, in order to avoid application of the ademption doctrine. The cases turn on whether the testator made a gift of "200 shares" or "*my* 200 shares."

Examples: 1) Tom's will bequeaths "my 200 shares of Acme common stock to my cousin Bill." Thereafter, Tom sells the Acme stock, and does not own any such stock at his death. Since the bequest is of "*my* 200 shares" of Acme stock, this is a specific bequest of the shares that Tom owned at the time the will was executed. Ademption applies, and Bill takes nothing.

2) Tom's will also bequeaths "500 shares of Baker common stock to my niece Nora." Thereafter, Tom sells the Baker stock, and does not own any such stock at his death. Here, the courts seize on the absence of a possessive pronoun (he didn't say "*my* 500 shares") and conclude that Tom did not intend to make a gift of the 500 shares of Baker stock that he owned. Rather, Tom's will made a *general legacy* of the *value* of 500

shares of Baker stock. Since ademption does not apply to general legacies, Nora is entitled to the date-of-death value of 500 shares of Baker stock. (The courts would reach this result even if Tom owned exactly 500 shares of Baker stock at the time the will was executed!) The only way this strained "reasoning" can be explained is that the courts want to avoid application of the ademption doctrine in cases such as this. [Bostwick v. Hurstel, 364 Mass. 282 (1973)]

4. Interest on General Legacies

If a general legacy is not paid within one year after the testator's death, beginning with the second year, the beneficiary is entitled to interest at 4% per annum. [Mass. Gen. L. ch. 197, §20]

5. Corporate Reorganizations, Mergers, Etc.

A specific devisee of stock is entitled to securities of another corporation owned by the testator as a result of a takeover, merger, consolidation, reorganization, or other similar action. [Mass. Gen. L. ch. 191, §1A(3)]

Example: T's will bequeaths 100 shares of Acme Company common stock to B. Thereafter, Acme is acquired by Gulf Industries. Under the terms of the acquisition, each Acme shareholder gets one share of Gulf Industries stock for every two shares of Acme stock. At T's death, B is entitled to 50 shares of Gulf Industries stock.

C. SPECIFIC BEQUEST OF STOCK INCLUDES STOCK SPLITS AND STOCK DIVIDENDS

A specific devisee of stock is entitled to any additional or other securities owned by the testator because of action initiated by the entity, other than securities acquired by the exercise of a purchase option. [Mass. Gen. L. ch. 191, §1A(3)]

Examples: 1) T's will bequeaths "my 200 shares of Redeye Company common stock" to B. One year later, Redeye Company declares a two-for-one stock split that gives T an additional 200 shares. Two years after that, Redeye Company declares a 10% stock dividend that gives T an additional 40 shares. Under the statute, B is entitled to all 440 shares of Redeye stock owned by T at his death.

2) T's will includes a bequest of "500 shares (not "*my* 500 shares") of Baker common stock to my niece Nora." Thereafter, Baker Company declares a two-for-one stock split. Despite the absence of a possessive pronoun, this was a specific bequest of Baker common stock, and Nora takes the additional 500 shares produced by the stock split. Wait a minute! When the issue was ademption (*see* B.3., *supra*), a bequest of "500 shares of Baker common stock" was classified as a general legacy! How can the same form of bequest be classified as specific when a stock split has occurred? Because, say the courts, different issues are involved. A bequest of stock can be classified as general for one purpose (ademption) and specific for another purpose (stock split). [Bostwick v. Hurstel, *supra*]

VIII. RESTRICTIONS ON THE POWER OF TESTATION— PROTECTION OF THE FAMILY

A. WAIVER OF WILL BY SURVIVING SPOUSE—ELECTIVE SHARE STATUTE

As is true of most states, Massachusetts has an elective share statute designed to protect surviving spouses against disinheritance. A spouse is given the right to waive any provision in her favor in the decedent's will and, instead, take a statutory share of the decedent's estate.

1. Amount of Elective Share

The amount of the surviving spouse's elective share depends on which other relatives also survived the decedent. [Mass. Gen. L. ch. 191, §15]

a. No Issue or Kindred Survive—First $25,000 Plus One-Half of Balance

If the decedent was not survived by issue or other kindred, the amount of the elective share is the first $25,000 of property owned by the decedent, plus one-half of any excess. Thus, if the decedent left a net estate of $425,000 and was not survived by issue or kindred, the spouse's elective share would be $225,000. This is the only case in which the spouse's share of the balance passes to the spouse outright, rather than in a life estate. This situation is rarely encountered, however, because it would apply only if the decedent were *not survived by any living relatives* by blood or adoption, and there is no limit on the degree of relationship needed to qualify as "kindred."

b. **Survived by Kindred But Not by Issue—First $25,000 Plus Life Estate in One-Half of Balance**
If the decedent was survived by kindred but not by issue, the amount of the elective share is the first $25,000 of property owned by the decedent, plus a *life estate in one-half* of any excess. The first $25,000 passes to the spouse outright. To the extent that the life estate in one-half of the balance involves personal property, it is held in trust for the spouse for life. To the extent that it involves real property, the spouse takes a "legal" life estate (*i.e.*, a life estate free of any trust). (*See* Real Property outline.)

c. **Survived by Issue—Up to $25,000 Plus Life Estate in One-Third of Balance**
If the decedent was survived by a spouse and issue (*i.e.*, lineal descendants) of this marriage or an earlier marriage, the amount of the elective share is *one-third of the first $75,000 of property* owned by the decedent (up to a maximum of $25,000), plus a *life estate in one-third* of any excess. The first (up to) $25,000 passes to the spouse outright. To the extent that the life estate in one-third of the balance involves personal property, it is held in trust for the spouse for life. To the extent that it involves real property, the spouse takes a "legal" life estate.
Example: Wilma dies leaving a net estate valued at $45,000, and a will that devises her estate in equal shares to her husband, Horace, and her good friend Sue Smith. Should Horace waive the will and file for an elective share? (i) If Wilma was not survived by issue or kindred, the amount of Horace's elective share would be the first $25,000 of property, plus one-half the balance, for a total of $35,000. Horace should take an elective share. (ii) If Wilma was survived by kindred but not by issue, the amount of Horace's elective share would be the first $25,000 of property outright, plus a life estate in one-half of the balance (*i.e.*, in property worth $10,000). Horace should take an elective share. (iii) If Wilma was survived by issue, the amount of Horace's elective share would be one-third of the $45,000 (or $15,000), plus a life estate in one-third of the balance of $30,000 (or $10,000). Thus, Horace's elective share is not as valuable as the gift under the will—one-half of $45,000 or $22,500 outright.

d. **First $25,000 Satisfied from Personal Property (to Extent Possible)**
In cases where the decedent was survived by issue or kindred, the share passing outright to the spouse (*i.e.*, the first $25,000) is satisfied first out of personal property in the decedent's estate. If the personal property is insufficient, the excess is raised by selling or mortgaging real property in the estate.

2. **Elective Share Applies to Revocable Dispositions**
Under the Uniform Probate Code and by statute in several states, the elective share fraction applies to certain nonprobate transfers as well as to property passing under the deceased spouse's will. In these states, the elective share applies to the "augmented estate," which includes dispositions in which the decedent retained economic controls and benefits (life insurance policies, certificates of deposit, joint and survivor bank accounts, etc.). The concern addressed by these statutes is that, otherwise, a person could disinherit his spouse through the use of such arrangements, and thereby thwart the policy underlying the elective share statute. However, in Massachusetts the elective share statute applies only to the decedent's probate estate, and does not apply to nonprobate transfers *unless* the decedent made a lifetime transfer in which he retained the power to revoke the disposition.

a. **Revocable Trusts**
In *Kerwin v. Donaghy,* 317 Mass. 559 (1945), the court ruled that assets placed in a revocable trust during marriage were not subject to the surviving spouse's elective share even though the purpose and effect of the trust was to undercut the elective share right, because the trust assets were not part of the decedent's probate estate. This continues to be the rule for revocable trusts created *before January 23, 1984*, as long as the trust was not amended or additional assets placed in the trust on or after that date. In *Sullivan v. Burkin,* 390 Mass. 864 (1984), the Supreme Court overruled *Kerwin v. Donaghy,* but did so *on a prospective basis only*. (The surviving spouse, who expended legal fees in actually "winning" the case, received no recovery; she just paved

the way for others!) As a result, the elective share applies to the decedent's probate estate *and* property in a trust created or amended by the decedent *on or after January 23, 1984*, in which the decedent retained either the power to revoke the disposition or a general power of appointment.

b. Totten Trust Bank Account

The elective share statute applies to a Totten trust bank account because the depositor has the power to withdraw the funds on deposit at any time. [Bongaards v. Millen, 440 Mass. 10 (2003)] (*See* Trusts outline.)

c. Revision of Elective Share Statute Left to Legislature

In *Bongaards v. Millen, supra,* the court held that the task of modernizing the elective share statute is left to the legislature. The court noted that "the current version of the statute is woefully inadequate to satisfy modern notions of a decedent spouse's obligation to support the surviving spouse" and it "does not authorize us to tinker with the statute's provisions in order to remedy those inadequacies. It is up to the Legislature to choose between the complex—and apparently controversial—options for modernizing this outdated scheme, not up to us to modernize it piecemeal according to our views of what remedies should be made available to a disinherited spouse."

3. Procedure for Making Election

a. Waiver and Election Must Be Made During Spouse's Lifetime

The right of election is personal to the surviving spouse and cannot be assigned by her. If the spouse dies before an election is made, the right to an elective share dies with her, and an election cannot be made on behalf of her estate by her personal representative. [Friedman v. Andrews, 293 Mass. 566 (1936)] This shows that the purpose of an elective share is to protect the surviving spouse from disinheritance, not her heirs.

b. Election on Behalf of Incapacitated Spouse Requires Court Approval

If the spouse is legally incapacitated, on petition by the spouse's guardian, the election to waive the decedent's will may be made by order of the court upon a showing that the election is needed for the spouse's welfare. [Old Colony Trust Co. v. Coffman, 342 Mass. 153 (1961)]

c. Election Must Be Made Within Six Months After Probate of Will

To take an elective share, the surviving spouse must file, within six months after the will is admitted to probate, a written, signed instrument that waives all provisions in the will in her favor and claims a statutory share.

1) Time May Be Extended If Will Challenged

If legal proceedings are instituted challenging the validity or effect of the will (*e.g.,* a will contest or a suit to construe the will's terms), the probate court may, on petition, extend the time for filing the claim and waiver until six months after the termination of such proceedings.

4. Effect of Spouse's Waiver and Election—Will Read as Though Spouse Predeceased Testator

If the surviving spouse waives the decedent's will and claims an elective share, the spouse relinquishes all testamentary gifts in his favor. The decedent's will is read as though the spouse had predeceased the testator. If the will gave the spouse a life estate in property with the remainder to others, the remainder is "accelerated" and the beneficiaries take a present interest. [Hesseltine v. Partridge, 236 Mass. 77 (1920)] In making up the spouse's elective share, the abatement rules apply (*see* X.F., *infra*): It is first taken from intestate property (if there was a partial intestacy), then from the residuary estate (with each residuary beneficiary contributing pro rata), and so on. [Crocker v. Crocker, 230 Mass. 478 (1918)]

Example: H's father had created a trust: "income to H for life, remainder to such persons, including H's estate, as he appoints by will [a general testamentary power of appointment]; in default of appointment, to H's heirs at law." H died leaving a will that exercised the power of appointment in favor of his wife, W. W filed a waiver of the will and claimed an elective share. *Held:* Since the will is read as though the electing spouse predeceased the decedent, by waiving the will, W relinquished the benefits of the exercise of the power of appointment. The trust property passed to H's heirs as takers in default of appointment. [Fiske v. Fiske, 173 Mass. 413 (1899)]

5. **Waiver of Right of Election**
   A spouse may waive the right to an elective share by written contract before or during marriage after full notice of the extent of the right to be waived, provided that the contract is supported by adequate consideration.

6. **When Spouse Estopped from Waiving Will**
   If the spouse accepts a benefit under the will (*e.g.,* accepts a distribution), she is estopped from waiving the will and claiming an elective share. However, the spouse is not precluded from taking an elective share merely because she accepted benefits under a life insurance policy or employee retirement plan. These interests pass to the spouse entirely independent of the will as nonprobate transfers, and do not affect the elective share entitlement in any way. [Miller v. Miller, 339 Mass. 262 (1959)]

7. **When Spouse Disqualified—Desertion or Living Apart for Justifiable Cause**
   The surviving spouse is not entitled to take an elective share if he deserted the decedent, or if the decedent had been living apart from the surviving spouse for justifiable cause (*e.g.,* spousal abuse). [Mass. Gen. L. ch. 209, §36] The same conduct disqualifies the spouse from taking dower, a spouse's allowance, or as an omitted spouse.

B. DOWER

In lieu of taking under the will, waiving the will and taking an elective share, or taking an intestate share if the decedent left no will, the surviving spouse can elect to take an estate called tenancy by dower. This estate is *a life estate in one-third of all real property* owned by the deceased spouse at death. [Mass. Gen. L. ch. 189, §1] Unlike common law dower, Massachusetts does not recognize inchoate dower (*i.e.,* an estate in land conveyed without the spouse's joinder during the decedent's lifetime). It is important to note that encumbrances on the land take precedence over tenancy by dower. Because a life estate in the decedent's real property is invariably less than the amount of the spouse's elective share or intestate share, the dower election is rarely made. Dower would be an attractive option only if the decedent's estate consisted of real property free of any encumbrances, but other obligations to creditors would exhaust the estate's assets. An election to take dower must be made within six months after approval of the executor's bond.

C. OTHER RIGHTS OF SURVIVING SPOUSE

1. **Surviving Spouse's Allowance**
   Upon petition, the surviving spouse is entitled to receive an allowance in an amount needed "for the reasonable sustenance of the family." [Mass. Gen. L. ch. 196, §2] The purpose of the spouse's allowance is to provide for "necessaries" for the decedent's family for a short time until they have had an opportunity to adjust to the new situation. [Estate of Abely, 489 F.2d 1327 (1st Cir. 1974)—$50,000 allowance held excessive] The amount of the allowance is in the court's discretion, in view of all the circumstances of the case, and taking into account the standard of living to which the spouse was accustomed, her living expenses and other sources of income, and the cost of maintaining the family home. [Townsend v. Wood, 342 Mass. 481 (1961)] The allowance is payable from personal property in the estate or, if the personalty is insufficient, from the sale or mortgage of real property. If the decedent was not survived by a spouse, his minor children are entitled to an allowance, not to exceed $100 per child (!).

   a. **Takes Precedence Over All Creditors' Claims**
      The spouse's allowance is not charged against any benefit or share passing to the spouse by will, intestate succession, or as an elective share. The allowance takes precedence over all creditors' claims, expenses of administration, expenses of last sickness, and even over funeral expenses. [Kingsbury v. Wilmarth, 84 Mass. 310 (1861)]

2. **Homestead**
   A homestead to the extent of $100,000 in the decedent's home is exempt from the laws of conveyance, descent, devise, attachment, levy on execution, and sale for payment of debts or legacies except in the following cases: (i) sale for taxes; (ii) for a debt contracted prior to acquisition of the homestead; (iii) for a debt contracted for the purchase of the home; and (iv) for execution for court-ordered spousal or child support. [Mass. Gen. L. ch. 188, §1]

   a. **Surviving Spouse's Right of Occupancy**
      On the homestead owner's death, in addition to granting an exemption from creditors' claims, the statute gives the surviving spouse and minor children the right to continue

to occupy the homestead until the youngest unmarried child is 18, and until the marriage or death of the spouse. [Mass. Gen. L. ch. 188, §4] The homestead right of occupancy does not depend upon the existence of outstanding debts and is over and above any other entitlements of the surviving spouse. [Silloway v. Brown, 12 Allen (Mass.) 30 (1866)] "The manifest objective of the statute is to provide a home for the householder's widow and children during their widowhood or minority, or for such of them as choose to occupy it, to be held and enjoyed by them together." [Abbott v. Abbott, 97 Mass. 136 (1867)] There appear to be no cases discussing the spouse's entitlement where the value of the property exceeds $100,000.

1) Scope

The homestead right of occupancy becomes relevant only if the owner devised his residence to someone other than his spouse or minor children. If the decedent devised the residence to his spouse, as owner she would have the exclusive right of occupancy without the need to assert her homestead occupancy right. Similarly, if the residence was held in joint tenancy or a tenancy by the entirety, the residence is exempt from creditors' claims to the extent of $100,000, but title passes to the spouse by right of survivorship.

3. Right to Occupy Residence Rent-Free for Six Months

The surviving spouse is entitled to remain in the house of the deceased spouse, and to use the furniture, furnishings, and provisions therein, for six months after the decedent's death without being chargeable for rent. [Mass. Gen. L. ch. 196, §1] Unlike the spouse's right to occupy the homestead, *supra,* there is no dollar limit on the value of the residence that is subject to the six-month right to occupy. This provision has no application if the residence was held as a tenancy by the entirety, as title would pass to the spouse by right of survivorship.

D. NO RESTRICTIONS ON TESTAMENTARY GIFTS TO CHARITY

Unlike some states, Massachusetts does not have a "mortmain" statute restricting the amount of testamentary gifts to charity. A testator can bequeath her entire estate to charity if she wants to.

IX. WILL CONTESTS

A. IN GENERAL

1. Grounds for Contesting a Will

In addition to the assertion that the will was not properly executed, grounds for denial of probate of a will include: lack of testamentary capacity, undue influence, fraud, and mistake.

2. Only Interested Party May File Will Contest

Only an interested party has standing to contest a will. An interested party is a person who has an economic interest that would be adversely affected by the will's admission to probate. Thus, "interested party" includes the testator's heirs, as well as legatees under an earlier will who would take if the contested will is set aside. [Sheldone v. Marino, 398 Mass. 817 (1986)] Creditors of a decedent do not have standing, as their right to collect from the decedent's estate is not affected by whether the decedent left a will or died intestate.

B. LACK OF TESTAMENTARY CAPACITY

1. Age—Must Be Eighteen

In Massachusetts, a person must be 18 years of age or older to make a will. The requirement is applied as of the date of the execution of the will, not as of the date of the decedent's death.

2. Testamentary Capacity

To have mental capacity to make a will, the testator must have sufficient capacity to:

(i) Understand the nature of the act he is doing (*i.e.,* that he is writing a will);

(ii) Know the nature, condition, and extent of his property;

(iii) Know the names of, and his relationship to, the natural objects of his bounty; and

(iv) Understand the scope and meaning of the provisions of his will.

[Santry v. France, 327 Mass. 174 (1951)]

a. **Facts that Do Not Destroy Mental Capacity**
The fact that the testator was very old, physically frail, or ill, or that he possessed a failing memory, was a habitual drinker, or addicted to drugs, does not mean that he lacked the requisite mental capacity and was not able to comprehend the nature of his act. [Palmer v. Palmer, 23 Mass. App. Ct. 245 (1986)] Likewise, the fact that a testator was scheduled to have life-threatening surgery the day after executing a new will was not sufficient to indicate that she was not of sound mind. [Wimberly v. Jones, 403 Mass. 1103 (1988)] A testator's belief that she frequently communicated with the spirits of her deceased husband and nephew, and her signing her husband's name on a letter that she believed was from her husband, did not require granting a jury issue as to capacity in view of the testator's belief in spiritualism. [Donovan v. Sullivan, 296 Mass. 55 (1936)]

b. **Adjudication of Incapacity Not Conclusive**
A person who has been adjudicated incapacitated and for whom a conservator has been appointed does not necessarily lack testamentary capacity. While such an adjudication is admissible as bearing upon testamentary incapacity, it does not raise a presumption of incapacity and will not support a directed verdict. [Clifford v. Taylor, 204 Mass. 358 (1910)]

c. **Insane Delusion**
A person may have sufficient mental capacity to conduct his affairs and to make a will, but may be suffering from an insane delusion so as to require a particular provision in the will to fail on the ground of testamentary incapacity. An insane delusion may invalidate the entire will or only a portion (such as a particular gift) thereof.

1) **Will Set Aside to Extent Delusion Caused Testamentary Disposition**
A will can be set aside on the ground of insane delusion only if and to the extent it can be shown that the delusion caused the testamentary disposition. The contestant must show that the testator would not have made the disposition in question *but for* the insane delusion.

2) **Delusion Must Be "Insane"**
A "delusion" is a conception of reality that has no foundation in reality and is not supported by evidence of any kind. If there is any factual reason for his belief, it is not a delusion and not disqualifying, notwithstanding the fact the testator may actually have been in error in drawing his conclusions or have made unwarranted accusations. The fact that a testator suffers from delusions with respect to matters unrelated to his will does not destroy his capacity to leave his property as he sees fit.

d. **Burden of Proof on Contestants**
The Massachusetts courts recognize a presumption that the testator was of sound mind. The burden of proof is on the contestant, who must establish lack of capacity by a preponderance of the evidence. If the contestant introduces evidence sufficient, if believed, to warrant a finding of incapacity, the presumption drops and the proponent must now introduce evidence of capacity. [Clifford v. Taylor, *supra*]

C. **UNDUE INFLUENCE**
A will is invalid if it is obtained through undue influence. To establish undue influence, it must be shown that the testator was subjected to mental coercion, or duress, the effect of which was to destroy the free will of the testator so as to produce an instrument that reflects the desires, not of the testator, but of the party exerting the influence. [Neill v. Brackett, 234 Mass. 367 (1920)] "Undue influence involves some form of compulsion which coerces a person into doing something the person does not want to do." [Heinrich v. Silvernail, 23 Mass. App. Ct. 218 (1986)]

1. **Contestant Has Burden of Proof to Establish Undue Influence**
Unless a fiduciary relationship is involved, the contestant has the burden of proof to establish undue influence. [Tarricone v. Cummings, 340 Mass. 758 (1960)] The contestant must show:

(i)   The *existence* and exertion of *influence*;

(ii) The *effect* of the influence was to *subvert or overpower* the mind and will of the testator; and

(iii) The *product* of the influence was a will (or a gift therein) that would not have been made *but for* such influence.

a.   Surmise, Conjecture, Opportunity Are Not Sufficient to Establish Undue Influence
Mere suspicion, surmise, or conjecture, or proof that a party had the opportunity to influence the testator is not enough to warrant a finding of undue influence. [Flynn v. Prindeville, 327 Mass. 266 (1952)] Also, flattery, pleading with, or begging the testator to make a gift does not constitute undue influence. There must be *affirmative evidence* that undue influence was exerted. [Wellman v. Carter, 286 Mass. 237 (1934)]

2.   Fiduciary Has Burden of Proof to Show No Undue Influence
The burden of proof shifts when a fiduciary benefits from a transaction with his principal. One acting in a fiduciary capacity has the burden of proving that a transaction between the principal and himself was not the product of undue influence. The fiduciary must show that the transaction was fair and that his principal was fully informed. This burden is generally met if the fiduciary shows that his principal made the bequest with full knowledge and intent or with the advice of independent legal counsel. [Pollock v. Marshall, 391 Mass. 543 (1984)] The fact that the fiduciary is a close family relative does not shift the burden of proof back to the contestant. Relative or no relative, "[t]he first question in such a case is whether the beneficiary owed a fiduciary duty to the decedent." [Cleary v. Cleary, 427 Mass. 286 (1998)]

a.   What Constitutes Fiduciary Relationship
For purposes of this rule, a fiduciary relationship includes such relationships as attorney-client, insurance agent, attorney-in-fact under power of attorney, and financial confidant. [Cleary v. Cleary, *supra*]

b.   Compare—Confidential Relationship
If a beneficiary occupied a confidential relationship but not a fiduciary relationship with the decedent (*e.g.*, a nurse, friend, brother, sister, etc.), it generally takes less evidence to establish undue influence. [Tetrault v. Mahoney, Hawkes & Goldings, 425 Mass. 456 (1997)] However, the *burden of proof does not shift*, but remains with the contestant.

D.   FRAUD
If the execution of a will, or the inclusion therein of a particular gift, is the result of fraud, the will or the particular gift is invalid. Fraud consists of making that which is false appear to the testator to be true, thereby affecting his will. The elements of fraud are:

(i)   False representations that the speaker knew to be false;

(ii) Made with the intent to deceive the testator;

(iii) The testator's ignorance of the falsity; and

(iv) Reliance upon such representations resulting in a different will than the testator otherwise would have made.

1.   Fraud in the Execution (Fraud in the Factum)
In fraud in the factum, there is a *misrepresentation as to the nature or the contents* of the instrument.
Examples: 1) A presents an instrument to T, telling T that it is a power of attorney which, upon being signed by T and two witnesses, will enable A to pay T's hospital bills. In fact, the instrument is a will that devises T's entire estate to A.

2) T, an elderly widow, has a daughter (B) and three sons. B's husband, an attorney, prepares a will for T and tells T that the will leaves T's estate in equal shares to her children. T signs the will without reading it. In fact, the will devises the bulk of T's estate to B.

2. Fraud in the Inducement

In fraud in the inducement, the testator intends to execute the instrument as his will and to include the particular contents of that instrument, but he is *fraudulently induced into making this will* or some particular gift therein by misrepresentations as to facts which influence his motivation. The will or the particular gifts affected by the fraud can be set aside upon proof of the fraudulent inducement.

Example: T had a son C (who lived with T) and a daughter D. Although D and her husband had a good relationship with T, the relationship between C and D was strained. Over a period of time, C persuaded his father that D and her husband were thieves and had stolen from T, and that in the purchase of a farm years before, D and her husband had cheated T. Relying on these representations, which were false, T became embittered toward D and her husband and severed all friendly relations with them. T's will, which bequeathed $5 to D and the rest of his estate to C, was set aside on grounds of fraud.

E. MISTAKE

1. Mistake in Execution of Will

a. Mistake as to Nature of Instrument—Extrinsic Evidence Admissible

Extrinsic evidence is admissible to show that the testator was unaware of the nature of the instrument she signed (*e.g.,* she believed it to be a power of attorney). Such a mistake relates to the issue of whether the testator had the requisite testamentary intent, without which the will would be invalid.

b. Wrong Will Signed—Courts Divided on Relief Question

In cases where the testator has signed the wrong will, the courts are divided on the question of whether relief should be granted. Suppose that reciprocal wills are prepared for H and W, under which each devises his or her estate to the other. By mistake, H signs the will prepared for W, and W signs the will prepared for H. Thus, the will signed by H reads, "I, Rose Snide, leave all my property to my husband, Harvey Snide." Some courts have denied relief on the ground that H lacked testamentary intent because he did not intend to execute the document that he signed. [Pavlinko's Estate, 148 A.2d 528 (Pa. 1959)] However, the better and modern view is that the court should grant relief since both the existence and the nature of the mistake are so obvious. The court should substitute "Harvey" for "Rose" and "husband" for "wife" (and vice versa), as appropriate. [Matter of Snide, 418 N.E.2d 656 (N.Y. 1981)] No Massachusetts case has considered this question.

2. Mistake in Inducement—No Relief Granted

If the alleged mistake involves the reasons that led the testator to make the will (or the reasons for making or not making a particular gift therein), and the mistake was not fraudulently induced, no relief is granted. *Rationale:* To allow evidence as to the alleged mistake would open the door to fraudulent testimony, since the testator is dead and cannot contradict the testimony as to the supposed mistake. Moreover, even if the alleged mistake were shown, this would not establish that the testator would have made a different disposition had the true facts been known.

Example: T's nephew Ron is a prisoner of war. Assuming that Ron is dead, T revokes a will that left everything in equal shares to Ron and T's other nephew, Don, and executes a new will leaving everything to Don. After T's death, Ron returns alive. Evidence of the mistake is not admissible, and Don takes T's estate under the second will.

a. Exception If Mistake Appears on Face of Will

The courts have recognized (more often in dictum than in actual holdings) that if the mistaken inducement appears on the face of the will, relief will be granted.

Example: Same facts as above, except that T's new will says, "Since my nephew Ron is dead, I revoke my earlier will and leave all my property to my nephew Don." Several courts have stated in dictum that since the mistake is shown on the face of the will and extrinsic evidence need not be relied on to show the mistake, the court should deny probate of the second will and instead probate the will that benefits Ron and Don equally.

3. Mistake as to Contents of Will

a.   **Mistaken Omission—No Relief Granted**
Extrinsic evidence is not admissible to show that a provision was mistakenly omitted from a will, or that a provision contained in the will is not what the testator intended. Absent evidence of fraud, duress, or suspicious circumstances, it is conclusively presumed that the testator understood and approved the terms of the new will when she signed it. "Courts have no power to reform wills. Hypothetical or imaginary mistakes of testators cannot be corrected. Omissions cannot be supplied. Language cannot be modified to meet unforeseen changes in conditions. The only means for ascertaining the intent of the testator are the words written and the acts done by him." [Gove v. Hammond, 385 Mass. 1001 (1982)]

Example: T executes a will that makes only minor changes from an earlier will (which was revoked by the new will). Unlike the earlier will, the new will does not contain a residuary clause. The attorney who prepared the new will makes a sworn affidavit stating that the omission was inadvertent and was contrary to T's instructions. The affidavit is not admissible, and the new will must be probated. Since the will is clear as to its meaning and is not ambiguous, extrinsic evidence as to T's intent is inadmissible. Correction would require the addition of a new provision, and *the courts cannot reform a decedent's will*.

b.   **Plain Meaning Rule—Evidence Not Admissible to Contradict Plain Language**
If there is no patent or latent ambiguity in the provisions of a will, the words used by the testator must be given their ordinary meaning. Evidence is not admissible to show that the testator made a mistake in describing a beneficiary or the property that was to be the subject of the gift, or that the testator used a word in other than its clear meaning. [Flannery v. McNamara, 432 Mass. 665 (2000)] *Rationale:* The testator signed the will and is conclusively presumed to have read, understood, and intended its contents. To allow oral testimony to contradict the will's plain meaning would open the door to fraud.

Examples: 1) T's will bequeaths "200 shares of IBM stock" to B. Evidence, no matter how compelling, is *not* admissible to show that T actually owned 300 shares of IBM stock and intended to bequeath all 300 shares to B.

2) T's will bequeathed property to her brother Enoch "or his heirs." Enoch predeceased T, survived by his wife, Martha, but not by descendants. T's attorney testified that T intended for "heirs" to include only "descendants," and that T told the attorney that she did not want Martha to take anything if Enoch predeceased T. On that basis, the probate court entered an order directing that Martha took nothing. *Reversed.* It was error to admit the attorney's testimony. "Where the will is unambiguous, extrinsic evidence to aid in interpretation of its provisions is inadmissible even though the language involved has a legal meaning which is not likely to have been understood by the testator or which does not correspond to an oral statement of his intention." [Gustafson v. Svenson, 373 Mass. 273 (1977)]

4.   **Extrinsic Evidence Admissible to Cure Ambiguity**

a.   **Latent Ambiguity**
A latent ambiguity exists when the language of the will, although clear on its face in describing a beneficiary or property, results in a misdescription when applied to the facts to which it refers. The language and its meaning are clear, but some extrinsic fact creates the possibility of more than one meaning. Generally, there are two types of latent ambiguity. The first type occurs when a will clearly describes a person or thing, and two or more persons or things exactly fit that description. The second type of latent ambiguity exists when no person or thing exactly fits the description, but two or more persons or things partially fit. [Phipps v. Barbera, 23 Mass. App. Ct. 1 (1986)] Extrinsic evidence is admissible to cure the ambiguity. *Rationale:* Reliance on extrinsic evidence does not have the effect of "rewriting" the will or adding to its terms. Instead, the evidence is being received to give meaning to the words the testator actually used. *But note:* If the extrinsic evidence does not resolve the ambiguity, the gift fails.

Examples: 1) T's will devises Blackacre "to my niece Nellie." T has two nieces named Nellie. Parol evidence is admissible to show which niece T intended to benefit.

2) Same facts as above, except that T does not have a niece named Nellie. He does, however, have a niece named Norrie and a cousin named Nellie. Extrinsic evidence is admissible to show whether T intended to make a gift to cousin Nellie or to niece Norrie. But if the evidence does not establish which one T had in mind, the gift fails.

3) T's will made bequests "to my nephews and nieces." T had no brothers and sisters (and thus had no nephews and nieces), raising a latent ambiguity. Evidence that T was close to her former husband's nephews and nieces, and had contributed to their education, supported a finding that they were the intended beneficiaries. [Clymer v. Mayo, 393 Mass. 754 (1984)] But if the testator actually had blood nephews and nieces, the "plain meaning" rule would apply, and evidence would **not** be admissible to show that she intended to include nephews and nieces by marriage. [Goddard v. Amory, 147 Mass. 71 (1888)]

b. Patent Ambiguity

A patent ambiguity exists when the uncertainty appears on the face of the will because of defective, obscure, or insensible language (*e.g.,* where the will mentions two cousins, Mary Jones and Mary Smith, and then makes a gift "to my cousin Mary"). The traditional view was that extrinsic evidence is not admissible to correct a patent ambiguity, and that the gift fails because of the misdescription. However, the modern and better view is that such evidence is admissible.

Example: T's will bequeathed one-third of his business to A and B, but the will was unclear as to whether A and B were to receive one-third each or whether, instead, the one-third share was to be divided between A and B (giving them one-sixth each). This is a patent ambiguity, and extrinsic evidence is admissible to cure the ambiguity.

F. NO CAUSE OF ACTION FOR TORTIOUS INTERFERENCE WITH INHERITANCE RIGHTS

Massachusetts does not recognize a cause of action for tortious interference with inheritance rights. Where someone allegedly has interfered with an inheritance right by improperly converting a person's property, sufficient remedies are available under current law: (i) a guardian could be appointed for the person to bring suit to recover the property; or (ii) after the person's death, her executor or administrator could bring an action to recover the property; or (iii) the aggrieved will beneficiary could contest the will on grounds of duress, fraud, or undue influence. [Labonte v. Giordano, 426 Mass. 319 (1997)]

G. NO-CONTEST CLAUSES ARE GIVEN FULL EFFECT

Suppose H dies leaving a will that devises $10,000 to his son, Sam, and the rest of his substantial estate to his housekeeper, Hilda. The will contains a no-contest clause (sometimes called an *in terrorem* clause): "Should any beneficiary named herein contest this will or any part thereof, he shall forfeit all interests given to him by the will." Sam brings a will contest on grounds of undue influence and lack of testamentary capacity. Sam loses the will contest, and H's will is admitted to probate. Does Sam forfeit his legacy?

1. Majority Rule—No Forfeiture If Probable Cause for Contesting Will

In most states, it is held that if the beneficiary had probable cause for bringing the contest (*i.e.,* it was not a strike suit whose sole purpose was to provoke a settlement), the no-contest forfeiture clause is not given effect. Whether Sam had probable cause is a question of fact.

2. Massachusetts—No-Contest Clause Given Full Effect Regardless of Probable Cause

Massachusetts has rejected the "probable cause" defense to enforcement of no-contest clauses. A provision that triggers a forfeiture if a beneficiary contests the will is given full effect, regardless of whether there was probable cause for challenging the will. *Rationale:* Will contests "frequently, if not invariably, result in minute examination into the habits, manners, beliefs, conduct, idiosyncracies, and all the essentially private and personal affairs of the testator, when he is not alive and cannot explain what may without explanation be given a sinister appearance. To most persons such exposure to publicity of their own personality is distasteful, if not abhorrent. [Also,] a will contest not infrequently engenders animosities and arouses hostilities among kinfolk of the testator, which may never be put to rest and which contribute to general unhappiness. Thus a will contest may bring sorrow and suffering to many concerned. A [no-contest clause] may contribute to the fair reputation of the dead and to the peace and harmony of the living." [Rudd v. Searles, 262 Mass. 490 (1928)]

3. **Not Triggered by Suit to Construe Will**
A suit to construe a will's provision is not a "contest" that will trigger an in terrorem clause. In such an action the validity of the will is not challenged. Rather, the issue is to determine what interests were created by the will.

X. PROBATE AND ESTATE ADMINISTRATION

A. PROBATE
"Probate" refers to the proceeding in which an instrument is judicially established as the duly executed last will of the decedent (or, if there is no will, the proceeding in which the decedent's heirs are judicially determined). After the will is admitted to probate (or the heirs are determined), the court issues "letters" to the *personal representative*, who administers the estate. If named in the decedent's will, the representative is called an *executor* and is issued *letters testamentary*. If appointed by the court, the representative is called an *administrator* and is issued *letters of administration*. The letters are the personal representative's evidence of his authority to take possession of the decedent's property, and to act on behalf of the estate in dealing with third parties. Technically, you *probate* a decedent's will and you *administer* the decedent's estate. However, the term "probate" is commonly used to refer to all steps in the process of estate administration ("probate administration" or "the probate process").

1. **Venue**
A petition for admitting a will to probate must be filed in the county in which the testator was domiciled at the time of his death. [Brignati v. Medenwald, 315 Mass. 636 (1944)]

B. APPOINTMENT OF PERSONAL REPRESENTATIVE

1. **Persons Eligible for Appointment**
If a will nominates an executor, the nominated person will usually be appointed. If the person named is not competent or declines the appointment, the court will appoint a person who would be entitled to administer the estate if it were an intestate estate. Administration of the estate of a person dying intestate must be granted in the following order: (i) to the *surviving spouse*; (ii) to the decedent's *next of kin*; (iii) to a *creditor* of the decedent; or (iv) to a *public administrator*. [Mass. Gen. L. ch. 193, §1]

   a. **Persons *Not* Eligible for Appointment—Murder or Manslaughter of Decedent**
   A person cannot be appointed personal representative of a decedent's estate if she has been convicted of *murder or manslaughter* of the decedent, or as *accessory before the fact* to the murder or manslaughter of the decedent. [Mass. Gen. L. ch. 193, §§1, 7]

2. **Letters of Authority**
When the personal representative is appointed, "letters testamentary" (if a will) or "letters of administration" are issued. These letters state the fiduciary's duties and authority, and are sufficient to entitle the fiduciary to secure and take possession of the property belonging to the estate. They are his evidence of official and representative authority in dealing with third persons.

C. DUTIES OF PERSONAL REPRESENTATIVE
The personal representative, whose functions are generally analogous to those of a receiver of a defunct corporation or a trustee in bankruptcy, is charged with the duty of marshalling the decedent's assets, giving notice to creditors and paying valid claims, filing the decedent's final income tax return and an estate tax return (if required), taking whatever other steps are necessary to wind up the decedent's affairs, and distributing the remaining assets according to the decedent's will or the intestacy statutes.

1. **Collection of the Decedent's Assets**
The personal representative must collect all assets properly belonging to the estate. This means he must process any claims that the decedent had that survived his death. All claims in contract and tort (*i.e.,* those tort claims relating to injury to person or property) survive. Additionally, wrongful death actions survive and must be pursued by the personal representative. Title to the decedent's personal property passes to the personal representative, while title to real property vests immediately in the heirs. However, upon court order the personal representative may sell real property to pay the decedent's creditors. Also, property passing outside of probate (right of survivorship property, life insurance, etc.) is not part of the estate.

2. Continuation of Decedent's Business

It is not part of the regular function of a personal representative to carry on a trade or business, even though a business comes to him as one of the assets of the estate. He should not attempt to carry on the business of the decedent or to embark in any new one, unless pursuant to a power expressly conferred upon him by will, by agreement of all interested parties, or after obtaining express court authority.

3. Inventory

Within three months of appointment, the personal representative must file an inventory setting forth all of the assets of the estate and their estimated value.

4. Sale of Real Property—Requires Court Authorization

An executor or administrator can sell real property in the estate only for the purpose of *paying debts and expenses*, and then only after being granted express authority ("license") by the probate court. [Mass. Gen. L. ch. 202, §1] (This rule, and the exception set out below, have been tested several times in recent years.)

a. Exception—Will Gives Executor Power of Sale

If a will gives the executor a power of sale, the executor can sell real property without court authorization, but only for the purposes specified in the will. [Justice v. Soderlund, 225 Mass. 320 (1916)]

D. LIABILITY OF PERSONAL REPRESENTATIVE

A fiduciary is liable for *any loss to the estate* arising from embezzlement; commingling of estate funds with his own; negligence or wanton and willful mishandling of funds; self-dealing; failure to account for or terminate the estate when it is ready for termination (and no extension of time has been granted); premature distribution of estate assets; and for any misfeasance, malfeasance, nonfeasance, or other breach of duty.

A fiduciary is also liable for (i) neglect or unreasonable delay in raising money by collecting the debts or selling the real or personal estate of the deceased, or (ii) neglect to pay over money in his hands, lessening the value of the estate.

E. CREDITORS' CLAIMS—ACTION MUST BE FILED WITHIN ONE YEAR

Until 1990, Massachusetts had a "nonclaim" statute applicable to claims against a decedent's estate. Under the former statute, the personal representative was required to give notice by publication in a newspaper of general circulation. Creditors had nine months in which to file their claims; otherwise the claims were barred. A similar Oklahoma nonclaim statute (under which creditors had two months from the publication of notice to file their claims) was held unconstitutional in *Tulsa Professional Collections, Inc. v. Pope,* 485 U.S. 478 (1988). The Court held that the Due Process Clause required personal notice to known or reasonably ascertainable creditors before their claims could be barred. This decision raised doubts as to the constitutionality of the Massachusetts nonclaim statute, even though the time for filing claims was much longer. In response, the legislature enacted a *one-year statute of limitations* on all actions against a decedent's estate. If the action is not filed within one year, the claim is barred regardless of whether the creditor was given notice of the decedent's death or the estate's administration. [Mass. Gen. L. ch. 197, §9] Dictum in the *Tulsa Professional Collections* opinion indicates that the one-year statute of limitations is constitutional. Since the limitation period is automatic and self-executing, there is *no state action* because no court involvement starts the limitation period running.

1. Exception—New Assets Discovered

A creditor may file a claim if the estate receives new assets more than one year after the decedent's death. [Mass. Gen. L. ch. 197, §11] The rationale for the exception is that creditors of a known insolvent frequently do not bother to file claims, and they should have a chance to file when the estate receives additional assets. The usual source of such assets is a successful lawsuit on the decedent's behalf.

2. Exception—Action Accrues More than One Year After Death

If a cause of action against the decedent does not accrue until after one year, the creditor may file any time prior to the final decree closing the estate. [Mass. Gen. L. ch. 197, §13; Flannery v. Flannery, 429 Mass. 55 (1999)]

Example: Attorney commits malpractice during his representation of Client. Attorney dies in March 1999. Client discovers the malpractice when consulting another lawyer in April 2000. Since the cause of action did not accrue until April 2000, Client may file suit against the attorney's estate if the estate is not yet closed.

3. **Exception—Claim for Personal Injury or Death Covered by Liability Insurance**

An action for personal injury or death can be filed more than one year after the decedent's death (but in any event, the action must be filed within three years after the cause of action accrued), in which case the recovery is limited to the amount covered by liability insurance. [Mass. Gen. L. ch. 197, §9A] This rule shows that the purpose of the one-year statute of limitations is to protect a decedent's estate from late-filed claims, not to protect insurance companies. If no executor or administrator has been appointed to administer the decedent's estate, the action is maintained by naming the decedent as defendant.

Example: Mary was killed in an automobile accident while driving home from a New Year's Eve party. The other driver (Paul), who was seriously injured, brings an action against Mary's estate, alleging that Mary was driving under the influence of alcohol and was negligent. Mary had a $500,000 liability policy issued by Allstate. If Paul files his action within one year of Mary's death and recovers a judgment of $700,000, he will collect $500,000 from Allstate and $200,000 from Mary's estate. If Paul files his action more than one year after Mary's death, his recovery is limited to the amount of the insurance coverage.

4. **Exception—"Where Justice and Equity Require It"**

The court may authorize payment of a late-filed claim "where justice and equity require it," as long as the creditor was not chargeable with "culpable neglect" in not filing the action within one year. [Mass. Gen. L. ch. 197, §10] Even under the former nonclaim statute, very few cases granted relief under this exception. It was invoked only in situations where the creditor was induced to forgo an action based on misleading assurances [McMahon v. Miller, 192 Mass. 241 (1906)—promise that creditor would be paid as soon as land was sold], or when a creditor with a limited education and a limited command of English relied on an experienced attorney's assurances that his claim was being properly handled [Hastoupis v. Gargas, 9 Mass. App. Ct. 27 (1980)]. It is difficult to imagine a situation where relief would be granted under the current self-executing statute of limitations, especially since the courts have consistently ruled that lack of knowledge of the decedent's death [Thompson v. Owen, 249 Mass. 229 (1924)] or of the rules governing payment of claims [First Portland National Bank v. Taylor, 323 Mass. 492 (1949)] are not grounds for relief.

F. ORDER OF PAYMENT OF CLAIMS

1. **Priority for Payment of Claims**

Priorities are important when the estate is partially insolvent. Charges and claims against a decedent's estate are classified and paid in the following order: (i) the *surviving spouse's allowance* (*see* VIII.C.1., *supra*); (ii) *administration expenses*; (iii) *funeral expenses* and expenses of last sickness; (iv) *debts entitled to preference* under the laws of the United States; (v) *child support arrearages* and *taxes*; (vi) *debts due the Division of Medical Assistance*; (vii) *debts up to $100 for labor* performed within one year of death; (viii) *debts up to $100 for necessaries* furnished within one year of the decedent's death; (ix) *secured debts* up to the value of the collateral; and (x) *unsecured debts* (and secured debts to extent debt exceeds value of the collateral). [Mass. Gen. L. ch. 198, §1]

2. **Abatement of Legacies**

In the typical cases in which there are sufficient assets to pay all death costs and still satisfy all gifts made by the will, debts and expenses are charged against the residuary estate. But suppose that the assets owned by the testator at death are not sufficient to pay all of her debts and also satisfy all of the specific, demonstrative, and general legacies made by the will. Which legacies must be sacrificed first in order to pay debts and expenses of administration? In Massachusetts, legacies are subject to *abatement* in the following order (absent a contrary will provision):

(i)   Residuary estate. (A residuary gift is a gift of what remains of the testator's property after first paying debts, expenses and taxes, and then satisfying the general, demonstrative, and specific gifts made by the will.)

(ii) General and demonstrative legacies.

(iii) Specific devises and bequests.

(iv) Last to be abated are legacies to satisfy legal obligations of the decedent; a legacy in lieu of dower, curtesy, or antenuptial agreement; or a legacy to a minor child. [Bailey v. Milligan, 256 Mass. 90 (1926)]

Within each category, legacies and devises *abate pro rata*, with no distinction between real and personal property in that category. [Mass. Gen. L. ch. 191, §26; Farnum v. Bascom, 122 Mass. 292 (1877)] The rules of abatement also apply in satisfying the share taken by a spouse as an elective share. If the residuary estate is exhausted and debts remain unpaid, general and demonstrative legacies abate pro rata, and so on.

Example: T's will devises Blackacre (worth $10,000) to A, her Cadillac (worth $5,000) to B, makes general legacies of $5,000 to C and $1,000 to D, and bequeaths her residuary estate to E. After paying all claims against the estate and administration expenses, there remains in the estate Blackacre, the Cadillac, and $3,000 cash. E takes nothing, because the residuary estate has been exhausted. The general legacies to C and D abate pro rata; C takes $2,500, and D takes $500. Since all claims now have been satisfied, the specific gifts are not abated. A takes Blackacre, and B takes the Cadillac.

a. Contrary Will Provision

The above order of abatement is applicable unless the will makes a contrary provision. A testator can always specify a different formula for abatement of legacies.

3. Devise of Encumbered Property—No Exoneration of Liens

At common law and in many states, a specific beneficiary of encumbered property is entitled to have the lien exonerated. That is, the beneficiary is entitled to demand that the obligation be paid out of the residuary estate, so that title passes to him free of the lien. Massachusetts has abolished the "exoneration of liens" doctrine by statute. Liens on specifically bequeathed property are not exonerated unless the will explicitly directs exoneration. [Mass. Gen. L. ch. 191, §23]

Example: Frank's will devises Greenacre to George, and his residuary estate to Gladys. At Frank's death, Greenacre is subject to a mortgage that secures a $24,000 note on which Frank was personally liable. Under the common law rule, George would be entitled to have the lien discharged by having the $24,000 paid out of the residuary estate. Since, however, Massachusetts has abolished the exoneration of liens doctrine, George takes exactly what Frank owned: Title subject to a mortgage lien.